Contemporary ECONOMICS 3e

William A. McEachern

SOUTH-WESTERN CENGAGE Learning

Australia • Brazil • Japan • Korea • Mexico • Singapore • Spain • United Kingdom • United States

Contemporary Economics, Third Edition
William A. McEachern

Vice President of Editorial, Business: Jack W. Calhoun

Vice President/Editor-in-Chief: Karen Schmohe

Executive Editor: Eve Lewis

Sr. Developmental Editor: Karen Caldwell

Consulting Editor: Hyde Park Publishing Services

Editorial Assistant: Anne Merrill

Marketing Manager: Kara Bombelli

Sr. Marketing Communications Manager: Libby Shipp

Sr. Content Project Managers: Diane Bowdler, Martha Conway

Sr. Media Editor: Sally Nieman

Manufacturing Planner: Kevin Kluck

Production Service: Integra Software Services Pvt. Ltd.

Sr. Art Director: Michelle Kunkler

Internal Design: Ke Design, Mason, Ohio

Internal Infographics: Rob Schuster

Cover Design and Illustration: Rob Schuster, Tippy McIntosh

Cover Images, bottom and clockwise: © Cristian Baitg, iStock; © Talshiar, iStock; © Geanina Bechea, Shutterstock; © Konstantin Sutyagin, Shutterstock; © SVLuma, Shutterstock; © Raygun, Getty Images; © WillSelarep, iStock

All Infographics, Illustrations, and Tables: © Cengage Learning 2013

Rights Acquisition Specialist, Text and Images: Amber Hosea

Text Permissions Researcher: PreMedia Global

Photo Researcher: Darren Wright

Student Edition ISBN-13: 978-1-111-58018-6
Student Edition ISBN-10: 1-111-58018-9

South-Western
5191 Natorp Boulevard
Mason, OH 45040
USA

Cengage Learning products are represented in Canada by Nelson Education, Ltd.

For your course and learning solutions, visit **www.cengage.com/school**
Visit our company website at **www.cengage.com**

Printed in the United States of America
1 2 3 4 5 6 7 16 15 14 13 12

ABOUT THE AUTHOR

FROM THE AUTHOR

Hello Colleagues,

Because there can be no real learning without student interest, my first priority in *Contemporary Economics* is to generate interest. How do I know what interests students? Much experience in the classroom at the University of Connecticut has helped me figure out what works and what doesn't.

My approach in *Contemporary Economics* is to remind students how much they already know since they make economic decisions every day. Never has there been a better time to learn economic principles. As the world grows more competitive, your students need the market advantage that economic insight provides.

I use timely, relevant examples to stimulate student interest. My examples build bridges from what students already know to what they need to learn—moving from the familiar to the new. Examples should be self-explanatory, conveying their meaning quickly and directly. Having to explain an example is like having to explain a joke. The point gets lost.

Interest also flows from variety—variety in the way material is presented. My explanations of economic theory, economic events, and economic institutions include not only examples, but also anecdotes, analogies, parables, case studies, facts, statistics, photographs, web links, questions, graphs, tables, exercises, and other vehicles that keep the presentation fresh and lively.

I show students how economic theory helps them understand a changing world. But the intuition behind the theory is introduced as something familiar, often reflected by common expressions. For example, the idea of diminishing marginal utility is captured by the expression "Been there. Done that."

I'm not afraid to use graphs, but I use them judiciously. A graph should make things clearer, not become an obstacle to teaching and learning. Some textbooks use graphs the way a drunk uses a lamppost—more for support than for illumination.

Photo courtesy of William A. McEachern

I believe I can help you help your students learn economics. I am new enough to the task to keep it fresh but experienced enough to get it right.

Will McEachern

About the Author

William A. McEachern was born in Portsmouth, NH, earned an undergraduate degree in the honors program from College of the Holy Cross, served three years as an Army officer, and earned an M.A. and a Ph.D. in economics from the University of Virginia. He won the University of Connecticut's Excellence in Teaching Award. He offers teaching workshops around the country and is Founding Editor of *The Teaching Economist,* a newsletter that focuses on making teaching more effective and more fun.

Professor McEachern has advised federal, state, and local governments on policy matters. His research has been published in book form and in scholarly journals. He has been quoted in media such as the *New York Times, Times* of London, *Wall Street Journal, USA Today,* and *Reader's Digest.*

REVIEWERS

Carol M. Ardito
Business Department Teacher
North Haven High School
North Haven, Connecticut

Brian Bergin
Instructor
Alton High School
Alton, Illinois

Jeffrey W. Biersach
Upper School Faculty
Durham Academy
Durham, North Carolina

Shauna Demers
Business Department Teacher
Mountain Pointe High School
Phoenix, Arizona

Rick La Greide
Teacher
Portland Public Schools
Portland, Oregon

Angela Hartman
Business Instructor
Underwood School District
Underwood, Minnesota

Marc S. Hechter
Social Studies Department Chair
Palo Verde High School
Las Vegas, Nevada

Holly Jones
AP Economics Instructor
The Pennington School
Pennington, New Jersey

Jeffrey L. Leard
Social Studies Teacher
West-Oak High School
Westminster, South Carolina

Paul Limpert
Business Education Teacher
Cedarcliff Local Schools
Cedarville, Ohio

Norman B. McCabe
Teacher
Gilbert School District
Gilbert, Arizona

Susan D. Miller
Social Studies Department Teacher
Eleanor Roosevelt High School
New York, New York

Cheryl M. Morrow
Economics, AP Macroeconomics, and AP Government and Politics Teacher
Spain Park High School
Hoover, Alabama

Todd K. Siler
Social Studies Department Teacher
Wyoming High School
Cincinnati, Ohio

Donna Stubbe
Business Department Teacher
Two Rivers High School
Two Rivers, Wisconsin

Thomas A. Trosko
Economics Teacher
Portland Public Schools
Portland, Oregon

Kenneth Ward
Business Department Teacher
Martin Luther King Jr. Senior High School
Detroit, Michigan

BRIEF CONTENTS

CONTENTS

Comstock/Jupiter Images

© Rob Crandall/Alamy

© Jeff Greenberg/Alamy

Unit 4 Personal Financial Literacy

oliverong/Shutterstock.com

Unit 5 The National Economy

© Russell Kord/Alamy

Unit 6 Public Policy and the U.S. Economy

Sportstock/Shutterstock.com

Digital Vision/Getty Images

FEATURES TABLE OF CONTENTS

ASK THE EXPERT

CONNECT TO HISTORY

INVESTIGATE YOUR LOCAL ECONOMY

ESSENTIAL QUESTION

MOVERS AND SHAKERS

NET BOOKMARK

21ST CENTURY SKILLS

SPAN THE GLOBE

FIGURES TABLE OF CONTENTS

VOLUNTARY NATIONAL CONTENT STANDARDS IN ECONOMICS

Standard	Chapter Coverage in *Contemporary Economics*
1. **Scarcity** Productive resources are limited. Therefore, people cannot have all the goods and services they want; as a result, they must choose some things and give up others.	1, 2, 3, 4, 5, 8, 9, 14, 21
2. **Decision Making** Effective decision making requires comparing the additional costs of alternatives with the additional benefits. Many choices involve doing a little more or a little less of something: few choices are "all or nothing" decisions.	1, 2, 3, 4, 5, 6, 8, 9, 10, 11, 12, 14, 16
3. **Allocation** Different methods can be used to allocate goods and services. People acting individually or collectively must choose which methods to use to allocate different kinds of goods and services.	1, 2, 3, 21
4. **Incentives** People usually respond predictably to positive and negative incentives.	1, 2, 3, 4, 5, 6, 7, 8, 9, 10, 14, 15, 17, 18, 19, 20, 21
5. **Trade** Voluntary exchange occurs only when all participating parties expect to gain. This is true for trade among individuals or organizations within a nation, and among individuals or organizations in different nations.	2, 3, 6, 10, 13, 18, 20, 21
6. **Specialization** When individuals, regions, and nations specialize in what they can produce at the lowest cost and then trade with others, both production and consumption increase.	1, 2, 3, 5, 6, 7, 18, 20, 21
7. **Markets and Prices** A market exists when buyers and sellers interact. This interaction determines market prices and thereby allocates scarce goods and services.	1, 2, 4, 5, 6, 7, 11, 12, 15, 20, 21
8. **Role of Prices** Prices send signals and provide incentives to buyers and sellers. When supply or demand changes, market prices adjust, affecting incentives.	4, 5, 6, 9, 11, 12
9. **Competition and Market Structure** Competition among sellers usually lowers costs and prices, and encourages producers to produce what consumers are willing and able to buy. Competition among buyers increases prices and allocates goods and services to those people who are willing and able to pay the most for them.	3, 6, 7, 8, 14
10. **Institutions** Institutions evolve and are created to help individuals and groups accomplish their goals. Banks, labor unions, markets, corporations, legal systems, and not-for-profit organizations are examples of important institutions. A different kind of institution, clearly defined and enforced property rights, is essential to a market economy.	2, 3, 7, 8, 9, 10, 11, 12, 13, 14, 15, 17, 18, 19, 20, 21
11. **Money and Inflation** Money makes it easier to trade, borrow, save, invest, and compare the value of goods and services. The amount of money in the economy affects the overall price level. Inflation is an increase in the overall price level that reduces the value of money.	2, 3, 8, 10, 11, 12, 18, 19, 20

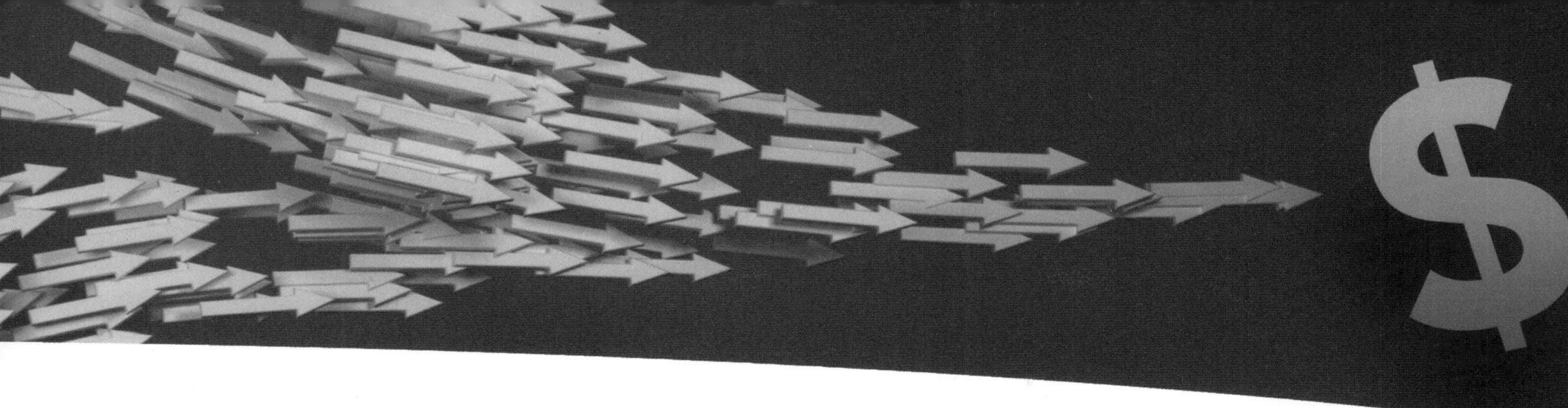

Standard	Chapter Coverage in *Contemporary Economics*
12. **Interest Rates** Interest rates, adjusted for inflation, rise and fall to balance the amount saved with the amount borrowed, which affects the allocation of scarce resources between present and future uses.	3, 10, 11, 12, 13, 15, 17, 18, 19
13. **Income** Income for most people is determined by the market value of the productive resources they sell. What workers earn primarily depends on the market value of what they produce.	1, 3, 5, 9, 13, 14, 15, 17, 21
14. **Entrepreneurship** Entrepreneurs take on the calculated risk of starting new businesses, either by embarking on new ventures similar to existing ones or by introducing new innovations. Entrepreneurial innovation is an important source of economic growth.	1, 3, 5, 8, 10, 12, 14, 21
15. **Economic Growth** Investment in factories, machinery, new technology, and in the health, education, and training of people stimulates economic growth and can raise future standards of living.	1, 2, 3, 8, 9, 10, 12, 13, 14, 15, 17, 19, 21
16. **Role of Government and Market Failure** There is an economic role for government in a market economy whenever the benefits of a government policy outweigh its costs. Governments often provide for national defense, address environmental concerns, define and protect property rights, and attempt to make markets more competitive. Most government policies also have direct or indirect effects on peoples' incomes.	2, 3, 6, 7, 8, 11, 14, 16, 16, 17, 18, 19, 20, 21
17. **Government Failure** Costs of government policies sometimes exceed benefits. This may occur because of incentives facing voters, government officials, and government employees, because of actions by special interest groups that can impose costs on the general public, or because social goals other than economic efficiency are being pursued.	3, 7, 15, 16, 20, 21
18. **Economic Fluctuations** Fluctuations in a nation's overall levels of income, employment, and prices are determined by the interaction of spending and production decisions made by all households, firms, government agencies, and others in the economy. Recessions occur when overall levels of income and employment decline.	1, 13, 15, 17, 21
19. **Unemployment and Inflation** Unemployment imposes costs on individuals and the overall economy. Inflation, both expected and unexpected, also imposes costs on individuals and the overall economy. Unemployment increases during recessions and decreases during recoveries.	12, 13, 15, 17, 19, 21
20. **Fiscal and Monetary Policy** Federal government budgetary policy and the Federal Reserve System's monetary policy influence the overall levels of employment, output, and prices.	15, 16, 17, 18, 19, 20

READING SKILLS

Your textbook is a guide to help you learn new information, but you cannot retain that information without reading the text effectively. The following reading skills strategies can help you get the most out of your reading.

BEFORE YOU READ

Set a Purpose for Reading

- ✓ Think about what you will be reading and what you hope to learn from the reading. Consider how the topic might relate to your daily life and what you already know about the topic.

Preview

- ✓ Look over the headings and visuals in the reading, including the chapter title, subheads, photos, graphs, charts, and maps. Look over any "preview" items the chapter provides, such as lists of bold-faced terms.

Predict

- ✓ Using the information you examined in your preview, predict what you will learn from it.
- ✓ Use the following graphic organizer to help you prepare to read new materials.

Purpose for Reading	Preview	Prediction(s)
I will be reading about ____.	The chapter title is ________________.	Based on what I have previewed, I will probably learn ____.
I hope to learn ____.	The subheads are ____.	
The topic relates to my daily life in that ____.	Chapter visuals include ____.	
I already know ____.	Chapter preview items include ____.	

AS YOU READ

Find the Main Idea

The main idea is the most important idea in a reading passage. Sometimes the main idea of a passage is stated clearly, often in the first one or two sentences of a paragraph. But sometimes it is not stated so clearly, and you must read carefully to infer the main idea. You can test whether or not you have identified the correct main idea by offering details from the reading that support this idea. Using a graphic organizer like the one below can help you in this process.

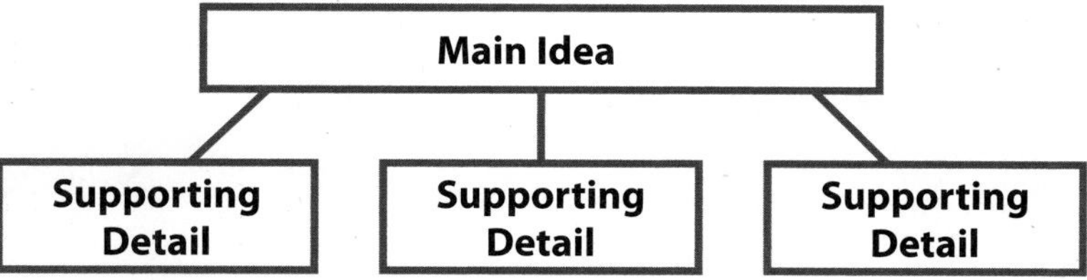

Draw Connections Between Items

As you read, pay particular attention to the relationships between people, places, events, and ideas. These relationships can include cause and effect, differences and similarities, sequencing, and problems or solutions. It also contains some lists of clue words that can help you spot some relationships. Recognizing relationships between items can help you understand complicated information.

Analyze Visual Information

Pay attention to the visual information in the text. Ask yourself why it is included and what it adds to the text. Think about how your understanding of the visuals as you read may have changed from when you looked at the visuals in your preview exercise.

AFTER YOU READ

Summarize

Once you have finished your reading, try to summarize, or state in the simplest way possible, what the reading passage is all about. The process of summarizing a reading passage is very similar to finding the main idea. As you prepare to summarize a passage, look at your notes on the most important details mentioned in the reading. Use these details to state what happened in the passage in the simplest way possible. Using a graphic organizer like the one below can help you in this process.

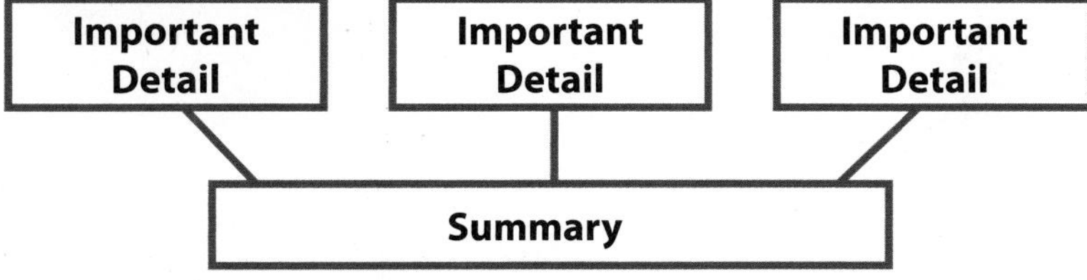

Assess

After you have finished reading and summarizing, look back at your predictions about the chapter and analyze whether you learned what you thought you were going to learn. Consider how the information you learned may be put to use in your daily life.

Where Real Life and Economics Intersect!

Bring economics to life with practical examples that make concepts clear and intriguing. *Contemporary Economics, 3e* blends economic expertise and educational insights with comprehensive content, sound instructional design, and extensive print and media teaching tools.

Make the connection between economics and real life as you move from the basics of supply and demand to the role of market institutions. Timely, rich examples help you link what you already know—economics happening in the world around you—to what you need to learn about today's economics theories, events, and institutions. To ensure comprehension, the book covers CEE (Council for Economic Education) Standards completely and repeatedly. In addition, this text includes two chapters covering personal finance, including information on managing money and being a responsible consumer.

NEW! Each **Essential Question** correlates to one of the CEE Standards. The Essential Question reinforces student comprehension by highlighting core concepts within the text.

Take a look at how the connected structure of this dynamic text brings economics to life. A sound instructional design with strong pedagogy, real-world connections, and assessment ensures mastery of economic concepts.

Prepare to master concepts with clearly identified **Learning Objectives**, **Key Terms**, and the **In Your World** overview.

1.1 THE ECONOMIC PROBLEM

Learning Objectives

LO1 Recognize the economic problem, and explain why it makes choice necessary.

LO2 Identify productive resources and list examples.

LO3 Define goods and services, list examples, and explain why they are scarce.

In Your World

Economics is always in the news. Newspapers, television, and the Internet bombard you with information about the economy. The media report on economic issues because they are important in people's lives. People like you want to know the latest about job opportunities for the summer, sales at the mall, the best cell-phone plan, and other matters that affect your income, spending, and lifestyle. Economics is concerned with identifying and clarifying the choices you face now and in the future.

Key Terms

scarcity 5
productive resources 5
economics 6
human resources 7
labor 7
entrepreneur 7
natural resources 8
capital goods 8
good 8
service 8

"'In Your World' is a good way to help students relate to the material. It provides a framework."

~SUSAN D. MILLER
ELEANOR ROOSEVELT HIGH SCHOOL, NEW YORK, NY

...OICES

...onomic choices ...rt-time

how people use their scarce resources to satisfy their unlimited wants

unlimi... knowledge of the city, driving skills, ... come, in turn, buys housing, groceries, clothing, trips to Disney World, ... goods and services that help satisfy some of the driver's unlimited wants.

CHECKPOINT What is the economic problem, and why does it make choice necessary?

Checkpoints throughout the chapter relate back to each learning objective and provide opportunities for informal evaluation of learning.

ASSESSMENT

Think Critically

1. What is the central problem you face when you make economic choices?
2. What are examples of productive resources you use in your life?
3. How can you tell whether the food you eat from your refrigerator is scarce?
4. Identify each of the following as a human resource, natural resource, or capital good:
   a. a hammer used to build a wooden box
   b. the tree that was cut down to make lumber to build a wooden box
   c. the effort used to nail lumber together to make a wooden box

Graphing Exercise

5. Draw a pie chart that demonstrates how you spend your money that is similar to the one below. To construct a pie chart, draw a circle and divide it into slices. Each slice represents the percentage the spending category is of your income. Label each slice with a spending category, and identify it as either a good or a service.

Make Academic Connections

6. **Government** Identify a good or service provided by the government that has no apparent cost for you. Why is this good or service not really free?

...nWork Working in small teams, make a list of household tasks that different members of the team are expected to complete regularly. Examples could include cleaning their room or vacuuming their home each Saturday. The team should then work together to identify types of human and capital resources used when they complete the tasks on their list. These could include effort and skills (human resources) and a broom and vacuum (capital resources) used to produce a clean home.

Apply Economics Concepts

34. **Circular-Flow Model** Sketch a copy of the circular-flow model on your own paper. Place each of the following in the correct location on your model.
   a. Brad has a pizza delivered as he watches Monday night football.
   b. The Sony Corporation produces a new TV.
   c. Brad works at a local drugstore.
   d. Brad buys a new TV from a Sears store.

35. **Opportunity Cost** Your uncle has offered to buy you either a new computer or a good-quality bicycle as a graduation present. The prices of both items are the same. Write an essay that identifies which gift you would choose and describes the opportunity cost that would result from your choice. Why might other people make a different choice? Why might you be at least as well off if, as an additional option, your uncle also offers you the cash?
36. **Rational Self-Interest** Describe something you have recently done to help someone else. Explain how the action you took was based on rational self-interest. What opportunity cost did you pay for your action? If the value of your opportunity cost had been much greater, would you have still taken the action? Why or why not?
37. **21st Century Skills: Critical Thinking and Problem Solving** A bakery purchased a new oven that allowed it to eliminate six of its employees and still produce as many loaves of bread as it had in the past. Write a paragraph that describes this change in a way that makes it clear you understand the terms *productive resources*, *human resources*, and *capital goods*.

Assessments appear at the end of every lesson and chapter, allowing frequent evaluation of comprehension and progress.

"The end-of-lesson assessments are a good mix of written, graphing, and research questions."

~BRIAN BERGIN
ALTON HIGH SCHOOL, ALTON, IL

Economics—Always Relevant, Always Real.

Digging Deeper
with Economics e-Collection

Economics is always in the news. This Digging Deeper activity provides you the opportunity to research the Gale Economics e-Collection, a database of articles about economic topics from popular newspapers, magazines, and journals. Access this e-Collection through the URL below. To see the broad scope of economics topics covered in the media, type in the word "economics" under the Keyword or Subject tab. Refine your results by typing one of the key terms from Chapter 1. (The key terms appear at the beginning of each lesson and are printed in blue on the pages.) Choose an article, read it, and then write a one-paragraph summary about it. Also look through the table of contents of your textbook to find where it addresses this topic. Be prepared to discuss your article in class.

www.cengage.com/school/contecon

NEW! The **Digging Deeper with Economics e-Collection** allows a further investigation of topics with access to the online Gale Economic Database. This unique tool provides online access to numerous articles from economics-focused magazines and academic journals such as NewsUSA and the Economist (U.S.). Each Digging Deeper is accompanied by an activity or follow-up question.

Span the Globe

Entrepreneurial Gaming

In 2007 Harvard Business School (HBS) students Daniel Kafie, Mario Schlosser, and Joshua Kushner created Vostu, a social networking site for the Latin American market, specifically Brazil. The venture was inspired by Facebook, also started by a Harvard student. Launched with an initial investment by Intel Capital, the company struggled to make a profit. Within two years, the student entrepreneurs had gone through three versions of the idea. Following their first attempt, they switched to a platform designed to host other social networks. By 2009, the company focused specifically on creating social games. Since then Vostu has grown from 12 to 400 employees, most involved in designing games in the company's Buenos Aires office. Concentrating on social games played on Orkut, the popular social networking site in Brazil and Latin America Google's equivalent of Facebook, the company now claims 22 million players.

The career goals of the three co-founders differed from those of typical HBS students. Most HBS students aspire to "taking the big job or following what other people have done," Schlosser said. For Kafie, HBS was a place "to meet really interesting people and to see if there's an opportunity to work on some sort of entrepreneurship idea." According to Kafie, "Entrepreneurship is not about being smart, analytical (or) being the best in one field. It's about being persistent."

Think Critically **Was there an opportunity cost to the three founders of Vostu because they did not follow the more traditional route upon graduating from Harvard Business School? How does their persistence illustrate the concept of sunk cost?**

Span the Globe brings an international focus to economic principles by drawing connections between global interactions and their impact on local, regional, and national economies.

admission cost you $10. The irrelevance of sunk costs is underscored by the proverb,

Math in Economics

Common Core The Number System

In most jobs, when you work more than 40 hours a week, you are paid a premium hourly rate. The overtime premium is a factor of your regular hourly wage. You can calculate the amount you will earn for working overtime by multiplying the number of hours worked (greater than 40) times your regular hourly wage times the overtime premium. (1.5 in most situations)

EXAMPLE Calculate the amount an employee will make if her regular wage rate is $12.20 per hour and she works 6 hours of overtime with an overtime premium of 1.5.

SOLUTION Multiply 6 times $12.20 times 1.5.

$6 \times \$12.20 \times 1.5 = \$109.80$

Practice the Skill Calculate the amount earned for working overtime hours in each of the following exercises. Write answers to the nearest cent.

1. William worked 7 hours of overtime. His regular wage rate is $9.70 per hour and the overtime premium is 1.5.
2. Tiesha worked 5.5 hours of overtime. Her regular wage rate is $13.30 per hour and the overtime premium is 1.5
3. How much would you want to be paid per hour to give up your Saturday

NEW! Math in Economics is a new feature that addresses Common Core Standards and reinforces math skills that are essential to the study of economics. Concepts such as averaging, calculating percentages, compounding, and discounting are covered and applied.

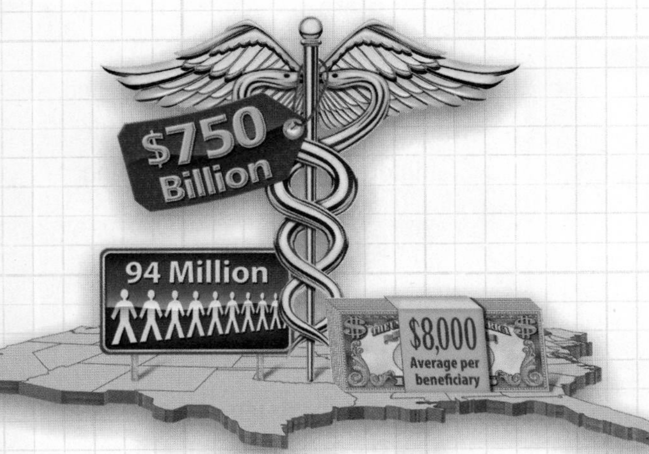

Information graphics or **infographics** bring information, data, or key concepts to life with a vivid visual representation.

NEW! 21st Century Skills highlights the skills, knowledge, and expertise needed to succeed in work and life as established by the Partnership for 21st Century Skills.

Partnership for 21st Century Skills

21st Century Skills

CRITICAL THINKING AND PROBLEM SOLVING

Managers Choose Between Human and Capital Resources

Most products can be produced in more than one way. A clay flowerpot, for example, may be created by hand on a potter's wheel, by robotic machines on a production line, or in a variety of other ways that use different combinations of human and capital resources. When managers choose the specific combination of resources to produce a product, they must evaluate a variety of questions, including the following:

- What quantities can be produced per unit of time using various combinations of resources?
- How much will qualified workers cost to employ for each possible method of production?
- How much will the tools and supplies needed to create the product for each possible method of production cost to purchase, maintain, and operate?
- Will the quality of products produced in each possible way compare? Will any product be significantly better or worse?

Existing Production

If production is already taking place using a particular method, managers who are considering adopting a new method of production should evaluate additional factors, such as:

- What costs must be paid if current production methods are replaced?
- Can qualified workers be found or trained to use this different method?
- How much will these workers cost?
- If the new method fails to work what costs may need to be paid?

Weighing Marginal Costs and Benefits

Virtually all decisions involve a tradeoff between costs and benefits. Managers should realize that some costs must be paid regardless of the number of products that are made or the way they are produced. For example, if a business has borrowed money to build a factory that is large enough for 100 workers, the firm must pay its mortgage each month even if the workers are replaced with a machine that uses only half of the space. Managers may make poor choices if they only consider the *marginal benefits* of a business decision without weighing them against *marginal costs* that may result from their decision.

Apply the Skill

Assume that you are the manager of a printing company. You employ 20 workers who do much of their work by hand. A new printing press has been invented that would allow you to eliminate these workers although you would still need to hire or retrain four workers to operate the new machine. The new press would cost $8 million to purchase. Make a list of five specific questions you would need to answer before you could make a rational decision about whether or not to purchase the new technology. Explain why each question is important. Compare and contrast the benefits and costs of using both production techniques.

For a strong cross-curricular emphasis, **Connect to History** takes an historical viewpoint of economics, exploring how economic principles relate to American history.

Connect to History

Glassmaking in Jamestown

Despite failed attempts to establish a colony in the New World, in 1606 King James I of England granted a charter for this purpose to the Virginia Company of London. Because earlier enterprises had been expensive, the required funds were raised through a joint stock company. Colonists were instructed to settle land between the 34th and 41st parallels. The three ships carrying 104 "colonists" arrived at the site of Jamestown Island on May 13, 1607.

Colonists provided labor for the company. Lured by the promise of easy gold, many of them were not prepared for the ordeal that followed. Many of the colonists were younger sons of wealthy families who were not used to hard work, and they struggled to survive. Still, these men perceived their opportunity cost as being small because they stood to inherit little at home. The colony seemed a way for them to gain the land and prominence they could not obtain in England. Wealthy colonists who provided their own armor and weapons were paid in land, dividends, or additional shares of stock. Less-well-off colonists received clothes, food, and arms from the company, and then after seven years, they received land.

The Virginia Company was still recruiting colonists when Captain Christopher Newport returned to England, bringing word of a struggling colony. Although disappointed that gold and silver did not lie on the beach or grow on the trees, the entrepreneurs of the Virginia Company still saw profitable opportunities in various industries. They believed the colony could take advantage of the land's natural resources and manufacture products for sale in England. One such product was glass. Demand for glass products in England in the early seventeenth century was growing. However, scarce resources in England limited the growth of industry. England's forests were being depleted, a took a lot of wood—about a week of burning tw three cords per day—to get the furnaces hot en to produce glass. The New World, with its unlim forests, appeared an ideal spot for a glassmakin industry.

Glassmaking in England also suffered from a s age of labor, as few people were skilled in the Although some glassmakers had come from countries, England could not meet the dem glass. Much of it had to be imported, leadin pany to believe that a Virginia-based enter produce glass more cheaply. Because glas England were doing very well, their oppo of leaving the country for the uncertainty dangerous land was too high.

Countries that exported large amounts better places to recruit workers. Among settlers in Virginia in the summer of 16 Germans and Poles for the glassmakin colony produced some glass, but the short lived. Workers had little time to industry because they were too bus When the newly appointed govern on May 24, 1610, he found that 90 nists had died, and with them, Am

Think Critically Devise that could have guided the Virgini to begin a colony in the New Worl variables might these entrepren What might their assumptions h their hypotheses have been?

Movers and Shakers introduces individuals who have made a significant impact on economics with their entrepreneurial ideas.

MOVERS AND SHAKERS

J. K. Rowling

Author, Harry Potter Series

Author J. K. Rowling's rise to success with her series of books about boy wizard Harry Potter began in 1990. The idea came to her while traveling on a train in England. She began writing the story immediately and continued working on it for years. After a failed marriage and her return to London with her infant daughter, she was determined to finish it. On welfare and struggling financially, she sent the first three chapters to an agent, who returned them immediately without comment. A second agent wrote back asking to see the rest of the manuscript. Rowling found a publisher the next year. What followed was a fast rise to success. By age 41, she had sold more than 325 million books. Rowling's personal fortune is estimated at close to $1 billion.

A Rags-to-Riches Story

Rowling's rags-to-riches story has some valuable lessons for entrepreneurs:

- Make sure your product is ready for the market. Rowling worked on her book for years.
- Don't be afraid to work with a big idea. She recognized the value of her idea and developed it. She said, "I just wrote the sort of thing I liked reading when I was younger—and still enjoy now."
- Don't get sidetracked, and never give up. She said, "It is our choices . . . that show what we truly are, far more than our abilities." Her choice to stay with her idea, her perseverance, and her dedication helped make her books successful. Even though one publisher advised her to get a day job because she "had little chance of making money in children's books," Rowling refused to get sid

Bros. to produce a series of movies based on the books.

Charities also have benefited from Rowling's success. She donated $15 million to establishing a neurology clinic at the University of Edinburgh. The clinic will be devoted to the research and treatment of multiple sclerosis, a disease from which her mother, Anne Rowling, died at the age of 45. She also supports AIDS and cancer research, children's issues, human rights, and hunger and literacy programs.

Rowling's refusal to give up on her idea has done more than sell books. In addition to enriching her person ally, her work h

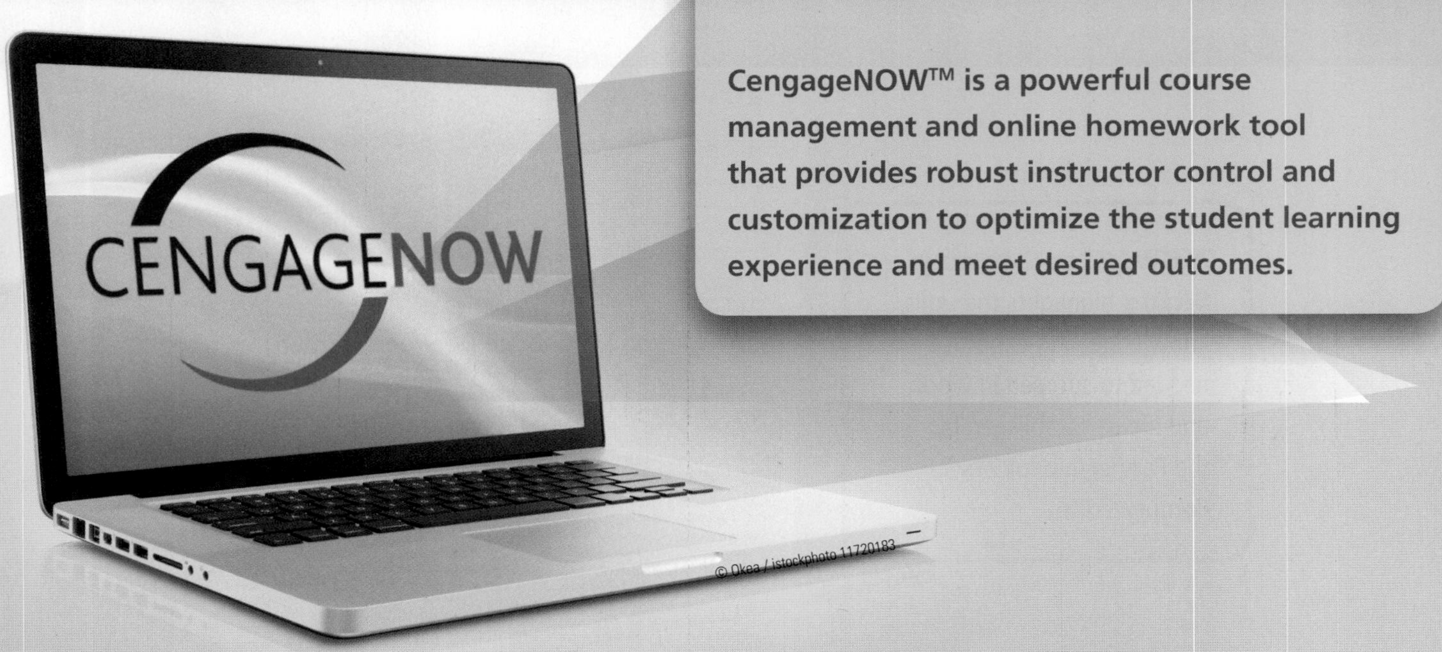

CengageNOW™ is a powerful course management and online homework tool that provides robust instructor control and customization to optimize the student learning experience and meet desired outcomes.

CengageNOW for *Contemporary Economics, 3e* offers:

- **CLeBook** With this enhanced eBook, it is easy to highlight, take notes, and search the textbook easily and efficiently.

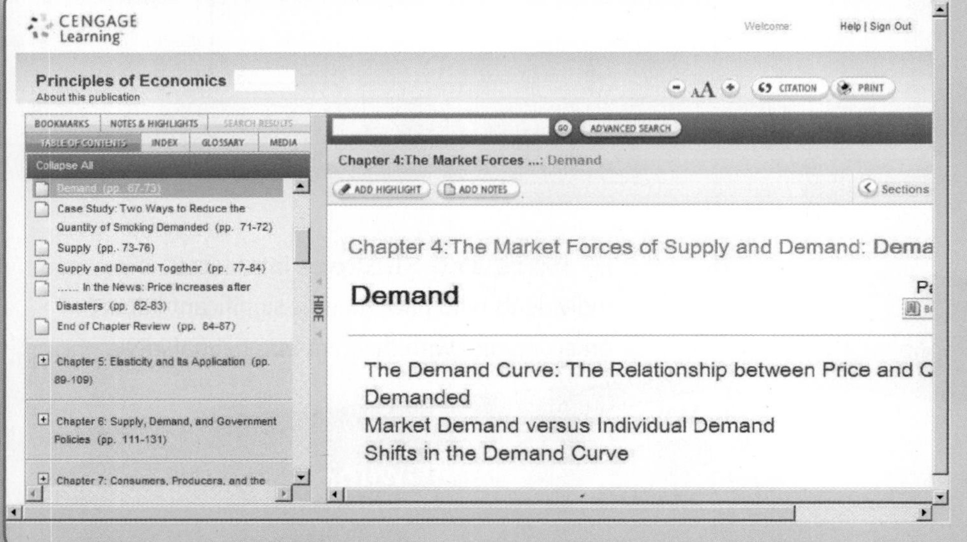

- **Auto-graded Homework**, including end-of-lesson, end-of-chapter, and workbook activities.
- A **Personalized Study Plan** is a diagnostic tool with Pre-Test, Customized Study Plan, and Post-Test activities for each chapter, including
  - Text material
  - Learning objectives
  - Ask the Expert videos
  - PowerPoint® slides
  - Crossword puzzles
  - Flashcards
  - Net Bookmarks
  - Quizzing games
- **Test Bank**, including **Exam*View*®**, Chapter Tests, and Unit Tests.

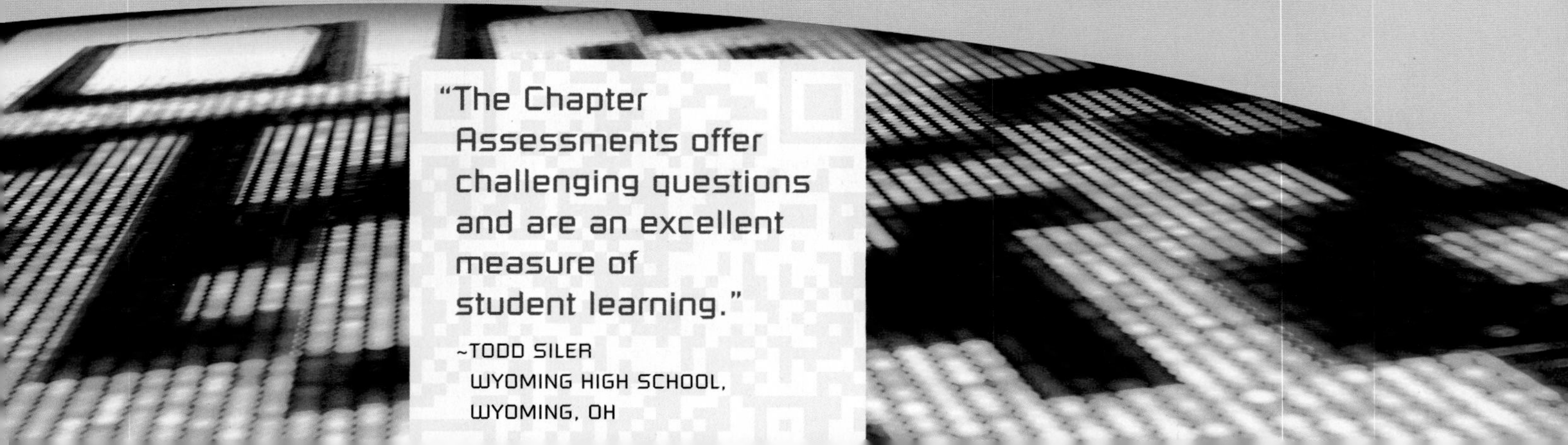

"The Chapter Assessments offer challenging questions and are an excellent measure of student learning."

~TODD SILER
WYOMING HIGH SCHOOL,
WYOMING, OH

Complete the *Contemporary Economics Connection* with Comprehensive Support.

The powerful package that accompanies *Contemporary Economics, 3e* includes a wealth of student and teacher resources with a common thread of built-in flexibility and proven effectiveness.

Instructor's Wraparound Edition

ISBN: 978-1-133-49417-1

The Instructor's Wraparound Edition provides comprehensive instructional support for *Contemporary Economics, 3e*. The lesson-plan format is incorporated in the margins, providing the tools to lead students from learning, to applying, to owning the economic material. All solutions are included in the margins, as well as additional ideas, background, and projects for different learning styles and ability levels. Unit Overviews contain pacing guides and identify coverage of CEE Standards in the upcoming chapters. References in the Instructor's Wraparound Edition tie the textbook content to problem-based learning material from the Buck Institute for Education, a nonprofit educational research and development organization.

Workbook

ISBN: 978-1-133-56161-3

The supplemental Workbook provides a pen-and-paper method for reviewing chapter material with objective questions and activities.

Exam*View*®

ISBN: 978-1-133-49420-1

Building customized assessments with **Exam***View*® is a snap! It is easy to edit and add questions, customize tests (scramble answers & questions), and test online.

Chapter and Unit Tests

ISBN: 978-1-133-56160-6

Printed chapter tests, unit tests, and a final exam.

Instructor's Resource CD (IRCD)

ISBN: 978-1-133-49419-5

Everything needed to teach the course in one handy location. Ancillaries on the IRCD include:

- PDF of Instructor's Wraparound Edition
- Lesson Plans
- PowerPoint® Presentations
- Instructor's Edition of Chapter and Unit Tests
- Instructor's Edition of Student Workbook
- Reading Study Guide
- Personal Finance Activities
- Spanish Resources
- Developing Interpersonal and Leadership Skills
- Developing Reading, Writing, and Math Skills
- Developing Social Studies and Economic Measurement Skills
- Teaching Tools that include topics such as Ethics, Block Scheduling, International Business, and more

Instructor's Resource Box

ISBN: 978-1-133-49418-8

Keep all of the teaching materials and solutions you need for your course in one handy location! This box includes:

- Student Edition
- Instructor's Wraparound Edition
- Instructor's Edition of the Workbook
- Instructor's Edition Chapter and Unit Tests
- Demo CD

Companion Website—

www.cengage.com/school/contecon

You and your students can access this free website to find a wealth of online learning tools, including:

- ***Interactive Quizzes***
- ***Graphing Workshops***—Animated tutorials that guide students through explanations of the economics concepts behind certain graphs. (Noted in the textbook by an icon.)
- ***Ask the Expert***
- ***NetBookmark***
- ***Digging Deeper with Economics e-Collection***

Comstock/Jupiter Images

© Alexey Dudoladov

UNIT 1

Introduction to Economics

Last Saturday you earned $50 helping a neighbor move some furniture. What will you do with that money? There are many possibilities. You could spend it on movies, pizza, music downloads, gasoline, or a favorite brand of jeans. Or you could save the money toward a trip to Europe or a college education. You could even give the money to a worthy charity or to a friend in need. Whatever you decide, you are making an economic choice. Economics focuses on how your choices, and the choices of millions of others, affect individual markets—such as the market for pizza—and shape the economy as a whole.

CONSIDER ...

- Why are you reading this book right now rather than doing something else?
- Why are some comic strip and cartoon characters like Cathy, the Simpsons, and Family Guy missing a finger on each hand?
- Why is there no sense crying over spilt milk?
- In what way are people who pound on vending machines relying on a theory?
- Why is a good theory like a closet organizer?

CHAPTER 1

What Is Economics?

Point your browser

www.cengage.com/school/contecon

Antonio Jorge Nunes/Shutterstock.com, Background image: dibrova/Shutterstock.com

1.1 THE ECONOMIC PROBLEM

Learning Objectives

LO1 Recognize the economic problem, and explain why it makes choice necessary.

LO2 Identify productive resources and list examples.

LO3 Define goods and services, and explain why they are scarce.

Key Terms

In Your World

Economics is always in the news. Newspapers, television, and the Internet bombard you with information about the economy. The media report on economic issues because they are important in people's lives. People like you want to know the latest about job opportunities for the summer, sales at the mall, the best cell-phone plan, and other matters that affect your income, spending, and lifestyle. Economics is concerned with identifying and clarifying the choices you face now and in the future.

ECONOMIC CHOICES

LO1
Recognize the economic problem, and explain why it makes choice necessary.

Economics is about making choices. You make economic choices every day. You make choices about whether to get a part-time job or focus on your studies, buy a car or save for college, pack a lunch or buy the school lunch. You already know more about economics than you realize. You bring to the subject a rich personal experience. This experience will help you reinforce your understanding of the basic ideas.

The Economic Problem

Would you like a new car, a nicer home, better meals, more free time, more spending money, more sleep? Who wouldn't? And even if you can satisfy some of these desires, others keep popping up. Here's the economic problem: *Although your wants, or desires, are virtually unlimited, the productive resources available to help satisfy these wants are scarce.* Scarcity creates the economic problem. **Scarcity** is the condition facing all societies because there are not enough productive resources to satisfy people's unlimited wants.

Productive resources, or *factors of production*, are the inputs used to produce the goods and services that people want. *Because productive resources are scarce, goods and services are scarce, too.* A productive resource is *scarce* when it is not freely available. Because productive resources are scarce, you must choose from among your

scarcity A condition facing all societies because there are not enough productive resources to satisfy people's unlimited wants

productive resources The inputs used to produce the goods and services that people want

ESSENTIAL QUESTION

Standard: CEE 1 Scarcity
Productive resources are limited. Therefore, you cannot have all the goods and services you want; as a result, you must choose some things and give up others.

What must you do in the face of scarcity?

Photos courtesy of Shutterstock.com; teen: Elena Elisseva; popcorn: colia; purse: laola; gauge: leonardo255; pup: Utekhina Anna; racket: zimmtws

many wants. Whenever you make a choice, you must go without satisfying some other wants. The problem of scarce resources but unlimited wants exists for each of the seven billion people on the planet.

Because you cannot have all the goods and services you would like, you must choose among them continually. Making choices means you must pass up some alternatives. Going to a basketball game on Saturday night means you must pass up a movie or a babysitting job.

Economics Defined

economics The study of how people use their scarce resources to satisfy their unlimited wants

Economics examines how people use their scarce resources to satisfy their unlimited wants. A taxicab driver uses the cab and other scarce resources, such as knowledge of the city, driving skills, gasoline, and time, to earn income. That income, in turn, buys housing, groceries, clothing, trips to Disney World, and other goods and services that help satisfy some of the driver's unlimited wants.

CHECKPOINT What is the economic problem, and why does it make choice necessary?

PRODUCTIVE RESOURCES

LO2
Identify productive resources, and list examples.

Productive resources, also called *factors of production, inputs,* or simply *resources,* sort into three broad categories: human resources, natural resources, and capital goods.

Human Resources

The first category, **human resources**, is the broad category of human efforts, both physical and mental, used to produce goods and services. *Labor,* such as the labor of a cab driver or a brain surgeon, is the most important of the human resources. **Labor** is the physical and mental effort used to produce goods and services. Labor itself comes from a more fundamental human resource: time. Without time you accomplish nothing. You allocate your time to alternative uses: You can sell your time as labor to earn a *wage,* or you can spend your time doing other things, such as sleeping, eating, studying, playing sports or video games, going online, watching TV, or just hanging out with friends.

Human resources also include the special skills of an **entrepreneur**, who tries to earn a profit by developing a new product or finding a better way to produce an existing one. An entrepreneur seeks to discover profitable opportunities by purchasing resources and assuming the risk of business success or failure. *Profit* equals the *revenue* from sales minus the *cost* of production. If production costs exceed revenue, the entrepreneur suffers a loss. Profit provides the incentive that makes entrepreneurs willing to accept the risk of losing money. Each company in the world today began as an idea of an entrepreneur.

Creatas/Jupiter Images

What incentive makes entrepreneurs willing to accept the risk of losing money?

human resources The broad category of human efforts, both physical and mental, used to produce goods and services

labor The physical and mental effort used to produce goods and services

entrepreneur A profit-seeker who develops a new product or process and assumes the risk of profit or loss

Natural Resources

Natural resources are so-called "gifts of nature." They include land, forests, minerals, oil reserves, bodies of water, and even animals. Natural resources can be divided into renewable resources and exhaustible resources. A *renewable resource* can be drawn on indefinitely if used wisely. Thus, timber is a renewable resource if felled trees are replaced to provide a steady supply. The air and rivers are renewable resources if they are allowed sufficient time to recover from a certain level of pollution. More generally, biological resources such as fish, game, livestock, forests, rivers, groundwater, grasslands, and agricultural soil are renewable if managed properly.

An *exhaustible resource*—such as oil or coal deposits—does not renew itself and so is available in a limited amount. Each barrel of oil or ton of coal, once burned, is gone forever. Sooner or later, all deposits of oil and coal will be will be tapped out. The world's oil and coal deposits are exhaustible.

Capital Goods

Capital goods include all human creations used to produce goods and services. Capital goods consist of factories, tools, trucks, machines, computers, buildings, airports, highways, and other manufactured items employed to produce goods and services. Capital goods include the taxi driver's cab, the farmer's tractor, the surgeon's scalpel, the interstate highway system, and your school.

CHECKPOINT **Name the three categories of productive resources, and provide examples of each.**

GOODS AND SERVICES

LO3
Define goods and services, and explain why they are scarce.

Resources are combined in a variety of ways to produce goods and services.

Goods

A farmer, a tractor, 50 acres of land, seeds, and fertilizer come together to grow the good *corn*. Corn is a **good** because it is tangible—something you can see, feel, and touch. It requires scarce resources to produce, and it satisfies human wants. This book, the chair you are sitting in, the clothes you are wearing, and your next meal are all goods.

Services

One hundred musicians, musical instruments, chairs, a conductor, a musical score, and a music hall combine to produce the service *Beethoven's Fifth Symphony*. The performance of the Fifth Symphony is a **service** because it is intangible—that is, not physical—yet it uses scarce resources to satisfy human wants. Movies, concerts, cell-phone service, Internet connections, guitar lessons, dry cleaning, and your next haircut are all services. Rather than say "goods and services" all the time, this book usually will use the term "goods" to mean both goods and services.

natural resources So-called "gifts of nature" used to produce goods and services; includes both renewable and exhaustible resources

capital goods All human creations used to produce goods and services; for example, factories, trucks, and machines

good An item you can see, feel, and touch that requires scarce resources to produce and satisfies human wants

service Something not physical that requires scarce resources to produce and satisfies human wants

Ferenc Szelepcsenyi/Shutterstock.com

In the example of the service Beethoven's Fifth Symphony, *what are the musicians, instruments, chairs, conductor, and music hall called?*

No Free Lunch

You may have heard the expression "There is no such thing as a free lunch." This is so because all goods involve a cost to someone. The lunch may seem free to you, but it draws scarce resources away from the production of other goods. Also, whoever provides the free lunch often expects something in return. A Russian proverb makes a similar point but with a bit more bite: "The only place you find free cheese is in a mousetrap."

Because goods and services are produced using scarce resources, they are themselves scarce. A good or service is scarce if the amount people desire exceeds the amount available at a zero price. But not everything is scarce. In fact, we would prefer to have less of some things. For example, we would prefer to have less garbage, less spam email, and less pollution. Things we want none of even at a zero price are called *bads*. Think of a bad as the opposite of a good.

A few goods seem free because the amount freely available (that is, available at a zero price) exceeds the amount people want. For example, air and seawater often seem free because you can breathe all the air you want and have all the seawater you can haul away. Yet, despite the old saying, "The best things in life are free," most goods are scarce, not free. Even those that appear to be free come with strings attached. For example, *clean* air and *clean* seawater have become scarce. *Goods that are truly free are not the subject matter of economics. Without scarcity, there would be no need for prices and no economic problem.*

Sometimes you may mistakenly think of certain goods as free because they involve no apparent cost to you. For example, paper napkins appear to be free at Starbucks. Nobody stops you from taking a fistful. Providing napkins, however, costs Starbucks millions each year and the company's prices include that cost. Some other restaurants try to keep napkin use to a minimum—by, for example, requiring you to ask for them at the counter.

CHECKPOINT Define goods and services, provide examples, and explain why goods and services are scarce.

1.1 ASSESSMENT

© Alexey Dudolado

Think Critically

1. What is the central problem you face when you make economic choices?
2. What are examples of productive resources you use in your life?
3. How can you tell whether the food you eat from your refrigerator is scarce?
4. Identify each of the following as a human resource, natural resource, or capital good:
    a. a hammer used to build a wooden box
    b. the tree that was cut down to make lumber to build a wooden box
    c. the effort used to nail lumber together to make a wooden box

Graphing Exercise

5. Draw a pie chart similar to the chart shown here that demonstrates how you spend your money. To construct your pie chart, draw a circle and divide it into slices. Each slice represents the spending categories of your income, by percentages. Label each slice with a spending category, and identify it as either a good or a service.

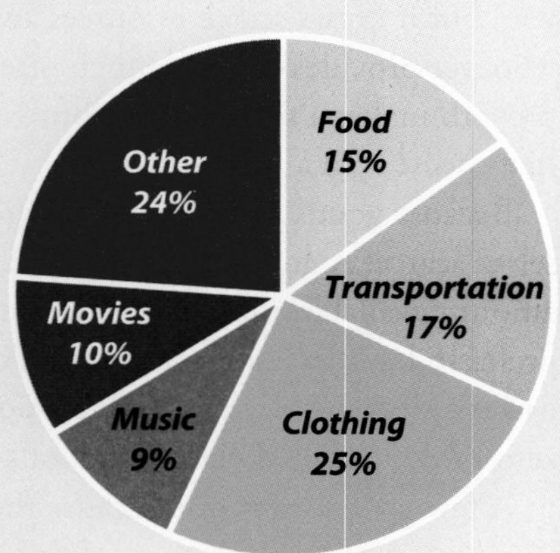

Make Academic Connections

6. **Government** Identify a good or service provided by the government that has no apparent cost to you. Why is this good or service not really free?

TeamWork

Working in small teams, make a list of household tasks that different members of the team are expected to complete regularly. Examples could include cleaning their room or vacuuming their home each Saturday. The team should then work together to identify types of human and capital resources used when they complete the tasks on their list. These could include effort and skills (human resources) and a broom and vacuum (capital resources) used to produce a clean home.

MOVERS AND SHAKERS

J. K. Rowling

Author, Harry Potter Series

Author J. K. Rowling's rise to success with her series of books about boy wizard Harry Potter began in 1990. The idea came to her while traveling on a train in England. She began writing the story immediately and continued working on it for years. After a failed marriage and her return to London with her infant daughter, she was determined to finish it. On welfare and struggling financially, she sent the first three chapters to an agent, who returned them immediately without comment. A second agent wrote back asking to see the rest of the manuscript. Rowling found a publisher the next year. What followed was a fast rise to success. By age 41, she had sold more than 325 million books. Rowling's personal fortune is estimated at close to $1 billion.

A Rags-to-Riches Story

Rowling's rags-to-riches story has some valuable lessons for entrepreneurs:

- Make sure your product is ready for the market. Rowling worked on her book for years.
- Don't be afraid to work with a big idea. She recognized the value of her idea and developed it. She said, "I just wrote the sort of thing I liked reading when I was younger—and still enjoy now."
- Don't get sidetracked, and never give up. She said, "It is our choices . . . that show what we truly are, far more than our abilities." Her choice to stay with her idea, her perseverance, and her dedication helped make her books successful. Even though one publisher advised her to get a day job because she "had little chance of making money in children's books," Rowling refused to get sidetracked from her goal.

Her stories about Harry Potter grew into an empire that has enriched every company involved in producing them. Bloomsbury, a London publishing house, decided to publish Rowling's books after the firm's top executive tested the manuscript on his daughter. Bloomsbury's profits increased fivefold from 1995 to 2002. A small London filmmaking company, Heyday Films, also benefited from the magic of Harry Potter. Heyday partnered with American movie studio Warner Bros. to produce a series of movies based on the books.

Charities also have benefited from Rowling's success. She donated $15 million to establishing a neurology clinic at the University of Edinburgh. The clinic will be devoted to the research and treatment of multiple sclerosis, a disease from which her mother, Anne Rowling, died at the age of 45. She also supports AIDS and cancer research, children's issues, human rights, and hunger and literacy programs.

Rowling's refusal to give up on her idea has done more than sell books. In addition to enriching her personally, her work has benefited many people around the world. It will continue to do so for years to come.

Think Critically **Like you, entrepreneurs make choices based on their own self-interests. J. K. Rowling chose to become a children's book author because she had a passion for writing. What are you passionate about? How would you channel your passion into a career? Write a paragraph to answer these questions.**

Sources: http://www.looktothestars.org/celebrity/171-jk-rowling#ixzz1JzQNJg4j; The Economist: http://www.economist.com/node/15108711; http://www.streetdirectory.com/travel_guide/193298/entrepreneurship/top_five_tips_small_business_owners_can_learn_from_j_k_rowling.html; J. K. Rowling's official website: http://www.jkrowling.com/textonly/en/biography.cfm

1.2 ECONOMIC THEORY

Key Terms

economic theory 12
marginal 15
microeconomics 16
macroeconomics 17
markets 17

Learning Objectives

LO1 Explain the goal of economic theory.

LO2 Understand the role of marginal analysis in making economic choices.

LO3 Explain how market participants interact.

In Your World

An economy results from the choices that millions of people like you make in attempting to satisfy their unlimited wants. Because choices lie at the very heart of the economic problem—coping with scarce resources but unlimited wants—they deserve a closer look.

THE GOAL OF ECONOMIC THEORY

LO1 Explain the goal of economic theory.

Economists develop theories, or models, to help explain economic behavior. An **economic theory**, or *economic model*, is a simplification of economic reality *used to make predictions about the real world*. Thus the goal of economic theory is to make predictions about the real world, such as what happens to the consumption of Pepsi when its price increases.

Simplify the Problem

A theory captures the important elements of the problem under study. It need not spell out every detail and relationship. In fact, the more detailed a theory gets, the more confusing it becomes, and the less useful it may be. The world is so complex that simplifying often is necessary to make sense of things. For example, a wristwatch is a model that tells time. However, a watch loaded with extra features and dials is harder to read at a glance and is therefore less useful as a time-telling model. Store mannequins simplify the human form (some even lack arms and heads). Comic-strip and cartoon characters are simplified, missing fingers (in the case of Cathy, the Simpsons, and Family Guy) or even a mouth (in the case of Dilbert). You might think of economic theory as a stripped-down, or streamlined, version of economic reality. One way to strip down reality is with simplifying assumptions.

Simplifying Assumptions

To help develop a theory, economists make simplifying assumptions. One category of assumptions is the *other-things-constant assumption*. The idea is to identify the variables of interest and then focus exclusively on the relations among them, assuming that nothing else of importance changes—that other things remain constant.

economic theory
A simplification of economic reality used to make predictions about the real world

Suppose you are interested in how a change in the price of Pepsi affects the amount purchased. To isolate the relationship between these two variables—price and quantity purchased—you assume for purposes of the model that there are no changes in other relevant variables such as consumer income, the price of Coca-Cola and the average outdoor temperature.

Economists also make assumptions about what motivates people—how people behave. These are called *behavioral assumptions*. Perhaps the most basic behavioral assumption is that people make choices based on self-interest.

Rational Self-Interest

A key assumption about behavior is that, in making choices, you rationally select alternatives you perceive to be in your best interests. By *rational,* economists mean that you try to make the best choices you can, given the information available. *In general, rational self-interest means that you try to maximize the expected benefit achieved with a given cost or to minimize the expected cost of achieving a given benefit.*

Rational self-interest does not necessarily mean selfishness or greed. You probably know people who are tuned to radio station WIIFM (What's In It For Me). For most of you, however, self-interest often includes the welfare of your family, your friends, and perhaps the poor of the world. Even so, your concern for others is influenced by your personal cost of that concern. You may volunteer to drive a friend to the airport on Saturday afternoon but are less likely to offer a ride if the flight leaves at 6:00 A.M. When you donate clothes to charitable organizations such as Goodwill Industries, these clothes are more likely to be old than new. People tend to give more to a favorite charity if contributions are tax deductible.

The assumption of rational self-interest does not rule out concern for others. It simply means that concern for others is influenced to some extent by the same economic forces that affect other economic choices. The lower your personal cost of helping others, the more help you will offer. We don't like to think that our behavior reflects our self-interest, but it usually does. As Jane Austen wrote in *Pride and Prejudice*, "I have been a selfish being all my life, in practice, though not in principle."

Rationality implies that each consumer buys the products expected to maximize his or her level of satisfaction. Rationality also implies that each firm supplies the products expected to maximize that firm's profit. These kinds of assumptions are called *behavioral assumptions* because they specify how economic decision makers are expected to behave.

cnicbc/iStockphoto.com

How would choosing to volunteer your time tutoring young students fit in with the concept of rational self-interest?

Everybody Uses Theories

Many people don't understand the role of theory. Perhaps you have heard, "Oh, that's fine in theory, but in practice it's another matter"—meaning that the theory provides little aid in practical matters. People who say this do not realize that they are merely substituting their own theory for a theory they either do not believe or do not understand. They really are saying, "I have my own theory, which works better."

Everyone uses theories, however poorly defined or understood. Someone who pounds on a vending machine that just ate a quarter has a crude theory about how that machine works and what went wrong. One version of that theory might be, "The quarter drops through a series of whatchamacallits, but sometimes the quarter gets stuck. *If* I pound on the machine, *then* I can free up the quarter and send it on its way." This theory seems to be used so widely that many people continue to pound on vending machines that fail to perform. (This is a real problem for that industry and one reason why newer vending machines are fronted with glass.) Yet, if you asked any of these mad pounders to explain their "theory" of how the machine works, he or she would look at you as if you were crazy.

A good theory helps us understand a messy and confusing world. Lacking a theory of how things work, your thinking can become cluttered with facts, one piled on another, as with clothes in a messy closet. You could think of a good theory as a closet organizer for the mind. A good theory serves as a helpful guide to sorting, saving, and understanding information.

Economists Tell Stories

Economists explain their theories by telling stories about how they think the economy works. To tell a convincing story, an economist relies on case studies, anecdotes, parables, the listener's personal experience, and supporting data. Throughout this book, you will read stories that shed light on the ideas under consideration. Stories, such as the one about the vending machine, breathe life into economic theory.

Normative Versus Positive Statements

Economists try to explain how the economy works. Sometimes they focus on how the economy *should* work rather than on how it *does* work. Compare these two statements: "The U.S. unemployment rate should be lower" versus "The U.S. unemployment rate is 9 percent." The first is called a *normative economic statement* because it reflects someone's opinion. An opinion cannot be shown to be true or false by reference to the facts. The second is called a *positive economic statement* because it is a statement about economic reality that can be supported or rejected by reference to the facts.

Positive statements concern what *is*. Normative statements concern what, in someone's opinion, *should be*. Positive statements need not be true, but you should be able to find out whether they are true or false by referring to the facts. Economic theories are expressed as positive statements such as, "If the price increases, then the quantity purchased will decrease."

Most of the disagreement among economists involves normative debates—for example, what should be the appropriate role of government—rather than statements of positive analysis. To be sure, many theoretical issues remain unresolved. However, economists do agree on most basic theoretical principles—that is, about positive economic analysis.

Normative statements, or personal opinions, are relevant in debates about public policy (such as the proper role of government) provided that opinions are distinguished from facts. In such debates, you are entitled to your own opinions, but you are not entitled to your own facts.

Explain the goal of economic theory. **CHECKPOINT**

MARGINAL ANALYSIS

LO2 Understand the role of marginal analysis in making economic choices.

Economic choice usually involves some adjustment to the existing situation, or the status quo. Your favorite jeans are on sale, and you must decide whether to buy another pair. You have just finished dinner at a restaurant and are deciding whether to eat dessert. Amazon.com must decide whether to add a new line of products. The school superintendent must decide whether to hire another teacher.

Compare Marginal Cost with Marginal Benefit

Economic choice is based on a comparison of the expected marginal benefit and the expected marginal cost of the action under consideration. **Marginal** means incremental, additional, extra, or one more. Marginal refers to a change in an economic variable, a change in the status quo.

marginal Incremental, additional, extra, or one more; refers to a change in an economic variable, a change in the status quo

A rational decision maker will change the status quo as long as the expected marginal benefit from the change exceeds the expected marginal cost. For example, you compare the marginal benefit you expect from eating dessert (the additional satisfaction) with its marginal cost (the additional dollar cost, time, and calories). Likewise, Amazon.com compares the marginal benefit expected from adding a new product line (the additional sales revenue) with the marginal cost (the additional cost of resources required).

Typically, the change under consideration is small, but a marginal choice can involve a major economic adjustment, as in your decision whether or not to go to college. For a firm, a marginal choice might mean building a factory in Mexico or even filing for bankruptcy protection.

Focusing on the effect of a marginal adjustment to the status quo cuts the analysis of economic choice down to a manageable size. Rather than confront a puzzling economic reality head-on, economic analysis can begin with a

Martin KubÃ?Â¡t/Shutterstock.com

When strawberries are in season, local markets offer them for a low price. What would be the marginal benefit of purchasing twice as many strawberries as you normally would? What would be the marginal cost of this decision?

marginal choice and then show how that choice affects a particular market and shapes the economy as a whole.

To the noneconomist, *marginal* usually means inferior, as in "a movie of marginal quality." Forget that meaning for this course. Instead, think of *marginal* as meaning incremental, additional, extra, or one more.

Choice Requires Time and Information

Rational choice takes time and requires information, but time and information are scarce and therefore valuable. If you have any doubts about the time and information required to make choices, talk to someone who recently purchased a home, car, or personal computer. Talk to a corporate official deciding whether to introduce a new product, sell online, build a new factory, or buy another firm. Or consider your own decision about going to college. You already may have talked to friends, relatives, teachers, and guidance counselors about it. You might review school catalogs, college guides, and websites. You might even visit some campuses. The decision will take time and money, and probably will involve some hassle and worry.

Because information is costly to acquire, you often are willing to pay others to gather and digest it for you. College guides, travel agents, real estate brokers, career counselors, restaurant reviews, movie critics, specialized websites, and *Consumer Reports* magazine all offer information to help improve your economic choices. *Rational decision makers will continue to acquire information as long as the marginal benefit expected from that information exceeds the marginal cost of gathering it.*

microeconomics Study of economic behavior in particular markets, such as the market for computers or for unskilled labor

Microeconomics and Macroeconomics

Although you have made thousands of economic choices, you probably seldom think about your economic behavior. For example, why are you reading this book right now rather than doing something else? **Microeconomics** focuses on your economic behavior and the economic behavior of other individuals and firms who make choices involving what to buy and what to sell, how much to work and how much to play, how much to borrow and how much to save. Microeconomics examines the factors that influence individual economic choices and how markets coordinate the choices of various decision makers. For example, microeconomics explains how price and output are determined in an individual market, such as the market for breakfast cereal, sports equipment, or unskilled labor.

Golden Pixels LLC/Shutterstock.com

Which branch of economics, macro or micro, focuses on the factors that influence your family's economic choices?

You probably have given little thought to what influences your own economic choices. You likely have given even less thought to how your choices link up with those made by hundreds of millions of others in the U.S. economy to determine measures such as total production, employment, and economic growth. **Macroeconomics** focuses on the performance of the economy as a whole, especially the national economy.

Thus microeconomics looks at the individual pieces of the economic puzzle. Macroeconomics fits all the pieces together to look at the big picture.

Describe the role of marginal analysis in making economic choices.

CHECKPOINT

MARKET PARTICIPANTS

LO3 Explain how market participants interact.

There are four types of decision makers in the economy: households, firms, governments, and the rest of the world. Their interaction determines how an economy's resources get allocated.

Four Types of Participants

Households play the leading role in the economy. As consumers, households demand the goods and services produced. As resource owners, households supply the resources used to produce goods and services.

Firms, governments, and *the rest of the world* demand the resources that households supply. They then use these resources to supply the goods and services that households demand. The rest of the world includes foreign households, foreign firms, and foreign governments that supply resources and products to U.S. markets and demand resources and products from U.S. markets.

Markets

Markets are the means by which buyers and sellers carry out exchange. By bringing together the two sides of exchange, demand and supply, markets determine price and quantity. Markets may be physical places, such as supermarkets, department stores, shopping malls, or flea markets. Markets also involve other ways for buyers and sellers to communicate, such as the stock market, telephones, bulletin boards, classified ads, the Internet, and face-to-face bargaining.

Markets provide information about the quantity, quality, and price of products offered for sale. Goods and services are bought and sold in *product markets.* Resources are bought and sold in *resource markets.* Many economists believe that the most important resource market is the labor, or job, market.

A Circular-Flow Model

Now that you have learned a bit about economic decision makers, consider how they interact. Such a picture is conveyed by the *circular-flow model,* which describes the flow of resources, products, income, and revenue among economic decision makers. A simple circular-flow model focuses on the interaction between households and firms in a market economy. Figure 1.1 shows households on the left and firms on the right.

Households supply human resources, natural resources, and capital goods to firms through resource markets, shown in the lower portion of the figure. In return, households demand goods and services from firms through product

macroeconomics Study of the economic behavior of the economy as a whole, especially the national economy

markets The means by which buyers and sellers carry out exchange

markets, shown in the upper portion of the figure. Viewed from the business end, firms supply goods and services to households through product markets, and firms demand human resources, natural resources, and capital goods from households through resource markets.

The flows of resources and products are supported by the flows of income and expenditure—that is, *by the flow of money*. The supply and demand for resources come together in resource markets to determine what firms pay for resources. These resource prices—wages, interest, rent, and profit—flow as income to the households. The supply and demand for products come together in product markets to determine what households pay for goods and services. The prices paid for goods and services flow as revenue to firms.

Resources and products flow in one direction—in this case, counterclockwise—and the corresponding payments flow in the opposite direction—clockwise.

FIGURE 1.1 Circular-Flow Model for Households and Firms

Households earn income by supplying resources to the resource markets, as shown in the lower left portion of the model. Firms demand these resources in order to produce goods and services, which they supply to the product markets. This is shown in the right-hand portion of the model. Households spend their income to demand these goods and services. This spending flows through the product market to become revenue to firms.

CHECKPOINT How do market participants interact?

1.2 ASSESSMENT

Think Critically

1. How are economic theories used in the real world?
2. Why do economists often use the other-things-constant assumption when they develop economic theories?
3. What does rational self-interest suggest that people want to achieve?
4. When Anthony went to watch another school's basketball team he saw that their center was nearly seven-feet tall. He immediately decided that this person would be that team's best rebounder. What theory did he use to draw this conclusion?
5. Identify each of the following as an example of either a positive or normative statement.
   a. Kerry Anne earns $7.50 per hour at her job.
   b. $250 is too much to pay for a prom dress.
   c. Schools should hire more math teachers.
   d. The U.S. unemployment rate in September 2011 was 9.1%.
   e. The minimum wage ought to be increased.
6. Tomás bought two pairs of shoes for $60 each. He chose not to purchase a third pair at this price. What do you know about the marginal value of a third pair of shoes for Tomás?

Graphing Exercise

7. Latischa works for a business that produces pocket calculators. She spends $100 on phone service from the $2,000 she earns each month. She also pays rent of $800 per month. Draw and label a simple circular-flow model. Use the figure to the right as a guide. Place her income and both expenditures described on your model, and describe the flows between households and firms that result.

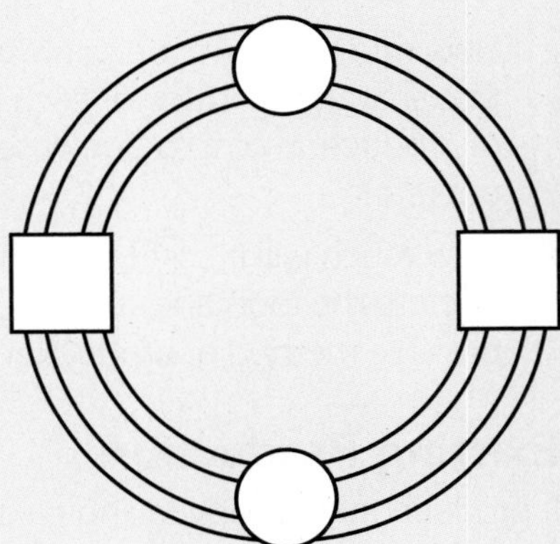

Make Academic Connections

8. **Research** Find the number of new claims for unemployment insurance compensation filed in a recent week in your state at www.dol.gov. Explain how unemployment relates to both macroeconomics and microeconomics.

TeamWork

Organize into teams of four students to study how market participants interact. One pair of students will work together to make a list of transactions that cause a flow in the circular model from households to firms. The other pair will make a similar list of transactions that cause a flow from firms through the product markets. Each pair of students will then explain the flow they have studied to the other pair.

21st Century Skills

CRITICAL THINKING AND PROBLEM SOLVING

Managers Choose Between Human Resources and Capital Goods

Most products can be produced in more than one way. A clay flowerpot, for example, may be created by hand on a potter's wheel, by robotic machines on a production line, or in a variety of other ways that use different combinations of human resources and capital goods. When managers choose the specific combination of resources to produce a product, they must evaluate a variety of questions, including the following:

- What quantities can be produced per unit of time using various combinations of resources?
- How much will qualified workers cost to employ for each possible method of production?
- How much will the tools and supplies needed to create the product for each possible method of production cost to purchase, maintain, and operate?
- How much will it cost to purchase, maintain, and operate the tools and supplies needed in each possible method of production?

Existing Production

If production is already taking place using a particular method, managers who are considering adopting a new method of production should evaluate additional factors, such as:

- What costs must be paid if current production methods are replaced?
- Can qualified workers be found or trained to use this different method?
- How much will these workers cost?
- If the new method fails to work, what costs may need to be paid?

Weighing Marginal Costs and Benefits

Virtually all decisions involve a tradeoff between costs and benefits. Managers should realize that some costs must be paid regardless of the number of products that are made or the way they are produced. For example, if a business has borrowed money to build a factory that is large enough for 100 workers, the firm must pay its mortgage each month even if the workers are replaced with a machine that uses only half of the space. Managers may make poor choices if they only consider the *marginal benefits* of a business decision without weighing them against *marginal costs* that may result from their decision.

Apply the Skill

Assume you are the manager of a printing company. You employ 20 workers who do much of their work by hand. A new printing press has been invented that would allow you to eliminate these workers, although you would still need to hire or retrain four workers to operate the new machine. The new press would cost $8 million to purchase. Make a list of five specific questions you would need to answer before you could make a rational decision about whether or not to purchase the new technology. Explain why each question is important. Compare and contrast the benefits and costs of using both production techniques.

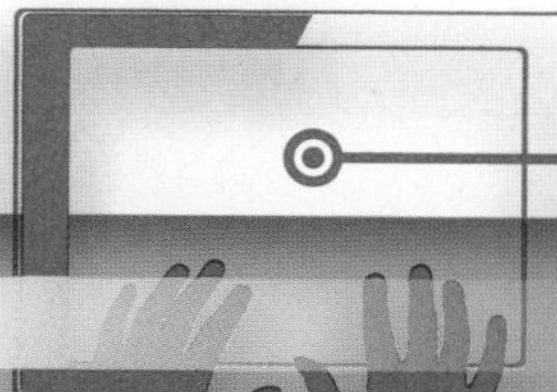

1.3 OPPORTUNITY COST AND CHOICE

Learning Objectives

LO1 Define opportunity cost.

LO2 Follow guidelines for making choices.

LO3 Analyze the opportunity cost of attending college.

Key Terms

In Your World

Think about a decision you just made: the decision to read this chapter rather than study for another course, hang out with friends, play sports, play video games, watch TV, go online, get some sleep, or do something else. Suppose your best alternative to reading this now is getting some sleep. The cost of reading this chapter is passing up the opportunity to sleep. Because of scarcity, whenever you make a choice, you must pass up another opportunity. You experience an opportunity cost.

OPPORTUNITY COST

LO1 Define opportunity cost.

What do you mean when you talk about the cost of something? Isn't it what you must give up or go without to get that thing? The **opportunity cost** of the chosen item or activity is *the value of the best alternative you must pass up*. You can think of opportunity cost as the *opportunity lost*. Sometimes opportunity cost can be measured in dollar terms. However, as you shall see, money usually captures only part of opportunity cost.

Nothing Better to Do?

How many times have you heard people say they did something because they "had nothing better to do"? They actually mean they had no alternative more attractive than the one they chose. Yet, according to the idea of opportunity cost, people *always* do what they do because they had nothing better to do. The choice selected seems, at the time, preferable to any other possible alternative. You are reading this page right now because you have nothing better to do.

Estimate Opportunity Cost

Only the individual decision maker can select the most attractive alternative. You, the chooser, seldom know the actual value of the best alternative you gave up, because that alternative is "the road not taken."

If you give up an evening of pizza and conversation with friends to work on a term paper, you will never know exactly what you gave up. You know only what you *expected*. You expected the value of working on that paper to exceed the value of the best alternative.

opportunity cost The value of the best alternative passed up for the chosen item or activity

Opportunity Cost Varies

Your opportunity cost depends on your alternatives. This is why you are less likely to study on a Saturday night than on a Tuesday night. On Saturday night, the opportunity cost of studying is higher because your alternatives are more attractive than they are on a Tuesday night when there's less to do.

What if you go to a movie on Saturday night? Your opportunity cost is the value of the best alternative you gave up, which might be attending a basketball game. Studying on Saturday night might rank well down the list of alternatives for you—perhaps ahead of cleaning your room but behind watching TV.

Opportunity cost is a personal thing, but in some cases, estimating a dollar cost for goods and services may provide a good measure. For example, the opportunity cost of a personal DVD player is the benefit of spending that $100 on the best alternative. In other cases, the dollar cost may omit some important elements, particularly the value of the time involved. For example, going to a movie costs not just the ticket price but the time and travel expense to get there, watch the movie, and get home.

CHECKPOINT What is opportunity cost, and why does it vary with circumstances?

CHOOSE AMONG ALTERNATIVES

LO2 Follow guidelines for making choices.

You now have some idea what opportunity cost is and how it can vary depending on the situation. To apply this concept to the specific economic decisions you make, follow these guidelines: calculate opportunity cost, consider your time involved, and ignore sunk costs.

Calculate Opportunity Cost

Economists assume that your rational self-interest will lead you to select the most valued alternative. This does not mean you must calculate the value of all possible alternatives. Because acquiring information about alternatives is costly and time-consuming, you usually make choices based on limited or even faulty information. Indeed, some choices may turn out to be poor ones: You went for a picnic but it rained. Your new shoes pinch your toes. The movie was terrible.

Regret about lost opportunities is captured in the common expression "coulda, woulda, shoulda." At the time you made the choice, however, you believed you were making the best use of all your scarce resources, including the time required to gather information and assess your alternatives. You assess alternatives as long as the expected marginal benefit of gathering more information about your options exceeds the expected marginal cost. In other words, you try to do the best you can for yourself.

Consider Your Time

The sultan of Brunei is among the world's richest people, with wealth estimated at $20 billion based on huge oil revenues that flow into his tiny country. He built two palaces, one for each wife. Supported by his great wealth, the sultan appears to have overcome the economic problem caused by scarcity. However, although he can buy just about whatever he wants, his time to enjoy these goods and services is scarce. If he pursues one activity, he cannot at the same time do something else. Each activity he undertakes has an opportunity cost. The sultan must choose from among the competing uses of his scarcest resource, time. You, too, face a time constraint, especially when term papers and exams claim your time.

Ignore Sunk Cost

Suppose you have just finished shopping and are wheeling your shopping cart to the checkout. How do you decide which line to join? You pick the one you think will take less time. What if, after waiting ten minutes in a line that barely moves, you notice a cashier has opened another line and invites you to check out. Do you switch to the open line, or do you think, "I've already spent ten minutes in this line. I'm staying here"?

The ten minutes you waited represents a **sunk cost**, which is a cost you have already incurred and cannot recover, regardless of what you do now. You should ignore sunk cost in making economic choices and should switch to the newly opened line.

Economic decision makers should consider only those costs that are affected by their choice. Sunk costs are not recoverable. Therefore, sunk costs are irrelevant and should be ignored. Likewise, you should walk out on a boring movie, even if admission cost you $10. The irrelevance of sunk costs is underscored by the proverb,

sunk cost A cost you have already paid and cannot recover, regardless of what you do now

Math in Economics

Common Core The Number System

In most jobs, when you work more than 40 hours a week, you are paid a premium hourly rate. The overtime premium is a multiple of your regular hourly wage. You can calculate the amount you will earn for working overtime by multiplying the number of hours worked (in excess of 40) times your regular hourly wage times the overtime premium (1.5 in most situations).

EXAMPLE Calculate the total amount an employee will earn if her regular wage rate is $12.20 per hour and she works 6 hours of overtime with an overtime premium of 1.5.

SOLUTION Multiply 6 times $12.20 times 1.5.

6 × $12.20 × 1.5 = $109.80

Practice the Skill Calculate the total amount earned for working overtime hours in each of the following exercises. Write answers to the nearest cent.

1. William worked 7 hours of overtime. His regular wage rate is $9.70 per hour and the overtime premium is 1.5.
2. Tiesha worked 5.5 hours of overtime. Her regular wage rate is $13.30 per hour and the overtime premium is 1.5.
3. How much would you need to be paid per hour to give up your Saturday and work an extra eight hours? How much would you earn? How does this question demonstrate the concept of opportunity cost?

"There's no sense crying over spilt milk." The milk has already spilled. What you do now cannot change that fact. Or, as Shakespeare's Lady Macbeth put it: "Things without all remedy should be without regard: what's done is done." Get over it.

CHECKPOINT Explain the guidelines for choosing among alternatives.

THE OPPORTUNITY COST OF COLLEGE

LO3 Analyze the opportunity cost of attending college.

You can apply the concepts you have learned about opportunity cost and choice in deciding whether or not to go to college. What will be your opportunity cost of attending college full-time? What will be the most valued alternative you must give up to attend college? If you already know what kind of job you can get with a high school education, you have a fair idea of the income you must give up to attend college.

Forgone Earnings

You may think that if you do not go to college, you could find a job paying $20,000 a year, after taxes. But wait a minute. Don't many college students also work part-time during the school year and full-time during the summer? If you do the same, suppose you could earn $8,000 a year, after taxes.

Thus, by attending college you give up the $20,000 you could earn from a full-time job, yet you could still earn $8,000 from part-time and summer work. Your annual earnings would be $12,000 lower ($20,000 minus $8,000) if you attend college. One part of your opportunity cost of college is the value of what you could have purchased with that additional $12,000 in income.

Direct Costs of College

You also need to consider the direct costs of college itself. Suppose you must pay $9,000 a year for tuition, fees, and books at a public college (paying out-of-state rates would add about $10,000 to that, and attending a private college would add about $20,000). The opportunity cost of paying for tuition, fees, and books is the value of the goods and services that money could have purchased otherwise.

NET Bookmark

To examine whether college would be a sensible investment for you, try Professor Jane Leuthold's College Choice program. This program will guide you through applying economic tools such as cost-benefit analysis to determine whether it makes economic sense to enroll in a college program of your choosing. Access the website shown below and click on the link for Chapter 1.

www.cengage.com/school/contecon

Other College Costs

What about room and board? Expenses for room and board are not an opportunity cost of college because, even if you did not attend college, you would still need to live somewhere and eat something, though these costs could be higher at college. Likewise, whether or not you attend college, you and your family would still pay for your personal items such as movies, cell-phone service, clothing, toiletries, and laundry. Such expenses are not an opportunity cost of attending college. They are personal expenses that arise regardless of what you do. So, for simplicity, assume that room, board, and personal expenses will be the same whether or not you attend college.

The forgone earnings of $12,000 plus the $9,000 for tuition, fees, and books yield an opportunity cost of $21,000 per year for a student paying in-state rates at a public college. The opportunity cost jumps to about $31,000 for those paying out-of-state rates at a public college and to about $41,000 for those at a private college. Scholarships, but not loans, would reduce your opportunity cost.

Other-Things-Constant Assumption

This analysis assumes that all other things are constant. If you expect college to be more painful than your best alternative, then the opportunity cost of attending college is even higher. In other words, if you expect to find college difficult, boring, and in most ways more unpleasant than a full-time job, then your money cost understates your opportunity cost. You not only pay the dollar cost of college, but you also must give up a more pleasant quality of life. If, however, you think college will be more enjoyable than a full-time job, then the dollar cost overstates your opportunity cost—the next best alternative involves a less satisfying quality of life.

Investigate Your Local Economy

Compare your opportunity cost for attending the community college that is nearest to your home with that of attending the nearest four-year state university. List the assumptions you make for each alternative such as the cost of driving to school or living on campus. Compare your findings with those of other students in your class.

Digital Vision/Getty Images

Have you made your decision about whether or not to attend college? If not, applying this section of the textbook to your own situation will help you weigh more carefully the opportunity costs of this important decision.

Evidently, many young people view college as a wise investment in their future, even though college is costly and perhaps even difficult for some. College graduates on average earn about twice as much per year as high-school graduates.

Still, college is not for everyone. Some find the opportunity cost too high. For example, Tiger Woods, once an economics major at Stanford University, dropped out after two years to earn a fortune in professional golf. Some college athletes who believe they are ready for professional basketball leave college after their first year. Most pro tennis players and many singers and actors skip college. However, for most of you, the opportunity cost of attending college isn't nearly as high.

CHECKPOINT **How do you measure the opportunity cost of attending college?**

© mustafahacalaki / istockphoto_11915252

Span the Globe

Entrepreneurial Gaming

In 2007 Harvard Business School (HBS) students Daniel Kafie, Mario Schlosser, and Joshua Kushner created Vostu, a social networking site for the Latin American market, specifically Brazil. The venture was inspired by Facebook, also started by a Harvard student. Launched with an initial investment by Intel Capital, the company struggled to make a profit. Within two years, the student entrepreneurs had gone through three versions of the idea. Following their first attempt, they switched to a platform designed to host other social networks. By 2009, the company focused specifically on creating social games. Since then Vostu has grown from 12 to 400 employees, most involved in designing games in the company's Buenos Aires office. Concentrating on social games played on Orkut, the popular social networking site in Brazil and Latin America Google's equivalent of Facebook, the company now claims 22 million players.

The career goals of the three co-founders differed from those of typical HBS students. Most HBS students aspire to "taking the big job or following what other people have done," Schlosser said. For Kafie, HBS was a place "to meet really interesting people and to see if there's an opportunity to work on some sort of entrepreneurship idea." According to Kafie, "Entrepreneurship is not about being smart, analytical (or) being the best in one field. It's about being persistent."

Think Critically **Was there an opportunity cost to the three founders of Vostu because they did not follow the more traditional route upon graduating from Harvard Business School? How does their persistence illustrate the concept of sunk cost?**

Source: Dizik, Alina, "Entrepreneurs learn the rule s of the game – Using business knowhow gained at Harvard, three alumni have founded a thriving online venture," *The Financial Times* (London, England) March 21, 2011.

1.3 ASSESSMENT

Think Critically

1. Why must there be an opportunity cost for every choice you make?
2. Why isn't the opportunity cost of using your time to do homework always the same?
3. What factor forces even people who are very wealthy to face opportunity costs?
4. Why should consumers ignore costs they have already paid when making decisions?
5. What is the greatest cost of attending college at in-state public institutions?

Graphing Exercises

6. Harold sells snowblowers at his hardware store in North Dakota. Although he never changes his price, his sales vary throughout the year. The following table shows his sales in each month of last year. Draw a line graph that demonstrates these data.
7. Explain how the graph you drew for exercise 6 shows that the value of buying a snowblower changes over time. What does this have to do with the opportunity cost of other uses for limited funds?

HAROLD'S SNOWBLOWER SALES

Month	Sales	Month	Sales
January	13	July	0
February	11	August	0
March	3	September	8
April	0	October	32
May	0	November	38
June	0	December	21

Make Academic Connections

8. **Entrepreneurship** Wilma owns a 200-acre farm. She could plant either beans or tomatoes. If the weather is sunny and there is enough rain, she can earn $400 per acre of tomatoes. However, if it is dry or cloudy, tomatoes may earn her no profit at all. Beans are hardy and will grow well unless the weather is truly awful. Wilma can count on earning $200 per acre from beans. Explain why Wilma cannot be sure of the opportunity cost of any decision she might make. What do you think she will choose to do? Why?
9. **Office Technology** Ms. Morra teaches classes in office technology. Her school board has approved $10,000 to buy new computers to replace her old, outdated models. For this amount she can buy 20 low-end computers that just meet her student's current needs, or she can purchase 10 computers with greater speed and capabilities that she would like her students to learn to use. What is her opportunity cost for either of these choices?

TeamWork

Working in small teams, identify and list the opportunity cost you would pay to accept a babysitting job next Saturday evening. You will be paid $30 but must give up other uses for your time. Compare the opportunity costs identified. Are they of equal value? Why are some team members likely to accept the job while others won't? Report your results to the class.

Glassmaking in Jamestown

Despite failed attempts to establish a colony in the New World, in 1606 King James I of England granted a charter for this purpose to the Virginia Company of London. Because earlier enterprises had been expensive, the required funds were raised through a joint stock company. Colonists were instructed to settle land between the 34th and 41st parallels. The three ships carrying 104 colonists arrived at the site of Jamestown Island on May 13, 1607.

Colonists provided labor for the company. Lured by the promise of easy gold, many of them were not prepared for the ordeal that followed. Many of the colonists were younger sons of wealthy families who were not accustomed to hard work, and they struggled to survive. Still, these men perceived their opportunity cost as being small because they stood to inherit little at home due to the inheritance custom in England at the time. Following this custom, called primogeniture, the eldest son would inherit the family's entire estate, so younger sons would leave the country in search of their own land. The colony seemed a way for them to gain the land and prominence they could not obtain in England. Wealthy colonists who provided their own armor and weapons were paid in land, dividends, or additional shares of stock. Less-well-off colonists received clothes, food, and arms from the company, and then after seven years, they received land.

The Virginia Company was still recruiting colonists when Captain Christopher Newport returned to England, bringing word of a struggling colony. Although disappointed that gold and silver did not lie on the beach or grow on the trees, the entrepreneurs of the Virginia Company still saw profitable opportunities in various industries. They believed the colony could take advantage of the land's natural resources and manufacture products for sale in England. One such product was glass. Demand for glass products in England in the early seventeenth century was growing. However, scarce resources in England limited the growth of the industry. England's forests were being depleted, and it took a lot of wood—about a week of burning two to three cords per day—to get the furnaces hot enough to produce glass. The New World, with its unlimited forests, appeared an ideal spot for a glassmaking industry.

Glassmaking in England also suffered from a shortage of labor, as few people were skilled in the craft. Although some glassmakers had come from foreign countries, England could not meet the demand for glass. Much of it had to be imported, leading the company to believe that a Virginia-based enterprise could produce glass more cheaply. Because glassmakers in England were doing very well, their opportunity cost of leaving the country for the uncertainty of a new and dangerous land was too high.

Countries that exported large amounts of glass were better places to recruit workers. Among the early settlers in Virginia in the summer of 1608 were eight Germans and Poles for the glassmaking industry. The colony produced some glass, but the enterprise was short lived. Workers had little time to devote to their industry because they were too busy trying to survive. When the newly appointed governor of Virginia arrived on May 24, 1610, he found that 90 percent of the colonists had died; with them had died America's first industry.

Think Critically **Devise an economic theory that could have guided the Virginia Company's decision to begin a colony in the New World. What questions and variables might these entrepreneurs have considered? What might their assumptions have been? What might their hypotheses have been?**

Chapter 1 Summary

1.1 The Economic Problem

A. Economic choices are necessary because of our unlimited desires and the scarce supply of productive resources available to satisfy them.

B. There are three basic types of productive resources. Human resources is the broad category of human efforts, both physical and mental, used to produce goods and services. Natural resources, so-called "gifts of nature, can be divided into renewable resources and exhaustible resources. Capital goods include all human creations used to produce goods and services.

C. Both goods and services are able to satisfy some human desires. Goods can be seen, felt, and touched but services cannot. Goods and services are scarce if their price exceeds zero. Because goods and services are produced using scarce resources, they are themselves scarce. Goods or services that are truly free are not a concern of economics.

ASK THE EXPERT

www.cengage.com/school/contecon

Why are economists always talking about money and wealth?

1.2 Economic Theory

A. Economic theories, or economic models, are simplifications of economic reality that are used to make predictions about the real world. When economic theories are constructed, they are based on simplifying assumptions that include other things remaining constant and rational self-interest.

B. Economic choice usually involves a change in the status quo. The only relevant factors are the additional benefits and additional costs resulting from that change. Focusing on the effects of a change to the status quo is called marginal analysis. A rational decision maker will change the status quo as long as the expected marginal benefit from the change exceeds the expected marginal cost. Economics can be seen from two perspectives. Microeconomics concerns how choices by individuals determine the price and quantity in particular markets. Macroeconomics focuses on the condition of the economy as a whole. There are four types of participants in the economy: households, firms, governments, and the rest of the world.

C. Markets are the means by which buyers and sellers carry out exchange. By bringing together the two sides of exchange, demand and supply, markets determine price and quantity.

D. An economic system can be represented by a simple circular-flow diagram that includes households, firms, resource markets, and product markets. There are flows of goods, services, and resources that move in one direction through this model, and flows of money that move in the opposite direction.

1.3 Opportunity Cost and Choice

A. Whenever an economic decision is made, an opportunity cost is involved. Opportunity cost is the value of the best alternative to a choice that is made. It is often impossible to know the true value of the best alternative not selected. Decisions are based on the expected opportunity cost of a choice. Opportunity costs of a decision vary with circumstances. Calculating the value of an opportunity cost requires time and information. Even the wealthiest people in the world still face a scarcity of time. Their use of time involves an opportunity cost.

B. When making economic choices, calculate opportunity cost, consider your time involved, and ignore sunk costs.

CHAPTER 1 ASSESSMENT

Review Economic Terms

a. capital goods
b. economics
c. entrepreneur
d. good
e. human resources
f. marginal
g. markets
h. natural resources
i. opportunity cost
j. productive resources
k. scarcity
l. service
m. sunk cost

Match the terms with the definitions. Some terms will not be used.

_____ 1. An item you can see, feel, and touch that requires scarce resources to produce and satisfies human wants

_____ 2. The means by which buyers and sellers carry out exchange

_____ 3. The broad category of human efforts, both physical and mental, used to produce goods and services

_____ 4. The value of the best alternative passed up for the chosen item or activity

_____ 5. The study of how people use their scarce resources to satisfy their unlimited wants

_____ 6. All human creations used to produce goods and services

_____ 7. Something not physical that requires scarce resources to produce and satisfies human wants

_____ 8. A profit-seeker who develops a new product or process and assumes the risk of profit or loss

_____ 9. So-called "gifts of nature" used to produce goods and services

_____ 10. Incremental, additional, extra, or one more; refers to a change in an economic variable, a change in the status quo

Review Economic Concepts

11. **True or False** Scarcity exists because our supplies of productive resources are limited.

12. Which of the following is an example of a natural resource?
    a. lumber used to build a house
    b. a tree standing in a forest
    c. a carpenter who installs new cabinets
    d. gasoline you put in your car

13. A(n) ________?________ is a person who tries to earn a profit by dreaming up a new product or finding a better way to produce an existing one.

14. When a firm's revenue from sales exceeds its cost of production, it will earn a(n) ________?________.

15. **True or False** Services are different from goods because they are not able to satisfy human desires.

16. Which of the following is an exhaustible resource?
    a. crude oil in the ground
    b. corn growing in a field
    c. water in the ocean
    d. fish in the ocean

17. **True or False** When you play football in a public park you receive a free good because you do not pay to use the park.

18. A(n) ________?________ is a simplification of economic reality that is used to make predictions about the real world.

19. When economists use the other-things-constant assumption they are trying to
    a. consider only variables that interest them.
    b. duplicate reality in their ideas.
    c. establish economic laws that will last indefinitely.
    d. combine several ideas into one.

20. **True or False** In general, the assumption of rational self-interest means that individuals try to maximize the expected benefit achieved with a given cost.

21. ________?________ statements concern what is.

22. **True or False** The assumption of rational self-interest rules out concerns for others.

23. Which of the following is a normative statement?
    a. On average, Rose works 30 hours a week.
    b. Rose is paid $8.00 per hour for her labor.
    c. Rose pays 7.65 percent of her earnings in Social Security tax.
    d. Rose's hourly pay is too low.

24. **True or False** Most of the disagreement among economists involves debates over positive statements.

25. A rational decision maker will change the status quo as long as the expected ________?________ benefit from the change exceeds the expected ________?________ cost.

26. Which of the following is an example of microeconomics?
    a. Tyrone received a 5 percent raise in his wage last year.
    b. On average, prices in the economy increased by 2.3 percent last year.
    c. The federal government borrowed more than $1,000 billion last year.
    d. U.S. businesses invested 3.1 percent more last year than in the previous year.

27. **True or False** Opportunity cost is the value of the best alternative that you pass up when you make a choice.

28. Which of the following is Yo-chee's opportunity cost of spending $10 to go to a movie with her friends?
    a. the value of the $10 she spent
    b. the value of the time she worked to earn the $10
    c. the value of the enjoyment she received from seeing the movie
    d. the value of the pizza she would have bought if she had not gone to the movie

29. **True or False** If you have nothing better to do when you make a choice, there is no opportunity cost of your decision.

30. Which of the following would not be part of the opportunity cost of attending college?
    a. other uses of the money used to pay college tuition
    b. other uses of the time used to study and attend classes
    c. other uses of extra income earned because of the college education
    d. other uses of funds used to pay higher costs for room and board while attending college

31. **True or False** The value of the opportunity cost of a particular choice is the same for all people.

32. **True or False** The opportunity cost you would incur for cleaning your room would probably be different on Saturday evening than on Tuesday afternoon.

33. Which of the following is a sunk cost that should be ignored when deciding whether or not to buy a new computer over the Internet?
    a. the $50 delivery charge
    b. the $40 monthly payment you already agreed to make to connect to the Internet
    c. the extra $200 you might pay to get a large monitor
    d. the $150 two-year service contract you could decide to buy

Apply Economic Concepts

34. **Circular-Flow Model** Sketch a copy of the circular-flow model on your own paper. Place each of the following in the correct location on your model.
    a. Brad has a pizza delivered as he watches Monday Night Football.
    b. The Sony Corporation produces a new TV.
    c. Brad works at a local drugstore.
    d. Brad buys a new TV from a Sears store.

Circular-Flow Model

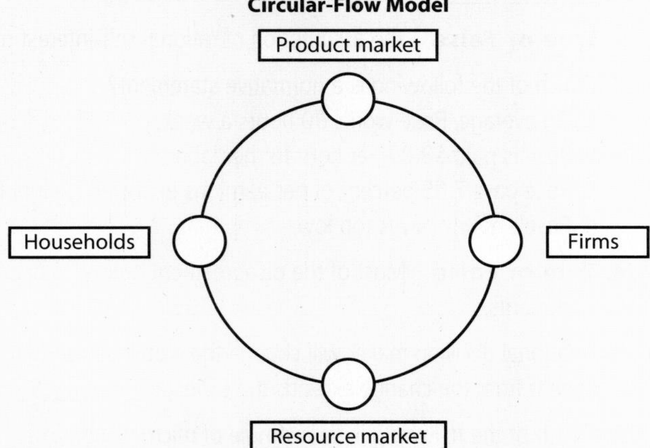

35. **Opportunity Cost** Your uncle has offered to buy you either a new computer or a good-quality bicycle as a graduation present. The prices of both items are the same. Write an essay that identifies which gift you would choose and describes the opportunity cost that would result from your choice. Why might other people make a different choice? Why would you be at least as well off if, as an additional option, your uncle also offers you the cash?

36. **Rational Self-Interest** Describe something you have recently done to help someone else. Explain how the action you took was based on rational self-interest. What opportunity cost did you incur? If the value of your opportunity cost had been much greater, would you have still taken the action? Why or why not?

37. **21st Century Skills: Critical Thinking and Problem Solving** A bakery purchased a new oven that allowed it to eliminate six of its employees and still produce as many loaves of bread as it had in the past. Write a paragraph that describes this change in a way that makes it clear you understand the terms *productive resources, human resources,* and *capital goods.*

Digging Deeper

with Economics e-Collection

Economics is always in the news. The Digging Deeper activity provides you the opportunity to research the Gale Economics e-Collection, a database of articles about economic topics from popular newspapers, magazines, and journals. Access this e-Collection through the URL below. To see the broad scope of economics topics covered in the media, type in the word "economics" under the Keyword or Subject tab. Refine your results by typing one of the key terms from Chapter 1. (The key terms appear at the beginning of each lesson and are printed in blue on the pages.) Choose an article, read it, and then write a one-paragraph summary about it. Also look through the table of contents of your textbook to find where it addresses this topic. Be prepared to discuss your article in class.

www.cengage.com/school/contecon

CHAPTER 2

Economic Systems and Tools

CONSIDER ...

- Can you save time by applying economic principles to your family chores?
- Why are economies around the world becoming more market oriented?
- How much can an economy produce with the resources available?
- Why is experience a good teacher?
- Why is fast food so fast?

Point your browser

www.cengage.com/school/contecon

Stockbyte/Jupiter Images; Background image: dibrova/Shutterstock.com

2.1 ECONOMIC QUESTIONS AND ECONOMIC SYSTEMS

Key Terms

economic system 34
pure market economy 35
pure command economy 38
mixed economy 39
market economy 39
transitional economy 40
traditional economy 41

Learning Objectives

LO1 Identify the three questions all economic systems must answer.

LO2 Describe a pure market economy, and identify its problems.

LO3 Describe a pure command economy, and identify its problems.

LO4 Compare mixed, market, transitional, and traditional economies.

In Your World

What should the economy produce? How should it produce this output? For whom should it produce? More than 200 countries around the world attempt to answer these three economic questions, all using somewhat different economic systems. One way to distinguish among economic systems is to focus on the role of government. Imagine a range from the most free to the most government-controlled economic system. A pure market economy stands at one end of the range, and a pure command economy stands at the other. Although no economy in the world reflects either extreme, knowing the features and problems of each will help you understand differences in economies around the world.

THE THREE ECONOMIC QUESTIONS

LO1 Identify the three economic questions.

All economies must answer three questions:

1. What goods and services will be produced?
2. How will they be produced?
3. For whom will they be produced?

An **economic system** is the set of mechanisms and institutions that resolves the *what, how,* and *for whom* questions. Some standards used to distinguish among economic systems are

1. Who owns the resources?
2. What decision-making process is used to allocate resources and products?
3. What types of incentives guide economic decision makers?

What Goods and Services Will Be Produced?

economic system The set of mechanisms and institutions that resolves the what, how, and for whom questions for an economy

Most people take for granted the many choices that go into deciding what gets produced—everything from which new kitchen appliances are introduced and which novelists get published, to which roads are built. Although different economies resolve these and millions of other questions using different decision-making rules and mechanisms, all economies must somehow decide what to produce.

How Will Goods and Services Be Produced?

The economic system must determine how output is to be produced. Which resources should be used, and how should they be combined to make each product? How much labor should be used and at what skill levels? What kinds of machines should be used? What type of fertilizer grows the best strawberries? Should the office complex be built in the city or closer to the interstate highway? Millions of individual decisions determine which resources are employed and how these resources are combined.

For Whom Will Goods and Services Be Produced?

Who will consume the goods and services produced? The economic system must determine how to distribute the fruits of production among the population. Should equal amounts be provided to everyone? Should it be first-come, first-served, so those willing to wait in line the longest get more? Should goods be allocated according to height? Weight? Religion? Age? Gender? Race? Looks? Strength? Lottery? Majority rule? Political connections? The value of resources supplied? The question "For whom will goods and services be produced?" often is referred to as the *distribution* question.

Interdependent Questions

The three economic questions are closely related. The answer to one depends very much on the answers to the others. For example, an economy that distributes goods and services in uniform amounts to everyone will, no doubt, answer the what-will-be-produced question differently from an economy that allows each person to choose a unique bundle of goods and services.

CHECKPOINT

What three questions must all economic systems answer?

PURE MARKET ECONOMY

LO2
Describe a pure market economy, and identify its problems.

In a **pure market economy**, private firms account for all production. There is no government. Features of this economic system include the private ownership of all resources and the coordination of economic activity based on the prices generated in free, competitive markets. Any income from selling resources goes exclusively to the resource owners.

pure market economy
An economic system with no government so that private firms account for all production

The Invisible Hand of Markets

Resource owners have *property rights* to the use of their resources and are free to supply those resources to the highest bidder. Producers are free to make and sell whatever they believe will be profitable. Consumers are free to buy whatever they can afford. All this voluntary buying and selling is coordinated by competitive markets that are free from any government regulations.

HultonArchive/iStockphoto.com

Adam Smith

Market prices guide resources to their most productive use and channel goods to those consumers who value them the most. Markets answer the what, how, and for whom questions. Markets transmit information about relative scarcity, provide incentives to producers and consumers, and distribute income among resource suppliers.

No single individual or small group coordinates these activities. Rather, the voluntary choices of many buyers and sellers responding only to their individual incentives direct resources and products to those who value them the most.

According to Adam Smith (1723–1790), market forces coordinate production as if by an "invisible hand." Smith argued that *although each individual pursues his or her self-interest, the "invisible hand" of market competition promotes the general welfare.* Voluntary choices in competitive markets answer the questions *what, how,* and *for whom.*

Problems with Pure Market Economies

A pure market economy offers resource owners the freedom and the incentive to get the most from their resources. However, markets do not always work well on their own. The most notable *market failures* include

ESSENTIAL QUESTION

Standard CEE 3: Allocation

Different methods can be used to allocate goods and services. People acting individually or collectively must choose which methods to use to allocate different kinds of goods and services.

Pharmacy: Photodisc/Getty Images; Grocery store: iofoto/Shutterstock.com

With what activity is the economic question "For whom will goods and services be produced?" typically associated?

1. **Difficulty Enforcing Property Rights** Market activity depends on people using their scarce resources to maximize their satisfaction. However, what if you were repeatedly robbed of your paycheck on your way home from work? What if, after you worked a week in a new job, your employer refused to pay you? Markets would break down if you could not safeguard your property or enforce contracts. In a pure market economy, there is no government, so there is no central authority to protect property rights, enforce contracts, and otherwise ensure that the "rules of the game" are followed.
2. **Some People Have Few Resources to Sell** Due to poor education, disability, discrimination, the time demands of caregiving, or bad luck, among many other reasons, some people have few resources to sell in a market economy. Because markets do not guarantee even a minimum level of income, some people would have difficulty surviving.
3. **Some Firms Try to Monopolize Markets** Although the "invisible hand" of market competition usually promotes the general welfare, some producers may try to monopolize the market by either unfairly driving out competitors or by conspiring with competitors to increase prices. With less competition, firms can charge a higher price to earn more profit. Thus, firms have a profit incentive to monopolize a market.
4. **No Public Goods** Private firms do not produce so-called *public goods*, such as national defense. Once produced, public goods are available to all, regardless of who pays and who does not pay for them. Suppliers cannot easily prevent those who fail to pay for a public good from benefiting from the good. Because firms cannot sell public goods profitably, they are not produced in a pure market economy.
5. **Externalities** Market prices reflect the benefits to buyers and the costs to sellers. However, some production and consumption affect third parties—those not directly involved. For example, a paper mill fouls the air local residents must breathe, but the market price of paper fails to reflect such costs. Because the pollution costs are outside—or external to—the market transaction, they are called *externalities*. Private markets fail to account for externalities. Because of this type of market failure, even market economies allow a role for government.
6. **Economic Fluctuations** Market economies experience alternating periods of expansion and recession, especially in employment and production. *Economic fluctuations* reflect the rise and fall of economic activity relative to the long-term growth trend of the economy. During recessions, jobs disappear and unemployment increases, as happened during the recession of 2008–2009.

Photodisc/Getty Images

Why does the market system fail to account for problems such as the health effects of air pollution from a paper mill? How can such problems be solved for a society?

What is a pure market economy, and what are its problems? **CHECKPOINT**

PURE COMMAND ECONOMY

LO3 Describe a pure command economy, and identify its problems.

In a **pure command economy** all resources are government-owned and government officials coordinate production. At least in theory, ownership of all resources is public, or communal. That is why a command economy is sometimes called *communism.* Central planners answer the three economic questions by spelling out how many missiles, how many homes, and how much bread to produce. Central planners also decide how to produce these goods and who should get them.

The Visible Hand of Central Planners

Rather than rely on competitive markets, central planners direct the allocation of resources and products. Central planners may believe that market economies produce too many consumer goods and too few capital goods, especially military hardware. They also may believe that central planning yields a fairer distribution of goods across households than does a market economy.

In a pure command economy, the central authority, or state, controls all resources, including labor. Central planners direct production through state-run enterprises, which usually face no competition. Some goods and services are rationed, meaning that each household gets a certain amount. For example, each household gets so many square feet of living space. Other products are allocated based on prices central planners set. Prices, once set, tend to be inflexible.

Problems with Command Economies

A pure command economy ideally produces the combination of products that society desires. But this economic system has serious flaws. Because of these flaws, countries have modified command economies to allow a greater role for private ownership and market competition. Most notable are the following six failures.

1. **Consumers Get Low Priority** Central plans may reflect the preferences of central planners rather than those of consumers. Central planners decide what gets produced and who should consume the goods. When goods are rationed or offered for an inflexible price, severe shortages can result. Evidence of a consumer goods shortage includes empty store shelves, long waiting lines, and the "tips"—or bribes—shop operators expect for supplying scarce goods.

2. **Little Freedom of Choice** Because central planners are responsible for all production decisions, the variety of products tends to be narrower than in a market economy. Households in command economies not only have less choice about what to consume, they also have less freedom in other economic decisions. Central planners, who in many cases are unelected dictators, may decide where people live and where they work. For example, North Koreans need government permission to travel outside their own town.

3. **Central Planning Can Be Inefficient** Running an economy is so complicated that central planners often end up directing resources inefficiently. Consider all that's involved in growing and distributing farm products. Central planners must decide what to grow, what resources to employ (who, for example, should

pure command economy An economic system in which all resources are government-owned and all production is directed by the central plans of government

become farmers), and who gets to consume the harvest (should it be rationed or sold for a set price). Mistakes along the way result in inefficiencies and waste. For example, the former Soviet Union had a command economy. About one-third of the harvest there reportedly rotted on its way to consumers.

4. **Resources Owned by the Central Authority Are Sometimes Wasted** Because resources are owned by the central authority, or government, nobody in particular has an incentive to see that resources are employed in their highest-valued use. Some resources are wasted. For example, Soviet workers usually had little regard for government equipment. Workers would dismantle new trucks or tractors for parts, or send working equipment to scrap plants. In contrast, Soviet citizens had much more incentive to take good care of their personal property. For example, personal cars were so well maintained that they lasted more than 20 years on average—twice the official projected life of an automobile.
5. **Environmental Damage** In theory, a command economy, with its focus on "the common good," should take better care of the environment than a market economy. In practice, however, directors of state enterprises often are more concerned with meeting production goals set by the central planners. For example, in its drive for military dominance, the former Soviet government set off 125 nuclear explosions above ground. The resulting bomb craters filled with water, forming contaminated lakes. Thousands of barrels of nuclear waste were dumped into Soviet rivers and seas.
6. **No Role for Entrepreneurs** In a system where government owns the resources and makes the decisions, there is no role for profit-seeking entrepreneurs. Because there is no private property, there are no private firms and no profit. With no profit incentive, no individual has a reason to develop new products or find more efficient ways to make existing products. Lacking entrepreneurs, a command economy tends to be less innovative, less efficient, and offers fewer consumer choices than a market economy.

CHECKPOINT

What is a pure command economy, and what are its problems?

MIXED, TRANSITIONAL, AND TRADITIONAL ECONOMIES

LO4 Compare mixed, market, transitional, and traditional economies.

No country on Earth represents either a market economy or command economy in its pure form. Economic systems have become more alike over time. The role of government has increased in market economies, and the role of markets has increased in command economies. As a result, most economies now mix central planning with competitive markets and are called **mixed economies**.

mixed economy An economic system that mixes central planning with competitive markets

market economy Describes the U.S. economic system, where markets play a relatively large role

Mixed Economy

The United States is a mixed economy. Because markets play a relatively large role, it also is considered a **market economy**. Government accounts for about one-third of all U.S. economic activity.

NET Bookmark

The *CIA World Factbook* provides brief descriptions of all the world's economies. Access this website through the URL shown below. Choose one country and identify its economy. Write a paragraph explaining the characteristics of the country's economy.

www.cengage.com/school/contecon

Government also regulates the U.S. private sector in a variety of ways. For example, local zoning boards determine lot sizes, home sizes, and the types of industries allowed. Federal bodies regulate workplace safety, environmental quality, competition in markets, and many other activities.

Although both ends of the economic spectrum have moved toward the center, the market system has gained more converts in recent decades. Consider countries that have been cut in two by political and economic ideology. In such cases, the economies began with similar resources and income levels right after the split. Over time the market-oriented economies produced a much higher standard of living than the command economies. For example, income per capita in Taiwan, a market-oriented economy after it split from China, averages about four times that of China, a command economy. As another example, income per capita in market-oriented South Korea is about 15 times that of North Korea, perhaps the most centrally planned economy in the world and a country run by a dictator.

Consider the experience of the early colonists who in 1620 tried to establish Plymouth Colony. They first tried communal ownership of the land. That turned out badly. Crops were neglected and food shortages developed. After three years of near starvation, the system was changed so that each family was assigned its own private plot of land and allowed to keep whatever it grew. Crop yields increased sharply. The colonists learned that people take better care of what they grow individually. Common ownership often leads to common neglect.

Recognizing the power of property rights and markets to create incentives and provide information about scarcity, even some of the most diehard central planners now reluctantly accept some market activity. For example, about 20 percent of the world's population lives in China, which grows more market oriented each day. The former Soviet Union dissolved into 15 independent republics. Most are now trying to introduce more market incentives. Even North Korea has opened some special economic zones where market forces are allowed to operate with less government interference.

Transitional Economy

transitional economy
An economic system in the process of shifting from central planning to competitive markets

More than two dozen countries around the world are **transitional economies**, in the process of shifting from command economies to market economies. This transition involves converting government enterprises into private enterprises. This is a process called *privatization.* From Moscow to Beijing, from Hungary to Mongolia, the transition now under way will shape economies for decades to come.

Span the Globe

China's Latest Five-Year Plan

China began to reform its economy in 1978, moving from a closed, centrally planned command economy to one that embraces aspects of free enterprise. The reforms began in the agriculture sector and then moved to industry. They also affected the fiscal, banking, price-setting, and labor systems. Still, China's form of "state capitalism" retains major aspects of its old central planning system. It has continued its five-year plans and retained control over state-owned enterprises in sectors it considers important to economic security. Since beginning reform, China has sustained economic growth of more than 9 percent a year. It has become the world's largest exporter, and its economy has grown to become the second largest in the world. However, due to its large population, China's economy, in per capita terms, is still lower than average.

The Chinese government's latest five-year plan set a target of 7 percent growth a year. This is slightly down from previous plans and acknowledges the challenges that lie ahead. In the plan, China admitted the country relies too much on investment and not enough on consumer spending. It also acknowledged there is economic disparity between profits and wages, rich households and poor, coastal provinces and inland regions, and cities and countryside.

Think Critically **Have China's economic reforms succeeded in transforming it from a command economy to a mixed economy? Can China be classified as a transitional economy? Explain your answer.**

Source: "China's economic blueprint: Take five," *The Economist*, March 12, 2011.

Traditional Economy

Finally, some economic systems, known as **traditional economies**, are shaped largely by custom or religion. For example, caste systems in India restrict occupational choice. Charging interest is banned under Islamic law. Family relations also play significant roles in organizing and coordinating economic activity. In some countries, there is so little trust that businesses are reluctant to hire anyone who is not a family member. This restricts business growth.

Even in the United States some occupations still are dominated by women, and others by men, largely because of tradition. Your own pattern of consumption and choice of occupation may be influenced by some of these forces.

traditional economy An economic system shaped largely by custom or religion

CHECKPOINT

Compare mixed, market, transitional, and traditional economies.

2.1 ASSESSMENT

Think Critically

1. Compare the answers to the three basic economic questions in a pure market economy with the answers to these questions in a pure command economy. Present your answers using a spreadsheet or grid.
2. What did Adam Smith mean when he talked about an "invisible hand" that guides production in market economies?
3. Why are property rights important to the efficient working of a market economy?
4. In what sense are there traditional components in all types of economies, not just traditional economies? Provide examples.
5. What problems are likely to occur in command economies?
6. Why is the U.S. economic system sometimes called a "mixed market economy"?
7. What economic change is taking place in transitional economies?

Graphing Exercise

8. Draw a horizontal line. Label the left side of the line "Pure Market Economy" and the right side, "Pure Command Economy." Place each of the following nations on your line at a place that you think accurately represents the current state of its economy: United States, China, North Korea, Sweden, Russia, Mexico. Research the economies of the countries not familiar to you. Be prepared to explain your placements.

Make Academic Connections

9. **Government** When governments decide how to spend money, they often behave in a way similar to command economies. Investigate an important spending decision made by your local government. Write a one-page paper that identifies problems commonly encountered in command economies.
10. **Literature** Many novels have been written about the turmoil and difficulties associated with times of economic change. John Steinbeck's *The Grapes of Wrath* is a case in point. This book tells the story of poor Oklahoma farmers who were forced off their land to make way for large industrial farms during the Great Depression of the 1930s. Identify a literary work that describes how people have been affected by a recent economic change. Read either the book or a summary of it. Use it as an example to explain why important changes in the economy benefit some people more than others.

TeamWork

The United States is a mixed economy, containing features of both a market economy and a command economy. This textbook gives many examples of the central planning role of government in the U.S. economy. In small groups, brainstorm and list evidence of how the United States is a market economy. Compare the teams' results in class.

MOVERS AND SHAKERS

Steven Chu

U.S. Secretary of Energy

On December 11, 2008, President Barack Obama named Nobel Prize-winner Steven Chu, the son of Chinese immigrants, to be the U.S. Secretary of Energy. Confirmed by the Senate on January 20, 2009, Chu is the first Chinese-American to run the Department of Energy.

Chu's parents and other family members were outstanding scholars. Chu said. "Education in my family was not merely emphasized; it was our reason for living. Virtually all of our aunts and uncles had Ph.D.'s in science or engineering, and it was taken for granted that the next generation of Chu's were to follow the family tradition."

In college Chu, a self-proclaimed nerd, discovered he had a gift for physics. Later, while working at Bell Laboratories in Holmdel, New Jersey, he helped create the electron spectrometer. He also developed ways to cool and trap atoms using a laser. In 1997 Chu, Claude Cohen-Tannoudji, and William D. Phillips won the Nobel Prize in Physics for their work with atoms.

U.S. Department of Energy

Clean Energy Goals

Chu's work in renewable energy caught the attention of President Obama's administration. The administration made progress in energy conservation by establishing higher fuel economy standards and trying to restore America's leadership in the development of energy-efficiency technologies. Chu believes we need to take a "broad approach" to clean energy. His suggestions include

- Safely and responsibly produce more oil and gas from America's domestic resources.
- Provide consumers with choices that save money by saving energy.
- Invest in the next generation of innovative clean-energy technologies.
- Expand clean sources of electricity.

Chu said, "While we are on pace to double renewable energy generation, there is still much to be done. Our goal is to sponsor research and development that will lead to the deployment of renewable energy where the levelized cost of energy is competitive with the cost of any other form of energy."

Scientists like Chu are committed to helping reduce our dependence on foreign oil, increase our domestic energy production, and decrease energy waste.

Think Critically The U.S. Department of Energy is a federal agency that imposes regulations on the private sector. Its mission is to "promote America's energy security through reliable, clean, and affordable energy." Do you think this government agency is necessary? Why or why not?

Sources: http://nobelprize.org/nobel_prizes/physics/laureates/1997/chu-autobio.html; http://chineseculture.about.com/od/thechinesediaspora/p/Stevenchu.htm; http://www.theeestory.com/topics/8391?page=1#p188989

2.2 PRODUCTION POSSIBILITIES FRONTIER

Key Terms

production possibilities frontier (PPF) 45
efficiency 45
law of increasing opportunity cost 46
economic growth 47
rules of the game 49

Learning Objectives

LO1 Describe the production possibilities frontier, and explain its shape.

LO2 Explain what causes the production possibilities frontier to shift.

In Your World

To get an idea how well the economy works, you need some perspective. You can develop perspective using a simple model to help explain a more complicated reality. For example, what if you want to determine how much the U.S. economy can produce in a particular period if it uses its resources efficiently? In reality, the U.S. economy has millions of different resources that combine in all kinds of ways to produce millions of possible goods and services. You can use a simple model to describe the economy's production possibilities.

EFFICIENCY AND THE PRODUCTION POSSIBILITIES FRONTIER

LO1
Describe the production possibilities frontier.

How much can an economy produce with the resources available? What are the economy's production capabilities? To help consider these questions, you need a simple model of the economy, beginning with some simplifying assumptions.

Simplifying Assumptions

Here are the model's simplifying assumptions:

1. To reduce the analysis to manageable proportions, the model limits output to two broad classes of products: consumer goods, such as pizzas and haircuts, and capital goods, such as pizza ovens and hair clippers.
2. The focus is on production during a given period, in this case, one year.
3. The resources available in the economy are fixed in both quantity and quality during the period.
4. Society's knowledge about how best to combine these resources to produce output—that is, society's *technology*—does not change during the year.
5. The "rules of the game" that facilitate production and exchange are also assumed fixed during the period. These include the legal system, property rights, and the customs and conventions of the market.

The point of these simplifying assumptions is to freeze the economy's resources, technology, and rules of the game for a period of time to focus on what possibly can be produced during that time.

PPF Model

Given the resources, technology, and rules of the game, the **production possibilities frontier (PPF)** shows the possible combinations of two types of goods that can be produced when available resources are employed efficiently. **Efficiency** means producing the maximum possible output from available resources.

The economy's PPF for consumer goods and capital goods is shown by the curve *AF* in Figure 2.1. Point *A* identifies the amount of consumer goods produced per year if all the economy's resources are used efficiently to produce consumer goods. Point *F* identifies the amount of capital goods produced per year if all the economy's resources are used efficiently to produce capital goods.

Points along the curve between *A* and *F* identify possible combinations of the two goods that can be produced when the economy's resources are used efficiently. Resources are employed efficiently when there is no change that could increase production of one good without decreasing production of the other good.

production possibilities frontier (PPF) Shows the possible combinations of two types of goods that can be produced when available resources are employed efficiently

efficiency Producing the maximum possible output from available resources, meaning the economy cannot produce more of one good without producing less of the other good

FIGURE 2.1 Production Possibilities Frontier (PPF)

If the economy uses its available resources and technology efficiently to produce consumer goods and capital goods, it will be on its production possibilities frontier curve *AF*. The PPF is bowed out to illustrate the law of increasing opportunity cost: The economy sacrifices more and more units of consumer goods to produce equal increments of capital goods. More consumer goods must be given up in moving from *D* to *E* than in moving from *A* to *B*, although in each case the gain in capital goods is 10 million units. Points inside the PPF, such as *I*, represent inefficient use of resources. Points outside the PPF, such as *U*, represent unattainable combinations.

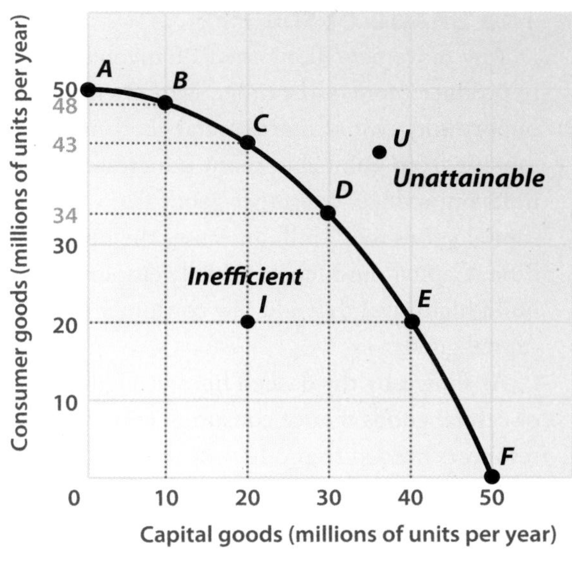

Inefficient and Unattainable Production

Points inside the PPF, including *I* in Figure 2.1, represent combinations that do not employ resources efficiently. Note that point *C* yields more consumer goods and no fewer capital goods than point *I*. Point *E* yields more capital goods

molten steel: 1971yes/Shutterstock.com; kitchen: Steve Holderfield/Shutterstock.com

Study the two images and decide which one represents capital goods and which one represents consumer goods. If these goods were represented on a PPF, what would happen to the production of one type of good if the production of the other good increased?

and no fewer consumer goods than point *I*. In fact, any point along the PPF between *C* and *E*, such as point *D*, yields both more consumer goods and more capital goods than *I*. So point *I* is inefficient. By using resources more efficiently, the economy can produce more of at least one good without reducing the production of the other good.

Points outside the PPF, such as *U* in Figure 2.1, represent unattainable combinations, given the resources, technology, and rules of the game. Thus *the PPF not only shows efficient combinations of production but also serves as the border between inefficient combinations inside the frontier and unattainable combinations outside the frontier.*

The Shape of the PPF

Any movement along the PPF involves producing less of one good in order to produce more of the other. Movement down the curve indicates that the opportunity cost of more capital goods is fewer consumer goods. For example, moving from point *A* to point *B* increases capital goods from none to 10 million units but reduces consumer goods from 50 million to 48 million units. Increasing capital goods to 10 million causes the production of consumer goods to fall only a little. Capital production initially employs resources (such as road graders used to build highways) that add few consumer goods but are quite productive in making capital goods.

As shown by the dashed lines in Figure 2.1, each additional 10 million units of capital goods reduce consumer goods by successively larger amounts. The resources needed to produce more capital are increasingly better suited to making consumer goods. *The resources in the economy are not all perfectly adaptable to the production of both types of goods. Therefore, the opportunity cost of producing more capital increases as the economy produces more of it.*

law of increasing opportunity cost Each additional increment of one good requires the economy to give up successively larger increments of the other good

The shape of the production possibilities frontier reflects the **law of increasing opportunity cost**. If the economy uses all resources efficiently, the law of increasing opportunity cost states that each additional increment of one good requires the economy to give up successively larger increments of the other good.

The PPF has a bowed-out shape due to the law of increasing opportunity cost. For example, whereas the first 10 million units of capital goods have an opportunity cost of only 2 million consumer goods, the final 10 million units of capital goods—that is, the increase from point *E* to point *F*—have an opportunity cost of 20 million consumer goods. As the economy moves down the curve, the curve becomes steeper, reflecting the higher opportunity cost of capital goods in terms of forgone consumer goods.

Graphing Workshop

The law of increasing opportunity cost also applies when switching from the production of capital goods to the production of consumer goods. When all resources in the economy are making capital goods, as at point *F*, certain resources, such as cows and farmland, are of little use in making capital goods. Thus, when resources switch from making capital goods to making consumer goods, few capital goods need be given up initially. As more consumer goods are produced, however, resources that are more productive in making capital goods must be used for making consumer goods, reflecting the law of increasing opportunity cost.

Incidentally, if resources were perfectly adaptable to the production of both types of goods, the amount of consumer goods sacrificed to make more capital goods would remain constant. In this case, the PPF would be a straight line, reflecting a constant opportunity cost along the PPF.

Describe the assumptions of the PPF model, and explain its shape. CHECKPOINT

SHIFTS OF THE PPF

LO2
Explain what causes the production possibilities frontier to shift.

The production possibilities frontier assumes that resources available in the economy, the technology, and the rules of the game remain constant during the period. Over time, however, the PPF may shift as a result of changes in any of these. An outward shift of the PPF reflects **economic growth**, which is an expansion of the economy's production possibilities, or ability to produce. The economy's ability to make stuff grows.

Changes in Resource Availability

If the labor force increases, such as through immigration, the PPF shifts outward, as shown in panel (A) of Figure 2.2. If people decide to work longer hours, retire later, or if the labor force becomes more skilled, this too would shift the PPF outward. An increase in the availability of other resources, such as new oil discoveries, also would shift the PPF outward.

economic growth An expansion of the economy's production possibilities, or ability to produce

FIGURE 2.2 Shifts of the Production Possibilities Frontier (PPF)

When the resources available to an economy change, the PPF shifts. If more resources become available, the PPF shifts outward, as in panel (A), indicating that more output can be produced. A decrease in available resources causes the PPF to shift inward, as in panel (B).

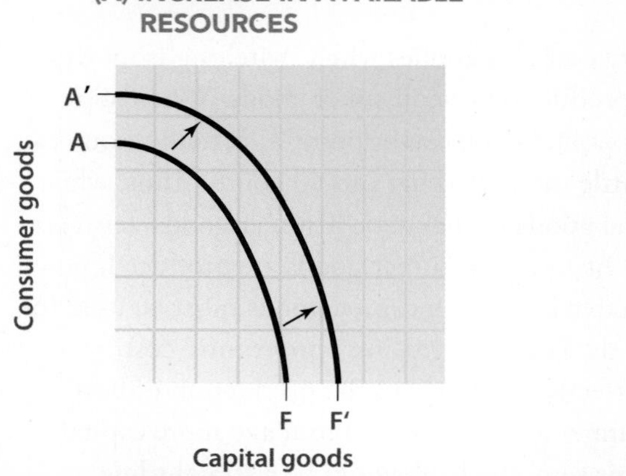

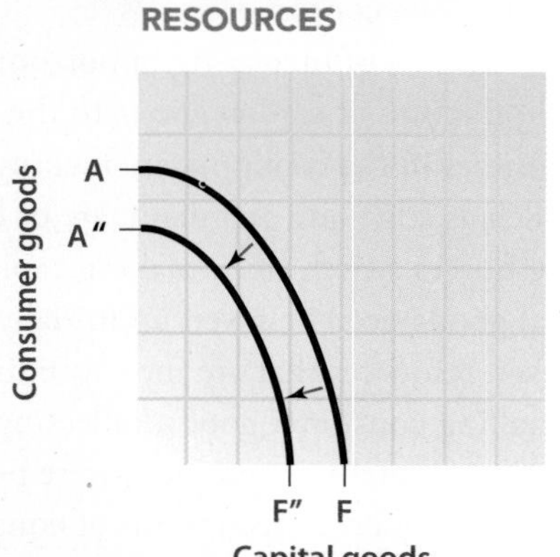

In contrast, a decrease in the availability or quality of resources shifts the PPF inward, as shown in panel (B). For example, in West Africa, the sands of the Sahara spread and destroy thousands of square miles of productive farmland each year, shifting the PPF of that economy inward. Likewise, in northwest China, wind-blown sands claim grasslands, lakes, and forests, and entire villages, forcing tens of thousands of people to flee.

Increases in Stock of Capital Goods

An economy's PPF depends in part on its stock of capital goods. The more capital goods an economy produces during one period, the more output it can produce the next period. Thus, producing more capital goods this period (for example, by building more factories) shifts the economy's PPF outward in the future.

The choice between consumer goods and capital goods is really between present consumption and future production. Again, the more capital goods produced this period, the greater the economy's production possibilities next period.

Technological Change

Another change that could shift the economy's PPF outward is a technological discovery that employs available resources more efficiently. For example, the Internet has increased the efficiency of resource markets by boosting each firm's ability to identify resource suppliers. Such an increase expands the economy's PPF, as shown in panel (A) of Figure 2.2 above.

Improvements in the Rules of the Game

The rules of the game are the formal and informal institutions that support the economy—the laws, customs, manners, conventions, and other institutional underpinnings that encourage people to pursue productive activity. A more stable political environment and more reliable property rights increase the incentive to work and to invest, and thus help the economy grow. This is shown in panel (A) of Figure 2.2. For example, people have more incentive to work if taxes claim less of their paychecks. People have more incentive to invest if they are more confident that their investment will not be taken over by government, stolen by thieves, destroyed by civil unrest, or blown up by terrorists. Improvements in the rules of the game shift the economy's PPF outward. On the other hand, greater political instability reduces the economy's productive capacity as reflected by an inward shift of the PPF. This is shown in panel (B) of Figure 2.2.

rules of the game
The laws, customs, manners, conventions, and other institutional underpinnings that encourage people to pursue productive activity

Lessons from the PPF

To recap, the PPF demonstrates several concepts. The first is *efficiency*: The PPF describes the efficient combinations of outputs possible given the economy's resources, technology, and rules of the game. The second is *scarcity*. Given the stock of resources, technology, and rules of the game, the economy can produce only so much. The PPF slopes downward, indicating that, as the economy produces more of one good, it must produce less of the other good. This tradeoff demonstrates *opportunity cost.*

The bowed-out shape of the PPF reflects the *law of increasing opportunity cost.* Not all resources are perfectly adaptable to the production of each type of good. A shift outward of the PPF reflects *economic growth.* Finally, because society must somehow choose a specific combination of output along the PPF, the PPF also emphasizes the need for *choice.* That choice will determine both current consumption and the capital stock available next period.

Each point along the economy's production possibilities frontier is an efficient combination of output. Whether the economy produces efficiently and how the economy selects the most preferred combination depend on the economic system.

Photodisc/Getty Images

What happens to the PPF when technological change, such as a change in the way computer chips are manufactured, results in a more efficient production process?

What causes the production possibilities frontier to shift? **CHECKPOINT**

2.2 ASSESSMENT

Think Critically

1. Explain why each of the following assumptions is made when a production possibilities frontier (PPF) is constructed.
   a. Only two goods or services are considered.
   b. The time considered is limited.
   c. The available resources are fixed in terms of quality and quantity.
   d. The available technology does not change during the period considered.
   e. The "rules of the game" are fixed during the period.
2. Explain why the law of increasing opportunity cost causes the PPF to bow out from the origin (corner) of the graph.
3. Using consumer goods and capital goods in a production possibilities frontier, what conditions would produce a straight-line PPF? What does this indicate about opportunity cost along the PPF, and why?

Graphing Exercise

4. The nation of Iberia can produce either digital cameras or DVD players. The more it makes of one product, the less it is able to make of the other. The table shows combinations of the two products it could make from available resources. Use these data to construct and label a production possibilities frontier for this economy. Why isn't there a one-for-one tradeoff between production of the two products?

POSSIBLE COMBINATIONS OF DIGITAL CAMERAS AND DVD PLAYERS FOR IBERIA

Combination	DigitalCameras	DVD Players
A	0	5,000
B	2,000	4,500
C	3,400	3,400
D	4,500	2,000
E	5,000	0

Make Academic Connections

5. **Math** Consider the table in exercise 4 above. Suppose digital cameras sell on the world market for $300 each, while DVD players sell for $200 each. How much revenue would producers in Iberia earn from selling each of the combinations of production indicated on the table? Which combination would maximize revenue from the nation's output?

TeamWork

In a small team, make a list of resources in the economy that are better suited to the production of consumer goods and resources that are better suited to the production of capital goods. Use this list to explain the shape of the PPF. Identify still other resources that could be equally productive in producing consumer goods and capital goods.

21st Century Skills

SOCIAL AND CROSS-CULTURAL SKILLS

New Technologies and Economic Transition

Some people think that economic transition occurs only in nations shifting from command to market economies. However, the advancement of technology compels all economies, their people, and their institutions to change. Consider, for example, how the Internet has altered the economy since it first became widely available in the early 1990s. The Internet has changed the way in which people communicate, buy and sell products, complete homework, and use their free time.

Not Everyone Benefits Equally from Technological Change

Although most people benefit from technological advancements, they do not all benefit equally. Among those who are less able to benefit from new technologies are

- People who have less education or are afraid of new technologies
- People who cannot afford new technologies
- People employed in old technologies and who lose their jobs
- People who are not able to learn easily about new technologies

Prepare for Change

It is important to recognize that technology does advance and that the changes can affect your life. The best way to avoid problems when new technologies are developed is to prepare for them. This does not mean you need to purchase every new technology as soon as it becomes available. (Usually the first generation of a new technology has the most bugs.) It does mean, however, that you should keep up with developments in technology and recognize when advancements are likely to affect your life. You may do this by reading newspapers or magazines, watching television, or searching the Internet. Evaluate important new technologies and use them when the marginal benefit they offer is greater than their marginal cost.

Help Others Benefit from New Technology

People who have learned how to use a technological advancement usually can recognize and help others who have not. Although people may take formal classes to learn about new technologies, some individuals or groups may be unable or reluctant to take advantage of these opportunities. Responsible members of society may choose to help these people learn about new technologies by offering to help them on a one-on-one or group basis.

Apply the Skill

Think of a new technology that has become important in your life. Now, think of a person or group of people in your community who do not currently have this technology but who could benefit from it. Identify the person or group and the technology. Describe three specific steps you could take as an individual that would help these people learn to use the new technology. Then explain how the person or group you help could benefit from this knowledge.

2.3 COMPARATIVE ADVANTAGE AND SPECIALIZATION

Key Terms

Learning Objectives

LO1 Explain the law of comparative advantage.

LO2 Understand the gains from specialization and exchange.

In Your World

The law of comparative advantage helps explain why, even if you are talented at many things, you can get more done by specializing and then trading with other specialists. For example, even if you are talented at both washing cars and mowing lawns, you will likely get more done by specializing in just one of those tasks. The division of labor allows an economy to increase production by having each worker specialize. Specialization occurs not only among individual workers, but also among firms, regions, and entire countries.

COMPARATIVE ADVANTAGE

LO1 Explain the law of comparative advantage.

You probably are expected to do certain chores at home on a regular basis. What if it is your responsibility each week to wash the two family cars and to mow the lawn? It takes you 45 minutes to wash a car and one hour to mow the lawn. Altogether, you spend two and a half hours a week washing two cars and mowing the lawn.

Your high school friend David lives next door. He happens to face the same weekly chores—washing two family cars identical to yours and mowing a lawn identical to yours. David, however, is not nearly as quick as you. It takes him one hour to wash a car and three hours to mow the lawn. Altogether, David spends five hours a week on these chores.

Absolute Advantage

Compared to David, you have an absolute advantage in each task, because you can do each using fewer resources. The resource here is your labor time. More generally, having an **absolute advantage** means being able to produce something using fewer resources than other producers require.

absolute advantage The ability to make something using fewer resources than other producers require

When you and David each do your own weekly chores, you take two and a half hours and he takes five hours. Because you can complete each task in less time than David can, you see no advantage in cooperating with him to save time. However, is this the best you can do?

The Law of Comparative Advantage

Absolute advantage is not the best guide for deciding who should do what. The best guide is comparative advantage. According to the **law of comparative advantage**, the worker with the lower opportunity cost of producing a particular output should specialize in that output. **Specialization**, then, occurs when individual workers focus on single tasks, enabling each worker to become more efficient and productive. Note that for the definitions of both the law of comparative advantage and specialization, the term *worker* may be replaced by the terms *firm*, *region*, or *country.*

What is your opportunity cost of washing each car? In the 45 minutes you take to wash a car, you could instead mow three-fourths of the lawn. So your opportunity cost of washing a car is mowing three-fourths of a lawn.

In the hour David takes to wash a car, he could instead mow one-third of the lawn. So his opportunity cost of washing a car is mowing one-third of a lawn. Because your opportunity cost of washing a car is mowing three-fourths of a lawn and David's is mowing one-third of a lawn, he faces the lower opportunity cost of washing cars.

Again, the law of comparative advantage says that the person with the lower opportunity cost should specialize in producing that output. In this example, David should specialize in washing cars.

Because David has a lower opportunity cost for washing cars, you must have a lower opportunity cost for mowing lawns. So you should specialize in mowing lawns.

Gains from Specialization

If you each specialize, David will wash your family's cars, and you will mow his family's lawn. David washes the four cars in four hours, saving himself an hour. You cut both lawns in two hours, saving yourself a half hour. Through specialization and exchange, each of you saves time. Even though you can complete each task in less time than David can, your comparative advantage is mowing lawns. Put another way, David, although not as fast as you at either task, is not as slow at washing cars as he is at mowing lawns. He has a comparative advantage in washing cars. You each specialize based on comparative advantage, and you each save time.

Absolute advantage focuses on which of you uses the fewest resources, but comparative advantage focuses on what else those resources could have produced—that is, on the opportunity cost of those resources. The law of comparative advantage indicates who should do what.

Exchange

In this example, you and David specialize and exchange your output. No money is involved. In other words, you two engage in **barter**, a system of exchange in which products are traded directly for other products. Barter works best in simple economies that have little specialization and few types of goods to trade. For economies with greater specialization, *money* plays an important role in facilitating exchange. **Money**—coins, bills, and checking accounts—serves as a medium of exchange because it is the one thing that everyone is willing to accept in exchange for all goods and services.

Investigate Your Local Economy

Working in small teams, brainstorm a list of possible resources that provide your local economy with a comparative advantage. After five minutes of brainstorming, each group will present its results to the class.

law of comparative advantage The worker, firm, region, or country with the lowest opportunity cost of producing an output should specialize in that output

specialization Occurs when individual workers focus on single tasks, enabling each worker to become more efficient and productive

barter A system of exchange in which products are traded directly for other products

money Anything that everyone is willing to accept in exchange for goods and services

Wider Application

Due to such factors as climate, an abundance of labor, workforce skills, natural resources, and capital stock, certain parts of the country and the world have a comparative advantage in producing particular goods. From software in California's Silicon Valley to oranges in Florida, from DVD players in Taiwan to bananas in Honduras, *resources are allocated most efficiently across the country and around the world when production and trade conform to the law of comparative advantage.*

CHECKPOINT What is the law of comparative advantage?

SPECIALIZATION

LO2 Understand the gains from specialization and exchange.

Because of specialization based on comparative advantage, most people consume little of what they produce and produce little of what they consume. People specialize in particular activities, such as plumbing or carpentry. They then exchange their products for money which, in turn, is exchanged for goods and services. Specialization and exchange create more interdependence in an economy.

Did you make anything you are wearing? Probably not. Think about the specialization that went into making your cotton shirt. Some farmer in a warm climate grew the cotton and sold it to someone who spun it into thread, who sold it to someone who wove it into fabric, who sold it to someone who sewed the shirt, who sold it to a wholesaler, who sold it to a retailer, who sold it to you. Figure 2.3 illustrates the many specialists who produced your shirt.

FIGURE 2.3 Specialization in the Production of Cotton Shirts

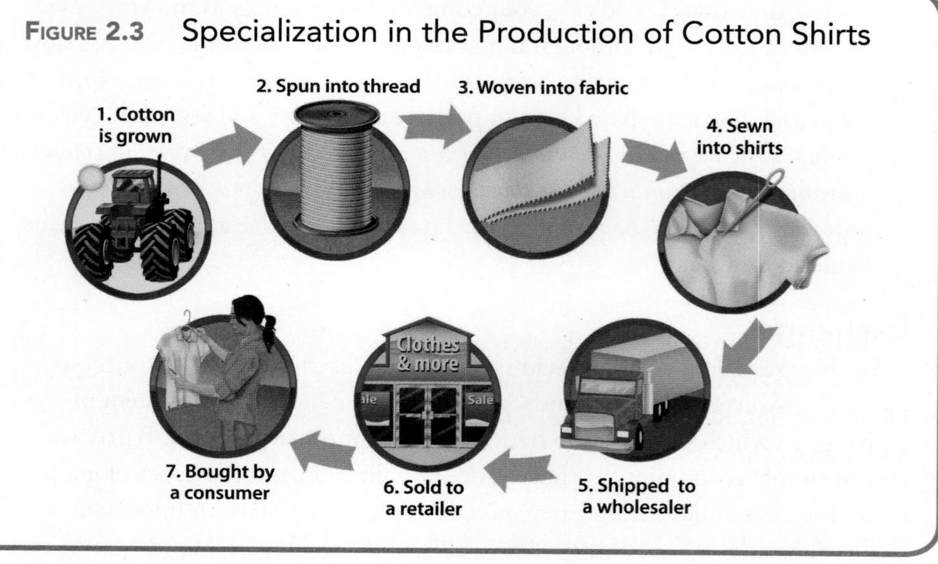

Evidence of specialization is all around us. Shops at the mall specialize in products ranging from luggage to lingerie. Restaurants range from subs to sushi. Search through the help-wanted ads or Yellow Pages®, where you will find thousands of specializations. The degree of specialization is perhaps most obvious online, where the pool of potential customers is so vast that individual sites become sharply focused, from toe rings to cat bandanas. Without moving a muscle, you can observe the division of labor within a single industry by watching the credits roll at the end of a movie. The credits show scores of specialists—from gaffer (lighting electrician) to assistant location scout. As an extreme example, thousands of names appear in the credits at the end of the movie *Avatar*.

Division of Labor

Picture a visit to McDonald's: "Let's see, I'll have a Big Mac, an order of fries, and a chocolate shake." Less than a minute later, your order is ready. It would take you much longer to make a homemade version of this meal. Why is a McDonald's meal faster, cheaper, and—for some people—tastier than one you could make yourself? Why is fast food so fast?

McDonald's takes advantage of the gains resulting from the division of labor. The **division of labor** organizes the production process so that each worker specializes in a separate task. This allows the group to produce much more.

How is this increase in productivity possible? First, the manager can assign tasks according to individual preferences and abilities—that is, according to the law of comparative advantage. The worker with the nice smile and good personality can handle the customers up front. The muscle-bound worker with fewer social graces can do the heavy lifting in the back room.

Second, a worker who performs the same task again and again gets better at it: Experience is a good teacher. The worker filling orders at the drive-through, for example, learns how to deal with special problems that arise there. Third, because a worker stays with the same task, no time is lost in moving from one task to another.

Finally, and perhaps most important, the division of labor allows for the introduction of more sophisticated production techniques that would not make sense on a smaller scale. For example, McDonald's large milkshake machine would be impractical in your home. The division of labor allows for the introduction of specialized machines, and these machines make each worker more productive.

To review, the division of labor (a) takes advantage of individual preferences and natural abilities, (b) allows workers to gain experience at a particular task, (c) reduces the need to shift between different tasks, and (d) permits the introduction of labor-saving machinery. The specialization that results with the division of labor does not occur among individuals only. It also occurs among firms, regions, and entire countries.

division of labor
Organizes the production process so that each worker specializes in a separate task

What are the gains from specialization and exchange? **CHECKPOINT**

Math in Economics

Common Core Number and Operations in Base Ten

You can calculate the number of units of one product that would be given up to obtain additional units of another product by subtracting values on the Production Possibilties Frontier (PPF).

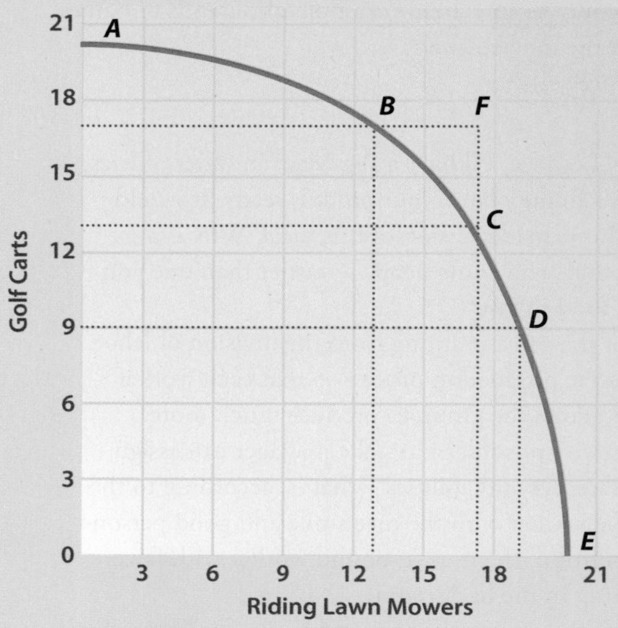

EXAMPLE Find the number of lawn mowers that must be given up to move from point *D* to point *B* on the PPF.

SOLUTION Subtract the number of lawn mowers that could be produced at point *B* from the number that could be produced at point *D*.

$19 - 13 = 6$

Production of 6 lawn mowers must be given up to produce more golf carts.

Practice the Skill Answer the following questions.

1. How many more golf carts could be produced by moving from point *D* to point *B* on the PPF?
2. How many fewer golf carts could be produced by moving from point *C* to point *D* on the PPF?
3. How many more lawn mowers could be produced by moving from point *B* to point *E* on the PPF?
4. How many units of each product would be produced at point *F*? Explain why this level of production is currently not possible.

2.3 ASSESSMENT

Think Critically

1. Why does specialization require people to carry out exchanges?
2. How does money help people carry out exchanges?
3. How is the division of labor accomplished?
4. What advantages are offered by the division of labor in addition to allowing workers to become more accomplished at the tasks they complete?

Graphing Exercises

5. Joel and Jamal work together at a bakery. In one hour Joel can ice ten cakes or prepare five pies. In the same time Jamal can ice eight cakes or prepare only one pie. Draw bar graphs to represent production of iced cakes and prepared pies for each of the following situations. Explain how your graphs demonstrate the law of comparative advantage.

   Situation A Joel spends one hour icing cakes and three hours preparing pies. Jamal does the same.

   Situation B Joel spends four hours preparing pies, while Jamal spends four hours icing cakes.

Make Academic Connections

6. **Research** Investigate the division of labor and specialization on a high-school sports team, such as basketball, football, or field hockey. Write a paragraph explaining the different positions, and how each one contributes to the team effort.
7. **Sociology** At one time people in India were divided into castes that, among other things, determined what sort of work they were allowed to do. For example, if their parents were farmers, they would be required by society to be farmers, too. Write a paragraph that explains why this practice limited the Indian economy's ability to take advantage of specialization and a division of labor.

TeamWork

Working in small teams, outline how you would divide tasks required to produce and sell pizzas to customers in a small neighborhood restaurant. What would the tasks be? How would you decide which students were responsible for which tasks? How would the division of labor created increase your productivity through specialization? Report your results to the class.

Jamestown and the English Mercantile System

In 1612, John Rolfe began growing tobacco in Jamestown from seeds he obtained from the Spanish colonies. Rolfe acquired the seeds despite the Spaniards' threat of death to anyone selling tobacco seeds to a non-Spaniard. The local Indians may have aided Rolfe's acquisition of the seeds, as he was engaged to marry the chief's daughter, Pocahontas. By 1614, the first tobacco from Virginia was sold in London. Despite the disapproval of King James I, this "stinking weed" came into high demand in England and throughout Europe. With tobacco as a cash crop, the Virginia colony established the basis for its economic success.

With the success of tobacco, the demand for labor in the colony increased. Labor was first supplied by indentured servants, who sold their labor not for wages but for passage to Virginia plus food, clothing, and other necessities. After filling the terms of the contract, usually three to seven years, the indentured servant would be given land, tools, and perhaps a small amount of money. A 20 percent death rate on the voyage over, and further exposure to demanding work and disease, made it difficult to recruit indentured laborers. As time passed and the survival rate increased, more were willing to come. After indentured servants proved finally to be an unsatisfactory labor resource, slavery developed. Slaves initially were more expensive to purchase than indentured servants, but slaves proved to be a cheaper form of labor because their work was bought for life.

Although Virginia could grow crops other than tobacco, such as wheat, the opportunity cost was high. By specializing in tobacco, a farmer could increase his profits over what he could make from growing other crops. Tobacco was profitable on any size farm. However, specializing in tobacco depleted the soil. As the plantation system developed, so did the division of labor. Virginia's comparative advantage lay in growing tobacco.

Virginia tobacco farmers were part of the English mercantile system. The object of the system was to increase a nation's wealth, as defined by the amount of gold the national treasury accumulated. A nation could acquire gold by possessing a territory that mined gold. It also could acquire gold by developing a positive balance of trade that brought in gold payments in return for exported goods. For England, tobacco was an ideal mercantilist product. It was easy to ship and could replace the imports of tobacco from Spain. England did not allow Virginia to ship or sell its tobacco anywhere but back to England, where it became a large source of import duties for the English treasury. By 1639, Virginia had shipped at least 750 tons of tobacco to England. After taking a profit, England re-exported the tobacco to Europe. England's enforcement of this system became a contributing factor to the American Revolution.

Think Critically **The Jamestown colonists faced the choice of producing food for consumption or producing tobacco for sale. Draw a production possibilities frontier for producing food on the horizontal axis and tobacco on the vertical axis. Label the points where the PPF intersects the axes, as well as several other points along the frontier. What would it mean for the colonists to move upward and to the left along the PPF? Under what circumstances would the PPF shift outward?**

Chapter 2 Summary

2.1 Economic Questions and Economic Systems

A. All economic systems answer three basic questions: (1) What goods will be produced? (2) How will these goods be produced? (3) For whom will these goods be produced?

B. In a pure market economy, all resources are privately owned and controlled. Competition forces businesses to serve the interest of consumers as these businesses try to earn a profit. Property rights must be protected for a market economy to work. Business owners would not bother trying to produce if any profit earned was taken from them.

C. Pure market economies have some problems. These include the difficulty in enforcing property rights, the possibility that people who produce little of value will fall into poverty, the possibility of businesses monopolizing markets, and a lack of public goods. Also, externalities impose costs on people not directly involved in a transaction. Market economies also experience economic fluctuations, which can increase unemployment.

D. In a pure command economy, all resources are publicly owned and controlled. Government planners answer the three basic economic questions according to their own priorities or those of government leaders. Problems associated with these economies include a low priority given to consumer preferences, little consumer freedom of choice, inefficient use of resources, and no incentive for entrepreneurs.

E. The problems of pure market and pure command economies have caused some nations to reorient their economies. Many command economies have increased the role of markets while some market economies have increased the role of governments. Nations moving from command economies to market economies have transitional economies. In some economies, resources are allocated according to traditions that are passed from one generation to the next.

2.2 Production Possibilities Frontier

A. The production possibility frontier (PPF) demonstrates different combinations of two goods that can be produced from a given amount of resources. Simplifying assumptions include focusing on a specific time period, such as a year, and holding technology, resources, and the rules of the game fixed during that period.

B. The law of increasing opportunity cost states that producing each additional unit of one good requires successively larger sacrifices of the other good. This happens because resources are not perfectly adaptable to the production of both goods.

C. Any point inside a PPF indicates inefficiency because more goods could be produced from the available resources. Any point outside a PPF indicates a level of production not currently attainable. A PPF will shift outward if more or better resources become available, technology improves, or a change in the rules of the game boosts production incentives.

2.3 Comparative Advantage and Specialization

A. According to the law of comparative advantage, workers should specialize in output where their opportunity cost is the lowest.

B. When people specialize, they must exchange what they produce for other goods they desire. These exchanges are easier when carried out through the use of money.

C. A division of labor results in greater efficiency because workers become more skilled in their tasks, lose no time switching between tasks, and are able to use more sophisticated production techniques.

ASK THE EXPERT

www.cengage.com/school/contecon

Have computers affected worker productivity?

CHAPTER 2 ASSESSMENT

Review Economic Terms

a. absolute advantage
b. barter
c. division of labor
d. economic growth
e. economic system
f. efficiency
g. law of comparative advantage
h. law of increasing opportunity cost
i. market economy
j. mixed economy
k. money
l. production possibilities frontier (PPF)
m. pure command economy
n. pure market economy
o. specialization
p. traditional economy
q. transitional economy

Match the terms with the definitions. Some terms will not be used.

_____ 1. The set of mechanisms and institutions that resolve the what, how, and for whom questions for an economy

_____ 2. Organizes the production process so that each worker specializes in a separate task

_____ 3. Ability to make something using fewer resources than other producers require

_____ 4. Anything that everyone is willing to accept in exchange for goods and services

_____ 5. The worker, firm, region, or country with the lowest opportunity cost of producing an output should specialize in that output

_____ 6. Producing the maximum possible output from available resources

_____ 7. An economic system with no government so that private firms account for all production

_____ 8. Shows the possible combinations of two types of goods that can be produced when available resources are employed efficiently

_____ 9. An economic system that mixes aspects of central planning with competitive markets

_____ 10. An expansion of the economy's ability to produce

Review Economic Concepts

11. **True or False** According to the law of comparative advantage, only people with an absolute advantage can benefit from specialization.

12. ________?________ is a system of exchange in which products are traded directly for other products.

13. Which of the following is the best example of a division of labor?
    a. Todd lives in a cabin in the woods where he does most things for himself.
    b. Julia works as a doctor, while her husband Ted is an automobile mechanic.
    c. Benito washes dishes after lunch, while his wife dries them and puts them away.
    d. Brenda reads the front page of the newspaper, while her husband studies the comics.

14. **True or False** The law of comparative advantage applies not only to individuals, but also to firms, regions of countries, and entire nations.

15. **True or False** All economic systems must decide what goods will be produced from the resources available.

16. The economic question ________?________ often is referred to as the distribution question.

17. Points ________?________ the PPF represent unattainable combinations given the resources, technology, and rules of the game available.

18. Which of the following is not a simplifying assumption made when a production possibilities frontier (PPF) is created?
    a. Only two goods are considered.
    b. The prices of the goods produced do not change.
    c. Production is limited to a fixed period of time.
    d. There is a given amount of resources available in the economy.
19. Movement along the PPF indicates that the ________?________ of producing more capital goods is producing fewer consumer goods.
20. According to the law of increasing opportunity cost, each additional increment of one good requires the sacrifice of
    a. successively larger increments of the other good.
    b. equal increments of the other good.
    c. successively smaller increments of the other good.
    d. the productive efficiency.
21. **True or False** In a pure market economy, resources are publicly owned and controlled.
22. Adam Smith argued that although each individual pursues his or her self-interest in a market economy, the "invisible hand" of ________?________ promotes the general welfare.
23. **True or False** One problem with command economies is too much focus on consumer needs and wants.
24. **True or False** In command economies, government enterprises often are more concerned with meeting the production goals set by government planners than they are about environmental quality.
25. ________?________ is a process that involves converting government-owned enterprises into private enterprises.
26. An economic system in which the means and methods of production are passed from one generation to the next is a
    a. pure market economy.
    b. pure command economy.
    c. transitional economy.
    d. traditional economy.

Apply Economic Concepts

27. **Apply Production Possibilities** Draw a production possibilities frontier for consumer goods and capital goods, assuming that some resources are not perfectly adaptable to the production of each type of good. Label your curve *AF*. Explain how the PPF you have drawn demonstrates (a) efficiency, (b) opportunity cost, and (c) the law of increasing opportunity cost.
28. **Create a Division of Labor** Make a list of five friends who you know well. Assume that the six of you have decided to open a small restaurant. Assign each of your friends, and yourself, to one of the following job descriptions in the way that you believe would result in the most efficient

operation of your restaurant. Briefly explain the reasons for each of your assignments. How does this demonstrate the advantages of specialization and a division of labor?

a. Greet customers and take them to their tables
b. Take customer orders and bring food to their tables
c. Be the chief cook in the kitchen
d. Clear tables and wash dishes
e. Keep the books, accept payments, order supplies, and pay the bills
f. Be the chief cook's assistant

29. **Apply Shifts of Production Possibilities** Determine whether each of the following would cause the economy's PPF to shift inward, outward, or not at all.
a. Increase in average vacation length
b. Increase in immigration
c. Decrease in the average retirement age
d. Migration of workers to other countries

30. **21st Century Skills: Social and Cross-Cultural Skills** Imagine that the leaders of a developing nation have seen how production in developed nations has grown through the use of the Internet. They decide that installing fiber optic Internet cables throughout their nation will help their businesses expand production of both capital and consumer goods. After spending billions of dollars over five years they are dissapointed to discover that their PPF curve has remained essentially unchanged. Although the fiber optic network exists, few people have the desire, training, or equipment needed to use it. What mistakes did the leaders of this nation make? What could they do to correct their mistake? Why doesn't a new technology that brings about growth in one economic system necessarily guarantee increased production in another?

Digging Deeper

with Economics e-Collection

Access the Gale Economics e-Collection through the URL below to research an economy in transition. Use the name of the country as your search term. Countries with economies in transition include Cambodia, China, Lithuania, Russia, and Vietnam. Your teacher can provide you with a more complete list. Find an article that deals with an aspect of the country's economy, such as property rights, public goods, central planning, the role of entrepreneurs, or privatization, among others. Conduct your initial search by entering the country's name as either a Key Word or a Subject. Narrow your search using the Refine Results box by entering "economy" or one of the topics listed above. Be sure to search all Content Types, including Magazines, Academic Journals, News, and Audios. Write a short report on the economic aspect of the country. Be prepared to present your report in class.

www.cengage.com/school/contecon

CHAPTER 3

U.S. Private and Public Sectors

CONSIDER ...

- Why did households go from self-sufficiency to relying on markets?
- How did firms evolve to take advantage of large-scale production?
- Why do countries trade?
- If the "invisible hand" of competitive markets works so well, why must governments get into the act?
- Why are some people poor even in the world's most productive economy?
- How is poverty measured?

digitalskillet/iStockphoto.com; Background image: dibrova/Shutterstock.com

Point your browser

www.cengage.com/school/contecon

3.1 THE U.S. PRIVATE SECTOR

Key Terms

household 64
utility 65
firm 66
Industrial Revolution 67

Learning Objectives

LO1 Describe the evolution of households.

LO2 Explain the evolution of the firm.

LO3 Understand why international trade occurs.

In Your World

The private sector includes three types of economic decision makers: households, firms, and the rest of the world. To develop a better feel for how the economy works, you must become more acquainted with these key players. You already know more about them than you may realize. You grew up as a member of a household, and households are the key economic decision makers. And, you have interacted with firms, from Walmart to Taco Bell, all your life. You have a growing awareness of the rest of the world, from imports to international websites.

HOUSEHOLDS

LO1 Describe the evolution of households.

Households play the starring role in a market economy. All those who live together under one roof are considered part of the same **household**. Households' demand for goods and services determines what gets produced. The human resources, natural resources, and capital goods they sell help to produce that output. As buyers of goods and services and sellers of resources, households make all kinds of economic choices. These choices include what to buy, how much to save, where to live, and where to work.

Evolution of the Household

In 1850 about two-thirds of America's labor force worked on farms. The economy was primarily agricultural, and each farm household was largely self-sufficient. Individual family members specialized in specific farm tasks—preparing meals, sewing clothes, tending livestock, growing crops, mending fences, and so on. These households produced most of what they consumed and consumed most of what they produced.

With the introduction of labor-saving machinery, disease-resistant seeds, and better fertilizers, farm productivity increased sharply. Because each farmer produced much more, fewer farmers were needed to grow enough food to feed the nation. At the same time, the growth of urban factories increased the demand for factory labor. As a result, many workers and their families moved from farms to cities, where they worked in factories but became less self-sufficient. Now, only about 2 percent of the U.S. labor force works on farms.

household The most important economic decision maker, consisting of all those who live together under one roof

U.S. households have evolved in other important ways. For example, in 1950 only about 15 percent of married women with children under 18 years old were in the labor force. Since then, higher education levels among married women and a growing need for workers increased women's earnings. It also raised their opportunity cost of staying home. Today, more than half of married women with young children are in the labor force.

The rise of two-earner households has affected the family as an economic unit. Less production occurs in the home. More goods and services are purchased in markets. Reduced household production has led to increased availability of child-care services and greater varieties of restaurants. The rise of two-earner families has reduced the importance of specialization in household production.

Households Maximize Utility

The United States has more than 116 million households. Economists consider each household to be a single decision maker. Households, like other economic decision makers, are assumed to pursue their rational self-interest. This means they try to select products they expect will make them better off.

But what exactly do households attempt to accomplish in making decisions? Economists assume that households attempt to maximize their **utility**—their level of satisfaction, happiness, or sense of well-being. Maximizing utility depends on each household's personal goals, not on some objective standard. For example, some households maintain neat homes with well-groomed lawns. Other households pay little attention to the maintenance of their homes and yards.

utility A household's level of satisfaction, happiness, or sense of well-being

menu: Chubykin Arkady/Shutterstock.com; box office: Photo Intrigue/Shutterstock.com; add to cart: diego_cervo/iStockphoto.com; shopper: thepraetorian/iStockphoto.com

ESSENTIAL QUESTION

Standard CEE 2: Decision Making

Effective decision making requires comparing the additional costs of alternatives with the additional benefits. Many choices involve doing a little more or a little less of something: few choices are "all or nothing" decisions.

What should you compare when faced with an economic decision?

CHECKPOINT How has the household evolved over time?

FIRMS

LO2 Explain the evolution of the firm.

Household members once built their own homes, made their own clothes and furniture, grew their own food, and entertained themselves. Over time, however, the efficiency arising from comparative advantage resulted in more specialization among resource providers. Resource providers often organize as firms. A **firm** is an economic unit formed by a profit-seeking entrepreneur who combines resources to produce goods and services and who accepts the risk of profit and loss. What led to the development of the firm as we know it today?

Investigate Your Local Economy

Research to find how many households there are in your community. How many of those are two-earner families? How many are headed by a single parent? What is the average annual income of households in the community? What conclusions can you draw from your research?

Evolution of the Firm

Specialization and comparative advantage help explain why households are no longer self-sufficient. But why is a firm the natural outgrowth? For example, rather than make a woolen sweater from scratch, couldn't a consumer take advantage of specialization by hiring someone to produce the wool, another person to spin the wool into yarn, and a third to knit the yarn into a sweater? Why is a firm even necessary?

Here's the problem with that model: If the consumer had to visit and make agreements with each of these specialists, the resulting *transaction costs*—the cost of time and information required for exchange—could easily erase the efficiency gained from specialization. Instead of visiting and dealing with each specialist, the consumer can pay someone else to do this. The consumer can pay an entrepreneur to hire all the resources necessary to make the sweater. *An entrepreneur, by hiring specialists to make many sweaters rather than just one, is able to reduce the transaction costs per sweater.* During the seventeenth and eighteenth centuries, entrepreneurs provided raw material, such as wool and cotton, to rural households. The entrepreneur hired households to turn this raw material into finished products, such as woolen goods made from yarn. This system developed in the British Isles, where workers' rural cottages served as tiny factories. Production usually occurred during the winter months, when farming tasks were few, so the opportunity cost for farm workers was lower.

This approach, which came to be known as the *cottage industry system*, still exists in some parts of the world. You can view this system as the bridge between the self-sufficient farm household and the modern firm.

The Industrial Revolution

As the economy expanded in the eighteenth century, entrepreneurs began organizing the stages of production under one factory roof. Technological developments, such as water power and later steam power, increased the productivity of each worker. They also contributed to the shift of employment from rural farm to urban factory.

firm A business unit or enterprise formed by a profit-seeking entrepreneur who combines resources to produce goods and services

Work, therefore, became organized in large, centrally powered factories that

1. promoted a more efficient division of labor
2. allowed for the direct supervision of production
3. reduced transportation costs
4. facilitated the use of specialized machines far larger than anything that had been used in the home

The development of large-scale factory production, known as the **Industrial Revolution**, began in Great Britain around 1750. The Industrial Revolution then spread to the rest of Europe, North America, and Australia. Figure 3.1 shows the evolution of production from self-sufficient rural households; to the cottage industry system, where specialized production occurred in the household; to the Industrial Revolution of handling most production under one factory roof; to a modern, large-scale facility.

Firms Maximize Profit

Today, entrepreneurs combine resources in firms such as factories, mills, offices, stores, and restaurants. The entrepreneurs accept the risk of profit and loss from the enterprise. Just as households attempt to maximize utility, firms attempt to maximize profit. Profit is the entrepreneur's reward for accepting the

Industrial Revolution
Development of large-scale production during the eighteenth century

Figure 3.1 Evolution of Production

The production process evolved from self-sufficient rural households to the cottage industry system, where specialized production occurred in the household. From there, the Industrial Revolution saw the organization of the various stages of production under one roof with the eventual development of large-scale factory production.

fotomedia/iStockphoto.com

Photodisc/Getty Images

Stockbyte/Getty Images

Stockbyte/Getty Images

risks involved. Profit equals revenue (the money received from selling goods and services) minus the cost of production:

Profit = Revenue − Cost of Production

The United States has more than 30 million profit-seeking firms. Two-thirds of these are small retail businesses, small service operations, part-time home-based businesses, and small farms. Each year more than a million new businesses start up and nearly as many go out of business. Despite the challenges, the lure of profit provides entrepreneurs with the incentive to keep trying.

CHECKPOINT **How have production processes changed over time?**

THE REST OF THE WORLD

LO3 **Understand why international trade occurs.**

So far the focus has been on private-sector institutions within the United States—that is, U.S. households and firms. This focus has been appropriate because your primary objective is to understand the workings of the U.S. economy, the largest in the world.

The rest of the world affects what U.S. households consume and what U.S. firms produce. For example, firms in Japan and South Korea supply U.S. markets with autos, electronic equipment, and other goods, thereby affecting U.S. prices, employment, wages, and profit. Political unrest in the Middle East can drive up the price of oil, increasing U.S. production costs.

Foreign decision makers have a significant effect on the U.S. economy—on what Americans consume and on what they produce. The *rest of the world* consists of the households, firms, and governments in the more than 200 nations throughout the world.

International Trade

The gains from comparative advantage and specialization explain why households stopped trying to do everything for themselves and began to sell their resources to specialized firms. International trade arises for the same reasons. *Gains from international trade occur because the opportunity cost of producing specific goods differs across countries.*

Trade allows the countries involved to specialize and thereby increase production. Americans buy raw materials (such as crude oil, metals, and coffee beans) and finished goods (such as cameras, DVD players, and automobiles) from other countries. U.S. producers sell to other countries sophisticated products such as computer hardware and software, aircraft, and movies, and raw materials such as agricultural products.

International trade between the United States and the rest of the world has increased in recent decades. In 1970, only about 6 percent of U.S. production was sold to other countries. That figure has doubled to 12 percent.

Trade in Raw Materials

To understand how international trade works, consider the trade in raw materials. Figure 3.2 shows U.S. production as a percent of U.S. consumption for 14 key commodities. If production exceeds consumption, Americans sell the difference to other countries. If production falls short of consumption, Americans buy the difference from other countries. For example, because the United States grows little coffee, it imports nearly all the coffee consumed here. U.S. production of coffee is only 1 percent of U.S. consumption.

The figure also shows that U.S. production falls short of consumption for oil and for metals such as lead, zinc, copper, and aluminum. At the other extreme, U.S.-grown wheat is nearly double U.S. wheat consumption. Nearly half of the U.S. wheat crop is exported, and U.S.-grown cotton is more than triple U.S. cotton consumption. Thus, U.S. cotton exports are more than double the U.S. consumption of cotton. When it comes to raw materials, the United States is a net importer of energy and metals and a net exporter of crops. Farm exports are why America has long been called the "breadbasket of the world."

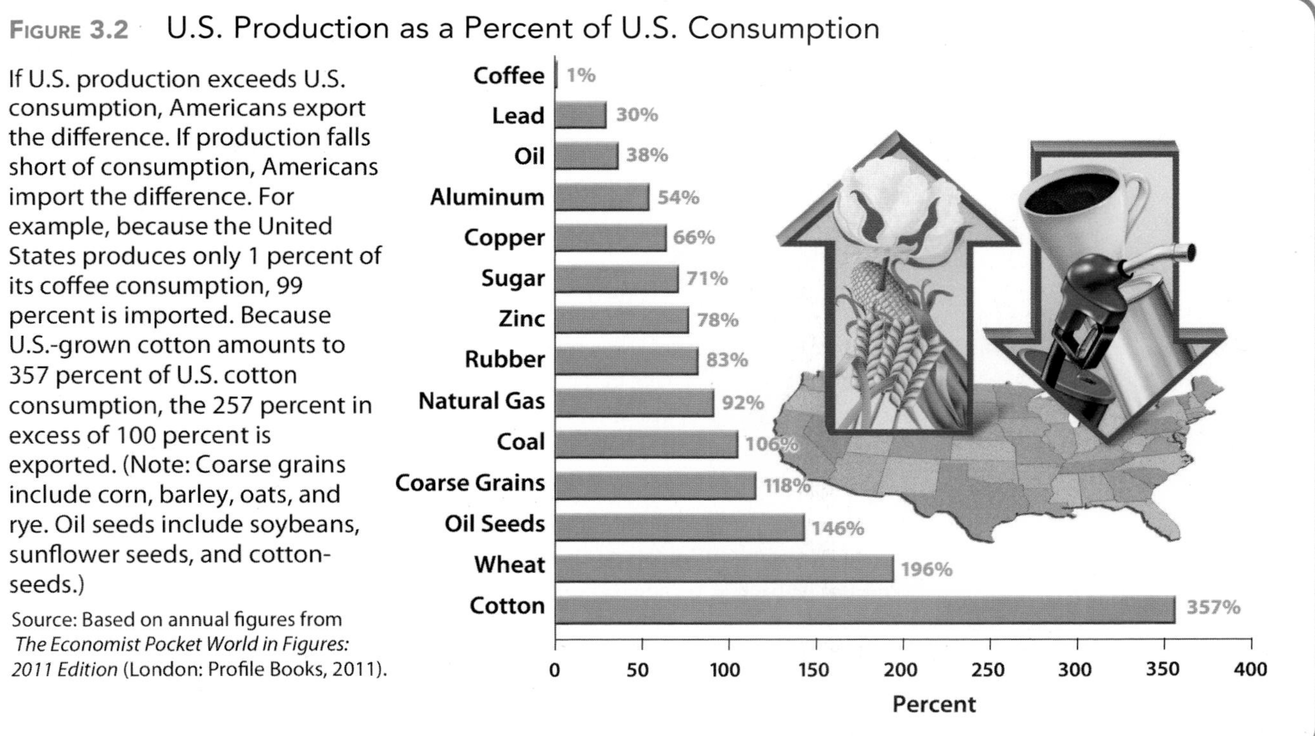

FIGURE 3.2 U.S. Production as a Percent of U.S. Consumption

If U.S. production exceeds U.S. consumption, Americans export the difference. If production falls short of consumption, Americans import the difference. For example, because the United States produces only 1 percent of its coffee consumption, 99 percent is imported. Because U.S.-grown cotton amounts to 357 percent of U.S. cotton consumption, the 257 percent in excess of 100 percent is exported. (Note: Coarse grains include corn, barley, oats, and rye. Oil seeds include soybeans, sunflower seeds, and cottonseeds.)

Source: Based on annual figures from *The Economist Pocket World in Figures: 2011 Edition* (London: Profile Books, 2011).

Why does international trade occur? **CHECKPOINT**

3.1 ASSESSMENT

Think Critically

1. Describe three tasks that would probably have been done within most households 100 years ago that your family now pays others to do.
2. In what ways is working at home on a computer today similar to, and different from, the cottage industry system that existed in the seventeenth century?
3. Identify a product that you often buy and use. Describe the steps that are taken to produce this good. Explain why you do not produce this product for yourself.
4. Think of a recent event that took place in a different part of the world that had an impact on the U.S. economy. Explain how the event affected the U.S. economy.

Graphing Exercise

5. Draw a bar graph that demonstrates the declining size of the average U.S. household, based on the data in the table. Explain why smaller households might purchase more of the goods and services they use rather than produce them.

Year	Average Size of U.S. Household
1950	3.38 members
1960	3.29
1970	3.11
1980	2.75
1990	2.63
2000	2.62
2009	2.57

Source: *Statistical Abstract of the United States: 2011*, Table 61 at http://www.census.gov/compendia/statab/cats/population.html.

Make Academic Connections

6. **History** In 1825 Robert Owen bought a community called New Harmony in Indiana. He told people who lived there to contribute whatever they produced to a community storehouse. They could also take whatever they needed from this storehouse for free. Look up New Harmony and find out how Owen's experiment worked out. Why weren't residents of New Harmony able to benefit from their comparative advantages?
7. **Research** Choose a foreign country that one of your ancestors came from or one that interests you. Investigate this nation's economy and identify products it exports. Explain how this nation benefits from trade by using its comparative advantage.

TeamWork

Working in small teams, brainstorm to identify an item you own that is typically imported from another country. List and explain possible reasons why this product was not manufactured in the United States. How do your answers demonstrate the principle of comparative advantage? Report your team's findings in class.

AND MOVERS SHAKERS

Paul Tudor Jones

Founder, Tudor Investment Corporation

Paul Tudor Jones is the founder of Tudor Investment Corporation. *Forbes* magazine ranks him as one of the richest men in the world. Jones earned an undergraduate degree in economics from the University of Virginia and began working as a trader for broker E. F. Hutton in 1976. After becoming bored with trading, his cousin William Dunavant, Jr., sent him to New Orleans to work for commodity broker Eli Tullis. Tullis taught Jones how to trade cotton futures on the New York Cotton Exchange. Jones said Tullis "…taught me that trading is very competitive and you have to be able to handle getting your butt kicked. No matter how you cut it, there are enormous emotional ups and downs involved."

Tudor Investment Corporation

In 1980 Jones founded Tudor Investment Corporation. The company and its affiliates actively trade, invest, and research in the global marketplace. The company also is involved in the venture capital, currency, debt, and commodity markets.

Jones is famous for his prediction of Black Monday, a devastating stock market crash in 1987. He was able to turn the crash into a success for his company, and he tripled his money. In describing his investment philosophy, Jones said, "I think I am the single most conservative investor on earth in the sense that I absolutely hate losing money…I'd say that my investment philosophy is I don't take a lot of risk. I look for opportunities with tremendously skewed reward-risk opportunities."

He says the secret to being a successful trader is to have "…an undying and unquenchable thirst for information and knowledge." He says over the years his perceptions and priorities have changed, "I think there's a natural progression that everyone goes through. The older you get, the more you realize that a quality life is one that has an extraordinary balance in it. In my twenties all I cared about was being financially successful, and today I look to strive for a more balanced life."

Venture Philanthropy

Jones is more than a successful trader. The Robin Hood Foundation, which Jones founded, is one of the most innovative philanthropic organizations in the United States. Robin Hood does what the name suggests—takes from the rich and gives to the poor. However, whereas in the legend, Robin Hood steals from the rich to give to the poor, Jones networks with wealthy would-be donors to persuade them to give to his foundation, whose mission is to fight poverty in New York City. The foundation follows a "venture philanthropy" approach in that it applies venture capital strategies, skills, and resources to charitable giving. Venture capital refers to funds provided by private investors to start-up companies.

Some of the projects Robin Hood has funded in New York City include:

- The Excellence Charter School for boys, a school focused on educating minority youth and preparing them for college
- Soup kitchens
- Prison education and job training for ex-cons
- Housing for the homeless
- Financial service centers for the poor

Jones has shown it is possible to be as successful in philanthropy as in business. He said, "Poverty is a growth business. The good news is it seems that the best and brightest minds on Wall Street and in business are starting to do something about it."

Think Critically **Comment on Paul Tudor Jones' innovative "venture philanthropy." Why do you think this approach is successful?**

Sources: http://money.cnn.com/magazines/fortune/fortune_archive/2006/09/18/8386204/index.htm; http://nyphilanthropist.com/philanthropists-individuals-paul-tudor-jones.htm; and http://chinese-school.netfirms.com/Paul-Tudor-Jones-interview.html

3.2 REGULATING THE PRIVATE SECTOR

Key Terms

Learning Objectives

LO1 Explain how government can improve operation of the private sector.

LO2 Distinguish between regulations that promote competition and those that control natural monopolies.

LO3 Describe how fiscal policy and monetary policy try to stabilize economic fluctuations.

In Your World

The private sector would not run smoothly on its own in a pure market economy. With no government, there would be no laws to protect your life and property. People could rob your earnings and possessions and steal your inventions and ideas. Contracts, such as insurance policies or cell phone plans, would have no binding force without laws and the authority to enforce those laws. Some firms could drive their competitors out of the market. Firms also might try to sell you unsafe or defective products or otherwise cheat you. These actions could bring about reduced economic activity and result in high unemployment. Government intervention in the economy aims to address these market shortcomings.

RULES FOR A MARKET ECONOMY

LO1
Explain how government can improve operation of the private sector.

The effects of government regulations are all around you. Government-required labels that provide washing instructions are stitched into your clothes. The condition of the vehicle you drive to school is regulated by the government. The government also regulates how fast you can drive and prohibits you from driving under the influence of alcohol. Government has an influence on many aspects of your life, as well on as the economy.

Establishing Property Rights

In a market system, specific individuals usually own the rights to resources. **Private property rights** guarantee individuals the right to use their resources as they choose or to charge others for the use. Owners therefore have a strong incentive to get the most value from their resources. This ensures that resources will find their most productive use.

However, if people could not safeguard their property, they would have less incentive to work, to save, to invest, to buy things, or to pursue other market activity. Markets could break down. You would have less incentive to work if your employer refused to pay you or if you were repeatedly robbed of your earnings.

private property rights Legal claim that guarantees an owner the right to use a resource or to charge others for its use

Governments play a role in safeguarding private property by establishing legal rights of ownership. They then enforce these rights through national defense, police protection, legal contracts, and the judicial system.

Photodisc/Getty Images

Which intellectual property right protects the compositions of this young musician?

Intellectual Property Rights

Laws also grant property rights to the creators of new ideas and new inventions. Inventors reap the rewards of their creations so they have more incentives to create.

Patent laws encourage inventors to invest the time and money required to discover and develop new products and processes. If others could simply copy successful products, inventors would be less willing to incur the initial costs of invention. The limited life of patents also provide the stimulus to turn inventions into marketable products, a process called *innovation.* Abraham Lincoln once observed that "the patent system added the fuel of interest to the fire of genius."

Thus, the patent system establishes property rights to inventions and other technical advances. Likewise, a *copyright* assigns property rights to original expressions of an author, artist, composer, or computer programmer. A *trademark* establishes property rights to unique commercial marks and symbols, such as McDonald's Golden Arches and the Nike Swoosh.

Measurement and Safety

Much market exchange involves products sold by weight, such as a pound of hamburger, or by volume, such as a gallon of gasoline. To ensure that buyers don't get cheated, governments test and certify the accuracy of various measuring devices. For example, the U.S. Bureau of Weights and Measures is responsible for the annual inspection and testing of all commercial measuring devices used to buy, sell, and ship products.

Consumers also want to be confident that the products they buy are safe. The U.S. Food and Drug Administration (FDA) regulates the safety of foods, prescription and over-the-counter drugs, and medical devices. The U.S. Department of Agriculture helps the FDA by inspecting and grading meat and poultry for freshness and quality. The Consumer Product Safety Commission, a federal agency, monitors the safety of all consumer products, from baby cribs to dishwashers.

CHECKPOINT

How can laws and regulations improve the operation of the private sector?

MARKET COMPETITION AND NATURAL MONOPOLIES

LO2
Distinguish between regulations that promote competition and those that control natural monopolies.

It's been said that businesspeople praise competition, but they love monopoly. Their praise of competition echoes Adam Smith's argument that the invisible hand of market competition harnesses self-interest to promote the general good. However, competition imposes a discipline that most businesses would rather avoid. A business owner would prefer to be a monopolist—that is, to be the only seller of a product. As an only seller, a monopolist usually can charge a higher price and earn a greater profit than when facing competition.

Promoting Market Competition

Although competition typically ensures the most efficient use of resources, an individual firm would prefer the higher price and higher profit of monopoly. Here's the problem. When a few firms account for most of the sales in a market, such as the market for steel, those firms may join together to fix a price that is higher than one that would result from greater market competition. These firms try to act like a monopolist to boost their prices and profits. An individual firm also may try to become a monopolist by driving competitors out of business or by merging with competitors.

Thus, a monopoly or a group of firms acting as a monopoly tries to charge a higher price than would result through competition. This higher price hurts consumers more than it benefits producers, making society worse off. Monopoly may harm social welfare in other ways as well. If a monopoly does not have to face market competition, it may be less innovative. Worse still, monopolies may try to influence the political system to protect and enhance their monopoly power.

antitrust laws Laws that reduce anticompetitive behavior and promote competition in markets where competition is desirable

Antitrust laws attempt to promote competition and reduce anticompetitive behavior. These laws prohibit efforts to create a monopoly in a market in which competition is desirable. Antitrust laws are enforced in the courts by government attorneys. They also are enforced by individual firms bringing lawsuits against other firms for violating these laws.

Losevsky Pavel/Shutterstock.com

Why do you think it's more efficient to have one producer build and operate a subway system?

Regulating Natural Monopolies

Competition usually forces the price lower than it would be if the product were sold by a monopoly. In rare instances, however, a monopoly can produce and sell the product for less than could several competing firms. For example, a city's subway service is delivered more efficiently by a single firm digging one tunnel system than by competing firms each digging its own. The cost per rider is lower if the city is served by a single subway system.

When it is cheaper for one firm to serve the market than for two or more firms to do so, that firm is called a **natural monopoly**. But a natural monopoly, if unregulated by government, maximizes profit by charging a higher price than is optimal from society's point of view. Government can increase social welfare by forcing the monopolist to lower its price. To do this, the government can either operate the monopoly itself, as it does with most urban transit systems, or regulate a privately owned monopoly, as some other cities do with their urban transit systems. Government-owned or government-regulated monopolies are called *public utilities.*

CHECKPOINT

Why does government promote competition in some markets and control natural monopolies in others?

GROWTH AND STABILITY OF THE U.S. ECONOMY

LO3
Describe how fiscal policy and monetary policy try to stabilize economic fluctuations.

The U.S. economy and other market economies have alternating periods of growth and decline in their level of economic activity, especially employment and production. *Economic fluctuations* reflect the rise and fall of economic activity relative to the long-term growth trend of the economy. Governments try to reduce these fluctuations, making the bad times not so bad and the good times not quite so good. Pursuing these objectives through taxing and spending is called *fiscal policy.* Pursuing them by regulating the money supply is called *monetary policy.*

Fiscal Policy

Fiscal policy uses taxing and public spending to influence macroeconomic variables such as how much is produced, how many people have jobs, and how fast the economy grows. The idea behind fiscal policy is that when economic activity in the private sector slows down, the government should offset this by cutting taxes to stimulate consumption and investment. The government also may increase its own spending to offset a slumping private sector, as occurred during the 2008–2009 recession.

On the other hand, the economy may be growing so fast it causes higher *inflation*, which is an increase in the economy's average price level. In this case the government should increase taxes and reduce its spending to cool down the economy. This will keep inflation from getting too high.

When economists study fiscal policy, they usually focus on the federal government, although governments at all levels affect the economy. The federal, state, and local governments in the United States spend about $5 trillion per year, making the public sector a significant part of the country's $15 trillion economy.

natural monopoly One firm that can serve the entire market at a lower per-unit cost than two or more firms can

fiscal policy The federal government's use of taxing and public spending to influence the macroeconomy

Monetary Policy

Just as oil makes the gears in a car operate more smoothly, money reduces the friction—the transaction costs—of market exchange. Too little money can leave parts creaking. Too much money can gum up the works.

Monetary policy aims to supply the appropriate amount of money to help stabilize economic fluctuations and promote healthy long-term economic growth. In the United States, monetary policy is the responsibility of the Board of Governors of the Federal Reserve System, the U.S. central bank established by Congress in 1913. The Federal Reserve System, or Fed, used monetary policy to try to stabilize the economy after the 2008 financial crisis. By increasing the money supply, the Fed reduced a key interest rate in the economy. The interest rate is the cost of borrowing money and the reward for lending it. The Fed's action was intended to encourage borrowing and spending and thereby to prevent a deeper recession.

Too much money in circulation results in higher inflation. For example, in 1994 huge increases in Brazil's money supply resulted in wild inflation. Prices in Brazil were on average about 3.6 million times higher in 1994 than in 1988.

monetary policy The Federal Reserve System's attempts to control the money supply to influence the macroeconomy

At the other extreme, too little money in an economy can make market exchange more difficult. For example, people tried to cope with a severe money shortage in the early American colonies by maintaining very careful records, showing who owed what to whom. However, the transaction costs of all this record keeping used up scarce resources and reduced output in the economy.

Span the Globe

Bamboo Capitalism

China began adopting what it called its "bamboo economic policy" when it moved away from a pure command economy and started to embrace aspects of capitalism. In so doing, its economy grew to be the second largest on the globe. As part of this reform, the Chinese government allowed the development of private entrepreneurs. According to some economic analysts, these entrepreneurs are the backbone of the Chinese economy and the reason for its success. Because so many operate outside of the official economy, accurate figures are hard to determine. One estimate is that 90 percent of China's 43 million companies are private, and these companies produce 70 percent of the country's GDP.

The right of many of these companies to exist in China is not clear. Some fear that as the companies become more successful, the government will feel pressured to exert more control.

Think Critically **Which rules for its market economy should China embrace? Can it do this while still officially embracing its brand of "state capitalism"?**

Source: "Bamboo capitalism: China's success owes more to its entrepreneurs than its bureaucrats. Time to bring them out of the shadows," *The Economist*, March 10, 2011); and "The state and the economy: Re-enter the dragon," *The Economist*, June 5, 2010, http://www.economist.com/node/18332610

How do fiscal policy and monetary policy reduce economic fluctuations?

CHECKPOINT

3.2 ASSESSMENT

Think Critically

1. Describe one way your life might be different if the government did not protect individual property rights.
2. Study the contents label of a cereal box. Explain how the government attempts to protect consumers when it requires manufacturers to place these labels on food products.
3. During the economic expansion of the early 2000s, the Federal Reserve System took steps to reduce the rate of growth of money in the U.S. economy. Was this an example of monetary policy that was intended to slow the growth of production? Why or why not?

CHANGES IN THE MONEY SUPPLY AND INTEREST RATES, 2001–2010

Year	% change in money supply	% interest charged to businesses
2001	8.7%	6.9%
2002	3.2	4.7
2003	7.1	4.1
2004	5.4	4.3
2005	-0.1	6.2
2006	-0.6	8.0
2007	0.5	8.1
2008	16.7	5.1
2009	5.7	3.3
2010	8.2	3.3

Source: *Economic Indicators*, March 2011, pp. 26 & 30.

Graphing Exercise

4. Draw a double line graph of changes in the money supply and interest rates charged to large businesses in the U.S. economy, based on the data in the top table at the right. Describe if and how these two sets of data appear to be related to each other.

FEDERAL SPENDING AND REVENUE, 2001–2010 AMOUNTS IN BILLIONS OF DOLLARS

Year	Spending	Revenue	Difference
2001	1,863	1,991	___
2002	2,012	1,853	___
2003	2,160	1,783	___
2004	2,293	1,880	___
2005	2,472	2,154	___
2006	2,655	2,407	___
2007	2,729	2,568	___
2008	2,982	2,524	___
2009	3,518	2,105	___
2010	3,456	2,162	___

Source: *Economic Report of the President*, February 2011, Table B-80.

Make Academic Connections

5. **Math** Calculate the amount of the federal government's surplus or deficit in different years, using data in the bottom table. Are you concerned about the government spending more than it receives in taxes? Explain your point of view.

TeamWork

Working in small teams, identify a natural monopoly from which your family purchases goods or services (electric, natural gas, or water utilities, for example). Describe what would happen if the government forced the creation of one or more businesses to compete with this firm. Compare your findings with other teams.

3.3 PUBLIC GOODS AND EXTERNALITIES

Key Terms

private goods 78
public goods 78
open-access goods 79
negative externalities 81
positive externalities 81

Learning Objectives

LO1 Describe and provide examples of four types of goods.

LO2 Define negative and positive externalities.

In Your World

Government tries to improve the performance of the private sector—enforcing property rights, promoting competition, regulating natural monopolies, and smoothing out the business cycle. However, the private sector cannot profitably supply some goods that you and other people want. The government is in a better position to supply goods such as national defense and a system of justice. What's more, the private sector sometimes affects people not involved in a market transaction, such as the factory that pollutes the air you breathe. In such cases, the government often intervenes to improve the market's performance.

PRIVATE GOODS, PUBLIC GOODS, AND IN BETWEEN

LO1
Describe and provide examples of four types of goods.

So far this book has been talking mostly about private goods, such as tacos, toasters, and cell phone service. Other categories of goods exist as well. At the other extreme are public goods, with various categories in between, including natural monopoly goods and open-access goods.

Private Goods

Private goods have two important features. First, they are *rival in consumption.* This means that the amount consumed by one person is unavailable for others to consume. For example, when you and some friends share a pizza, each slice they eat is one less available for you. A second key feature of a private good is that suppliers can easily exclude those who don't pay, so a private good is said to be *exclusive.* Only paying customers get a pizza. Thus a private good is both *rival in consumption* and *exclusive.*

private goods Goods with two features: (1) the amount consumed by one person is unavailable to others, and (2) nonpayers can easily be excluded

public goods Goods that, once produced, are available to all, but the producer cannot easily exclude nonpayers

Public Goods

In contrast to private goods, **public goods**, such as national defense, the Centers for Disease Control, or a neighborhood mosquito-control program, are nonrival in consumption. One person's benefit does not reduce the amount available to others. Such goods are available to all in equal amount. Once the good is produced, the marginal cost of providing the good to an additional consumer is zero.

Public goods are not provided through the market system because of the problem of who would pay for them. Public goods are both nonrival and nonexclusive. Once produced, public goods are available for all to consume, regardless of who pays and who doesn't. As a consequence, for-profit firms cannot profitably sell public goods. For example, if a private firm were to spray a neighborhood for mosquitoes, all of the households in the neighborhood would benefit. However, many households might not be willing to pay, figuring that they would still benefit from the spraying. These households would be called *free riders.*

The government provides public goods and funds them through enforced taxation. Sometimes nonprofit agencies also provide public goods, funding them through charitable contributions and other revenue sources.

Natural Monopoly Goods

The economy consists of more than just private goods and public goods. Some goods are nonrival but exclusive. For example, numerous households can tune to the same TV show without harming the TV reception of other viewers. TV signals are nonrival in consumption. Yet the program's producer can make viewers "pay" for the show, either by adding commercials or by charging each household for the show, as with cable TV and pay-per-view. So the TV signal is nonrival but exclusive. Likewise, as noted earlier, additional passengers can ride a subway without reducing the benefits of other riders. Until the subway becomes crowded, the service is nonrival (once the subway draws a crowd, space in the cars becomes scarce and the service becomes rival, like a private good). Goods that are nonrival but exclusive result from *natural monopolies*, a term introduced earlier.

Open-Access Goods

Finally, some other goods are rival but nonexclusive. The fish in the ocean are rival because every fish caught is not available for others to catch. The same goes for migratory game, like wild geese. Ocean fish and migratory game are nonexclusive in that it would be costly or impossible for a private firm to prevent access to them. Goods that are rival but nonexclusive are called **open-access goods** because it would be difficult and costly to block access to these goods.

In the absence of regulations, open-access goods are overfished, overhunted, and overused. For example, the United Nations reports that 11 of the world's 15 primary fishing grounds are seriously depleted.

By imposing restrictions on open-access resources, governments try to keep renewable resources from becoming depleted. Regulators try to reduce resource use to a sustainable rate. For example, governments now impose a variety of restrictions on the fishing industry to reduce the tendency to overfish.

Summary Table

Figure 3.3 summarizes the four types of goods in the economy. Across the top, goods are either *rival* or *nonrival*, and along the left margin, goods are either *exclusive* or *nonexclusive*. Private goods usually are provided by the private sector.

open-access goods
Goods that are rival in consumption but exclusion is costly

FIGURE 3.3 Categories of Private and Public Goods

The four types of goods—private, natural monopoly, open-access, and public—are characterized as being either rival or nonrival in consumption and either exclusive or nonexclusive. Think of two more examples for each type of good.

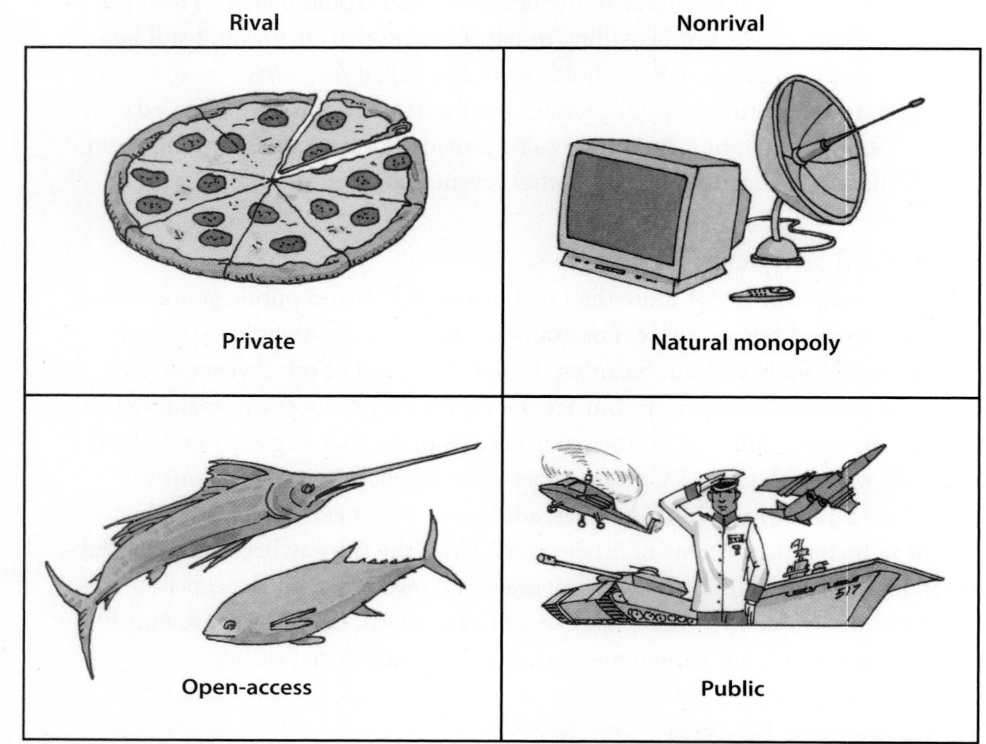

Natural monopoly goods are sometimes provided by government, as with an urban transit system. Other times they are provided by the private sector, as with a government-regulated but privately owned urban transit system. Government also usually regulates open-access goods, such as with fishing licenses and fishing seasons. Government usually funds public goods with taxes.

CHECKPOINT **Name the four categories of goods, and provide an example of each.**

EXTERNALITIES

LO2 Define negative externalities and positive externalities.

The rivers in Jakarta, Indonesia, are dead—killed by acid, alcohol, and oil. Some coral reefs in the South Pacific have been ripped apart by dynamite fishing. The air in some U.S. cities does not meet health standards. These are all examples of *negative externalities*, which are by-products of production and consumption. Some externalities are positive. For example, if you get vaccinated, you reduce your chances of contracting that disease. However, you also reduce the chances that others will catch it from you, so they benefit, too. *The private sector, operating on its own, produces too many negative externalities and too few positive externalities.* Government intervenes in the market to improve the outcomes.

Negative Externalities

A renewable resource can be used indefinitely if used conservatively. Some renewable resources also are open-access resources. This creates a special problem for the environment. The atmosphere and waterways are renewable resources to the extent they can absorb and neutralize a certain level of pollutants yet still remain relatively clean. **Negative externalities** generally are by-products of production or consumption that impose costs on third parties. (Third parties are those who are neither the buyer nor the seller in a transaction.)

Market prices can direct the allocation of resources as long as property rights are well defined and can be enforced at a reasonable cost. But private property rights to open-access resources cannot be easily defined and enforced. Therefore, pollution of open-access resources such as air, land, water, peace and quiet, and scenery arises due to overuse.

Polluters of an open-access resource tend to ignore the impact of their pollution on other people and on the resource's ability to renew itself. Therefore, the quality and quantity of an open-access resource tends to decline over time.

Government restrictions can improve the allocation of open-access resources. For example, antipollution laws limit the kind and amount of gases that can be released into the atmosphere from factories, automobiles, and other pollution sources. Restrictions aimed at maintaining water quality limit what can be dumped into the nation's rivers, lakes, and oceans. Noise restrictions aim at maintaining peace and quiet. Local zoning laws limit where firms can locate and in what condition homes must be maintained. In short, government restrictions try to reduce negative externalities.

Positive Externalities

Some externalities are positive, or beneficial. **Positive externalities** occur when the by-products of consumption or production benefit third parties. For example, education generates positive externalities. Society as a whole benefits from education. Those who acquire more education become better citizens, can read road signs, and become more productive workers who are better able to support themselves and their families. Educated people also are less likely to require public assistance or to resort to violent crime for income. Thus, education benefits those getting the education, but it also confers benefits on others.

When there are positive externalities, governments aim to increase the level of production beyond what would be chosen privately. For example, governments try to increase the level of education by providing free primary and secondary education, by requiring students to stay in school until they reach 16 years of age, by subsidizing public higher education, and by offering tax breaks for some education expenditures.

negative externalities
By-products of production or consumption that impose costs on third parties

positive externalities
By-products of consumption or production that benefit third parties

CHECKPOINT What are negative externalities and positive externalities, and why does government intervene to regulate them?

3.3 ASSESSMENT

Think Critically

1. Most public school districts require students to be vaccinated before they are allowed to attend school. Are vaccinations an example of a public good? Why or why not?
2. Identify and describe an example of each of the following types of goods that you encounter in your life.
   a. private good
   b. good resulting from a natural monopoly
   c. open-access good
   d. public goods
3. Describe an example of a negative externality that has been a problem in your community. Describe steps your community has taken to try to eliminate or reduce the negative externality you identified.

Graphing Exercise

4. Construct a pie chart for 2000 and another for 2010 that show federal spending on natural resources and the environment. Base your charts on the data in the table. What parts of this spending may have been dedicated to trying to reduce negative externalities?

FEDERAL SPENDING FOR NATURAL RESOURCES AND THE ENVIRONMENT, 2000 AND 2010 (AMOUNTS IN BILLIONS OF DOLLARS)

Type of Spending	2000	% of total	2010	% of total
Water resources	$ 5.1	20.6%	$12.4	26.4%
Conservation	5.9	23.8	12.1	25.7
Recreation	3.4	13.7	4.0	8.5
Pollution control	7.4	29.8	11.5	24.4
Other	3.0	12.1	7.0	14.9
Total	$24.8	100.0	$47.0	100.0

Source: *Statistical Abstract of the United States: 2011*, p. 312.

Make Academic Connections

5. **Business Management** Although trucks powered by natural gas are expensive to purchase, they create little pollution when operating. Why do you think some states give tax reductions to businesses that use natural gas-powered trucks? Explain how this is an effort by these states to reduce a negative externality. Do you think this is a good idea? Why or why not?

In small teams, brainstorm a list of public goods that you and your families consume. Make sure that each good you list is both nonrival and nonexclusive. Have groups compare their work.

21st Century Skills

Media Literacy

Express Yourself

In the United States, consumers may obtain goods or services from the government or businesses. They also may provide the goods and services for themselves. Education is a good example of this. Most students in this country attend public schools. Others attend private or religious schools or are home-schooled. No matter where education takes place, it requires an allocation of scarce resources.

In recent years individuals and groups in many communities have worked to reduce the growth in spending on public education. Others have encouraged a greater expansion of this spending. Convincing decision makers that one point of view or the other is correct has involved the use of many types of media, including

- Reports of public demonstrations on television, radio, or the Internet
- Printed signs on private property or in public locations
- Letters or e-mails to politicians
- Print, television, radio, or other media advertisements
- Appearances on talk radio or television shows
- Text messages to individuals

Different Media Reach Different People

Different people pay attention to different types of media. The number of subscribers to newspapers, for example, has been falling as people have turned to television and the Internet for news and information. As a group, newspaper readers tend to be older and often wealthier than people who do not read newspapers. A message to convince grandparents to encourage their grandchildren to attend a certain university would probably be more successful using print media than by placing advertisements on the Internet. The same message would better reach graduating high school seniors through use of electronic media.

Is It True?

Just because a statement appears in the media does not make it is true. When you receive media communications on an issue you care about, take time to investigate their validity. Steps you might take include

- Look for evidence from other sources that either support or refute the message.
- Evaluate whether the message is based on facts and logic or on opinion.
- Ask people whom you respect for their perspective on the message.

A final step you should take is to consider the message in relation to other information you already have about the issue. Ask yourself whether it fits in with what you know or makes little sense when placed in this perspective.

Apply the Skill

Assume that members of your town council will decide next week whether to spend $100,000 in tax money to install lights at a local little league baseball park. This would allow eight more teams to join the league that now has a waiting list of more than 200 children.

Decide whether you would support or oppose this expenditure. Then describe three ways you could use media to convince others your point of view is correct. Identify the group you would target with each method of communication. Explain why you believe each message would be successful for that group.

3.4 PROVIDING A SAFETY NET

Key Terms

median income 84
social insurance 88
income-assistance programs 89

Learning Objectives

LO1 Determine why household incomes differ, and identify the main source of poverty in the United States.

LO2 Describe government programs that provide a safety net for poor people.

In Your World

Operating on its own, the private sector offers no guarantee that you will earn enough to survive. What if you have few resources that are valued in the market? Because markets do not guarantee even a minimum level of income, society has made the political decision that poor families should receive short-term public assistance, or welfare. This aid reflects society's attempt to provide a social safety net. However, public assistance could reduce a recipient's incentive to work, because welfare benefits decrease as earnings from work increase.

INCOME AND POVERTY

LO1 Determine why household incomes differ, and identify the main source of poverty in the United States.

In a market economy, income depends primarily on earnings, which depend on the value of each person's contribution to production. The problem with allocating income according to productivity is that some people are not very productive. Individuals born with mental or physical disabilities tend to be less productive and may be unable to earn a living. Others may face limited job choices and low wages because of advanced age, poor health, little education, discrimination, bad luck, or the demands of caregiving, among other reasons. Consider first why incomes differ across households.

Why Household Incomes Differ

The **median income** of all households in the economy is the middle income when incomes are ranked from lowest to highest. In any given year, half of the households are above the median income and half are below it.

The main reason household incomes differ is that the number of household members who are working differs. For example, the median income for households with two earners is nearly double that for households with only one earner and about four times that for households with no earners. Household incomes also differ for all the reasons that labor earnings differ, including differences in education, ability, job experience, and so on.

median income The middle income when a group of incomes is ranked from lowest to highest

On average, people with more education earn more, at every age. For example, those with a professional degree earn about four times more than those who only have a high school education. Age itself has an important effect on income. As workers mature, they typically acquire valuable job experience, get promoted, and earn more.

NET Bookmark

Data and reports about income distribution can be found at the U.S. Census Bureau's website. Access this website through the URL shown below. Click on the link to Frequently Asked Questions. Write down five statistics you learned about income in the United States.

www.cengage.com/school/contecon

Differences in earnings based on age and education reflect a normal life-cycle pattern of income. In fact, most income differences across households reflect the normal workings of resource markets, whereby workers are rewarded according to their productivity. Because of these lifetime patterns, the same households do not necessarily remain rich or poor over time. There is much income mobility among households.

Despite this mobility over time, generalizations can be made. High-income households typically consist of well-educated couples with both spouses employed. Low-income households typically are headed by single mothers who are young, poorly educated, and not in the labor force.

Young, single motherhood is a recipe for poverty. Often the young mother drops out of school, which reduces her future earning possibilities when and if she seeks work outside the home. Even a strong economy is little aid to households with nobody in the labor force.

Official Poverty Rate

Because poverty is such a relative concept, how can it be measured objectively over time? The federal government determines the official poverty level and adjusts this benchmark over time to account for inflation. For example, the official poverty level for a family of four was $22,350 in 2011.

U.S. poverty since 1959 is presented in Figure 3.4 on page 86. Poverty is measured both in millions of people living below the official poverty level and in the percent of the U.S. population below that level. Periods of U.S. recession are shaded as vertical pink bars. A recession is defined as a decline in the nation's total production that lasts at least six months. Note how poverty increases during recessions.

The biggest decline in U.S. poverty occurred before 1970. The poverty rate dropped from 22 percent in 1959 to 12 percent in 1969. During that period, the number of poor people decreased from about 40 million to 24 million. More recently, the poverty rate declined from 15.1 percent in 1993 to 11.3 percent in 2000. It then rose to 14.3 percent by 2009. The 43.6 million people in poverty in 2009 was the highest total on record.

Poverty is a relative term. The U.S. official poverty level of income is many times greater than the average income for most of the world's population. Some other countries set a much lower income level as their poverty level. For example, the poverty level for a family of four in the United States in 2009 was $15.31 per person per day. The poverty level used in many developing countries around the world is $1 or $2 per person per day.

FIGURE 3.4 **Number and Percent of U.S. Population in Poverty: 1959–2009**

On the line graph, the "number in poverty" line shows how many millions of people were living below the official poverty level. The "poverty rate" line shows the percent of the U.S. population below that level. Periods of U.S. recessions are shaded. What happens to the number in poverty and the poverty rate during a recession?

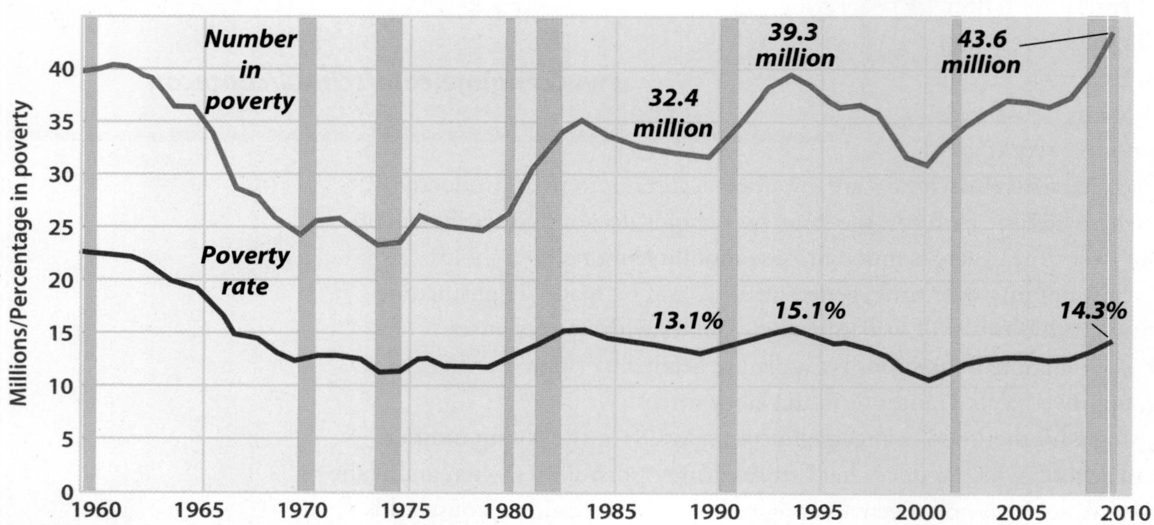

Source: U.S. Census Bureau, *Income, Poverty, and Health Insurance Coverage in the United States: 2009*, Current Population Reports, September 2010, Fig. 4, p. 14, www.census.gov/prod/2010pubs/p60-238.pdf.

Angela Farley/Shutterstock.com

Why do you think babies born to teenage mothers are more likely than other children to be poor?

Poverty and Marital Status

One way to measure poverty is based on the marital status of the household head. Figure 3.5 compares poverty rates since 1973 for

1. families headed by females with no husband present.
2. families headed by males with no wife present.
3. married couples.

Three trends are clear. First, poverty rates among female-headed families are five to six times greater than rates among married couples. Second, poverty rates among female-headed families are two to three times greater than those for male-headed families. And third, poverty rates trended down for all types of families beginning in the mid-1990s, but began rising in 2000 and continued to increase during the recession of 2008–2009.

FIGURE 3.5 **U.S. Poverty Rates and Types of Households**

Female-headed families have the highest poverty rate in the United States, followed by male-headed families and married couples.

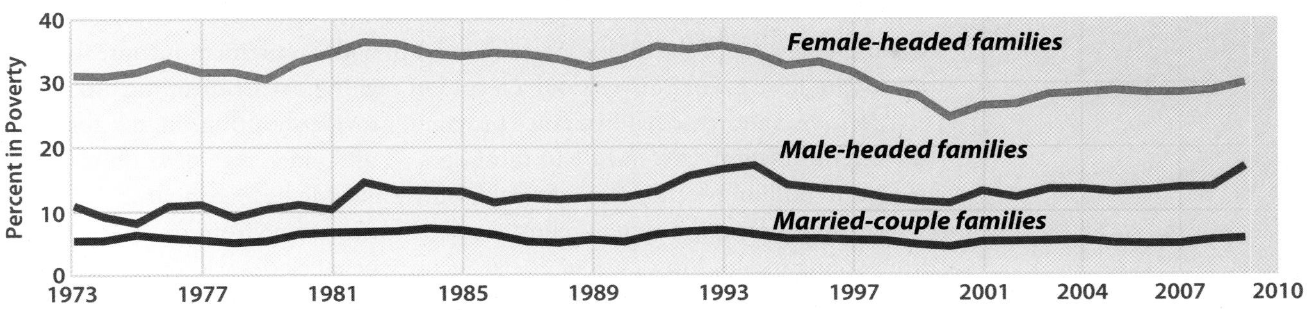

Source: Developed from U.S. Census Bureau, *Income, Poverty, and Health Insurance Coverage in the United States: 2009*, Current Population Reports, September 2010, Table B-3 at www.census.gov/prod/2010pubs/p60-238.pdf.

The percent of births to unmarried mothers is five times greater today than in 1960. Many of these births are to teenage mothers. The United States has the highest teenage pregnancy rate in the developed world—twice the rate of Great Britain and more than 12 times that of Japan. Because fathers in such cases typically assume little responsibility for child support, children born outside marriage are much more likely to be poor than other children are. Births to single mothers make up the primary source of poverty in the United States.

CHECKPOINT

Why do incomes differ across households, and what is the main source of poverty in the U.S. economy?

PROGRAMS TO HELP THE POOR

LO2
Describe government programs that provide a safety net for poor people.

How should society respond to poverty? Families with a full-time worker are nine times more likely to escape poverty than families with no workers. Thus, the government's first line of defense in fighting poverty is to promote job opportunities. Yet even when the unemployment rate is low, some people remain poor.

Since the 1960s, spending for income redistribution at all levels of government has increased sharply. These programs divide into two broad categories: social insurance and income assistance.

Social Insurance Programs

Social insurance programs are designed to help people who lose income due to retirement, temporary unemployment, or inability to work resulting from a work-related injury or disability. The U.S. government funds all these programs. The major social insurance program is Social Security, established during the Great Depression of the 1930s. *Social Security* provides retirement income for those who have a work history and a record of making payments to the program.

Medicare, another social insurance program, provides health insurance for short-term medical care, mostly to those ages 65 and older, regardless of income. About 50 million people receive Social Security and Medicare benefits.

The social insurance system tends to redistribute income from rich to poor and from young to old. Most current Social Security beneficiaries will receive far more in benefits than they paid into the program, especially those with a brief work history or a record of low wages.

social insurance Cash transfers for retirees, the unemployed, and others with a work history and a record of contributions to the program

Other social insurance programs include unemployment insurance and workers' compensation, which supports workers injured on the job. Both programs require that beneficiaries have a prior record of employment.

Kzenon/Shutterstock.com

Providing social insurance programs takes a large portion of the country's annual budget and has been a target of reform by many legislators. Do you think the federal government should be responsible for providing these programs? Why or why not?

Income-Assistance Programs

Income-assistance programs—typically called welfare programs—provide money and in-kind assistance to poor people. Programs that give money directly to recipients are called *cash transfer programs.* Non-cash forms of assistance, such as for housing and healthcare, are provided through *in-kind transfer programs.*

Unlike social insurance programs, income-assistance programs do not require a work history or a record of contributions. Instead, income-assistance programs are means tested. In a *means-tested program,* a household's income and assets must fall below a certain level to qualify for benefits. The federal government funds two-thirds of welfare spending, and state and local governments fund one-third.

Cash Transfer Programs The two main cash transfer programs are *Temporary Assistance for Needy Families (TANF),* which provides cash to poor families with dependent children, and *Supplemental Security Income (SSI),* which provides cash to the elderly poor and the disabled. Cash transfers vary inversely with family income from other sources. The federal government gives each state a fixed grant to help fund TANF programs. Each state determines eligibility standards.

The SSI program helps the elderly and disabled poor, including people addicted to drugs and alcohol, children with learning disabilities, and, in some cases, the homeless. SSI is the fastest-growing cash transfer program, with outlays of $56 billion in 2011, double the TANF outlays that year.

In-Kind Transfer Programs A variety of in-kind transfer programs provide goods and services such as food vouchers, healthcare, housing assistance, and school lunches to the poor. Medicaid funds medical care for those with incomes below a certain level who are elderly, blind, disabled, or are living in families with dependent children. *Medicaid is the largest welfare program, costing nearly twice as much as all cash transfer programs combined.* It has grown more than any other poverty program, quadrupling in the past decade and accounting for nearly one-fifth of the typical state's budget. States get federal grants covering half or more of their Medicaid budget.

Each state sets the qualifying level of income. Some states are quite strict. Therefore, the proportion of poor covered by Medicaid varies greatly across states. In 2011, nearly 60 million people received free medical care under Medicaid at a total cost of about $400 billion. Outlays averaged about $7,000 per recipient.

In all, there are about 75 means-tested federal welfare programs. To get some idea of federal spending on programs to help the poor, also called *income redistribution programs,* look at Figure 3.6, on the next page. This figure shows the composition of federal outlays since 1960. As you can see, income redistribution, including Social Security, Medicare, and various welfare programs, increased from about one-fifth of all federal outlays in 1960 to about half by 2011. Conversely, defense spending fell from more than half of all federal outlays in 1960 to about one-fifth by 2011. Thus, income redistribution claims a growing share of the federal budget and accounts for half of federal outlays.

income-assistance programs Government programs that provide money and in-kind assistance to poor people

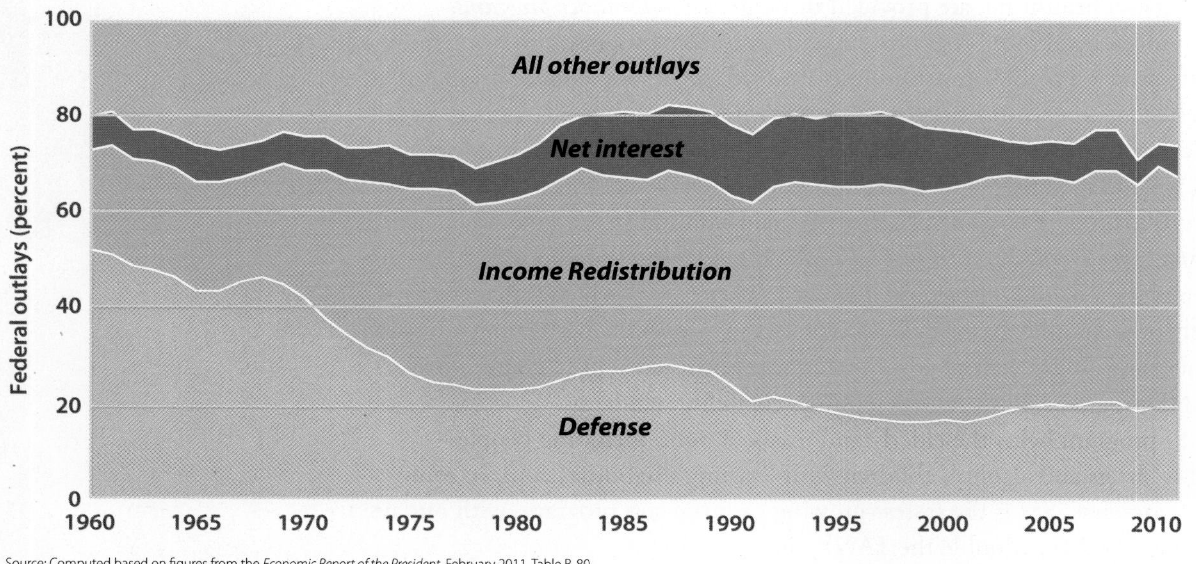

FIGURE 3.6 Income Redistribution as a Percentage of All Federal Outlays, 1960–2011

Since 1960, spending on income redistribution has increased and spending on defense has decreased as a share of federal outlays.

Source: Computed based on figures from the *Economic Report of the President*, February 2011, Table B-80

Earned-Income Tax Credit

The *earned-income tax credit* supplements wages of the working poor. For example, a family with three children that earned $21,000 in 2010 paid no federal income tax and received a cash transfer of about $5,700. The idea is to increase income and to provide incentives for people to work. More than 20 million working families received such transfers in 2010, requiring federal outlays exceeding $40 billion. Many states also have their own programs.

Welfare Reform

The biggest reform of the welfare system in the past 60 years came with 1996 legislation that created the current system, Temporary Assistance for Needy Families (TANF). The earlier program established eligibility rules that guaranteed the federal government would pay most of the cost. Families could stay on welfare for a decade or more. Under the new system, states get a fixed amount of aid from the federal government and can run their own welfare programs. The system requires welfare recipients to look for jobs and limits cash transfers to five years.

About half the states impose time limits shorter than five years. Some observers fear that states now have an incentive to keep welfare costs down by cutting benefits. To avoid becoming destinations for poor people—that is, to avoid becoming "welfare magnets"—states may be tempted to offer relatively low levels of benefits.

Welfare reform has reduced welfare rolls and increased employment. However, because most people on welfare are poorly educated and have few job skills, wages for those who find jobs remain low. Part-time work also is common, as are job losses among those who find jobs.

On the plus side, the earned-income tax credit provided up to $5,700 in 2010 in additional income to low-income workers with some states adding to that total. Most of those getting off welfare by finding jobs also can continue to receive food vouchers, child care, and Medicaid.

What are the main government programs created to offer a safety net? **CHECKPOINT**

Math in Economics

Common Core Statistics and Probability

You can find the average, or mean, income for a group of people by adding their individual incomes together and dividing that total by the number of incomes.

EXAMPLE Find the mean income for five students who earn the following amounts each week: $57.62, $34.21, $82.23, $19.50, $62.44.

SOLUTION $57.62 + $34.21 + $82.23 + $19.50 + $62.44 = $256.00

$256.00 ÷ 5 = $51.20

The average, or mean, income of the students is $51.20.

Practice the Skill Find the mean income for each group of student incomes.

1. $14.36, $28.92, $43.13, $81.95
2. $73.90, $92.04, $53.55, $66.89, $71.02
3. $12.72, $16.47, $127.08
4. Consider the third problem. Explain why the mean income for the group is not close to the incomes in the problem. What conclusion can you make about how the mean income may have limited meaning when one income in a group is very different from the other incomes?

3.4 ASSESSMENT

Think Critically

1. Explain why a pure market economy would not work well if all people were guaranteed the same income by the government.
2. Why is poverty a relative term?
3. Think of a person you know who you believe lives in poverty. What steps could the government take to help this person escape poverty? Do you think the government should do these things? Would you be willing to pay more taxes to support this type of help?
4. Why do you think spending for Medicare is the most rapidly growing part of the social insurance program?
5. After the U.S. welfare system was reformed 1996 the number of welfare cases fell by more than half. Explain why this does not necessarily mean that the number of people living in poverty was also cut in half during these years.

Graphing Exercise

6. Draw a double line graph of the percent of U.S. residents and children who were officially designated as living in poverty from 2000 through 2008, based on the data in the table below. As a percent, why do more children than adults live in poverty?

PERCENT OF U.S. RESIDENTS AND CHILDREN LIVING IN POVERTY, 2000–2008

Year	% of total population living in poverty	% of children living in poverty
2000	11.3%	15.6%
2002	12.1%	16.3%
2004	12.7%	17.3%
2006	12.3%	16.9%
2008	13.2%	18.5%

Source: *Statistical Abstract of the United States: 2011*, pp. 464, 465.

Make Academic Connections

7. **Sociology** In the years following the recession of 2008–2009, many low-income families moved from northern cities such as Detroit, Cleveland, and Chicago to southern states where their families had originally come from. Investigate this migration and explain how changes in government assistance programs may have contributed to it.

TeamWork

Working in small teams, brainstorm a list of ways in which low-income families could be helped to escape poverty. Agree on the one that members of your team think would be both effective and affordable for society. How difficult is it to form a plan that meets both these criteria? Explain your team's suggestion to the class.

Connect to History

The Commerce Clause

In September, 1786, at a meeting held in Annapolis, Maryland, delegates from five states met to discuss the problems of interstate commerce. Realizing that the problems were beyond their power to resolve, the Virginia delegation and Alexander Hamilton called for a general convention to be held in Philadelphia the next year. When the convention met on May 25, it was with the purpose of revising the Articles of Confederation. The delegates decided to abandon the Articles and write a new plan of government. By September 17, the 55 delegates representing 12 of the 13 states had drafted the U.S. Constitution. Although inspired by economic circumstances, the U.S. Constitution is not just an economic document. Even so, the Constitution contains the basis of the country's economic success.

Much of the federal government's regulatory power comes from Article 1, Section 8—the Commerce Clause—of the U.S. Constitution. This section states that Congress shall have the power to "regulate commerce with foreign nations, and among the several states, and with Indian tribes." The first major case involving the Commerce Clause was *Gibbons v. Ogden*. In this 1824 decision the U.S. Supreme Court, led by Chief Justice John Marshall, established the government's right to regulate interstate commerce. However, Marshall didn't stop there. He used the case as an opportunity to expand the power of the federal government by broadening the definition of commerce. Reading the phrase "to regulate commerce . . . among the several states," Marshall rejected the notion that "commerce" meant only the transportation of goods across state lines for sale. In his opinion, the term "commerce" came to include nearly every commercial activity that eventually would include the transportation of persons, things, services, or power across state lines. This opinion was confirmed by subsequent Court rulings.

The 1887 Interstate Commerce Act, which created the Interstate Commerce Commission (ICC), and the Sherman Antitrust Act (1890) were the federal government's first major use of the Commerce Clause as the authority for regulating the economy. This introduced the Progressive Era of the early twentieth century, which saw the government increase its regulatory power with the Hepburn Act (1906), the Mann-Elkins Act (1910), and the creation of the Federal Trade Commission (1914). The Commerce Clause has been used to justify the expansion of government into many aspects of the national life and economy. For example, it has been used to justify laws prohibiting child labor, to regulate business-labor relations, to create a federal minimum wage, and to prosecute gangsters.

Between 1789 and 1950, more Supreme Court cases dealt with the Commerce Clause than any other Constitutional clause. The Court's actions have made it an important, if not *the most important*, source of government power over the economy. President Ronald Reagan tried to roll back some of that power in the 1980s, when he attempted to abolish the Interstate Commerce Commission (ICC). He argued that deregulation had made the agency unnecessary. Congress refused to go along. Today the power of the federal government to regulate any business activity that even remotely affects interstate commerce seems well established.

Think Critically **Read and analyze the Fifth Amendment and the rest of the Commerce Clause of the U.S. Constitution. What parts of these affect the U.S. economic system, and how?**

Chapter 3 Summary

ASK THE EXPERT

www.cengage.com/school/contecon

Will there always be poverty?

3.1 The U.S. Private Sector

A. There are four types of decision makers in the U.S. economy: households, firms, government, and the rest of the world.

B. Firms gained importance in the economy during the Industrial Revolution. By gathering resources into one location, a firm created a more efficient division of labor.

3.2 Regulating the Private Sector

A. The private sector of the U.S. economy would not run smoothly without some government regulation. Economic rules created and enforced by the government set standards for quality and weights and measures, and protect property rights and consumer safety.

B. The federal government promotes market competition and limits monopoly power by enforcing antitrust laws and regulating natural monopolies.

C. The government promotes economic growth and stability through fiscal and monetary policies. Fiscal policy uses taxes and public spending to influence economic conditions. Monetary policy adjusts the amount of money in the economy to influence interest rates, borrowing, spending, and production.

3.3 Public Goods and Externalities

A. Goods can be classified as private goods, public goods, natural monopoly goods, or open-access goods.

B. Public goods are nonrival and nonexclusive. Use of a public good by one person does not prevent another person from benefiting from it.

C. Natural monopoly goods are nonrival but exclusive. The use of a subway by one person does not prevent others from using it, too, unless it becomes very crowded. The subway owner, however, may charge for entry, which limits access only to those who choose to pay.

D. Open-access goods are rival but nonexclusive. If you collect seashells at the beach, the shells you gather cannot be collected by others. However, you are free to collect as many as you can find.

E. Negative externalities are costs of production that are imposed on people who are neither the producer nor the consumer of a product.

3.4 Providing a Safety Net

A. In a pure market economy, people would receive income in proportion to the value of their contribution to production. Individuals unable to work could fall into poverty and starve. Government provides assistance to those who otherwise might live in poverty.

B. The official poverty rate in the United States declined in most years since the government began to measure poverty. It increased during the 2008–2009 recession. Poverty is most common for households headed by single mothers.

C. The government has established many programs to help specific groups of people. Among these are social insurance programs, income-assistance programs, and the earned-income tax credit. The nation's welfare programs were reformed in 1996, with the creation of the Temporary Assistance for Needy Families Program.

CHAPTER 3 ASSESSMENT

Review Economic Terms

Match the terms with the definitions. Some terms will not be used.

_____ 1. A household's level of satisfaction, happiness, or sense of well-being

_____ 2. Laws that prohibit anticompetitive behavior and promote competition

_____ 3. Legal claims that guarantee an owner the right to use a good or resource exclusively or to charge others for its use

_____ 4. The federal government's use of taxing and public spending to influence the macroeconomy

_____ 5. The Federal Reserve System's attempts to control the money supply to influence the macroeconomy

_____ 6. One firm that can serve an entire market at a lower per-unit cost than two or more firms can

_____ 7. A good with two features: (1) the amount consumed by one person is unavailable to others, and (2) nonpayers can be excluded easily

_____ 8. A good that, once produced, is available for all to consume, but the producer cannot easily exclude nonpayers from consuming it

_____ 9. A good that is rival in consumption but exclusion is costly

_____ 10. By-products of consumption or production that benefit third parties

a. antitrust laws
b. firm
c. fiscal policy
d. household
e. income-assistance programs
f. Industrial Revolution
g. median income
h. monetary policy
i. natural monopoly
j. negative externalities
k. open-access good
l. positive externalities
m. private good
n. private property rights
o. public good
p. social insurance
q. utility

Review Economic Concepts

11. All those who live together under one roof are considered to be part of the same ________?________.

12. Firms organizing production in large, centrally powered factories did all of the following except
    a. promote a more efficient division of labor.
    b. reduce transportation costs.
    c. reduce consumer reliance on trade.
    d. enable the use of specialized machines.

13. In the evolution of the firm, the ________?________ was the bridge between the self-sufficient farm household and the modern firm.

14. Which of the following is correct?
    a. Revenue = Profit − Cost of Production
    b. Profit = Cost of Production − Revenue
    c. Profit = Revenue − Cost of Production
    d. Cost of Production = Revenue + Profit

15. **True or False** International trade occurs because the opportunity cost of producing specific goods differs among countries.

16. A(n) ________?________ awards an inventor the exclusive right to produce a good for a specific period of time.

17. Which of the following is not a true statement about monopolies?
    a. Monopolies try to charge higher prices than would result through competition.
    b. By maximizing profits, monopolies ultimately benefit social welfare.
    c. Antitrust laws attempt to reduce monopoly power.
    d. Monopolies may try to influence the political system in order to protect and enhance their monopoly power.

18. Which of the following is the best example of the government regulating a natural monopoly?
    a. emission standards for automobiles
    b. required testing and approval to market new drugs
    c. rules for selling new shares of corporate stock
    d. setting prices for distributing electricity to homes

19. **True or False** Public goods can be used by all consumers and have no economic cost.

20. Goods that result from ________?________ are nonrival but exclusive, such as a subway system.

21. **True or False** Poverty is a relative term that has different meanings at different times and in different locations.

22. Which of the following would be an example of an attempt by the Federal Reserve System to stimulate the economy through monetary policy?
    a. a 5 percent reduction in federal income tax rates
    b. an increase in government spending for road construction
    c. an increase in the amount of money in the economy
    d. an increase in the tax on goods purchased from other countries

23. Another term for welfare is
    a. job-placement program.
    b. income-assistance program.
    c. social insurance program.
    d. tax rebate program.

Apply Economic Concepts

24. **Your Share of the Cost** In 2010, the cost of national defense for the United States was just over $710 billion. At that time, there were approximately 310 million people living in this country. Calculate the cost of national defense per person in 2010. Explain why it is difficult to charge individuals their "fair share" of the cost of national defense.

25. **Identifying Goods** Copy the graphic organizer. Place the following items in the correct box on the organizer.

a. Police protection
b. Shrimp in the ocean
c. Public vaccinations
d. Picnic tables in a national park
e. Your television set
f. An unused public tennis court
g. Seashells on a beach
h. Your uncle's fishing boat

	Rival	**Nonrival**
Exclusive		
Nonexclusive		

26. **Examples in Your Community** Make a second copy of the figure in exercise 25. Place two examples of each type of good that exists in your community in the appropriate boxes. Use examples that are different from those in exercise 25.

27. **21st Century Skills: Media Literacy** Identify an example of a negative externality that exists in or near your community. What steps have been taken by the government to try to reduce this externality? How effective have they been? Explain what you could do to help improve or eliminate this situation. How could you use three different types of media to encourage others to share your point of view?

Digging Deeper

with Economics e-Collection

The federal government's funding of social insurance and income-assistance programs is a source of controversy as political leaders work to pull the economy out of a recession and balance the federal budget. Some leaders think the "big three" programs—Social Security, Medicare, and Medicaid—should be cut, while others believe they should not be touched. Access the Gale Economics e-Collection through the URL below to research the current status of this debate and these programs. Read several articles on both sides of the issue, and then write a letter to the editor of your local newspaper stating your opinion. Make sure you support your opinion with facts. Be prepared to discuss the issue in class.

www.cengage.com/school/contecon

GELARTI
HSBC
LG
Life's Good
SALIDA
STEELERS
Tie City
Island

UNIT 2

The Market Economy

In 1962, Sam Walton opened his first store in Rogers, Arkansas, with a sign that read: "Wal-Mart Discount City. We sell for less." Walmart now sells more than any other retailer in the world because its prices are the lowest around. As a consumer, you understand why people buy more at a lower price. Walmart, for example, sells on average more than 20,000 pairs of shoes an hour. Buyers love a bargain, but sellers must make sure their prices cover the costs of supplying the goods. Differences between the desires of buyers and sellers are sorted out by competitive pressures in a market economy.

CHAPTER 4

Demand

CONSIDER ...

- Why are newspapers sold in vending machines that allow you to take more than one copy?
- How much chocolate do you eat when you can eat all you want?
- What cures spring fever?
- What economic principle is behind the saying, "Been there, done that"?
- Why do higher cigarette taxes cut smoking by teenagers more than by other age groups?

Point your browser

www.cengage.com/school/contecon

4.1 THE DEMAND CURVE

Learning Objectives

LO1 Explain the law of demand.

LO2 Interpret a demand schedule and a demand curve.

Key Terms

demand 101
law of demand 101
marginal utility 103
law of diminishing marginal utility 103
demand curve 105
quantity demanded 106
individual demand 107
market demand 107

In Your World

The primary building blocks of a market economy are demand and supply. Consumers demand goods and services that maximize their utility, and producers supply goods and services that maximize their profit. As a consumer in the U.S. market economy, you demand all kinds of goods and services. You buy less of a good when its price increases and more when the price decreases. This section draws on your own experience as a consumer to help you understand demand, particularly the demand curve.

LAW OF DEMAND

LO1 Explain the law of demand.

How many 12-inch pizzas do people buy each week if the price is $12? What if the price is $9? What if it's $6? The answers reveal the relationship between the price of pizza and the amount purchased. Such a relationship is called the *demand* for pizza.

Demand indicates how much of a product consumers are both *willing* and *able* to buy at each price during a given time period, other things constant. Because demand pertains to a specific period—a day, a week, a month—you should think of demand as the *amounts purchased per time period* at each price. Also, notice the emphasis on *willing* and *able.* You may be able to buy a rock concert ticket for $50 because you can afford one. However, you may not be *willing* to buy one if the performers don't interest you enough.

This relation between price and quantity demanded reflects an economic law. The **law of demand** says that quantity demanded varies inversely or negatively, with price, other things constant. Thus, the higher the price, the smaller the quantity demanded. The lower the price, the greater the quantity demanded.

demand A relation showing the quantities of a good that consumers are willing and able to buy per period at various prices, other things constant

law of demand The quantity of a good demanded per period relates inversely to its price, other things constant

Demand, Wants, and Needs

Consumer demand and consumer wants are not the same thing. Wants are unlimited. You may want a new Mercedes-Benz SL600 Roadster convertible,

RyanJLane/iStockphoto.com

The law of demand applies even to personal choices, such as whether or not to own a pet. For example, after New York City passed an anti-dog-litter law, owners had to follow their dogs around the city with scoopers and plastic bags. The law raised the cost, or price, of owning a dog. What do you think happened to the quantity of dogs demanded as a result of this law, and why?

but the $139,100 price tag is likely beyond your budget. (The quantity you demand at that price is zero.) Nor is demand the same as need. You may have outgrown your winter coat and need a new one. But if the price is $200, you may decide your old coat will do for now. If the price drops enough—say, to $100—then you become both willing and able to buy a new one.

Substitution Effect

What explains the law of demand? Why, for example, does the quantity demanded increase when the price falls? The explanation begins with unlimited wants meeting scarce resources. Many goods and services help satisfy your particular wants. For example, you can satisfy your hunger with pizza, tacos, burgers, chicken, sandwiches, salads, or hundreds of other foods. Similarly, you can satisfy your desire for warmth in the winter with warmer clothing, a home-heating system, a trip to Hawaii, or in other ways.

Some ways of satisfying your wants are more appealing to you than others. A trip to Hawaii is more fun than warmer clothing. In a world without scarcity, everything would be free, so you would always choose the most attractive alternative. Scarcity, however, is a reality, and the degree of scarcity of one good relative to another helps determine each good's relative price.

Notice that the definition of *demand* includes the other-things-constant assumption. Among the "other things" assumed to remain constant are the prices of other goods. For example, if the price of pizza declines while other prices remain constant, pizza becomes *relatively* cheaper. Consumers are more *willing* to buy pizza when its relative price falls. People tend to substitute pizza for other goods. This is called the *substitution effect of a price change.* On the other hand, an increase in the price of pizza, other things constant, increases its relative price. Pizza's opportunity cost increases—that is, the amount of other goods you must give up to buy pizza increases. This higher opportunity cost causes some consumers to substitute other goods for the now higher-priced pizza, thus reducing their quantity of pizza demanded.

Remember that the *change in the relative price—the price of one good relative to the prices of other goods—causes the substitution effect.* If all prices changed by the same percent, there would be no change in relative prices and no substitution effect.

Income Effect

A fall in the price increases the quantity demanded for a second reason. If you take home $36 a week from a Saturday job, your money income is $36 per week. Your *money income* is simply the number of dollars you receive per period, in this case, $36 per week. Suppose you spend all your income on pizza, buying four a week at $9 each. What if the price falls to $6? At that lower price you can now afford six pizzas a week.

Your money income remains at $36 per week, but the drop in the price increases your *real income*—that is, your income measured in terms of how much it can buy. The price reduction, other things constant, increases the purchasing power of your income, thereby increasing your ability to buy pizza and, indirectly, other goods. The quantity of pizza you demand likely increases because of this *income effect of a price change.* You may not increase your quantity demanded to six pizzas, but you can now afford six. If you purchase five pizzas a week when the price drops to $6, you would still have $6 left to buy other goods.

Thus, the income effect of a lower price increases your real income and thereby increases your *ability* to purchase pizza and other goods, making you better off. The income effect of a lower price is underscored in Walmart's slogan, which emphasizes the benefits of low prices: "Save money. Live better." Because of the income effect, consumers typically increase their quantity demanded after a price decrease. Conversely, an increase in the price of pizza, other things constant, reduces your real income, thereby reducing your ability to buy pizza. Because of the income effect of a price increase, consumers typically reduce their quantity demanded after a price increase.

Diminishing Marginal Utility

After a long day of school, studies, and sports, you are starved, so you visit a local pizzeria. That first slice tastes great and puts a serious dent in your hunger. The second is not quite as good as the first. A third is just fair. You don't even consider a fourth slice. The satisfaction you derive from an additional unit of a product is called your **marginal utility**. For example, the additional satisfaction you get from a second slice of pizza is your marginal utility of that slice.

The marginal utility you derive from each additional slice of pizza declines as your consumption increases. Your experience with pizza reflects the **law of diminishing marginal utility**. This law states that the more of a good an individual consumes per period, other things constant, the smaller the marginal utility of each additional unit consumed.

Diminishing marginal utility is a feature of all consumption. A second foot-long submarine sandwich at one meal would probably yield little or no marginal utility. You might still enjoy a second movie on Friday night, but a third one is probably too much to take. In fact, almost anything repeated enough can become torture, such as being forced to watch the same movie or listen to the same song over and over. Yes, variety is the spice of life.

marginal utility The change in total utility resulting from a one-unit change in consumption of a good

law of diminishing marginal utility The more of a good an individual consumes per period, other things constant, the smaller the marginal utility of each additional unit consumed

Photodisc/Getty Images

How does the law of diminishing marginal utility apply to pizza consumption?

Consumers buy things to increase their satisfaction, or utility. In deciding what to buy, people make rough estimates about the marginal utility, or marginal benefit, they expect from the good or service. Based on this expected marginal benefit, people then decide how much they are willing and able to pay. Because of diminishing marginal utility, you would not be willing to pay as much for a second slice of pizza as for the first. This is why it takes a decrease in price for you to increase your quantity demanded.

Suppose each slice of pizza sells for $2. How many slices do you buy? You increase consumption as long as the marginal benefit you expect from another slice exceeds $2. You won't buy an additional slice if you expect its marginal benefit is less than $2. Simply put, you aren't willing to pay $2 for something that's worth less than that to you.

What if the price of pizza drops to $1 a slice? You buy more as long as the marginal benefit of another slice exceeds $1. *The law of diminishing marginal utility helps explain why people buy more when the price declines.*

Diminishing marginal utility has wide applications. Restaurants depend on the law of diminishing marginal utility when they offer all-you-can-eat specials. People at all-you-can-eat specials continue to eat as long as the marginal benefit of another bite is greater than zero. And no doggie bags—the deal is all you can eat now, not all you can eat now and for as long as the doggie bag holds out.

After a long winter, that first warm day of spring is something special and is the cause of "spring fever." The fever is cured by many warm days like the first. By the time August rolls around, most people get much less marginal utility from yet another warm day.

For some goods, the drop in marginal utility after the first unit is dramatic. For example, a second copy of the same daily newspaper would likely provide you with no marginal utility. In fact, the design of newspaper vending machines relies on the fact that you won't take more than one.

More generally, the expressions "Been there, done that" and "Same old, same old" convey the idea that, for many activities, things start to get old after the first time. Your marginal utility, or marginal benefit, declines.

CHECKPOINT **Explain the law of demand in your own words.**

DEMAND SCHEDULE AND DEMAND CURVE

LO2 Interpret a demand schedule and a demand curve.

Demand can be expressed as a *demand schedule* and as a *demand curve*. Panel (A) of Figure 4.1 shows a hypothetical demand schedule for pizza. When you describe demand, you must specify the units being measured and the period considered. In this example, the price is for a 12-inch regular pizza and the period is a week. The schedule in panel (A) lists prices, along with the quantity demanded at each price.

At a price of $15, for example, consumers in this market demand 8 million pizzas per week. As you can see, the lower the price the greater the quantity demanded, other things constant. If the price drops as low as $3, consumers demand 32 million per week. As the price falls, consumers substitute pizza for other goods. As the price falls, the real income of consumers increases, causing them to increase the quantity of pizza they demand. As pizza consumption increases, the marginal utility of pizza declines, so quantity demanded increases only if the price falls.

The *demand schedule* in panel (A) of Figure 4.1 appears as a **demand curve** in panel (B), with price measured on the vertical axis and the quantity demanded per week on the horizontal axis. Each combination of price and quantity listed in the demand schedule becomes an individual point on the market demand curve. Point *a*, for example, indicates that if the price is $15, consumers demand 8 million pizzas per week. These points connect to form the market demand curve for pizza, labeled *D*. Note that some demand curves are straight lines, some are crooked lines, and some are curved lines, but all of them are called demand curves, and they all slope downward.

demand curve A curve or line showing the quantities of a particular good demanded at various prices during a given time period, other things constant

FIGURE 4.1 Demand Schedule and Demand Curve for Pizza

Market demand curve *D* shows the quantity of pizza demanded, at various prices, by all consumers.

(A) DEMAND SCHEDULE

	Price per pizza	Quantity demanded per week (millions)
a	$15	8
b	12	14
c	9	20
d	6	26
e	3	32

(B) DEMAND CURVE

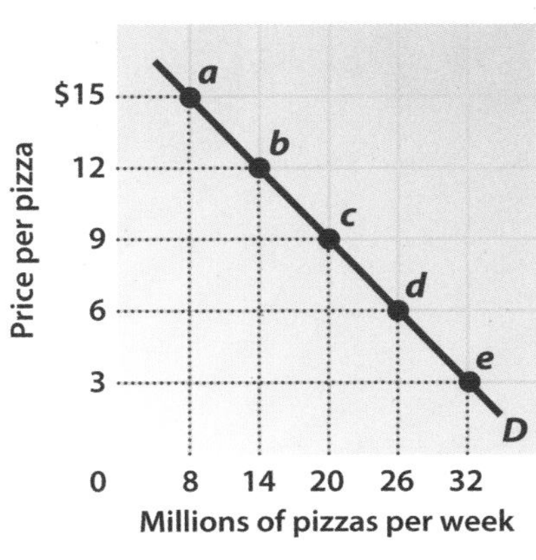

A demand curve slopes downward from left to right, reflecting the *law of demand*—that is, price and quantity demanded are inversely, or negatively, related, other things constant. Several things are assumed to remain constant along the demand curve, including the prices of other goods. Thus, along the demand curve, the price of pizza changes *relative to the prices of other goods.* The demand curve shows the effect of a change in the *relative price* of pizza—that is, relative to other prices, which do not change.

Demand Versus Quantity Demanded

Be careful to distinguish between *demand* and *quantity demanded.* An individual point on the demand curve shows the **quantity demanded** at a particular price. For example, point *b* on the demand curve in Figure 4.1 indicates that 14 million pizzas are demanded when the price is $12. The *demand* for pizza is not a specific quantity, but the *entire relation* between price and quantity demanded. This relation is represented by the demand schedule or the demand curve. To recap, quantity demanded refers to a specific amount of the good on the demand schedule or the demand curve, whereas demand refers to the entire demand schedule or demand curve.

quantity demanded
The amount demanded at a particular price

ESSENTIAL QUESTION

Standard CEE 7: Markets and Prices
A market exists when buyers and sellers interact. This interaction determines market prices and thereby allocates scarce goods and services.

Digital Vision/GettyImages

What is the result of the interaction between buyers and sellers?

Individual Demand and Market Demand

It is also useful to distinguish between **individual demand**, which is the demand of an individual consumer, such as you, and **market demand**, which sums the individual demands of all consumers in the market. *The market demand curve shows the total quantities demanded per period by all consumers at various prices.*

In most markets, there are many consumers, sometimes millions. To give you some feel for how individual demand curves sum to the market demand curve, assume that there are only three consumers in the market for pizza: Hector, Brianna, and Chris. Figure 4.2 shows how three individual demand curves are summed across to get the market demand curve. When the price of a pizza is \$8, for example, Hector demands two pizzas a week, Brianna demands one, and Chris demands none. The quantity demanded at a price of \$8 is therefore three pizzas. At a price of \$4, Hector demands three per week, Brianna two, and Chris one, for a quantity demanded of six. Panel (D) sums horizontally each individual's demand curve to arrive at the market demand curve.

The market demand curve is simply the sum of the individual demand curves for all consumers in the market. Unless otherwise noted, this book focuses on market demand.

individual demand The demand of an individual consumer

market demand The sum of the individual demands of all consumers in the market

FIGURE 4.2 Market Demand for Pizza

The individual demand curves of Hector, Brianna, and Chris are summed across to get the market demand curve. At a price of \$8 per pizza, Hector demands 2 per week, Brianna demands 1, and Chris demands none. Quantity demanded at a price of \$8 is 2 + 1 + 0 = 3 pizzas per week. At a lower price of \$4, Hector demands 3, Brianna demands 2, and Chris demands 1. Quantity demanded at a price of \$4 is 6 pizzas. The market demand curve D is the horizontal sum of individual demand curves d_H, d_B, and d_C.

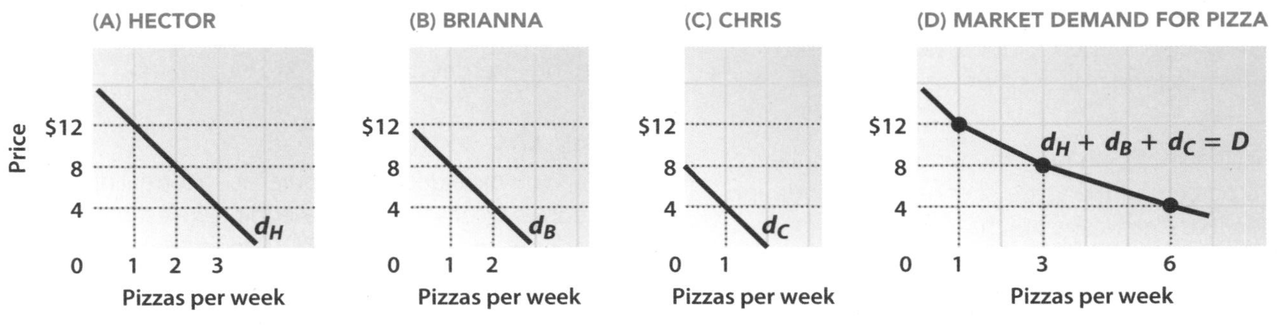

What do a demand schedule and a demand curve show? **CHECKPOINT**

21st Century Skills

Communication and Collaboration

Technological Progress and Quantity Demanded

At one time, people who lived in rural areas had little choice about where they shopped or the amount they paid for many products they purchased. For example, a woman living in Fargo, North Dakota, in 1870 had very few shopping alternatives. She probably bought cloth for her family's clothing at a local store where she paid the price the shopkeeper asked. If the same fabric cost half as much 400 miles away in Chicago, she would have had no way of knowing this. Even if she did, she could not have traveled the 400 miles to take advantage of the lower price. This situation no longer exists. Modern technology and transportation provide rural residents with almost as many shopping alternatives as urban dwellers.

Consider how the following facts have affected the quantity of consumer goods and services people demand in the United States today.

- The prices charged for most goods and services are similar regardless of where they are offered for sale.
- Online shopping now accounts for roughly 20 percent of the value of consumer goods and services Americans purchase.
- Many online retailers offer free shipping for consumer products.

The ability to easily compare prices over the Internet ensures consumers that they are being asked to pay a fair price for the goods and services they want and need.

Finding Lower Prices

Also thanks to the Internet, consumers who wish to buy deeply discounted goods or services have an alternative. They may purchase many products through websites such as eBay, Priceline, or Overstock.com. These online services offer consumers a way to buy goods or services from businesses that are willing to accept lower prices than consumers might normally expect to pay. Hotels.com, for example, offers advantages to both consumers and hotel owners by helping people rent hotel rooms at a discounted price that would otherwise remain empty. This collaboration between the online service and the retailer allows each party to the transaction to benefit: The consumer is able to pay less for the hotel room; the hotel owners receive at least some income for their unsold rooms; and Hotels.com earns a fee for providing its service. Transactions such as these would have been difficult, if not impossible, before the Internet was created.

Apply the Skill

Imagine you have decided to purchase a formal dress or tuxedo to wear to a friend's wedding. Investigate prices for this product offered by local retailers, online merchants, and discount services on the Internet. Identify two retailers of each type, list the prices they ask for similar products, and explain why you would choose a particular retailer. Explain how the Internet has increased the options of goods and services demanded in the United States.

4.1 ASSESSMENT

Think Critically

1. Many students would like to own an expensive sports car. Is this considered demand? Why or why not?
2. Homeless people need warmer clothes for the winter. Is this considered demand? Why or why not?
3. How would the income effect of a price change be demonstrated by a $10 reduction in the price of tickets to a concert that resulted in a sell-out crowd?
4. Joe is willing to pay $1.50 for one taco after basketball practice but chooses not to purchase a second taco for the same price. How does this illustrate the law of diminishing marginal utility?
5. What is the average price of a lunch in the cafeteria at your school? What, approximately, is the market quantity demanded at that price?

Graphing Exercise

6. The owners of a local shoe store surveyed their customers to determine how many pairs of running shoes they would buy each month at different prices. The results of the survey appear in the demand schedule below. Use these data to draw a demand curve for running shoes. Explain how your graph demonstrates the law of diminishing marginal utility.

DEMAND FOR RUNNING SHOES

Price	Quantity Demanded
$70	40
$60	50
$50	60
$40	70
$30	80

Make Academic Connections

7. **Marketing** Nancy is the sales manager of the shoe store described above. The owner has told her that she must set a price that allows the store to sell at least 50 pairs of running shoes next month. What price should she set? If another local store has a big sale and lowers its price for running shoes by 25 percent, will Nancy's employer reach the sales goal? Why or why not?
8. **History** When television sets first became available to consumers in the late 1940s, many people wanted one. Still, very few sets were sold at first. Explain why people's desire to own televisions did not result in a great demand for this product.

TeamWork

Working in small teams, brainstorm a list of products that most members of the team consume in a typical week. Then, working on your own, apply the law of diminishing marginal utility to each item. How many units of each item would you consume per week before the marginal benefit is less than the price of each unit? Compare your answers with those of other teams members.

4.2 ELASTICITY OF DEMAND

Key Terms

elasticity of demand 110

total revenue 112

Learning Objectives

LO1 Compute the elasticity of demand, and explain its relevance.

LO2 Discuss the factors that influence elasticity of demand.

In Your World

Knowing the law of demand is useful, but a demand curve can offer you even more information. It can show you how sensitive quantity demanded is to a change in price. For example, suppose you manage a fast-food restaurant and would like to know what happens to total revenue if you introduce a dollar menu. The law of demand indicates that a lower price increases the quantity demanded, but by how much? Your success or failure as a manager depends on how much you know about the demand for your product. This section measures how sensitive quantity demanded is to a change in price.

COMPUTING ELASTICITY OF DEMAND

LO1 Compute the elasticity of demand, and explain its relevance.

Figure 4.3 shows the market demand curve for pizza developed earlier. As you can see, if the price of a pizza falls from \$12 to \$9, quantity demanded increases from 14 million to 20 million. Is such a response in quantity demanded a little or a lot? Demand elasticity measures consumer responsiveness to the price change. *Elasticity* is another word for *responsiveness.* Specifically, **elasticity of demand** measures the percent change in quantity demanded divided by the percent change in price, or

$$\text{Elasticity of demand} = \frac{\text{Percent change in quantity demanded}}{\text{Percent change in price}}$$

What's the demand elasticity when the price of pizza falls from \$12 to \$9? The percent increase in quantity demanded is the change in quantity, 6 million, divided by 14 million. So, quantity demanded increases by 43 percent. The percent change in price is the price change of \$3 divided by \$12, which is 25 percent. Elasticity of demand is the percent increase in quantity demanded, 43 percent, divided by the percent decrease in price, 25 percent, which equals 1.7.

elasticity of demand
Measures how responsive quantity demanded is to a price change; the percent change in quantity demanded divided by the percent change in price

FIGURE 4.3 The Demand for Pizza

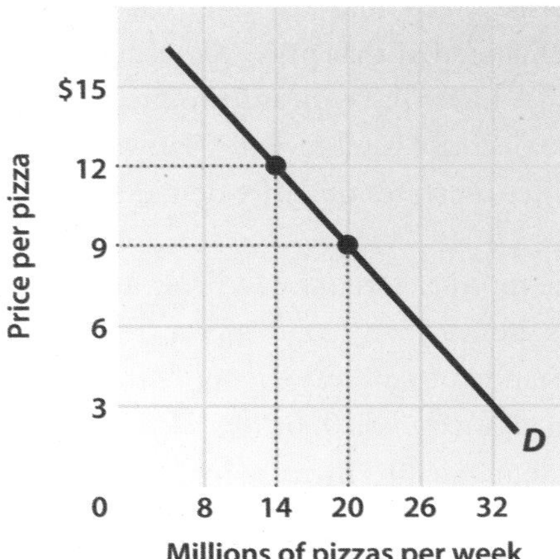

If the price falls from $12 to $9, the quantity of pizza demanded increases from 14 million to 20 million per week.

Elasticity Values

Does an elasticity of 1.7 indicate that consumers are sensitive to the price change? To offer some perspective, economists sort elasticity into three general categories. If the percent change in quantity demanded exceeds the percent change in price, the resulting elasticity exceeds 1.0. Such a demand is said to be *elastic*, meaning that quantity demanded is relatively responsive to a change in price. The demand for pizza is elastic when the price falls from $12 to $9.

If the percent change in quantity demanded just equals the percent change in price, the resulting elasticity is 1.0, and this demand is called *unit elastic.* Finally, if the percent change in quantity demanded is less than the percent change in price, the resulting elasticity lies between 0 and 1.0, and this demand is said to be *inelastic*, or relatively unresponsive to a change in price.

In summary, *demand is elastic if greater than 1.0, unit elastic if equal to 1.0, and inelastic if between 0 and 1.0.* Also, the elasticity usually varies at different points on a demand curve. Demand is almost always more elastic at higher prices and less elastic at lower prices. This is particularly true when the demand curve is a straight line that slopes down from left to right.

Elasticity expresses a relationship between two amounts: the percent change in price and the resulting percent change in quantity demanded. Because the focus is on the percent change, you don't need to be concerned with how output or price is measured. For example, suppose the good in question is apples. It makes no difference in the elasticity formula whether you measure apples in pounds, bushels, or even tons. All that matters is the percent change in quantity demanded. Nor does it matter whether you measure price in U.S. dollars, Mexican pesos, Swiss francs, or Zambian kwacha. All that matters is the percent change in price.

Elasticity and Total Revenue

Knowledge of elasticity is especially valuable to producers, because elasticity also indicates how a price change affects total revenue. **Total revenue** is price multiplied by the quantity demanded at that price. What happens to total revenue when price decreases? A lower price means producers are paid less for each unit sold, which tends to decrease total revenue. However, according to the law of demand, a lower price increases quantity demanded, which tends to increase total revenue.

The impact of a lower price on total revenue can be estimated using elasticity of demand. When elasticity is greater than 1.0, or *elastic*, reducing the price by 5 percent causes quantity demanded to increase by more than 5 percent. Thus the total revenue increases. When elasticity is 1.0, or *unit elastic*, reducing the price by 5 percent causes quantity demanded to increase by 5 percent. In this case total revenue remains unchanged. When elasticity is less than 1.0, or *inelastic*, reducing the price by 5 percent causes the quantity demanded to increase, but by less than 5 percent. So, total revenue falls.

Knowing a product's elasticity can help businesses with their pricing decisions. If demand is inelastic, producers will never willingly cut the price because doing so would reduce their total revenue. The percent increase in quantity demanded would be less than the percent decrease in price. Why cut the price if selling more reduces total revenue?

CHECKPOINT **What does the elasticity of demand measure?**

DETERMINANTS OF DEMAND ELASTICITY

LO2 **Discuss factors that influence elasticity of demand.**

So far you have explored the link between elasticity of demand and what happens to the total revenue of producers when the price changes. However, you have not yet considered why elasticity differs for different goods. Several characteristics influence the elasticity of demand.

Availability of Substitutes

Your individual wants can be satisfied in a variety of ways. A rise in the price of pizza makes other food relatively cheaper. If close substitutes are available, an increase in the price of pizza prompts some people to buy those substitutes. But if nothing else satisfies like pizza, the quantity of pizza demanded does not decline as much. *The greater the availability of substitutes for a good and the more similar these are to the good in question, the greater that good's elasticity of demand.*

total revenue Price multiplied by the quantity demanded at that price

The number and similarity of substitutes depend on the definition of the good. *The more broadly a good is defined, the fewer substitutes there are and the less elastic the demand.* For example, everyone needs some sort of shoes, so the demand for shoes in general tends to be inelastic. If shoe prices go up 20 percent, most people will still buy shoes eventually. If you consider one particular brand of shoes, however, the demand will be more elastic because there are many other brands of shoes you could buy instead. For example, if only one shoe manufacturer raises its price by 20 percent, many shoe buyers will switch to other brands, which have not increased in price.

Certain goods—many prescription drugs, for instance—have no close substitutes. The demand for such goods tends to be less elastic than for goods with close substitutes, such as Bayer Aspirin. Much advertising is aimed at establishing in the consumer's mind the uniqueness of a particular product—an effort to convince consumers "to accept no substitutes."

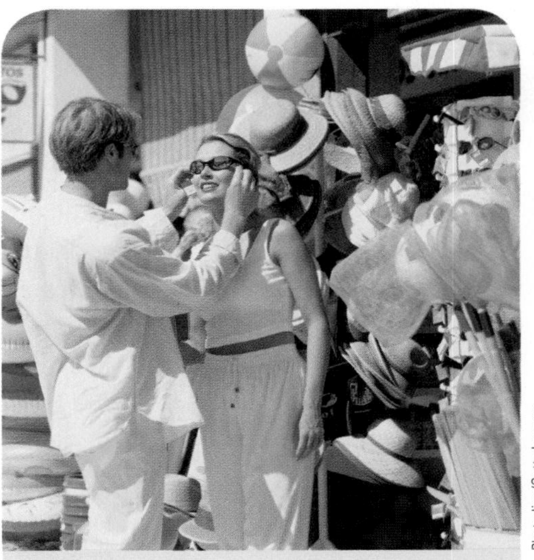

Photodisc/Getty Images

Do you think demand for sunglasses is elastic or inelastic? Identify the determinant of demand elasticity that supports your answer.

Share of Consumer's Budget Spent on the Good

Recall that a higher price reduces quantity demanded in part because a higher price lowers the real spending power of consumer income. A demand curve reflects both the consumer's *willingness* and *ability* to purchase a good at alternative prices. Because spending on some goods represents a large share of the consumer's budget, a change in the price of such a good has a substantial impact on the amount consumers are able to purchase.

An increase in the price of housing, for example, reduces the ability to purchase housing. The income effect of a higher price reduces the quantity demanded. In contrast, the income effect of an increase in the price of, say, paper towels is less significant because paper towels represent such a tiny share of any budget. *The more important the item is as a share of the consumer's budget, other things constant, the greater is the income effect of a change in price, so the more elastic is the demand for the item.* This explains why the quantity of housing demanded is more responsive to a given percent change in price than is the quantity of paper towels demanded.

Duration of the Adjustment Period

Consumers can substitute lower-priced goods for higher-priced goods, but finding substitutes takes time. For example, between 1973 and 1974, the OPEC oil cartel raised the price of oil sharply. The initial result was a 45-percent increase in the price of gasoline, but the quantity demanded decreased only 8 percent. As more time passed, however, people purchased smaller cars and made greater use of public transportation. Because the price of oil used to generate electricity and to heat homes increased as well, people bought more energy-efficient appliances and insulated their homes better. As a result, the decline in the amount of oil demanded was greater over time as consumers adjusted to the price hike.

The longer the adjustment period, the easier it is to find lower-priced substitutes. Thus, the longer the period of adjustment, the more responsive the change in quantity demanded is to a given change in price.

Figure 4.4 shows how the demand for gasoline becomes more elastic over time. Given an initial price of \$3.00 a gallon, let D_w be the demand curve one week after a price change; D_m, one month after; and D_y, one year after. Suppose the price increases to \$3.50. The more time consumers have to adjust to the price increase, the greater the reduction in quantity demanded. The demand curve D_w shows that one week after the price increase, the quantity demanded has not declined much—in this case, from 100 million to 95 million gallons per day. The demand curve D_m indicates a reduction to 75 million gallons per day after one month, and demand curve D_y shows a reduction to 50 million gallons per day after one year.

FIGURE 4.4 **Demand Becomes More Elastic Over Time**

D_w is the demand curve one week after a price increase from \$3.00 to \$3.50 per gallon. Along this curve, quantity demanded falls from 100 million to 95 million gallons per day. One month after the price increase, quantity demanded has fallen to 75 million gallons per day along D_m. One year after the price increase, quantity demanded has fallen to 50 million gallons per day along D_y. At any given price, D_y is more elastic than D_m, which is more elastic than D_w.

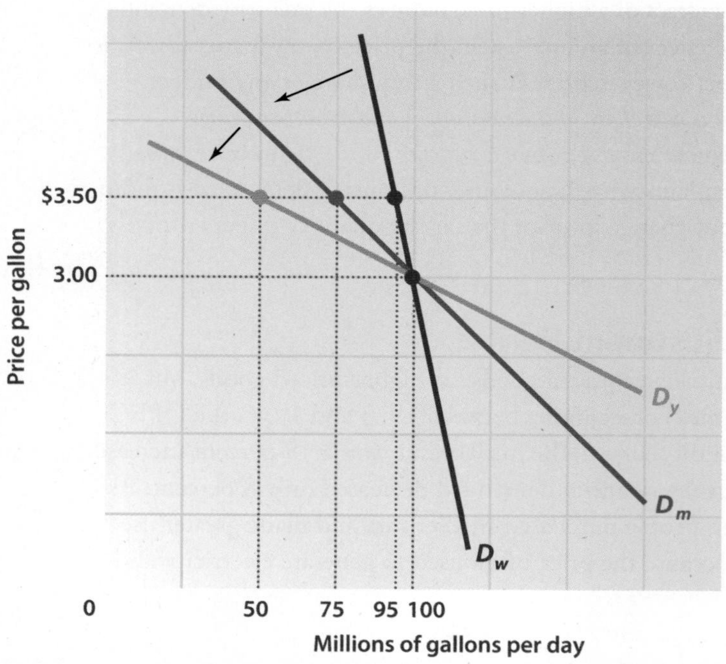

Span the Globe

We Ate Most of the Big Fish

About 80 percent of the big fish—such as giant tuna, swordfish and Chilean seabass—are gone from the world's oceans mainly due to overfishing to satisfy world demand. The Whole Foods Market grocery chain is partnering with Blue Ocean Institute and Monterey Bay Aquarium to drive down demand for these endangered fish. The company is the first national grocer to institute a color-coded sustainability-rating program for wild-caught seafood and plans to phase out the sale of some species. This will complement Whole Foods' ongoing partnership with the Marine Stewardship Council (MSC), the world's leading certifier of sustainable wild-caught seafood. The colors will range from "Green," a best choice that is relatively abundant, to "Yellow" signifying a good alternative but with some sustainability concerns, to "Red" for species that should be avoided due to overfishing.

Another MSC partner is Canada's largest supermarket chain, Loblaws. This has resulted in customers being greeted by empty trays in the deep-sea fish counters. Many have seen a note suggesting they consider tilapia or sole instead. Like Whole Foods, Loblaws is committed to offering only seafood coming from sustainable sources. It already has stopped selling Chilean seabass, orange roughy, bluefin tuna, and shark. Loblaws hopes its decisions will have a real impact on seafood supplies as well as raise awareness and improve worldwide fishing practices.

Think Critically **How does the commitment by Whole Foods and Loblaws to selling sustainable seafood affect the demand for those products?**

Sources: "Take a Pass on Chilean Sea Bass," U.S. Newswire, April 21, 2006; Kenneth R. Weiss, *Los Angeles Times*, "Study Finds Industrial Fleets Have Stripped Oceans of Big Fish," *Las Vegas Review Journal*, May 15, 2003; "Whole Foods Market - Empowers Shoppers to Make Sustainable Seafood Choices with Color-Coded Rating System- Partners with Monterey Bay Aquarium and Blue Ocean Institute to Create Science-based Wild-caught Seafood Rating Program; Plans to Phase Out Red-rated Species," PR Newswire (USA) September 13, 2010; and "Loblaw Modifies Select Fresh Fish and Seafood Counters to Highlight "at risk" Fish and Suggested Alternatives," Canada Newswire, February 4, 2010.

Some Elasticity Estimates

Let's look at some estimates of the elasticity of demand for particular goods and services. As noted earlier, the switch to lower-priced substitutes usually takes time. Thus, when estimating elasticity, economists often distinguish between a period during which consumers have little time to adjust—call it the *short run*—and a period during which consumers can more fully adjust to a price change—call it the *long run*. Figure 4.5 provides some short-run and long-run elasticity estimates for selected products.

The elasticity of demand is greater in the long run because consumers have more time to adjust. For example, if the price of electricity rose today, consumers in the short run might cut back a bit on their use of electrical appliances. Those in homes with electric heat might lower the thermostat in winter. Over time, however,

Figure 4.5 Selected Elasticities of Demand

When estimating elasticity, economists distinguish between the short run (a period during which consumers have little time to adjust to a price change) and the long run (a period during which consumers can more fully adjust to a price change). Demand is more elastic in the long run because consumers have more time to adjust.

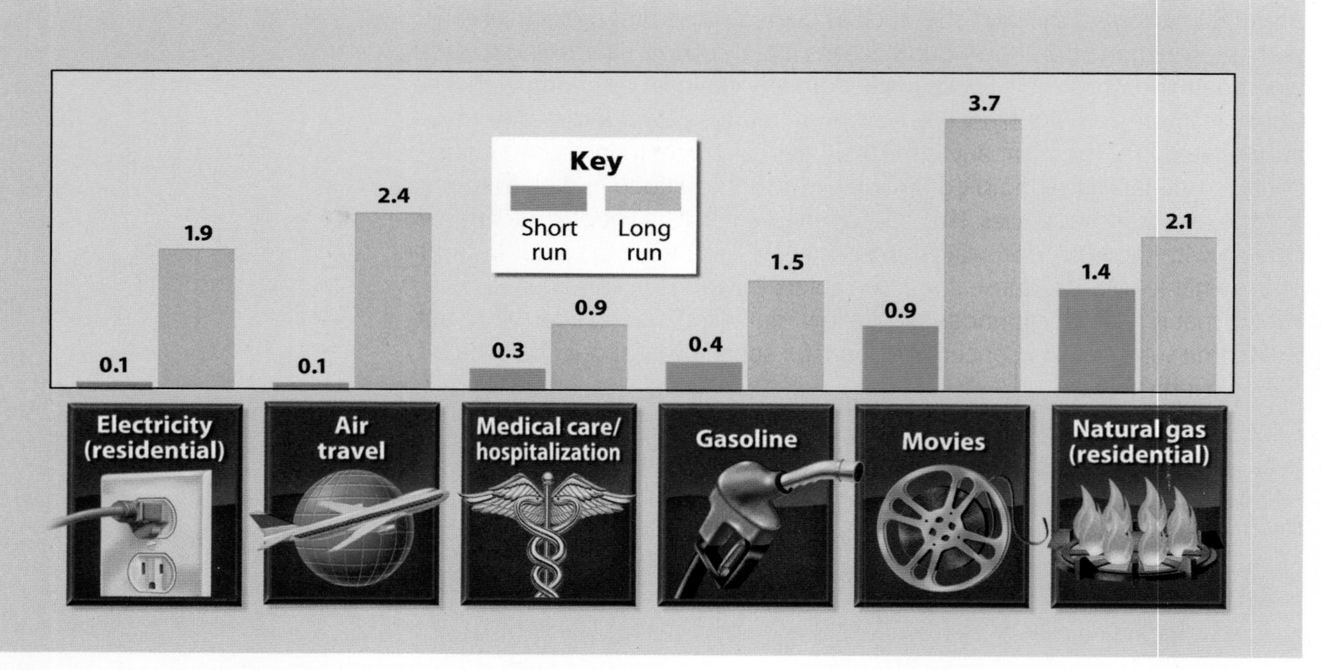

consumers would switch to more energy-efficient appliances, insulate their homes better, and might convert from electric heat to oil, natural gas, or solar heat. So the demand for electricity is more elastic in the long run than in the short run, as noted in Figure 4.5. In fact, for each product listed, demand is more elastic in the long run than in the short run.

An Application: Teenage Smoking

As the U.S. Surgeon General warns on each pack of cigarettes, smoking cigarettes can be hazardous to your health. Researchers estimate that smoking causes more than 440,000 deaths a year in the United States—more than 10 times the fatalities from traffic accidents.

One way to reduce smoking is to raise the price of cigarettes through higher cigarette taxes. Economists estimate the demand elasticity for cigarettes among teenage smokers to be about 1.3, so a 10 percent increase in the price of cigarettes would reduce teen smoking by 13 percent. Among adult smokers, the estimated elasticity is only 0.4, or only about one-third that of teenagers.

Why are teenagers more sensitive to price changes than adults? First, recall that one of the factors affecting the elasticity of demand is the importance of the item in the consumer's budget. The share of income that a teenage smoker spends on cigarettes usually exceeds the share for adult smokers. Second, peer pressure is more influential in a young person's decision to smoke than in an adult's decision to continue smoking. (If anything, adults face peer pressure not to smoke.) The effects of a higher price get multiplied among young smokers because a higher price reduces smoking by peers. With fewer peers smoking, there is less pressure to smoke. And third, because smoking is addictive, young people who are not yet hooked are more sensitive to price increases than are adult smokers, who are already hooked.

What are the determinants of demand elasticity? **CHECKPOINT**

Math in Economics

Common Core Ratios and Proportional Relationships

You can calculate the percent change in a value by dividing the amount of the change by the original value changed and then converting the quotient to a percent. To make the conversion, multiply by 100, or move the decimal point two places to the right.

EXAMPLE Find the percent change in the price of eggs if the price increased from $1.50 a dozen to $1.68 per dozen.

SOLUTION Subtract the smaller price from the larger price. Divide the result by the original price. Convert that answer to a percent by moving the decimal point two places to the right.

$1.68 − $1.50 = $0.18

$0.18 ÷ $1.50 = 0.12

0.12 = 12%

The price of eggs increased by 12%.

Practice the Skill For each situation, find the percent change in price and the resulting percent change in quantity demanded.

1. The quantity of milk demanded by consumers depends on the price. When the price of a gallon of milk rose from $3.25 to $3.51, sales fell from 200 gallons per day to 190 gallons per day.
2. The quantity of pizzas ordered changes when the price of pizza changes. When a pizza sold for $8 instead of $10, sales grew from 80 pizzas per day to 120 pizzas per day.
3. One of these products has elastic demand, while the other demonstrates inelastic demand. Identify which is which. Explain your answer.

4.2 ASSESSMENT

Think Critically

1. What would a shoe store need to do to calculate the elasticity of demand for the running shoes it sells if it decides to raise its price by 10 percent?
2. If the shoe store finds a demand elasticity for its running shoes of 1.3, is this elastic, unit elastic, or inelastic demand?
3. If the shoe store increases its price for running shoes by 10 percent, what would happen to the store's total revenue from these products?
4. Why should you expect the demand for a particular brand of cake mix to be more elastic than the demand for cake mix in general?

Graphing Exercise

5. Consider this graph, at right, for running shoes. Note that if the store's manager increases the price from $60 to $70 (16.7%), the quantity demanded would fall from 50 to 40 pairs per month (20.0%). What is the elasticity of demand? Is demand elastic, unit elastic, or inelastic? Will the store's total revenue increase, decrease, or remain unchanged as a result of the price increase?

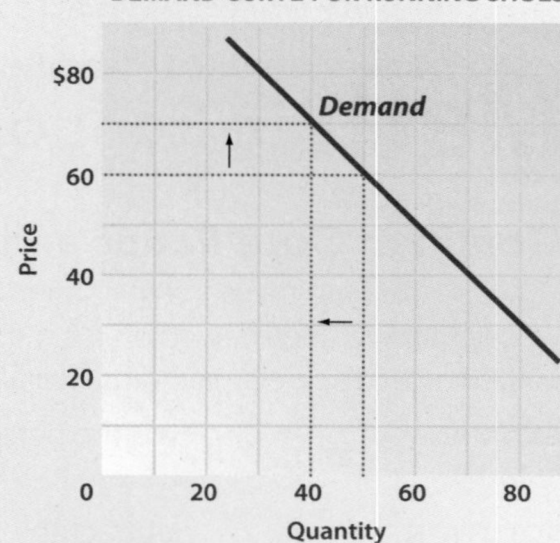

Make Academic Connections

6. **Sociology** The elasticity of demand for some products is affected by the personal values of potential customers. Consider devout practitioners of the Hindu religion who believe it is wrong to eat meat. In Hindu communities, the elasticity of demand for meat products is 0.0, or completely inelastic—consumers won't buy meat no matter what happens to its price. Describe several other situations where other factors are more important to the buying decision than is the price.
7. **Entrepreneurship** If there are 10 bakeries in a small city, why might the elasticity of demand for the products any one of them supplies be high? Why might this small city not be a good location for you to open another bakery?

TeamWork

Working in small teams, brainstorm a list of products that most members of the team consume and indicate the average price for each. Estimate how a 10 percent increase in each product's price would change the quantity demanded. Which products have elastic demand? Which have inelastic demand? Compare your results with those of other teams.

MOVERS AND SHAKERS

Bonita Stewart

Vice President, Sales, Google

Google's Vice President of Sales, Bonita Stewart, knows that the four Ps of marketing are not just for marketing products. She discovered how to apply them to her career path as well. The Google executive has a bachelor's degree from Howard University and an MBA from Harvard. She also has worked at IBM and DaimlerChrysler.

Stewart originally majored in journalism, hoping to become a broadcaster like Katie Couric. However, she quickly became more interested in her minor—business.

Stewart interned at IBM during college and then left to get her Master's degree, returning to the company after her Harvard graduation. She said, "…when I came back [to IBM], I came up with my own [career] path. I was going to follow the four P's of marketing: pricing, product, place, promotion."

To learn "pricing" she worked pricing IBM printers and software. She implemented "product" by working on developing IBM's personal computer business. When she took her first managerial position and moved to Detroit, she had the opportunity to focus on "place," learning the ins and outs of the distribution aspect of marketing. Later, while working at DamilerChrysler, she learned how to formulate and drive consumer strategy and how to effectively "promote" and launch products. When Stewart realized she was not working within her strongest skill set or interest, she chose to return to product marketing with Google.

Stewart carefully built a career that did not follow a straight and traditional path. When asked how she knew it was time to change jobs she said, "Throughout my career, I've always been more of an entrepreneur, trying to drive new ideas and being part of change." By working for Google, Stewart has added finance, media, entertainment, and travel to her career portfolio—all industries where advanced digital strategies are part of everyday business.

Stewart stresses the importance of mentors, acknowledging "it takes a village" to build a career. She said, "You're going to meet people along the way. I believe that if you do your best, you're inquisitive, you have the desire and you have an audacious goal, others will recognize you. That's what's happened to me." She knows it takes a lot of work for a woman to rise to the top but thinks change is coming. She said, "I see so many talented women and minorities…. That diversity is what drives innovation."

She suggests that people beginning their careers make a development plan much like they would for marketing a product. She said, "It doesn't have to be a novel. It could just be a few bullet points that you keep on a piece of paper. It's your thoughts on your career. If you don't step back and have that conversation with yourself from time to time, it's difficult to move through your career with some degree of focus and passion."

Digital marketing is the wave of the future. When Stewart left DaimlerChrysler the company had become an aggressive digital marketer. Google, however, was focusing on the search aspect of its business model instead of going after "brand dollars." Since Stewart has joined Google, the company has integrated YouTube, DoubleClick, AdMob, and Invite Media into its marketing model.

Think Critically **Bonita Stewart applied marketing principles to her career development. How can you apply the principles of demand to your career development?**

Sources: http://sales-jobs.fins.com/Articles/SBB0001424053111903520204576480710777456084/Being-a-Googler-Beats-Being-Katie-Couric; http://adage.com/article/special-report-women-to-watch/women-watch-bonita-stewart-google/227799/; http://www.google.com/events/thinkauto/bios.html; and http://atlantapost.com/2011/08/11/tech-spotlight-bonita-coleman-stewart-vp-us-sales-at-google/

4.3 CHANGES IN DEMAND

Key Terms

tastes 123
movement along a given demand curve 124
shift of a demand curve 124

Learning Objectives

LO1 Identify the determinants of demand, and explain how a change in each affects the demand curve.

LO2 Distinguish between the money price and the time price of a good.

In Your World

So far the discussion of demand has been limited to the relationship between price and quantity demanded. That is, your focus has been on movements along a particular demand curve. A demand curve isolates the relation between the price of a good and the quantity demanded when other factors that could affect demand remain unchanged. Here you will be introduced to these other determinants of demand and will learn how changes in them affect demand.

CHANGES THAT SHIFT THE DEMAND CURVE

LO1 Identify the determinants of demand, and explain how a change in each affects the demand curve.

A demand curve isolates the relationship between price and quantity demanded when other factors that could affect demand are assumed constant. These other factors are often referred to as *determinants of demand.* The determinants of demand include the following:

1. Consumer income
2. The prices of related goods
3. The number and composition of consumers
4. Consumer expectations
5. Consumer tastes

How does a change in each affect demand?

Changes in Consumer Income

Figure 4.6 shows the market demand curve *D* for pizza. Consumers' money income is assumed to remain constant along a demand curve. Suppose money income increases. Some consumers are then willing and able to buy more pizza at each price, so market demand increases. The demand curve shifts to the right from *D* to *D′*. For example, at a price of $12, the amount demanded per week increases from 14 million to 20 million, as indicated by the movement from point *b* on demand curve *D* to point *f* on demand curve *D′*. In short, *an increase*

FIGURE 4.6 **An Increase in the Market Demand for Pizza**

An increase in the market demand for pizza is shown by a rightward shift of the demand curve. After the increase in demand, the quantity of pizza demanded increases at each price level. For example, the quantity demanded per week at a price of $12 increases from 14 million (point *b*) to 20 million (point *f*).

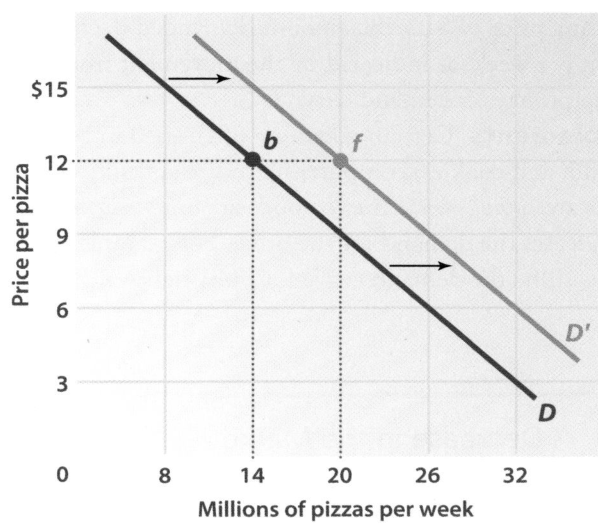

in demand—that is, a rightward shift of the demand curve—means that consumers are more willing and able to buy pizza at each price.

Normal Goods Goods are classified into two broad categories depending on how the demand for the good responds to changes in money income. The demand for a *normal good* increases as money income increases. Because pizza is a normal good, its demand curve shifts rightward when money income increases. Most goods are normal goods.

Inferior Goods In contrast, the demand for an *inferior good* actually decreases as money income increases. Examples of inferior goods include bologna sandwiches, used furniture, used clothing, trips to the Laundromat, and bus rides. As money income increases, consumers switch from these inferior goods to normal goods—such as roast beef sandwiches, new furniture, new clothing, a washer and dryer, and automobile or plane rides.

Changes in the Prices of Related Goods

As you've seen, the prices of other goods are assumed to remain constant along a given demand curve. Now you are ready to consider the impact of changes in the prices of other goods.

Substitutes Products that can be used in place of each other are called *substitutes*. Consumers choose among substitutes partly on the basis of relative prices. For example, pizza and tacos are substitutes, though not perfect ones. An increase in the price of tacos prompts some consumers to buy pizza instead. This is shown in Figure 4.6 by a rightward shift of the demand curve. Two goods are *substitutes* if an increase in the price of one shifts the demand curve for the other rightward.

On the other hand, a decrease in the price of tacos would reduce the demand for pizza, as shown in Figure 4.7, where the demand curve for pizza shifts to the left from *D* to *D''*. As a result, consumers demand less pizza at every price. For example, at a price of $12, the amount demanded decreases from 14 million to 10 million per week, as indicated by the movement from point *b* on demand curve *D* to point *j* on demand curve *D''*.

Complements Certain goods are often used in combination. Pizza and soft drinks, milk and cookies, computer hardware and software, and airline tickets and rental cars are *complements.* If two goods are *complements*, a decrease in the price of one increases the demand for the other. For example, a decrease in the price of soft drinks shifts the demand curve for pizza rightward.

FIGURE 4.7 A Decrease in the Market Demand for Pizza

A decrease in the demand for pizza is shown by a leftward shift of the demand curve. After the decrease in demand, the quantity of pizza demanded decreases at each price level. For example, quantity demanded per week at a price of $12 decreases from 14 million (point *b*) to 10 million (point *j*).

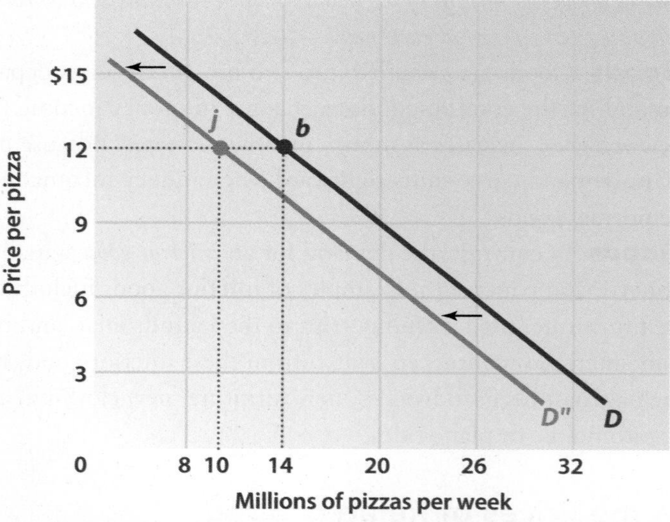

Changes in the Size or Composition of the Population

The market demand curve is the horizontal sum of the individual demand curves of all consumers in the market. If the population grows, the number of consumers in the market increases, so demand increases. For example, if the population grows, the demand curve for pizza shifts rightward. Even if the total population remains unchanged, demand could shift as a result of a change in the composition of the population. For example, an increase in the teenage population could shift pizza demand rightward. A baby boom would increase the demand for car safety seats and baby food. A growing Latino population increases the demand for Latino foods.

To learn more about the economics of consumption, read Jane Katz's "The Joy of Consumption" in the Federal Reserve Bank of Boston's Regional Review. Access this article through the URL shown below. What evidence does Katz cite about how the rising value of time has affected consumer spending patterns?

www.cengage.com/school/contecon

Changes in Consumer Expectations

Another factor assumed to be constant along a given demand curve is consumer expectations about factors that influence demand, such as incomes and prices. A change in consumer expectations can shift the demand curve. For example, your demand for some goods may increase after you line up a summer job, even before that job begins.

Changes in price expectations also can shift demand. For example, if you expect pizza prices to jump next week, you may buy an extra one today for the freezer, thereby shifting the demand curve for pizza rightward. Or if consumers come to believe that home prices will climb next year, some increase their demand for housing this year, shifting the demand curve for housing rightward. The expectation of lower prices has the opposite effect. For example, during the recession of 2008–2009, people expected home prices to continue falling, so they put off buying one, shifting the demand for housing leftward.

Investigate Your Local Economy

Examine changes or trends in the composition of the population of your city or town. What products or categories of products might these changes affect?

Changes in Consumer Tastes

Do you like anchovies on your pizza? How about sauerkraut on a hot dog? Is music to your ears more likely to be rock, country, heavy metal, hip-hop, reggae, jazz, Latin, gospel, New Age, or classical? Choices in food, music, clothing, reading, movies, TV shows—indeed, all consumer choices—are influenced by consumer tastes.

Tastes are your likes and dislikes as a consumer. Tastes are assumed to remain constant along a given demand curve. What determines your tastes? Your desire to eat when hungry and to drink when thirsty are largely biological. So, too, is your desire for shelter, comfort, rest, companionship, personal safety, and a pleasant

tastes A consumer's likes and dislikes

ImagesbyTrista/iStockphoto.com

When analyzing changes in demand for specific goods and services, why do you think changes in consumers' tastes are difficult for economists to isolate?

environment. Your family background, surrounding culture, and peer influence all shape many of your tastes.

Generally, economists claim no special expertise in understanding how tastes develop and can change over time. Economists recognize, however, that tastes are important in shaping demand. For example, although pizza is popular, some people just don't like it and others might be allergic to the cheese, tomatoes, or the gluten in the pizza dough. Thus, most people like pizza but some don't. A change in tastes for a particular good would shift the demand curve. For example, a discovery that the combination of cheese and tomato sauce on pizza promotes overall health could affect consumer tastes, shifting the demand curve for pizza to the right.

But a change in tastes is difficult to isolate from other economic changes. That's why economists attribute a change in demand to a change in tastes only as a last resort, after ruling out other possible explanations.

movement along a demand curve Change in quantity demanded resulting from a change in the price of the good, other things constant

shift of a demand curve Increase or decrease in demand resulting from a change in one of the determinants of demand other than the price of the good

Movement Along a Demand Curve Versus a Shift of the Curve

Remember the distinction between a movement along a demand curve and a shift of a demand curve. A change in price, other things constant, causes a **movement along a demand curve**, changing the quantity demanded. A change in one of the determinants of demand other than price causes a **shift of a demand curve**, changing demand.

CHECKPOINT

What are the five determinants of demand, and how do changes in each shift the demand curve?

THE ROLE OF TIME IN DEMAND

LO2
Distinguish between the money price and the time price of a good.

Because consumption does not occur instantly, time plays a role in demand analysis. Consumption involves a *money price* and a *time price.* It is not the microwave oven, personal computer, airline trip, or pain medicine that you value but the services each provides. Other things constant, you would pay more to get the same benefit in less time, as with faster ovens, computers, airline trips, or pain relief. That's also why you are willing to pay more for ready-to-eat foods that you don't need to prepare yourself.

Your willingness to pay more for time-saving goods and services depends on the opportunity cost of your time. Differences in the value of time among consumers help explain differences in the consumption patterns observed in the economy. For example, a retired couple has more leisure time than a working couple. The retired couple may clip discount coupons and search the newspapers for bargains, sometimes even going from store to store for particular grocery items on sale that week. The working couple may ignore the coupons and sales, eat out more often, and purchase more at convenience stores, where they are willing to pay extra for the convenience. The retired couple is more inclined to drive across country on vacation, whereas the working couple flies to a vacation destination.

Differences in the opportunity cost of time among consumers shape consumption patterns. This adds another dimension to demand analysis.

CHECKPOINT

What's the difference between the money price of a good and its time price?

apomares/iStockphoto.com

Are there goods and services for which you would be willing to pay more money? Explain your answer.

4.3 ASSESSMENT

Think Critically

1. What would happen to the demand curve for bus tickets if the price of gasoline increased to $6 per gallon? Which of the determinants of demand would this affect?
2. What would happen to the demand curve for a particular brand of shampoo if a famous movie actress with beautiful hair announces that it is the best shampoo she has ever used? Which of the determinants of demand would this affect?
3. What would happen to the demand curve for towels today if a large store announces a 50-percent-off sale on towels next week? Which of the determinants of demand would this affect?
4. Why might the demand for quick oats that cook in 2.5 minutes be greater than the demand for regular oats that take 10 minutes?

Graphing Exercise

5. Make a copy of the demand curve for running shoes at a local retailer as shown here. Draw the shift of the demand curve on your copy that would result from each of the following events. Label each shift of the demand curve.
   a. Many people decide to buy new running shoes to run in a local marathon.
   b. Three months of almost uninterrupted rain keeps most people inside.
   c. Income tax rates for most workers are increased by 10 percent.
   d. A new housing development is built near the store.

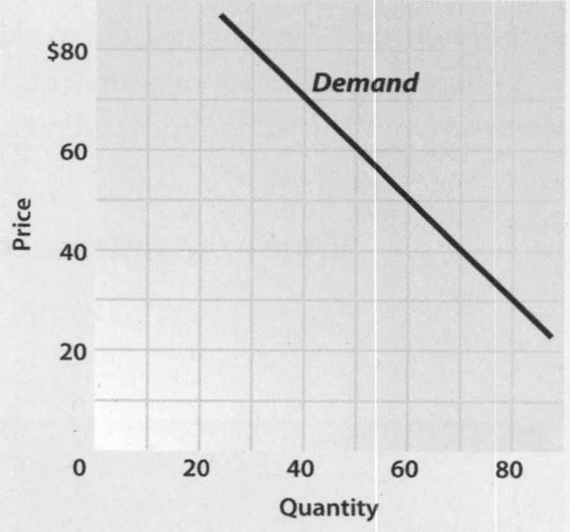

Make Academic Connections

6. **History** When the stock market crashed in 1929, demand for normal goods fell. Explain why this happened and how it contributed to the Great Depression. What types of goods sell better in hard times?
7. **Health** For decades, cigarette manufacturers have been required to place health warnings on their products. What are these warnings intended to do to the demand curves for cigarettes?

Working in small teams, brainstorm a list of TV advertisements you believe are particualrly persuasive. Explain how each is designed to shift consumer demand curves for the product. To which of the determinants of demand do the ads appeal? Compare your work with that of other teams.

Connect to History

The Industrial Revolution in England: The Demand for Cotton

The Industrial Revolution began with England's textile industry in the mid-1700s. Cotton had been around since the 1630s, when it was introduced to Europe from India. Although popular, cotton was considered a threat to the British wool, linen, and silk industries. To protect these industries, Parliament restricted cotton imports. The restrictions lasted until 1736, when Great Britain changed the laws allowing the manufacture and sale of cotton. This marked the beginning of cotton manufacturing in the West.

The two basic stages of manufacturing cotton textiles were spinning and weaving. Typically these tasks were done in the home in what was called a cottage industry. Entrepreneurs supplied raw materials, such as raw cotton or thread, to a household. Then members of the household would produce thread or cloth for the entrepreneur. Of the two tasks, spinning thread from cotton was simpler, and the spinners produced more thread than the weavers could weave. John Kay's 1733 invention, the Flying Shuttle, changed much of that. It allowed one weaver rather than two to operate a loom and produce more cloth. As the weaving industry grew, so did the demand for thread.

To satisfy this demand, James Hargreaves invented the Spinning Jenny in the 1760s. With his invention, a single worker could spin multiple threads but produce a relatively weak product. Richard Arkwright invented the Water Frame in 1769. This innovation produced a stronger, coarser thread. Finally, Samuel Crompton's 1779 Spinning Mule produced a strong yet fine thread. Once again spinners were producing more than weavers could use.

Edmund Cartwright's Power Loom, patented in 1785, enabled the British cotton textile production to explode. In 1796, the country manufactured 21 million yards of cotton cloth. That increased to 347 million yards by 1830. The technological advances, coupled with cotton from the United States, caused the price of cotton cloth to drop. By the early part of the nineteenth century, Britain was even able to sell cotton cloth in India. With this increased technology and growing exports, the demand for raw cotton increased. Great Britain found in the United States a willing and able supplier.

wynnter/iStockphoto.com

18th century English textile mill

Think Critically **Indicate how the demand curve for raw cotton would shift with each of the Industrial Revolution's technological inventions. Use D_1 for the cottage industry demand, D_2 for John Kay's Flying Shuttle, D_3 for Samuel Crompton's Spinning Mule, and D_4 for Edmund Cartwright's Power Loom.**

Chapter 4 Summary

ASK THE EXPERT

www.cengage.com/school/contecon

Why do consumers buy less of an item when its price rises?

4.1 The Demand Curve

A. Demand indicates how much of a product consumers are willing and able to buy at each price during a given period, other things remaining constant. The law of demand states that the higher the price, the smaller the quantity demanded, and vice versa.

B. The quantity demanded increases as the price falls because of the substitution effect, the income effect, and diminishing marginal utility. The law of diminishing marginal utility states that each additional unit of a product consumed normally provides less additional utility than the previous unit.

C. Demand for a product can be expressed as a demand schedule or as a graph called a demand curve. Most demand curves slope down from left to right, indicating an inverse relationship between price and quantity demanded. This means that as the price declines, the quantity demanded increases.

4.2 Elasticity of Demand

A. Elasticity of demand measures the responsiveness of quantity demanded to a change in price. Elasticity is calculated by dividing the percent change in the quantity demanded by the percent change in price.

B. Demand may be elastic, unit elastic, or inelastic. Elastic demand has an elasticity value greater than 1.0. When demand is elastic, a percent change in price results in a larger percent change in the quantity demanded. Unit elastic demand has a value of 1.0. When demand is unit elastic, a percent change in price results in an identical percent change in the quantity demanded. Inelastic demand has a value less than 1.0. When demand is inelastic, a percent change in price results in a smaller percent change in the quantity demanded.

C. Elasticity of demand can be used to predict what happens to a firm's total revenue when the price changes. When demand is elastic, a price increase reduces total revenue. When demand is unit elastic, a price increase does not change total revenue. When demand is inelastic, a price increase boosts total revenue.

D. A good with many substitutes or that represents a large proportion of the consumer's budget tends to have elastic demand. A good with few substitutes or that represents a small proportion of the consumer's budget, tends to have inelastic demand. As a general rule, demand is more elastic the more time consumers have to adjust to a price change.

4.3 Changes in Demand

A. There are five general categories of economic events that can cause a demand curve to shift. These are: (1) a change in the money income of consumers, (2) a change in the price of a related good, (3) a change in the number or composition of consumers, (4) a change in consumer expectations, and (5) a change in consumer tastes.

B. Substitute products are used somewhat interchangeably. An increase in the price of one causes demand for the other to increase. Complementary products are normally used together. An increase in the price of one causes the demand for the other to decrease.

C. The demand for products can be influenced by time. Customers who must wait in line to buy a product may decide not to wait. Consumers are usually willing to pay more for goods that offer the same benefit but in less time.

CHAPTER 4 ASSESSMENT

Review Economic Terms

Match the terms with the definitions. Some terms will not be used.

_____ 1. The sum of the individual demands of all consumers in the market

_____ 2. A line that shows the quantities of a particular good demanded at various prices during a given time period, other things constant

_____ 3. The demand of a single consumer in the market

_____ 4. The amount of a product that is demanded at a particular price

_____ 5. An increase or decrease in demand that results from a change in a determinant of demand

_____ 6. A change in the quantity demanded that results from a change in the product's price

_____ 7. The change in total utility resulting from a one-unit increase in consumption of a good

_____ 8. The more of a good a person consumes per period, the smaller the marginal utility of each additional unit consumed, other things constant

_____ 9. The quantity of a good demanded per period is inversely related to its price, other things constant

_____ 10. Price multiplied by the quantity demanded at that price

_____ 11. A relation showing the quantities of a good consumers are willing and able to buy at various prices per period, other things constant

_____ 12. Measures how responsive quantity demanded is to a price change

_____ 13. Consumer preferences; assumed to be constant along a given demand curve

a. complements
b. demand
c. demand curve
d. elasticity of demand
e. individual demand
f. inelastic
g. law of demand
h. law of diminishing marginal utility
i. marginal utility
j. market demand
k. movement along a given demand curve
l. quantity demanded
m. shift of a demand curve
n. substitutes
o. tastes
p. total revenue
q. unit elastic

Review Economic Concepts

14. **True or False** A change in the price of a product will not cause that product's demand curve to shift.

15. The ________?________ is demonstrated by the fact that people will buy more hot dogs and hamburgers when the price of pizza increases.

16. Elasticity expresses a relationship between the percent change in ________?________ and the resulting percent change in ________?________.

17. Which of the following is false about demand curves?
    a. They normally slope down from left to right.
    b. They show the relationship between price and the quantity demanded.
    c. They can be used to calculate a product's elasticity of demand.
    d. They show how much profit is earned by businesses that sell the product.

18. **True or False** Quantity demanded at a particular price is represented by an individual point on a demand curve.

19. **True or False** A firm's total revenue will increase if it raises the price of a product that has an elasticity of demand equal to 0.7.

20. If the total revenue from selling a product declines when the product's price is increased, the demand for that product is ________?________.

21. **True or False** A business is more likely to increase the price of its product if the demand for the product is elastic than if the demand is inelastic

22. Which of the following is the correct formula for the elasticity of demand?

a. $\frac{\text{change in the price of the product}}{\text{change in the quantity demanded}}$

b. $\frac{\text{change in the quantity demanded}}{\text{change in the price of the product}}$

c. $\frac{\text{\% change in the price of the product}}{\text{\% change in the quantity demanded}}$

d. $\frac{\text{\% change in the quantity demanded}}{\text{\% change in the price of the product}}$

23. **True or False** Market demand is the demand of an individual consumer.

24. Which of these products is most likely to have elastic demand?
   a. cable television service
   b. a particular brand of hand soap
   c. ground black pepper
   d. taxi service in a large city

25. **True or False** When consumers earn more income, their demand for normal products will increase.

26. Which of the following is not a determinant of demand?
   a. consumer income
   b. prices of related goods
   c. consumer expectations and tastes
   d. all of the above are determinants of demand

27. **True or False** Demand for a normal good decreases as money income increases.

28. One purpose of advertising is to
   a. shift a product's demand curve to the right.
   b. shift a product's demand curve to the left.
   c. make a product's demand more elastic.
   d. help consumers identify the product's substitutes

Apply Economic Concepts

29. **Market Demand** Working in small groups, determine your group's market demand for gasoline. Make up a chart listing a variety of prices per gallon of gasoline, such as \$3.50, \$3.75, \$4.00, \$4.25, \$4.50, \$4.75. Each group member should determine how many gallons per week they would purchase at each price. Then do the following:
   a. Plot each group member's demand curve. Check to see whether each person's responses are consistent with the law of demand.
   b. Derive the "market" demand curve by adding the quantities demanded by all students at each price.
   c. What do you think will happen to that market demand curve after your class graduates and your incomes rise?

30. **Graphing Shifts of Demand Curves** The owner of Rita's Tacos bought ads in a local newspaper. As a result, the demand for her tacos increased as demonstrated in the demand schedule below. Draw a graph of her demand as it was before the ads were printed. On the same graph, draw the new demand curve for tacos. Explain why many businesses advertise their products.

OLD AND NEW DEMAND SCHEDULE FOR RITA'S TACOS

Price Per Taco	Old Quantity Demanded	New Quantity Demanded
$2.00	25	75
$1.75	50	100
$1.50	75	125
$1.25	100	150
$1.00	125	175
$0.75	150	200

31. **21st Century Skills: Communication and Collaboration** Working with a partner, identify a specific product you both do not own but would like to purchase. Write down the most you would be willing to pay for this product. Investigate three businesses that sell the product by using the Internet or a local newspaper. Summarize your findings in a few sentences that identify the businesses and list the prices they charge. With your partner, discuss how you would choose which business to buy from. Remember, price may not be the only factor you consider when making your choice.

Digging Deeper

with Economics e-Collection

Access the Gale Economics e-Collection through the URL below to find an article about a new product recently introduced to the market. Research a product you already have in mind, or use the search term "new product" to find a product that interests you. Analyze the market for this new product in terms of the determinants of demand: (1) consumer income, (2) the prices of related goods, (3) the number and composition of consumers, (4) consumer expectations, and (5) consumer tastes. Based on your analysis, predict whether or not the product will be successful. Prepare a PowerPoint presentation or create handouts to present your analysis and findings.

www.cengage.com/school/contecon

CHAPTER 5
Supply

CONSIDER ...

→ Why would a firm decide to store its products in a warehouse rather than offer them for sale?

→ When might hiring another worker actually reduce a firm's output?

→ Can a firm shut down without going out of business?

→ Why do movie theaters have so many screens?

→ Why is bigger not always better when it comes to the size of a firm?

Point your browser

www.cengage.com/school/contecon

moodboard/Jupiter Images; background image: Lukiyanova Natalia/frenta/Shutterstock.com

5.1 THE SUPPLY CURVE

Learning Objectives

LO1 Explain the law of supply.

LO2 Describe the elasticity of supply, and explain how it is measured.

Key Terms

In Your World

Just as consumer behavior shapes the demand curve, producer behavior shapes the supply curve. When studying demand, you should think like a consumer, or a demander. When studying supply, however, you must think like a producer, or a supplier. You may feel more natural as a consumer—after all, you are one. But you know more about producers than you may realize. Either online or in person, you have been around them all your life—Walmart, Subway, Best Buy, Exxon, McDonald's, Microsoft, Apple, KFC, Pizza Hut, Ford, Home Depot, Target, Gap, Google, Facebook, local businesses, and thousands more. You will draw on your knowledge to develop an understanding of supply and the supply curve.

LAW OF SUPPLY

LO1 Explain the law of supply.

With demand, the assumption is that consumers try to maximize utility, the incentive that motivates their behavior. With supply, the assumption is that producers try to maximize profit. Profit is the incentive that motivates the behavior of suppliers.

Role of Profit

A firm tries to earn a profit by transforming resources into products. Profit equals total revenue minus total cost. Recall that total revenue equals the price times the quantity sold at that price. Total cost includes the cost of all resources used by a firm in producing goods or services, including the entrepreneur's opportunity cost.

$$\text{Profit} = \text{Total revenue} - \text{Total cost}$$

When total revenue just covers total cost, a firm *breaks even.* Over time, total revenue must cover total cost for the firm to survive. If total revenue falls short of total cost year after year, the firm will fail.

Each year, millions of new firms enter the U.S. marketplace and nearly as many leave. Most of the more than 30 million profit-seeking firms in the United States consist of just an owner-operator, such as a plumber or an accountant, with no hired employees. And, as you can see from the Figure 5.1 on page 134, among firms that have employees, more firms may close their doors than enter the market in a given year. Firms must decide what goods and services to produce and what

FIGURE 5.1 Starts and Closures of Employer Firms, 2005–2009*

In the U.S. economy, the supply of goods and services is constantly changing. This is reflected by the number of firms which start, close, or go bankrupt in a year.

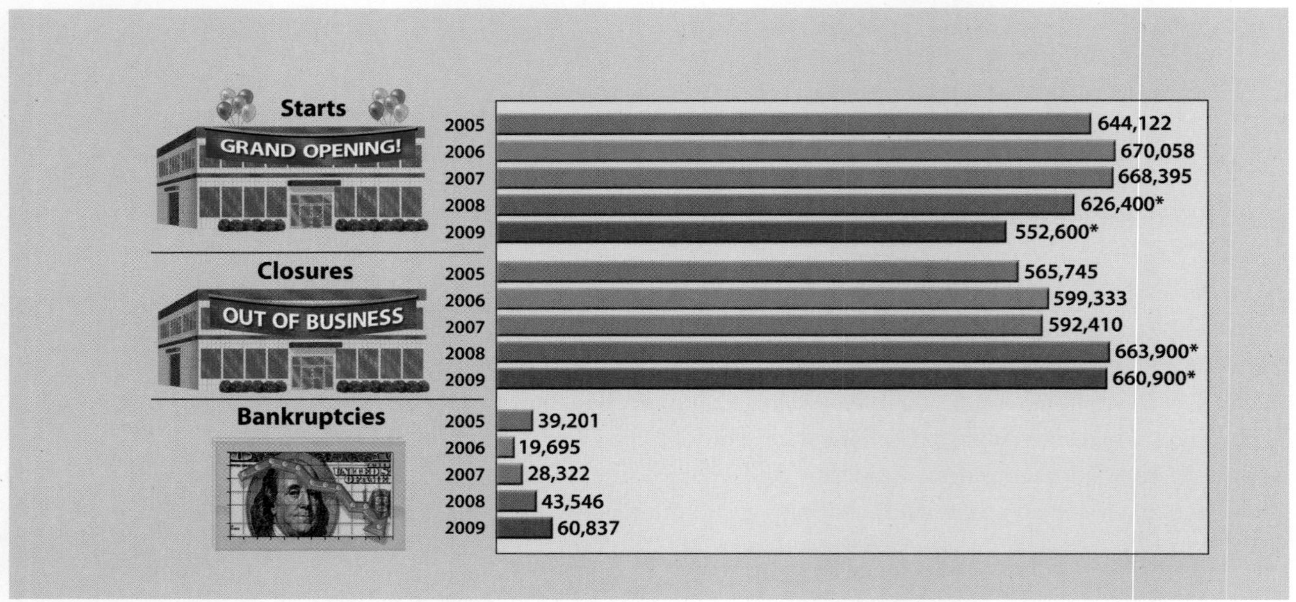

Source: U.S. Dept. of Commerce, Census Bureau, Administrative Office of the U.S. Courts, U.S. Dept. of Labour, Business Employment Dynamics (BED).
*Estimates based on Census data and BED trends

resources to employ. Firms must make plans while facing uncertainty about consumer demand, resource availability, and the intentions of other firms in the market. Despite the uncertainties, the profit incentive is strong enough to motivate entrepreneurs to pursue their dreams.

Supply

Just as demand is a relation between price and quantity demanded, supply is a relation between price and quantity supplied. **Supply** indicates how much of a good producers are *willing* and *able* to offer for sale per period at each price, other things constant. The **law of supply** says that the quantity supplied is usually directly, or positively, related to its price, other things constant. Thus, the lower the price, the smaller the quantity supplied. The higher the price, the greater the quantity supplied.

Figure 5.2 presents the market *supply schedule* and market **supply curve** *S* for pizza. A supply curve shows the quantities of a particular good supplied at various prices during a given time period, other things constant. Both show the quantities of 12-inch pizzas supplied per week at various prices by the many pizza makers in the market. As you can see, price and quantity supplied are directly related, other things constant. The supply curve shows, for example, that at a price of $6 per pizza, the quantity supplied is 16 million per week. At a price of $9, the quantity supplied increases to 20 million.

supply A relation showing the quantities of a good producers are willing and able to sell at various prices during a given period, other things constant

law of supply The quantity of a good supplied during a given time period is usually directly related to its price, other things constant

supply curve A curve, or line, showing the quantities of a particular good supplied at various prices during a given time period, other things constant

FIGURE 5.2 Supply Schedule and Supply Curve for Pizza

Market supply curve *S* shows the quantity of pizza supplied, at various prices, by all pizza makers.

(A) SUPPLY SCHEDULE

Price per pizza	Quantity supplied per week (millions)
$15	28
12	24
9	20
6	16
3	12

(B) SUPPLY CURVE

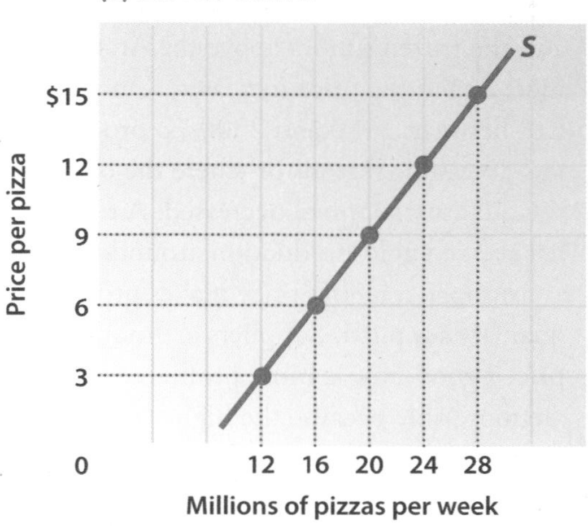

Like the demand curve, the supply curve reflects a particular period of time. It shows quantity supplied per period. For any supply curve, it is assumed that the prices of other goods the business could produce using these same resources remain unchanged. Thus, along the supply curve for pizza, the price of pizza changes *relative to other prices*, which do not change. The supply curve shows the effect of a change in the relative price of pizza—that is, relative to the prices of other goods the resources could supply. Producers have a profit incentive to supply more pizza at a higher price than at a lower price, so the supply curve slopes upward, from left to right.

More Willing to Supply

Producers offer more for sale when the price rises for two reasons. First, as the price increases, other things constant, a producer becomes more willing to supply the good. Prices act as signals to existing and potential suppliers about the rewards for producing various goods. An increase in the price of pizza, with other prices remaining constant, creates a profit incentive to shift some resources out of producing other goods, whose prices are now relatively lower, and into pizza, whose price is now relatively higher. *A higher pizza price makes supplying pizza more profitable and attracts resources from lower-valued uses.*

More Able to Supply

Higher prices also increase the producer's *ability* to supply the good. The cost of producing an additional unit of a good usually rises as output increases—that is, the *marginal cost* of production increases as output increases. (You will learn more about marginal cost in Lesson 5.3.) Because suppliers face a higher marginal cost of producing the good, they need to get a higher price to be able to increase the quantity supplied. *A higher price makes producers more able to increase quantity supplied.*

For example, a higher price for gasoline in recent decades increased producers' ability to search for oil in less-accessible areas, such as the remote jungles of the Amazon, the oil-sands of the Canadian West, the stormy waters of the North Sea, and the frozen tundra above the Arctic Circle. Thus, the quantity of oil supplied increased as the price increased. On the other hand, gold prices fell by more than half between 1980 and 2000, so producers were no longer able to mine gold in less-accessible regions or where the ore contained less gold. As the price declined, the quantity supplied decreased. A rebound in gold prices since 2000, however, has revived gold production around the world, increasing the quantity supplied.

In short, a higher price makes producers more *willing* and more *able* to increase quantity supplied. Suppliers are more willing because production of the higher-priced good now is more profitable than the other uses of the resources. Suppliers are more able because the higher price allows them to cover the higher marginal cost that typically results from increasing production.

Supply Versus Quantity Supplied

As with demand, economists distinguish between *supply* and *quantity supplied. Supply* is the entire relation between the price and quantity supplied, as shown by the supply schedule or supply curve. *Quantity supplied* refers to the amount offered for sale at a specific price, as shown by a point on a given supply curve. Thus, it is the *quantity supplied* that increases with a higher price, not supply. The term supply by itself refers to the entire supply schedule or supply curve.

ESSENTIAL QUESTION

Standard CEE 4: Incentives

People usually respond predictably to positive and negative incentives.

VasilySmirnov/iStockphoto.com

How does a producer respond when the price of its product increases?

Individual Supply and Market Supply

Economists also distinguish between *individual supply* (the supply from an individual producer) and *market supply* (the supply from all producers in the market for that good). *The market supply curve shows the total quantities supplied by all producers at various prices.*

In most markets, there are many suppliers, sometimes thousands. Assume for simplicity, however, that there are just two suppliers in the market for pizza: Pizza Palace and Pizza Castle. Figure 5.3 shows how the supply curves of two producers in the pizza market are added together to yield the market supply curve for pizza. Individual supply curves are summed across to get a market supply curve.

For example, at a price of $9, Pizza Palace supplies 400 pizzas per week and Pizza Castle supplies 300. Thus, the quantity supplied in the market for pizza at a price of $9 is 700. At a price of $12, Pizza Palace supplies 500 and Pizza Castle supplies 400, for a market quantity of 900 pizzas per week. The market supply curve in panel (C) of Figure 5.3 shows the horizontal sums of the individual supply curves in panels (A) and (B).

The market supply curve is simply the horizontal sum of the individual supply curves for all producers in the market. Unless otherwise noted, when this book talks about supply, you can take that to mean market supply.

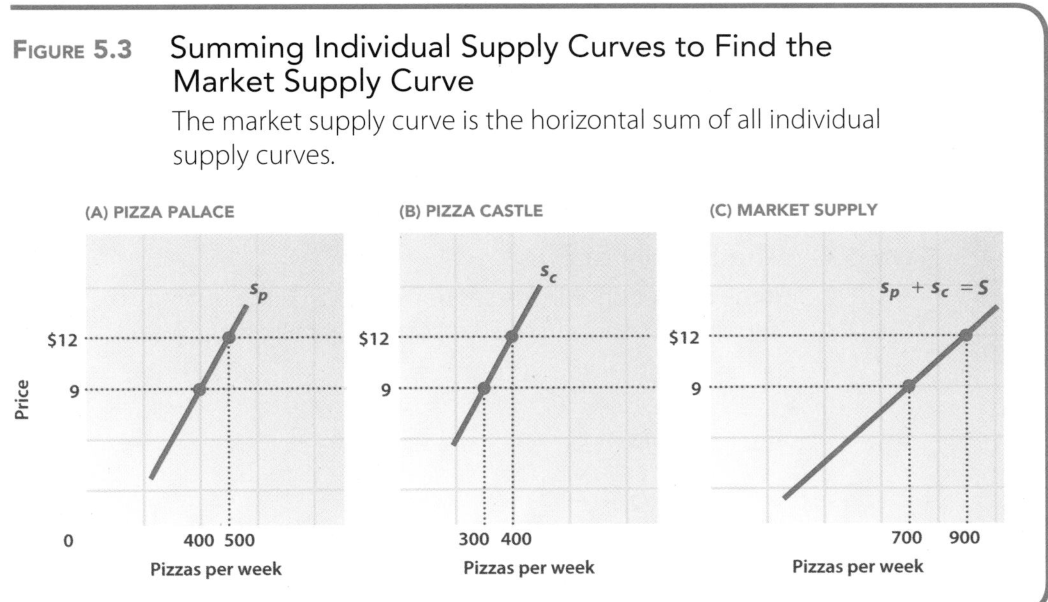

FIGURE 5.3 Summing Individual Supply Curves to Find the Market Supply Curve

The market supply curve is the horizontal sum of all individual supply curves.

Explain the law of supply in your own words. **CHECKPOINT**

ELASTICITY OF SUPPLY

LO2 Describe the elasticity of supply.

Prices are signals to both sides of the market about the relative scarcity of products. High prices discourage consumption but encourage production. Low prices encourage consumption but discourage production. Elasticity of demand measures how responsive consumers are to a price change. Likewise, elasticity of supply measures how responsive producers are to a price change.

Measurement

Elasticity of supply is calculated similarly to elasticity of demand. **Elasticity of supply** equals the percent change in quantity supplied divided by the percent change in price.

$$\text{Elasticity of supply} = \frac{\text{Percent change in quantity supplied}}{\text{Percent change in price}}$$

Suppose the price increases. Because a higher price makes production more attractive, the quantity supplied increases as the price increases.

Figure 5.4 depicts the typical upward-sloping supply curve presented earlier. As you can see, if the market price of pizza increases from $9 to $12, the quantity supplied increases from 20 million to 24 million. What is the elasticity of supply between these two points? The percent change in quantity supplied is the change in quantity supplied—4 million—divided by 20 million. So quantity supplied increases by 20 percent. The percent change in price is the change in price—$3—divided by $9, which is 33 percent.

elasticity of supply
A measure of the responsiveness of quantity supplied to a price change; the percent change in quantity supplied divided by the percent change in price

FIGURE 5.4 The Supply of Pizza

If the market price increases from $9 to $12, the quantity of pizza supplied increases from 20 million to 24 million per week.

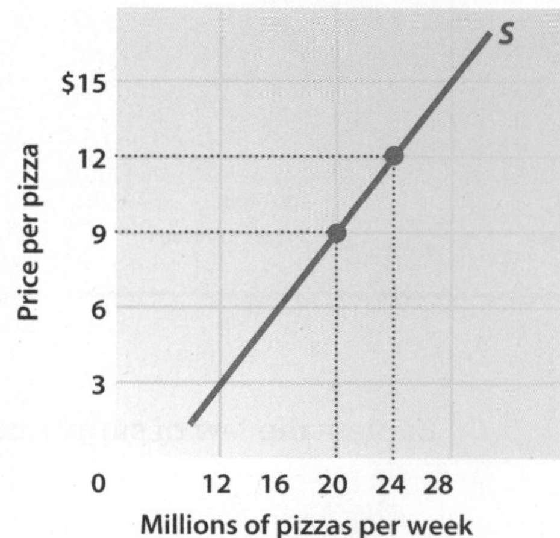

Elasticity of supply is, therefore, the percentage increase in quantity supplied—20 percent—divided by the percentage increase in price—33 percent—which equals 0.6.

Categories of Supply Elasticity

The terms for supply elasticity are the same as for demand elasticity. If supply *elasticity* exceeds 1.0, supply is *elastic.* If it equals 1.0, supply is *unit elastic.* If supply elasticity is less than 1.0, it is *inelastic.* Because 0.6 is less than 1.0, the supply of pizza is inelastic when the price increases from $9 to $12. Note that elasticity usually varies along a supply curve.

Determinants of Supply Elasticity

Elasticity of supply indicates how responsive producers are to a change in price. Their response depends on how costly it is to alter output when the price changes. If the cost of supplying an additional unit rises sharply as output expands, then a higher price causes little increase in quantity supplied. In this case, supply tends to be inelastic. However, if the cost of an additional unit rises slowly as output expands, the profit lure of a higher price prompts a relatively large boost in output. In this case, supply is more elastic.

One important determinant of supply elasticity is the length of the adjustment period under consideration. Just as demand becomes more elastic over time as consumers adjust to price changes, supply also becomes more elastic over time as producers adjust to price changes. The longer the adjustment period under consideration, the more easily producers can adapt to price changes. For example, a higher oil price prompts suppliers to pump more from existing wells in the short run. However, in the long run, suppliers can explore for more oil.

Figure 5.5 on page 140 demonstrates how the supply of gasoline becomes more elastic over time, with a different supply curve for each of three periods of adjustment. S_w is the supply curve when the period of adjustment is a week. As you can see, a higher gasoline price generates little response in quantity supplied because firms have little time to adjust. This supply curve is inelastic between $3.00 to $3.50 per gallon.

S_m is the supply curve when the adjustment period under consideration is a month. Firms have more time to vary output. Thus, supply is more elastic when the adjustment period is a month than when it's a week. Supply is yet more elastic when the adjustment period is a year, as is shown by S_y. A given price increase in gasoline prompts a greater quantity supplied as the adjustment period lengthens. Research confirms the positive link between the elasticity of supply and the length of the adjustment period. *The elasticity of supply is typically greater the longer the period of adjustment.*

The ability to increase quantity supplied in response to a higher price differs across industries. For example, oil was discovered on Alaska's North Slope in 1967, but that oil did not reach the market until a decade later. The long run is longer for oil and timber (where expansion may take a decade) than for window washing and hot-dog vending (where expansion may take only days).

FIGURE 5.5 Market Supply Becomes More Elastic Over Time

The supply curve one week after a price increase, S_w, is less elastic, at a given price, than the curve one month later, S_m, which is less elastic than the curve one year later, S_y. In response to a price increase from $3.00 to $3.50, quantity supplied per day increases to 110 million gallons after one week, to 140 million gallons after one month, and to 200 million gallons after one year.

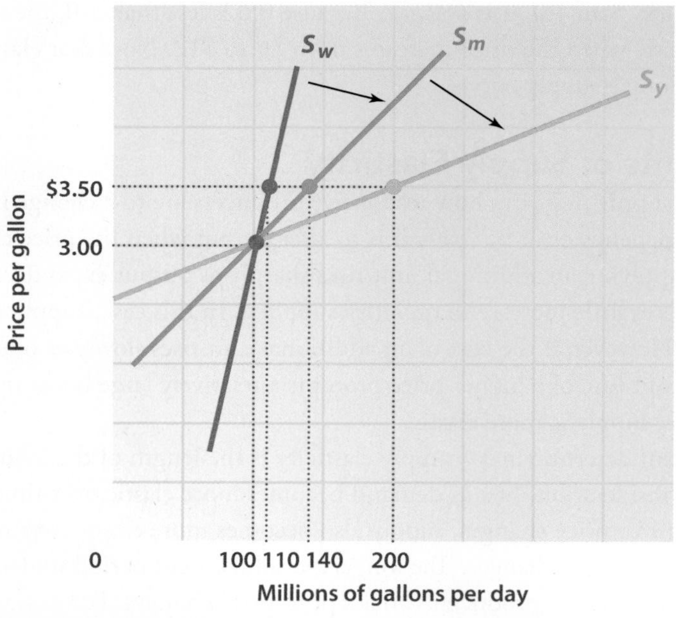

CHECKPOINT What does the elasticity of supply measure, and what factors influence its numerical value?

Bork/Shutterstock.com

Passant/iStockphoto.com

Why do you think the "long run" is longer for a business that produces windows than it is for a business that washes windows?

5.1 ASSESSMENT

Think Critically

1. In what ways do the motives of a pizza restaurant owner differ from the motives of customers who buy the restaurant's pizza?
2. Why should the quantity of winter jackets supplied increase when there is an increase in the price of these jackets?

Graphing Exercise

3. The owner of a shoe store reviewed her costs to determine how many pairs of running shoes she would be willing to supply each month at different prices. The results of her research appear in the supply schedule shown here. Use these data to draw her supply curve for running shoes. Explain how the graph demonstrates the law of supply.

SUPPLY OF RUNNING SHOES

Price	Quantity Supplied
$70	100
$60	80
$50	60
$40	40
$30	20

Make Academic Connections

4. **Mathematics** The table below shows how much cheese three dairies in a small community supply each month at the current price of $3.00 per pound. It also shows how much each one would supply if the price increased to $4.00. Calculate the percent changes in price and in quantity supplied that would result from this price increase. What is the elasticity of supply for cheese in this market? Is supply elastic, unit elastic, or inelastic?

SUPPLY OF CHEESE AT $3.00 AND $4.00 PER POUND

Dairy	Quantity Supplied at $3.00	Quantity Supplied at $4.00
A	1,000 pounds	1,300 pounds
B	1,700 pounds	2,600 pounds
C	2,300 pounds	3,100 pounds
Total Production	5,000 pounds	7,000 pounds

TeamWork

Working in small teams, think of five industries other than those given as examples in this lesson. For each industry, describe the product or services sold, as well as the means of distribution, such as retail stores, online, or wholesale. Rank these industries in order of the time the industry needs to adjust to a price change. Give a ranking of 1 to industries that would require the least amount of time to adjust fully to a price change and a 5 to those that would require the most time. Provide an explanation for each of your rankings. Discuss your team's rankings in class.

MOVERS AND SHAKERS

John Schnatter

Founder, Papa John's

Incorporated in 1984 and headquartered in Louisville, Kentucky, Papa John's is a franchised fast-food restaurant chain that specializes in pizza. It is the third largest pizza take-out and delivery company in the United States. Papa John's has more than 3,360 franchises in the United States and an additional 500 in more than 30 other countries.

Papa John's founder, John Schnatter, began his restaurant career at Rocky's Sub Pub during high school. During college he delivered pizzas for Greek's Pizza in Muncie, Indiana. After graduation, he began to work for his father, co-owner of a nearly bankrupt pub in Jeffersonville, Indiana. In 1983 he sold his treasured 1971 Chevrolet Camaro Z28 to buy out his father's partner. He then knocked out a closet, installed an oven, and began selling pizza to the pub's customers. Schnatter made his pizzas using fresh dough and superior-quality ingredients.

The pizza sold so well that in 1984 he opened the first Papa John's in a retail space next to the pub. Schnatter began offering Papa John's franchises in 1986. In 2002 Papa John's began online ordering throughout the United States. To maintain product consistency and quality, he opened regional commissaries from which fresh dough and other ingredients are delivered twice weekly to the restaurants.

Schnatter offers advice to potential franchisers on how to manage people:

- "You need to listen to the managers so you know what's working and what's not working and can take care of problems as soon as they happen."
- "You have to entrust people to make decisions if you are going to lead people."
- "If a manager or anyone has an idea, I want them to deploy that better way to do something."
- "There are only so many good people out there running restaurants. If you can recruit and retain those people, you will do well. Your competitors will get the leftovers."

SHANNON STAPLETON/Reuters/Landov.

In 2009, Schnatter began a campaign to find the Z28 Camaro he sold to finance his first store, offering a $250,000 reward. The car was traced to a man in Flatwoods, Kentucky, who had kept it in excellent condition. Schnatter bought the car back for $250,000 and paid a $25,000 reward to the family who had tipped him off to its whereabouts. To celebrate, he announced he would give a free pizza to anyone who drove a Camaro to a Papa John's location on August 26.

Schnatter is generous to the community that is home to his corporate headquarters. He has made donations in the Louisville area that include a $10 million pledge in 2007 toward Louisville's Papa John's Cardinal Stadium expansion and a $1 million contribution to the Louisville Zoo's Glacier Run expansion.

As Papa John's founder and Chairman of the Board, Schnatter continues to be enthusiastic about making superior-quality pizzas that can be delivered directly to the customer. "I love the product, I like the people, I love the business . . . It's all I know."

Think Critically **Analyze the quotations attributed to John Schnatter. From these statements, what qualities do you think he possesses that made him a successful entrepreneur?**

Sources: http://findarticles.com/p/articles/mi_m3190/is_n40_v30/ai_18779124/; U.S. Franchising Opportunities - Requirements & Fees - Papa John's Pizza; http://www.mrpizzaiolo.com/2008/06/04/online-ordering-riches/; http://www.allamericanspeakers.com/sportspeakers/printerbio.php?speaker_id=10358; and http://investing.businessweek.com/research/stocks/people/person.asp?personId=325396&ticker=PZZA:US

5.2 SHIFTS OF THE SUPPLY CURVE

Learning Objectives

LO1 Identify the determinants of supply, and explain how a change in each affects the supply curve.

LO2 Contrast a movement along the supply curve with a shift of the supply curve.

Key Terms

movement along a supply curve 147

shift of a supply curve 147

In Your World

Supply curves indicate the price and variety of goods available to you—from the latest social network sites to the smartest phones. Assumed constant along a supply curve are the determinants of supply other than the good's price. As you will see, there are five such determinants of supply. A change in any of these could cause a supply curve to shift. This contrasts with a change in price, other things constant, which causes a movement along a supply curve.

DETERMINANTS OF SUPPLY

LO1
Identify the determinants of supply, and explain how a change in each affects the supply curve.

Each firm's supply curve is based on the cost of production and profit opportunities in the market. Anything that affects production costs and profit opportunities helps shape the supply curve. Following are the five determinants of market supply other than the price of the good:

1. The cost of resources used to make the good
2. The price of other goods these resources could make
3. The technology used to make the good
4. Producer expectations
5. The number of sellers in the market

Change in the Cost of Resources

Any change in the cost of resources used to make a good will affect the supply of the good. For example, suppose the cost of mozzarella cheese falls. This reduces the cost of making pizza. Producers are therefore willing and able to supply more pizza at each price. This is reflected by a rightward shift of the supply curve from *S* to *S′* in Figure 5.6. After the shift, the quantity supplied is greater at each price. For example, at a price of $12, the quantity supplied increases from 24 million to

FIGURE 5.6 An Increase in the Supply of Pizza

An increase in the market supply of pizza is reflected by a rightward shift of the supply curve, from *S* to *S′*. After the increase in supply, the quantity supplied per week increases at each price. For example, the quantity of pizza supplied at a price of $12 increases from 24 million pizzas (point *g*) to 28 million pizzas (point *h*).

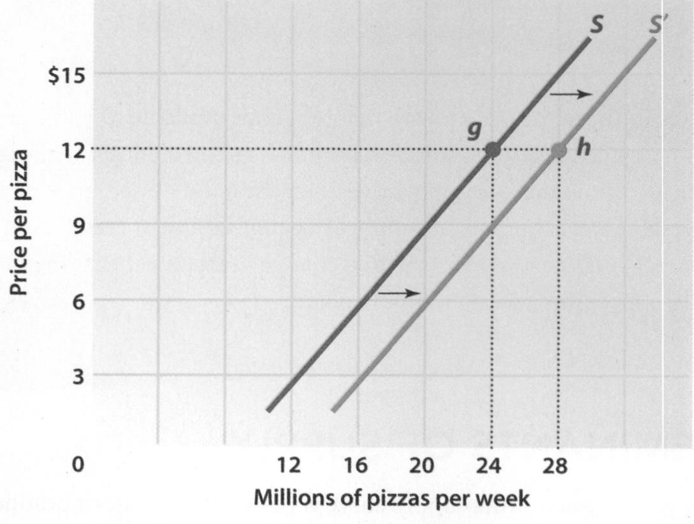

28 million pizzas per week, as shown by the movement from point *g* to point *h*. In short, *an increase in supply—that is, a rightward shift of the supply curve—means that producers are willing and able to supply more pizza at each price.*

What about an increase in the cost of a resource used to make pizza? This means that at every level of output, the cost of supplying pizza increases. An increase in the cost of a resource will reduce the supply of pizza, meaning a leftward shift of the supply curve. For example, if the wage paid to pizza workers increases, the higher labor cost would increase the cost of production, so pizza becomes less profitable.

Higher production costs decrease supply, so pizza supply shifts leftward, as from *S* to *S″* in Figure 5.7. Producers supply less at each price. For example, at a price of $12, the quantity supplied declines from 24 million to 20 million per week. This is shown in Figure 5.7 by the movement from point *g* to point *i*.

Change in the Prices of Other Goods

Nearly all resources have alternative uses. The labor, building, machinery, ingredients, and knowledge needed to make pizza could produce other products, such as calzones, bread sticks, rolls, and other baked goods.

A change in the price of another good these resources could make affects the opportunity cost of making pizza. For example, if the price of calzones falls, the opportunity cost of making pizza declines. These resources are not as profitable in their best alternative use, which is making calzones. So pizza production

FIGURE 5.7 A Decrease in the Supply of Pizza

A decrease in the supply of pizza is reflected by a leftward shift of the supply curve, from *S* to *S″*. After the decrease in supply, the quantity supplied per week decreases at each price level. For example, the quantity of pizza supplied at a price of $12 decreases from 24 million pizzas (point *g*) to 20 million pizzas (point *i*).

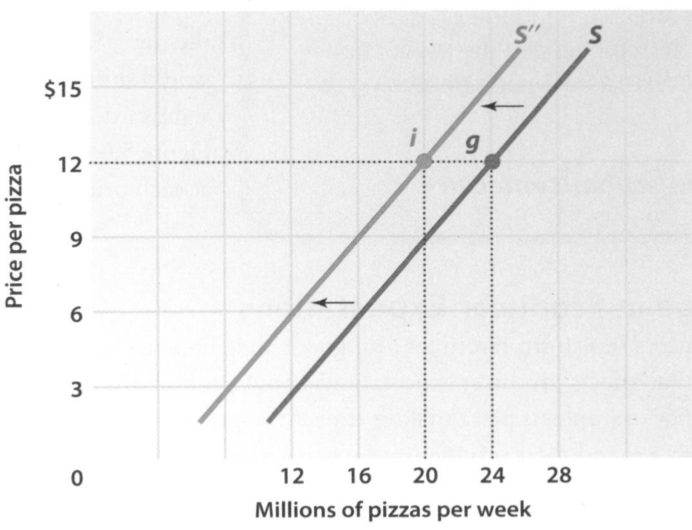

becomes relatively more attractive. As some resources shift from baking calzones to making pizza, the supply of pizza increases, or shifts to the right, as shown in Figure 5.6.

On the other hand, if the price of calzones increases, so does the opportunity cost of making pizza. Some pizza makers may bake more calzones and less pizza, so the supply of pizza decreases, or shifts to the left, as in Figure 5.7. A change in the price of another good these resources could produce affects the profit incentives of pizza makers.

Change in Technology

Technology represents the economy's stock of knowledge about how to combine resources efficiently. Discoveries in chemistry, biology, electronics, and many other fields have created new products, improved existing products, and lowered the cost of production. For example, the first microprocessor, the Intel 4004, could execute about 400 computations per second when it hit the market in 1971. Today a standard PC can handle more than 6 billion computations per second, or *15 million times* what the Intel 4004 could handle. Technological change—in this case, faster computers—lowers the cost of producing goods that involve computers, from automobile manufacturing to document processing.

Along a given market supply curve, technological know-how is assumed to remain unchanged. If better technology is discovered, the cost of production falls, making this market more profitable. Improvements in technology make firms willing and able to supply more of the good at each price. Consequently, supply increases, as reflected by a rightward shift of the supply curve. For example, suppose a new high-tech oven that costs the same as existing ovens bakes pizza in half the time. Such a breakthrough would shift pizza supply rightward, as from *S* to *S′* in Figure 5.6, so more is supplied at each price.

NET Bookmark

Changes and advances in computer technology have lowered the production costs of many goods and services in recent years. Since the year 2000, many major developments have occurred. Access a timeline that covers developments in computer technology from 2000 to 2011 by clicking on the URL below. After scanning the list, click on one of the links for a development you think influenced the production of goods and services in some way. Write a paragraph describing the development and its influence.

www.cengage.com/school/contecon

Change in Producer Expectations

Producers transform resources into goods they hope to sell for a profit. Any change that affects producer expectations about profitability can affect market supply. For example, if pizza makers expect the price to increase in the future, some may expand their production capacity now. This would shift the supply of pizza rightward, as shown in Figure 5.6.

Some goods can be stored easily. For example, crude oil can be left in the ground and grain can be stored in a silo. Expecting higher prices in the future might prompt some producers to reduce their current supply while awaiting the higher price. This would shift the current supply curve to the left, as shown in Figure 5.7. Thus, an expectation of higher prices in the future could either increase or decrease current supply, depending on the good.

Investigate Your Local Economy

Businesses generally pay taxes to the local, state, and federal governments. Contact your local government's bureau of taxation. Find out what taxes are paid by local businesses. Also find out if business taxes have changed in the past five years. Has an increase or decrease in tax rates affected supply in your area? Write a paragraph to explain your findings.

Change in the Number of Suppliers

Any change in the market environment also can affect the number of suppliers in that market. For example, government regulations may influence market supply. As a case in point, for decades government strictly regulated the prices and entry of new firms in a variety of industries including airlines, trucking, and telecommunications. During that era, the number of firms in each market was artificially limited by these government restrictions. When these restrictions were eased, more firms entered these markets, increasing supply. More generally, any government action that affects a market's profitability, such as a change in business taxes, could shift the supply curve. Lower taxes on a particular industry will attract more firms to that market, thereby increasing supply. Higher taxes will have the opposite effect.

CHECKPOINT **What are the five determinants of supply, and how does a change in each affect the supply of a product?**

A MOVEMENT ALONG A SUPPLY CURVE VERSUS A SHIFT OF A SUPPLY CURVE

LO2
Contrast a movement along the supply curve with a shift of the supply curve.

Note again the distinction between *a movement along a supply curve* and *a shift of a supply curve.* A change in *price*, other things constant, causes a **movement along a supply curve** from one price-quantity combination to another. A change in one of the determinants of supply other than the price causes a **shift of a supply curve**, changing supply. A shift of the supply curve means a change in the quantity supplied at each price.

A change in price, other things constant, changes quantity supplied along a given supply curve. A change in a determinant of supply other than the price of the good—such as the cost of resources used to make the good, the price of other goods these resources could produce, technology used to make the good, producer expectations, or the number of firms in the market—shifts the entire supply curve to the right or left.

movement along a supply curve Change in quantity supplied resulting from a change in the price of the good, other things constant

shift of a supply curve Increase or decrease in supply resulting from a change in one of the determinants of supply other than the price of the good

CHECKPOINT

Explain the difference between a movement along a supply curve and a shift of a supply curve.

Span the Globe

Oil for One and One for Oil

The Organization of the Petroleum Exporting Countries (OPEC) is a 12-nation, international group that works to control the output and price of oil. OPEC pumps about one-third of the world's crude oil. Its production policies can have a major effect on the price consumers pay for fuel to drive their cars and heat their homes.

Representatives of 12 countries meet periodically and agree to increase, decrease, or hold constant the number of barrels of crude oil they supply to achieve the price level they desire. If the market price drops, OPEC can cut production to increase the price to the desired level. If the market price rises, OPEC can increase production to lower the price to the desired level. OPEC has no control over the world demand for oil or what other oil producers supply. When OPEC reaches its productive capacity, it can still reduce output to increase the price, but it can't increase output much if it wants to lower the price.

Think Critically **As OPEC nears its productive capacity, why can it more easily raise the world price of oil than lower the world price?**

Sources: Berkman, Ouliaris, & Samiei, "The Structure of the Oil Market and Causes of High Prices," International Monetary Fund, September 21, 2005.

5.2 ASSESSMENT

Think Critically

1. One year a farmer grows corn on his 200 acres of land. He sells his corn in September for $3.00 per bushel. Early the next spring he notices that the price of soybeans has gone up 50 percent while the price of corn has remained the same. What might happen to his supply curve for corn? Explain your answer.
2. The Apex Plastics Corp. finds a new way to produce plastic outdoor furniture from recycled milk bottles at a low cost. What will happen to the supply curve for plastic furniture? Explain your answer.
3. A big storm destroys most of the sugarcane crop in Louisiana. Most people expect this to cause a large increase in the price of sugar in a few months. What will happen to the supply curve for sugar today?

Graphing Exercise

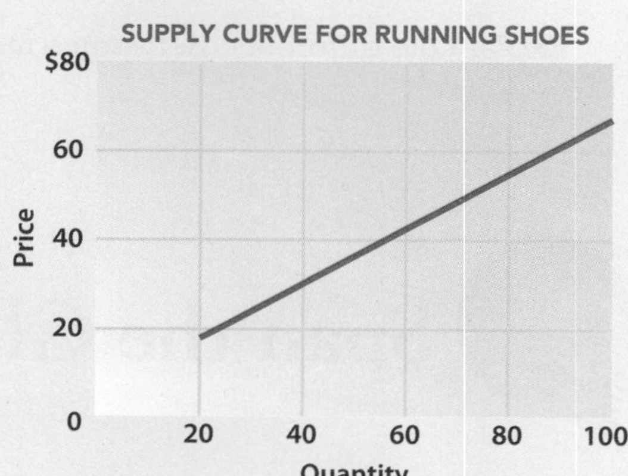

4. Make a copy of the supply curve shown here. Draw and explain the shifts of the market supply curve on your copy that would result from each of the following events. Label each shift of the supply curve.
   a. There is an increase in the cost of rubber used to produce the soles of running shoes.
   b. There is a decrease in the market price of rubber tires.
   c. A new machine is invented that produces running shoes using only one-third as many workers.
   d. A new mall is built in town with three stores that sell running shoes.

Make Academic Connections

5. **Research** Use newspapers, magazines, or the Internet to research a world event that could have an impact of the supply of a product consumed in the United States. Describe this event and explain how it might shift the U.S. supply curve.
6. **Technology** Choose a single product many consumers buy, and write a paragraph that discusses whether the creation of the Internet has shifted the supply curve for this product.

TeamWork

Working in small teams, identify five products that have experienced either an increase or decrease in supply over the past year. Explain what event(s) caused the shift in supply for each of the products and which of the five determinants of supply the shift demonstrates. Discuss your team's work with the class.

5.3 PRODUCTION AND COST

Learning Objectives

LO1 Explain how marginal product varies as a firm hires more labor in the short run.

LO2 Explain the shape of the firm's marginal cost curve and identify what part of that is the firm's supply curve.

LO3 Distinguish between economies of scale and diseconomies of scale in the long run.

Key Terms

In Your World

Suppose you manage a firm, such as a fast-food restaurant. How much should you supply in order to maximize profit? The answer requires a brief introduction to how a firm converts productive resources into outputs. In general, a profit-maximizing firm increases the quantity supplied as long as the marginal revenue from each unit sold exceeds its marginal cost. But no firm is guaranteed a profit in a market economy. Some firms just break even and others suffer losses that could eventually drive them out of business. Still, just the promise of profit attracts a steady stream of entrepreneurs.

PRODUCTION IN THE SHORT RUN

LO1
Explain how marginal product varies as a firm hires more labor in the short run.

A firm tries to earn a profit by converting productive resources, or *inputs*, into goods and services, or *outputs*. Consider production by a hypothetical moving company called Hercules.

Fixed and Variable Resources

All producers, including Hercules, use two categories of resources: fixed and variable. Resources that cannot be altered easily—the size of a building, for example—are called *fixed resources*. Hercules' fixed resources consist of a warehouse, a moving van, and some moving equipment. Resources that can be varied quickly to change output are called *variable resources*. In this example, suppose labor is the only variable resource.

When considering the time required to change the quantity of resources employed, economists distinguish between the short run and the long run. In the **short run**, at least one resource is fixed. In the **long run**, all resources can be varied. Hercules is operating in the short run because some resources are fixed. In this example, labor is the only resource that varies in the short run. A firm can enter or leave a market in the long run but not in the short run.

short run A period during which at least one of a firm's resources is fixed

long run A period during which all of a firm's resources can be varied

Figure 5.8 relates the amount of labor employed to the amount of furnishings moved. Labor is measured in worker-days, which is one worker for one day. Output is measured in tons of furnishings moved per day. The first column shows the number of workers employed per day. The second column shows the total product per day, measured in tons of furniture moved. **Total product** is the total output of the firm per period—in this case, tons of furniture moved per day. The third column shows the **marginal product** of each worker—that is, the amount by which the total product changes with each additional worker, assuming other resources remain unchanged.

FIGURE 5.8 **Short-Run Relationship Between Units of Labor and Tons of Furniture Moved**

As each of the first three workers is hired, the firm experiences increasing returns from labor. Marginal product increases as more labor is hired. Beginning with the fourth worker, the law of diminishing returns takes hold. This law states that as more units of one resource are added to all other resources, marginal product eventually declines.

Units of the Variable Resource (worker-days)	Total Product (tons moved per day)	Marginal Product (tons moved per day)
0	0	—
1	2	2
2	5	3
3	9	4
4	12	3
5	14	2
6	15	1
7	15	0
8	14	–1

Increasing Returns

total product The total output of the firm per period

marginal product The change in total product resulting from a one-unit change in a particular resource, all other resources constant

Without labor, nothing gets moved, so total product is zero when no workers are hired. If one worker is hired, that person must do all the driving, packing, and moving. A single worker cannot easily move some of the larger items. Still, one worker manages to move 2 tons per day. When a second is hired, some division of labor occurs, and two can move the big stuff more easily, so production more than doubles to 5 tons per day. The marginal product of a second worker is 3 tons per day.

Adding a third worker allows for an even better division of labor, which contributes to increased production. For example, one worker can pack fragile items while the other two do the heavy lifting. The total product of three workers climbs to 9 tons per day, 4 tons more than with two workers. The firm experiences *increasing returns* from labor as each of the first three workers is hired, meaning that marginal product increases as more labor is hired.

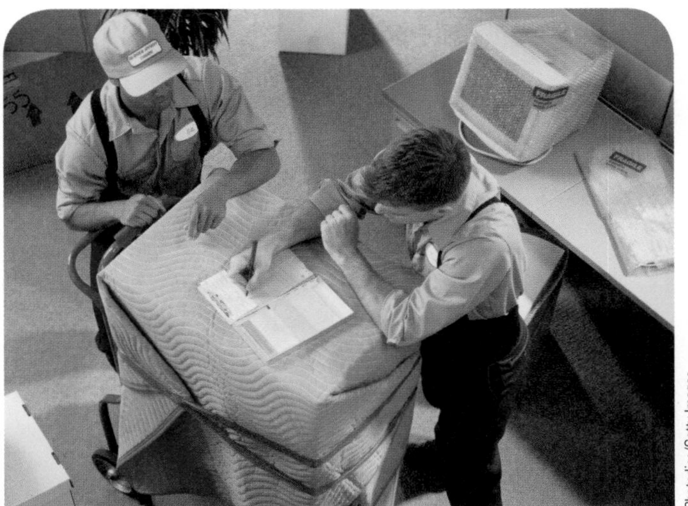
Photodisc/Getty Images

When Hercules hires a second worker, division of labor occurs, and production more than doubles. What is total product and marginal product with two workers? With three workers? What happens when a fourth worker is hired?

Law of Diminishing Returns

Hiring a fourth worker adds to the total product but not as much as was added by a third. Hiring still more workers increases total product by successively smaller amounts, so the marginal product in Figure 5.8 declines after three workers. Beginning with the fourth worker, the **law of diminishing returns** takes hold. This law states that as more of one resource is added to a given amount of other resources, marginal product eventually declines. *The law of diminishing returns is the most important feature of production in the short run.*

As long as marginal product is positive, total product continues to increase. However, as more workers are hired, total product may eventually decline. For example, an eighth worker would crowd the work area so much that people start getting in each other's way. As a result, total output would drop, meaning a negative marginal product. Likewise, a restaurant can hire only so many cooks before congestion and confusion in the kitchen cut total product.

Marginal Product Curve

Figure 5.9 shows the marginal product of labor, using data from Figure 5.8. Note that because of increasing returns, marginal product increases with each of the first three workers. Beginning with the fourth worker, diminishing returns cut marginal product. Marginal product turns negative if an eighth worker is hired. Figure 5.9 identifies three ranges of marginal product:

1. Increasing marginal returns
2. Diminishing but positive marginal returns
3. Negative marginal returns.

Firms normally produce in the range of diminishing but positive marginal returns.

law of diminishing returns As more of a variable resource is added to a given amount of other resources, marginal product eventually declines and could become negative

FIGURE 5.9 The Marginal Product of Labor

The marginal product of the first three workers shows increasing returns. The next three workers show diminishing returns, the seventh shows a zero return, and the eighth shows negative returns.

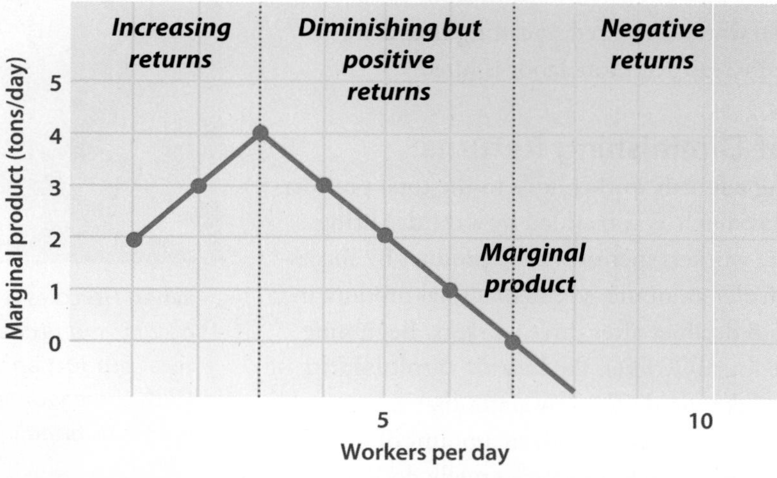

CHECKPOINT How does marginal product vary as a firm employs more labor in the short run?

COSTS IN THE SHORT RUN

LO2
Explain the shape of the firm's marginal cost curve and identify what part of that is the firm's supply curve.

Now that you have some idea about production in the short run, consider how the firm's costs vary with output. A firm faces two kinds of costs in the short run: fixed cost and variable cost.

Fixed and Variable Costs

A **fixed cost** is one that does not change in the short run, no matter how much is produced. A firm must pay a fixed cost even when nothing gets produced. Even if Hercules hires no labor and moves no furniture, the firm must pay for the warehouse, property taxes, insurance, vehicle registration, and equipment. By definition, fixed cost is just that—fixed. It does not vary with output in the short run. Fixed cost is sometimes called *overhead.* Hercules' fixed cost is $200 per day.

Variable cost varies with the amount produced. With Hercules, only labor varies in the short run, so labor is the only variable cost. For example, if Hercules hires no labor, output is zero, so variable cost is zero. As more labor is employed, output increases, as does variable cost. Variable cost depends on the amount of labor employed and on the wage. If the firm can hire each worker for $100 per day, variable cost equals $100 times the number of workers hired.

fixed cost Any production cost that is independent of the firm's output

variable cost Any production cost that changes as output changes

Total Cost

Figure 5.10 offers cost information for Hercules. The table lists the daily cost of moving furniture. Column 1 shows the number of tons moved per day. Column 2 shows the quantity of labor needed to produce each level of output. For example, moving 2 tons per day requires one worker, 5 tons requires two workers, and so on. Only the first six workers are listed, because additional workers would add nothing to total product.

Column 3 lists variable cost, which equals $100 times the number of workers employed. For example, the variable cost of moving 9 tons of furniture per day is $300 because this output rate requires three workers. Column 4 indicates the fixed cost for each output total. By definition, fixed cost remains at $200 per day regardless of the amount moved. Column 5 lists the **total cost**, which sums the variable cost and fixed cost—that is, columns 3 plus 4. As you can see, when output is zero, variable cost is zero, so total cost consists entirely of the fixed cost of $200.

total cost The sum of fixed cost and variable cost

FIGURE 5.10 Short-Run Cost Data for Hercules

Column 7 shows the marginal cost of moving another ton of furnishings. It is the change in total cost divided by the change in tons moved.

1 Tons Moved per Day	2 Workers Per Day	3 Variable Cost	4 Fixed Cost	5 Total Cost	6 Change in total cost ÷ Change in tons moved =	7 Marginal Cost
0	0	$ 0	$200	$200	—	
2	1	$100	$200	$300	$100 ÷ 2	$ 50.00
5	2	$200	$200	$400	$100 ÷ 3	$ 33.33
9	3	$300	$200	$500	$100 ÷ 4	$ 25.00
12	4	$400	$200	$600	$100 ÷ 3	$ 33.33
14	5	$500	$200	$700	$100 ÷ 2	$ 50.00
15	6	$600	$200	$800	$100 ÷ 1	$100.00

Marginal Cost

Of special interest to the firm is how much total cost changes with output. In particular, what is the marginal cost of moving another ton? As shown in columns 6 and 7 of Figure 5.10, the **marginal cost** of production is simply the change in total cost divided by the change in quantity, or

$$\text{Marginal cost} = \frac{\text{Change in total cost}}{\text{Change in quantity}}$$

For example, increasing output from 0 to 2 tons increases total cost by $100. The marginal cost of each of the first 2 tons is the change in total cost, $100, divided by the change in output, 2 tons, or $100/2, which equals $50. The marginal cost of each of the next 3 tons is the change in total cost, $100, divided by the change in output, 3 tons, or $100/3, which equals $33.33.

Notice in column 7 that marginal cost first decreases and then increases. Changes in marginal cost reflect changes in the productivity of the variable resource, labor. The first three workers show increasing returns. This rising marginal product of labor reduces marginal cost for the first 9 tons moved. Beginning with the fourth worker, the firm experiences diminishing returns from labor, so the marginal cost of output increases. Thus, marginal cost in Figure 5.10 first falls and then rises, because returns from labor first increase and then decrease.

Marginal Cost Curve

Figure 5.11 shows the marginal cost curve for moving furniture based on the data in Figure 5.10. Because of increasing returns from labor, the marginal cost curve at first slopes downward. Because of diminishing marginal returns from labor, the marginal cost curve slopes upward after 9 tons. Keep in mind that economic analysis is marginal analysis. Marginal cost is a key to the firm's production decision.

marginal cost The change in total cost resulting from a one-unit change in output; the change in total cost divided by the change in output

FIGURE 5.11 Marginal Cost Curve for Hercules

Marginal cost first declines, reflecting increasing marginal returns, and then increases, reflecting diminishing marginal returns.

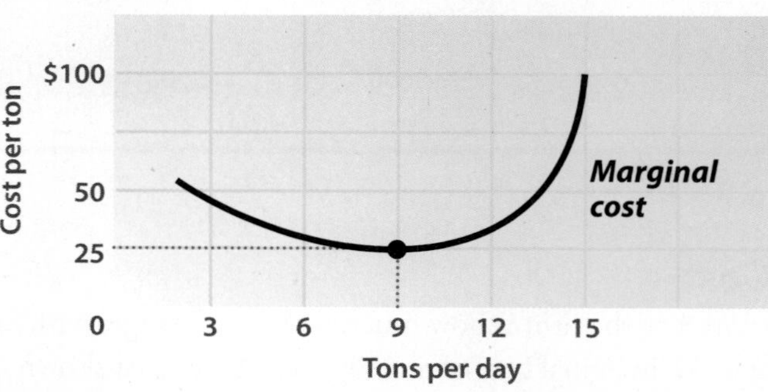

Marginal Revenue

To understand how firms work, it may help to draw on your knowledge of demand. Remember that demand is based on the marginal benefit that consumers get from buying each additional unit of the good. Likewise, supply is based on the marginal benefit that producers get from selling each additional unit of a good. The marginal benefit that producers get from supplying another unit is the **marginal revenue** they receive. This is the change in total revenue from selling that unit. In competitive markets, the firm's marginal revenue is the market price. A competitive firm receives the market price for selling one more unit.

Maximizing Profit and Minimizing Loss

In general, producers sell additional units as long as the marginal revenue they receive exceeds the marginal cost. In competitive markets, the firm supplies additional units as long as the price exceeds marginal cost. The firm's profit-maximizing level of output occurs where *marginal revenue equals marginal cost.* Thus, for a firm in competitive markets, the profit-maximizing level of output occurs where the market price equals marginal cost.

There is one qualification to this profit-maximizing rule. Sometimes the market price may be so low that production makes no economic sense. At the level of output where marginal revenue equals marginal cost, the firm's total revenue must at least cover its variable cost. A firm that can't cover variable cost should shut down.

Here's the logic behind the shutdown decision. Even if the firm produces nothing in the short run, it must still pay fixed cost. If nothing is produced, the firm's loss equals fixed cost. For example, Hercules would lose $200 per day if no labor is hired and no furniture gets moved.

What if the market price is relatively low, say $25 per ton, but the firm decides to produce anyway, hiring three workers for $100 each to move 9 tons per day? The total revenue from supplying 9 tons at $25 per ton is $225. That's $75 less than the variable cost of $300. The firm loses $75 in variable cost plus $200 in fixed cost, for a total loss of $275. The firm would lose less—only $200—by shutting down. Why produce when doing so only increases the loss?

A firm's *minimum acceptable price* is a price high enough to ensure that total revenue at least covers variable cost. If the market price is below that minimum, the firm shuts down in the short run. Note that shutting down is not the same as going out of business. A firm that shuts down keeps its productive capacity intact—paying the rent, fire insurance, and property taxes, keeping water pipes from freezing in the winter, and so on. For example, auto factories sometimes shut down temporarily when sales are slow. Businesses in summer resorts often shut down for the winter. These firms do not escape fixed cost by shutting down, because fixed cost by definition is not affected by changes in output.

If in the future demand increases enough, the firm will resume production. If market conditions look grim and are not expected to improve, the firm may decide to leave the market. But that's a long-run decision. The short run is defined as a period during which some resources and some costs are fixed. A firm cannot escape those costs in the short run, no matter what it does. A firm cannot enter or leave the market in the short run.

marginal revenue The change in total revenue from selling another unit of the good

The Firm's Supply Curve

To produce in the short run, the price must be high enough to ensure that total revenue covers variable cost. The *competitive firm's supply curve* is the upward sloping portion of its marginal cost curve at and above the minimum acceptable price. This supply curve shows how much the firm will supply at each price.

In the Hercules example, a price of $33.33 allows the firm to at least cover variable cost of moving 12 tons per day. Hercules's short-run supply curve is presented in Figure 5.12 as the upward-sloping portion of the marginal cost curve starting at $33.33. At that price, Hercules supplies 12 tons of moving per day. At a price of $50 per ton, the company moves 14 tons, and at a price of $100 per ton, the company moves 15 tons. At a price of $100, the firm's total revenue from supplying 15 tons is $1,500. Figure 5.10 indicated that the total cost of supplying 15 tons is $800, leaving the Hercules with a profit of $700 per day.

Figure 5.12 shows the supply curve for an individual firm in the short run. The market supply curve sums the individual supply curves for all firms in the market.

FIGURE 5.12 Short-Run Supply Curve for Hercules

A competitive firm's supply curve shows the quantity supplied at each price. The supply curve is the upward-sloping portion of its marginal cost curve, beginning at the firm's minimum acceptable price. The minimum acceptable price, in this case $33.33 per ton, is the lowest price that allows the firm's total revenue to cover its variable cost.

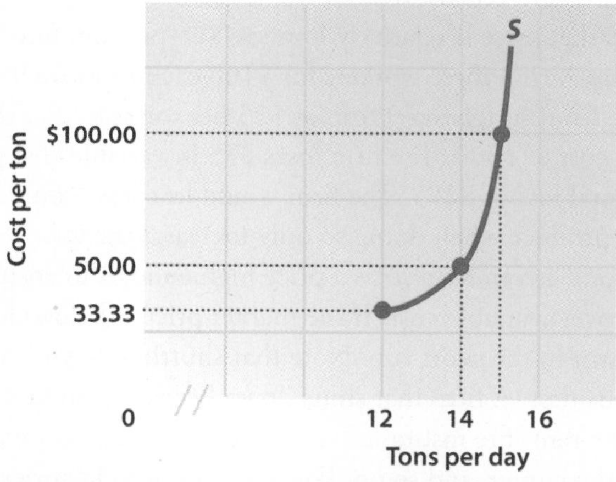

CHECKPOINT Why does the firm's marginal cost curve slope upward in the short run?

PRODUCTION AND COSTS IN THE LONG RUN

LO3 Distinguish between economies and diseconomies of scale in the long run.

So far, the analysis has focused on how short-run costs vary with output for a firm of a given size. In the long run, all inputs can be varied, so there are no fixed costs. What should be the size of the firm?

Economies of Scale

A firm's owner would like to know how the average cost of production varies as the size, or scale, of the firm increases. *Average cost* equals total cost divided by output. A firm's *long-run average cost* indicates the lowest average cost of producing each output when the firm's size is allowed to vary.

If the firm's long-run average cost declines as the firm size increases, this reflects economies of scale. Consider some reasons for economies of scale. *A larger firm often allows for larger, more specialized machines and greater specialization of labor.* Typically, as the scale of the firm increases, capital substitutes for labor. Production techniques such as the assembly line can be introduced only if the firm is sufficiently large.

Diseconomies of Scale

As the scale of the firm continues to increase, however, another force may eventually take hold. If the firm's long-run average cost increases as production increases, this reflects *diseconomies of scale.* For example, Oasis of the Seas is the world's largest cruise liner. The ship can accommodate 6,300 guests, but it's too large to visit some of the globe's most popular ports such as Venice and Bermuda.

More generally in a firm, as the amount and variety of resources employed increase, so does the *task of coordinating all these inputs.* As the workforce grows, additional layers of management are needed to monitor production. Information may not be correctly passed up or down the chain of command.

Movie theaters experience both economies and diseconomies of scale. A theater with one screen needs someone to sell tickets, usually another to sell popcorn, and yet another to run the movie projector. If a second movie screen is added, the same staff can perform these tasks for both screens. What's more, contruction costs per screen are reduced because only one lobby and one set of rest rooms are required. By adding more screens, which have increased to an average 13 per theater in the United States, theaters take advantage of economies of scale.

Beyond some number, adding still more screens creates deseconomies of scale. Traffic congestion around the theater may become gridlocked. The limited supply of popular films will not support that many screens. Finally, scheduling becomes a challenge because only certain times are popular with the public.

economies of scale
Forces that reduce a firm's average cost as the firm's size, or scale, increases in the long run

It is possible for long-run average cost to neither increase nor decrease with changes in firm size. If neither economies of scale nor diseconomies of scale occur as the scale of the firm expands, a firm experiences *constant returns to scale* over some range of production.

Long-Run Average Cost Curve

Figure 5.13 presents a firm's **long-run average cost curve**, showing the lowest average cost of producing each rate of output. The curve is marked into segments reflecting economies of scale, constant returns to scale, and diseconomies of scale. Production must reach quantity *A* for the firm to achieve its *minimum efficient scale*, which is the smallest scale, or size, that allows the firm to take full advantage of economies of scale. At the minimum efficient scale, long-run average cost is at a minimum. From output *A* to output *B*, the firm experiences constant returns to scale. Beyond output rate *B*, diseconomies of scale increase long-run average cost.

long-run average cost curve A curve that indicates the lowest average cost of production at each rate of output when the firm's size is allowed to vary

Firms try to avoid diseconomies of scale. Competition weeds out firms that grow too large. To avoid diseconomies of scale, IBM divided into six smaller decision-making groups. Other large corporations have spun off parts of their operations to create new companies. HP started Agilent Technologies, and AT&T started Lucent Technologies.

FIGURE 5.13 A Firm's Long-Run Average Cost Curve

Average cost declines until production reaches output level *A*. The firm is experiencing economies of scale. Output level *A* is the minimum efficient scale—the lowest rate of output at which the firm takes full advantage of economies of scale. Between *A* and *B*, the economy has constant returns to scale. Beyond output level *B*, the long-run average cost curve reflects diseconomies of scale.

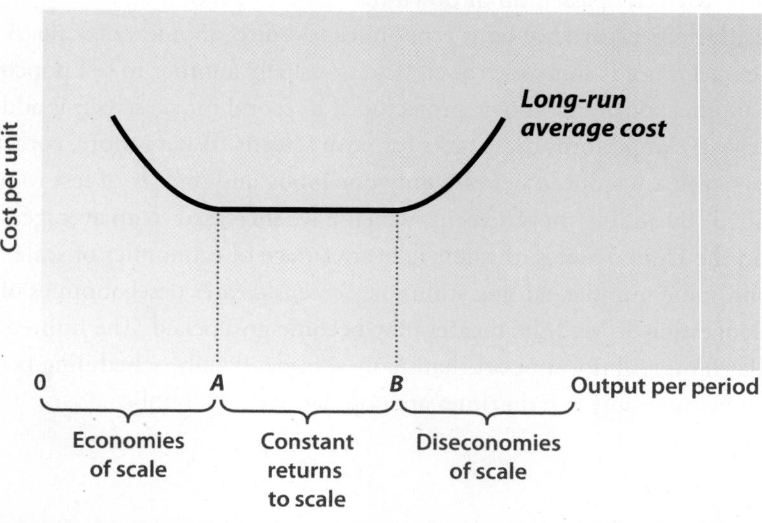

The long-run average cost curve guides the firm toward the most efficient plant size for a given rate of output. However, once a plant of that scale is built, the firm has fixed costs and is operating in the short run. A firm in the short run chooses the output rate where marginal revenue equals marginal cost. Firms plan for the long run, but they produce in the short run.

How are economies of scale and diseconomies of scale reflected in a firm's long-run average cost curve?

Math in Economics

Common Core Number and Operations—Fractions

When adding or subtracting fractions, the fractions must have a common denominator. If one of the fractions is 1, you can write it as a fraction of the common denominator over itself (Example: 1 = 5/5). Once the fractions have a common denominator, the answer is the sum or difference in the numerator over the common denominator. If the fraction is not in simplified form, rewrite it in its simplest form.

EXAMPLE

A business buys 1/5 of the coal it needs from one supplier and 2/5 from a different supplier. What fraction of the coal the business needs must be bought from other sources?

SOLUTION

The value 1 represents the amount of coal the business needs. Write a problem where each known fraction of coal purchased from suppliers is subtracted from 1.

1 – 1/5 – 2/5

The denominator of both fractions in the problem is 5. Write 1 as a fraction with the common denominator 5 in its numerator and denominator. Then subtract the numerators of the fractions. The denominator is 5.

5/5 – 1/5 – 2/5 = (5 – 1 – 2)/5 = 2/5

The business needs to purchase 2/5 of the coal it needs from other suppliers.

Practice the Skill

Answer the following questions.

1. If it requires 3/4 of a ton of coal to produce 500 pounds of steel and 1/4 of a ton of coal to reheat the steel before it is rolled into bars, how much coal is required to produce 500 pounds of steel bars?
2. If 7/10 of a firm's costs are variable, what fraction of its costs are fixed?
3. If a firm's variable labor costs equal 4/7 of its total cost of production and its fixed costs equal 1/7 of its total cost of production, what fraction of its costs are variable?
4. Why will the fraction of a firm's costs that are fixed costs decline as it produces more output?

5.3 ASSESSMENT

Think Critically

1. Tanya runs a computer repair business in a small room in her basement. Many people wanted her to fix their computers so she hired another worker, who doubled the number of computers she could fix each day. But when she hired a third worker, she found that the total number of computers she could service hardly changed at all. Explain how this demonstrates the law of diminishing returns.
2. Tanya has borrowed more than $10,000 to buy special equipment she needs in order to repair computers. Is the $750 she pays each month to repay her loan a fixed or a variable cost? Explain your answer.

Graphing Exercise

3. Draw a graph of fixed cost, variable cost, and total cost, and then draw a second graph of marginal cost for Tony's Pizza, using the data in the table shown. What other information does Tony need in order to determine how many pizzas he should produce per week? Explain your answer.

WEEKLY COST DATA FOR TONY'S PIZZA

Output	Fixed Cost	Variable Cost	Total Cost	Marginal Cost
0	$500	0	$ 500	—
10	$500	$1, 000	$1, 500	$100
20	$500	$1, 500	$2, 000	$ 50
30	$500	$1, 800	$2, 300	$ 30
40	$500	$2, 100	$2, 600	$ 30
50	$500	$2, 600	$3, 100	$ 50
60	$500	$3, 600	$4, 100	$100

Make Academic Connections

4. **Entrepreneurship** You own a gas station. You have found that the cost of keeping your store open is $35 per hour for labor and electricity. Between midnight and 5:00 a.m., you sell only 100 gallons of gas per hour. Your markup on gas is $0.25 per gallon. Should you keep your business open all night? Explain your answer.

TeamWork

Working in small teams, make two lists of costs that a pizza restaurant might have. One should include its fixed costs and the other, its variable costs. Explain why an increase in wages or in the cost of flour might cause the business to close in the short run. Compare your team's work with that of other teams.

21st Century Skills

PARTNERSHIP FOR 21ST CENTURY SKILLS

PRODUCTIVITY AND ACCOUNTABILITY

Making Decisions for the Long Run

You can think of your experience in school as an investment in your future. The more you learn now, the more you will be able to produce and earn in the future. But education is not free. The following are examples of costs you or your family pay for you to attend school.

- The cost of school supplies such as a graphing calculator or gym shoes
- The cost of transportation to and from school
- The forgone value of alternative uses of your time and effort

Society's Costs for Education

Although students and their families pay significant costs for education, society in general pays even more. Consider the following public costs of education.

- The cost of building, equipping, and supplying schools
- The cost of heating, cooling, cleaning, and maintaining schools
- The cost of hiring teachers, administrators, and other school employees

Short-Run Costs and Long-Run Benefits

When resources are allocated to schools, they result in short-run costs but yield long-run benefits. Imagine, for example, that enrollments in many classes at your school are very large. Your school could spend $1 million to hire 15 new teachers to reduce class size, but how much difference would this make? How could taxpayers know they would receive a reasonable benefit in the future for their expenditure today? One solution that has been tried is to make students and teachers accountable for their work. In recent years many states and the federal government have instituted testing programs to evaluate student progress. Additional resources have been allocated to those schools with higher student achievement as measured by the tests. Although this plan provides more resources to schools with higher scores, does this guarantee that students who attended these schools will be more productive members of society? Or is it possible that schools with students who did not score as well need additional resources even more? Unfortunately, it is difficult to measure the value of future benefits. We can only make choices based on logic and the best information available.

Long-Run Decisions in Your Life

The skills that employers look for today are not likely to be the same skills they will seek 20 years from now. Today's students will be forced to adapt to change throughout their lives. To accomplish this, it makes sense to learn fundamental skills such as reading, writing, mathematics, and communications—skills that can help you adjust to change and be productive in tomorrow's economy.

Apply the Skill

Imagine you are selecting your classes for next year. You have one more class to choose and have narrowed your choice down to two possibilities. One is a class in pre-calculus to prepare you to take other classes in higher mathematics. The other would teach you how to use a new operating system for home and office computers. Decide which class would serve you best over the long run and explain three reasons for your choice.

The Industrial Revolution in England: The Supply of Cotton

The increases in the production of cotton textiles in the late 1700s contributed to the Industrial Revolution. As production became more industrialized, suppliers of raw cotton were faced with heavy demand. In the United States, growing cotton was profitable only along narrow coastal strips of Georgia and the Carolinas. These were the only locations in which Sea Island cotton could be grown. Another strain of cotton, which could be grown in the interior, was unprofitable because it produced too many seeds, which had to be removed by hand. It took a day's work to separate the seeds from the lint, making production too slow and too expensive to satisfy the demands of the industry.

Eli Whitney changed all this in 1793 with his invention of the cotton gin. Whitney's invention allowed one worker to produce what it had previously taken 50 workers, mostly slaves, to produce. Cotton now could be grown where it formerly had been cost prohibitive, enabling the American South to supply Great Britain's growing demand for raw cotton. Within two years, cotton exports from the United States to Great Britain rose from 487,000 pounds to 6,276,300 pounds. Because Great Britain's textile mills were demanding ever-increasing amounts of cotton, Southern planters were willing to move inland and devote more land and resources to producing cotton. The quantity of cotton supplied increased rapidly, keeping pace with the growing British cotton textile industry.

The British government, protective of its textile industry, passed laws preventing anyone with working knowledge of a textile mill from leaving the country. Despite that prohibition, an English textile mechanic, Samuel Slater, was attracted by a prize being offered for information about the English textile industry. He disguised himself as a farm laborer and came to the United States. Slater established a mill at Pawtucket, Rhode Island. Building machinery entirely from memory, he started the American textile industry on December 20, 1790. Still, American mills had a difficult time competing with British imports and could afford only cheaper cotton imported from the West Indies. Southern states sold all of their cotton at a higher price to English mills.

Walter G Arce/Shutterstock.com

Think Critically **What variable cost did the invention of the cotton gin allow Southern cotton producers to lower? How were the growers able to create "economies of scale"? Why do you think the American cotton mills, using essentially the same equipment, had difficulty competing with the British cotton imports?**

Chapter 5 Summary

5.1 The Supply Curve

A. Firms are motivated to supply products out of their desire to earn profit. The supply curve indicates how much of a good producers are willing and able to offer for sale per period at each price, other things constant. The law of supply states that the quantity supplied is greater at a higher price than at a lower price, other things constant.

B. Businesses supply more as the price increases because they can shift resources from other products that now have relatively lower prices. Further, higher prices help producers cope with the higher marginal cost that results from increasing the quantity supplied. Individual supply is the relation between price and the quantity supplied by one firm in a market. Market supply is the relation between price and quantity supplied by all firms in a market.

C. Elasticity of supply is the relationship between a percent change in the price of a product and the resulting percent change in the quantity supplied. Supply may be elastic, unit elastic, or inelastic. As a general rule, the more difficult and costly it is to increase the quantity supplied, the less elastic is supply.

ASK THE EXPERT

www.cengage.com/school/contecon

Why can't we feed the world from a flower pot?

5.2 Shifts of the Supply Curve

A. There are five determinants of supply that can shift the location of a supply curve. They are (1) a change in the cost of resources used to make the good, (2) a change in the price of other goods these resources could make, (3) a change in the technology used to make the good, (4) a change in the producers' expectations, and (5) a change in the number of sellers in the market.

B. A change in the price of a product causes a movement along a supply curve. This is called a change in the quantity supplied. A change in a determinant of supply other than price causes the supply curve to move, or shift, to the left or right. This is called a change in supply.

5.3 Production and Cost

A. The short run is a period during which at least one resource cannot be changed, or is fixed. Variable resources can be changed in the short run. In the long run, all resources are variable.

B. The marginal product of an additional worker is the change in total production that results from employing that worker. As workers are added, a firm experiences first increasing returns and then diminishing returns.

C. Fixed cost does not change with the amount produced. Variable cost is zero when output is zero and increases when output increases.

D. Marginal cost is the change in total cost when the firm produces one more unit of output. Marginal revenue is the change in total revenue when the firm sells one more unit of output. Businesses sell more output as long as the marginal revenue exceeds the marginal cost. In the short run, a firm's supply curve is that portion of its marginal cost curve rising above the minimum acceptable price.

E. In the short run, a firm that is losing money will continue to produce as long as total revenue exceeds variable cost. A firm will shut down in the short run if variable cost exceeds total revenue.

F. In the long run, firms face economies and diseconomies of scale. The long-run average cost curve first slopes downward as the size, or scale, of the firm expands, reflecting economies of scale. At some point the long-run average cost curve may flatten out, reflecting constant returns to scale. As the size of the firm increases, the long-run average cost curve may begin to slope upward, reflecting diseconomies of scale.

CHAPTER 5 ASSESSMENT

Review Economic Terms

Match the terms with the definitions. Some terms will not be used.

a. economies of scale
b. elasticity of supply
c. fixed cost
d. law of diminishing returns
e. law of supply
f. long run
g. long-run average cost curve
h. marginal cost
i. marginal product
j. marginal revenue
k. short run
l. supply
m. supply curve
n. total cost
o. total product
p. variable cost

_____ 1. A period of time during which at least one of a firm's resources is fixed

_____ 2. The change in total revenue from selling another unit of a product

_____ 3. Any cost that does not change with the amount produced in the short run

_____ 4. A period of time during which all of a firm's resources can be varied

_____ 5. The change in total cost resulting from producing one more unit of output

_____ 6. Any production cost that changes as output changes

_____ 7. A measure of the responsiveness of quantity supplied to a change in price

_____ 8. The change in total product that results from a one-unit increase of a resource

_____ 9. As more of a variable resource is added to a given amount of fixed resources, marginal product eventually declines and could become negative

_____ 10. Forces that reduce a firm's average cost of production as the firm's size grows

_____ 11. The total output of a firm

_____ 12. A line showing the quantities of a particular good supplied at various prices during a given time period, other things constant

Review Economic Concepts

13. A shift of a product's supply curve will be caused by each of the following except
    a. an increase in the cost of the resources used to produce the product.
    b. an improvement in the technology used to produce the product.
    c. an increase in consumer demand for the product.
    d. a decrease in the price of other products that resources could be used to produce.

14. **True or False** If a product's elasticity of supply is 0.8, a 2 percent increase in price will cause a greater than 2 percent increase in the quantity supplied.

15. Typically, the longer the period of time allowed for firms to adjust to a price change, the ________?________ a product's supply curve will be.

16. An increase in the price of a firm's product will cause ________?________ the firm's supply curve.

17. Which of the following events would cause the supply curve to shift to the left?
    a. A firm's employees negotiate a 5 percent increase in their wages.
    b. A firm's managers buy new, more efficient machinery for workers to use.
    c. A firm provides its workers with training to better use their tools.
    d. A firm finds a new, less expensive source of raw materials.

18. **True or False** In the long run, all costs of production are variable.

19. An increase in the cost of a product's raw materials will cause the supply curve for that product to ________?________.

20. If a firm experiences diminishing returns, it finds that
    a. there will be no increase in production when it hires another worker.
    b. the next worker hired will add less to production than the previous worker hired.
    c. it will earn no profit if it hires additional workers.
    d. it must lay off workers to earn a profit.

21. Which of the following is an example of a variable cost?
    a. the cost or wages for night security guards
    b. the cost of fire insurance for a firm's factory
    c. the cost of raw materials used to produce goods
    d. the cost of electricity to operate a security alarm.

22. In the short run, ________?________ cost does not change as a firm produces additional output.

23. **True or False** When a firm experiences diminishing returns, its marginal cost of production decreases as output increases.

24. If a 1 percent change in price results in a 2 percent change in the quantity of the product that is supplied, the supply of that product is
    a. elastic.
    b. unit elastic.
    c. inelastic.
    d. none of the above.

25. ________?________ are forces that reduce a firm's average cost of production as the firm grows in size.

26. In the long run, a firm will
    a. experience economies of scale if its long-run average cost curve slopes upward.
    b. experience diseconomies of scale if its long-run average cost curve slopes downward.
    c. experience diseconomies of scale if its long-run average cost curve slopes upward.
    d. experience constant returns to scale if its long-run average cost curve slopes upward.

27. **True or False** According to the law of supply, the quantity supplied will increase as the price of that product increases.

Apply Economic Concepts

28. **Accounting** Classify each of the following costs as variable or fixed. Explain your decision for each cost.
    - The cost of a leased delivery truck
    - The cost of a night security service
    - The cost of delivering finished products
    - The cost of fire insurance
    - The cost of electricity used to run production machinery

29. **Calculating Elasticity of Supply** Complete the table below by calculating each missing elasticity of supply value. Is the supply elastic or inelastic?

SUPPLY ELASTICITY OF BAGELS

Price per Dozen	Percent Change	Quantity Supplied	Percent Change	Elasticity	Elastic/ Inelastic
$8	—	100	—	—	—
$7	12.5%	90	10.0%	_____	_____
$6	14.3%	80	11.1%	_____	_____
$5	16.6%	70	12.5%	_____	_____
$4	20.0%	60	14.3%	_____	_____
$3	25.0%	50	16.6%	_____	_____

30. **21st Century Skills: Productivity and Accountability** Most young people today are able to use a wide variety of electronic devices. In most cases they acquired the necessary skills without completing any formal classes. Write a few paragraphs that describe how you learned to use a specific electronic device. Discuss how you could have learned these skills more easily. Why will learning how to use new electronic devices continue to be important in your future?

Digging Deeper

with Economics e-Collection

Technology used to make goods and services affects production costs and profit opportunities for suppliers of goods. Access the Gale Economics e-Collection through the URL below to find articles that identify trends in production technology. Make a list of three to five new technologies. For each technology, name the industries that will use the technology and the specific products or services it will produce.

www.cengage.com/school/contecon

CHAPTER 6

Market Forces

CONSIDER ...

- How is market competition different from competition in sports?
- Why do car dealers usually locate together on the outskirts of town?
- What's the difference between making stuff right and making the right stuff?
- Why do government efforts to keep rents low usually lead to a housing shortage?
- Why do consumers benefit nearly as much from a low price as from a zero price?
- What have economists learned from psychologists about the limits of rational self-interest?

Point your browser

www.cengage.com/school/contecon

Comstock/Jupiter Images; background image: Lukiyanova Natalia/frenta/Shutterstock.com

6.1 PRICE, QUANTITY, AND MARKET EQUILIBRIUM

Key Terms

market equilibrium 168
surplus 168
shortage 168
transaction costs 172

Learning Objectives

LO1 Understand how markets reach equilibrium.

LO2 Explain how markets reduce transaction costs.

In Your World

You participate in the market economy every time you buy or sell something. Markets allow you to buy or sell for a price. Price is the amount you pay if you buy a good and the amount you receive if you sell it. As a buyer, or demander, you like lower prices. As a seller, or supplier, you like higher prices. How are these differing views about the price sorted out? Market forces resolve the differences.

MARKET EQUILIBRIUM

LO1 Understand how markets reach equilibrium.

When the quantity that consumers are willing and able to buy equals the quantity that producers are willing and able to sell, that market reaches **market equilibrium**. In equilibrium, the independent plans of buyers and sellers exactly match, and there is no incentive for change. Therefore, market forces exert no further pressure to change price or quantity.

A Surplus Forces the Price Down

To understand how a particular market reaches equilibrium, you need to consider demand *and* supply. Figure 6.1 shows the market for pizza, using schedules in panel (a) and curves in panel (b). What if the price initially is $12? At that price, producers supply 24 million pizzas per week, but consumers demand only 14 million, resulting in an *excess quantity supplied*, or a **surplus**, of 10 million pizzas per week. This surplus means that suppliers are stuck with 10 million pizzas they can't sell at $12.

Suppliers' desire to eliminate the surplus puts downward pressure on the price. The arrow pointing down in the graph represents this pressure. As the price falls, producers reduce their quantity supplied and consumers increase their quantity demanded. As long as quantity supplied exceeds quantity demanded, the surplus forces the price lower.

market equilibrium When the quantity consumers are willing and able to buy equals the quantity producers are willing and able to sell

surplus At a given price, the amount by which quantity supplied exceeds quantity demanded; a surplus usually forces the price down

shortage At a given price, the amount by which quantity demanded exceeds quantity supplied; a shortage usually forces the price up

A Shortage Forces the Price Up

What if the initial price of pizza is $6? Figure 6.1 shows that at that price, consumers demand 26 million pizzas per week, but producers supply only 16 million. This results in an *excess quantity demanded*, or a **shortage**, of

FIGURE 6.1 Equilibrium in the Pizza Market

Market equilibrium occurs at the price at which the quantity demanded by consumers is equal to the quantity supplied by producers. This is shown at point *c*. At prices above the equilibrium price, the quantity supplied exceeds the quantity demanded. At these prices there is a surplus, which puts downward pressure on the price. At prices below equilibrium, quantity demanded exceeds quantity supplied. The resulting shortage puts upward pressure on the price.

(A) MARKET SCHEDULES (MILLIONS OF PIZZAS PER WEEK)

Price per Pizza	Quantity Demanded	Quantity Supplied	Surplus or Shortage	Effect on Price
$15	8	28	Surplus of 20	Falls
12	14	24	Surplus of 10	Falls
9	20	20	Equilibrium	Remains the same
6	26	16	Shortage of 10	Rises
3	32	12	Shortage of 20	Rises

(B) MARKET CURVES

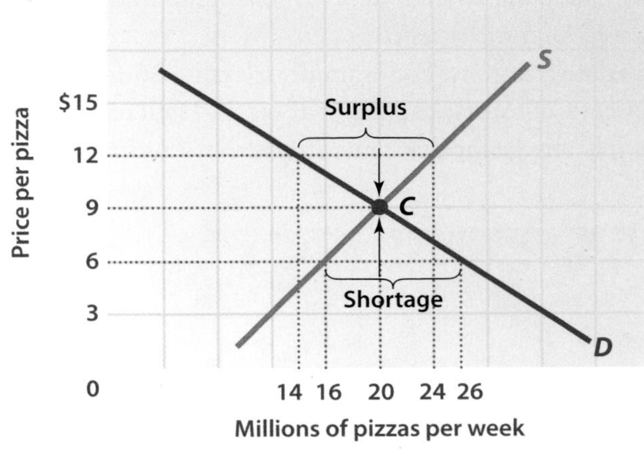

10 million pizzas per week. Consumers compete to buy the product, which is in short supply. Competition among buyers creates market pressure for a higher price. The arrow pointing up in the graph represents this pressure. As the price rises, producers increase their quantity supplied and consumers reduce their quantity demanded. The price continues to rise as long as quantity demanded exceeds quantity supplied.

Investigate Your Local Economy

Go to a local shopping center. Look for evidence of specific goods that seem to be experiencing a surplus and those that seem to be experiencing a shortage. Make a list of at least four examples of each. Share your list of goods in class, and discuss the evidence that led you to choose each one.

Thus, *a surplus puts downward pressure on the price, and a shortage puts upward pressure*. As long as quantity demanded and quantity supplied differ, this difference forces a price change. Note that a shortage or a surplus is always measured at a particular price. There is no such thing as a general shortage or a general surplus.

Market Forces Lead to Equilibrium Price and Quantity

In Figure 6.1, the demand and supply curves intersect at the *equilibrium point*, identified as point *c*. The *equilibrium price*, which equates quantity demanded with quantity supplied, is $9 per pizza. The *equilibrium quantity* is 20 million per week. The demand and supply curves form an "X" at the intersection. The equilibrium point is found where "X" marks the spot. At that price and quantity, the market is said to *clear*. That's why the equilibrium price is also called the *market-clearing price*. Because there is no shortage and no surplus, there is no longer pressure for the price to change. The equilibrium price remains at $9 unless there is some change that shifts the demand or supply curve.

A market finds equilibrium through the independent and voluntary actions of thousands, or even millions, of buyers and sellers. In one sense, the market is personal because each consumer and each producer makes a personal decision about how much to buy or sell at a given price. In another sense, the market is impersonal because it requires no conscious communication or coordination among consumers or producers. The price does all the talking. *The independent decisions of many individual buyers and many individual sellers cause the price to reach equilibrium in competitive markets.*

Prices reflect relative scarcity. For example, to rent a 26-foot truck one-way from San Francisco, California, to Austin, Texas, U-Haul recently charged $3,236. Its one-way charge for that same truck from Austin to San Francisco was

Fuse/Jupiter Images

What does this display tell you about the relative scarcity of the fruit for sale?

just $399. Why the difference? Many more people wanted to move from San Francisco to Austin than vice versa, so U-Haul had to pay its own employees to drive the empty trucks back from Texas. Rental rates reflected that extra cost.

How do markets reach equilibrium? **CHECKPOINT**

MARKET EXCHANGE

LO2
Explain how markets reduce transaction costs.

To repeat, buyers prefer a lower price and sellers prefer a higher price. Thus, buyers and sellers have different views about the price of a particular good. Markets help sort out those differences. Markets answer the questions *what to produce, how to produce it,* and *for whom to produce it.*

Adam Smith's Invisible Hand

Market prices guide resources to their most productive uses and channel goods to those consumers who value them the most. Market prices transmit information about relative scarcity and provide incentives to producers and consumers. Markets also distribute earnings among resource owners.

The coordination that occurs through markets takes place because of what Adam Smith called the "invisible hand" of market competition. No individual or small group coordinates market activities. Rather, it is the voluntary choices of many buyers and sellers responding only to their individual incentives. Although each individual pursues his or her own self-interest, the "invisible hand" of competition promotes the general welfare.

Market Exchange Is Voluntary

Your experience with competition probably comes from sports and games, where one side wins and the other loses. Market exchange is not like that. Market exchange is a voluntary activity in which both sides of the market expect to benefit and usually do. Neither buyers nor sellers would participate in the market unless they expected to become better off. A buyer values the product purchased at least as much as the money paid for it. A seller values the money received at least as much as the product sold.

For example, a consumer pays $9 for a pizza only if he or she expects the marginal benefit of that pizza to be worth at least the best alternative use of that $9. The producer supplies a pizza for $9 only if he or she expects its marginal cost to be no more than $9. Again, voluntary exchange usually makes both sides better off. Voluntary exchange is typically win-win.

Market prices serve as signals to buyers and sellers about the relative scarcity of the good. A higher price encourages consumers to find substitutes for the good

ESSENTIAL QUESTION

Standard CEE 8: Role of Prices

Prices send signals and provide incentives to buyers and sellers. When supply or demand changes, market prices adjust, affecting incentives.

What is the role of prices in a market economy?

or even go without it. A higher price also encourages producers to allocate more resources to the production of this good and fewer resources to the production of other goods.

In short, prices help people recognize market opportunities to make better choices as consumers and as producers. The beneficial effects of market exchange include trade between people or organizations in different parts of the country, and among people and organizations in different countries.

Markets Reduce Transaction Costs

A market sorts out the conflicting views of price between demanders and suppliers. Markets also reduce **transaction costs**, or the costs of time and information needed to carry out market exchange. The higher the transaction cost, the less likely it is that an exchange takes place. For example, the car business needs acres of land so car dealers locate on the outskirts of town, where land is cheaper. Dealers also tend to locate near each other because, grouped together, they become a more attractive destination for car buyers. Any dealer who makes the mistake of locating away from the others will miss out on a lot of business from comparison shoppers. In this way, car dealers reduce the transaction costs of car shopping. This is also why stores locate together downtown and in suburban malls. More generally, *markets reduce transaction costs.*

transaction costs The costs of time and information needed to carry out market exchange

CHECKPOINT How do markets reduce transaction costs?

6.1 ASSESSMENT

Think Critically

1. How would the owner of a dress shop react if she found she had 30 extra prom dresses that she could not sell at the current price?
2. How would the owners of a nursery react if hundreds of customers wanted to buy yucca plants at the current price of $15 when the nursery has 25 plants to sell?
3. How is it possible for both you and the owner of a fast-food restaurant to benefit when you choose to buy a hamburger for $5.00?
4. What are the transaction costs involved in purchasing a pair of shoes at your local mall?
5. What is it reasonable to conclude about the quantity of a product that is demanded and the quantity that is supplied if the price of the product does not change over many months?
6. Explain Adam Smith's "invisible hand" concept.

Graphing Exercise

7. Draw a graph of the demand and supply for running shoes from the data in the demand and supply schedules below. What is the equilibrium price? What would happen to the price and quantity demanded and supplied if the current price was $60?

DEMAND AND SUPPLY OF RUNNING SHOES

Price	Quantity Demanded	Quantity Supplied
$70	40	100
$60	50	80
$50	60	60
$40	70	40
$30	80	20

Make Academic Connections

8. **Science** Scientists have created tomatoes through genetic engineering that are resistant to many diseases. Over time this has caused the equilibrium price of tomatoes to fall. Explain why this has happened.

TeamWork

Working in small teams identify and explain five different ways in which the Internet has helped reduce the transaction costs of buying and selling goods and services in the U.S. economy. Compare your team's work with that of other teams in your class.

AND MOVERS SHAKERS

Leonardo DiCaprio

Hollywood Actor and Environmental Activist

JONATHAN REBBOAH/Maxpp/Landov

Leonardo DiCaprio might be one of Hollywood's biggest stars, but he has never conformed to Hollywood's expectations. Born in 1974 in Los Angeles, California, DiCaprio began his acting career at the age of five on the children's television show *Romper Room*. He is known for his portrayals of unconventional, complex characters. His first big hit was *This Boy's Life* with Robert De Niro. His acting has earned him rave reviews and roles in acclaimed films such as *What's Eating Gilbert Grape, Romeo and Juliet, Titanic, Catch Me If You Can, Blood Diamond, Revolutionary Road, Shutter Island, Inception* and *J. Edgar*.

DiCaprio also has become one of America's hardest-working environmentalists. He interviewed former President Bill Clinton on environmental issues while Clinton was still in the White House. He also made a documentary film, *The 11th Hour*, that highlights the serious problems facing planet Earth, such as global warming, deforestation, mass species extinction, and depletion of the oceans' habitats.

Although DiCaprio has been called a "Learjet liberal" and an "alarmist," he takes the criticism in stride admitting he's not entirely environmentally friendly because he must fly frequently for work. He said, "I try to live a green lifestyle. I've done things that I can do in my house to make my house green: energy-efficient appliances, I drive a hybrid car, I have solar panels—but I don't walk to work." The point, he said, is to make small but powerful changes.

DiCaprio also is a strong advocate of securing a sustainable future for the planet. In 2004 he joined the boards of the Natural Resources Defense Council and Global Green USA. In addition to the award-winning documentary *11th Hour*, he has produced a Discovery Network show called *Eco-Town*, which documents the reconstruction of Greensburg, Kansas, a town that was almost entirely destroyed by a tornado in 2007. He also has launched leonardodicaprio.org, an "eco website."

DiCaprio uses his wealth in other ways to be an advocate for change, including donating $1 million dollars each to the Wildlife Conservation Society and Haitian earthquake relief and donating $35,000 for a Leonardo DiCaprio Computer Center at the Los Feliz branch of the Los Angeles Public Library.

DiCaprio believes that people in the United States need to get the word out to the rest of the world about the dangers to our global environment. He says, "We are the leading consumers, the biggest producers of waste around the world and, unless we're the ones to set an example for less industrialized countries, how is the rest of the world going to follow?" He says people need to become more aware. "This is a cultural and global shift that needs to happen on a massive level. These things should be integrated into everyone's lives. Things should be made more efficient. They should have a concern for the planet and global emissions, and it should be integrated into everything we buy."

Think Critically **What is the significance of celebrities such as Leonardo DiCaprio taking the lead in social issues?**

Sources: 11thhour.com; http://luxuryholistics.com/2011/03/leonardo-dicaprio-environmental-activist/; http://dicapriocom.free.fr/news/post/22-leonardo-dicaprio-why-i-m-now-a-green-campaigner; http://www.buzzinefilm.com/interviews/film-leonardo-dicaprio-interview-12252008

6.2 SHIFTS OF DEMAND AND SUPPLY CURVES

Learning Objectives

LO1 Explain how a shift of the demand curve affects equilibrium price and quantity.

LO2 Explain how a shift of the supply curve affects equilibrium price and quantity.

Key Terms

In Your World

You should be interested in equilibrium price because that's usually what you pay for the thousands of goods and services you consume. An equilibrium lasts until something shakes up the market in question. This lesson examines what sorts of things will shake up the market. In other words, it examines what will shift the demand curve or the supply curve and, in the process, change the equilibrium price and quantity.

SHIFTS OF THE DEMAND CURVE

LO1 Explain how a shift of the demand curve affects equilibrium price and quantity.

In Figure 6.2, demand curve *D* and supply curve *S* intersect at the equilibrium price of $9 and the equilibrium quantity of 20 million 12-inch pizzas per week. What happens to equilibrium price and quantity if the demand curve shifts? A shift of the demand curve means that quantity demanded changes at each price.

What Could Shift the Demand Curve?

If one of the factors that determine the demand for pizza changes in a way that increases demand, this would shift the demand curve to the right from *D* to *D'*. Any of the following could shift the demand for pizza rightward:

1. An increase in the money income of consumers (because pizza is a normal good)
2. An increase in the price of a substitute, such as tacos, or a decrease in the price of a complement, such as beverages
3. A change in expectations that encourages consumers to buy more pizza
4. An increase in the number of pizza consumers
5. A change in consumer tastes in favor of pizza

An Increase in Demand

Any one of those five changes could increase the demand for pizza. An **increase in demand** means that consumers are now willing and able to buy more of the product at every price. Note that none of these changes shifts the supply curve.

After the demand curve shifts rightward to *D′* in Figure 6.2, the amount demanded at the initial price of $9 increases from 20 million to 30 million pizzas. Because producers supply only 20 million pizzas at that price, there is a shortage of 10 million pizzas. Millions of consumers are frustrated because they can't find pizza for $9. Producers realize that they can charge more than $9 for pizza. The shortage puts upward pressure on the price.

increase in demand
Consumers are willing and able to buy more of the product at each price

As price increases, quantity demanded decreases along the new demand curve, *D′*, and quantity supplied increases along the supply curve, *S*, until the two quantities are once again equal. The new equilibrium price is $12, and the new equilibrium quantity is 24 million pizzas per week. *As long as the supply curve slopes upward, a rightward shift of the demand curve increases both price and quantity.*

FIGURE 6.2 Effects of an Increase in Demand

Prices send signals and provide incentives to buyers and sellers. When demand changes, market prices adjust, affecting buyers' incentives. After an increase in demand shifts the demand curve from *D* to *D′*, quantity demanded exceeds quantity supplied at the initial price of $9 per pizza. As the price rises, quantity supplied increases along supply curve *S*, and quantity demanded decreases along demand curve *D′*. When the new equilibrium price of $12 is reached, the quantity demanded once again equals the quantity supplied. Both price and quantity are higher following the increase in demand.

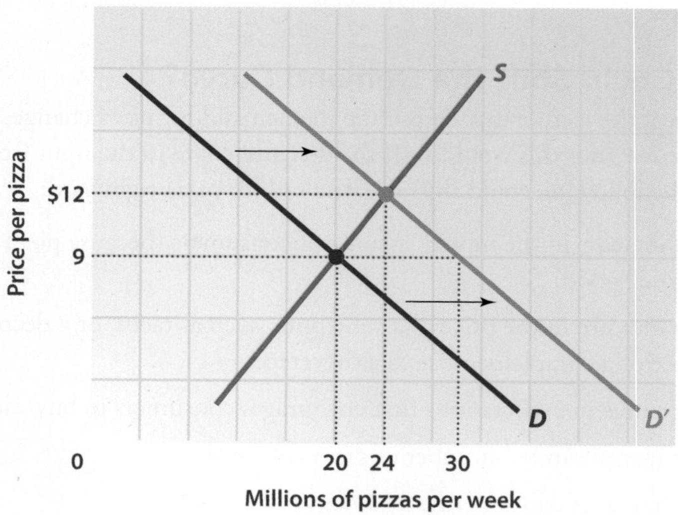

A Decrease in Demand

What if one of the determinants of demand changed in a way that reduced demand—such as a decrease in consumer income, a decrease in the price of a substitute, or a reduction in the number of consumers? This would result in a **decrease in demand**, and consumers are now willing and able to buy less of the product at every price.

The effect of a decrease in demand is shown in Figure 6.3. The demand curve for pizza shifts leftward from *D* to *D″*. The amount demanded at the initial price of $9 declines from 20 million to 10 million pizzas. Because producers supply 20 million at that price, there is a surplus of 10 million pizzas. To eliminate the surplus, the price must fall. Thus, this surplus puts downward pressure on the price.

As the price falls, quantity demanded increases along the new demand curve *D″* and quantity supplied decreases along the supply curve *S* until the two quantities are equal once again. The new equilibrium price drops to $6, and the new equilibrium quantity is 16 million pizzas per week. *As long as the supply curve slopes upward, a leftward shift of the demand curve reduces both price and quantity.*

decrease in demand
Consumers are willing and able to buy less of the product at each price

FIGURE 6.3 Effects of a Decrease in Demand

After a decrease in demand shifts the demand curve from *D* to *D″*, quantity supplied exceeds quantity demanded at the initial price of $9 per pizza. As the price falls, quantity supplied decreases along supply curve *S*, and quantity demanded increases along demand curve *D″*. When the new equilibrium price of $6 is reached, the quantity demanded once again equals the quantity supplied. Both price and quantity are lower following the decrease in demand.

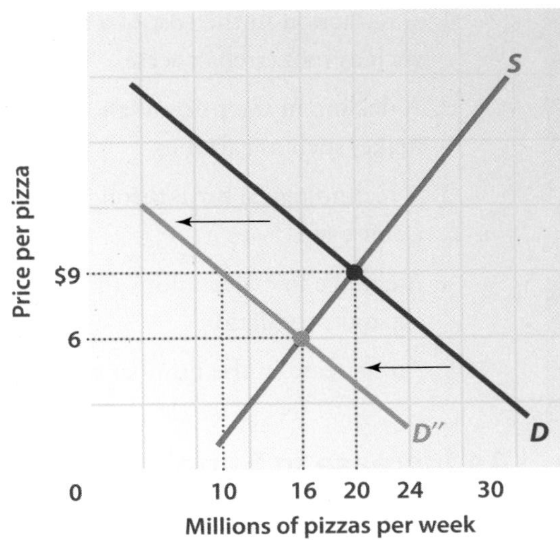

Summary of Demand Shifts

Given an upward-sloping supply curve, a rightward shift of the demand curve increases both price and quantity and a leftward shift of the demand curve decreases both price and quantity. One way to remember this is to picture the demand curve shifting along an upward-sloping supply curve. If the demand curve shifts rightward, price and quantity increase. If the demand curve shifts leftward, price and quantity decrease.

CHECKPOINT **How does a shift of the demand curve affect equilibrium price and quantity?**

SHIFTS OF THE SUPPLY CURVE

LO2 Explain how a shift of the supply curve affects equilibrium price and quantity.

In Figure 6.4, demand curve *D* and supply curve *S* intersect to yield the initial equilibrium price of $9 and the initial equilibrium quantity of 20 million 12-inch pizzas per week. What happens to equilibrium price and quantity if the supply curve shifts? A shift of the supply curve means that quantity supplied changes at each price.

increase in supply
Producers are willing and able to sell more of the product at each price

What Could Shift the Supply Curve?

If one of the factors that determine supply changes in a way that increases supply, this would shift the supply curve to the right from *S* to *S′* in Figure 6.4. Any of the following could shift the pizza supply curve rightward:

1. A reduction in the cost of a resource used to make pizza, such as mozzarella cheese
2. A decline in the price of another good these resources could make, such as calzones
3. A technological breakthrough in pizza production, such as a faster oven
4. A change in expectations that encourages pizza makers to expand production
5. An increase in the number of pizzerias

Photodisc/Getty Images

What would happen to the supply curve for pizza in your area if many of the pizza restaurants bought cheaper, faster pizza ovens?

An Increase in Supply

Any of the above changes shifts the supply curve, but none shifts the demand curve. An **increase in supply** means that producers are willing and able to supply more pizza at each price. After the supply curve shifts rightward to *S′* in Figure 6.4, the amount supplied at the initial price of $9 increases from 20 million to

FIGURE 6.4 **Effects of an Increase in Supply**

An increase in supply is depicted as a rightward shift of the supply curve, from *S* to *S′*. At the new equilibrium point, quantity is greater and price is lower than before the increase in supply.

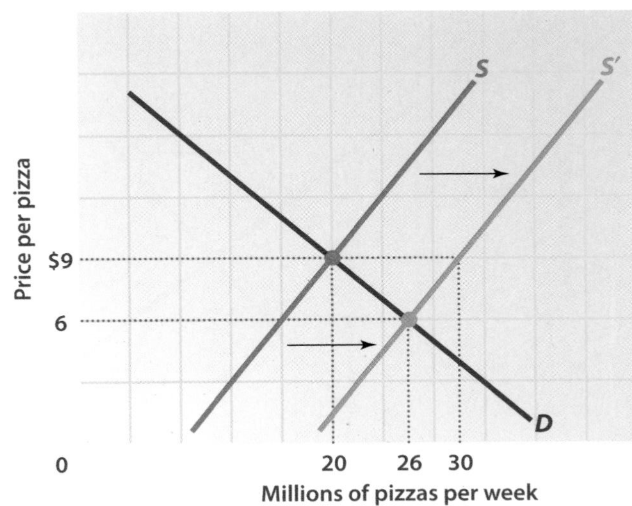

30 million. Producers supply 10 million more pizzas than consumers demand. The buildup of unsold pizzas frustrates producers stuck with pizzas they can't sell for $9 each. This surplus forces the price down.

As the price falls, quantity supplied declines along the new supply curve and quantity demanded increases along the demand curve until a new equilibrium point is reached. The new equilibrium price is $6, and the new equilibrium quantity is 26 million pizzas per week. *As long as the demand curve slopes downward, a rightward shift of the supply curve reduces price but increases quantity.*

A Decrease in Supply

What if one of the determinants of supply changed in a way that reduced supply? For instance, what if there were an increase in the cost of a resource used to make pizza, an increase in the price of another good these resources could make, or a decrease in the number of pizzerias?

A **decrease in supply** means that producers are willing and able to supply less pizza at each price. After the supply curve shifts leftward to *S″* in Figure 6.5,

decrease in supply Producers are willing and able to sell less of the product at each price

FIGURE 6.5 Effects of a Decrease in Supply

A decrease in supply is depicted as a leftward shift of the supply curve, from *S* to *S''*. At the new equilibrium point, quantity is lower and price is higher than before the decrease in supply.

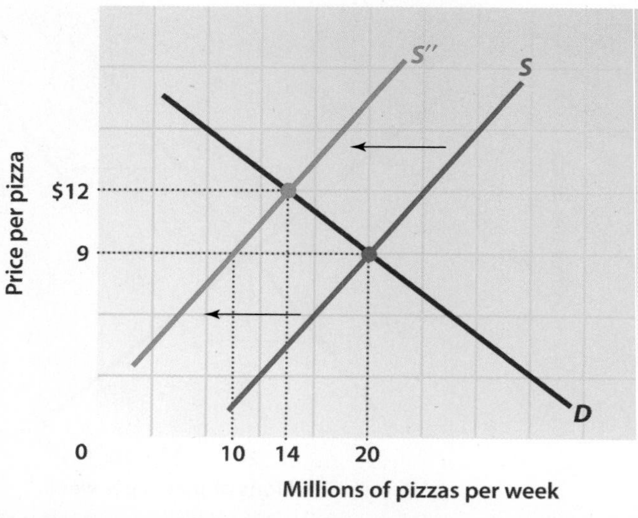

the amount supplied at the initial price of $9 decreases from 20 million to 10 million. Producers supply 10 million fewer pizzas than consumers demand. This shortage forces the price up.

As the price rises quantity supplied increases along the new supply curve and quantity demanded decreases along the demand curve until a new equilibrium point is reached. The new equilibrium price is $12, and the new equilibrium quantity is 14 million pizzas per week. *As long as the demand curve slopes downward, a leftward shift of the supply curve increases price but reduces quantity.*

Summary of Supply Shifts

Thus, *given a downward-sloping demand curve, a rightward shift of the supply curve decreases price but increases quantity, and a leftward shift of the supply curve increases price but decreases quantity.* Picture the supply curve shifting along a downward-sloping demand curve. If the supply curve shifts rightward, price decreases but quantity increases. If supply shifts leftward, price increases but quantity decreases.

How does a shift of the supply curve affect equilibrium price and quantity?

Math in Economics

Common Core Expressions and Equations

You can read values from line graphs by following perpendicular lines from points on the graph to corresponding values on their vertical and horizontal axes. These values may be subtracted from each other to calculate change.

EXAMPLE If the price of a gallon of gasoline is $3.75, how many gallons per week will be demanded and supplied using demand curve D_1, and supply curve S_1?

SOLUTION Follow the dashed line from $3.75 on the *y* axis to the intersection of D_1 and S_1. Then follow the dashed line down to the *x* axis.

At $3.75 per gallon, the quantity demanded and supplied is about 2,750 gallons.

WEEKLY DEMAND AND SUPPLY OF GASOLINE

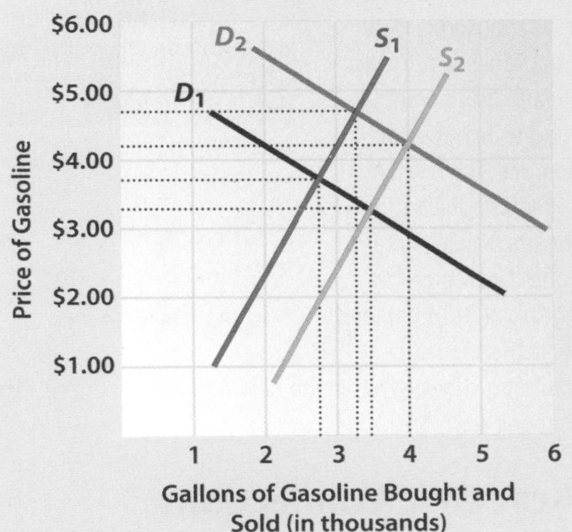

Practice the Skill Answer the following questions.

1. Start with supply curve S_1. If many people trade their fuel-efficient cars for large SUVs and the demand curve shifts from D_1 to D_2, what will happen to the quantity of gasoline demanded and supplied? What will be the market price of gasoline?
2. If OPEC increases its supply of oil, causing the supply curve to shift from S_1 to S_2 while the demand curve remains at D_2, what will be the market price of gasoline? What will happen to the quantity demanded and supplied?
3. If the economy declines and people don't drive as much, causing the demand curve to shift from D_2 back to D_1 while the supply curve remains at S_2, what will happen to the price of gasoline? What will happen to the quantity demanded and supplied?

6.2 ASSESSMENT

Think Critically

1. What would happen to the demand curve for movie tickets if the cost of making movies increased sharply?
2. What would happen to the demand curve for movie tickets if the price of DVD movie rentals increased by $4.00 each?
3. What would happen to the equilibrium price and the supply curve for loaves of bread if the bakery agreed to give its workers a 10 percent raise in pay?

Graphing Exercise

4. Suppose that running becomes much more popular. As a result, consumers are willing and able to purchase 30 thousand more pairs of running shoes at each possible price. The demand and supply schedules to the right show this increase in demand. Draw a graph showing this shift of demand and the unchanged supply for running shoes. What is the new equilibrium price? Explain why the equilibrium price changed from $50.

DEMAND AND SUPPLY SCHEDULES FOR RUNNING SHOES (THOUSANDS OF PAIRS PER MONTH)

Price	Quantity Demanded		Quantity Supplied
	Old	New	
$70	40	70	100
$60	50	80	80
$50	60	90	60
$40	70	100	40
$30	80	110	20

Make Academic Connections

5. **Advertising** Find an advertisement for a well-known brand of candy. Explain what the firm is trying to do to the location of the demand curve for its product. If the firm is successful, what will probably happen to its total revenue?
6. **History** During 1974, there was a war in the Middle East that caused many petroleum-exporting nations to stop shipping oil to the United States. Explain what this did to the location of the supply curve and price of gasoline in the United States.

TeamWork

Working in small teams, identify five products that have experienced either an increase or decrease in supply over the past year. Explain what event(s) caused the shift in supply for each of the products and which of the five determinants of supply the shift demonstrates. Discuss your team's work with other teams in class.

21st Century Skills

Flexibility and Adaptability

Making the Right Stuff

The products consumers demand now are not likely to be the same products they will demand in the future. Consider the Apple iPad as an example. This product first became available in April of 2010 at a base price of $499. Apple sold more than 80 million iPads in 2010. Less than one year later, production of the original iPad was halted and replaced with the iPad 2, which had greater capabilities for the same base price. By 2011 the original model was selling for as little as $99.

Keeping Up With Change

Businesses can make a profit only if they can sell goods and services for more than their cost of production. To achieve this, they need to control their costs and produce what consumers are willing to buy at prices they are willing to pay.

To keep up with the times, companies must be aware of changes in their market and be flexible enough to adapt to the changes as they occur. Consider the following strategies businesses use to keep up with their competition.

- Employ specialists who are assigned to monitor developments in their markets and actions of their competitors.
- Limit the number of products kept in inventory to no more than what is required for current sales.
- Survey customers on a regular basis to determine whether they are satisfied with the firm's products and expect to continue purchasing them in the future.
- Monitor new products offered by other firms to determine whether they offer opportunities to market similar or complementary goods or services.

Consumers Need to Be Flexible, Too

Consumers who don't anticipate changes in the market are likely to purchase goods or services that are out-of-date or will soon be available at lower prices. Again, think of the Apple iPad. It was first offered at $499. One month later its price was lowered to $299. How would you have felt if you had paid the higher price? Would you have been willing to wait if you had known the price would fall? What would you have done if you owned an original iPad when the iPad 2 was introduced? Would you have replaced your old model with the new, or would you have decided to wait for a yet newer model?

When you consider buying a new product, you should weigh the marginal benefits and marginal costs of your decision. This requires you to investigate alternatives that are or soon will be available. In this way you can increase the probability that you will make a rational decision.

Apply the Skill

Imagine you are considering the purchase of a new car. A model recently has come to market that is 100 percent electric-powered. It has a range of 200 miles per charge and gets the equivalent of 85 miles per gallon. The car costs 50 percent more than a similar gas-powered automobile. List and explain four specific questions you should answer before deciding to buy this product.

6.3 MARKET EFFICIENCY AND THE GAINS FROM EXCHANGE

Key Terms

productive efficiency 184
allocative efficiency 185
disequilibrium 185
price floor 186
price ceiling 187
consumer surplus 189

Learning Objectives

LO1 Distinguish between productive efficiency and allocative efficiency.

LO2 Explain what happens when government imposes price floors and price ceilings.

LO3 Identify the benefits that consumers get from market exchange.

In Your World

As you have learned, demand and supply are the foundations of a market economy. Although a market usually involves the interaction of many buyers and sellers, few markets are consciously designed. Just as the law of gravity works whether or not you understand Newton's principles, market forces operate whether or not buyers and sellers understand the laws of demand and supply. Market forces arise naturally without central coordination, much the way car dealers gather together on the city's outskirts, or the way fruits and vegetables from all over the world find their way to the produce section of your local grocer.

COMPETITION AND EFFICIENCY

LO1 Distinguish between productive efficiency and allocative efficiency.

How do competitive markets stack up in terms of efficiency? To judge market performance, economists employ two measures of efficiency. The first, called *productive efficiency*, refers to producing output at the lowest possible cost. The second, called *allocative efficiency*, refers to producing the goods that consumers value the most. Market competition promotes both productive efficiency and allocative efficiency.

Productive Efficiency: Making Stuff Right

Productive efficiency occurs when a firm produces at the lowest possible cost per unit. The firms that survive and thrive in a competitive market are those that supply the product at the lowest cost. *Competition ensures that firms produce at the lowest possible cost per unit.* Firms that are not efficient must either shape up or leave the market.

productive efficiency Occurs when a firm produces at the lowest possible cost per unit

Allocative Efficiency: Making the Right Stuff

Producing at the lowest possible cost per unit is no guarantee that firms are producing what consumers most prefer. This situation is like the airline pilot who announces to passengers that there's some good news and some bad news: "The good news is that we're making record time. The bad news is that we're lost!" Likewise, firms may be producing goods efficiently but producing the wrong goods—that is, making stuff right but making the wrong stuff.

Allocative efficiency occurs when firms produce the output that is most valued by consumers. How do economists know that market competition guarantees allocative efficiency? The answer lies with the market demand and supply curves. The demand curve reflects the marginal benefit that consumers attach to each unit of the good, so the market price is the amount of money people are willing and able to pay for the final unit they purchase.

Supri Suharjoto/Shutterstock.com

Competition in the music industry encourages companies to supply the types of music that consumers want to hear. What type of efficiency does this statement suggest?

In like fashion, equilibrium price equals the marginal cost of supplying the final unit sold. Marginal cost measures the opportunity cost of resources employed by the firm to produce that final unit sold. Thus the supply curve reflects the opportunity cost of producing the good.

The supply and demand curves intersect at the combination of price and quantity at which *the marginal benefit that consumers attach to the final unit purchased just equals the marginal cost of the resources employed to produce that unit.*

As long as marginal benefit equals marginal cost, that last unit purchased is worth as much as, or more than, any other good that could have been produced using those same resources. There is no way to reallocate resources to increase the total value of output to society. Thus, there is no way to reallocate resources to increase the total benefit consumers reap from production.

When the marginal benefit that consumers derive from a good equals the marginal cost of producing that good, that market is said to be allocatively efficient. Competition among sellers encourages producers to supply more of what consumers value the most. Firms not only are making stuff right, they are also making the right stuff.

CHECKPOINT

Distinguish between productive efficiency and allocative efficiency.

DISEQUILIBRIUM

LO2
Explain what happens when government imposes price floors and price ceilings.

One way to understand markets is to examine instances when they are slow to adjust or where they are not free to work. A surplus of goods exerts downward pressure on price, and a shortage of goods exerts upward pressure. But markets don't always reach equilibrium quickly. During the time required to adjust, the market is said to be in disequilibrium. **Disequilibrium** is usually a temporary condition when the plans of buyers do not match the plans of sellers. Sometimes, usually as a result of government intervention in markets, disequilibrium can last a while, even years.

allocative efficiency Occurs when a firm produces the output most valued by consumers

disequilibrium A mismatch between quantity demanded and quantity supplied as the market seeks equilibrium; usually temporary, except when government intervenes to set the price

Span the Globe

Mongolian Goats and the Price of Cashmere Sweaters

Do you think there is a connection between the price tag on a four-ply cashmere sweater and a herd of Mongolian goats? You bet there is. A decade ago there were fewer goats, and a cashmere sweater could cost as much as $500. Today you can purchase a cashmere sweater at Walmart for as little as $19.95. So why has the price of this product, which is difficult to produce, dropped so drastically?

Cashmere comes from the hair of Kashmir goats, the majority of which are raised in Mongolia and northern China. It takes two or three goats to produce enough usable cashmere fiber to make a sweater. The fiber must go through a labor-intensive process of cleaning and de-hairing. As a result of inexpensive Chinese cashmere flooding the market, the price has dropped, making what was formerly a luxury item one for the masses. China's dominance of the cashmere market has forced the Mongolian sellers to accept far less than what they could demand in a more diverse market. This, in turn, depresses the income of the herders. Unfortunately for the Mongolian people, a product that once commanded a price of $27.50 a pound is down to half that figure.

To try and make up for the loss, the herders have increased the number of goats from 10 million in 2002 to nearly 20 million in 2010. The Mongolian government has set up a marketing agency to help producers compete on quality and brand, not price.

Think Critically **Why might a Mongolian herder believe that increasing his goat herd will make up for lower prices? Is he correct? How can the Mongolian government's approach affect both supply and demand?**

Sources: Wachter, Sarah J., "Pastoralism Unraveling in Mongolia," *The New York Times*, December 8, 2009; Gibbs, Susan, "The True Cost of Cheap Cashmere," *Huffington Post*, April 12, 2010

Price Floor

At times public officials set the price above its equilibrium level. For example, the federal government often regulates the prices of agricultural products in an attempt to ensure farmers a higher and more stable income than they would earn otherwise. To achieve higher prices, the federal government establishes a price floor for a product, such as a gallon of milk, making it illegal to sell below the floor price. A **price floor** is a *minimum* legal price. To have an impact, the price floor must be set above the equilibrium price. Price floors distort markets and reduce economic welfare.

price floor A minimum legal price below which a product cannot be sold

FIGURE 6.6 **Effects of a Price Floor and a Price Ceiling**

If a price floor is established above the equilibrium price as in panel (A), a permanent surplus results. A price floor established at or below the equilibrium price has no effect. If a price ceiling is established below the equilibrium price as in panel (B), a permanent shortage results. A price ceiling established at or above the equilibrium price has no effect.

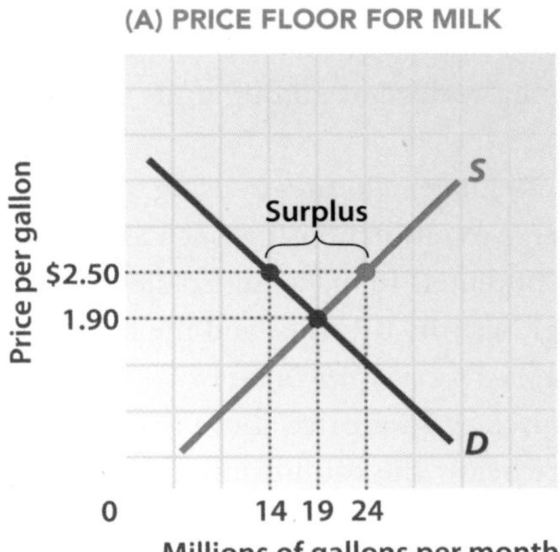

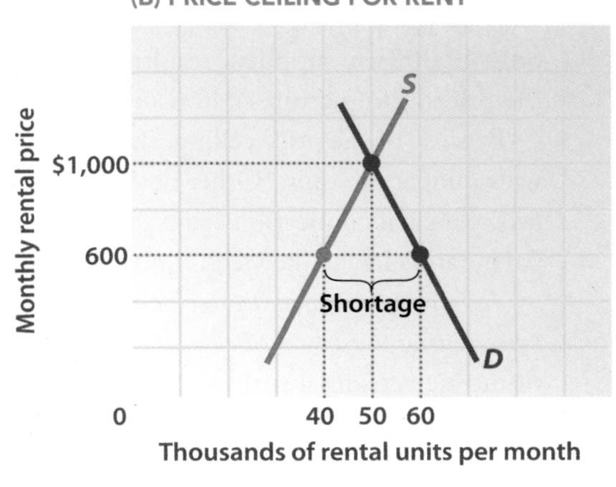

Panel (A) of Figure 6.6 shows the effect of a $2.50 per gallon price floor for milk. At that price, farmers supply 24 million gallons per week, but consumers demand only 14 million gallons. Thus, the price floor results in a surplus of 10 million gallons. This surplus milk will accumulate on store shelves and eventually sour. So, as part of the price-support program, the government usually agrees to buy up the surplus milk to take it off the market. The federal government, in fact, has spent billions buying and storing surplus agricultural products.

NET Bookmark

The *minimum wage* is a price floor in the market for labor. The government sets a minimum price per hour of labor in certain markets, and no employer is permitted to pay a wage lower than that. Access the Department of Labor website through the website shown below to learn more about the mechanics of the program. Then use a supply and demand graph to illustrate the effect of a minimum wage above equilibrium on a particular labor market. What happens to quantity demanded and quantity supplied as a result?

www.cengage.com/school/contecon

Price Ceiling

price ceiling A maximum legal selling price above which a product cannot be sold

Sometimes public officials try to keep a price below the equilibrium level by establishing a **price ceiling**, or a *maximum* legal price. For example, concern about the rising cost of rental housing in some U.S. cities prompted local officials to impose rent ceilings, making it illegal to charge more than the ceiling price. Panel (B) of Figure 6.6 represents the demand and supply for rental housing. The vertical axis shows the monthly rent, and the horizontal axis shows the quantity of rental units. The equilibrium, or market-clearing, rent is $1,000 per month. The equilibrium quantity is 50,000 housing units.

Suppose city officials are concerned that rents of $1,000 per month are not affordable to enough households. They pass a law setting a maximum legal rent of $600 per month. At that ceiling price, 60,000 rental units are demanded, but only 40,000 are supplied, resulting in a housing shortage of 20,000 units. Thus, the price ceiling creates a housing shortage.

Because of the price ceiling, the rental price no longer allocates housing to those who value it the most. Other devices must emerge to ration housing, such as waiting lists, personal connections, and the willingness of renters to make under-the-table payments, such as "key fees," "finder's fees," high security deposits, and the like.

To have an impact, a price floor must be set above the equilibrium price, and a price ceiling must be set below the equilibrium price. A floor price above the equilibrium price creates a surplus, and a ceiling price below the equilibrium price creates a shortage. Various nonprice devices must emerge to cope with the disequilibrium resulting from the market interference.

Price controls distort market prices and interfere with the market's ability to allocate resources efficiently. Prices no longer provide consumers and producers accurate information about the relative scarcity of goods. The good intentions of government officials create shortages and surpluses that often are economically wasteful.

Other Sources of Disequilibrium

Government intervention in the market is not the only source of disequilibrium. Sometimes, when new products are introduced or when demand or supply changes suddenly, the market takes a while to adjust. For example, popular toys, bestselling books, the latest smartphone, and chart-busting CDs often sell out and are temporarily unavailable while suppliers produce more. In these cases, there are temporary shortages.

On the other hand, some new products attract few buyers and pile up unsold on store shelves. In these cases, there are temporary surpluses, awaiting a "clearance sale."

What happens when governments impose price floors and price ceilings?

CONSUMER SURPLUS

LO2
Identify the benefits that consumers get from market exchange.

In equilibrium, the marginal benefit of pizza just equals its marginal cost. The cost to the economy of bringing that final pizza onto the market just equals the marginal benefit that consumers get from that pizza. Does this mean that consumers get no net benefit from the good? No. Market exchange usually benefits both consumers and producers.

Market Demand and Consumer Surplus

A demand curve shows the marginal benefit consumers attach to each unit of the good. For example, based on the demand curve for pizza presented earlier, consumers demand 8 million pizzas at a price of $15. Apparently, those consumers believe the marginal benefit of a pizza is worth at least $15. Consumers demand 14 million at a price of $12. At a price of $9, consumers demand 20 million, even though some are willing to pay $15 each for 8 million pizzas and $12 each for 14 million pizzas.

If the price is $9 per pizza, consumers enjoy a surplus, or a bonus, because they get to buy all 20 million pizzas for $9 each, even though some are willing to pay more for lesser amounts. **Consumer surplus** is the difference between the most that consumers would be willing and able to pay for a given quantity and the amount they actually do pay.

To get a clearer idea of consumer surplus, refer to the demand curve in Figure 6.7. If the price is $2 per unit, each person adjusts his or her quantity demanded until the marginal benefit of the final unit he or she purchases equals at least $2. Each consumer gets to buy all other units for $2 each as well. The dark-shaded area bounded above by the demand curve and below by the price of $2 depicts the consumer surplus if the price is $2.

The lighter-shaded area shows the increase in consumer surplus if the price drops to $1. If this good were free, the consumer surplus would be the entire area under the demand curve. Notice that at a price of zero, the consumer surplus is not that much greater than when the price is $1. Competitive markets maximize the amount of consumer surplus in the economy.

consumer surplus The difference between the most that consumers are willing and able to pay for a given quantity of a good and what they actually pay

FIGURE 6.7 Market Demand and Consumer Surplus

Consumer surplus at a price of $2 is shown by the darker green area. If the price falls to $1, consumer surplus increases to include the lighter green area between $1 and $2. If the good is free, consumer surplus would increase by the lightest green area under the demand curve.

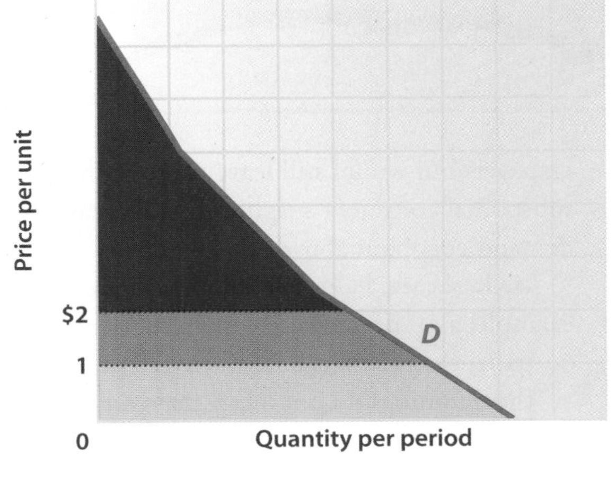

An Application of Consumer Surplus: Free Medical Care

Certain Americans, such as the elderly and those receiving public assistance, are provided government-subsidized health care. As shown in Figure 6.8, taxpayers spent more than $750 billion in 2011 providing health care to 94 million Medicare and Medicaid recipients, for an average annual cost of more than $8,000 per beneficiary. Medicaid is the largest and fastest-growing spending category in most state budgets. The dollar cost to most beneficiaries is usually little or nothing. The problem with giving something away is that beneficiaries consume it to the point where their marginal benefit from the final unit is zero. However, the marginal cost to taxpayers can be substantial.

FIGURE 6.8 Medicaid/Medicare Average Annual Cost per Beneficiary

Why would the average annual cost of Medicaid or Medicare decrease if beneficiaries were required to pay a small amount for each service they receive?

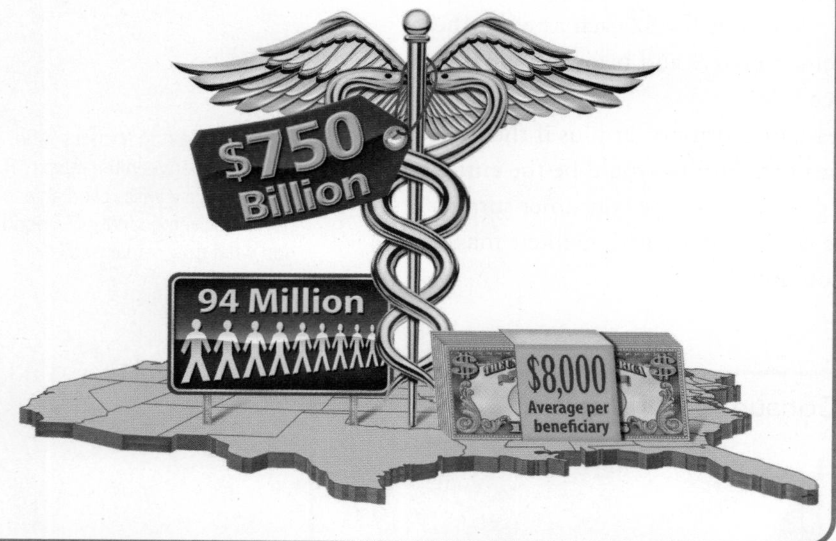

This is not to say that beneficiaries derive no benefit from free health care. Although they may not value the final unit consumed all that much, most derive a large consumer surplus from the other units they consume. For example, suppose that Figure 6.7 represents the demand for health care by Medicaid beneficiaries. Because the dollar price to them is zero, they consume medical care up to the point where the demand curve intersects the horizontal axis. Their consumer surplus is the entire area under the demand curve.

The cost to taxpayers of providing that final unit of health care may be $100 or more. One way to reduce the cost to taxpayers of such programs without really harming beneficiaries is to charge a small price—say, $1 per physician visit. Beneficiaries would eliminate visits they value less than $1. This would yield significant savings to taxpayers but would still leave those in the program with good health care and a substantial consumer surplus. This is measured in Figure 6.7 as the area under the demand curve but above the $1 price.

Medical care, like other goods and services, is also sensitive to a time price. For example, a 10 percent increase in the average travel time required to visit a free outpatient clinic reduced visits by 10 percent.

These findings do not mean that certain groups shouldn't receive low-cost health care. The point is that when something is provided for free, people consume it until their marginal benefit is zero—that is, until their marginal cost equals their marginal benefit. Even a modest money cost or time cost would reduce program costs yet still leave beneficiaries with a substantial consumer surplus.

How do consumers benefit from market exchange? CHECKPOINT

6.3 ASSESSMENT

Think Critically

1. How does market competition ensure that consumers will be offered a selection of low-priced foods?
2. How does market competition ensure that a firm is making the products that consumers value the most?
3. If the minimum wage were increased to $20 per hour, how many of your classmates do you think would look for a job? How many jobs do you expect they would find? How is this an example of a price floor?
4. If the government set a price ceiling of $5 per month to subscribe to an Internet Service Provider (ISP), what would happen to the number of ISPs that offer Internet access and the number of people who wished to purchase their service?
5. Suppose you buy a salad for lunch every day for $2.75. This is the most you would be willing to pay for that salad. One week there is a special on salads and the price is reduced to $2.00. What is the value of the consumer surplus you will receive if you buy five salads during that week?

DEMAND AND SUPPLY SCHEDULES FOR RUNNING SHOES (THOUSANDS OF PAIRS PER MONTH)

Price	Quantity Demanded	Quantity Supplied
$70	40	100
$60	50	80
$50	60	60
$40*	70	40
$30	80	20

(* government price ceiling)

Graphing Exercises

6. Suppose the government became concerned about the high price of running shoes and imposed a price ceiling of $40 per pair. Given the demand and supply schedules shown here, what would the results of such a regulation be? Why would many consumers and producers be upset with this result? Draw a graph that demonstrates the result of such a regulation.

Make Academic Connections

7. **History** In the early 1900s, many businesses produced horse-drawn wagons at very low cost. Still, many of these firms were forced out of business due to a lack of consumer demand. Many people chose to purchase automobiles instead of wagons. Explain how this fact demonstrates the importance of allocative efficiency.

TeamWork

In small teams, discuss the pros and cons of "clearance sales" with regard to consumers and suppliers. Who wins? Who loses? What impact do you think these sales have on the prices of other goods the store sells? Compare your team's answers with those of other teams.

6.4 BEHAVIORAL ECONOMICS

Key Terms

behavioral economics 192
bounded rationality 193
limited willpower 194
neuroeconomics 195

Learning Objectives

LO1 Understand the limits of rational self-interest.

LO2 Explain the effects of bounded rationality on making economic decisions.

LO3 Understand the effects of limited willpower on making economic decisions.

LO4 Explain why some economists are mapping brain activity in the laboratory.

In Your World

Economists generally assume that you and other economic decision makers act rationally to maximize your overall well-being. You know what you want, you respond to incentives, and you follow through with those choices. In short, *the standard economic approach assumes that you and others pursue your rational self-interest.* According to Adam Smith, the pursuit of self-interest in competitive markets promotes the general good. In the extreme, this standard approach views the economy as populated by calculating, unemotional maximizers who make choices consistent with rational self-interest and then follow through on those choices. This standard approach has limitations, however.

PEOPLE AREN'T ROBOTS

LO1 Understand the limits of rational self-interest.

Viewing people as robot-like maximizers is a simplifying assumption that can be defended on the grounds that this approach is easy to spell out in a theoretical model and is supported by many empirical studies. On the other hand, psychologists have come to believe that people are not as good at making decisions as economists assume. Psychologists have found that people are prone to mistakes, are fickle and inconsistent, and often do not get the best deal for themselves when making choices. Psychologists have investigated the biases, faulty assumptions, and errors that affect how people make decisions in all aspects of life.

In recent decades, some economists have begun to draw on findings from psychology to reconsider instances where people do not act according to standard economic theory. The convergence of economics and psychology eventually created a new field of study called *behavioral economics*, a field pursued by a small but growing band of economists. **Behavioral economics** borrows insights from psychology to better explain some economic decisions. This approach questions some assumptions of traditional economics, particularly the assumptions of unbounded rationality and unlimited willpower.

behavioral economics An approach that borrows insights from psychology to help explain economic choices

What problem with standard economics does behavioral economics try to address?

CHECKPOINT

BOUNDED RATIONALITY

LO2
Explain the effects of bounded rationality on making economic decisions.

Psychologists have long argued that people have limited information-processing capabilities. The term *bounded rationality* describes a more realistic conception of human problem-solving ability. **Bounded rationality** is the idea that there are limits on the amount of information people can comprehend and act on. Because humans have only so much brainpower and only so much time, they cannot be expected to solve complex production or consumption problems optimally. When faced with lots of information that they aren't sure how to process, most people rely on simple rules of thumb for guidance.

Psychologists find that people, when facing complex financial decisions, are prone to inertia, even when making no decision may cost them money. The simplest rule of thumb in the face of a difficult decision is to avoid making it. In the face of uncertainty, doing nothing or doing little also means that people are inclined to accept whatever option is presented to them. For example, employees have a strong tendency to stick to whatever retirement savings option an employer presents, even when they are free to choose better options.

bounded rationality
There are limits to the amount of information people can comprehend and act on

Songquan Deng/Shutterstock.com

What do psychologists suggest as the reason people do not always make wise economic decisions?

Companies are trying to help their employees overcome inertia about retirement savings. Under the old system, the company would send a letter to employees inviting them to participate in the retirement program, whereby the company would match a certain amount of employee savings. To participate, the employee would have to fill out and return a form choosing an option. An employee who failed to act would not be enrolled. Many failed to act, thus passing up free matching money from the company. To help their employees overcome this intertia, most companies now automatically enroll an employee in the program unless that employee explicitly opts out. By simply switching the default option—that is, what happens if you do nothing—companies increased employee participation dramatically.

Inertia is also why, once people make a decision or allow a decision to be made for them, they tend to stick with that option even when circumstances change. In short, people try to avoid making hard choices even when the consequences of no decision are costly to them. In that regard, people do not seem to be pursuing their rational self-interest.

What rule of thumb do some people follow when faced with a complex and difficult decision?

LIMITED WILLPOWER

LO3 Understand the effects of limited willpower on making economic decisions.

A second assumption of traditional economics is that people, once they make a decision, have unlimited willpower. This means they have complete self-control and can follow through with every decision. But even when they know what's best for them, people often lack the discipline to follow through. People have **limited willpower**, which is limited self-discipline in following through with decisions that are in their self-interest, especially in their long-term interest.

Most people, despite their best intentions, end up eating, drinking, or spending too much, and exercising, saving, or studying too little. For example, nearly two-thirds of American adults are overweight. You may find yourself watching TV instead of studying for an exam or spending impulsively now rather than saving for something that really matters.

Market and nonmarket solutions have evolved to help people overcome self-discipline problems. From morning weigh-ins to New Year's resolutions, people use devices to help boost their willpower. Those who want to study more, save more, exercise more, quit smoking, lose weight, quit drinking, shop less impulsively, get off drugs, or stop gambling often are willing to pay time and money for help, as with tutors and enforced study hours, payroll-savings plans, fitness trainers and club memberships, nicotine gum and patches, diet plans and weight-loss surgery, Alcoholics Anonymous, Shopaholics Anonymous, drug rehab treatment, and Gamblers Anonymous. Some casinos allow problem gamblers to ban

limited willpower
Limited self-discipline in following through with decisions that are in one's self-interest, especially one's long-term interest

themselves from the premises. They will be turned away if they show up and can be denied any winnings if they do manage to gamble and win.

To pursue long-term goals, people must be able to postpone at least some immediate gratification. More economists are now looking at willpower issues.

What are some market and nonmarket approaches to help people overcome self-discipline problems to achieve their goals? **CHECKPOINT**

NEUROECONOMICS

LO4 Explain why some economists are mapping brain activity in the laboratory.

Traditional economics looks at how people react to a change in their incomes, in prices, or in some other factor affecting their choices. Thus, traditional economics is based on what people *do* in response to a change in circumstances. Some behavioral economists are now digging deeper into economic choices by drawing on advances in brain imaging technology. This new subfield of behavioral economics, called **neuroeconomics**, examines how economic decision-making affects areas of the brain.

In a typical experiment, a test subject is asked to make an economic decision. The experimenter, using magnetic resonance imaging (MRI), then measures activity in the parts of the brain associated with that choice. By mapping brain activity, these researchers hope to develop more realistic models of economic decision-making.

Here are three types of choices test subjects have been asked to make:

1. Choices involving uncertainty and risk (for example, would you prefer having $100 for certain or, instead, having a 50 percent chance of $300 and a 50 percent chance of zero)
2. Choices involving present versus future outcomes (for example, would you prefer receiving $100 today or $125 one year from today)
3. Social choices involving strategic interactions with other people (for example, how much of a $100 reward would you be willing to share with someone you didn't know)

The findings of neuroeconomists have challenged the traditional view that economic choices boil down to a simple process of utility maximization. Their laboratory results suggest a more complex interaction among competing objectives. For example, your rational self-interest is sometimes in conflict with your ethical sense of fairness. You often feel concern for others and may try to help them even if that conflicts with your rational self-interest.

neuroeconomics The mapping of brain activity while subjects make economic choices to develop better models of economic decision making

How does neuroeconomics explore economic decision making? **CHECKPOINT**

6.4 ASSESSMENT

Think Critically

1. Gina always wants to wear the latest fashions. She subscribes to several fashion magazines and dresses as much like the models as her budget will allow. Explain why she is likely to make decisions that are not in her best economic interest.
2. Gina does almost all of her clothing shopping at her favorite boutique. Although she sometimes learns that she could have purchased the same garments at a lower price somewhere else, she continues to shop at the boutique. Explain what inertia may have to do with her choice of where to shop.
3. Gina almost always spends more for clothing than she intends to spend. As a result, she can't buy other things she needs and has run up a substantial balance on her credit card. Explain how this demonstrates her limited willpower.

Graphing Exercise

4. An entrepreneur has operated a shoe store in a mall for many years. Last year she opened another store at a mall in a different community. The two communities are similar in terms of population, income, and shopping habits. Still, the new store's sales were much lower. The owner commisioned a market survey to determine the quantity of shoes that would be demanded per week at each store at different prices. Use these data to construct a graph showing the demand curves for each of the stores. Explain what bounded rationality may have to do with the greater quantities demanded at the old store.

DEMAND SCHEDULE FOR SHOES

Price	Old Store Quantity Demanded	New Store Quantity Demanded
$60	400	125
$70	390	100
$80	390	75
$90	370	50

Make Academic Connections

5. **Entrepreneurship** You own the boutique where Gina likes to shop. You would like to encourage Gina and other shoppers to buy many of your garments but not so many that they are unable to pay their bills. How would you encourage your salespeople to deal with Gina?

Working in small teams, make a list of shopping decisions that members of your team have made that they later came to regret. Identify reasons why each decision was made and how similar decisions could be avoided in the future. Compare your work with that of other teams.

Connect to History

The Rocky Mountain Fur Company

On March 20, 1823, an ad appeared in the *Missouri Republican:*

> ". . . to enterprising young men. The subscriber wishes to engage one hundred young men to ascend the Missouri River to its source, there to be employed for one, two, or three years. For particulars enquire of Major Henry, near the lead mines in the county of Washington, who will ascend with, and command, the party of the subscriber near St. Louis."
>
> *William H. Ashley*

This call for young men began the era of the Mountain Men and the fur trade in the American Far West. To the north, the French and the British had long established a profitable fur trade in North America. However, Americans did not reach the Far West until after the Lewis and Clark expedition. The trade was driven by the demand for furs in the eastern United States and in Europe, but the Napoleonic Wars and the War of 1812 closed many of these markets. When the wars ended, the demand once again rose in the United States and Europe.

With the establishment of trading posts, most furs were obtained by trading with Native Americans. Some were obtained by company-employed hunters and trappers. Furs also could be purchased from independent hunters and trappers. The Rocky Mountain Fur Company cut costs by taking an innovative approach that would send groups of trappers into the wilderness. Each would trade or trap furs and then meet at the end of the season at a predetermined location. At that rendezvous, the Mountain Men would sell their furs and obtain supplies for the next season. This method allowed the company to avoid the cost of building and maintaining of expensive trading posts.

Think Critically

Using supply and demand curves, demonstrate the following situations:

1. **The effects of the end of the War of 1812 on the market for fur**
2. **The effects of depleting the stock of fur-bearing animals on the supply of furs**
3. **The effect of substituting wool for fur in men's hat**

Sources: Ann M. Carlos, *The North American Fur Trade, 1804–1821: A Study in the Life-Cycle of a Duopoly*, New York: Garland Publishing, Inc., 1986; Hiram Martin Chittenden, *American Fur Trade of the Far West*, Vols. 1 & 2, Lincoln, Nebraska: University of Nebraska Press, 1987; Victor R. Fuchs, *The Economics of the Fur Industry*, New York: Columbia University Press, 1957; Jon E. Lewis, *The Mammoth Book of the West*, New York: Carrol & Graf Publishers, Inc., 1996; and *Oxford History of the American West*, Clyde A. Milner, Carol A. O'Connor, Martha A. Sandweiss, eds., New York: Oxford University Press, 1994.

Chapter 6 Summary

6.1 Price, Quantity, and Market Equilibrium

A. In a competitive market, the forces of demand and supply push the price to its equilibrium level, where quantity demanded equals quantity supplied.

B. Any price above the equilibrium level creates a surplus, which forces the price down to its equilibrium level. Any price below the equilibrium level creates a shortage, which forces the price up to its equilibrium level.

C. In competitive markets, buyers and sellers are free to exchange goods for money. Because this exchange is voluntary, neither party would bother unless it expected to gain.

D. Transaction costs are the costs of time and information involved in carrying out market exchanges—that is, the costs of bringing together buyers and sellers and working out a deal. By reducing transaction costs, markets promote exchange.

ASK THE EXPERT

www.cengage.com/school/contecon

Why do some prices adjust more slowly?

6.2 Shifts of Demand and Supply Curves

A. A change in any one of five factors can shift the demand curve for a product: (1) the money income of consumers, (2) the prices of substitute or complementary products, (3) consumer expectations, (4) consumer population, and (5) consumer tastes.

B. A change in any one of five factors can shift the supply curve for a product. These factors are (1) cost of a resource used to make the product, (2) prices of other goods that these resources could make, (3) technology, (4) producer expectations, and (5) number of producers.

C. A shift of the demand curve or the supply curve changes the equilibrium price and quantity.

6.3 Market Efficiency and the Gains from Exchange

A. Competitive markets result in productive and allocative efficiency. Productive efficiency occurs when goods are produced at the lowest possible cost per unit. Allocative efficiency occurs when firms produce the goods consumers most value.

B. Disequilibrium occurs when the quantity consumers demand does not equal the quantity producers supply. Government-imposed price floors are likely to create product surpluses, while government-imposed price ceilings usually create shortages.

C. Consumer surplus is the difference between the most that consumers would have been willing to pay for a product and what they actually pay for it. Competitive markets typically maximize consumer surplus, which is good for consumers.

6.4 Behavioral Economics

A. Behavioral economics uses insights from psychology to explain some economic decisions. Psychologists have found that people are prone to mistakes, are fickle and inconsistent, and often do not seek the best deal when making choices.

B. Bounded rationality is the idea that there are limits to the amount of information that people can comprehend and act on.

C. Because of limited willpower, many people have difficulty following through with decisions that are in their self-interest, especially their long-term interest.

D. To develop better models of how people make economic decisions, neuroeconomists map brain activity as test subjects make such choices.

CHAPTER 6 ASSESSMENT

Review Economic Terms

Match the terms with the definitions. Some terms will not be used.

_____ 1. The quantity of a product demanded is not equal to the quantity supplied

_____ 2. Quantity demanded equals quantity supplied and the market clears

_____ 3. A situation achieved when a firm produces output most valued by consumers

_____ 4. A minimum legal price below which a product cannot be sold

_____ 5. The amount of a product that remains unsold at a given price

_____ 6. An approach that borrows insights from psychology to help explain economic choices

_____ 7. A maximum legal price above which a product cannot be sold

_____ 8. A situation achieved when a firm produces output at the lowest possible cost per unit

_____ 9. The amount by which the quantity demanded exceeds the quantity supplied at a particular price

_____ 10. The cost of time and information needed to carry out market exchange

_____ 11. The idea that there are limits on the amount of information that people can comprehend and act on

a. allocative efficiency
b. behaviorial economics
c. bounded rationality
d. consumer surplus
e. decrease in demand
f. decrease in supply
g. disequilibrium
h. increase in demand
i. increase in supply
j. limited willpower
k. market equilibrium
l. neuroeconomics
m. price ceiling
n. price floor
o. productive efficiency
p. shortage
q. surplus
r. transaction costs

Review Economic Concepts

12. **True or False** A price below a product's equilibrium price will result in a surplus of the product.

13. When there is a voluntary exchange, it is reasonable to believe that
    a. both the buyer and seller gained.
    b. neither buyer nor seller gained.
    c. the buyer gained more than the seller.
    d. the seller gained more than the buyer.

14. **True or False** A market is always in a state of equilibrium.

15. **True or False** A price ceiling has an impact only if ceiling price is set above its equilibrium level.

16. Given an upward-sloping supply curve, a rightward shift of the demand curve
    a. decreases both equilibrium price and quantity.
    b. increases both equilibrium price and quantity.
    c. decreases equilibrium price only.
    d. increases equilibrium price only.

17. **True or False** A shift of the supply curve results from a change in quantity demanded at all prices.

18. ________?________ are the costs of time and information required to carry out market exchange.

19. A market will stay in equilibrium until
    a. one of the factors that determines demand changes.
    b. one of the factors that determines supply changes.
    c. all the suppliers go out of business.
    d. both a and b

20. Each of the following will cause the demand for butter to increase except
    a. an increase in the price of margarine.
    b. a scientific study that shows butter is good for people's health.
    c. an increase in the number of people who are unemployed.
    d. an increase in the number of people who might purchase butter.

21. **True or False** Limited willpower is more of a problem when decisions are made for the short run than for the long run.

22. Each of the following will cause supply to increase except
    a. workers are trained to be more efficient.
    b. a new, lower-cost source of electric power is found.
    c. firms invest in new technology that reduce their costs of production.
    d. a number of experienced workers retire and are replaced by new workers.

23. **True or False** If firms' costs of production fall while the demand for their product grows, you can be sure the equilibrium price for the product will fall.

24. There is ________?________ when a firm produces products at the lowest possible cost per unit.

25. Which of the following demonstrates the problem of bounded rationality?
    a. Ted buys the only used car he can afford.
    b. Ted forgets to take a towel when he goes to the beach.
    c. Ted often buys groceries at the store that is nearest to his home.
    d. Ted bought the first computer a salesperson recommended to him.

Apply Economic Concepts

26. **Make Predictions** Predict how the equilibrium price of coffee would be affected by the following changes:
    a. Poor growing conditions for coffee beans (demand remains constant)
    b. A major advertising campaign in the United States by a group of the world's coffee growers (supply remains constant)
    c. The publication of a new medical study warning against coffee consumption in excess of one cup per week (supply remains constant)
    d. Trade prohibition against a country in South America that produces a significant share of the U.S. coffee supply (demand remains constant)

27. **Equilibrium** On a separate sheet of paper, complete the table below:

DEMAND AND SUPPLY SCHEDULE FOR TACOS

Price Per Taco	Quantity Demanded	Quantity Supplied	Surplus/ Shortage	Will the price rise or fall?
$2.00	25	175		
$1.75	50	150		
$1.50	75	125		
$1.25	100	100		
$1.00	125	75		
$0.75	150	50		

28. **Graphing Demand and Supply** Construct a graph of the demand and supply for tacos from the data provided in the table in exercise 27.

29. **Graphing Shifts in Demand and Supply** On your graph, draw and label the shifts of demand and supply curves for tacos that would result from each of the following events.
    a. The cost of corn meal increases 50 percent.
    b. The price of pizza goes down 25 percent.
    c. The number of people who like tacos increases by 30 percent.
    d. A new machine is invented that makes tacos automatically.

30. **21st Century Skills: Flexibility and Adaptibility** When new products first become available, customers for certain products line up outside the store and are willing to wait sometimes days to be the first to purchase them. Make a list of three or more rules you would set to help you decide when to join such a line. Explain your reasoning for each rule you set.

Digging Deeper

with Economics e-Collection

The field of behavioral economics applies concepts from psychology to explain how people make some economic decisions. Access the Gale Economics e-Collection through the URL below to find articles that discuss behavioral economics. Choose one of the articles. Write a paragraph explaining the aspect or aspects of behavioral psychology the article discusses. Be prepared to share and discuss what you learned in class.

www.cengage.com/school/contecon

CHAPTER 7

Market Structure

CONSIDER ...

- What does a share of Google stock have in common with a bushel of wheat?
- What's so perfect about perfect competition?
- Why don't most monopolies last?
- Why is some drinking water sold in green, tear-shaped bottles?
- Why was OPEC created?
- Is the U.S. economy becoming more competitive?

Point your browser

www.cengage.com/school/contecon

shotbydave/iStockphoto.com; Background image: Lukiyanova Natalia/frenta/Shutterstock.com

7.1 PERFECT COMPETITION AND MONOPOLY

Learning Objectives

LO1 Identify the features of perfect competition.

LO2 Describe the barriers to entry that can create a monopoly.

LO3 Compare the market structures of monopoly and perfect competition in terms of price and quantity.

Key Terms

In Your World

At this point you already know something about competitive markets and how they work, but there are other types of markets besides competitive markets. Market structure describes the important features of a market, including the number of buyers and sellers, the product's uniformity across suppliers, the ease of entry into the market, and the forms of competition among firms. To get a better feel for the economy, you need to learn more about different types of market structures. All firms that supply output to a particular market—such as the market for cars, shoes, or wheat—are referred to as an industry. Therefore, the terms *industry* and *market* are used interchangeably. The first two market structures you will consider are perfect competition and monopoly.

PERFECT COMPETITION

LO1 Identify the features of perfect competition.

To begin your study of market structures, familiarize yourself with the four market features shown in Figure 7.1. The term **market structure** describes the important characteristics, or features, of a market. The first market structure to consider is **perfect competition**. Perfectly competitive markets are assumed to have the following features:

1. There are many buyers and sellers—so many that each buys or sells only a tiny fraction of the total market output. This assumption ensures that no individual buyer or seller can influence the price.
2. Firms produce a standardized product, or a **commodity**. A commodity is a product that is identical across suppliers, such as a bushel of wheat, a bushel of corn, or a share of Google stock. Because all suppliers offer an identical product, no buyer is willing to pay more for one particular supplier's product.
3. Buyers are fully informed about the price, quality, and availability of products, and sellers are fully informed about the availability of all resources and technology.
4. Firms can easily enter or leave the industry. There are no obstacles preventing new firms from entering profitable markets or preventing existing firms from leaving unprofitable markets.

market structure Important features of a market, including the number of buyers and sellers, product uniformity across sellers, ease of entering the market, as well as forms of competition

perfect competition A market structure with many fully informed buyers and sellers of an identical product and ease of entry

commodity A product that is identical across sellers, such as a bushel of wheat

Figure 7.1 Market Structure

MARKET STRUCTURE DESCRIBES THE IMPORTANT CHARACTERISTICS OF A MARKET.

Market Feature	Questions to Ask
1. Number of buyers and sellers	Are there many, only a few, or just one?
2. Product's uniformity across suppliers	Do firms in the market supply identical products or are products differentiated across firms?
3. Ease of entry into the market	Can new firms enter easily, or do natural or artificial barriers block them?
4. Forms of competition among firms	Do firms compete based only on prices, or are advertising and product differences also important?

If these conditions exist in a market, individual buyers and sellers have no control over the price. Price is determined by market demand and market supply. Once the market establishes the price, each firm is free to supply whatever quantity maximizes its profit or minimizes its loss. *A perfectly competitive firm is so small relative to the size of the market that the firm's quantity decision has no effect on the market price.* Any profit in this market attracts new firms in the long run, which increases the market supply. This reduces the market price. The lower price drives down the profit in this market.

Examples of Perfectly Competitive Markets

Examples of perfect competition include markets for the shares of large corporations such as Google or General Electric; markets for foreign exchange, such as yen, euros, and pounds; and markets for most agricultural products, such as livestock, corn, and wheat. In these markets, there are so many buyers and sellers that the actions of any one cannot influence the market price.

In the perfectly competitive market for wheat, for example, an individual supplier is a wheat farm. In the world market for wheat, there are tens of thousands of wheat farms, so any one supplies just a tiny fraction of market output. For example, the thousands of wheat farmers in Kansas together grow less than 3 percent of the world's supply of wheat. No single wheat farmer can influence the market price of wheat. Any farmer is free to supply any amount he or she wants to supply at the market price.

Market Price

In Figure 7.2, the market price of wheat of $5 per bushel is determined in panel (A) by the intersection of the market demand curve *D* and the market supply curve *S*. Once the market price is established, each farmer can sell however much he or she wants to sell at that market price.

Each farm is so small relative to the market that each has no impact on the market price. Because all farmers produce an identical product—bushels of wheat—any farmer who charges more than the market price sells no wheat. For example, if a farmer charged $5.25 per bushel, wheat buyers simply buy from other sellers.

Of course, any farmer is free to charge less than the market price. But why do that when all wheat can be sold at the market price? *The demand curve facing an individual farmer is, therefore, a horizontal line drawn at the market price.* In this example, the demand curve in panel (B) is drawn at the market price of $5 per bushel.

FIGURE 7.2 **Market Equilibrium and Firm's Demand Curve: Perfect Competition**

In panel (A), the market price of $5 is determined by the intersection of the market demand and supply curves. Each perfectly competitive firm can sell any amount at that price. The demand curve facing each perfectly competitive firm is horizontal at the market price, as shown by demand curve *d* in panel (B).

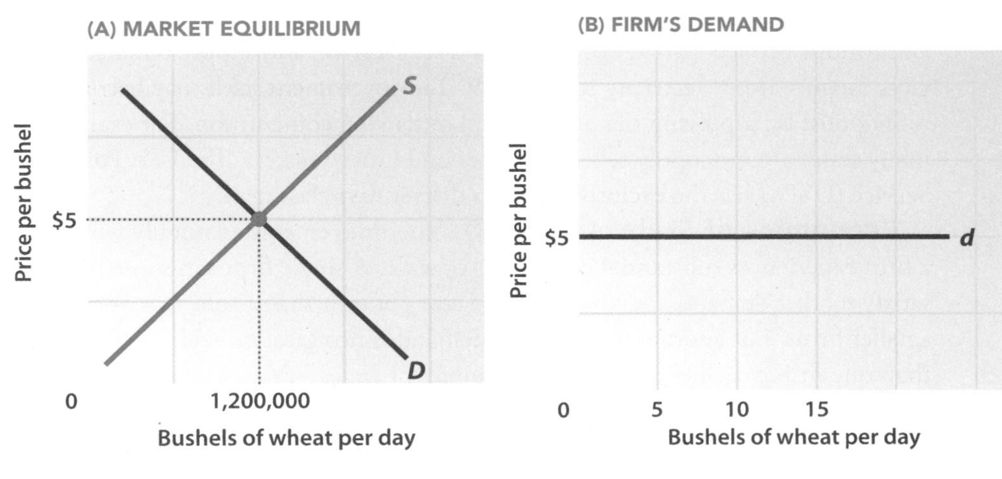

It has been said, "In perfect competition there is no competition." Two neighboring wheat farmers in perfect competition are not really rivals. They both can sell all they want at the market price. The amount one sells has no effect on the market price or on the amount the other can sell. Likewise, no two buyers compete for the product because they both can buy all they want at the market price. Each farm, or firm, tries to maximize profit. Firms that ignore this strategy don't survive.

What are the features of perfect competition? **CHECKPOINT**

MONOPOLY

LO2 Describe the barriers to entry that can create a monopoly.

The monopoly market structure is the opposite of the perfect competition structure. A **monopoly** is the sole supplier of a product with no close substitutes. The term *monopoly* comes from a Greek word meaning "one seller." A monopolist has more market power than does a business in any other market structure. **Market power** is the ability of a firm to raise its price without losing all its sales to rivals. A perfect competitor has no market power.

monopoly The sole supplier of a product with no close substitutes

market power The ability of a firm to raise its price without losing all sales to rivals

barriers to entry Restrictions on the entry of new firms into an industry

Barriers to Entry

A monopolized market has high **barriers to entry**, which are restrictions on the entry of new firms into an industry. Barriers to entry allow a monopolist to charge a price above the competitive price. If other firms could easily enter the market, they would increase the market supply and thereby drive the price down to the competitive level. There are three types of entry barriers: legal restrictions, economies of scale, and control of an essential resource.

Legal Restrictions Governments can prevent new firms from entering a market by making entry illegal. Patents, licenses, and other legal restrictions imposed by the government provide some producers with legal protection against competition.

Governments in some cities confer monopoly rights to sell hot dogs at civic auditoriums, collect garbage, offer bus and taxi service, and supply other services ranging from electricity to cable TV. The government itself may become a monopolist by supplying the product and outlawing competition. For example, many states are monopoly sellers of liquor and lottery tickets. The U.S. Postal Service (USPS) has the exclusive right to deliver first-class mail.

Economies of Scale A monopoly sometimes emerges naturally when a firm experiences substantial economies of scale. A single firm can sometimes satisfy market demand at a lower average cost per unit than could two or more smaller firms. Put another way, market demand is not great enough to allow more than one firm to achieve sufficient economies of scale.

Span the Globe

Flower Auction Holland

Five days a week in a huge building 10 miles outside Amsterdam, some 2,000 buyers gather to participate in Flower Auction Holland. At this auction, more than 19 million flowers and 2 million plants from 5,000 growers around the globe are auctioned off each day. The auction is held in the world's largest commercial building, and it is spread across the equivalent of 100 football fields. Flowers are grouped and auctioned off by type—long-stemmed roses, tulips, and so on. Hundreds of buyers sit in theater settings with their fingers on buttons. Once the flowers are presented, a clock-like instrument starts ticking off descending prices until a buyer stops it by pushing a button. The winning bidder gets to choose how many and which items to take. The clock starts again until another buyer stops it, and so on, until all flowers are sold. Buyers also can bid from remote locations. Flower auctions occur swiftly—on average one transaction occurs every four seconds. This is an example of a *Dutch auction,* which starts at a high price and works down. Dutch auctions are common where multiple lots of similar, though not identical, items are sold, such as flowers in Amsterdam, tobacco in Canada, and fish in seaports around the world.

Think Critically Is Flower Auction Holland a perfect example of a perfectly competitive market? Why or why not?

Thus, a single firm emerges from the competitive process as the sole supplier in the market. For example, the transmission of electricity involves economies of scale. Once wires are run throughout a community, the cost of linking additional households to the power grid is relatively small. The cost per household declines as more and more households are wired into the system.

A monopoly that emerges due to the nature of costs is called a *natural monopoly.* A new entrant cannot sell enough output to experience the economies of scale enjoyed by an established natural monopolist. Therefore, entry into the market is naturally blocked.

In less-populated areas, natural monopolies include the only grocery store, movie theater, or restaurant for miles around. These are geographic monopolies for products sold in local markets.

Control of Essential Resources Sometimes the source of monopoly power is a firm's control over some resource critical to production. Following are some examples of the control of essential resources barrier to entry.

- For decades, Alcoa controlled the world's supply of bauxite, the key raw material in aluminum.
- China is a monopoly supplier of pandas to the world's zoos. The National Zoo in Washington, D.C., for example, rents a pair of pandas from China for $1 million per year. As a way of controlling the panda supply, China stipulates that any offspring from the Washington pair becomes China's property. Other zoos have similar deals with China.
- A key resource for any professional sports team is a large stadium. Pro teams typically sign exclusive, long-term leases for stadiums in major cities. These leases help block the formation of another league in the sport.

Monopolists May Not Earn a Profit

Because a monopoly, by definition, supplies the entire market, the demand curve for a monopolist's output also is the market demand curve. That demand curve, therefore, slopes downward, reflecting the law of demand. Price and quantity demanded are inversely, or negatively, related.

Even a monopolist with iron-clad barriers to entry may go broke. Although a monopolist is the sole supplier of a good with no close substitutes, the demand for that good may not be great enough to keep the firm in business. After all, many inventions are protected from direct competition by patents, yet most patented products never get produced and many that are produced fail to attract enough customers to survive.

True Monopolies Are Rare

Long-lasting monopolies are rare because a profitable monopoly attracts competitors and substitutes. Even where barriers to entry are initially high, technological change tends to create substitutes. For example, railroads at one time enjoyed a natural monopoly in shipping goods across country. The monopoly ended when the trucking industry was born. The development of wireless transmission of long-distance telephone calls created competitors for the monopolist AT&T and is erasing the monopoly held by some local cable TV providers and some local phone services. Likewise, fax machines, email, the Internet, text messaging, and delivery firms such as FedEx and UPS have all cut into the U.S. Postal Service's monopoly on first-class mail delivery.

CHECKPOINT **Name and describe the three barriers to entry into a market.**

MONOPOLY AND EFFICIENCY

LO3 Compare the market structures of monopoly and perfect competition.

Monopolists are not guaranteed a profit. Monopolies can lose money. Monopolies are relatively rare. So, then, what's the problem?

Monopoly vs. Perfect Competition

One way to understand the problem is to compare monopoly to perfect competition. Competition forces firms to be *efficient*—that is, to produce the maximum possible output from available resources—and to supply that output at the lowest possible price. Consumers get a substantial consumer surplus from this low price. However, a successful monopolist typically charges more than competitive firms do. Thus, the biggest problem with monopolies is they charge higher prices, so fewer consumers can afford the product.

To compare monopoly and perfect competition, suppose D in Figure 7.3 is the *market demand curve* for a product sold in perfect competition. Suppose the market supply curve (which is not shown) intersects the market demand curve at point c. The market price is p_c and the market quantity is Q_c. Consumer surplus is the triangular area below the demand curve and above the price, measured by acp_c. (Recall that *consumer surplus* is the difference between the most that consumers are willing to pay for a given quantity of a good and what they actually pay.)

What if one firm buys up all the individual firms in the perfectly competitive market, creating a giant monopoly? In this case, the market demand curve becomes the monopolist's demand curve. Suppose the average cost per unit is the same with monopoly as with perfect competition. What we can say for sure is that a monopoly supplies less output and at a higher price than would a perfectly competitive market. To maximize profit, the monopolist restricts quantity to Q_m and increases the price to p_m. With monopoly, consumer surplus shrinks to the blue triangle, which is much smaller than with perfect competition.

Other Problems With Monopoly

Monopolies may reduce social welfare for other reasons besides higher prices to consumers. These include a possible waste of resources and inefficiencies that may develop in their operation.

Resources Wasted Securing Monopoly Privilege Because of their size and economic importance, monopolies may have too much influence on the political system, which they use to protect and strengthen their monopoly power.

Figure 7.3 Monopoly, Perfect Competition, and Consumer Surplus

Suppose the market supply curve (which is not shown) intersects the market demand curve at point *c*. A perfectly competitive industry would produce output Q_c and sell at a price p_c. A monopoly that could produce at that same average cost would supply output Q_m and sell at price p_m. Output is lower and price is higher under monopoly than under perfect competition. With perfect competition, consumer surplus is the entire triangle acp_c. With monopoly, consumer surplus shrinks to the blue-shaded triangle.

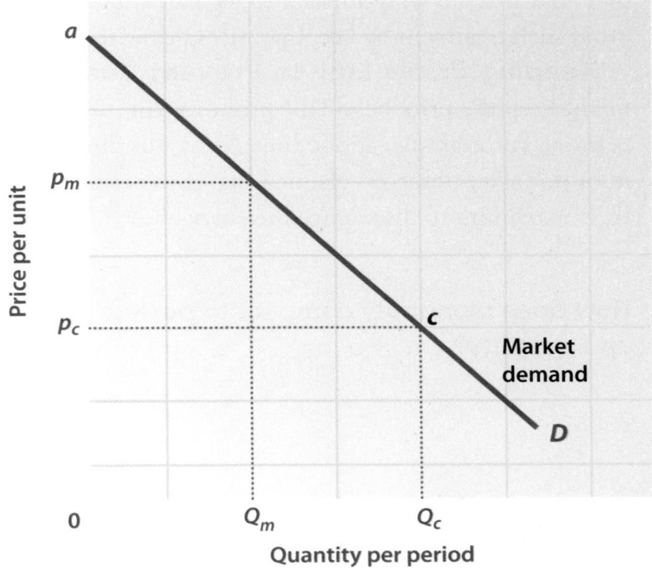

Lawyers' fees, lobbying expenses, and other costs associated with gaining a special privilege from government are largely a social waste because they use up scarce resources but add not one unit to output.

Monopolies May Grow Inefficient The monopolist, insulated from the rigors of market competition, could grow fat and lazy, and thus become inefficient. Executives might waste resources by creating a more comfortable life for themselves. Lavish salaries and company perks could boost the average cost of production above the competitive level. Monopolists also have been criticized for being slow to adopt the latest production techniques, reluctant to develop new products, and generally lacking in innovation.

Why Monopoly Might Not Be So Bad

For several reasons, some monopolies may not be as socially wasteful as was just described.

Economies of Scale If economies of scale are substantial, a monopolist might be able to produce output at a lower average cost than competitive firms could. Therefore, the price, or at least the cost of production, could be lower with monopoly than with perfect competition.

Government Regulation Government intervention can increase social welfare by forcing the monopolist to lower the price and increase output. The government can either operate the monopoly itself, as it does with most urban transit systems, or it can regulate a privately owned monopoly, as it does with local phone services and electricity transmission. You will read more about government regulation later in this chapter.

Keeping Prices Low to Avoid Regulation A monopolist might keep prices below the profit-maximizing level to avoid government regulation. For example, the prices and profits of drug companies, which individually are monopoly suppliers of patented medicines, come under scrutiny from time to time by public officials who threaten to regulate drug prices. Drug firms might try to avoid such treatment by keeping prices below the level that would maximize profit.

Keeping Prices Low to Prevent Competition Finally, a monopolist might keep the price below the profit-maximizing level to avoid attracting competitors. For example, at one time Alcoa was the only U.S. producer of aluminum. Industry observers claimed that the company kept prices and profits below their maximum to discourage the entry of new firms.

CHECKPOINT How does monopoly compare to perfect competition in terms of price and quantity?

ESSENTIAL QUESTION

Standard CEE 9: Competition and Market Structure

Competition among sellers usually lowers costs and prices, and encourages producers to produce what consumers are willing and able to buy. Competition among buyers increases prices and allocates goods and services to those people who are willing and able to pay the most for them.

store row: ©PCL/Alamy; T-Mobile: George Nikitin/AP Images/T-Mobile

What are the effects on the economy of competition among sellers and competition among buyers?

7.1 ASSESSMENT

Think Critically

1. What characteristics of farms suggest that these firms operate in perfectly competitive markets?
2. One decade ago, the town of Mt. Utopia had five fast-food restaurants. The town's population has grown rapidly since then. As the town grew, the sales and profits of these restaurants increased. There now are 15 fast-food restaurants in Mt. Utopia. None of them earns a large profit. What feature of competitive markets does this demonstrate? Explain your answer.
3. Identify a firm that operates in your community that you think has a significant amount of market power. Explain why you chose this firm.
4. At one time, the American Telephone and Telegraph Corp. (AT&T) had a great deal of monopoly power and earned large profits. The growth in the use of cellular technology caused AT&T to lose money. What happened to AT&T's monopoly power?

Graphing Exercise

5. Use data in the table to draw two graphs: the market demand and supply curves, and the individual demand curve for the Apex Coal Mine. Assume this is a perfectly competitive market, and that Apex is one firm in that market. What is the market equilibrium price? How did you derive the individual demand curve for Apex?

MARKET COAL DEMAND AND SUPPLY SCHEDULE PER MONTH

Price per Ton	Market Demand (tons)	Market Supply (tons)
$200	4,000,000	8,000,000
$175	5,000,000	7,000,000
$150	6,000,000	6,000,000
$125	7,000,000	5,000,000
$100	8,000,000	4,000,000

Make Academic Connections

6. **History** Between 1880 and 1900, the Standard Oil Company came to control almost 90 percent of oil production in the United States. It did this by buying up or driving other firms out of business. With this monopoly power, the firm's owners were able to earn as much as a 20 percent profit on the value of the firm's assets, such as its refineries, pipelines, etc. Much of the firm's profit was used to develop new technologies that, according to the owners, contributed to lower prices. In your opinion, is it possible for monopolies to be good for consumers? Explain your answer.

TeamWork

Working in small teams, identify two local businesses that have a significant amount of market power. Describe the barrier(s) to entry that allows these firms to set prices. Are consumers better served or harmed by these businesses? Compare your team's answers with the work of other teams.

21st Century Skills

LEADERSHIP AND RESPONSIBILITY

To Protect and Serve

Throughout history, some individuals have enjoyed greater income and wealth than most other people. In the United States names such as Andrew Carnegie, John D. Rockefeller, and Cornelius Vanderbilt come to mind. More recently, Bill Gates and Warren Buffet have made vast fortunes by leading successful businesses. What is interesting is the fact that, having made their fortunes, these men chose to use much of their wealth to help others who were less fortunate. Consider the following.

- Carnegie used his wealth to establish more than 3,000 public libraries in the United States, Canada, and England.
- Rockefeller gave funds to educational organizations including $80 million to the University of Chicago.
- Vanderbilt donated funds to establish Vanderbilt University in Tennessee.
- Gates pledged $50 billion to the Bill and Melinda Gates Foundation that is dedicated to bringing innovations in health, development, and learning to the global community.
- Buffet pledged roughly $30 billion in Berkshire Hathaway stock to the Bill and Melinda Gates Foundation.

Wealth and Responsibility

It has been said that with great wealth goes great responsibility. Each of the men cited above gained wealth by leading successful firms. Carnegie dominated steel production. During the 1890s Rockefeller's Standard Oil produced most of the petroleum in the United States. Vanderbilt controlled several railroads. Gates created Microsoft. And, Buffet became wealthy as the head of Berkshire Hathaway, a conglomerate, multi-industry holding company.

Some people believe most of these men took unfair advantage of market power to accumulate their wealth. Antitrust laws were used against several of them in an attempt to limit their power. In 1911, for example, Rockefeller's Standard Oil Co. was dissolved into 34 smaller firms. In 1998, the U.S. Department of Justice brought suit against Microsoft, accusing the firm of monopolizing the computer software market. Regardless of how these men accumulated their wealth, history shows that they ultimately used a large part of their fortune to help others. If you had been in their situations, what would you have done with your wealth and power?

Leadership and Responsibility on a Smaller Scale

On a smaller scale, most people have the opportunity to use the wealth and power they accumulate to help others. Millions of Americans choose to share their wealth with people who are in need. Which of these factors would you weigh when you decide whether to contribute part of your wealth to people who are less fortunate than you?

- The need of the people you might help
- Your ability to sacrifice
- Contributions made by others
- Whether you are related to those who are in need

Apply the Skill

Imagine that a natural disaster has occurred in a foreign nation. You have seen TV reports that show thousands of victims who are suffering from a lack of food, shelter, water, and medical care. Describe three specific factors you would consider in order to decide whether or not to help. Would you work to encourage others to contribute? Explain why or why not.

7.2 MONOPOLISTIC COMPETITION AND OLIGOPOLY

Learning Objectives

LO1 Identify the features of monopolistic competition.

LO2 Identify the features of oligopoly, and analyze firm behavior when these firms cooperate and when they compete.

Key Terms

monopolistic competition 213
oligopoly 214
cartel 216

In Your World

You are now aware of the extreme market structures of perfect competition and monopoly. Next you will learn about monopolistic competition and oligopoly, the two structures between the extremes in which most firms operate. Firms in monopolistic competition are like golfers in a tournament in which each player strives for a personal best. Firms in oligopoly are more like players in a tennis match, where each player's actions depend on how and where the opponent hits the ball.

MONOPOLISTIC COMPETITION

LO1 Identify the features of monopolistic competition.

In monopolistic competition, many firms offer products that differ slightly. As the expression **monopolistic competition** suggests, this structure contains elements of both monopoly and competition. The "monopolistic" element is that each firm has some market power. In other words, a firm can raise its price without losing all its customers. Because the products of different suppliers differ slightly, each firm's demand curve slopes downward. The "competition" element of monopolistic competition is that barriers to entry are so low that any short-run profit attracts new competitors, and this will erase profit in the long run.

Market Characteristics

Because barriers to entry are low, firms in monopolistic competition can, in the long run, enter or leave the market with ease. Consequently, there are enough sellers that they behave competitively. There also are enough sellers that each tends to get lost in the crowd, like a golfer in a tournament who is striving for a personal best. A particular firm, in deciding on a price, does not worry about how other firms in the market will react. For example, in a large city, an individual restaurant, gas station, drugstore, dry cleaner, or convenience store tends to act *independently* from its many competitors—it tends to get lost in the crowd.

Product Differentiation

In perfect competition, the product is identical across suppliers, such as a bushel of wheat. In monopolistic competition, the product differs slightly among sellers, as with the difference between one rock radio station and another. Sellers differentiate their products in four basic ways.

monopolistic competition A market structure with low entry barriers and many firms selling products differentiated enough that each firm's demand curve slopes downward

Photodisc/Getty Images

Would you be willing to pay more for food if it means you would have more restaurant choices?

Physical Differences The most obvious way products differ is in their physical appearance and their qualities. The differences among products are seemingly endless. Shampoos, for example, differ in color, scent, thickness, lathering ability, and bottle design. Packaging also is designed to make a product stand out in a crowded field, such as drinking water in green, tear-shaped bottles or potato chips in a can.

Location The number and variety of locations where a product is available also are a means of differentiation. Some products seem to be available everywhere, including the Internet. Finding other products requires some search and travel.

Services Products also differ in their accompanying services. For example, some restaurants offer home delivery. Others don't. Some retailers offer product demonstrations by a well-trained staff. Others are mostly self-service.

Product Image A final way products differ is in the image the producer tries to foster in the consumer's mind. For example, some products use celebrity endorsements to boost sales.

Costs of Product Differentiation

Firms in monopolistic competition spend more on marketing to differentiate their products than do firms in perfect competition. This increases average cost. Some economists argue that monopolistic competition results in too many firms and in product differentiation that is artificial. Others argue that consumers are willing to pay a higher price for a wider choice.

Investigate Your Local Economy

Brainstorm a list of markets in your area in which firms seem to be operating with excess capacity. Cite evidence for each market.

Excess Capacity

Firms in monopolistic competition are said to operate with *excess capacity,* which means that a firm could lower its average cost per unit by selling more. Such excess capacity exists, for example, with gas stations, banks, convenience stores, motels, bookstores, and flower shops. As a specific example, industry analysts argue that the nation's 21,000 funeral homes could efficiently handle 4 million funerals a year, but only about 2.5 million people die each year. So the industry operates at about 60 percent capacity. This results in a higher average cost per funeral because most resources remain idle much of the time.

CHECKPOINT What are the important features of monopolistic competition?

OLIGOPOLY

oligopoly A market structure with a small number of firms whose behavior is interdependent

LO2 Identify the features of oligopoly.

Oligopoly is a Greek word meaning "few sellers." When you think of "big business," you are thinking of **oligopoly**, a market that is dominated by just a few firms. Perhaps three or four firms account for most market output. Because this market has only a few firms, each must consider the effect of its own actions on competitors' behavior. Oligopolistic industries include the markets for steel, oil, automobiles, breakfast cereals, and tobacco.

In some oligopolies, such as steel or oil, the product is identical, or undifferentiated, across producers. Thus, an *undifferentiated oligopoly* sells a commodity, such as an ingot of steel or a barrel of oil. In other oligopolies, such as automobiles or breakfast cereals, the product is differentiated across producers. A *differentiated oligopoly* sells products that differ across producers, such as Ford versus Toyota or General Mills' Wheaties versus Kellogg's Corn Flakes.

Firms in an oligopoly are interdependent, like tennis players. Therefore, each firm knows that any changes in its price, output, or advertising may prompt a reaction from its rivals. Each firm may react if another firm alters any of these features.

Barriers to Entry

Why have some industries evolved into an oligopolistic market structure, dominated by only a few firms, whereas other industries have not? Although the reasons are not always clear, *an oligopoly often can be traced to some barrier to entry, such as economies of scale or brand names built up by years of advertising*. Most of the entry barriers that apply to monopoly also apply to oligopoly.

Economies of Scale Perhaps the most significant barrier to entry is economies of scale. As noted in Chapter 5, the *minimum efficient scale* is the lowest rate of output at which a firm takes full advantage of economies of scale. If a firm's minimum efficient scale is large compared to industry output, then only a few firms are needed to produce the total amount demanded in the market. For example, an automobile factory of minimum efficient scale could make enough vehicles to supply nearly 10 percent of the U.S. market. To compete with existing producers, a new entrant must sell enough automobiles to reach a competitive scale of operation.

Figure 7.4 presents the long-run average cost curve for a typical firm in an industry with economies of scale. If a new entrant can expect to sell only *S* cars, the average cost per unit would be $50,000. This far exceeds the average cost of $10,000 for a manufacturer that sells *M* cars, which is the minimum efficient size. Because autos sell for less than $50,000, a potential entrant can expect to lose money on every car sold, and this prospect usually discourages entry. For example, John Delorean tried to break into the auto industry in the early 1980s with a modern design that was later featured in the *Back to the Future* movies. But his company managed to build and sell only 8,583 Deloreans before going bankrupt. If an auto plant costs $3 billion to build, just paying for the plant would have cost more than $300,000 per Delorean.

The High Cost of Entry The total investment needed to reach the minimum efficient size may be huge. A new auto factory or computer chip plant can cost more than $3 billion. The average cost of developing and testing a new drug exceeds $800 million. Advertising a new product to compete with established brands also could require enormous outlays. A failed product could bankrupt a new firm. That's why most new products usually come from large, existing firms, which can better withstand the possible loss. For example, McDonald's spent $100 million in its unsuccessful attempt to introduce the Arch Deluxe. Unilever lost $160 million when its new laundry detergent, Power, failed to catch on.

FIGURE 7.4 **Economies of Scale as a Barrier to Entry to Oligopoly**

At point *b*, an established firm can produce *M* or more automobiles at an average cost of $10,000 each. A new firm trying to break into this market that is able to sell only *S* automobiles would incur a much higher average cost of $50,000 at point *a*. If automobile prices are below $50,000, that new entrant would suffer a loss. In this market, economies of scale serve as a barrier to entry, insulating firms achieving minimum efficient scale from new competitors.

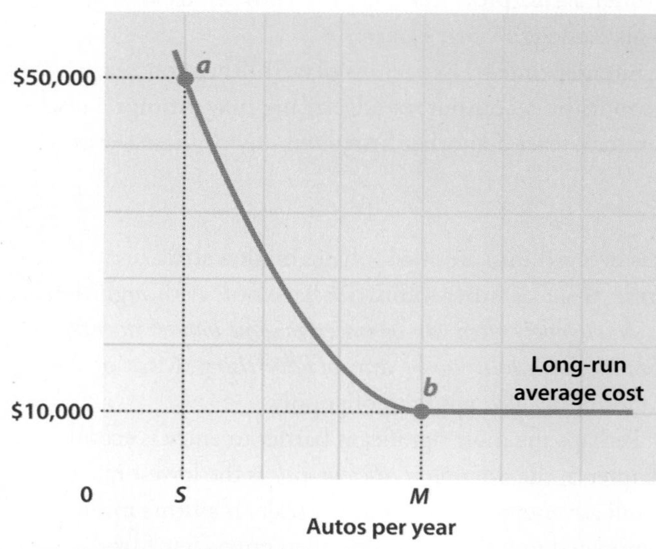

Product Differentiation Costs An oligopolist often spends millions and sometimes billions trying to differentiate its product. Some of this provides valuable information to consumers and offers them a wider array of products. However, some forms of product differentiation appear to be of little value. Slogans such as "It's the Cola" or "Open Happiness" convey little real information, yet Pepsi and Coke spend huge sums on such messages. For example, Coke spends more than $2 billion per year on advertising. Product differentiation expenditures create barriers to entry.

When Oligopolists Collude

To decrease competition and increase profit, oligopolistic firms, particularly those that offer identical products, may try to *collude*, or agree on a market price. *Collusion* is an agreement among firms in the industry to divide the market and fix the price. A **cartel** is a group of firms that agree to act as a single monopolist to increase the market price and maximize the group's profits.

Compared with competing firms, colluding firms usually produce less, charge more, earn more profit, and try to block the entry of new firms. Consumers lose consumer surplus because of the higher price, and potential entrants are denied the chance to compete in the market.

cartel A group of firms that agree to act as a single monopolist to increase the market price and maximize the group's profits

Collusion and cartels are illegal in the United States. However, monopoly profit can be so tempting that some firms break the law. Other countries are more tolerant of cartels. Some even promote them, as with the 12 nations of OPEC, the world oil cartel. If OPEC members were ever to meet in the United States, those officials could be arrested for price fixing. Even though they are outlawed in some countries, cartels still operate worldwide because there are no international laws banning them.

The biggest obstacle to maintaining a profitable cartel is the powerful temptation that each member has to cheat on the cartel agreement. By offering a price slightly below the established price, for example, individual firms in the cartel usually can increase their own sales and profit. A cartel collapses once cheating becomes widespread.

A second obstacle to cartel success is the entry of rival firms. The profit of the cartel attracts entry, entry increases market supply, and increased supply forces the market price down. A cartel's continued success therefore depends on the ability to block the entry of new firms or to get any new firms to join the cartel.

Finally, cartels, like monopolists, must be concerned that technological change can erode their market power. For example, hydrogen-powered fuel cells may eventually replace gasoline in automobiles. This could undermine OPEC.

OPEC's initial success with raising the price attracted so many other oil suppliers that OPEC now accounts for only about 40 percent of the world's oil output. As a result, OPEC has lost much of its market power. Efforts to form cartels in the world markets for bauxite, copper, coffee, and some other products have failed so far.

When Oligopolists Compete

Because oligopolists are interdependent, analyzing their behavior is complicated. At one extreme, the firms in the industry may try to coordinate their behavior so they act collectively as a single monopolist, forming a cartel, as was just discussed. At the other extreme, oligopolists may compete so fiercely that price wars erupt, such as those that flare up in markets for computers, airline fares, and long-distance phone service. Consumers benefit from the lower prices resulting from price wars.

You have now worked through the four market structures: perfect competition, monopolistic competition, oligopoly, and monopoly. Features of the four are summarized and compared in Figure 7.5.

FIGURE 7.5 Comparison of Market Structures

	Perfect Competition	Monopolistic Competition	Oligopoly	Monopoly
Number of firms	the most	many	few	one
Control over price	none	limited	some	complete
Product differences	none	some	none or some	none
Barriers to entry	none	low	substantial	insurmountable
Examples	wheat, shares of stock	convenience stores, bookstores	automobiles, oil, cereal	local electricity and phone service

What are the important features of oligopoly, and how do oligopolists that cooperate compare to those that compete? CHECKPOINT

7.2 ASSESSMENT

Think Critically

1. There are probably 20 or more brands of laundry detergent in the grocery store where your family shops. Make a list of different ways in which producers try to differentiate one detergent brand from another. Why can some brands have prices that are much higher than the price of others and still sell well?
2. Why would a new oil refinery have difficulty competing successfully with large oil refiners such as Chevron, Shell Oil, or ExxonMobil?
3. In the 1990s, many nations that grew coffee beans tried to set up a cartel that would have limited coffee production and stabilized prices at a higher level. This effort failed. Explain why it is so difficult to create a successful cartel when there are many producers.

Graphing Exercise

4. The graph shows the long-run average cost curve (discussed in Chapter 5) for Sleepwell Mattresses, one of several firms that manufacture mattresses. Suppose the firm maximizes profit in the short run by producing at the rate of output where its long-run average cost is $150 per mattress. The firm's owners realize they could reduce their long-run average cost by expanding output so as to benefit from economies of scale. Based on the graph, what is the smallest rate of output at which the firm would take full advantage of economies of scale? What, approximately, would be the long-run average cost at that output rate? Identify two ways the firm could try to increase the amount sold.

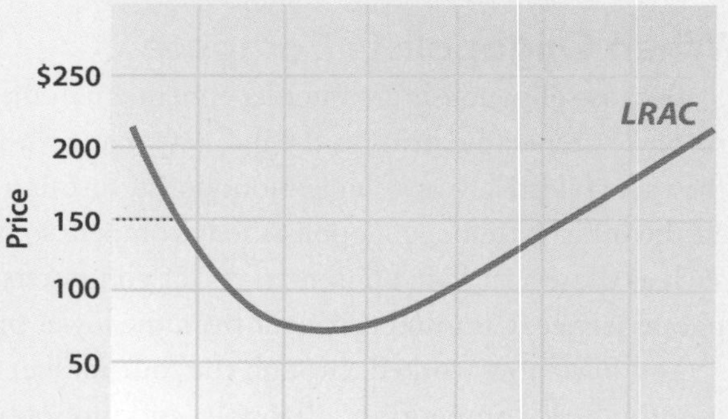

Make Academic Connections

5. **Research** In 2011 the cost of a 30-second TV advertisement during the Super Bowl was $3 million. Investigate the cost of this type of advertising during the most recent Super Bowl. Why are businesses willing to spend this amount for a 30-second advertisement? What are they trying to accomplish?

TeamWork

Working in small teams, brainstorm five additional examples to those given in Figure 7.5 on page 217 of industries that compete in each of the four market structures (perfect competition, monopolistic competition, oligopoly, and monopoly). For each example describe the specific characteristics of the industry's market structure that allowed your group to identify it. Compare your team's work with that of other teams.

Naveen Selvadurai

Co-Founder, FourSquare Labs Inc.

PARK JIN HEE/Xinhua/Landov

Geolocation applications are hot, high-tech additions to social networking platforms, and Naveen Selvadurai is leading the way. Together with partner Dennis Crowley, he invented the smartphone application FourSquare, which combines geolocation software and social networking.

FourSquare helps people get around their cities using the global positioning capabilities of their cell phone. It allows users to connect with friends and update their location via mobile phone or on social networking sites such as Twitter or Facebook. Users can earn points and badges for "checking in" at bars, restaurants, and other venues. With more than 7.5 million registered users, and growing at an estimated 100,000 new users per week, FourSquare is a hit. Of his motivation Naveen says, "I live in the East Village [of New York City], which has so much rich history and so much to do and I realized that I'd seen maybe 5 percent of it. I was looking for a way to get me and my friends to go out and do more things." Naveen says that people use FourSquare for three reasons:

- It has a game-like nature to it.
- It creates competition among friends.
- It keeps track of what you do.

Born in Tamil Nadu, India, into a family of engineers, Naveen grew up in an environment that encouraged tinkering with electronics. He said, "I knew I wanted to be an engineer. I knew I wanted to do something with computers. I got both my bachelor's and my master's [degrees]. My parents made me kind of have this wholesome education. They really wanted that on my résumé before I moved on to other things." Naveen graduated with degrees from King's College in London, England, and Worcester Polytechnic Institute in Massachusetts. He has worked at Sony Music Entertainment, Nokia, and Socialight. He is currently half-owner of FourSquare and an adjunct professor at The Cooper Union.

In explaining why he was driven to develop FourSquare, Naveen said, "I wanted to do and build

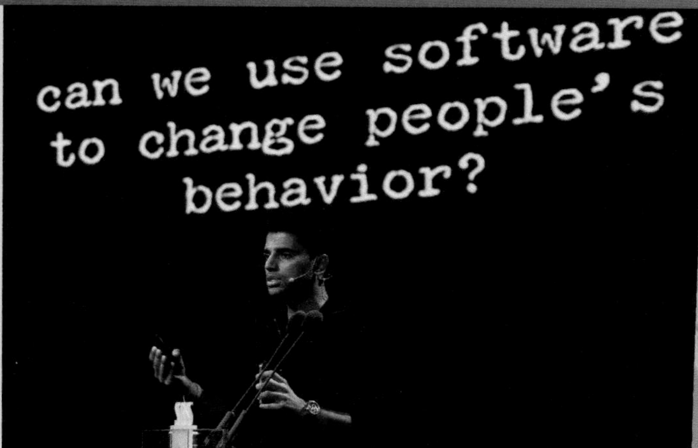

something that helps us learn more about where we live and learn more about locations to go where our friends go, and to learn more about the world in which we interact every day."

Naveen's advice to young entrepreneurs is:

- be passionate about what you do
- don't be afraid to take risks
- understand that you won't get it right the first time
- talk to people about your ideas, and get feedback.

The New York-based company FourSquare Labs Inc. is valued, at the time of this writing, at $600 million. The service attracts revenue from big brands and faces competition from location-based services such as Facebook Places and Twitter. By creating partnerships with local businesses, FourSquare hopes to increase profits. They want to give users recommendations on the hottest places to have dinner or have a snack after a concert or show. Selvadurai said, "Other sites want to keep you inside at the computer, while our entire goal is to get you out of the house."

Think Critically **Identify the structure of the market in which FourSquare's geolocation software competes. Justify your answer.**

Sources: http://www.encompasssocial.com/naveen-selvadurai-bio.html; http://www.zeitgeistminds.com/videos/founding-foursquare; http://www.fastcompany.com/100/2010/30/naveen-selvadurai; http://span.state.gov/nov-dec2010/eng/57-60-South-Asian.html; and http://www.bloomberg.com/news/2011-01-23/foursquare-valued-at-more-than-250-million-to-seek-new-funding.html

7.3 ANTITRUST, REGULATION, AND COMPETITION

Key Terms

Learning Objectives

LO1 Explain the goal of U.S. antitrust laws.

LO2 Distinguish between the two views of government regulation.

LO3 Discuss why U.S. markets have grown more competitive in recent decades.

In Your World

As a consumer, you have a special interest in buying products at competitive prices. Monopolists and colluding firms usually raise prices and this hurts you and other consumers. In 1776 Adam Smith wrote, "People of the same trade seldom meet together, even for merriment or diversion, but the conversation ends in a conspiracy against the public, or in some contrivance to raise prices." The tendency of firms to seek monopolistic advantage is predictable, given their drive to maximize profit. But monopoly power typically harms the economy. Public policy can promote competition in markets where competition seems desirable. It also can reduce the harmful effects of monopoly in markets where the output can be supplied most efficiently by only one or a few firms.

ANTITRUST

LO1 Explain the goal of U.S. antitrust laws.

Although competition typically promotes the most efficient use of the nation's resources, an individual firm would prefer to operate as a monopoly. If left alone, a firm might try to create a monopoly by driving competitors out of business, by merging with competitors, or by colluding with competitors to rig prices and increase profits. **Antitrust activity** attempts to prohibit efforts to monopolize markets in which competition is desirable.

U.S. Antitrust Activity

Antitrust activity tries to

1. Promote the market structure that leads to greater competition, and
2. Reduce anticompetitive behavior.

Antitrust Laws

Antitrust laws attempt to promote socially desirable market performance. Three early laws dealt with the growing problems of anticompetitive market structures and anticompetitive behavior. These included the Sherman Antitrust Act, the Clayton Act, and the Federal Trade Commission Act.

antitrust activity
Government efforts aimed at preventing monopoly and promoting competition in markets where competition is desirable

The Sherman Antitrust Act of 1890 outlawed the creation of trusts, restraint of trade, and monopolization. A trust is any firm or group of firms that tries to monopolize a market. The Clayton Act of 1914 was passed to outlaw certain practices not prohibited by the Sherman Act and to help government stop a monopoly before it develops. The Federal Trade Commission (FTC) Act of 1914 established a federal body to help enforce antitrust laws. The FTC has five full-time commissioners assisted by a staff of mostly economists and lawyers.

NETBookmark

Access the web page for the Federal Trade Commission's Bureau of Competition through the website shown below to view a slideshow about the history of antitrust laws. After viewing the slideshow, click on these questions: What's a monopoly? What's price fixing? and What's bid rigging? Be prepared to answer the questions in class.

www.cengage.com/school/contecon

These three laws provide the U.S. antitrust framework. This framework has been clarified and enhanced by amendments and by court decisions over the years.

Mergers and Antitrust

One way firms may try to reduce competition is by merging with competing firms. A **merger** is the combination of two or more firms to form a single firm. Much of what federal antitrust officials do today is approve or deny proposed mergers. These officials consider the merger's impact on the share of sales by the largest firms in the industry. If a few firms account for a large share of sales in the market (say, more than half), any merger that would increase that share may be challenged.

Federal guidelines sort all mergers into two broad categories. *Horizontal mergers* involve firms in the same market, such as a merger between competing oil companies. *Nonhorizontal mergers* include all other types of mergers. Horizontal mergers hold greater interest for antitrust officials. When determining whether to challenge a particular merger, officials consider factors such as the ease of entry into the market and possible efficiency gains from the merger. They would ask, for example, can the merger increase the resulting firm's economies of scale, or make the firm more competitive in the world market?

Flexible Merger Policy

In recent years, the government has shifted from rules that restrict big mergers to a more flexible approach. This new approach allows big companies to merge if the combination is more efficient or more competitive with other big firms in the market. For example, the government approved Whirlpool's $1.7 billion acquisition of Maytag even though Whirlpool at the time was the world's largest maker of major appliances and Maytag ranked third. Government officials noted that growing competition from Asia would keep prices down. As one antitrust official put it, "I do not believe that size alone is a basis to challenge a merger." However, just the threat of a legal challenge has stopped some potentially anticompetitive mergers.

merger The joining of two or more firms to form a single firm

What is the goal of antitrust laws? **CHECKPOINT**

REGULATION OF NATURAL MONOPOLIES

LO2 Distinguish between the two views of government regulation.

Antitrust laws try to prevent monopoly in those markets where competition seems desirable. On the other hand, the *regulation of natural monopolies* tries to control price, output, the entry of new firms, and the quality of service in industries in which monopoly appears inevitable or even desirable. *Natural monopolies*, such as local electricity transmission, local phone service, or a city subway system, are regulated. Several other industries, such as land and air transportation, were regulated in the past based on the same idea but have since been deregulated.

Two Views of Government Regulation

Why do governments regulate the price and output of certain markets? There are two views of regulation. The first view has been the one discussed so far—namely, such regulation is in the *public interest.* Regulation promotes social welfare by reducing the price and increasing the output when a market is served most efficiently by one or just a few firms.

A second view is that such regulation is not in the public interest but is in the *special interest* of regulated firms. According to this view, well-organized producer groups expect to profit from government regulation by persuading public officials to impose restrictions that these groups find attractive. Such restrictions include limiting entry into the industry and preventing price competition among existing firms.

Producer groups may claim that competition in their industry would hurt consumers. For example, the alleged problem of "cut-throat" competition among taxi drivers has led to regulations that eliminated price competition and restricted the number of taxis in many large metropolitan areas. The problem is that regulation has made taxis more expensive and harder to find. Thus, taxi regulations favor the special interest of the taxi industry rather than the public interest of consumers. Some economists argue that in this instance, government regulation is a failed policy. The special-interest theory may be valid even when the initial intent of the legislation was in the consumer interest. Over time, the regulators may start acting more in the special interests of producers.

Digital Vision/Getty Images

Why do you think it is desirable for local energy transmission to be regulated by government?

Compare the two views of government regulation. **CHECKPOINT**

COMPETITIVE TRENDS IN THE U.S. ECONOMY

LO3
Discuss why U.S. markets have grown more competitive in recent decades.

The U.S. economy has grown more competitive in the last half century. The number of industries judged to be competitive increased from about half of all industries in 1960 to more than three-fourths today. Causes of increased competition include antitrust activity, deregulation, international trade, and technological change. Consider the impact of each.

Antitrust Activity

As noted already, antitrust officials now spend most of their time evaluating the impact of proposed mergers on market competition. Perhaps the most significant antitrust action in recent years not involving a merger was the case antitrust officials from the U.S. Department of Justice brought against Microsoft. They charged Microsoft with having a monopoly in operating-system software and with attempting to extend this monopoly to the Web browser market. The settlement with Microsoft gives personal-computer makers greater freedom to install non-Microsoft software on new machines.

Deregulation

For most of the twentieth century, industries such as trucking, airlines, securities trading, banking, and telecommunications were regulated by the government to limit price competition and restrict entry. The trend in recent decades has been toward **deregulation**, which reduces or eliminates government regulations. For the most part, deregulation has increased competition and benefited consumers.

Take, for example, the regulation and deregulation of airlines. The Civil Aeronautics Board (CAB), established in 1938, once strictly regulated U.S. interstate airlines. Any potential entrant interested in serving an interstate route had to persuade the CAB that the route needed another airline, a task that proved impossible. During the 40 years of regulation, potential entrants submitted more than 150 applications for long-distance routes, *but not a single new interstate airline was allowed.* The CAB also forced strict compliance with regulated prices. Any airline seeking to lower its prices on any route would face a rate hearing, during which both the CAB and that airline's competitors would scrutinize the request. In effect, the CAB created a cartel that fixed prices among the 10 existing major airlines and blocked new entry.

deregulation A reduction in government control over prices and firm entry in previously regulated markets, such as airlines and trucking

In 1978, despite opposition from the established airlines and their labor unions, Congress passed the Airline Deregulation Act, which allowed price competition and new entry. By 2000, airfares averaged 27 percent below previously regulated prices. Passenger miles nearly tripled. Airlines became more productive by filling a greater percentage of seats. The net benefits of airline deregulation to consumers now exceed $25 billion per year, or more than $80 per U.S. resident.

Regulations that limited competition have also been repealed in trucking, securities trading, banking, and telecommunications. For the most part, these industries have become more competitive as a result of deregulation. Consumers benefit from lower prices and better products.

International Trade

Foreign imports increased competition in many industries, including autos, tires, and steel. Many imported goods were attractive to U.S. consumers because of their superior quality and lower prices. Finding themselves at a cost and technological disadvantage, U.S. producers initially asked for government protection from foreign competitors through trade barriers, such as quotas and tariffs. Despite their efforts to block foreign goods, U.S. producers still lost market share to imports.

For example, General Motors dominates U.S. auto manufacturing. GM's sales recently accounted for 47 percent of U.S. automobile sales by U.S. firms. However, as illustrated in Figure 7.6, when sales by non-U.S. producers are included, GM's share of the U.S. auto market falls to only about 22 percent. To survive in the market, U.S. producers improved quality and offered products at more competitive prices.

Figure 7.6 GM's Share of the Automobile Market in the United States vs. the Competition

What does this graphic suggest about the impact of international trade on General Motors and the U.S. market for automobiles?

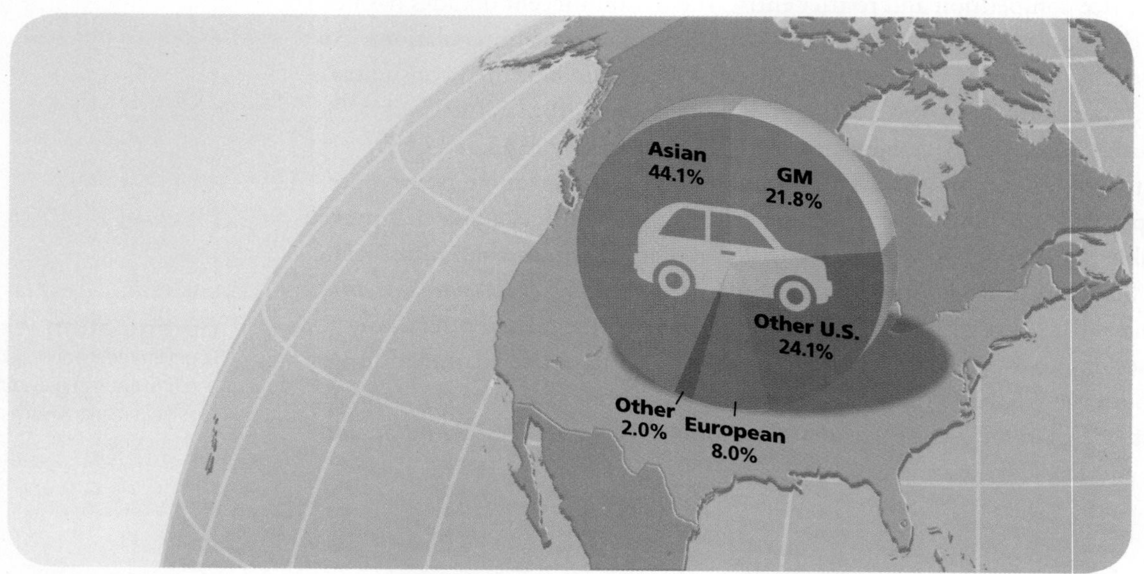

Technological Change

Some industries are growing more competitive as a result of technological change. Here are examples: In the past three decades, the prime-time audience share of the three major TV networks (NBC, CBS, and ABC) dropped from about 90 percent to less than 30 percent as satellite and cable technology delivered many more channels.

Despite Microsoft's dominance in operating systems, the packaged software market for personal computers barely existed in 1980. It now thrives in a technology-rich environment populated by thousands of software makers. Also, the Internet has opened possibilities for greater competition in a number of industries, from online stock trading to all types of electronic commerce and social networks. Some websites offer consumers information about the price and availability of products. This makes comparison shopping easier and lowers the transaction costs of buying and selling.

Why have U.S. markets grown more competitive in recent decades? **CHECKPOINT**

Math in Economics

Common Core Number and Operations—Fractions

When multiplying fractions, you multiply the numerators by each other and multiply the denominators by each other. Write the answer it its simplest form.

EXAMPLE Standard Products Inc. sells a pack of five DVD-R disks for $15. It offers a one-fifth discount to customers who buy online directly from the warehouse. What is the dollar value of the discount for purchasing online?

SOLUTION Write $15 as a fraction by placing it over 1. Multiply this fraction by 1/5 to find the amount of the discount when you buy online.

$$\frac{\$15}{1} \times \frac{1}{5} = \frac{\$15}{5} = \$3$$

A customer who buys a pack of DVD-R disks online saves $3.

Practice the Skill Find the discount for each situation in exercises 1–3.

1. A bicycle is offered for sale at 1/4 off its regular price of $240.
2. A computer is offered for sale at 1/10 off its regular price of $350.
3. A pair of shoes is offered at 2/3 off the regular price of $96.
4. Explain why large firms are often better able to offer discounts than smaller firms are.

7.3 ASSESSMENT

Think Critically

1. Imagine there are two large discount stores in a small town. Describe one way in which consumers might be harmed if these stores merged and one way they might benefit.
2. The basic antitrust laws in the United States have not changed very much in many years. Still, over time, there has been a significant difference in the way these laws have been enforced. What could explain this situation?
3. Fifty years ago, the vast majority of shoes sold in the United States were manufactured in this country. In recent years, U.S.-made shoes have accounted for less than 10 percent of this market. How has foreign competition reduced the monopoly power of U.S. shoe producers?
4. What would happen to the market power of a firm that found, patented, and received FDA approval to market a drug that prevents HIV infections? Why might such a firm not charge an extremely high price for this drug?

Graphing Exercises

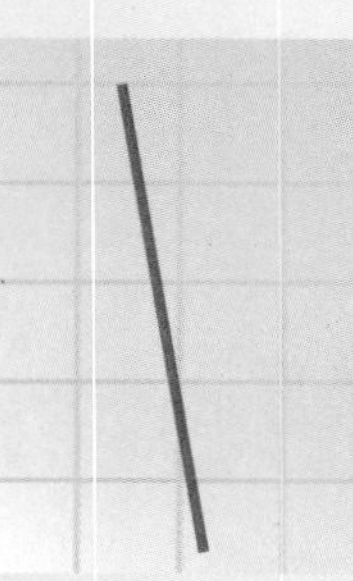

5. Study the demand curve shown at the right. First, identify what's measured on the horizontal axis and the vertical axis. The demand curve is either for a drug that thousands of people need to stay healthy, or it is for a particular brand of shampoo. Decide which product the demand curve represents and explain how you know this. How much power does the firm have to set its own price?

Make Academic Connections

6. **Technology** The U.S. Postal Service once had a government-enforced monopoly on delivering first-class mail. The USPS earned a profit but was not always known for efficiency. Then the Internet and other delivery systems created competition that drastically reduced the number of first-class letters the post office delivered. It began to lose money and was threatened with bankruptcy, after reporting a 2010 loss of more than $5 billion. Investigate what has happened to the USPS since 2011. What impact did its loss of monopoly power have?

Working in small teams, identify a firm that operates in your community under government regulation. List and evaluate reasons for this regulation. Describe what your team believes would happen if the government regulation for this firm was eliminated. Compare your team's answers with those of other teams.

Connect to History

The North American Fur Trade

From 1804 to 1816, two companies—the Hudson Bay Company (HBC) headquartered in London and the Northwestern Company (NWC) of Montreal—dominated the North American fur trade. Both companies operated over large areas of the Canadian wilderness. For the most part, each respected the other's territory and business operation without a formal market-sharing agreement.

With the start of the Napoleonic Wars in Europe, the demand for furs declined sharply because British traders could no longer sell North American furs to Europeans. The HBC suffered greater losses than its rival, because the HBC's charter prohibited it from trading anywhere but England. The NWC, on the other hand, was able to find markets in China, the United States, and even Europe. Despite the drop in demand, the HBC refused to slow down its operations because it hoped that the war would be short. It also did not want to jeopardize its business relations with the Native Americans, from whom it purchased the pelts. Instead, in an attempt to control supply and maintain prices, it chose to store the furs it collected.

However, while the two companies previously had respected each other's territory, the HBC's financial problems led it to end their informal agreement. It began to move into the area in which the NWC had been trapping exclusively. The cost of obtaining furs rose as competition between the companies drove up the price each had to pay the Native Americans. Both companies also attempted to disrupt the other's operation by employing "bully boys." This harmful competition ended in 1821, when the companies agreed to merge and form a monopoly. The new company brought an end to the destructive practices and lowered costs by taking advantage of the economies of scale. The combined company also provided a unified front in purchasing from the Native Americans.

Think Critically **Referring to the characteristics of monopolistic competition and oligopoly, analyze the behavior of the Hudson Bay Company and the Northwest Company during the period from 1804 to 1821. What effect do you think the merger of the two companies had on the price of fur?**

Library of Congress, Prints & Photographs Division, 3b40570u

Chapter 7 Summary

7.1 Perfect Competition and Monopoly

A. Perfectly competitive markets share four features: (1) they involve many buyers and sellers; (2) producers supply the same standard product; (3) buyers are fully informed about the price, quality, and availability of products, and sellers are fully informed about all resources and technology used to make them; and (4) firms and resources are free to enter or leave the market.

B. The price that individual producers in perfect competition charge is determined by market supply and market demand.

C. A monopoly is the only supplier of a product that has no close substitutes. For monopolies to exist in the long run, there must be barriers to entry. These may include legal restrictions, economies of scale, and control of essential resources not available to other firms.

D. The demand curve facing a monopoly slopes downward from left to right. This means that the firm must lower its price to sell more.

E. Many people believe that monopolies harm the general welfare because they may waste resources, exert undue influence on the government, or grow lazy and inefficient. Others believe that monopolies may have lower costs and prices because of economies of scale and that government regulation can prevent them from exploiting consumers.

ASK THE EXPERT

www.cengage.com/school/contecon

Why are cable TV rates so high?

7.2 Monopolistic Competition and Oligopoly

A. Monopolistic competition is a market structure with many firms offering similar but not identical products. Each competitor tries to attract customers by differentiating its product.

B. Oligopoly is a market structure in which a few firms dominate the market and are interdependent. Oligopolies typically exist in markets where there are economies of scale and high costs of entry.

C. Oligopolists sometimes cooperate with each other in pricing their products. When they mutually agree to set prices, they collude, though collusion is illegal in the United States.

ASK THE EXPERT

www.cengage.com/school/contecon

What are the major differences among the four market structures?

7.3 Antitrust, Regulation, and Competition

A. The federal government has passed three basic antitrust laws intended to limit the monopoly power of large businesses: (1) the Sherman Antitrust Act, (2) the Clayton Act, and (3) the Federal Trade Commission Act.

B. Mergers are either horizontal—when firms supplying the same market join—or nonhorizontal—when firms not supplying the same product join. Many of the firms that came to dominate their markets gained their power through horizontal mergers. Much of federal antitrust activity today is directed toward limiting the ability of firms to merge if doing so would create a firm with significant market power.

C. An alternative to limiting the ability of firms to merge is to regulate those that have a significant amount of market power. The federal government and all states have regulatory agencies that are supposed to protect the public's interests, but some instead benefit the special interest of the regulated industry.

D. In recent years, there has been a trend toward deregulation of many parts of the economy. U.S. markets have grown more competitive in the past few decades because of deregulation, antitrust activity, technological change, and foreign trade.

CHAPTER 7 ASSESSMENT

Review Economic Terms

Match the terms with the definitions. Some terms will not be used.

_____ 1. A market structure with many fully informed buyers and sellers of an identical product and with no barriers to entry

_____ 2. A sole supplier of a product with no close substitutes

_____ 3. Restrictions on the entry of new firms into an industry

_____ 4. The ability of a firm to raise its price without losing all its sales

_____ 5. A market structure with no entry barriers and many firms selling products differentiated enough that each firm's demand curve slopes downward

_____ 6. A market structure with a small number of firms whose behavior is interdependent

_____ 7. A group of firms that agree to act as a monopolist to increase the market price and maximize the group's profits

_____ 8. Government efforts aimed at preventing monopoly and promoting competition in markets where competition is desirable

_____ 9. The combination of two or more firms into a single firm

_____ 10. A product that is identical across sellers

_____ 11. A reduction in government control over prices and firm entry in previously regulated markets

_____ 12. Important features of a market, including the number of buyers and sellers and the product's uniformity across sellers

a. antitrust activity
b. barriers to entry
c. cartel
d. commodity
e. collusion
f. deregulation
g. excess capacity
h. market power
i. market structure
j. merger
k. monopolistic competition
l. monopoly
m. oligopoly
n. perfect competition

Review Economic Concepts

13. Which of the following statements is not true of firms in perfect competition?
    a. All producers charge the same price.
    b. All producers make the same product.
    c. Each firm tries to sell more by reducing its price.
    d. There are no barriers to entry.

14. **True or False** The demand curve facing an individual firm in perfect competition is a horizontal line.

15. A firm operating in the ________?________ market structure has no market power.

16. **True or False** A monopoly may emerge naturally when a firm has substantial economies of scale.

17. A monopoly must lower the price of its product in order to
    a. sell more output.
    b. earn a profit.
    c. shift the demand curve.
    d. match the competition.

18. **True or False** By definition, all monopolies earn substantial profits.

19. **True or False** Most monopolies tend to last for a long time.

20. Suppose a giant monopoly is created when one firm buys up all the individual firms in a perfectly competitive market. In this case, the ________?________ curve becomes the monopolist's demand curve.

21. Firms in monopolistic competition
    a. all produce exactly the same product.
    b. all charge the same price.
    c. all earn the same profit.
    d. all work to differentiate their products.

22. **True or False** One problem for society resulting from monopoly is that the monopoly may have too much influence on the political system.

23. Which of the following is not a way in which sellers in monopolistic competition differentiate their products?
    a. physical differences
    b. location and services
    c. collusion
    d. product image

24. A firm that experiences ________?________ can lower its average cost by selling more of the good.

25. The demand curve facing a firm operating in monopolistic competition
    a. is a vertical line drawn at the number of units.
    b. is a horizontal line drawn at the market price.
    c. slopes downward from left to right.
    d. slopes upward from left to right.

26. In a(n) ________?________ oligopoly, the product is identical across producers.

27. Firms in an oligopoly
    a. are totally independent from each other.
    b. are interdependent.
    c. always have excess capacity.
    d. None of the above is true of an oligopoly.

28. **True or False** The minimum efficient scale is the greatest rate of output at which a firm takes full advantage of economies of scale.

29. Which of the following industries is most likely to be regulated by government?
    a. consumer products
    b. electrical service
    c. dry-cleaning service
    d. precious jewels

30. Each of the following is a basic federal antitrust law in the United States except
    a. the Fair Labor Standards Act of 1938.
    b. the Clayton Act of 1914.
    c. the Sherman Act of 1890.
    d. the Federal Trade Commission Act of 1914.

31. **True or False** Government regulatory agencies are supposed to protect the public's interests.

Apply Economic Concepts

32. **Analyze Pricing in Oligopoly** The two largest producers of commercial aircraft in the world are Airbus of Europe and the Boeing Corporation of the United States. Most economists regard the market for large commercial aircraft as a good example of an oligopoly. Describe what you think Boeing would do if Airbus decreased the price of its airplanes by 20 percent. How does this show the interdependence of these firms?

33. **Business Law** An important question today is whether limits should be placed on what consumers may download from the Internet. According to copyright law, those who produce literature, music, films, or works of art should be able to profit from what they create. They should, in effect, have a monopoly on their work. However, if their work can be placed on the Internet for others to copy for free, some may choose not to produce anything at all. Investigate the current status of this issue, and state your opinion of what should be done.

34. **History** There was a time when Nabisco, Post Cereals, Kellogg's, and General Mills sold nearly 75 percent of the breakfast cereal purchased in the United States. These firms were part of an oligopoly, but those days are now gone. Describe what has happened to reduce the monopoly power of these firms in the market. Think about the breakfast cereal shelves in your grocery store.

35. **Marketing** Although individual firms in perfect competition do not advertise their product, they sometimes form organizations that advertise on behalf of the entire industry. The Upstate Milk Cooperative, for example, in New York collects a fee from each of its member farmers and advertises dairy products on TV and in other media. What is this organization attempting to accomplish?

36. **21st Century Skills: Leadership and Responsibility** Suppose the largest employer in your community has significant monopoly power because it receives government protection from competition. The owners of this firm earn large profits by charging high prices but they also make many charitable contributions to your community. A recent study has suggested that the government should eliminate the protection from competition that this firm enjoys. This could lead to greater competition, lower prices, and reduced profits for the firm. Explain why people who live in your community might have mixed feelings about this proposal. Would you support or oppose this proposal? Explain your answer.

Digging Deeper

with Economics e-Collection

Governments undertake antitrust activity to promote competitive markets and to reduce anticompetitive behavior among firms. Access the Gale Economics e-Collection through the URL below to find articles that discuss specific antitrust lawsuits, either in the United States or abroad. Identify the following aspects of each lawsuit: (1) the country or countries and government agencies involved, (2) the industry and/or market, (3) the company or companies involved, (4) the specific issue, (5) the result of the lawsuit if it has been settled, and (6) the source citation for the article. If a resolution of the issue is not mentioned in the article, continue to research the database to find whether it has been resolved. Be prepared to discuss the lawsuit in class.

www.cengage.com/school/contecon

SUSIE'S
Alterations
140
VALENCIA CAMERA
150

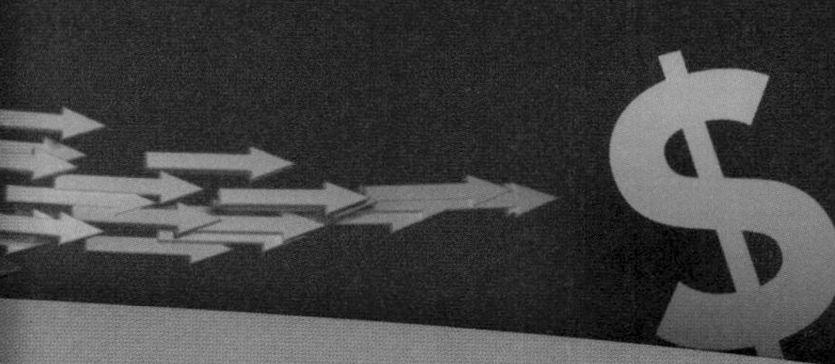

UNIT 3

Market Institutions

You are an important decision maker in our market economy. Your consumption choices and those of other consumers determine what is produced. To help supply the products that you and others demand, several institutions have developed to nurture a market economy. Among the most important are businesses, labor markets, and financial markets. You already know something about all three. You have interacted with businesses all your life. Most of you have participated in labor markets. You are even familiar with financial markets—from credit cards to bank accounts.

CHAPTER 8

Businesses

CONSIDER ...

- Why do some people decide to call themselves "boss"?
- Why start a business if most new ones don't last five years?
- What does your summer lawn-mowing operation have in common with Walmart?
- What do the abbreviations *Corp.* or *Inc.* in a company's name tell you about how the owners treat company debt?
- How is it possible that most U.S. businesses have no hired employees?

Point your browser

www.cengage.com/school/contecon

Blend Images/Jupiter Images; Background image: Pefkos/Shutterstock.com

8.1 ENTREPRENEURS

Learning Objectives

LO1 Understand the role of the entrepreneur in a market economy.

LO2 Distinguish entrepreneurs from people who perform a limited business role.

Key Terms

financial capital 237
innovation 238

In Your World

In a market economy, you are free to risk your time and savings to start a business. If the business succeeds, your reward is profit. If the business fails, you could lose a bundle. Chances of success are not great. Most new businesses don't last five years. On the other hand, some businesses survive, a few thrive, and a tiny few make their founders wealthy. Despite the high rate of business failure, the promise of profit attracts many prospective entrepreneurs. By putting their ideas into action, entrepreneurs drive the economy forward.

ROLE OF ENTREPRENEURS

LO1 Understand the role of the entrepreneur in a market economy.

An entrepreneur is the prime mover in the market economy—a visionary, someone who can see what others can't. The entrepreneur's role is to discover and introduce new and better products and more efficient ways of doing things. Because new products often involve long and costly development, they are risky. Entrepreneurs must have the confidence to accept that risk and must inspire confidence in others, such as resource suppliers and lenders. In short, *an entrepreneur comes up with an idea, turns that idea into a marketable product, accepts the risk of success or failure, and claims any resulting profit or loss.*

An entrepreneur tries to earn a profit by satisfying consumer wants. A business can consist simply of one self-employed person earning a few thousand dollars mowing lawns during the summer. Or, a business can be as complex as Walmart, with 2 million full-time employees, 8,400 stores around the world, and sales exceeding $440 billion per year. The lawn-mowing operation and Walmart are both businesses. There are more than 30 million for-profit businesses in the United States. Most consist of just one self-employed person often working part time in the business. Most of these self-employed enterprises will remain tiny. A handful will become the largest businesses in the world.

Entrepreneurs and Creative Change

The introduction of new or better products and new production methods are sources of technological progress and economic growth in the economy. Entrepreneurs initiate four types of creative changes in a market economy.

1. **Introduce New Products** Some entrepreneurs try to come up with new products, opening up markets that had not existed. For example, as a

Harvard undergraduate, Mark Zuckerberg was the primary creator of Facebook. By 2011, Facebook had more than 600 million active users and more than $2 billion in advertising revenue. Zuckerberg, the chief executive officer, owned 24 percent of the company, valued at more than $10 billion.

2. **Improve Quality of Existing Products** Some entrepreneurs begin with an existing product and make it better. For example, Howard Schultz took the simple cup of coffee and turned it into liquid gold by offering higher quality and greater variety in a more inviting atmosphere. Founded by Schultz in 1985, Starbucks Coffee now is a multibillion-dollar operation with 137,000 employees at 17,000 locations around the world. As another example, Guy Laliberté, at the age of 25, founded Cirque du Soleil in 1984 as a modern update on the circus. By 2011 he had created 21 different shows, some touring and some staying put. Through his creative efforts, he accumulated personal wealth of $3 billion.
3. **Introduce New Production Methods** Some entrepreneurs combine resources more efficiently to reduce production costs. They use less costly materials, employ better technology, or combine resources in more economical ways. Henry Ford, for example, introduced the assembly line, where automobiles move along a conveyer and the workers stay put. Ford didn't invent the automobile, but his assembly line made owning one affordable to millions of households. Similarly, Ray Croc did not invent the hamburger or the hamburger stand, but he applied the principles of mass production to make McDonald's hamburgers quickly and cheaply, first across the nation and then around the world.
4. **Introduce New Ways of Doing Business** Some entrepreneurs step outside existing business models to create a new way of doing business. For

Span the Globe

Some Chinese Strike It Rich

One way to measure the success of the Chinese economy's transition to a free market system is to look at the wealth of its new entrepreneurs. *Forbes* magazine, which in 2003 showed no Chinese billionaires, now lists 115 among the world's 1,210 billionaires. An additional 36 reside in Hong Kong. While the wealth of a quarter of the nation's billionaires comes from real estate, the wealth of the others comes from a wide range of businesses, from the Internet and solar energy to manufacturing and retail. The number is expected to rise as the Chinese economy continues to evolve.

Think Critically **If you lived in China and wanted to start a business, what field would you choose and why?**

Source: Flannery, Russell, "China's Billionaire Boom: Will It Last," *Forbes*, March 14, 2011

example, Michael Dell began in 1984 with $1,000 and the idea to sell computers directly to customers rather than through retailers. His made-to-order computers are sold by phone and over the Internet. Dell is now the world's largest computer seller, with sales exceeding $170 million a day.

Financing the Business

A good idea in itself does not guarantee profit. To succeed, entrepreneurs must figure out how best to transform their ideas into reality. They must obtain **financial capital**, that is, the money needed to start or expand the business. They must then acquire the necessary resources, including hiring employees and buying supplies.

Financial capital comes from various sources. One source is a loan from a bank. Another is *venture capitalists*—individuals or companies that specialize in financing start-up firms. Entrepreneurs also often draw from their own savings to invest in the new enterprise. Some even sell everything they own to get the business off the ground. For example, filmmaker Michael Moore sold all his possessions to finance his first documentary film, *Roger and Me.* To accept such risks, entrepreneurs must have confidence in their ideas. Moore's movie cost $160,000 and sold $6.7 million in tickets at the box office.

Profit Attracts Competitors

If an innovation succeeds in the market, many people benefit. The entrepreneur is rewarded with profit and the satisfaction of creating something of value. Workers are rewarded with more and better jobs. Consumers are rewarded with new and better products. The government benefits from higher tax revenue, which can be used to fund public goods and services or to lower other taxes. Overall the economy reaches a higher level of business activity. This translates into a higher standard of living for the people who live in the economy.

Entrepreneurs may earn profit in the short run. However, profit attracts competitors and substitutes. Others will enter the market in the long run and try to duplicate the success of the original entrepreneur. Competitors try to offer a better product or a lower price. Because these copycats must be creative and take risks, they, too, are considered entrepreneurs.

The original entrepreneur must fight to remain profitable in the long run. Ultimately, the pursuit of profit can lead to a chain of events that creates new and better products, more competition, more production, higher quality, and lower prices. Entrepreneurs are the key players in a market economy. They supply the creative sparks that drive the economy forward.

Profits tell entrepreneurs that they are on the right track. Losses tell them to change tracks. If the new business loses money and has no prospects for a turnaround, this tells the entrepreneur to find a better use for the resources. You could think of profits as a way of keeping score, a way of telling entrepreneurs whether they are winning or losing. When an entrepreneur wins, many others in the economy win as well. When an entrepreneur loses, it's primarily the entrepreneur who suffers.

financial capital Money needed to start or expand a business

Explain the role of entrepreneurs in a market economy.

WHO ISN'T AN ENTREPRENEUR?

LO2 Distinguish entrepreneurs from people who perform a limited business role.

Some people may carry out just one of the functions of an entrepreneur. For example, they may dream up a new product or process, they may manage resources, or they may assume the risk of success or failure. Carrying out just one of the roles alone does not make you an entrepreneur, however. A way of determining more about who is an entrepreneur is to learn more about people in business who are not entrepreneurs.

Invention, Innovation, and Entrepreneurs

Innovation is the process of turning an invention into a marketable product. Inventors are entrepreneurs if they bear the risk of success or failure. Most inventors work for firms as paid employees. For example, corporations such as Pfizer, Dow Chemical, or Intel employ thousands of scientists to improve existing products and develop new ones. These corporate inventors are paid even in years when their creative juices slow down. Because these inventors take no more risks than most other employees, they are not considered to be entrepreneurs.

Figure 8.1 shows the source of inventions since 1990 as measured by the number of U.S. patents awarded. The number of patents nearly doubled between 1990 and 2009. The share of patents awarded to individuals fell from 19 percent to only 8 percent, however. Some of these individual inventors are in the business of creating new products and then selling the ideas to others. Because they accept risks, self-employed inventors usually are entrepreneurs.

innovation The process of turning an invention into a marketable product

Managers and Entrepreneurs

Most entrepreneurs do not simply sell their good ideas to others. They try to bring their ideas to the market by going into business. Then they claim any profit or suffer any loss that results. Starting up a business does not necessarily mean

FIGURE 8.1 Sources of U.S. Patents Awarded for Inventions by Year

The number of patents grew from 89,400 in 1990 to 166,700 in 2009. In 1990, 19 percent of all patents were awarded to individuals. By 2009, only 8 percent went to individuals.

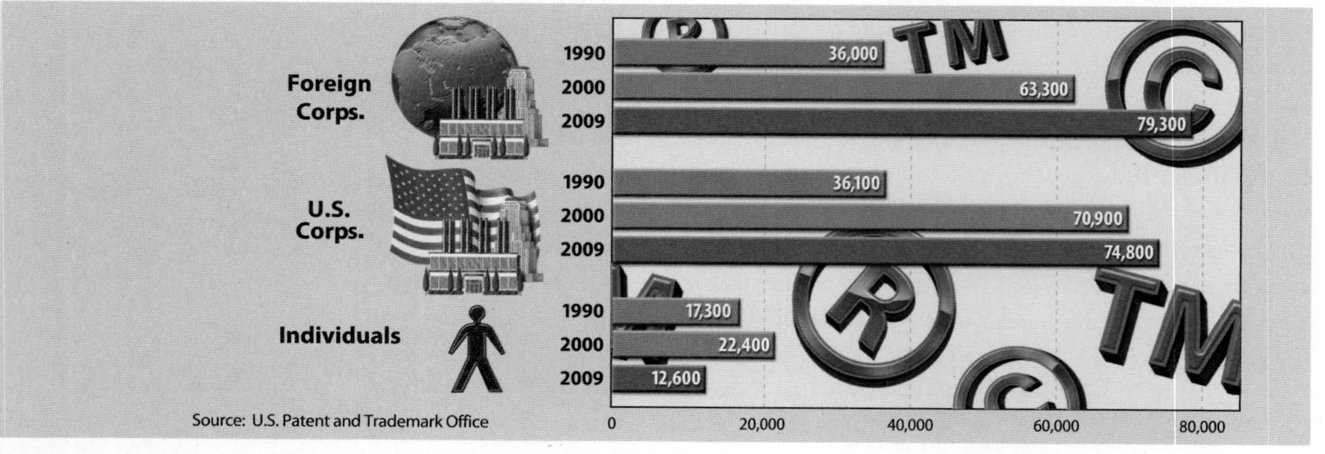

ESSENTIAL QUESTION

Standard CEE 14: Entrepreneurship

Entrepreneurs take on the calculated risk of starting new businesses, either by embarking on new ventures similar to existing ones or by introducing new innovations. Entrepreneurial innovation is an important source of economic growth.

bike shop: Creatas/Jupiter Images; digram: Andresr/iStockphoto.com

What is entrepreneurial innovation, and why is it an important source of economic growth?

the entrepreneur must manage the business. But the entrepreneur must have the power to hire and fire the manager.

For example, Dean Kamen, inventor of the Segway® Human Transporter, created a company to make and sell his invention. Kamen also hired a chief executive to run the business. Even though he didn't run the business himself, Kamen was still an entrepreneur because he had the power to hire and fire the manager. Kamen's chief executive was a well-paid employee, but not an entrepreneur. Kamen later sold his business.

Stockholders and Entrepreneurs

More than half of all households in the United States—about 60 million of them—own corporate stock. If a corporation fails, stockholders could lose the amount they paid for that particular stock. If the corporation thrives, the stock value will increase and stockholders will benefit.

People buy a corporation's stock because they believe in the managers' ability to increase the value of the business. They believe the managers can make more profitable use of their funds than they themselves can make. At the same time, the stockholders assume the risk of the company's success or failure. Does this make the stockholders entrepreneurs? No, it does not. True entrepreneurs do more than take the risk of success or failure. They decide what to produce and usually figure out how to produce it profitably. An individual stockholder, on the other hand, typically has little say in the firm's operation.

CHECKPOINT

What groups perform part of the entrepreneur's role but are not considered entrepreneurs?

8.1 ASSESSMENT

Think Critically

1. Which of the following describes an entrepreneur? (a) a person employed to mow lawns by a landscaping firm or (b) a person who buys a lawn mower to cut her neighbor's lawn for $20. Explain your answer.
2. What creative changes have fast-food restaurant owners used to distinguish their products from similar products offered by other firms?
3. Why aren't entrepreneurs likely to earn large profits from their businesses over many years?
4. Why aren't the engineers who developed the Apple iPad entrepreneurs?
5. What role do entrepreneurs play in the U.S. economy?

Graphing Exercise

6. Many entrepreneurs begin their businesses by inventing a product and then patenting it. Construct a bar graph from the data in the table that concerns patents granted by the federal government. What does your graph show about the number of inventions by individuals and by corporations? Why are only some of these inventions examples of entrepreneurship?

PATENTS GRANTED TO INDIVIDUALS AND CORPORATIONS, 1990–2009 (VALUES IN THOUSANDS)

Year	Patents Granted to Individuals	Patents Granted to U.S. Corporations
1990	17,300	36,100
1995	17,400	44,500
2000	22,400	70,900
2005	14,700	65,200
2009	12,600	74,000

Source: U.S. Bureau of the Census, *Statistical Abstract of the United States, 2011*, p. 510.

Make Academic Connections

7. **History** Review an American history textbook to identify a historical figure who was an important entrepreneur. Explain what this person did and the influence he or she had on the development of the U.S. economy.
8. **Marketing** Walmart sells the same products as many other discount stores, but it is much more successful than most. What did founder Sam Walton do differently that made him a successful entrepreneur?

Working in small teams, identify a local business that has been started in the past five years and has become successful. Describe the types of creative change it established that allowed it to prosper. How have other members of your community benefited from this business? Compare your team's answers with those of other teams.

MOVERS AND SHAKERS

Debbi Fields

Founder, Mrs. Fields Cookies®

Courtesy of Mrs. Fields Cookies

Cookie queen Debbi Fields enjoyed baking cookies as a young woman. After countless experiments, she hit on a recipe that would be the foundation of her success. By the time she was 18, Debbi's cookies were well known in her hometown of Oakland, California. Although she admits she was not an outstanding student, she proved to be a savvy businesswoman. At the age of 20, she married Randy Fields, a financial consultant. "Soon after that I started to think about what it was that I loved to do," she said, "and I realized I loved to make cookies. Six months later I had a business plan."

In 1977, with a $50,000 loan from her husband, Debbi decided to channel her baking skills into a business. She opened Mrs. Fields Chocolate Chippery. On her first day of business she did not make a single sale. She took a risk and went outside her shop handing out free cookies. Soon her shop was full of customers asking for more.

Mrs. Fields® opened 225 new stores between 1985 and 1988. By the late 1980s the company had grown to 425 cookie stores in the United States and had annual revenues of more than $87 million. Real success came with the introduction of software that handled supply-chain issues, enabling the company to keep production costs low. Debbi has high standards. Her motto is "Good Enough Never Is®". She once threw out a store's inventory for not being "soft and chewy" enough. She said her cookies, "have to be perfect. There's no word at Mrs. Fields for 'it's good enough.' I'll go in and throw away $600 worth of product. I don't think about what I'm throwing away, I just assume that there's been some reason why the people were not taught what the standards of the company are."

Mrs. Fields has many ideas for achieving success:

- **Success is innovation** Mrs. Fields Inc. was the first company in the food retailing business to consolidate operations and use a state-of-the-art computer system.
- **Success is believing in yourself** Debbi did not listen to the critic who told her, "A cookie store is a bad idea. Besides, the market research reports say America likes crispy cookies, not soft and chewy cookies like you make."
- **Success starts with a great recipe** "First, the recipe for success requires passion—you've got to love what you do. Second, you've got to persevere. There are many challenges, and it is a scary road out there—but you have to see it through. Finally, focus on perfection. To have a product or service that will last, you have to be the best, not 'me too'."
- **Success is accepting risk** "People talk about success, dream about success, and want to be successful. But to move to the next rung on the ladder, you've got to take risks. You've got to move out of your comfort zone."
- **Success is loving what you do and trying** "The important thing is not being afraid to take a chance. Remember, the greatest failure is to not try. Once you find something you love to do, be the best at doing it."

Think Critically **Using one or more of Debbi Fields' ideas for success, write a paragraph about how you could build a business around a special interest or ability you have.**

Sources: Debbi Fields, Overview, Personal Life, Career Details, Social and Economic Impact, Chronology: Debbi Fields - Cookies, Cookie, Stores, Business, Retail, and Standards, http://encyclopedia.jrank.org/articles/pages/6203/Fields-Debbi.html#ixzz1Qbqfwlt6; http://www.yeartosuccess.com/members/y2s/blog/VIEW/00000021/00000273/Inspiration-from-Debbi-Fields-Rose.html; and http://www.goodreads.com/quotes/show/71108

8.2 SOLE PROPRIETORSHIPS AND PARTNERSHIPS

Key Terms

sole proprietorship 242
liability 244
partnership 245
general partnership 245
limited partnership 245

Learning Objectives

LO1 Describe the advantages and disadvantages of sole proprietorships.

LO2 Describe the advantages and disadvantages of partnerships.

In Your World

Suppose you have decided to become an entrepreneur by opening a business next summer. As an entrepreneur starting a business, you must make all kinds of decisions. One of the first is to decide how to organize the business. What form of business would work best? You can organize your business in one of three basic ways: as a sole proprietorship, a partnership, or a corporation. Each has its advantages and disadvantages. Sole proprietorships and partnerships are the easiest to start, but they each also may pose certain risks for business owners.

SOLE PROPRIETORSHIP

LO1 Describe the advantages and disadvantages of sole proprietorships.

The simplest form of business organization is the sole proprietorship, which is a firm owned and run by a single individual like you. That person, the sole proprietor, earns all the firm's profits and is responsible for all the firm's losses. Although some **sole proprietorships** hire many employees, most do not. Most consist of just one person, the sole proprietor, who is self-employed. A self-employed person is not considered to be a hired employee.

Who Is a Sole Proprietor?

The majority of businesses in your community are owned by sole proprietors. These include self-employed plumbers, farmers, hairstylists, truckers, authors, lawyers, and dentists. Again, most sole proprietorships consist of just one self-employed person. A self-employed person may work at the business full time throughout the year, part of the year, or part time. For example, most self-employed farmers hold other jobs as their primary occupations.

Nearly three-quarters of all businesses in the United States are owned by sole proprietors. There are 22 million sole proprietorships. Because this type of business is typically small, however, sole proprietorships generate only 4 percent of all U.S. business sales.

sole proprietorship
The simplest form of business organization; a firm that is owned and run by one person who sometimes hires other workers

Figure 8.2 shows the distribution of sole proprietorships based on firm revenue and the type of industry in which the business operates. You can see in pie chart (A)

Figure 8.2 Distribution of Sole Proprietorships Based on Annual Sales and by Industry

Two-thirds of all sole proprietorships had annual sales of less than $25,000 per year. Most sole proprietorships are service businesses.

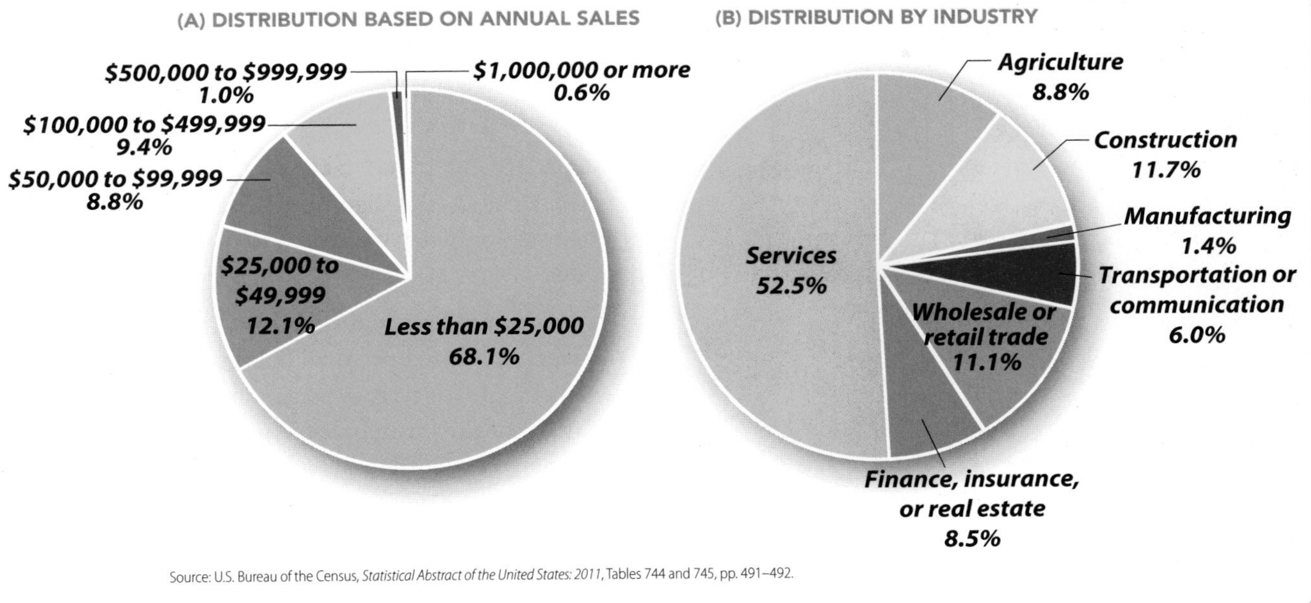

Source: U.S. Bureau of the Census, *Statistical Abstract of the United States: 2011*, Tables 744 and 745, pp. 491–492.

that nearly all sole proprietorships are small. About two-thirds reported annual sales, or revenue, of less than $25,000. Only 0.6 percent had sales of $1 million or more.

Pie chart (B) in Figure 8.2 shows the industry breakdown of sole proprietors. One-half supply services, such as health services and business services. Less than one in ten is in agriculture.

Advantages of Sole Proprietorships

The sole proprietorship is the most common type of business for a reason. It offers several advantages.

1. **Easy to Start** A sole proprietorship is easy to start. This form involves minimum red tape and legal expense. A sole proprietor might only need to get a business license and a permit to collect state or local sales taxes if those taxes apply.
2. **Few Government Regulations** Once established, a sole proprietorship faces few government regulations beyond maintaining tax records and complying with employment laws. Because most consist of only the self-employed sole proprietor with no hired employees, there are no employment laws to worry about.
3. **Complete Control** The sole proprietor is the boss, with complete authority over all business decisions, such as what to produce and how to produce it.
4. **Owner Keeps All Profit** The sole proprietor does not have to share profits with anyone.

Digital Vision/Getty Images

Do you think the advantages of organizing a business as a sole proprietor outweigh the disadvantages? Why or why not?

5. **Lower Taxes** Any profit generated by a sole proprietorship is taxed only once, as the owner's personal income. As you will learn later, most corporate profit is taxed twice.
6. **Pride of Ownership** Creating a successful business and watching it grow can provide a sole proprietor tremendous personal pride and satisfaction.

Disadvantages of Sole Proprietorships

There are also some significant disadvantages of sole proprietorships, when compared to other forms of business.

1. **Unlimited Personal Liability** A sole proprietor faces unlimited personal liability for any business losses. **Liability** is the legal obligation to pay any debts of the business. Sole proprietors are personally responsible for paying all their business debts. If the business goes bankrupt or is sued, the owner is personally responsible. To pay off debts, the sole proprietor may have to draw from personal savings or sell personal assets, such as a home or an automobile.
2. **Difficulty Raising Financial Capital** Because the sole proprietor has no partners or other financial backers, raising enough money to get the business going can be a problem. Banks are reluctant to lend to a new business with no track record and few assets. Even a sole proprietorship that's been around for a while may still seem risky to lenders.
3. **Limited Life** With a sole proprietorship, the business and the owner are one and the same. The business ends when the owner dies or leaves the business. The firm's assets can be sold or turned over to someone else, who may restart the business. The result is a new firm with new ownership.
4. **Difficulty Finding and Keeping Good Workers** Because of the lack of permanence and difficulty raising financial capital, sole proprietors have trouble offering workers the job security and opportunity for advancement available in larger businesses. Therefore, a sole proprietorship may have difficulty attracting and retaining talented employees.
5. **Broad Responsibility** Sole proprietors shoulder a great deal of responsibility. They usually must manage the firm, maintain financial records, oversee production, market the product, keep up with competition, and perform dozens

liability The legal obligation to pay any debts of the business

of other tasks. It is not likely that one person can do all of these things well. However, young firms typically cannot afford to hire experts to carry out each of these functions. This broad responsibility may lead to long work days—and a lot of stress—for the sole proprietor.

CHECKPOINT Explain the advantages and disadvantages of sole proprietorships.

PARTNERSHIPS

LO2 Describe the advantages and disadvantages of partnerships.

Another relatively simple form of business organization is the **partnership**, which involves two or more individuals who agree to contribute resources to the business in return for a share of any profit or loss. A partnership sometimes consists of one person who is talented at running the business and one or more who supply the money needed to get the business going. There are a little more than 3 million partnerships in the United States. They account for about 10 percent of all businesses and about 14 percent of all business sales.

Figure 8.3 shows the distribution of partnerships by annual revenue in pie chart (A) and by industry in pie chart (B). More than half of all partnerships had annual sales of less than $25,000. Only 8.4 percent had sales of $1 million or more. More than half of all partnerships are in finance, insurance, or real estate. Though not shown in the pie chart, real-estate firms alone account for about 45 percent of all partnerships.

Types of Partnerships

There are two broad types of partnerships: general partnerships and limited partnerships. Each divides responsibilities and liabilities differently.

General Partnerships The most common type of partnership is the **general partnership**, where partners share both in the responsibility for running the business and in any liability arising from its operation. Professional groups such as doctors, lawyers, and accountants often form general partnerships.

Limited Partnerships With a **limited partnership**, at least one partner must be a general partner. General partners manage the business and have unlimited personal liability for the partnership. The other partners don't manage the business. Their contribution is strictly financial. The most they can lose is the amount they invested in the firm. For example, limited partners in a real-estate business put up most of the money for a general partner to buy land, divide it into housing lots, build homes on those lots, and then sell the homes. Because their liability is limited, they are called *limited* partners. A limited partnership can have many limited partners but must have at least one general partner.

partnership Two or more people agree to contribute resources to the business in return for a share of the profit

general partnership Partners share both in the responsibility of running the business and in any liability from its operation

limited partnership At least one general partner runs the business and bears unlimited personal liability; other partners provide financial capital but have limited liability

Advantages of Partnerships

Partnerships offer several advantages.

1. **Easy to Start** As with the sole proprietorship, partnerships are easy to start. The partners need only agree on how to share business responsibilities, profits, and losses. Some partnerships are formed with articles of partnership, a legal agreement spelling out each partner's rights and responsibilities. In most states, partnerships that do not have their own agreement are governed by the Uniform Partnership Act (UPA), which established partnership rules.
2. **Few Government Regulations** Once the partnership has begun operating, it faces relatively few government regulations. Like the sole proprietorship, the partnership must maintain accurate tax records and comply with employment laws.
3. **Shared Decision Making and Increased Specialization** A sole proprietor makes all key business decisions. But general partners usually share decision-making responsibilities. On average, there are about six partners per partnership in the United States. By discussing important decisions, partners may make better decisions than a sole proprietor could make alone. By relying on the different skills of each partner, general partnerships also may be more efficient than sole proprietors. For example, one partner may be good at dealing with the public while another excels at record keeping and paperwork.
4. **Greater Ability to Raise Financial Capital** Partnerships often find it easier than sole proprietors to raise the financial capital needed to get a business

FIGURE 8.3 Distribution of Partnerships Based on Annual Sales and Industry

Most partnerships had annual sales of less than $25,000. More than half of all partnerships are in finance, insurance, or real estate.

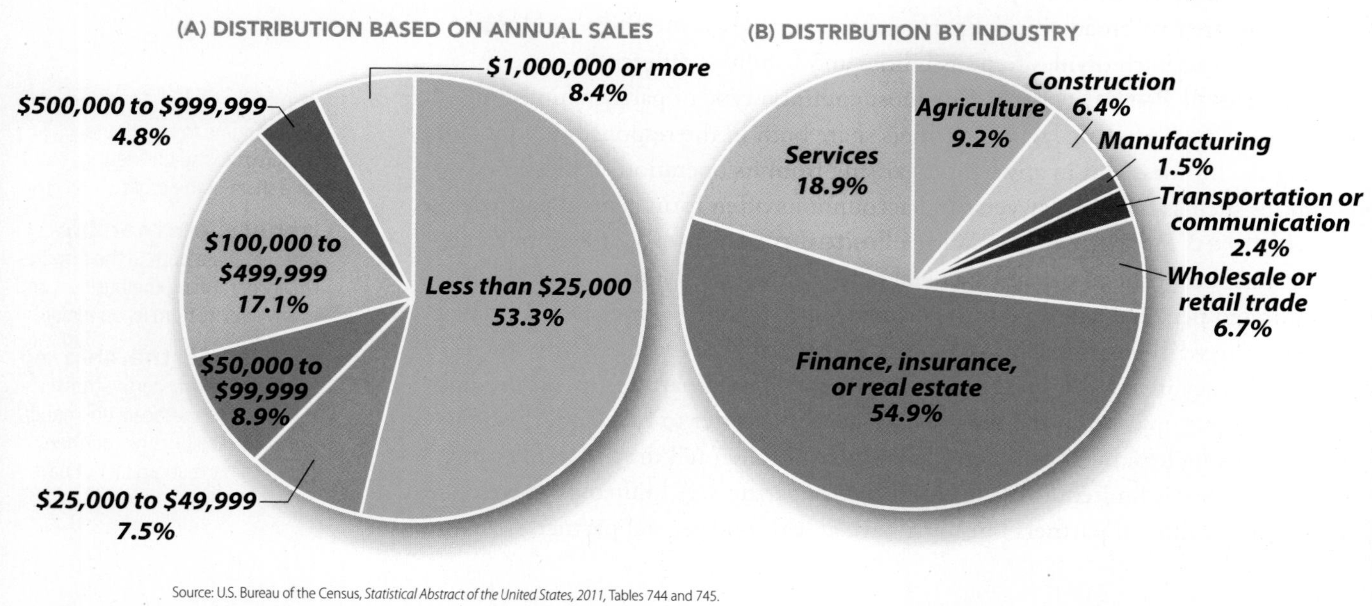

Source: U.S. Bureau of the Census, *Statistical Abstract of the United States, 2011*, Tables 744 and 745.

going. First, the partners themselves can come up with money from their own sources, such as a savings account. Second, banks may be more willing to lend money to a partnership than to a sole proprietor. With a partnership, the loans are backed by the promise and property of each general partner.

5. **More Able to Attract and Retain Workers** Compared to sole proprietors, partnerships offer employees more opportunities for advancement. For example, a partnership can make a key employee, such as a promising lawyer or accountant, a partner. A partnership typically is better able to attract and retain talented workers than is a sole proprietorship.
6. **Lower Taxes** Partners pay personal income taxes on their partnership income. The partnership itself does not have to pay a separate tax, as does a corporation.

Disadvantages of Partnerships

There also are disadvantages to partnerships. Some of these drawbacks are the same as for sole proprietorships.

1. **Unlimited Personal Liability** In a general partnership, each partner is personally responsible for paying business debts. If the business fails or is sued, the partners may have to draw from personal savings or sell personal assets, such as a home, to pay debts. This means one partner could lose everything because of another's blunder. In a limited partnership, the limited partners have less liability than the general partners. Their liability is limited to the amount of financial capital they invested.
2. **Limited Life of the Business** A partnership has no life of its own, independent of the partners. The partnership ends when one partner dies or leaves the business. A new partnership can be formed to continue the business, but the transition could be tricky. A partnership might end even if remaining partners would like it to continue.
3. **Partners May Disagree** Partners may not always agree on important decisions. Unlike a sole proprietorship, where the one owner makes all the

Digital Vision/Getty Images

In a general partnership with two partners, both are responsible for running the business and for any liability that results from its operation. If you were to start a business, would you rather be a partner or a sole proprietor? Give reasons for your answer.

decisions, partners must reach a consensus. Disagreements and disputes may hamper operations and could end the partnership.

4. **Profits Must Be Shared** Partners must share any profits according to the original partnership agreement. This may seem unfair to a partner who brings in most of the profit. Unless the sharing agreement is revised, the most productive partner may look for a better deal elsewhere. This could end the partnership. Some major law partnerships have dissolved recently because of this.

CHECKPOINT **What are the advantages and disadvantages of the partnership form of business?**

Math in Economics

Common Core Ratios and Proportional Relationships

You can calculate the value of an amount increased by a percentage by multiplying the original amount times the percent of the increase expressed as a decimal. Then add the original amount and the amount of the increase to find the new value.

EXAMPLE Find the value of $1,560.00 increased by 3%

SOLUTION 3% expressed as a decimal is 0.03. Multiply $1,560.00 times 0.03.

Add this amount to the original amount.

$1,560.00 × 0.03 = $46.80

$1,560.00 + $46.80 = $1,606.80

Practice the Skill Calculate the value of each amount when increased by the indicated percent. Write answers rounded to the nearest to cent.

1. $259.25 increased by 5%
2. $931.80 increased by 12%
3. Arnold recently started a business as a sole proprietor. His sales have not been as high as expected, and he needs to delay paying some of his expenses. His electric bill for last month was $428.10. If he does not pay it until next month, he will have to pay this amount plus a 2% penalty. How much will he be required to pay to satisfy this bill next month?

8.2 ASSESSMENT

Think Critically

1. Why are more restaurants organized as sole proprietorships than are industrial construction firms?
2. Why do some sole proprietorships become less efficient as they grow?
3. Why are many sole proprietorships run by part-time owners who earn most of their income as employees elsewhere?
4. Why do most partnerships last for only a few years or less?
5. Why do many new lawyers seek to become partners in established law firms?

Graphing Exercise

6. In 2007 all U.S. partnerships had a total of about $4.5 trillion in sales. The federal government classified partnerships into 19 categories. However, the bulk of the sales were by partnerships in seven of the federal classifications, as listed in the table below. Use the data in this table to construct a pie graph showing partnerships' sales. Why do you think some types of businesses lend themselves to being organized as partnerships?

GROSS SALES BY PARTNERSHIPS IN 2007 (VALUES IN BILLIONS OF DOLLARS)

Business Classification	Sales	Percent of Total
Manufacturing	$856	18.9%
Finance and insurance	$677	14.9%
Wholesale trade	$531	11.7%
Retail trade	$388	8.5%
Professional, scientific, and technical services	$345	7.6%
Real estate and rental and leasing	$315	6.9%
Construction	$305	6.7%
All other	$1,124	24.8%

Source: U.S. Bureau of the Census, *Statistical Abstract of the United States*, 2011, Table 743, p. 492.

Make Academic Connections

7. **Management** Make a list of all the management functions a sole proprietor must perform to be successful. What types of courses should a person who wants to own a business take? What types of experience should such a person look for in a job he or she might have while going to school?

TeamWork

Organize the class into small teams. Your team is starting a general partnership. Decide the type of business your team's partnership will run, and then decide the area of responsibility each team member will handle. Match each member's strengths and interests with the tasks to be done. Compare your team's choices with those of other teams.

21st Century Skills

Financial, Economic, Business, and Entrepreneurial Literacy

Build a Successful Business

Nearly one out of every ten adults in the United States is a sole proprietor. Although most of these businesses have sales of less than $10,000 per year, a few have sales that reach $1 million or more. About 670,000 sole proprietorships are created each year, while another 600,000 fail and cease operation.

The following is a list of steps entrepreneurs should take to increase the probability that their business will succeed.

- Create a detailed business plan based on realistic projections of costs and sales, not on wishful thinking.
- Survey the competition. Determine how to convince customers to purchase your products rather than those offered by the competition.
- Identify sources of funds to purchase resources you will need to start and maintain production. Remember to include enough to support yourself while your firm establishes itself in the market.
- Be sure you possess the skills necessary to operate the business or are able to hire employees who will carry out functions you are not able to provide.

Sources of Financial Capital

The biggest hurdle many new entrepreneurs face is gathering sufficient financial capital. Most new business do not generate much income when they begin. Their owners must have enough financial capital to pay for a place to operate, purchase raw materials, hire employees, market the product, and pay the firm's day-to-day operating expenses until all these costs can be covered from revenue generated by sales. The following are possible sources of financial capital new entrepreneurs might draw on and possible disadvantages of using each source.

- **Use personal savings.** This source is limited for most people and may leave too little money to pay for normal household expenses.
- **Ask friends or relatives to contribute funds.** This source may cause hard feelings among friends or family members and could lead others to interfere with managing the business.
- **Obtain a bank loan.** Banks lend funds to a business only if they are confident it will succeed and if the entrepreneur also comes up with a share of the financial capital. Banks usually charge higher interest rates for loans to a new business than to established firms.

Apply the Skill

Identify a technological advancement made in recent years. Describe an opportunity that it created for new entrepreneurs. List and explain four steps such an entrepreneur should take to create a sole proprietorship that would increase the probability of the firm's success.

8.3 CORPORATIONS AND OTHER ORGANIZATIONS

Learning Objectives

LO1 Describe how a corporation is established.

LO2 Understand why large businesses favor the corporate form.

LO3 Recognize other types of business organizations.

In Your World

Sole proprietorships and partnerships may suit small businesses, but they are not appropriate for larger, more complex businesses. Larger businesses need a more flexible organization that allows the firm to raise sufficient financial capital and cope with a changing business environment. The corporation is the most influential and complex form of business organization.

Key Terms

corporation 251
articles of incorporation 252
private corporation 253
publicly traded corporation 253
S corporation 255
limited liability company (LLC) 255
limited liability partnership (LLP) 255
cooperative 255
not-for-profit organizations 256

INCORPORATING

LO1
Describe how a corporation is established.

A **corporation** is a legal entity with an existence distinct from the people who organize it, own it, and run it. The corporation can earn a profit, lose money, be sued, and even be found guilty of a crime. There are about 6 million corporations in the United States, accounting for 18.3 percent of all businesses and 82.3 percent of all business sales. Figure 8.4 summarizes the share of businesses by each type of business organization and the share of sales by each.

corporation A legal entity with an existence that is distinct from the people who organize, own, and run it

FIGURE 8.4 Comparing Corporations with Sole Proprietorships and Partnerships

Sole proprietorships account for nearly three-quarters of all U.S. businesses, but corporations account for most business sales.

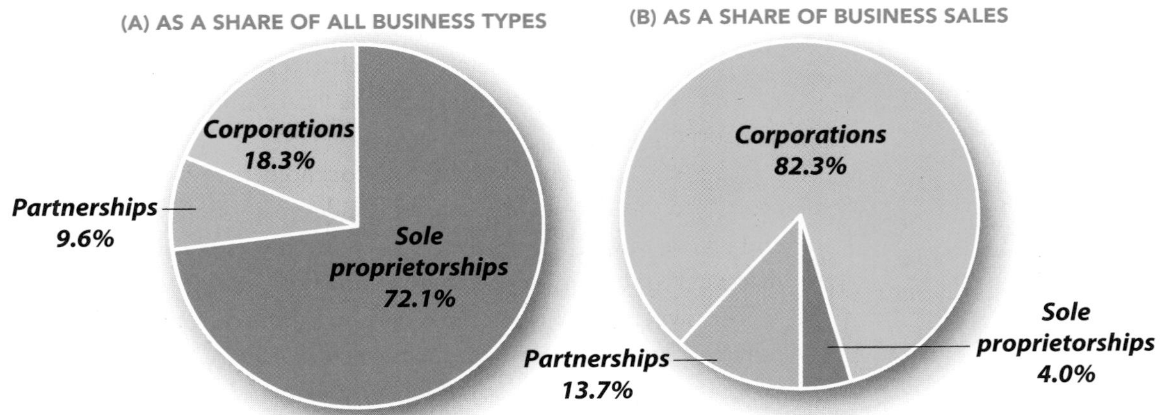

Source: U.S. Bureau of the Census, *Statistical Abstract of the United States, 2011*, Table 743.

FIGURE 8.5 Distribution of Corporations by Annual Sales and by Industry

Nearly one in five corporations had annual sales of $1 million or more. Four in ten corporations are in services, such as health care.

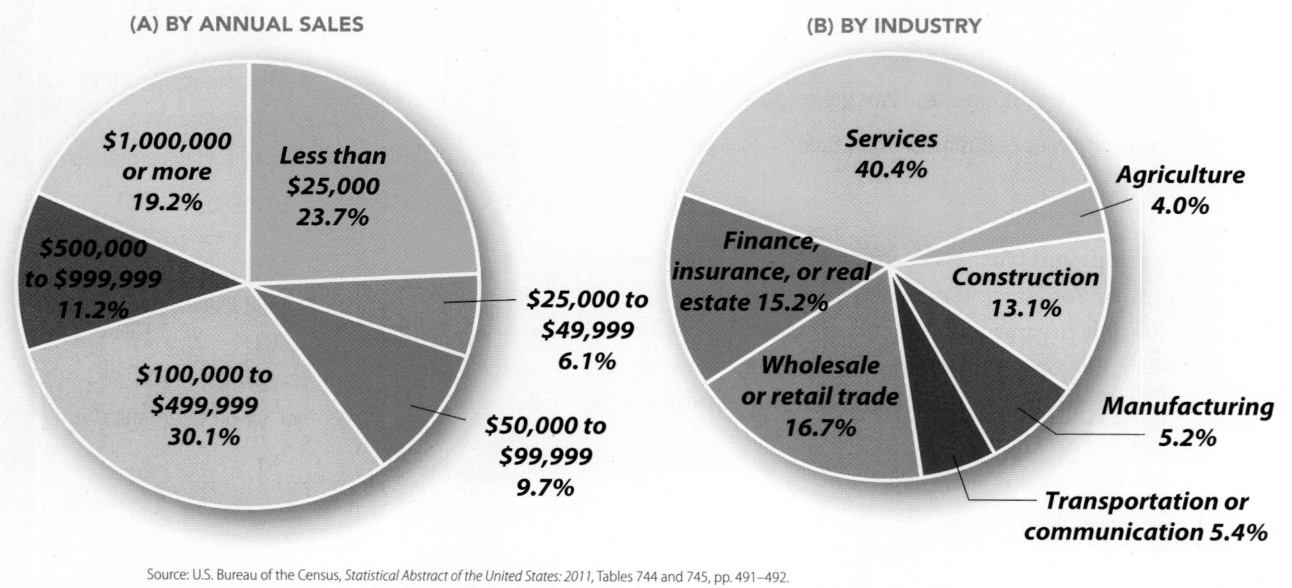

Source: U.S. Bureau of the Census, *Statistical Abstract of the United States: 2011*, Tables 744 and 745, pp. 491–492.

Figure 8.5 shows the distribution of corporations based on sales and on the industry. Whereas the median-sized sole proprietorship or partnership had annual sales of less than $25,000, the median-sized corporation had sales of $100,000 to $499,999. Virtually all the nation's large businesses are corporations. Compared with the other types of businesses, a smaller share of corporations is in agriculture and a larger share is in manufacturing.

Articles of Incorporation

A corporation is established through **articles of incorporation**, a written application to a state seeking permission to form a corporation. If these articles comply with state and federal laws, a charter is issued and the corporation becomes a legal entity. A *charter* offers the legal authorization to organize a business as a corporation.

A board of directors is elected by stockholders to oversee the firm's operation. The board sets corporate goals and decides major policy issues, and it appoints and sets salaries of top officers. Day-to-day duties of running the business are delegated to the corporate executives the board hires.

The owners of a corporation are issued *shares of stock*, entitling them to corporate profits and to vote for members of the board of directors and on various other issues in proportion to their stock ownership. For example, a stockholder who owns 1 percent of the stock has a right to 1 percent of the firm's profit paid in dividends and can vote 1 percent of the shares. *Dividends* are a share of profits a corporation pays to its stockholders.

articles of incorporation
A written application to the state seeking permission to form a corporation

Types of Corporations

A **private corporation** issues stock to just a few people, sometimes only family members. Such stockholders rarely sell their stock. Instead they pass it on within the family. Private corporations account for the overwhelming proportion of corporations in the United States.

In contrast, a **publicly traded corporation** has many shareholders—sometimes millions—who buy or sell shares. Stocks are bought and sold in stock exchanges. You will learn more about these in Chapter 12.

By any measure of size, whether by sales, employment, or market value, publicly traded corporations, on average, are much larger than private corporations. The 10,000 or so publicly traded corporations account for less than 1 percent of the 6 million U.S. corporations.

CHECKPOINT How is a corporation established?

ADVANTAGES AND DISADVANTAGES

LO3 Understand why large businesses favor the corporate form.

Here are the advantages and disadvantages of establishing a corporation.

Advantages of Incorporation

The corporate form offers advantages to the stockholders and to the business itself.

1. **Easier to Raise Financial Capital** The corporate form is the most effective structure for raising financial capital. This is especially true if large sums are needed to start or expand a business. Many investors—hundreds, thousands, even millions—can exchange their money for company shares, giving the firm a huge pool of funds. Corporations have more ways to raise money than either sole proprietors or partnerships.
2. **Limited Liability** In most cases, stockholders, the owners of the corporation can, at worst, lose no more than the value of their investment. Stockholders are said to have limited liability. Their personal assets cannot be seized to pay the debts of the business. Use of the abbreviations "Inc." or "Corp." in the name means this business has incorporated, which serves as a warning that stockholders will not accept personal liability for corporate debts.
3. **Unlimited Life** Unlike sole proprietorships and partnerships, a corporation does not cease to exist if a major stockholder dies or leaves the business. In fact, even if all stockholders die, the shares would pass on to heirs and the corporation would continue. Because stock is transferable—that is, it can be bought and sold or given to someone else—a corporation can exist indefinitely, independently of its owners.
4. **Specialized Management** In sole proprietorships and general partnerships, the firms' owners and managers often are the same people. Therefore,

private corporation Ownership limited to just a few people, sometimes only family members; shares are not publicly traded

publicly traded corporation Owned by many shareholders; shares can be bought or sold on stock exchanges

owners usually must possess management skills. However, the owners of a corporation—the stockholders—need no special management skills. Because ownership is often separated from management, a corporation can hire experts to manage the firm.

Disadvantages of Incorporation

The U.S. economy depends heavily on the corporate form. However, this business type also has some disadvantages when compared to sole proprietors and partnerships.

1. **Difficult and Costly to Start** Compared to the two other business forms, a corporation is more complicated to start. Articles of incorporation can be difficult and costly to draw up and get approved by government officials.
2. **More Regulated** Corporations, especially those publicly traded, face more regulations and red tape than other forms of business. For example, publicly traded corporations must issue financial reports every three months and issue annual reports prepared by an outside accounting firm. These reports must be made public and filed with the U.S. Securities and Exchange Commission (SEC), a federal agency that regulates trading of corporate stocks.
3. **Owners Have Less Control** The stockholders of a large, publicly traded corporation usually are far removed from the day-to-day operations of the business. These owners have little direct control over the corporation. Professional managers run the business, but they may not always act in the owners' best interests, as evidenced by some management failures in large corporations such as Enron, WorldCom, and Lehman Brothers.
4. **Double Taxation** In the eyes of the law, a corporation is a legal entity separate from its owners. The corporation therefore pays taxes on any earnings. Stockholders must then pay personal income taxes on any earnings they receive from the corporation as dividends. Thus, each dollar of corporate earnings gets taxed twice—first by the corporate income tax and then by the personal income tax.

CHECKPOINT **Why do large businesses favor the corporate form of business organization?**

OTHER ORGANIZATIONS

LO3 Recognize other types of business organizations.

So far you have considered the three basic business forms: sole proprietorships, partnerships, and corporations. Other ways of doing business have developed that combine attractive features of the basic forms.

Hybrid Businesses

A big advantage of sole proprietorships and partnerships is that business earnings are taxed only once—as income to the business owners. A big advantage of the corporation is that all owners are protected by limited liability. Some new business hybrid organizations offer the protection of limited liability while avoiding the double taxation of business income. Here are the most important new business types.

LLPs are governed by the Revised Uniform Partnership Act (RUPA). Access the text of this Act through the URL shown below. The LLP amendments to RUPA deal with four major issues. List these issues, and write a sentence summarizing each one.

www.cengage.com/school/contecon

S Corporation The S corporation was introduced about 30 years ago to combine the limited liability protection of the corporate form with the single taxation feature of a partnership. To qualify as an S corporation, a business must be incorporated in the United States, have no more than 100 stockholders, and have no foreign stockholders. Because of these restrictions, S corporations tend to be smaller than other corporations. About half of all U.S. corporations are S corporations.

Limited Liability Company (LLC) Like an S corporation, a limited liability company (LLC) combines the limited liability feature of the corporation with the single-tax provisions of a partnership. Company owners are called members, not partners or shareholders. An LLC does not have the ownership restrictions of the S corporation, making it ideal for a business with foreign investors. An LLC must have at least two members, and a member can personally guarantee certain obligations of the LLC. This gives a new business more financial flexibility. For example, a prospective landlord about to lease office space to a new business most likely would require a personal guarantee from a business owner. The LLC structure would allow one or more company members to make such a guarantee. Because of its more flexible management structure, the LLC has become a common way to own and operate a business.

Limited Liability Partnership (LLP) An existing partnership may find it difficult to convert to an LLC. This is why the limited liability partnership (LLP) was created. An LLP has the advantages of an LLC and is easier to establish, especially if a business needs to convert from a regular partnership. An existing partnership usually can be converted to an LLP simply by changing the partnership agreement and registering as an LLP. Both LLPs and LLCs are taxed as partnerships. The limited liability partnership differs from the limited partnership in that members of the LLP can take an active role in the business without exposing themselves to personal liability for the acts of others (except to the extent of their investment in the LLP).

Cooperatives A cooperative is a group of people who pool their resources to buy and sell more efficiently than they could independently. The government grants most cooperatives tax-exempt status. There are two types: consumer cooperatives and producer cooperatives.

A *consumer cooperative* is a retail business owned and operated by some or all of its customers in order to reduce costs. Some cooperatives require members to pay an annual fee and others require them to work a certain number of hours each year. Members sometimes pay lower prices than other customers or may share in any revenues that exceed costs. In the United States, consumer cooperatives operate credit unions, electric-power facilities, health plans, and grocery stores, among others. Many college bookstores are cooperatives.

S corporation Organization that offers limited liability combined with the single taxation of business income; must have no more than 100 stockholders and no foreign stockholders

limited liability company (LLC) Business with limited liability for some owners or members, single taxation of business income, and no ownership restrictions

limited liability partnership (LLP) Like a limited liability company but more easily converted from an existing partnership

cooperative An organization consisting of people who pool their resources to buy and sell more efficiently than they could independently

Investigate Your Local Economy

Identify a not-for-profit organization in your area. Research to discover how this organization affects your local economy. For example, find out what services the organization provides and how many paid employees and volunteers work for the organization. Share your findings in class.

In a *producer cooperative*, producers join forces to buy supplies and equipment and to market their output. Each producer's objective is to reduce costs and increase profits. For example, farmers pool their funds to purchase machinery and supplies. Farm cooperatives also provide storage facilities, processing, and transportation to market, thereby eliminating wholesalers. For example, Sunkist is a farm cooperative owned and operated by about 6,500 citrus growers in California and Arizona. Federal legislation allows farmers to cooperate in this way without violating antitrust laws. Firms in other industries could not do this legally.

Not-for-Profit Organizations So far, you have learned about organizations that try to maximize profits or, in the case of cooperatives, minimize costs. Some organizations have neither as a goal. **Not-for-profit organizations** engage in charitable, educational, humanitarian, cultural, professional, and other activities, often with a social purpose. Government agencies do not have profit as a goal either, but governments are not included in this definition of not-for-profit organizations.

Like businesses, not-for-profit organizations evolved to help people accomplish their goals. Examples include non-profit hospitals, private schools and colleges, religious organizations, the American Red Cross, charitable foundations, orchestras, museums, labor unions, and professional organizations such as the National Education Association. There are about 1.4 million not-for-profit organizations in the United States. They employ about 10 million workers, with hospitals accounting for about half this total.

Even not-for-profit organizations must pay their bills. Revenues typically include some combination of voluntary contributions and service charges, such as college tuition and hospital charges. In the United States, not-for-profit organizations usually are exempt from taxes. Figure 8.6 summarizes the purpose and ownership of each hybrid and offers examples.

CHECKPOINT Name and describe other types of business organizations.

not-for-profit organizations Groups that do not pursue profit as a goal; they engage in charitable, educational, humanitarian, cultural, professional, or other activities, often with a social purpose

FIGURE 8.6 Hybrid Business Organizations in the United States

Type	Purpose	Ownership	Examples
S corporation	Limited liability with single taxation	No more than 100 stockholders with no foreign stockholders	Nearly all small corporations
Limited liability company (LLC)	Limited liability with single taxation	No restrictions; one member can choose to be liable for debts	Law, accounting, real estate, medicine
Limited liability partnership (LLP)	Ideal for partnerships seeking limited-liability status	Partners can take active role without facing liability	Law, accounting, real estate, medicine
Cooperative	People cooperate to buy or sell more efficiently	Owned by members; producer cooperatives limited to agriculture	Banking and agriculture
Not-for-profit organization	Charitable, educational, humanitarian, cultural, and other goals	Profit is not a goal; no owners, so nobody can legally profit	Colleges, charities, labor unions, some hospitals

8.3 ASSESSMENT

Think Critically

1. Why would most people refuse to invest in corporations if there were no limited liability for stock owners?
2. Why might a family business organize as a private corporation rather than as a sole proprietorship?
3. Although stockholders do not need to be professional managers, they should remain aware of decisions made by the people who run the firm. Why is this true?
4. If publicly traded corporations account for less than 1 percent of all corporations, why should society care what they do?
5. Identify a local not-for-profit organization that operates in your community. In what ways does this firm differ from other businesses?

Graphing Exercises

6. In the years between 2006 and 2009, many publicly traded corporations in the United States reported falling profits. While they paid some of their profits to stockholders in dividends, they kept some as retained earnings. Use the data in the table to construct a double line graph that shows the change in corporate profits and dividends in these years. Why do you think many firms chose not to immediately pay a smaller share of their profits in dividends as profits fell in 2007?

CORPORATE AFTER-TAX PROFITS AND DIVIDENDS, 2005–2009 (VALUES IN BILLIONS OF DOLLARS)

Year	After-Tax Profits	Dividends	Dividends as a Percentage of After-Tax Profits
2005	$1,044	$557	53.4%
2006	$1,135	$705	62.1%
2007	$1,090	$768	70.5%
2008	$1,068	$690	64.6%
2009	$994	$576	57.9%

Source: U.S. Bureau of the Census, *Statistical Abstract of the United States,* 2011, Table 785, p. 516.

Make Academic Connections

7. **History** Investigate the history of a major U.S. corporation. How did it begin? What factors led to its growth? What impact has it had on the lives of American consumers?

TeamWork

Working in small teams, identify a local business that is organized as a corporation. List specific advantages and disadvantages of this form of business organization to the owners of this firm. Compare your group's work with that of other groups.

Andrew Carnegie—Entrepreneur and Philanthropist

When he was 12, Andrew Carnegie moved with his family from Scotland to the United States. Soon after arriving in this country, he got a job working in a cotton mill for $1.20 a week. At age 18, he took a job as a telegrapher for the Pennsylvania Railroad. While working there, he won the favor of Thomas A. Scott, a top official in the company. With Scott's help, Carnegie rose quickly through the company ranks. By age 24, he had become the superintendent of the western division of the railroad. He invested much of his earnings in stocks.

By age 30, Carnegie was earning $50,000 per year—a fortune at the time—and turned all his efforts and investments to the steel industry. This industry would make him the richest man in America. He believed that the new Bessemer process would cause the industry to grow. He hired good managers and plowed the profits back into his companies. He used what he learned from his railroad experience to lower costs and keep prices low. By controlling costs and reinvesting profits, he was able to take advantage of economies of scale. Smaller companies unable to undertake all the phases of production were at a disadvantage. Carnegie was able to increase his market share and expand his holdings. He purchased iron ore deposits and coke fields. Adding these to his steel mills, ships, and railroads, he was able to control the entire steel-making process, from ore to finished products.

When he sold his company to J.P. Morgan in 1901, Carnegie received $250 million—worth about $4.5 billion today. He then set out to give away most of his fortune. He wrote in an essay for the *American Review* that the man who dies rich, dies disgraced. Although at his death in 1919 he was worth more than $22 million, Carnegie did not die disgraced. He had given away 90 percent of his fortune—$350 million—to libraries, concert halls, and other public institutions across the nation and the world.

Think Critically **Research the life of another successful American entrepreneur. What were the keys to his or her success? What lessons can you learn from that success?**

jean morrison/Shutterstock.com

Chapter 8 Summary

8.1 Entrepreneurs

A. Entrepreneurs are the prime movers in our market economy. They bring about creative change through their effort to earn profits.

B. Entrepreneurs take risks when they operate businesses. They must obtain and risk financial capital to get their businesses off the ground. When entrepreneurs are successful, their success attracts other entrepreneurs to the same type of production. This creates competition that improves the quality of products and lowers prices for consumers.

C. Not all businesspeople are entrepreneurs. Many employees are paid to be innovative or to manage businesses. If they are not risking their own funds, they are not entrepreneurs.

ASK THE EXPERT

www.cengage.com/school/contecon

How do businesses raise cash to finance startups and expansions?

8.2 Sole Proprietorships and Partnerships

A. The three basic types of business organization in the United States are sole proprietorships, partnerships, and corporations.

B. Sole proprietorships are the most common type of business organization. A sole proprietorship is owned by someone who is totally responsible for its operation, and receives all of its profits or incurs all its losses. This business exists only as long as the owner controls it. Sole proprietorships are relatively easy to start, enjoy a lower level of government regulation, and are taxed only once on the profits they earn.

C. General partnerships are created when two or more people form a business by agreeing to share responsibilities for the firm and any resulting profits or losses. Limited partnerships are formed when at least one owner is a general partner and other owners contribute funds to become limited partners with limited liability.

D. Partnerships also are relatively easy to start, and general partners have unlimited liability for the debts of the firm. Partnerships are better able to raise financial capital than sole proprietorships, and their profits are taxed only once. The lives of partnerships are limited to the involvement of the partners.

8.3 Corporations and Other Organizations

A. Corporations are able to raise large amounts of financial capital by selling stock. They may either be private or publicly traded. Private corporations issue stock to a limited number of people, who often are members of a family and the stock usually remains in the family. Publicly traded corporations raise funds by selling stock to anyone who is willing to buy it. Stockholders receive a vote for each share owned for important business decisions that are made.

B. Corporations are established through articles of incorporation. Corporations are legal entities separate from the individual owners of their stock. The owners of corporate stock enjoy limited liability. They risk no more than the funds they use to purchase stock. Corporations have unlimited life. If a shareholder dies, the stock is sold or given to others. The corporation is unaffected.

C. Corporations are more difficult and costly to start than other forms. They are more closely regulated by the government, and their profits are taxed twice—once when earned by the firm and again when paid to stockholders in dividends or when shareholders gain by selling shares.

D. Some special forms of business organizations are called hybrid businesses. These ways of organizing help people accomplish their goals by filling the specific needs of a particular group of people.

CHAPTER 8 ASSESSMENT

Review Economic Terms

a. articles of incorporation
b. cooperative
c. corporation
d. financial capital
e. general partnership
f. innovation
g. liability
h. limited liability company (LLC)
i. limited liability partnership (LLP)
j. limited partnership
k. not-for-profit organization
l. partnership
m. private corporation
n. publicly traded corporation
o. S corporation
p. sole proprietorship

Match the terms with the definitions. Some terms will not be used.

_____ 1. The process of turning an invention into a marketable product

_____ 2. Two or more people agree to contribute resources to a business in return for a share of the profit

_____ 3. Ownership is limited to just a few people, sometimes only family members; shares are not publicly traded

_____ 4. An organization consisting of people who pool their resources to buy or sell more efficiently than they could independently

_____ 5. The legal obligation to pay any debts of a business

_____ 6. The simplest form of business organization; a firm owned and run by one person

_____ 7. A legal entity with an existence that is distinct from the people who organize, own, and run it

_____ 8. Owned by many shareholders; shares can be bought and sold

_____ 9. Limited liability combined with the single taxation of business income; must have no more than 100 stockholders and no foreign stockholders

_____ 10. Money needed to start or expand a business

_____ 11. Partners share both in the responsibility of running the business and in any liability from its operation

_____ 12. At least one general partner runs the business and bears unlimited personal liability; other partners provide financial capital but have limited liability

_____ 13. A written application to the state seeking permission to form a corporation

_____ 14. Business with limited liability for some owners (or members), single taxation of business income, and no ownership restriction

_____ 15. Group that does not pursue profit as a goal and often engages in activities with a social purpose

Review Economic Concepts

16. Entrepreneurs bring about creative change in each of the following ways except
    a. they improve the quality of existing products.
    b. they introduce new products.
    c. they find ways to eliminate competition.
    d. they introduce new production methods.

17. **True or False** Once established, most entrepreneurs are able to maintain a substantial profit on the products they produce and sell.

18. Competitors are attracted to a market that yields
    a. a profit.
    b. unlimited liability.
    c. lower prices for consumers.
    d. higher tax revenues.

19. Which of the following examples demonstrates entrepreneurship?
    a. A scientist invents a long-lasting paint and starts a business to produce it.
    b. A government official creates a new tax form that is easier to complete.
    c. A technician discovers a new type of wax that is used by the firm that employs her.
    d. A student cuts his elderly neighbor's lawn for free.
20. **True or False** Sole proprietorships are the most common form of business organization in the United States.
21. Sole proprietors enjoy each of the following advantages except
    a. they receive all the profit their businesses earn.
    b. it usually is easy for them to gather large amounts of financial capital.
    c. they can make business decisions quickly.
    d. it usually is easy for them to form their business.
22. Owners of sole proprietorships have ________?________ for the firm's debts if the firm fails to pay its bills.
23. Corporations are
    a. the most common type of business organization.
    b. the easiest form of business to start.
    c. the type of business organization that is best able to raise financial capital.
    d. the least-regulated form of business organization.
24. **True or False** Most large businesses in the United States are corporations.
25. **True or False** A corporation's stockholders are held responsible to pay off all the firm's debts if the firm files for bankruptcy.
26. A consumer cooperative generally is formed to
    a. earn a profit for its owners.
    b. reduce costs of buying goods or services for its members.
    c. avoid paying income tax on its profits.
    d. limit the type of people who can shop at specific stores.
27. **True or False** Almost all corporations in the United States are publicly traded corporations.
28. Which of the following types of business organizations cannot have a foreign owner?
    a. S corporation
    b. limited liability company
    c. limited liability partnership
    d. not-for-profit organization
29. Publicly traded corporations must issue financial reports and file them with the ________?________, a federal agency that regulates trading of corporate stocks.
30. **True or False** An important disadvantage of corporations is the fact that their profits are taxed twice.
31. **True or False** Use of the abbreviations "Inc." or "Corp." in a company name indicates that the owners are personally liable for the company's debts.
32. Which of the following describes an advantage of a corporation?
    a. difficult to start
    b. unlimited life
    c. owners have little control
    d. earnings are taxed twice

Apply Economic Concepts

33. **Entrepreneurship** Gretchen has invented a new lubricant that reduces friction between moving parts in an engine to almost nothing. This product should increase automobile gas mileage by at least 50 percent and make automobile engines last much longer. Explain how Gretchen could become an entrepreneur through her invention.

34. **Limited Liability** Gretchen has successfully tested her lubricant on small engines. She has not tried to use it in large engines or for extended periods of time. To complete these tests, she needs many thousands of dollars to buy equipment and run the tests. If the tests are successful, Gretchen thinks her product could earn millions of dollars in profit every year. If they fail, all the funds invested in the tests could be lost. Why would Gretchen want to limit her liability when she starts her business?

35. **Assess Limitations of Sole Proprietorships** Paul opened a florist business that marketed tropical flowers as a sole proprietorship. His idea was that by offering flowers that no other local store sold, he could charge high prices and earn a large profit. This may have been a good idea, but his business failed. First, he had only $30,000 to get started, so he was seldom able to keep many flowers in stock. Although he knew flowers, he didn't know much about advertising, accounting, or how to direct employees. Even when he put in 80-hour weeks, things didn't get done on time. When the business failed, he owed $40,000. The bankruptcy court took his house and car to pay his debts. Explain why Paul's business might have been more successful if it had been organized as a corporation or even a partnership.

36. **21st Century Skills: Building a Successful Business** After five years, Rita's business is successful. Her annual sales are $450,000 and she employs three workers. She is convinced she could double her sales if she hires more workers and invests $500,000 in new equipment. Rita has saved $100,000. Describe two methods she could use to raise the financial capital she needs to expand her business. Of these two, which would you recommend she choose? Explain your answer.

Digging Deeper

with Economics e-Collection

Entrepreneurs drive a market economy forward through initiating four types of creative change. They (1) introduce new products, (2) improve the quality of existing products, (3) introduce new production methods, and (4) introduce new ways of doing business. Access the Gale Economics e-Collection through the URL below. Type the word "entrepreneur" in the Keyword or Subject tab of the Basic Search screen to find articles about two entrepreneurs and the companies they operate. Classify each entrepreneur as to which type of creative change he or she has initiated. Note how the person came up with the idea for the business, the products or services it sells, and how the business was financed. Evaluate which of the two businesses you think will be more successful. Be prepared to discuss your entrepreneurs and evaluations in class.

www.cengage.com/school/contecon

CHAPTER 9

Labor Markets

Point your browser

www.cengage.com/school/contecon

CONSIDER...

- Why do truck drivers in the United States earn at least 20 times more than rickshaw drivers in Asia?
- Why do some professional basketball players earn 50 times more than others?
- Among physicians, why do surgeons earn twice as much as general practitioners?
- What's the payoff for a college education?
- In what sense have labor unions become victims of their own success?

R Carner/Shutterstock.com, Background image: Pefkos/Shutterstock.com

9.1 RESOURCE MARKETS

Key Terms

Learning Objectives

LO1 Determine the shapes of a resource demand curve and a resource supply curve.

LO2 Identify what can shift a labor demand curve.

LO3 Identify what can shift a labor supply curve.

In Your World

Some people earn much more than others because the resources they supply are more valuable. Your earnings depend on the market value of the resources you supply. In choosing a career—the labor market in which you will work—you probably will consider the income you could expect from alternative occupations. Earnings from productive resources—the inputs used to produce goods and services—are determined by the interaction of demand and supply.

DEMAND AND SUPPLY OF RESOURCES

LO1 Determine the shapes of a resource demand curve and a resource supply curve.

In the market for goods and services—the *product market*—households are demanders and firms are suppliers. Households demand the goods and services that maximize utility. Firms supply the goods and services that maximize profit. In the *resource market,* roles are reversed. Households are suppliers and firms are demanders. Households supply resources to maximize utility. Firms demand resources to maximize profit. Differences between households' utility-maximizing goals and firms' profit-maximizing goals are sorted out through voluntary exchange in markets.

Market Demand for Resources

Why do firms employ resources? Firms use resources to produce goods and services. They try to sell these products to earn a profit. A firm values not the resource itself but the resource's ability to produce goods and services. Because the value of any resource depends on the value of what it produces, the demand for a resource is said to be a *derived demand.* Another term for "derive" is "arise from." Thus, **derived demand** arises from the demand for the good or service produced by the resource. For example, demand for a carpenter arises, or derives, from the demand for the carpenter's output, such as a cabinet or a new deck. Demand for professional baseball players derives from the demand for ballgames. Demand for truck drivers derives from the demand for transporting goods.

derived demand The demand for a resource that arises from the demand for the product that resource produces

The derived nature of resource demand helps explain why professional baseball players usually earn more than professional hockey players, why brain surgeons earn more than tree surgeons, and why tractor-trailer drivers earn more than delivery-van drivers. *The more a worker produces and the higher the price of that product, the more valuable that worker is to a firm.* Thus, the demand for a resource is tied to the value of the output produced by that resource, or its **productivity**. The more productive a resource is, the more a firm is willing to pay for it.

The market demand for a particular resource sums the demands for that resource in all its different uses. For example, the market demand for *carpenters* adds together the demand for carpenters in residential and commercial construction, remodeling, cabinetmaking, and so on. Similarly, the market demand for the resource *timber* sums the demand for timber as lumber, furniture, railway ties, pencils, toothpicks, firewood, paper products, and so on. The demand curve for a resource, like the demand curves for the goods produced by that resource, slopes downward. This is depicted by the resource demand curve for carpenters, *D*, in Figure 9.1.

As the price of a resource falls, firms are more willing and more able to employ that resource. Consider first the firm's greater *willingness* to hire resources as the resource price falls. In developing the demand curve for a particular resource, the prices of other resources are assumed to remain constant. If the wage of carpenters falls, this type of labor becomes relatively cheaper compared with other resources the firm could employ to produce the same output. Firms, therefore, are willing to hire more carpenters and less of other, now relatively more costly, resources.

Firms may *make substitutions in production.* For example, a homebuilder can employ more carpenters and fewer factory-made sections. Likewise firms can substitute coal for oil as the relative price of coal declines.

A lower price for a resource also increases a firm's *ability* to hire that resource. For example, if the wage for carpenters falls, home builders can hire more carpenters for the same total cost. The lower resource price means the firm is *more able* to buy the resource. Because producers are more willing and more able to employ a resource when the price of that resource declines, the demand curve for a resource slopes downward, as shown in Figure 9.1.

productivity The value of output produced by a resource

FIGURE 9.1 **Labor Market for Carpenters**

The intersection of the upward-sloping resource supply curve of carpenters with the downward-sloping resource demand curve determines the equilibrium wage rate, *W*, and the equilibrium level of employment, *E*.

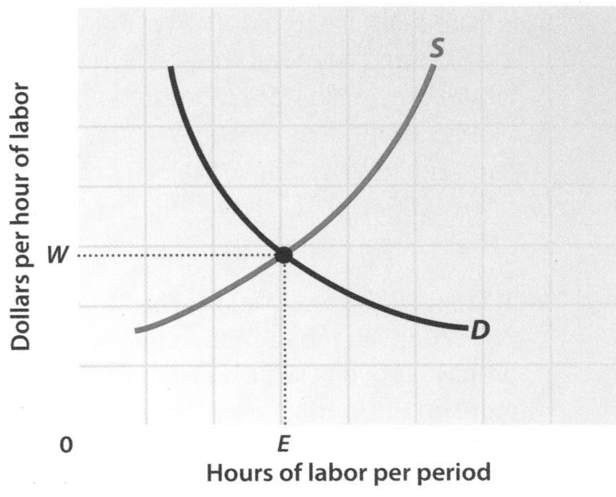

Market Supply of Resources

On the other side of the market, resource suppliers tend to be both more *willing* and more *able* to supply the resource as its price increases. This explains the upward-sloping market supply curve, as shown in Figure 9.1 by the resource supply curve of carpenters, *S*. Resource suppliers are more *willing* because a higher resource price, other things constant, means more goods and services can be purchased with the earnings from each unit of the resource supplied. Thus, they have an incentive to increase the quantity supplied.

Resource prices are signals about the rewards for supplying resources to alternative activities. A high resource price tells the resource owner, "The market really values your resource and is willing to pay you well for what you supply." Higher prices attract resources from lower-valued uses. For example, as the wage for carpenters increases, the hours of carpentry services supplied increases. Some carpenters give up leisure time to work more, because the opportunity cost of leisure has increased. Also, people in other lines of work are drawn to carpentry.

The second reason a resource supply curve slopes upward is that resource owners are more *able* to supply the resource at a higher price. For example, a higher carpenter's

Span the Globe

Is U.S. CEO Pay Excessive?

CEOs of the 200 largest U.S. corporations in 2010 earned, on average, more than 300 times the average production worker's pay. In other countries, including Germany and Japan, comparable multiples are much lower. Economists offer some possible explanations for the differences. First, they say U.S. businesses serve a wider market and are more efficient than those in other countries, so the U.S. CEO is potentially more productive and valuable. Next, top executives in U.S. firms often are recruited from outside the firm as compared to those in Germany and Japan, where they mainly are promoted from within the company. Therefore, the more highly competitive resource market for the top jobs in U.S. firms drives salaries up. Further, the stock market value of U.S. corporations has increased by a factor of six since 1980, and CEO pay has increased accordingly. Lastly, high salaries are more socially acceptable in the United States than they are in Japan and Germany.

Think Critically The 2010 Dodd-Frank Wall Street Reform and Consumer Protection Act required shareholders of publicly traded companies to have a "say-on-pay" vote on executive compensation. The intent was to have executive pay focus more on the long term and be tied more to the CEO's measurable performance. What effect do you think this law will have on a company's bottom line? How will this affect the economy in general?

Source: http://www.aflcio.org/corporatewatch/paywatch/ceopay.cfm; Xavier Gabaix and Augustin Landier, "Why Has CEO Pay Increased So Much?, " *Quarterly Journal of Economics,* 123 (February 2008): 49–100; *Economic Report of the President,* February 2010, at http://www.gpoaccess.gov/eop

wage means more apprentices will choose to undergo training to become carpenters. The higher wage *enables* resource suppliers to increase their quantity supplied. Similarly, a higher timber price enables loggers to harvest trees in less-accessible regions. A higher gold price enables miners to extract gold from lower grade ore. A higher oil price enables drillers to explore more remote parts of the world.

The interaction in Figure 9.1 of the resource demand curve, *D*, and the resource supply curve, *S*, determines the equilibrium wage for carpenters, *W*, and the equilibrium employment of carpenters, *E*. At the **equilibrium wage**, the quantity of labor that firms want to hire exactly matches the quantity carpenters want to supply. At the equilibrium wage, there is neither an excess quantity of carpenters demanded nor an excess quantity supplied. The interaction of labor demand and labor supply determines the market wage and thereby allocates the scarce resource, labor.

Explain the shapes of a resource demand curve and a resource supply curve. CHECKPOINT

NONWAGE DETERMINANTS OF LABOR DEMAND

LO2 Identify what can shift a labor demand curve.

The quantity of labor demanded increases as the wage decreases, other things constant, because a lower wage makes employers more willing and more able to hire workers. Thus the labor demand curve slopes downward, other things constant, as you saw in Figure 9.1. What are the things that are assumed to remain constant along a given labor demand curve? In other words, what are the nonwage factors that help shape the labor demand curve?

Demand for the Final Product

Labor demand is derived from the demand for the output produced by that labor. As noted already, the demand for carpenters derives from the demand for what they produce. Because the demand for labor is *derived* from the demand for that labor's output, any change in the demand for that output affects resource demand. For example, an increase in the demand for housing increases the demand for carpenters. As shown in Figure 9.2, this causes the demand curve for that labor to shift to the right, from *D* to *D'*. A rightward shift of the demand for carpenters increases the market wage and employment.

Prices of Other Resources

The prices of other resources are assumed to remain constant along the downward sloping demand curve for labor. A change in the price of other resources could shift the demand for labor. Some resources substitute for each other in production. For example, prefabricated home modules built mostly by machines at the factory substitute for on-site home construction by carpenters. Substitutes can replace each other in production. With **resource substitutes**, an increase in the cost of one increases the demand for the other. For example, an increase in the cost of prefabricated homes increases the demand for carpenters. This shifts the demand for carpenters to the right, as in Figure 9.2.

equilibrium wage The wage at which the quantity of labor firms demand exactly matches the quantity workers supply

resource substitutes One resource can replace another in production; an increase in the cost of one resource increases the demand for the other

FIGURE 9.2 An Increase in the Demand for Carpenters

An increase in the demand for carpenters is shown by a rightward shift of the labor demand curve. This shift increases the market wage and increases employment of carpenters.

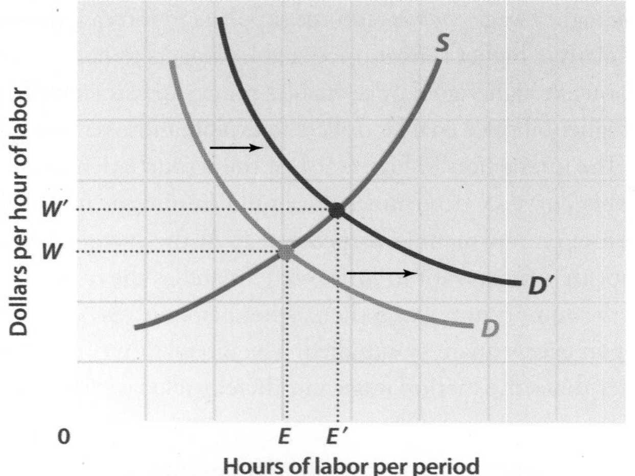

Some resources are complements in production—carpenters and lumber, for example. Complements go together in production. With **resource complements**, a decrease in the cost of one leads to an increase in the demand for the other. If the cost of lumber decreases, the quantity of lumber demanded increases, which increases the demand for carpenters, shifting the demand curve for carpenters to the right.

Technology

A labor demand curve assumes a given level of technology in that market. Thus, technology is assumed to be constant along a labor demand curve. A change in technology can shift the demand curve. More technologically sophisticated capital can increase the productivity of labor, thus increasing the demand for labor. For example, better power tools, such as a pneumatic nail driver, make carpenters more productive, thus shifting the demand curve for carpenters to the right. Alternatively, improved technology could make some carpenters unnecessary, thus shifting the demand for carpenters to the left. For example, if a more modern factory builds modular homes more efficiently, the demand for carpenters will decrease, or shift leftward.

Sometimes a technological improvement can increase the demand for some resources but reduce the demand for others. For example, the development of computer-generated animated movies increased the demand for computer programmers with that skill. At the same time, it decreased the demand for animators who drew each frame by hand.

Computer programs are changing job prospects in fields such as law, medicine, accounting, and architecture. For example, Quicken's WillMaker® software has written more wills than any lawyer alive. In accounting, software such as TurboTax® completes tax forms with ease. In architecture, three-dimensional programs such as 3D Home Architect® help configure all aspects of a structure. As software and hardware become better, cheaper, and easier to use, the demand for some professional services declines.

resource complements
One resource works with the other in production; a decrease in the cost of one increases the demand for the other

NONWAGE DETERMINANTS OF LABOR SUPPLY

LO3 Identify what can shift a labor supply curve.

The quantity of labor supplied increases as the wage rate increases, other things constant, so the labor supply curve slopes upward. What are the other things that are assumed to remain constant along a given labor supply curve? In other words, what are the nonwage factors that help shape the labor supply curve?

Worker Wealth

Although some jobs are rewarding in a variety of nonmonetary ways, the main reason people work is to earn money to buy goods and services. The wealthier people are, the less they need to work for a living. Thus, a person's supply of labor depends, among other things, on his or her wealth, including homes, cars, savings, securities, and other assets. A person's wealth is assumed to remain constant along the labor supply curve.

A decrease in wealth would prompt people to work more, thus increasing their supply of labor. For example, the stock market decline between 2008 and 2009 significantly reduced the wealth that many people planned to draw on during retirement. As a result, they had to put retirement plans on hold and instead work more and longer to rebuild their retirement nest egg. This increased the supply of labor, as shown by the rightward shift of the labor supply curve from S to S' in Figure 9.3. This reduced the wage and increased employment.

FIGURE 9.3 An Increase in the Supply of Carpenters

An increase in the supply of carpenters is shown by a rightward shift of the labor supply curve. This shift reduces the market wage and increases employment of carpenters.

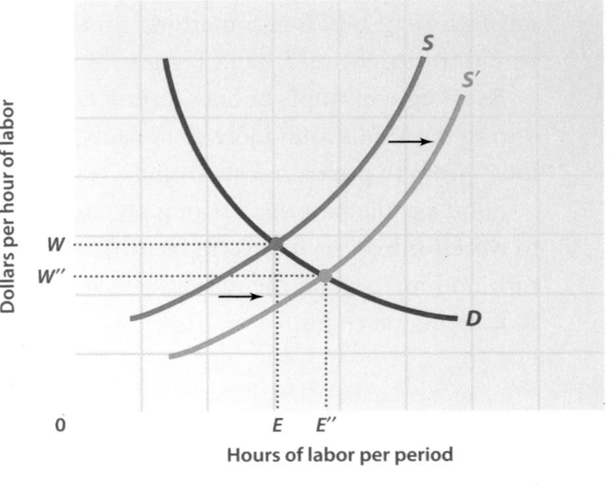

Photodisc/Getty Images

Based on working conditions, do you think that many people would like to supply their labor as steel workers? Why or why not?

As an example of the opposite effect, winners of multimillion-dollar lotteries often announce they plan to quit their jobs. This reduces their supply of labor in response to the increase in their wealth. In your own life, if you were to inherit a tidy sum, you might decide not to work this summer. This would decrease your labor supply.

Working Conditions

Labor supplied to a particular market depends on the working conditions, such as the difficulty of the job and the attractiveness of the work environment. Working conditions are assumed to remain constant along a given labor supply curve. Any improvement in working conditions would shift the labor supply curve rightward. For example, if employers offer carpenters more flexible hours, some will find this more attractive than a rigid work schedule. These carpenters will increase their supply of labor, shifting the labor supply curve to the right, as shown in Figure 9.3.

More generally, people supply less labor to jobs that are dirty, dangerous, dull, exhausting, illegal, low status, dead-end, and involve inconvenient hours. People supply more labor to jobs that are clean, safe, interesting, energizing, legal, high status, offer advancement opportunities, and involve convenient hours.

Tastes for Work

Just as consumer tastes for goods and services are assumed to remain constant along a demand curve, worker tastes for jobs are assumed to remain constant along a given labor supply curve. Job tastes are relatively stable. They don't change overnight. Still, over time, the supply of labor could change because of a change in the taste for a particular job. For example, suppose carpentry becomes more appealing because people become more attracted to jobs that provide exercise, fresh air, and the satisfaction of building something. In this case, the supply of labor to carpentry would shift rightward, as in Figure 9.3.

As another example of how worker tastes can change over time, most teenagers during the 1990s found jobs at fast-food restaurants relatively appealing. Teenagers today seem to prefer upscale employers such as Starbucks and the Gap.

Some people have such strong preferences for certain jobs that they are willing to work for free, such as volunteer firefighters. Likewise, most computer hackers earn nothing beyond the twisted satisfaction they get from spreading viruses and causing digital chaos.

Investigate Your Local Economy

In small groups, discuss job tastes among students at your high school. Do you see any trends? Are some jobs more desirable than others? Why do you think this is so?

What can shift the labor supply curve?

9.1 ASSESSMENT

Think Critically

1. What is the demand for workers in your school cafeteria derived from?
2. Why would the demand for roofers increase if the price of shingles fell by 50 percent?
3. Why would an increase in the price of crude oil along a given supply curve increase the quantity of oil supplied to the market?
4. What would happen to the demand for technicians who produce computer chips if a new chip-manufacturing process using only half as much raw material was introduced?
5. Why might the supply of high-school students who are willing to work in fast-food restaurants decrease if there were an economic boom and a huge increase in stock values?

Graphing Exercise

6. Draw a labor supply curve for students who are willing to work, based on the data in the table. Explain what would happen to the location of this labor supply curve as a result of each of the listed events.

Hourly Wage Rate	Quantity of Labor Students Supply
$6	5,000
$7	10,000
$8	15,000
$9	20,000
$10	25,000

a. Social networking becomes cheaper, easier, and more fun, so students spend much more time keeping in touch with friends.
b. Wearing old clothes becomes popular with students. This style causes many young people to stop buying new clothing.
c. The state board of education raises the grade requirement to graduate.

Make Academic Connections

7. **Management** Make a list of nonwage determinants of labor supply that could increase the supply of labor.
8. **Science** Identify scientific developments that have taken place in the past 50 years that have changed the demand for labor in the marketplace.

TeamWork

Working in teams, list events that might cause more young people to look for summer work. Make a similar list of things that might cause fewer young people to seek summer employment. What benefits beyond earning money might these young people gain from working? Discuss your team's lists in class.

21st Century Skills

CREATIVITY AND INNOVATION

New Technology Requires New Skills

Technological developments in the 21st century will allow you, as a member of the workforce, to be more productive. These developments also will require you to learn new skills so you can use these innovations. Think of the skills you have today that your parents did not have when they were looking for their first job. They likely did not have the ability to

- Search the Internet to find new or better ways to complete tasks.
- Use email or texting to communicate.
- Compare prices and the quality of goods or services marketed by firms on the Internet.
- Access data from the government and other sources over the Internet.

Keep Up With New Skills

Because new technologies require new skills, you need to commit yourself to lifelong learning. Consider the skills listed above. How did you learn to use them? Did you

- Use trial and error until you understood how to use the new technology?
- Ask friends or relatives who were already adept in using the new technology to help you learn how to use it?
- Search the Internet or print publications for instructions about how to use new technology?
- Register for and complete classes that taught you about the new technology?
- Sign up for on-the-job training if your employer offered instruction in how to use the new technology?

On-the-Job Training

Businesses that purchase new technologies need workers who are qualified to use them. Replacing workers who lack needed skills can be expensive. Firms may be required to provide economic assistance to workers they lay off, search for new workers who have the needed skills, and pay these new workers more to encourage them to accept their job offer. To avoid these costs, many employers offer on-the-job training to their current employees to help them learn new skills. The following are examples of ways in which such training might be offered:

- Formalized on-site training by experts either during or after regular working hours
- Mentoring of workers who lack the needed skills by other employees who already possess them
- Sending workers to a different location where they will attend training classes

Each of these alternatives involves significant costs to the employer, both in terms of paying for the training, and in lost production while employees are learning the skill. Still, these costs often are lower than those of finding and hiring new workers.

Apply the Skill

Assume your employer offers you the opportunity to learn how to use a new technology that it will begin using in the next six months. Although the training will be free, you will be required to attend six, eight-hour sessions on Saturdays, and you will not be paid for your time. State whether you would accept the offer and give three reasons for your decision.

9.2 WAGE DETERMINATION

Learning Objectives

LO1 Explain why wages differ across labor markets.

LO2 Describe minimum wage legislation.

Key Terms

minimum wage law 277

In Your World

What career will you pursue? Teacher? Builder? Lawyer? Physician? Retailer? Homemaker? Because of the division of labor and comparative advantage, the U.S. workforce is becoming more specialized. For example, the U.S. Census of 1850 identified 322 job titles. In the 2010 Census, there were about 100 times more job titles. The pay for each of these specialties is determined by the intersection of a labor demand curve and a labor supply curve. The resulting differences in pay across job specialties can be huge. These differences should interest anyone deciding on a career.

WHY WAGES DIFFER

LO1
Explain why wages differ across labor markets.

Wages differ substantially across labor markets. Figure 9.4 shows average hourly wages for the 131 million U.S. workers in 2009. Workers are sorted into 22 broad occupations from the highest to the lowest average wage. Management earns the highest wage, at $49 per hour, and food workers earn the lowest, at $10 per hour. Wage differences across labor markets can be attributed to differences in labor demand and labor supply.

Differences in Training, Education, Age, and Experience

Some jobs pay more because they require a long and expensive training period. Costly training reduces market supply because fewer people are willing to undergo the time and expense required, so the supply is smaller. However, extensive training increases the productivity of labor. This in turn increases the demand for workers with those skills. For example, certified public accountants (CPAs) earn more than file clerks because the extensive training for CPAs limits the labor supply to this field and because this training increases the productivity of CPAs compared to file clerks. Reduced supply and increased demand both increase the market wage. Even among physicians, some earn more than others because specialty training reduces supply and increases demand. This is why, for example, surgeons on average earn twice as much as general practitioners.

Figure 9.5 shows how education and experience affect earnings. Age groups are shown on the horizontal axis and average annual earnings, on the vertical axis. Earnings are for full-time, year-round workers. The lines are labeled to reflect the highest level of education achieved and range from "No high school degree" (bottom line)

Figure 9.4 Average Hourly Wage by Occupation

The average hourly wages for the 131 million U.S. workers in 2009 are sorted from the highest to the lowest in this bar graph. Wage differences across labor markets can be attributed to differences in labor demand, labor supply, or both.

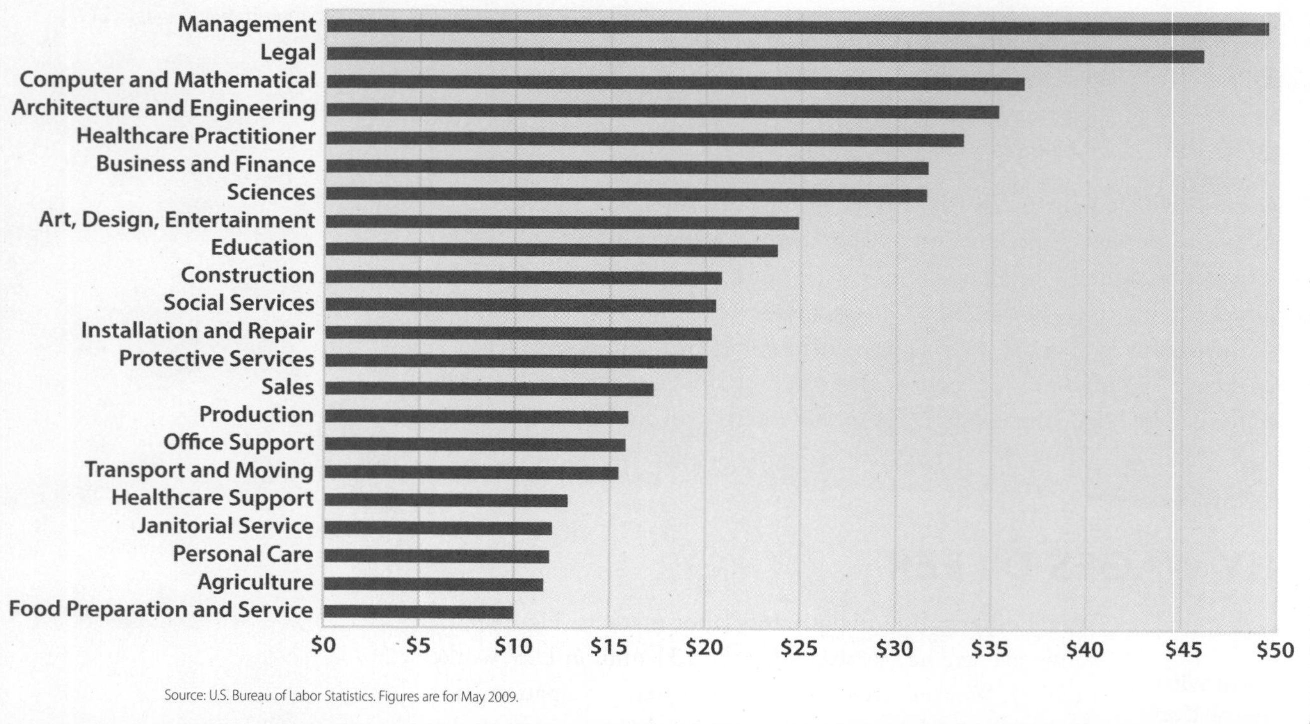

Source: U.S. Bureau of Labor Statistics. Figures are for May 2009.

up to "Professional degree" (top line). Professional degrees include graduate degrees in law, medicine, business administration, and the like.

The relationship between income and education is clear. At every age, those with more education earn more. For example, in the 35-to-44 age group, earnings for those with a professional degree average five times more than those with no high school degree. Age itself also can have an important effect on income. Earnings increase as workers gain more job experience and become more productive.

Notice that the pay increase based on age tends to be greater for more-educated workers. For example, among those with no high school degree, workers in the 55-to-64 age group earned about the same as those in the 25-to-34 age group. But among those with a professional degree, workers in the 55-to-64 age group earned nearly twice as much as those in the 25-to-34 age group. Thus, experience is rewarded more for those with more education.

These earnings differences reflect the normal operation of labor markets. More education and more job experience increase labor productivity, and more productive workers earn more.

FIGURE 9.5 Education Pays More for Every Age Group

At every age, those with more education earn more. Among more educated workers, earnings also increase as workers gain more job experience and therefore become more productive.

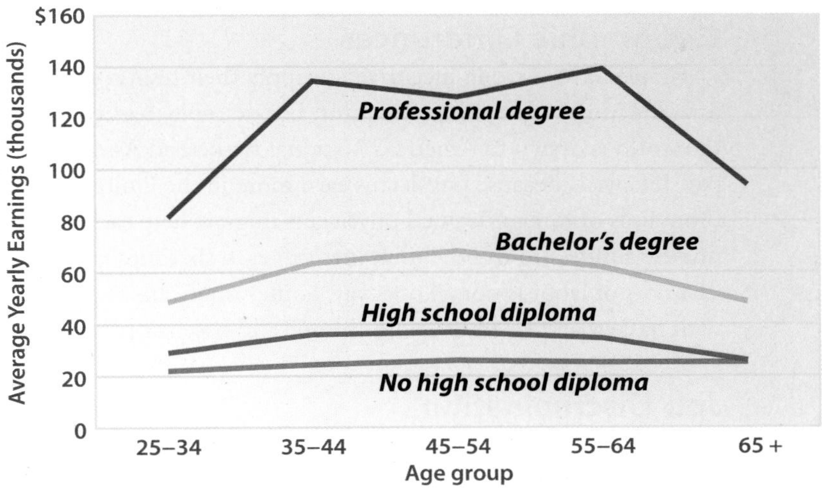

Source: U.S. Census Bureau, *Current Population Survey, 2010 Annual Social and Economic Supplement*. Figures are average earnings for all full-time, year-round workers in 2008.

Differences in Ability

Because they are more able and more productive, some workers earn more than others with the same training and education. For example, two college graduates majoring in economics may have identical educations, but one earns more because of greater ability and higher productivity. Most business executives have extensive training and business experience, but few get to head large corporations.

The same goes for professional athletes. In the National Basketball Association, for example, Kobe Bryant of the Los Angeles Lakers was paid $25 million in the 2010–2011 season (the season prior to the NBA labor dispute). Bryant's pay was about 50 times more than that of his two lowest-paid teammates.

Differences in Risk

Jobs with a higher probability of injury or death, such as coal mining and ocean fishing, pay more than safer jobs, other things constant. Workers also earn more, other things constant, in seasonal jobs such as construction and fishing. This is due to the higher risk of unemployment at certain times of the year.

Some jobs are both dangerous and seasonal. For example, deckhands on crab boats in the winter waters off Alaska can earn more than $10,000 for five days' work. But the job is dangerous, the temperature rarely gets above zero, and daily shifts allow for only three hours of sleep.

Geographic Differences

People have a strong incentive to supply their resources in the market where they earn the most, other things constant. For example, basketball talent from around the world is drawn to America's National Basketball Association because of the high pay. Likewise, because physicians earn more in the United States than elsewhere, thousands of foreign-trained physicians migrate here each year. The same goes for nurses (a nurse from the Philippines can earn six times more in the United States). The flow of labor is not all one way. Some Americans seek their fortune abroad, with basketball players going to Europe and baseball players heading to Japan.

Job Discrimination

Some people earn less because of discrimination in the job market based on race, ethnicity, or gender. Although such discrimination is illegal, history shows that certain groups—including African Americans, Hispanics, and women—have systematically been paid less than others of apparently equal ability.

Job-market discrimination can take many forms. An employer may fail to hire a minority job applicant because the applicant lacks training. But this lack of training can arise from discrimination in the schools, in union apprenticeship programs, or in employer-run training programs. For example, evidence suggests that black workers receive less on-the-job training than otherwise similar white workers.

The Equal Employment Opportunity Commission, established by the Civil Rights Act of 1964, monitors cases involving unequal pay for equal work and unequal access to promotion. Research suggests that civil rights legislation has helped narrow the black–white earnings gap.

The gap between male and female pay also has narrowed. For example, among all full-time, year-round U.S. workers, females in 1980 earned only 60 percent of what males earned. By 2009, females earned 80 percent of male pay. In addition to discrimination as a source of the pay gap, women do more housework and childcare than men do. This tends to reduce female job experience. It also causes some women to seek more flexible positions, which often pay less.

Union Membership

Finally, workers represented by labor unions earn more on average than other workers. The final section of this chapter discusses the effects of labor unions on the labor market.

CHECKPOINT **Why do wages differ across labor markets?**

THE MINIMUM WAGE

LO2 Describe minimum wage legislation.

In 2007, Congress and the president increased the minimum wage from $5.15 to $7.25. The **minimum wage law** establishes a minimum amount that an employer can pay a worker for an hour of labor.

Coverage of the Law

When the legislation was approved, only about 4 percent of the U.S. workforce earned less than $7.25 per hour and thus could have been affected by an increased minimum wage. This low-wage group included workers with few job skills. Most were young, the majority worked only part time, and they were employed primarily in service and sales occupations.

Effects of the Minimum Wage

Critics of minimum-wage legislation argue that a minimum wage established above the equilibrium wage causes employers either to reduce the quantity of labor employed or to change something else about the job. Advocates argue that the minimum wage increases the income of the poorest workers with little or no reduction in overall employment.

The U.S. Department of Labor provides information about the minimum wage on the Fair Labor Standards Act (FLSA) page of its website. Access the website shown below and click on the link for Chapter 9. Read the information on the FLSA page, and then answer these questions. Is the federal minimum wage still $7.25 per hour? If not, what is it? Which groups of workers are exempt from minimum wage and overtime pay requirements?

www.cengage.com/school/contecon

Most research on the effects of the minimum wage finds either no effect on employment or a negative effect, particularly among teenage workers. Employers often react to a minimum wage increase by

- substituting part-time jobs for full-time jobs
- substituting more-qualified minimum-wage workers (such as high school graduates) for less-qualified workers (such as high school dropouts)
- adjusting some nonwage features of the job to reduce employer costs or increase worker productivity.

Nonwage Job Features

Congress may be able to legislate a minimum wage, but employers can still adjust many other conditions of employment. Here are some of the nonwage job components that an employer could alter to offset the added cost of a higher minimum wage: the convenience of work hours, expected work effort, on-the-job training, time allowed for meals and breaks, wage premiums for night shifts and weekends, paid vacation days, paid holidays, sick leave policy, policies for arriving late or leaving early, healthcare benefits, and so on. For example, one study found that restaurants responded to a higher minimum wage by reducing fringe benefits, particularly vacation time, and reducing the higher wages offered for less-desirable shifts.

minimum wage law Establishes a minimum amount that an employer must pay a worker for each hour of labor

Math in Economics

Common Core Ratios and Proportional Relationships

You can read related values from bar and line graphs by locating the point on the graph and following a line parallel to the horizontal axis to the scale along the vertical axis.

EXAMPLE Find the change in percents of the minimum wage from 1996 to 2006. Compare this value to the percent change in price levels for these years.

SOLUTION Read the percent values for the minimum wages in 1996 and 2006. Subtract the 1996 value from the 2006 value. Do the same for the price level values.

21% – 12% = 9% change in the minimum wage

48% – 16% = 32% change in the price level

Practice the Skill Determine the percent change in each of the following relative to 1991 values.

1. What was the percent change in the price level between 2001 and 2011?
2. What was the percent change in the minimum wage level between 2001 and 2011?
3. Why might a person who only compared increases in these values between 2001 and 2011 draw a slightly different conclusion about their rates of change than someone who considered changes between 1991 and 2011?

Higher Opportunity Cost of School

A higher minimum wage also raises the opportunity cost of staying in school. According to one study, an increase in the minimum wage encouraged some 16- to 19-year-olds to quit school and look for work, though many failed to find jobs. Those who had already dropped out of school were more likely to become unemployed because of a higher minimum wage. Thus, an increase in the minimum wage may have the unintended consequence of encouraging some students to drop out of school. The unemployment rate is highest for high-school dropouts. For example, in 2011 the unemployment rate for those with no high school degree was four times that of college graduates.

CHECKPOINT

How might an increase in the minimum wage affect nonwage compensation for low-wage workers?

Photos courtesy of iStockphotos.com; office: bradwieland; pool: gchutka; roof: TerryJ

ESSENTIAL QUESTION

Standard CEE 13: Income

Income for most people is determined by the market value of the productive resources they sell. What you earn primarily depends on the market value of what you produce.

How does the market value of what you produce affect your income?

9.2 ASSESSMENT

Think Critically

1. Why are people who are trained to repair computers paid more than people who are trained to mend clothing?
2. Why does job discrimination harm not only the people who are discriminated against but also society in general?
3. Why might an increase in the minimum wage cause greater unemployment among low-skill workers?

Graphing Exercise

4. Data about labor supply is divided into several categories. Some people are not considered because they are too young or unable to work. The remaining people comprise the civilian noninstitutional population (CNP). Of this group, some people do not seek employment and are not in the labor force. The remaining people are either employed or unemployed. Use the data in the table to draw a multiple line graph that illustrates the data given below. What does your graph tell you about changes in labor supply in the United States?

U.S. LABOR FORCE DATA, 2001–2009 (MILLIONS OF PEOPLE)

Year	CNP	Not in Labor Force	In Labor Force	Employed	Unemployed
2001	215.1	71.4	143.7	136.9	6.8
2003	221.2	74.7	146.5	137.7	8.8
2005	226.1	76.8	149.3	141.3	8.0
2007	231.9	78.8	153.1	145.2	7.9
2009	235.8	83.7	152.1	139.9	12.2

Source: *Statistical Abstract of the United States, 2011*, p. 377.

Make Academic Connections

5. **Government** In 1968, the federal minimum wage was $1.60 per hour. This amount might seem very low; however, when adjusted for inflation, it had the same purchasing power as $10.06 per hour in 2009 dollars. In 2009, the federal minimum wage was $7.25 per hour. When adjusted for inflation, the minimum wage fell by about 28 percent between 1968 and 2009. Why do you think the federal government did not increase the minimum wage at the same rate as inflation?

TeamWork

Organize into teams of four students. Each team member should choose one of the occupation categories shown in Figure 9.4. Make sure that each member chooses a different occupation. As a team, discuss possible reasons for the wage differences among the four occupations. Report your conclusions to the class.

AND MOVERS SHAKERS

Beverly Kearney

Head Coach, University of Texas Women's Track and Field

Matt Szwajkos/Getty Images for Alan Taylor

As head coach of the women's track and field and cross country teams at the University of Texas, Beverly Kearney is one of the most successful coaches in the history of college athletics. In her 23 years as head coach, her teams have won 22 league titles and seven national championships. Since her arrival in Texas in 1993, Kearney has led the Longhorns to six NCAA National Championships and 19 league titles. Kearney has high expectations of her athletes, who have a 95 percent graduation rate and are among America's best athletes. Her enthusiasm and talent for coaching and mentoring also has motivated 12 Olympic athletes to win seven medals, three of them gold.

Kearney has been inducted into the International Women's Sports Hall of Fame. She is the first African American and the second woman to receive the "Lifetime Achievement Award" from Auburn University.

Kearney's success didn't come without challenges. In her senior year of high school, her mother died suddenly, leaving Kearney to take care of her six siblings. She said "I think everything we go through in life prepares us for the next thing…whether that is to get through the successes or the tragedies, we are prepared by life." It wasn't easy working and taking care of herself and her siblings, but she was driven. She said, "One thing that I think distinguishes [me] from everyone else around me is I wanted to be somebody. I didn't want to be nobody."

With the help of a mentor and despite all odds, Kearney graduated from high school and went on to college where she excelled at athletics and coaching. At 29, she was the youngest head coach of women's track and field in the history of the University of Florida. Kearney says she has faced racism and sexism, and experienced times where it would have been easier to give up on her dreams. But she never gave up. She said, "No matter what happens, celebrate it and move on." It was this fighting attitude that helped her overcome a devastating injury she received in a 2002 car crash. Kearney lost two of her friends in the accident, and was seriously injured herself. When paramedics found her she was barely breathing. Her skull was fractured and her spinal cord was badly injured, leaving her paralyzed below the waist. The doctors told her she would never walk again. But Kearney knew that through hard work, perseverance, and determination she could defy the odds. Within a year of the accident, she had abandoned the wheelchair and was able to walk again, with the assistance of a cane.

To help inspire others who have faced challenges similar to hers she founded "Pursuit of Dreams." This nonprofit foundation uses sports-based coaching methods and principles to help people in difficult situations fulfill their "total mental, physical and spiritual goals through the successful use of coaching principles and techniques."

She talks to young people about having dreams and never using the word "impossible." Her mantra is "believe it, speak it, do it." She says, "Don't give me a reality check because reality will tell you what you can't do… Once you find your passion, you are driven towards it. And once you get that, there isn't anything someone can tell you about what you can't do."

Think Critically **How do you think Beverly Kearney's record of success affects her earning power as a coach? Which of the factors listed under "Why Wages Differ" on pages 273–276 do you think most influence her earning power?**

Sources: http://www.letsredu.com/2010/09/track-coach-bev-kearney-on-decisions-from-the-roadtrip-nation-interview-archive/#fbid=bSzRaHmMCvn&wom=false; http://www.thesurvivorsclub.org/survivor-stories/extreme/its-a-place-of-healing; and http://www.bevkearneypursuitofdreams.com/?page_id=118.

9.3 LABOR UNIONS

Key Terms

Learning Objectives

LO1 Describe the history and tools of U.S. labor unions.

LO2 Analyze how labor unions try to increase wages.

LO3 Discuss recent trends in union membership.

In Your World

The aspect of labor markets that you read and hear about most frequently involves labor unions. Labor negotiations, strikes, picket lines, and heated confrontations between workers and employers all fit neatly into TV's "action news" format. But despite all the media attention, only about one in eight U.S. workers belongs to a labor union. Most union contracts are reached without a strike. The typical union member most likely is a government employee. Labor unions seek higher pay, job security, and more benefits for members.

ORGANIZED LABOR

LO1 Describe the history and tools of U.S. labor unions.

In the late nineteenth century, factory workers averaged 11-hour days, 6 days a week. Those in steel mills, paper mills, and breweries averaged 12-hour days, 7 days a week. Child labor was common, and working conditions were often dangerous. For example, according to one estimate, fatal accidents in the steel mills of Pittsburgh accounted for one-fifth of all male deaths in that city during the 1880s. Despite the long hours and dreadful working conditions, millions of immigrants entered the workforce, increasing the supply of labor and keeping wages low.

History of Labor Unions

Through a **labor union**, workers join forces to improve their pay and working conditions by negotiating a labor contract with their employers. The first labor unions in the United States were craft unions, where membership was limited to workers with a particular skill, or craft—such as carpenters, shoemakers, or printers. In 1886 craft unions formed their own national organization, the *American Federation of Labor (AFL).* The AFL was not a union itself but rather an organization of national unions, each retaining its own independence.

The Clayton Act of 1914 exempted labor unions from antitrust laws, meaning that *union members at competing companies could join forces legally in an effort to raise wages and improve working conditions.* Unions also were exempt from taxation. This favorable legislation encouraged the union movement.

labor union A group of workers who join together to seek higher pay and better working conditions by negotiating a labor contract with their employers

The *Congress of Industrial Organizations (CIO)* was formed in 1935 to serve as a national organization of unions in mass-production industries. Whereas the AFL organized workers in particular crafts, the CIO organized all workers in a particular industry. These *industrial unions* included all workers in an industry, such as all autoworkers or all steelworkers. The labor union still had to organize workers company by company, however. Workers at a company became unionized if a majority of them voted for union representation.

After World War II, economic conditions and public sentiment seemed to turn against labor unions. In 1947, Congress passed the *Taft-Hartley Act*, which authorized states to introduce right-to-work laws. A **right-to-work law** says that a worker at a union company does not have to join the union or pay union dues to hold a job there. Twenty-two states have passed right-to-work laws. These states are mostly in the South, the Plains, and the Mountain states. Union membership rates in the right-to-work states average only half the rates in other states. For more information on the history of labor unions, see the Connect to History feature on page 291.

right-to-work law State law that says a worker at a union company does not have to join the union or pay union dues to hold a job there

collective bargaining The process by which representatives of a union and an employer negotiate wages, employee benefits, and working conditions

mediator An impartial observer brought in when labor negotiations break down, to suggest how to resolve differences

binding arbitration When labor negotiations break down and the public interest is involved, a neutral third party is brought in to impose a settlement that both sides must accept

Collective Bargaining

Collective bargaining is the process by which union representatives negotiate with an employer about wages, employee benefits, and working conditions. Once a preliminary agreement is reached, union representatives present it to the membership for a vote. If the agreement is accepted, union representatives and the employer sign a labor contract. If the agreement is rejected, the union may strike or continue negotiations.

If the negotiators cannot reach an agreement, and if the public interest is involved, government officials may ask a mediator to step in. A **mediator** is an impartial observer who listens to both sides separately and then suggests a solution. The mediator has no power to impose a settlement on the parties.

In the provision of certain vital public services such as police and fire protection, a strike could harm the public. The government may impose **binding arbitration** in these cases. This means that a neutral third party evaluates both sides of the dispute and issues a ruling that both sides must accept. Some disputes skip the mediation and arbitration steps and go directly to a strike.

Photodisc/Getty Images

In your opinion, are labor unions necessary in today's economy? Why or why not?

The Strike

A major source of union power in the bargaining relationship is the threat of a **strike**. This is a union's attempt to withhold labor from the employer. The purpose of a strike is to force the firm to accept the union's position. But a strike also hurts union members, who suffer a drop in income and who could lose their jobs permanently. The threat of a strike hangs over labor negotiations and can encourage an agreement. *Although neither party usually wants a strike, rather than give in on key points, both sides act as if they could and would survive one.*

If a strike is called, union members usually picket the employer to prevent or discourage so-called strikebreakers from "crossing the picket lines." With non-striking employees and temporary workers, a firm sometimes can maintain production during a strike. That's bad news for the strikers.

Some industries are more vulnerable to strikes than others, such as those that involve perishable goods, like strawberries, and those where picket lines can turn away lots of customers, like Broadway theaters. In other industries, however, advances in technology have reduced the effectiveness of strikes. For example, striking workers in petroleum and chemical industries found that skeleton crews of supervisors could run computer-controlled refineries for a long time without union workers.

CHECKPOINT What tools do U.S. labor unions use?

UNION WAGES AND EMPLOYMENT

LO2 Analyze how labor unions try to increase wages.

The union's focus usually is on higher wages. Unions use two approaches to increase the wages of members: (1) reduce the supply of labor and (2) increase the demand for union labor.

Reduce the Supply of Labor

One way to increase wages is for the union to somehow reduce the supply of labor. This occurs with craft unions, such as unions of carpenters or plumbers. The effect of a supply restriction is shown as a leftward shift of the labor supply curve from S to S'' in panel (A) of Figure 9.6. The result is a higher wage and reduced employment.

Successful supply restrictions of this type require the union first to limit its membership and second to force all employers in the market to hire only union members. The union can restrict membership with high initiation fees, long apprenticeship periods, difficult qualification exams, restrictive licensing requirements, and other devices aimed at discouraging new membership. But, even if unions can restrict membership, they have difficulty requiring all firms in the market to hire only union workers. In right-to-work states, workers do not have to belong to a union even if the company workforce is unionized.

Professional groups—doctors, lawyers, and accountants, for example—also impose entry restrictions through education and examination requirements. These restrictions usually are defended by the professions on the grounds that they protect the public. Some observers, however, see the restrictions as attempts to increase pay among existing professionals by limiting the labor supply.

strike A labor union's attempt to withhold labor from a firm

Increase the Demand for Union Labor

Another way to increase the wage of union workers is to increase the demand for union labor. This strategy is reflected by a rightward shift of the labor demand curve from *D* to *D′* in panel (B) of Figure 9.6. This is an attractive alternative for union members because it increases both the wage and employment. Following are some ways unions try to increase the demand for union labor.

Increase Demand for Union-Made Products The demand for union labor may be increased through a direct appeal to consumers to buy only union-made products. Increasing the demand for union-made products increases the demand for union labor. Remember, the demand for any resource is derived from the demand for the good that resource produces.

Restrict Supply of Nonunion-Made Products Another way to increase the demand for union labor is to restrict the supply of products that compete with union-made products. The United Auto Workers, for example, has backed trade restrictions on imported cars. Fewer imported cars means greater demand and higher prices for cars produced by U.S. workers, who are mostly union members. This strategy became less effective as foreign automakers, such as Toyota, established nonunion plants in the United States.

Increase Productivity of Union Labor In the absence of a union, a dissatisfied worker may simply look for another job. Losing workers in this way is costly for an employer because the worker often leaves with on-the-job experience that makes that worker more productive and harder to replace. Unions also may try to keep workers from quitting or goofing off. This increases worker productivity, thus increasing the demand for union labor.

FIGURE 9.6 Reducing Labor Supply or Increasing Labor Demand

If a union can restrict labor supply to an industry, the supply curve shifts to the left from *S* to *S″*, as in panel (A). The wage rate rises from *W* to *W″*, but at the cost of a reduction in employment from *E* to *E″*. In panel (B), an increase in labor demand from *D* to *D′* raises both the wage and the level of employment.

(A) REDUCING LABOR SUPPLY

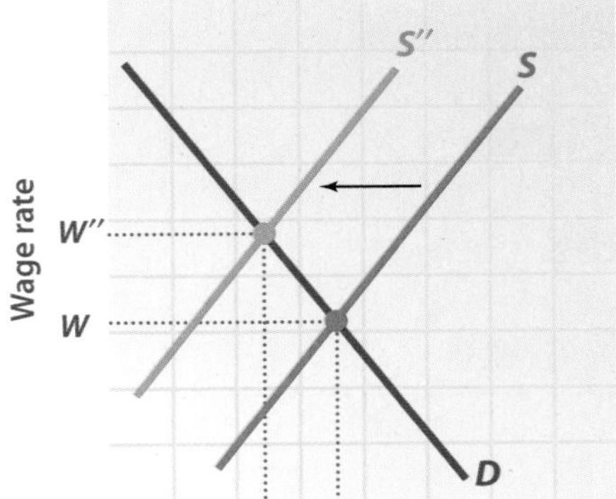

(B) INCREASING LABOR DEMAND

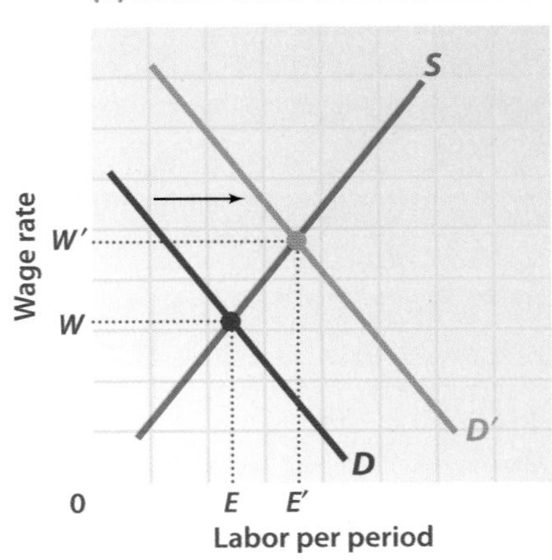

Featherbedding Another way unions try to increase the demand for union labor is by **featherbedding**. This is an attempt to ensure that more union labor is hired than the employer would prefer. For example, union rules require that each Broadway theater hire a permanent "house" carpenter, electrician, and property manager. Once the play begins, these workers appear only on payday to pick up their checks. In addition, the theater's box office must be staffed by at least three people. With featherbedding, the union tries to increase not only the wage but also the number of workers that must be hired at that wage. Featherbedding raises the prices that consumers face.

Union Pay Is Higher

featherbedding Union efforts to force employers to hire more union workers than demanded for the task

Studies have shown that union members earn an average of roughly 15 percent more than similarly qualified nonunion workers. Figure 9.7 compares the median weekly earnings of union and nonunion workers. Unions are more successful at raising wages in less-competitive industries. For example, unions have less impact on wages in the wholesale and retail trade, where markets tend to be more competitive. Unions have greater impact on wages in government, transportation, and

FIGURE 9.7 Median Weekly Earnings: Union vs. Nonunion

Median weekly earnings are higher for union workers than for nonunion workers.

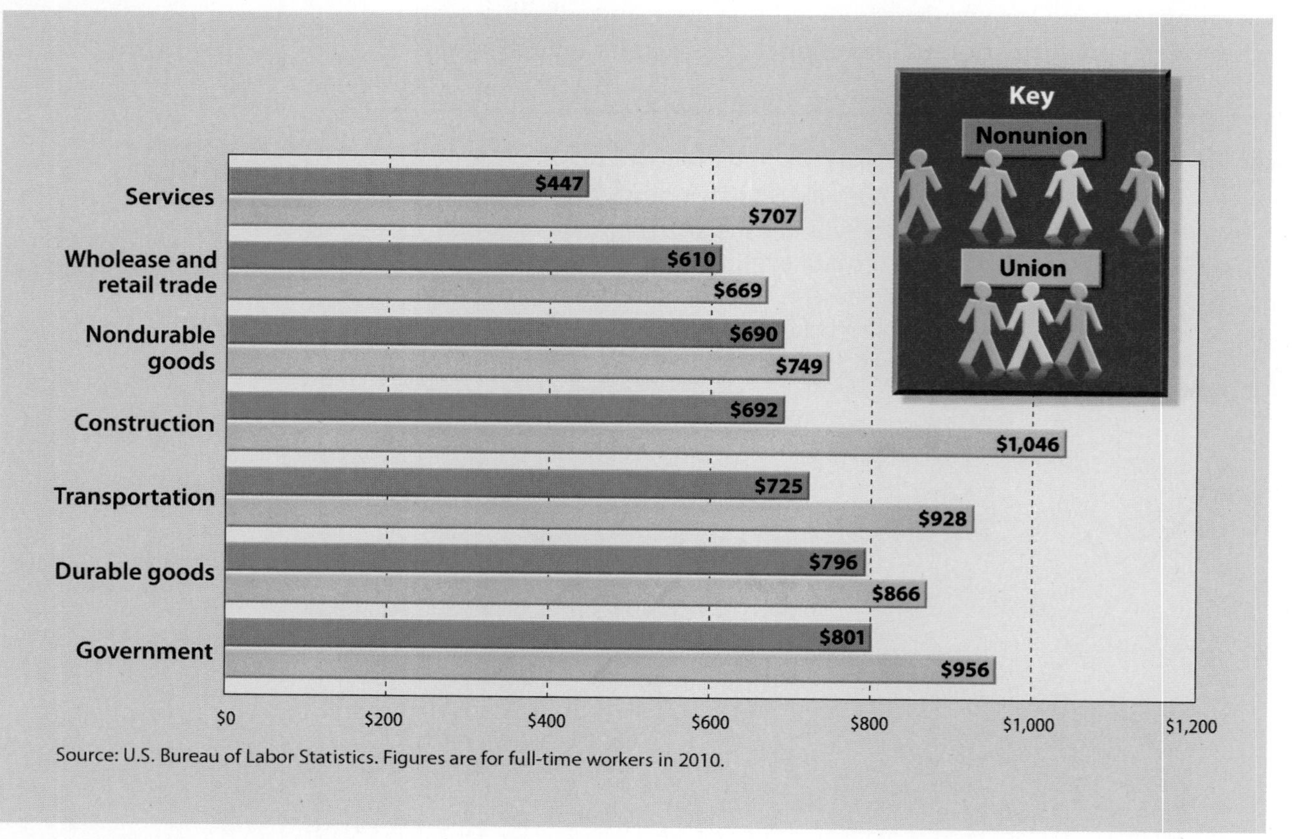

Source: U.S. Bureau of Labor Statistics. Figures are for full-time workers in 2010.

construction, which tend to be less competitive either because government plays more of a role or because firms have more market power. Recall that market power is the ability to raise prices without losing that many customers to other firms.

When there is more competition in the product market, employers cannot easily pass along higher union wages as higher product prices. Nonunion firms can enter the industry, pay lower wages, and sell the product for less. Competition among producers helps consumers but not union workers.

How do unions try to increase the wages of union workers? **CHECKPOINT**

TRENDS IN UNION MEMBERSHIP

LO3 Discuss recent trends in union membership.

In 1955, about one-third of workers in the United States belonged to unions. Union membership as a percentage of the workforce has since declined. Now only about one-eighth of all workers belong to a union. Government workers make up more than half of all union members, even though they account for just one-sixth of U.S. workers. Compared with other advanced economies, the United States ranks low in the share of workers who belong to a union. However, membership rates abroad have declined as well.

Membership by Gender and Age

The bar graph in Figure 9.8 indicates U.S. union membership rates by age and gender. The rates for men, shown by the green bars, are higher than the rates for women. This, in part, is because more men are employed in manufacturing, where

FIGURE 9.8 U.S. Union Membership for Men and Women by Age

Men in the United States have higher rates of union membership than women due to the nature of the work each group typically performs.

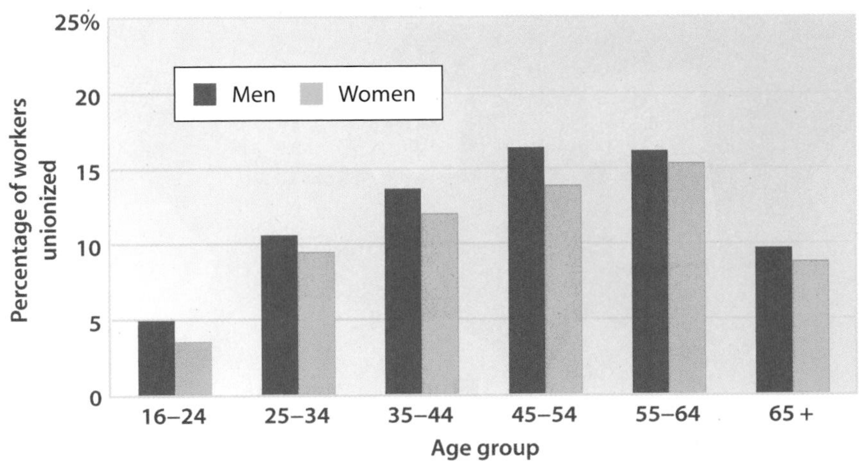

Source: U.S. Bureau of Labor Statistics, "Union Members," 21 January 2011, Table 1, at http://www.bls.gove/news.release/union2.t01.htm. Percentages are for 2010.

union membership tends to be higher. Women are employed more in the service sector, where union membership historically has been lower. The highest membership rate is for middle-aged men. The lowest rate is for young women.

Membership by State

Union membership rates also vary across states. Figure 9.9 shows union membership as a percent of those employed for each state. The figure also shades right-to-work states, where workers in unionized companies do not have to join the union or pay union dues. As noted earlier, unionization rates in right-to-work states average only half the rates in other states. New York has the highest unionization rate at 24.2 percent. North Carolina has the lowest, at 3.2 percent.

Reasons for Declining Membership

Improvements in the conditions of the average worker since the late nineteenth century have been remarkable. The average workweek in some industries has been cut in half. The workplace now is monitored more closely for health and

FIGURE 9.9 Right-to-Work States and Unionization Percentage by State

Shaded areas show right-to-work states, where workers in unionized companies do not have to join the union or pay union dues. Numbers indicate union membership as a percentage of all workers in each state. States that have right-to-work laws average only about half the percent of workers who belong to unions as other states.

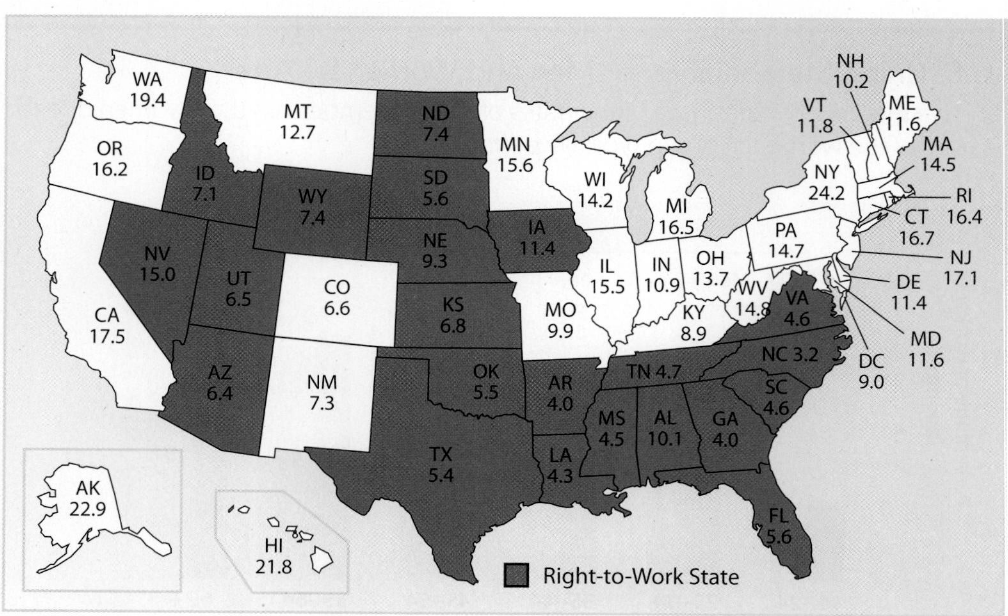

Source: U.S. Bureau of Labor statistics and the National Right to Work Committee, www.nrtwc.org/. Unionization rates are for 2010 and right-to-work states are as of 2011.

safety hazards. Child labor was outlawed decades ago. Wages have increased substantially.

These improvements cannot be entirely credited to labor unions. Competition among employers to attract qualified workers helps explain some of the improvements. The increase in wages can be traced mostly to an increase in labor productivity. This is because workers now have more education and training, and they benefit from more capital and better technology. However, unions played a crucial role in improving wages and working conditions, and in calling public attention to labor problems.

Photodisc/Getty Images

Assembly-line workers in factories often belong to unions. If you worked on an assembly line and had to decide whether or not to join the union, do you think you would join? Why or why not?

Because working conditions and wages are now much better, workers today feel less inclined to join a union, especially in those states where they need not join to enjoy union pay and benefits. Fewer union members mean fewer voters who belong to unions, so unions also have lost some political clout. Unions have, in a sense, become the victims of their own success. Here are some additional reasons why union membership has declined.

Changes in the Economy The decline in union membership is due partly to changes in the industrial structure of the U.S. economy. Unions have long been more important in the goods-producing sector than in the service-producing sector. But employment in the goods-producing sector, which includes manufacturing and construction, has fallen in recent decades as a share of all jobs.

Competition from Nonunion Firms Another factor in the decline of union membership is the growth in market competition, particularly from imports. Increased competition from nonunion employers, both foreign and domestic, has reduced the ability of unionized firms to pass higher labor costs on to consumers as higher prices.

Strikes Are Fewer and Less Effective Finally, the near disappearance of the strike has reduced union power. The 1970s averaged nearly 300 strikes per year involving 1,000 or more workers in the United States. Since 2000, there have been only about 20 such strikes per year. Many recent strikes ended badly for union workers because companies hired permanent replacements. Union members now are more reluctant to strike because of the increased willingness of employers to hire replacements and the increased willingness of some workers—both union and nonunion—to cross picket lines to work during a strike.

CHECKPOINT

In what sense is the union movement a victim of its own success?

9.3 ASSESSMENT

Think Critically

1. What are the potential costs and benefits of a strike for union members?
2. In what way were members of the AFL different from members of the CIO?
3. Why are unions more often successful in negotiating for higher wages with firms that have monopoly power than with firms that face strong competition?
4. What are two possible reasons for the lower share of female workers who join unions?
5. Why is union membership often lower in states that passed right-to-work laws? How did this affect the effectiveness of unions in these states?
6. What are three possible reasons for the decline in union membership in recent years?

Graphing Exercises

7. In the late 1950s, nearly one-third of all workers in the United States belonged to a labor union. Since then the share of union workers has declined steadily. Use the following data to draw a line graph to show the decline in the percent of union-organized workers in the labor force from 1985 to 2010: 1985, 18.0%; 1990, 16.1%; 1995, 14.9%; 2000, 13.5%; 2005, 12.3%; and 2010, 11.9%.

Make Academic Connections

8. **Research** Investigate a recent strike in your state. What issues were involved? What was the result of the strike?
9. **Government** In 2010 several states took legal steps to limit the power of public employee unions. This trend was caused at least in part by the financial difficulties many states faced at that time and their need to close large budget deficits. The ability to bargain collectively, for example, was abolished for many state workers in Wisconsin. Investigate this trend and prepare a report that describes what has happened to public employee unions since 2010.

TeamWork

Working in small teams, identify one local business that employs union workers and one that does not. List possible reasons and results for this situation and describe the results for workers and owners of each firm. Does the union help or reduce the organized firm's ability to compete successfully in the marketplace? Does the union restrict the number of workers available to this employer? If you had funds to invest in a business, which of these two firms would you choose? Which firm would you rather work for? Compare your team's answers with those of other teams.

Labor Unions

The U.S. labor movement had its roots in craft industries and skilled workers. The National Trades Union, the country's first national labor union, did not survive the economic panic of 1837. Only after the Civil War and the great boom in industrial growth in the United States did the union movement grow, as labor organizers realized the bargaining power of national organizations. The first major union to attempt a national reach was the National Labor Union. Started in 1866 in Baltimore, it grew to 60,000 members by 1872. Unwieldy with a diverse membership drawn from many industries, it failed to survive an economic downturn—the panic of 1873.

A third attempt at a national union was the Knights of Labor. Founded in 1869 in Philadelphia, the Knights had a goal of organizing all workers, skilled and unskilled, men and women. The union took a long-term view of labor reform with issues such as pay equity, the eight-hour workday, and the abolition of child labor. The Knights of Labor shied away from using the strike as a tool and played down higher wages as a goal. The broad reforms it sought, and its attempts to unite all segments of the workforce, proved difficult, as its members wanted more immediate results. Still, by 1886 it had grown to 750,000 members. In that year, the union was unjustly accused of the bombing of Haymarket Square in Chicago. This led to a public backlash against it and, ultimately, its demise.

Studies show that, unlike today's strikes, those of the 1880s rarely ended in compromise. Only about 10 percent led to something other than total victory for management or labor. The successful strikes for labor—about 50 percent of the total—occurred if the union was supported and the strikes were short. If strikebreakers were employed, the strike likely would fail.

National unions of skilled trades created the American Federation of Labor (AFL), the nation's oldest large-scale labor organization. Unlike the Knights, the AFL wanted to organize skilled workers by craft. Skilled workers were more difficult to replace than unskilled workers, giving the unions more bargaining power. It concentrated on small companies that were less likely to be able to bust the unions. Led by Samuel Gompers, the AFL emphasized basic issues such as higher wages, shorter hours, and better working conditions. It pressed for the "closed shop," a workplace where only union members could be hired.

Although the AFL questioned the effectiveness of strikes and boycotts, it did use those methods to force employers to engage in collective bargaining. Mediation also became more commonly used to settle labor disputes.

Think Critically **Using the concepts of supply and demand, explain how a closed shop could be used by a labor union to control the labor market within an industry.**

NY Dailey News via Getty Images

Samuel Gompers, President of the American Federation of Labor, 1920

Chapter 9 Summary

ASK THE EXPERT

www.cengage.com/school/contecon

What would happen if everyone were paid the same?

9.1 Resource Markets

A. The demand for a resource is a derived demand that arises from the demand for goods and services that resource produces. As the price of a resource falls, firms are more willing and able to employ that resource. Therefore, the resource demand curve slopes downward. The more productive a resource, the more a firm is willing to pay for it. On the other side, resource suppliers are more willing and able to supply the resource as the price increases. Therefore, the resource supply curve is upward sloping.

B. Nonwage determinants of labor demand include demand for the final product, costs of other resources, and the technology used in production.

C. Nonwage determinants of labor supply include workers' wealth and working conditions as well as current tastes for work.

9.2 Wage Determination

A. Wages differ among labor markets for a variety of reasons, including differences in education, training, and experience. More productive workers tend to be better paid.

B. The minimum wage law establishes a minimum amount that an employer can pay a worker for an hour of labor. Supporters of higher minimum wages say the laws can help low-paid workers improve their standards of living. Opponents argue that higher minimum wages reduce the number of jobs available to low-skill workers and cause employers to cut back on nonwage benefits, such as vacation days.

9.3 Labor Unions

A. Labor unions are formed when workers join together to improve their pay and working conditions by negotiating labor contracts with their employers. Union and management negotiations are carried out through a process called collective bargaining. Once a preliminary agreement is reached between the union bargaining team and management, union members vote to either ratify or reject the proposal. Negotiations can be assisted through mediation or binding arbitration, which involve a neutral third party. A labor strike is the last resort.

B. Unions work to improve wages and working conditions for their members by limiting union membership, increasing demand for union-made products, restricting the supply of nonunion-made products, or increasing the productivity of union workers. Featherbedding occurs when labor contracts require employers to hire more workers than they demand at that wage.

C. Union membership as a share of the workforce has been declining for the past 60 years. There are many possible reasons for this, including improved wages and working conditions, a reduction in the number of industrial jobs in the U.S. economy, competition from nonunion businesses either within or outside the United States, and the diminished effectiveness and reduced frequency of strikes in recent decades.

CHAPTER 9 ASSESSMENT

Review Economic Terms

Match the terms with the definitions. Some terms will not be used.

_____ 1. A labor union's attempt to withhold labor from a firm

_____ 2. An impartial observer brought in when labor negotiations break down to suggest how to resolve differences

_____ 3. The process by which representatives of a union and an employer negotiate wages, employee benefits, and working conditions

_____ 4. A state law that says workers do not have to join a union or pay union dues to hold a job

_____ 5. When labor negotiations break down and the public interest is involved, a neutral third party is brought in to impose a settlement both sides must accept

_____ 6. The demand for a resource that arises from the demand for the product that resource produces

_____ 7. One resource works with the other in production; a decrease in the price of one resource increases the demand for the other

_____ 8. One resource can replace another in production; an increase in the price of one resource increases the demand for the other

_____ 9. The wage at which the quantity of labor firms want to hire exactly matches the quantity workers want to supply

_____ 10. The value of output produced by a resource

_____ 11. Establishes a minimum amount that an employer must pay a worker for an hour of labor

a. binding arbitration
b. collective bargaining
c. derived demand
d. equilibrium wage
e. featherbedding
f. labor union
g. mediator
h. minimum wage law
i. productivity
j. resource complements
k. resource substitutes
l. right-to-work law
m. strike

Review Economic Concepts

12. The demand for resources is derived from
    a. the demand for products the resources are used to produce.
    b. the demand for higher wages for workers.
    c. the demand for profits by business owners.
    d. the demand for taxes to pay for government services.

13. **True or False** Resource prices provide information to producers that allows them to use resources in a way that maximizes their value.

14. If two resources are ________?________, an increase in the price of one will cause businesses to demand less of the other.

15. The market supply of labor will change as a result of each of the following except
    a. a change in the amount of wealth workers hold.
    b. a change in the conditions in which employees are expected to work.
    c. a change in the demand for products workers produce.
    d. a change in workers' tastes for being employed in a particular job.

16. **True or False** Some workers are better paid because they have acquired special training that makes their labor more valuable to employers.

17. Which of the following workers would be best paid?
    a. a worker who has not graduated from high school
    b. a worker who just completed a master's degree in English literature
    c. a worker who is willing to stay up all night to guard a bank's deposit box
    d. a worker who helped design Windows software for Microsoft
18. ________?________ takes place when a person is not employed because of his or her race, ethnicity, or gender.
19. **True or False** Membership in industrial unions is limited to workers with a particular skill.
20. When a labor settlement is imposed on management and on a union by a neutral third party,
    a. there is a right-to-work law.
    b. binding arbitration has taken place.
    c. there has been mediation.
    d. there is likely to be a strike.
21. ________?________ takes place when a contract requires management to hire more workers than it demands at the negotiated wage.
22. A craft union is formed when workers who all ________?________ join together to form a union.
    a. have the same employer
    b. work in the same location
    c. work in a particular industry
    d. have the same skill
23. ________?________ takes place when unions and management negotiate to reach a labor contract.
24. **True or False** In recent decades, union membership has declined.

Apply Economic Concepts

25. **Resource Substitutes** The Apex Pot company manufactures high-quality kitchen pans. Currently it employs 500 workers, who produce stainless steel pans one at a time on individual machines. It takes a worker six minutes to produce each pan. The workers are paid $12 per hour for their labor. Apex managers have found that they can purchase machines that will produce products with equal quality automatically. One machine costs $200,000 but can produce one pan per minute. So far, management has chosen not to purchase any of the machines. The workers' contract is due to expire next month. Their union has asked to have the wage rate increased to $14 per hour. Apex management has stated that the firm cannot afford to pay them any more than they currently receive. What factors should each side consider during collective bargaining?
26. **Minimum Wage Laws** Imagine that you own a fast-food restaurant, which is in a competitive industry. The restaurant employs 20 workers, who are paid the minimum wage. Next month, Congress passes a law that will increase the minimum wage you must pay your workers by $1 per hour. What steps could you take to control your production costs and remain competitive?

27. **Labor Unions** Interview a friend or relative who is a member of a labor union. Ask why this person joined a union. Ask what the biggest benefit is of union membership. Write a paragraph summarizing your interview.

28. **Binding Arbitration** You are the president of a firefighter's union in a large city. There is a law that provides for binding arbitration for vital public employees in your state. The current contract between your union and the city is about to expire. Your members want at least a 4 percent increase in their wages in each of the next three years. The city has offered a 2 percent raise per year. Negotiators have not been able to reach an agreement. The city has said it will call for binding arbitration unless the union accepts its "final offer." If an arbitrator is called in, he or she might award the union more than the city's 2 percent offer. But, you know the city is in a financial bind. The arbitrator could award less than the 2 percent. What recommendation would you make to your members? Explain your reasons for this recommendation.

29. **Assess a Strike** Garbage collectors in several cities in a state went on strike for better wages and a continuation of their employer-paid medical insurance coverage. At that time, the state and many of its local governments had large budget deficits. They argued that they could not afford to pay the garbage collectors more and demanded that these workers contribute to the cost of their medical coverage. Write an essay that addresses two issues: (1) Should garbage collectors be allowed to strike? Why or why not? (2) Should the garbage collectors be forced to pay part of the cost for their medical insurance when it has been totally paid by their employers in the past?

30. **21st Century Skills: Creativity and Innovation** Identify a product based on a new technology that has come on the market in the past two years. Describe the employment opportunities that this new product has created for workers. Explain what you could do to learn more about this product, the technology it is based on, and how this knowledge could help you gain employment in the future.

Digging Deeper

with Economics e-Collection

In choosing a career, one consideration will be the compensation you will earn for the work you do. To learn more about wage-related considerations, access the Gale Economics e-Collection through the URL below and type the keyword "wages and salaries" into the search box. Refine your search by typing in the name of a career you may want to pursue. Write a paper relating the article to one or more of the topics under "Why Wages Differ" on pages 273–276. Does this research support your decision to pursue this career? Why or why not?

www.cengage.com/school/contecon

CHAPTER 10

Financial Markets and Business Growth

CONSIDER...

- What's seed money, and why can't farmer Patel grow anything without it?
- Why is a movie download less than half the cost of a movie ticket?
- Why do you repeatedly burn your mouth eating pizza, despite knowing the risk?
- Why is a bank more likely to be called Security Trust than Benny's Bank?
- Why do banks charge more interest on car loans than on home loans?

Point your browser

www.cengage.com/school/contecon

jonya/iStockphoto.com; Background image: Pefkos/Shutterstock.com

10.1 PRODUCTION, CONSUMPTION, AND TIME

Learning Objectives

LO1 Explain why production requires saving.

LO2 Explain why people are willing to pay more to consume now rather than later.

LO3 Apply demand and supply analysis to the market for loans.

Key Terms

interest rate 299
demand for loans curve 301
supply of loans curve 302
market for loans 302
equilibrium interest rate 302

In Your World

Time plays an important role in both production and consumption. From an entrepreneur's bright idea for a new product to its delivery to market, production takes time. For example, consider the smartphone you now have or would like to have. As demonstrated on the cover of this textbook, some creative designers developed the rough idea of that phone with certain capabilities. They refined and tested that idea enough for drafting engineers to lay out precise manufacturing specifications. The phone was manufactured and, again, after rigorous testing and expensive marketing, it was shipped to distributors, who sold it to retailers, who sold it to you or to other consumers. During the long production process, how did these resource suppliers survive?

PRODUCTION AND TIME

LO1
Explain why production requires saving.

Patel is a primitive farmer in a simple economy. Isolated from any neighbors or markets, he literally scratches out a living on a plot of land, using only crude sticks. While the crop is growing, none of it can be eaten.

Production Takes Time

Because none of the crop can be consumed until it grows, Patel must rely on food saved from prior harvests to survive. The longer the growing season, the more Patel must have saved from prior harvests. In this simple example, it is clear that *production cannot occur without saving during prior periods.*

Investment Takes Time

With his current resources of land, labor, seed corn, fertilizer, and some crude sticks, suppose Patel grows about 200 bushels of corn per year. He soon realizes that if he had a plow—*a capital good*—his productivity would increase. Making a plow in such a primitive setting, however, would take time and keep him away

Farmer Patel must decide whether to invest his time in making a plow. Does adding 50 more bushels per year outweight the one-time cost of 200 bushels? If you were Patel, how would you decide?

from his fields for a year. Thus, the plow has an opportunity cost of 200 bushels of corn. Patel could not survive this drop in production unless he saved enough from prior harvests. The question is: Should he invest his time in the plow? The answer depends on the costs and benefits of the plow. You already know that the plow's opportunity cost is 200 bushels—the output given up to make the plow. The benefit depends on how much the plow increases production and how long the plow will last. Patel estimates that the plow will boost his yield by 50 bushels per year and will last his lifetime. In making the investment decision, he compares current costs to the future stream of benefits.

Capital Increases Labor Productivity

Rather than work the soil with his crude sticks, Patel produces capital to increase his future productivity. Making the plow is an investment of his time. For the economy as a whole, more investment means more capital goods, increasing the economy's ability to produce in the future. This growth can be shown by an expansion of the economy's production possibilities frontier. Advanced industrial economies invest more than other economies. These additions to capital accumulate over time. Figure 10.1 shows the value of capital goods in the United States in recent years. The value of business structures, which includes factories and office buildings, increased from \$6.4 trillion in 2000 to \$10.9 trillion in 2009. The value of business equipment and software increased from \$4.1 trillion in 2000 to \$5.6 trillion in 2009. This increase in capital of \$6.0 trillion between 2000 and 2009 makes U.S. workers more productive.

You can see from the farmer Patel example why most production cannot occur without prior saving. *Production depends on saving because production of both consumer goods and capital goods takes time.*

Financial Intermediaries

To modernize the example, suppose farmer Patel can borrow money. Many farmers visit their local banks each spring to borrow enough "seed money" to

FIGURE 10.1 **Value of Business Structures, Equipment, and Software in the United States**

The combined value of business structures and business equipment increased by $6.0 trillion between 2000 and 2009.

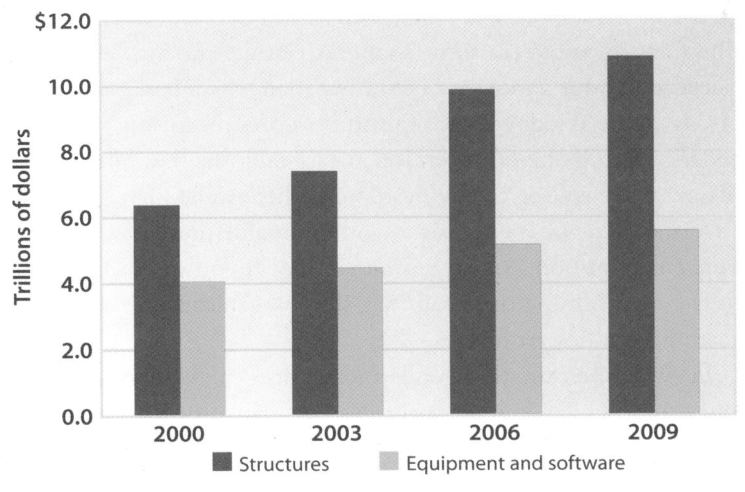

Source: Developed from estimates in the U.S. Department of Commerce, *Survey of Current Business*, September 2010, Table 1, p. 22. Structures include factories, buildings, and other permanent business fixtures. Figures are based on replacement value.

survive until the crops come in. Likewise, other businesses often borrow at least a portion of the financial capital needed until their output is sold.

The **interest rate** is the price of borrowing—the annual interest expressed as a percentage of the amount borrowed. For example, if the interest rate is 5 percent, the interest charged is $5 per year for each $100 borrowed. The lower the interest rate, the lower the price of borrowing. The lower the price of borrowing, the more farmer Patel and other producers are willing and able to borrow.

In a modern economy, producers need not rely exclusively on their own savings. To help finance a business, producers can borrow funds from other savers.

CHECKPOINT

Why does production require savings?

CONSUMPTION AND TIME

LO2
Explain why people are willing to pay more to consume now rather than later.

Did you ever burn the roof of your mouth biting into a slice of pizza that hadn't sufficiently cooled? Have you done this more than once? Why do you continue to do this when you know what is likely to happen? You continue because that bite of pizza is worth more to you now than the same bite two minutes from now. You are so anxious to eat that pizza that you are willing to risk burning your mouth rather than wait until it can no longer

interest rate Annual interest expressed as a percentage of the amount borrowed or saved

harm you. In a small way, this reflects the fact that you and other consumers usually value *present* consumption more than *future* consumption.

Paying More to Consume Now

When you value present consumption more than future consumption, you are willing to pay more to consume now rather than wait. Prices often reflect your greater willingness to pay to consume sooner. Consider the movies. You pay at least twice as much for a movie ticket rather than wait a few months for the movie to be available as a download. Furniture stores promising same-day delivery, dry cleaners offering one-hour service, and restaurants that offer food fast know that consumers are willing to pay more for earlier availability.

Thus, *impatience* is one reason you may value present consumption more than future consumption. Another is *uncertainty.* If you wait, something might prevent you from consuming the good. A T-shirt slogan captures this point best: "Life is uncertain. Eat dessert first."

One way to ensure that goods and services can be consumed now is to borrow money to buy now. Home mortgages, car loans, student loans, personal loans, and credit cards are examples of household borrowing. People borrow more when the interest rate declines, other things constant. For example, home purchases increase when mortgage rates decline.

CHECKPOINT **Why are people often willing to pay more to consume now?**

THE MARKET FOR LOANS

LO3
Apply demand and supply analysis to the market for loans.

You already know that producers are willing to pay interest to borrow money. This borrowing finances the production of consumer goods and capital goods. The simple principles developed for farmer Patel can be generalized to other producers.

The Demand for Loans

Firms borrow to help fund production and investment. They need money to pay for resources until output is produced and sold. Firms also need money to invest in capital goods, such as machines, trucks, and buildings. The interest rate is the cost of borrowing. The lower the interest rate, other things constant, the more firms are willing and able to borrow. So the demand for loans is a downward-sloping curve. It shows that firms borrow more when the interest rate declines.

Firms are not the only demanders of loans. Households borrow to pay for homes, cars, college tuition, and more. The lower the interest rate, the more willing and able households are to borrow. Therefore, households, like firms, borrow more when the interest rate declines, other things constant.

The downward-sloping **demand for loans curve**, labeled *D* in Figure 10.2, reflects the negative relationship between the interest rate and the quantity of loans demanded. The lower the interest rate, the greater the quantity of loans demanded, other things constant.

The Supply of Loans

What about the supply of loans? Because you and other consumers often value present consumption more than future consumption, you must be rewarded to postpone consumption. The amount saved during the year equals income minus consumption. When they save a portion of their incomes in financial institutions such as banks, households give up present consumption in return for interest. *Interest is the reward for not consuming now.*

People delay present consumption for a greater ability to consume in the future. The higher the interest rate, other things constant, the greater the reward

demand for loans curve A downward-sloping curve showing the negative relationship between the interest rate and the quantity of loans demanded, other things constant

FIGURE 10.2 Role of Interest Rates: Market for Loans

The quantity of loans demanded is inversely related to the interest rate. The quantity of loans supplied is directly related to the interest rate. The equilibrium interest rate, 5 percent, is determined at the intersection of the demand curve and supply curve for loans.

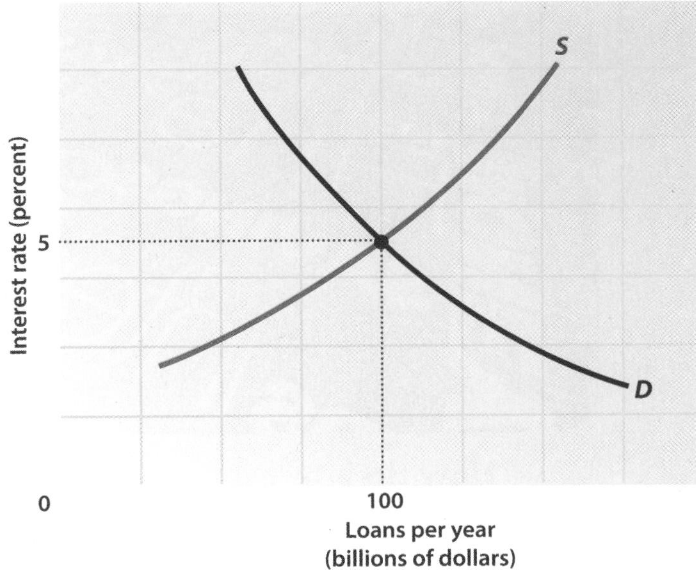

for saving, so the more people save. Savers are the suppliers of loans. The more saved, the greater the quantity of loans supplied.

The **supply of loans curve**, labeled *S* in Figure 10.2, shows the positive relationship between the interest rate and the quantity of loans supplied, other things constant. As you can see, this supply of loans curve slopes upward.

supply of loans curve An upward-sloping curve showing the positive relationship between the interest rate and the quantity of loans supplied, other things constant

market for loans The market that brings together borrowers (the demanders of loans) and savers (the suppliers of loans) to determine the market interest rate

equilibrium interest rate The only interest rate at which the quantity of loans demanded equals the quantity of loans supplied

Market Interest Rate

The demand for loans and the supply of loans come together in the market for loans to determine the market interest rate, as in Figure 10.2. The **market for loans** brings together borrowers (demanders of loans) and savers (suppliers of loans) to determine the market rate of interest. The interest rate is the price of borrowing and the reward for saving. In this case, the **equilibrium interest rate** of 5 percent is the only one that exactly matches the intentions of savers and borrowers. Here, the equilibrium quantity of loans is $100 billion per year.

Though not shown in Figure 10.2, you can easily imagine that an increase in the demand for loans, as reflected by a rightward shift of that curve, would increase the interest rate. An increase in the supply of loans, as reflected by a rightward shift of that curve, would reduce the interest rate.

CHECKPOINT How does demand and supply analysis apply to the market for loans?

ESSENTIAL QUESTION

Standard CEE 12: Interest Rates

Interest rates, adjusted for inflation, rise and fall to balance the amount saved with the amount borrowed, which affects the allocation of scarce resources between present and future uses.

eyeidea/Shutterstock.com

How do interest rates influence the allocation of scarce resources between present and future uses?

10.1 ASSESSMENT

Think Critically

1. Why couldn't you open up a pizza restaurant tomorrow if you wanted to?
2. Why were many more consumers willing to buy automobiles when manufacturers offered special zero percent interest rates?
3. Why do most people borrow funds to purchase a home or an automobile rather than wait until they can afford to pay cash?
4. What happens to the demand for loans that causes the equilibrium interest rate to fall during a downturn in the economy?

Graphing Exercise

5. Home mortgage interest rates change over time with changes in the demand and supply for loans. Use data given in the table to draw a line graph that shows the annual average for new-home mortgage interest rates from 2006 through 2011. How much did this interest rate fall from 2006 through 2011? How important is a change of 1 percent in the mortgage interest rate to a person who wants to borrow $100,000 to buy a home?

NEW HOME MORTGAGE INTEREST RATES, 2006–2011

Year	Interest Rate	Year	Interest Rate
2006	6.63%	2009	5.14%
2007	6.41%	2010	4.80%
2008	6.05%	2011	4.51%

Source: *Economic Indicators*, October, 2011, p. 30.

Make Academic Connections

6. **Financial Management** Most businesses rely on borrowed money. In the early 1980s, interest rates were very high in the United States, reaching levels of 20 percent or more. How would such high interest rates affect businesses, consumers and, therefore, the overall economy?
7. **Advertising** Businesses that market expensive consumer products typically include statements about "easy payment plans" in their ads. Why do they include this information? If more consumers borrow to finance their purchases, what will this do to the demand for loans and interest rates?

TeamWork

Divide your team into two groups. One should represent a business owner who wants to borrow $100,000 to buy new delivery trucks. The other group should represent people who have funds to lend. They should discuss the investment the owners wish to fund and the willingness of the lenders to extend them credit. Determine an interest rate that is acceptable to all. Compare your team's work with that of others.

21st Century Skills

INITIATIVE AND SELF-DIRECTION

Choosing New Technologies

Many new technologies will certainly be created in the 21st century. Devices based on new technologies typically are costly to purchase initially. Prices, however, can be expected to fall as production grows and other similar devices enter the market, creating competition. Additionally, significant improvements often are made soon after the introduction of a new technology. Choosing the exact time to implement a new technology can be a challenging decision for large and small enterprises.

When to Employ New Technologies

Business managers weigh the benefits and costs that will result from implementing new technologies. They should consider each of the following questions before making a purchase decision.

- How much will the technology cost to implement? This includes the purchase price and the cost of training or hiring workers to use the new technology.
- What benefits will the new technology provide in terms of product quality, costs of production, and quantity of goods that can be produced?
- What developments may occur in the future that could make it worth putting off a purchase decision until later?
- How will the firm pay for the new technology? Does the firm have sufficient funds set aside or must it find other sources of funding?

Financing the Purchase

If the managers decide that benefits offered by a new technology have greater value than their costs, they may need to find a way to finance its purchase. The following are sources of financing available to corporations. Possible costs of each alternative also are described.

- **Retained earnings** The firm may be able to rely on corporate profits. This means these funds will not be available for other capital investments and will not be paid out to shareholders as dividends.
- **Borrow from a bank** The firm must repay bank loans on a fixed schedule and pay interest that varies with the amount of the loan and its perceived risk.
- **Borrow from the public by selling corporate bonds** Although small corporations may find it difficult to sell bonds, the rate of interest required to borrow in this way typically is below that of bank loans. The firm must repay bondholders at a designated time in the future and must pay interest regularly until bondholders are repaid.
- **Issue additional stock** Funds raised through the sale of stock do not have to be repaid and dividends may be skipped if a firm is in financial difficulty. The sale of additional stock, however, dilutes the ownership and control of existing stockholders. It is costly to organize a new stock issue, making this impractical for smaller corporations.

Apply the Skill

Imagine you are the chief financial officer (CFO) of a small corporation ($15 million in annual sales) and a new computer-controlled process has been developed that could cut your firm's cost of production by 30 percent. The cost of buying and installing the process is $18 million. Identify and explain three steps you would take before you decide whether to recommend purchase of this process to your board of directors.

10.2 BANKS, INTEREST, AND CORPORATE FINANCE

Learning Objectives

LO1 Explain the role of banks in bringing borrowers and savers together.

LO2 Understand why interest rates differ across types of loans.

LO3 Identify and discuss sources of financial capital.

Key Terms

financial intermediaries 305
credit 305
line of credit 307
prime rate 307
collateral 308
initial public offering (IPO) 309
dividends 309
retained earnings 309
bond 310
securities 310

In Your World

You now understand why borrowers are willing to pay interest and why savers expect to be paid interest. Banks serve both groups. Banks are willing to pay interest to those who save because the banks can, in turn, charge more interest to those who borrow, such as farmers, home buyers, college students, and entrepreneurs looking to start or expand a business. Banks bring savers and borrowers together and try to earn a profit by serving both groups.

BANKS AS INTERMEDIARIES

LO1 Explain the role of banks in bringing borrowers and savers together.

Banks accumulate funds from savers and lend these funds to borrowers, thereby serving as **financial intermediaries** between the two groups. Savers need a safe place for their money. Borrowers need **credit**, which is the ability to borrow now, based on a promise to repay in the future.

Serving Savers and Borrowers

Savers are looking for a safe place for their money. Banks try to inspire confidence among savers. Banks usually present an image of trust and assurance. For example, banks are more likely to be called First Trust or Security National than Benny's Bank or Easy Money Bank and Trust.

Banks gather various amounts from savers and repackage these funds into the amounts demanded by borrowers. Some savers need their money back next week, some next year, and others, only after retirement. Likewise, different borrowers need credit for different lengths of time. Some need credit only for a short time, such as the farmer who borrows until the crop comes in. Homebuyers need credit for up to 30 years. Banks, as intermediaries, offer desirable durations to both savers and borrowers.

financial intermediaries Banks and other institutions that serve as go-betweens, accepting funds from savers and lending them to borrowers

credit The ability to borrow now, based on the promise of repayment in the future

Banks Specialize in Loans

As lenders, banks try to identify borrowers who are willing to pay enough interest and are able to repay the loans. Because of their experience and expertise, banks can judge the creditworthiness of loan applicants better than an individual saver

Investigate Your Local Economy

Identify three banks in your area. Contact the banks or access their websites to find the interest rates they currently apply to home mortgages, car loans, personal loans, business loans, and credit card balances. Compare the results in spreadsheet format. Share your results in class. Are the interest rates consistent among banks for each of the categories?

could. Because banks have experience in drawing up and enforcing contracts with borrowers, they can do so more efficiently than could an individual saver lending money directly to a borrower.

Thus, savers are better off dealing with banks than making loans directly to borrowers. The economy is more efficient because banks develop expertise in evaluating borrowers, structuring loans, and enforcing loan contracts. In short, *banks reduce the transaction costs of channeling savings to creditworthy borrowers.*

Reducing Risk Through Diversification

By lending funds to many borrowers rather than lending just to a single borrower, banks reduce the risk to each individual saver. A bank, in effect, lends a tiny fraction of each saver's deposit to each of the many borrowers. If one borrower fails to repay a loan, this failure hardly affects a large, diversified bank. However, if an individual were to lend his or her life's savings directly to a borrower who defaults on the loan, that would be a financial disaster for the lender.

Yet banks can get into financial trouble if many borrowers fail to repay their loans. For example, when housing prices collapsed in 2007 and 2008, many borrowers owed the bank more than their homes were worth. Some borrowers, particularly those who had lost their jobs, stopped making mortgage payments. These home went into foreclosure, and banks suffered heavy losses. The problems of these bad loans rippled through the economy and contributed to the national recession of 2008–2009.

Line of Credit

Businesses often need to borrow during the year to fund those stretches when sales are slow. For example, many retail businesses sell most of their output during the Christmas shopping season. These firms may need to borrow to get through

Comstock Images/Getty Images

What are the benefits of saving your money in a bank?

months when little is sold. Because of these fluctuations in cash needs, many businesses negotiate a **line of credit** with a bank. This allows the business to get cash as needed during the year. For example, the business applies for a line of credit of, say, $200,000. If the application is approved, the business can draw on that line of credit as needed without having to fill out a loan application each time. This line of credit is equivalent to a consumer's credit-card limit.

CHECKPOINT How and why do banks serve as financial intermediaries between borrowers and savers?

WHY INTEREST RATES DIFFER

LO2 Understand why interest rates differ across types of loans.

So far, the discussion has focused on the market rate of interest, as if there were only one interest rate in the economy. At any particular time, however, a range of interest rates may be available to borrowers. For example, different interest rates apply to home mortgages, car loans, personal loans, business loans, and credit card balances. Figure 10.3 shows interest rates for loans in various markets. The lowest is the so-called **prime rate**, the interest rate

line of credit An arrangement with a bank through which a business can quickly borrow cash as needed

prime rate The interest rate lenders charge for loans to their most trustworthy business borrowers

FIGURE 10.3 Interest Rates Charged for Different Types of Loans

Generally, the less collateral associated with a loan, the higher the interest rate will be. Personal loans and credit-card loans usually have no collateral and thus tend to have higher interest rates.

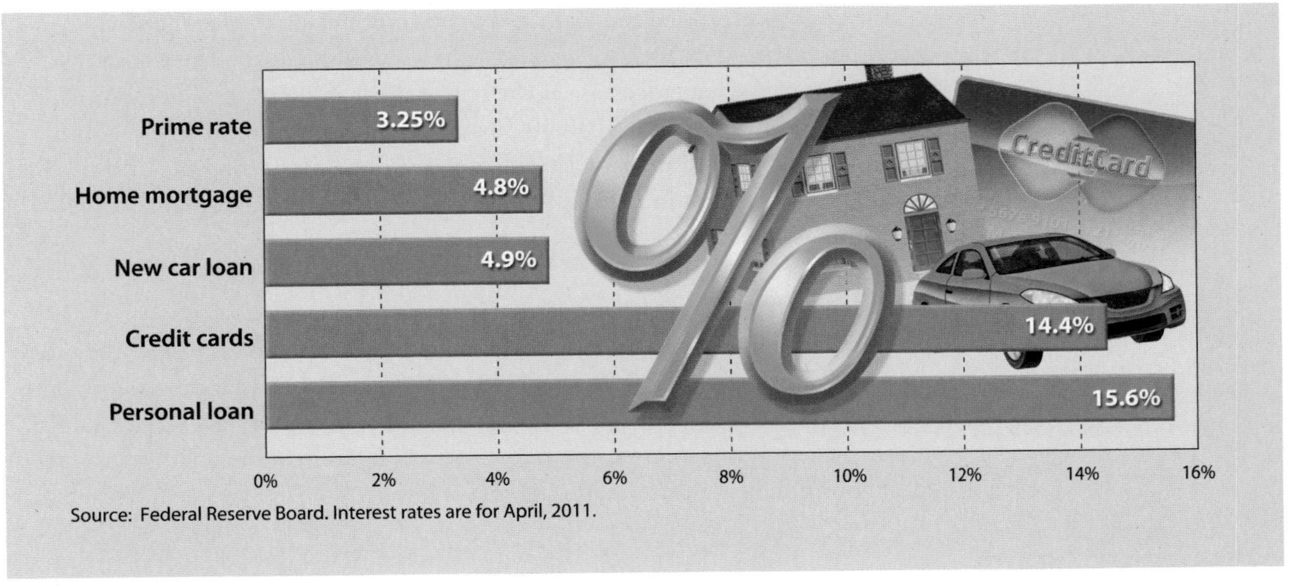

Source: Federal Reserve Board. Interest rates are for April, 2011.

lenders charge their most trustworthy business borrowers. Next lowest is the home mortgage rate, the rate charged those who borrow to buy a home. The highest is the rate charged on personal loans. Why do interest rates differ?

Risk

Some borrowers are more likely than others to *default* on their loans—that is, to not pay them back. Before a bank lends money, it usually requires that a borrower put up **collateral**. This is an asset owned by the borrower that can be sold to repay the loan in the event of a default. With business loans, any valuable assets owned by the firm serve as collateral. With a home mortgage, the home itself becomes collateral. With car loans, the car becomes collateral.

The more valuable the collateral backing up the loan, the less risky the loan for the lender, so the lower the interest rate charged on that loan. The interest rate charged on car loans is usually higher than on home loans. A car loses its value more quickly than a home, and it can be driven away by a defaulting borrower. Thus, a car is not as good collateral as a home. Interest rates are higher still for personal loans and credit cards, because there usually is no collateral for these loans.

Duration of the Loan

The future is uncertain, and the further into the future a loan is to be repaid, the more uncertain that repayment becomes. Thus, under normal circumstances, as the duration of a loan increases, the interest rate charged increases to compensate for the greater risk. For example, the annual interest rate on a ten-year loan typically is higher than on a one-year loan.

Cost of Administration

The costs of executing the loan agreement, monitoring the loan, and collecting payments are called the *administration costs* of the loan. These costs, as a proportion of the loan, decrease as the size of the loan increases. For example, the cost of administering a $100,000 loan is not much greater than the cost of administering a $10,000 loan. The relative cost of administering the loan declines as the size of the loan increases. This reduces the interest rate for larger loans, other things constant.

Tax Treatment

Differences in the tax treatment of different types of loans also affect the interest rate. For example, the interest earned on loans to state and local governments is not subject to federal income taxes. Because people do not have to pay federal income taxes on this interest, they are more willing to lend money to state and local governments. Thus, the interest rate is lower.

collateral An asset owned by the borrower that can be sold to pay off the loan in the event the loan is not repaid

CHECKPOINT Why do interest rates differ for different types of loans?

CORPORATE FINANCE

LO3 Identify and discuss sources of financial capital.

During the Industrial Revolution, labor-saving machinery made large-scale production more profitable. However, building huge factories filled with heavy machinery required substantial sums—more money than any single bank would lend. The corporate structure was the easiest way to finance such large-scale investments, and by 1920, corporations accounted for most employment and output in the U.S. economy.

As you may recall, a corporation is a legal entity, distinct from its shareholders. The corporation may own property, earn a profit, borrow, and sue or be sued. Stockholders, the owners of the corporation, are liable for company debts up to the amount of their investment in the firm.

Corporate Stock

Suppose you have developed a recipe for a spicy chili that your friends have convinced you will be a best seller. You start a sole proprietorship called Six-Alarm Chili. As the founder, you are an entrepreneur. Recall that entrepreneurs are profit-seeking decision makers. They begin with a good idea, organize a business to make that idea come to life, and then assume the risk of its operation.

Your chili company meets with early success. You believe, however, that you need to achieve economies of scale to remain competitive. To obtain the funds you need for expansion, you decide to incorporate the business. The newly incorporated company issues 1 million shares of stock. You award yourself 100,000 shares. You, in effect, pay for your shares with "sweat equity"—hard work you put into founding the company. The remaining 900,000 shares are sold to the public for $10 per share. This raises $9 million for what becomes a public corporation.

Corporations issue and sell stock to fund operations and to pay for new plants and equipment. The initial sale of stock to the public is called an **initial public offering (IPO)**. A share of corporate stock represents a claim on the net income and assets of a corporation. Each share also gives the shareholder one vote on important corporate issues.

Corporations must pay corporate income taxes on any profit they earn. After-tax profit is either paid as **dividends** to shareholders or reinvested in the corporation. Reinvested profit, or **retained earnings**, allows the firm to grow. A corporation is not required to pay dividends. Young firms usually don't. They prefer instead to put any profit back into the firm so it can grow faster. For example, Six-Alarm Chili might use any retained earnings to enter additional geographic markets.

Once shares of stock are issued, their price tends to fluctuate directly with the firm's profit potential. People buy stock because of the dividends they hope to receive. They also hope the stock price will increase over time.

initial public offering The initial sale of corporate stock to the public

dividends That portion of after-tax corporate profit paid out to shareholders

retained earnings That portion of after-tax corporate profit reinvested in the firm

Corporate Borrowing

Your corporation can acquire financial capital by issuing stock, retaining earnings, or borrowing. To borrow money, the corporation can go to a bank for a loan. Such loans usually are for short durations—from a matter of months to two or three years. For longer-term borrowing, corporations usually issue bonds. A **bond** is the corporation's promise to pay back the holder a fixed sum of money on the designated *maturity date* plus make annual interest payments until that date. For example, a corporation might sell bonds for $1,000 each, which promise the bond buyer annual interest of, say, $50 plus the $1,000 back at the end of 20 years. Corporate bonds have maturity dates as short as two years and as long as 30 years.

The payment stream to bondholders is more predictable than that for stockholders. Unless the corporation goes bankrupt, it must pay bondholders the promised amounts. On the other hand, stockholders are last in line when resource holders get paid. Because bondholders get paid before stockholders, bonds are considered less risky than stocks. Less risk means lower returns. Stocks usually yield a higher return than bonds.

Securities Exchanges

Both stocks and bonds are called **securities**. In the case of a share of stock, the security shows how much of the corporation the stockholder owns. In the case of a bond, it shows how much the corporation owes the bondholder. Ownership of securities is reflected by pieces of paper or by electronic entries in an online investment account.

bond A contract promising to repay borrowed money on a designated date and to pay interest along the way

securities Corporate stock and corporate bonds

Once corporations have issued stocks and bonds, buyers of these securities are usually free to resell them on *security exchanges*. In the United States, there are nine security exchanges registered with the *Securities and Exchange Commission (SEC)*, the federal body that regulates securities markets. The largest is the New York Stock Exchange, which trades the stock of more than 2,700 major U.S. corporations. All transactions occur on the trading floor in New York City. In addition there are more than a dozen electronic exchanges, the largest of which is the NASDAQ, which trades more than 3,200 corporate stocks, many of them technology companies. NASDAQ, like other electronic markets, is not a physical place, but a telecommunications network linking market traders.

BrendanMcDermid/Reuters/Landov

Buyers and sellers of securities come together through their representatives in the trading room of stock exchanges. Why are most securities transactions said to take place in the secondary market for securities?

Nearly all the securities traded each day are *secondhand securities* in the sense that they have already been sold by the corporation. Therefore, the bulk of daily transactions do not finance firms in need of investment funds. The money goes from a securities buyer to a securities seller, from one stockholder to another. By providing a *secondary market* for securities, exchanges enhance the *liquidity* of these securities—that is, the exchanges make the securities more easily sold for cash. This ready conversion into cash makes securities more attractive.

More than half the trading volume on major exchanges is done by *institutional investors*, such as banks, insurance companies, and mutual funds. A *mutual fund* issues stock to individual investors and with the proceeds buys a portfolio of securities.

The secondary market for stocks also determines the current market value of a corporation. The market value of a firm at any given time can be found by multiplying the share price by the number of shares outstanding. The share price reflects the current value of the expected profit. For example, Apple, the most valuable U.S. corporation, had a market value of $361.5 billion at the close of business on August 29, 2011. At that time, the market value of all publicly traded U.S. corporations exceeded $12 trillion.

CHECKPOINT What are the sources of financial capital for a corporation?

Math in Economics

Common Core Expressions and Equations

You can calculate the total cost of production by adding the costs of separate expenses. To find the costs of separate expenses, multiply individual costs by the number used.

EXAMPLE Calculate the total cost of producing a bicycle that requires six hours of labor paid at $12 per hour, two tires at $3 each, $33 of other parts, $7 in other variable costs (such as utilities), and $6 worth of fixed costs (such as rent and insurance).

SOLUTION Write an addition problem for each of the separate expenses.

labor	+	tires	+	other parts	+	other variable costs	+	fixed costs
($12 × 6)	+	($3 × 2)	+	$33	+	$7	+	$6
$72	+	$6	+	$33	+	$7	+	$6

$72 + $6 + $33 + $7 + $6 = $124

Practice the Skill Calculate the total cost of production in each item.

1. A wooden chair that requires four hours of labor paid at $15 per hour, seven wood boards (each 1 foot) at $5 per foot, other materials at a cost of $38, $14 in other variable costs, and $10 in fixed costs.
2. A coat that requires two hours of labor paid at $11 per hour, three yards of fabric at $8 per yard, $12 in other variable costs, and $9 in fixed costs.
3. Suppose a new machine that cost $500,000 could cut the time required to produce a coat in exercise 2 to one hour and would add $3 to the fixed costs of each coat. If the firm bought this machine, how much would the production costs of the coat total?
4. Why might a small business choose not to purchase the new machine even though it could cut its total cost for production per coat?

10.2 ASSESSMENT

Think Critically

1. Why are banks often unwilling to provide mortgage loans to people who want to purchase homes in urban neighborhoods with high crime rates and decreasing home values?
2. Would you rather lend a friend $50 until she gets paid tomorrow or until the end of the school year when she hopes to find a summer job? What does this tell you about the interest rates that are charged for short- and long-term loans?
3. Why might a corporation prefer to raise funds by selling stock than by borrowing money from a bank?

Graphing Exercise

4. Large corporations sell bonds to the public to finance expansion. Change in the amount of bonds outstanding is one indicator of how much business activity is taking place in the economy. Construct a line graph from the data in the table that shows the total value of U.S. corporate bonds outstanding between 2005 and 2009. What does your graph tell you about the U.S. economy during these years?

TOTAL CORPORATE BONDS OUTSTANDING, 2005–2009, IN BILLIONS OF DOLLARS

Year	New Stock Issues
2005	$3,032
2006	$3,248
2007	$3,559
2008	$3,764
2009	$4,145

Source: *Statistical Abstract of the United States*, 2011, p. 495.

Make Academic Connections

5. **History** Investigate the development of the NASDAQ market. Why have many high-tech corporations chosen to be listed on the NASDAQ rather than on a centralized exchange, such as the New York Stock Exchange?
6. **Communication** Identify a publicly traded corporation that does business in your community. Imagine that this firm wants to raise funds by issuing new stock. Write a letter that could be sent to potential investors that explains why they should consider buying this firm's newly issued shares.

Working in small teams, identify three local businesses of varying size. Pretend that your team operates a bank and that each of these businesses has applied for a $1 million loan. Explain which of these firms would be granted the loan and what interest rate would be charged. Make lists of reasons for your decisions. Compare your work with that of other teams.

MOVERS AND SHAKERS

Phillip Knight

Chairman of the Board and Co-Founder, NIKE, Inc.

Rick Wilking/Reuters/Landov

Philip Hampson Knight grew up in Portland, Oregon. He attended the University of Oregon, majoring in accounting. Knight was a member of the school's track team—at the time, one of the best college teams in the country. His coach, Bill Bowerman, was always experimenting with running shoes in order to make his team faster. Not happy with the shoes available, Bowerman began making his own shoes. "Since I wasn't the best guy on the team, I was the logical one to test the shoes," Knight explains.

After graduation and a year in the army, Knight enrolled in Stanford University's Graduate School of Business. While at Stanford, Knight came up with the idea for Blue Ribbon Sports. Once up and running, Blue Ribbon Sports operated by selling shoes from a van at high-school track meets and other athletic events. Within a few years, Knight secured a retail site, and renamed the company Nike. He paid a local designer $35 to create a logo, and the Nike "swoosh" was born. The new shoe, with its new logo, debuted at the 1972 U.S. Olympic trials in Eugene, Oregon. The launch was a success. That year $3.2 million of Nike shoes were sold. Profits doubled every year for the next ten years.

By the end of 1980, Nike completed its IPO and became a publicly traded company. Astronomical growth in the 1980s and 1990s resulted from Knight's idea to sign 21-year-old Michael Jordan to endorse a basketball shoe. It wasn't long before Air Jordans were must-have shoes among American youths. The company's success continued as star athletes including Tiger Woods, Bo Jackson, Gabrielle Reese, LeBron James, and Andre Agassi kept Nike sports shoes in the minds of aspiring athletes. When speaking of his company's advertising campaigns, Knight stated, "We didn't invent it [advertising], but we ratcheted it up several notches." The company typically budgets $200 million each year for advertising and celebrity endorsements.

Nike's sales goal for 2015 is $30 billion. The company employs more than 30,000 people and manufactures and sells shoes for baseball, cheerleading, golf, volleyball, and other sports. The company also sells Cole Haan dress and casual shoes, manufactures athletic apparel and equipment, and operates numerous retail outlets. Nike products are sold throughout the United States and around the world. The company's trademark "swoosh" is recognizable today even without the name.

Nike has faced some criticism for working conditions in its manufacturing operations in countries including China, Vietnam, Indonesia, and Mexico. It also was found to have contracted production to companies that used child labor. To address this criticism, Nike introduced a company Code of Conduct in 2002. The Code regulated working conditions and safety requirements in Nike's manufacturing facilities. In 2004, its Responsibility Report set forth additional health and labor standards and established plans for monitoring factories' adherence to the standards. Nike continues to be a target of anti-globalization groups.

Although shy and aloof, Knight is known as one of the smartest brand builders in history. He inspires employees with the "Nike Spirit" and motivates them to help take the company to the next level time after time. In addition to his trademark sunglasses—he is rarely seen without them—and wrinkled, casual wardrobe, one of Knight's trademark sayings is: "The trouble in America is not that we are making too many mistakes, but that we are making too few." His belief in learning from mistakes clearly has served him well.

Think Critically **Conduct Internet research to determine which securities exchange offers NIKE Inc. stock, the current price of NIKE Inc. stock, and analysts' forecasts for the stock. If you had $10,000 to invest right now, would NIKE Inc. be a good investment opportunity for you? Why or why not?**

10.3 BUSINESS GROWTH

Key Terms
horizontal merger 315
vertical merger 315
conglomerate merger 316
multinational corporation (MNC) 318

Learning Objectives
LO1 Recognize the role of profit and franchising in business growth.
LO2 Identify the types of corporate mergers and the four merger waves that occurred in the past.
LO3 Examine the multinational corporation as a source of corporate growth.

In Your World
Some business owners, such as grocers, plumbers, or pizza makers, are quite content running a small operation. However, many entrepreneurs want to see their business grow. Perhaps the business needs to grow to achieve economies of scale or to become more competitive. Maybe the owner believes the product could be profitably sold across the country or around the world. Whatever the reason, owners often consider growth as the desirable path to greater profits and, thus, to a more rewarding business.

PROFIT AND GROWTH

LO1 Recognize the role of profit and franchising in business growth.

Profitability is the surest path to a firm's growth. A profitable firm can reinvest earnings, and the more profit, the faster it can grow. Firm owners are more willing to invest their own savings in a business that is profitable. Profitable firms also find it easier to borrow the financial capital needed for expansion. Banks are more willing to lend to profitable businesses, because such firms are more able to pay back their loans.

To summarize, more profitable firms can grow faster because

1. more profit can be reinvested into the firm.
2. owners are willing to invest more of their own money in the firms.
3. banks are more willing to lend to them.

Corporate Profits and Growth
Corporate profitability opens up paths of growth that are not available to sole proprietorships or partnerships. The greater a corporation's profit, other things constant, the higher the price of shares on the stock market. The higher the share price, the more money a corporation can raise by issuing new shares. Unprofitable corporations cannot sell new shares easily. More profitable corporations also find it easier to borrow from banks or to sell bonds. The more profitable the corporation, the lower the interest rate it pays on bank loans and on corporate bonds.

Thus, financial markets allocate funds more readily to profitable corporations than to corporations in financial difficulty. Some corporations may be in such poor shape that they cannot issue stocks or bonds. *Securities markets promote the survival of the fittest by supplying financial capital to those firms that seem able to make the most profitable use of those funds.*

NET Bookmark

McDonald's maintains a web page entitled "Welcome to McFranchise" devoted to information about obtaining a franchise. Access the website shown below and click on the link for Chapter 10. Read the list of FAQs. How much cash does a potential franchisee need to qualify? How many partners can be involved in a franchise? Who selects the sites?

www.cengage.com/school/contecon

Franchises

One way a business with a successful product can grow quickly is by franchising that product. A *franchise* is a contract between a parent company (franchiser) and another business or individual (franchisee). For a fee, the parent company grants the franchisee the right to sell a certain product in a given region, such as Subway, Mrs. Fields, Dunkin' Donuts, or McDonald's.

The franchiser supplies the retailer with a brand name, production and marketing experience, and other expertise. The parent firm can achieve economies of scale in research and development, building design, business practices, and promoting the brand name. Franchises allow people with limited experience to enter a business. They are guided by the franchise plan, which can reduce their risk of failure. Most important is the brand name and reputation that comes with a franchise. Popular franchise programs also increase customer awareness of the business because many businesses operate in different locations using the same franchise name and promotions.

The franchise has been common for decades with gas stations and auto dealers. Of growing importance are franchises for hotels and restaurants. There are now more than 4,000 franchisers in the United States.

CHECKPOINT

Why do more profitable firms usually grow faster?

CORPORATE MERGERS

LO2
Identify the types of corporate mergers and the four merger waves that occurred in the past.

One way a firm can double its size overnight is to merge with a firm of equal size. Mergers represent the quickest path to growth.

Types of Mergers

Horizontal mergers occur when one firm combines with another firm making the same product, such as Exxon merging with Mobil. With a **vertical merger**, one firm combines with another from which it had purchased inputs

horizontal merger One firm combines with another firm making the same product

vertical merger One firm combines with another from which it had purchased inputs or to which it had sold output

or to which it had sold output. An example of a vertical merger would be one between a steel producer and an automaker. Finally, a **conglomerate merger** is a combination of firms in different industries, such as a merger between a plastics maker and an electronics firm. There have been four merger waves in this country over the past 125 years. They are summarized in Figure 10.4.

First Merger Wave: 1887–1904

In the last half of the nineteenth century, two important developments allowed some firms to grow large quickly. First, technological breakthroughs led to more extensive use of capital goods, increasing the minimum efficient size of manufacturing firms. Second, transportation costs declined as railroads increased from 9,000 miles of track in 1850 to 167,000 miles of track by 1890. *Economies of scale and lower transportation costs extended the geographical size of markets.* Firms grew larger to reach markets over a broader geographical area. Mergers offered an opportunity to quickly get bigger.

Mergers during this first wave tended to be horizontal. For example, the firm that is U.S. Steel today was created in 1901 through a billion-dollar merger that involved dozens of individual steel producers and two-thirds of the industry's production capacity. During this first wave, similar merger trends occurred in Canada, Great Britain, and elsewhere. This first merger wave created dominant firms, some of which survive to this day.

conglomerate merger One firm combines with another firm in a different industry

Second Merger Wave: 1916–1929

The first merger wave cooled with the introduction of antitrust laws. Because these laws restrained horizontal mergers, vertical mergers became more common during the second merger wave. This wave of mergers took place between 1916 and 1929. A vertical merger combines firms at different stages of the production process. For example,

FIGURE 10.4 Four U.S. Merger Waves in the Past 125 Years

Four distinct merger waves have taken place in the United States since 1887.

Wave	Years	Dominant Type of Merger	Examples	Stimulus
First	1887–1904	Horizontal	U.S. Steel, Standard Oil	Span national markets
Second	1916–1929	Vertical	Copper refiners with copper fabricators	Stock market boom
Third	1948–1969	Conglomerate	Litton Industries	Diversification
Fourth	1982–Present	Horizontal and vertical	Banking, telecommunications, health services, insurance	Span national and global markets, survive financial crisis

a copper refiner merges with a copper fabricator. The stock market boom of the 1920s fueled this second wave, but the stock market crash in 1929 stopped it cold.

Third Merger Wave: 1948–1969

The Great Depression and World War II slowed merger activity for two decades. The third merger wave began after the war. More than 200 of the 1,000 largest firms in 1950 disappeared by the early 1960s as a result of this merger wave. Between 1948 and 1969, many large firms were absorbed by other, usually larger, firms. The third merger wave peaked in a frenzy of activity between 1964 and 1969. During this time, conglomerate mergers accounted for four-fifths of all mergers.

Merging firms were looking to diversify their product mix and perhaps reduce costs by producing a variety of goods. For example, Litton Industries combined firms that made calculators, appliances, electrical equipment, and machine tools. As it turned out, this strategy didn't work that well. The firm resulting from a conglomerate merger no longer focused on producing a particular product efficiently. Instead, it tried to produce all kinds of different products efficiently, which proved too challenging for some corporate executives. Conglomerate mergers stretched management expertise and lost the efficiency gains from specialization and comparative advantage.

Fourth Merger Wave: 1982–Present

The fourth—and current—merger wave began in 1982 and involved both horizontal and vertical mergers. Some large conglomerate mergers of the 1960s were undone during this current wave as firms tried to focus on what they did best and sold off unrelated operations. About one-third of mergers during the 1980s resulted from *hostile takeovers*, where one firm would buy a controlling share of another against the wishes of the target firm's management. Hostile takeovers dwindled to less than one-tenth of mergers by the 1990s.

The break up of the Soviet Union in 1991 expanded markets around the world. Companies tried to achieve a stronger competitive position in global markets by merging with other firms here and abroad. Merger activity gained momentum during the latter half of the 1990s. Each time a record was set in the dollar value of a merger, it was soon broken by a bigger merger. Most mergers during the 1990s were financed by the exchange of corporate stock and were fueled by a booming stock market.

The largest mergers in history occurred during the late 1990s and in 2000. During this time, most merger activity took place in banking, radio and television, telecommunications, health services, and insurance. Not all these mergers turned out well. Corporate scandals engulfed some companies that had used mergers aggressively to grow, such as Enron and WorldCom. Another big merger that experienced difficulties was the $103 billion marriage of AOL and Time Warner. In 2002, the merged company lost $99 billion, a world record. The merged company split in 2009.

The current merger wave slowed down during the global financial crisis of 2008, but some troubled financial institutions had to merge to survive, such as Wachovia's merger with Wells-Fargo and Merrill Lynch's merger with Bank of America. The merger wave that began in 1982 continues today.

CHECKPOINT

What motivated the most recent wave of corporate mergers?

MULTINATIONAL CORPORATIONS

LO3 Examine the multinational corporation as a source of corporate growth.

The developer of a successful product has a profit incentive to sell it around the world. Because of high shipping costs and differences in labor costs, a firm often finds it more profitable to *make* products around the world as well. Many large corporations operate factories overseas and sell their products globally.

A corporation that operates globally is called a **multinational corporation (MNC)**. These companies also may be called transnational corporations, international corporations, or global corporations.

Running Multinationals

An MNC usually is headquartered in its country of origin and has affiliates in other countries. Most of the world's largest multinationals are headquartered in the United States, such as General Electric, General Motors, and Coca-Cola. Some are headquartered in Japan, such as Toyota, Honda, and Sony. Others are in Western Europe, such as Shell, BP, and Nestlé.

multinational corporation (MNC) A large corporation that makes and sells its products around the world

An MNC usually develops new products in its native country. It manufactures some or all of the goods abroad, where production costs usually are lower. For example, Whirlpool, the world's leading maker of major home appliances, is headquartered in Michigan but operates in more than 170 countries. The company motto is "Every home … Everywhere."

The multinational can take advantage of a successful brand by selling it around the world. Multinationals benefit consumers and workers worldwide by supplying products and creating jobs. Multinationals also spread the latest technology and the best production techniques around the globe. This allows some firms located in less-developed countries to adopt cutting-edge technologies.

Photodisc/Getty Images

Of the countries in which U.S. multinationals account for the largest share of output, most are advanced economies such as the Netherlands. Why do you think advanced economies benefit from the presence of U.S. multinationals?

Problems of Multinationals

Running a multinational is more complicated than running a domestic firm. It requires coordinating far-flung operations, adapting operations and products to suit local cultures, and coping with different business regulations, different tax laws, different currencies, and fluctuating exchange rates.

Union leaders in the United States have claimed that multinationals are hiring workers overseas because wages there are lower. It's true that wages are lower in poorer countries. However, reducing production costs makes U.S. firms more efficient. This lowers the price of U.S. goods, benefiting U.S. consumers and strengthening the firm's competitive position in world markets. Firms that fail to minimize average costs lose business to producers that do. No question some U.S. workers lose jobs when multinationals shift production overseas. On the other hand, some U.S. workers gain jobs because U.S. firms are more competitive. For example, if NIKE were not so competive on world markets, the company could not employ 14,000 workers in the United States. Some other U.S. workers gain jobs because many foreign multinationals manufacture here, such as Toyota, BMW, and Shell.

Some critics also charge that U.S. multinationals exploit workers overseas. However, the wages paid abroad by U.S. multinationals usually are higher than wages offered there by local employers.

CHECKPOINT

Why do firms become multinational corporations?

Span the Globe

Doing the Ford Shuffle

Ford, which once owned Jaguar, Land Rover, and Volvo, now owns none of these brands. Ford sold Jaguar and Land Rover to India's Tata Motors and sold Volvo to the Chinese automaker Geely. Volvo gives Geely access to foreign markets for less money than the Chinese company could capture on its own. Geely hopes the acquisition will help to improve its technology. When it bought Volvo, Geely promised to keep the company separate from its other operations, preserving Volvo's workforce, quality, and managerial independence. It pledged to continue to be a presence in Europe's high-cost, low-growth market.

Volvo's plan for where and how quickly to grow signals a shift in focus to fast-growing markets. While it will keep its plants in Sweden and Belgium, it now plans to build up to three factories in China. The cars produced there will be aimed at the Chinese market, which recently surpassed the United States as the world's largest.

Think Critically **Acquisitions such as Geely's purchase of Volvo haven't always succeeded. Often companies are for sale because they are in some way troubled and the emerging-market firms lack the expertise to run or benefit from them. What aspect of Geely's plans might help it deal with that possibility?**

Source: Reed, John, "Volvo Cars Plans New China Plants," *Financial Times* (London, England) February 25, 2011.

10.3 ASSESSMENT

Think Critically

1. Why are some people willing to invest in new firms that have not yet made any profit and do not expect to earn a profit for several years?
2. Do you think mergers are more often helpful or harmful for consumers? Explain your reasons.
3. When firms merge, they often lay off some workers to reduce their costs. Is it possible that this could be good for the economy?
4. Why have multinationals tended to "level the playing field" among workers and businesses in different nations?

Graphing Exercises

5. Mergers have an important impact on the U.S. economy, and they can be a sign of economic activity as well. More mergers tend to take place when the economy is booming and stock prices are high. They are less likely to occur when businesses are not earning good profits or when it is difficult to obtain funding to finance mergers. Use the data in the table to draw two bar graphs of merger activity in the U.S. economy from 2006 through 2009. One graph should show the number of mergers that took place each year. The other should show their total value. What do your graphs show about economic conditions in the United States during these years?

U.S. MERGERS AND TOTAL VALUE OF TRANSACTIONS BY YEAR: 2006–2009

Month	Number of Mergers	Value of Mergers in Billions of Dollars
2006	13,700	$1,950
2007	15,000	$2,500
2008	12,800	$1,800
2009	10,000	$1,250

Source: Institute on Mergers, Acquisitions and Alliances, http://www.imaa-institute.org.

Make Academic Connections

6. **Business Management** Many firms that offer franchise opportunities promote their organizations on the Internet. Identify a particular franchise business that exists in your community. Search the Internet for information about this franchise. What does the organization offer its members? What is the cost of becoming a franchisee? Would you consider starting this type of business? Why or why not?

TeamWork

Working in small teams, identify and debate the controversies involving multinational corporations. Do the benefits of multinationals to consumers and workers worldwide outweigh the problems associated with their operation? Explain your answer.

Connect to History

United States Steel

On December 12, 1900, Charles M. Schwab, president of the Carnegie Steel Company, spoke before a group of 80 industrial executives at the University Club of New York. He discussed the advantages of consolidation in such industries as steel. Whether Carnegie Steel owner Andrew Carnegie encouraged Schwab to make the speech—or if Carnegie was even in attendance—is not known. Within five months, however, the largest corporation in the world, United States Steel, was created.

The U.S. steel industry was growing quickly during the last two decades of the nineteenth century. In 1880, the United States produced only half as much crude pig iron as Britain. By 1900, it was making 50 percent more than Britain, as production rose from 4 to 14 million metric tons. Up to 1880, steel production was driven by the railroad industry, and 85 percent of production went to making rails. By 1900, rail production had increased almost 300 percent, but rails represented only 31 percent of the rolled steel output.

As demand grew, advantages in economies of scale became apparent. However, integrating the various stages of production and modernizing plants to achieve these economies were costly. Some in the industry viewed acquisition as a safer method of growth. Still, as long as steel prices remained high, success was insured for most steel producers. When competition grew fierce, however, prices dropped, causing the smaller, poorly financed companies to struggle.

Consolidation of the industry already had begun by 1900. Many of the companies that specialized in finished steel were combining horizontally as the product market diversified. Sheet making, wire making, and tube making were just a few of the activities subject to mergers. For these companies, most of the semi-finished steel was supplied along regional lines by one of two steel-producing giants—Federal or Carnegie Steel.

Two developments threatened to upset this arrangement. First, some of the companies that fabricated steel into products began trying to reduce costs by producing their own steel. Some new companies were formed just to supply steel to these finishing companies. The reaction of Federal Steel and Carnegie Steel was to go into the steel fabrication business as well. Facing cutthroat competition, smaller companies feared that lower prices would destroy them.

J.P. Morgan attended Schwab's University Club speech. Morgan had been involved in the formation of both Federal Steel and National Steel, and railroads were an important part of his business empire. Morgan recognized that he could secure the financial success of his companies by following Schwab's proposal. After the speech, Morgan pulled Schwab aside and spoke with him for half an hour. He followed up the conversation with a meeting a few weeks later. Morgan secured a list of the companies Schwab had proposed for consolidation in his speech. The list also included market values for what each company was worth. Morgan then asked Schwab to find out what Carnegie would sell his steel company for. Carnegie said $480 million. Morgan accepted Carnegie's price, and U.S. Steel was created on April 1, 1901.

Think Critically **Economies of scale were critical to the success of U.S. Steel. Still, some believe that the firm eventually became too large and difficult to manage. Its plants were spread over a large area. Also, because the company was profitable, it was harder to justify modernizing old plants. What kind of diagram would illustrate economies of scale? Draw a suitable diagram and show the effect of economies of scale in the long run. In the same diagram also show diseconomies of scale.**

Chapter 10 Summary

10.1 Production, Consumption, and Time

A. It takes time to produce goods and services. Investment in capital can increase labor productivity but also requires savings. Financial intermediaries help financial capital flow from savers to borrowers.

B. Consumers usually value current consumption more than future consumption. This can be seen in their willingness to pay interest to borrow funds that allow them to consume now. A demand for loans curve slopes downward. As the interest rate decreases, the quantity of loans demanded increases.

C. Loans are supplied by people willing to give up current consumption in order to consume more later. Interest is their reward for giving up current consumption. The higher the interest rate, the more money made available for loans. This is why the supply of loans curve slopes upward. As the interest rate increases, the quantity of loans supplied also increases.

ASK THE EXPERT

www.cengage.com/school/contecon

Why are some rates of interest so much higher than others?

10.2 Banks, Interest, and Corporate Finance

A. Banks act as financial intermediaries when they accumulate funds from savers and lend these funds to borrowers. By depositing funds in banks, savers earn interest. The banks then lend these funds at higher interest rates to borrowers who have been evaluated for their creditworthiness.

B. Interest rates differ for many reasons. The most important reason is the risk that a loan will not be repaid. Higher default risks require borrowers to pay higher rates of interest. Other factors that influence interest rates include the duration of the loan, the cost of administration, and the way in which interest is taxed.

C. Corporations raise financial capital in a variety of ways. They may sell corporate stock or bonds to the public. Funds received from the sale of stock do not have to be repaid. Dividends are paid on stock only when the corporation's board of directors chooses to do so. Bonds are debts of the business that must be repaid with interest, regardless of whether the firm earns a profit. Transactions of corporate stocks are carried out on stock exchanges.

10.3 Business Growth

A. Businesses that are profitable are better able to grow than those that are not profitable. Profits may be reinvested in a firm. Banks are more likely to make loans to firms that are profitable. Individual investors are more willing to purchase stocks or bonds issued by profitable firms. Some people go into business by purchasing a franchise. These businesses benefit from having an established name and a successful business plan.

B. There have been four waves of mergers in U.S. history. Although most mergers have created stronger, more successful businesses, some have not. Some giant mergers of the 1990s lost billions of dollars, and some of these mergers were later dissolved.

C. In recent years, many corporations have expanded beyond the borders of any individual nation. These multinationals often are able to market their products in many countries. It has been suggested that multinationals may exploit workers by producing goods and services in nations that have the lowest wage rates.

CHAPTER 10 ASSESSMENT

Review Economic Terms

Match the terms with the definitions. Some terms will not be used.

_____ 1. An asset owned by the borrower that can be sold to pay a loan in the event the loan is not repaid

_____ 2. The interest rate banks charge their most trustworthy business borrowers

_____ 3. Banks and other institutions that serve as go-betweens, accepting funds from savers and lending them to borrowers

_____ 4. A large corporation that makes and sells products around the world

_____ 5. An arrangement with a bank through which a business can quickly borrow needed cash

_____ 6. Corporate stock and corporate bonds

_____ 7. The portion of after-tax corporate profit that is reinvested in the firm

_____ 8. The initial sale of corporate stock to the public

_____ 9. The ability to borrow now, based on a promise of repayment in the future

_____ 10. Annual interest as a percentage of the amount borrowed or saved

a. bond
b. collateral
c. conglomerate merger
d. credit
e. demand for loans curve
f. dividend
g. equilibrium interest rate
h. financial intermediaries
i. initial public offering (IPO)
j. interest rate
k. line of credit
l. market for loans
m. multinational corporation (MNC)
n. prime rate
o. retained earnings
p. securities
q. supply of loans curve
r. vertical merger

Review Economic Concepts

11. **True or False** Production depends on saving because production takes time.

12. The fact that people generally prefer to consume now rather than in the future is shown by their willingness to
    a. pay tuition to attend college.
    b. pay interest for an automobile loan.
    c. pay for life insurance.
    d. deposit their savings in a bank account.

13. The _______?_______ brings together borrowers and savers to determine the market interest rate.

14. **True or False** The more valuable the collateral backing a loan, the higher the interest rate charged on the loan.

15. When the quantity of money supplied for loans exceeds the quantity of money demanded for loans, there will be a
    a. shortage of loans, and interest rates will soon fall.
    b. surplus of loans, and interest rates will soon grow.
    c. shortage of loans, and interest rates will soon grow.
    d. surplus of loans, and interest rates will soon fall.

16. A(n) ________?________ is extended to businesses by banks to provide them with funds during those months when their sales are low.

17. ________?________ are profits that a corporation earns but does not pay to its stockholders in dividends.

18. Which of the following situations will cause a bank to charge a lower interest rate?
   a. A loan is to be paid off in 60 days instead of 3 years.
   b. A loan is used to purchase an automobile instead of a house.
   c. A loan is made to a person who just changed jobs rather than a person who has been employed at the same job for 10 years.
   d. A loan is made to a small new business instead of a very large old business.

19. Which is not a form of merger used by U.S. firms in the past?
   a. vertical mergers
   b. conglomerate mergers
   c. horizontal mergers
   d. diagonal mergers

20. **True or False** A firm's profits have little to do with that firm's ability to grow.

21. A corporation that operates globally is called a(n) ________?________.

22. Which of the following statements about multinational corporations (MNCs) is not true?
   a. MNCs usually develop new products in their native countries.
   b. MNCs usually manufacture products in their native countries because costs usually are lower there.
   c. MNCs introduce new technologies to less-developed countries.
   d. MNCs usually benefit consumers and workers around the world by supplying products and creating jobs.

Apply Economic Concepts

23. **Lines of Credit** Justin and Carla own a ski resort. All of their income is earned in the months between November and April, but they have expenses throughout the year. During the summer, they must repair their equipment and clear their ski trails. The table shows their income and expenses from the end of last year's ski season through April of this year. Explain why Justin and Carla need a line of credit from their bank.

JUSTIN AND CARLA'S INCOME AND EXPENSES

Month	Income	Expenses
May	$ 0	$ 42,810
June	$ 0	$ 38,291
July	$ 0	$ 36,743
Aug.	$ 0	$ 34,805
Sept.	$ 0	$ 40,283
Oct.	$ 0	$ 52,939
Nov.	$ 10,832	$ 66,380
Dec.	$134,640	$103,592
Jan.	$288,902	$154,021
Feb.	$275,010	$152,831
March	$152,345	$100,438
April	$ 56,832	$ 83,921
Total	**$918,561**	**$907,054**

24. **Different Types of Mergers** Organize these businesses into three groups as they would form horizontal, vertical, and conglomerate mergers. You may not need to use all of the firms to complete this activity.

Ajax Trucking Co.	Dad's Ice Cream Co.	Mom's Detergent Co.
Apex Super Markets	Harold's Fruit Co.	Sue's Sandwich Co.
Clean Soap Co.	Joe's Wholesale Co.	XYZ Soap Co.

25. **21st Century Skills: Initiative and Self-Direction** Imagine you own a small carpet-cleaning business. A new dirt extractor has recently been invented that can clean carpets better and in half the time required by the machines you currently own. You would like to purchase ten of these new machines but they cost $8,000 each. How could you raise the $80,000 you need to buy these machines? What factors would you consider when you decide whether or not to make this purchase?

26. **Demand and Supply for Loans** On a separate sheet of paper, complete the table. In the box to the right of each event, indicate what would happen in each situation by placing a (1) for increase, (2) for decrease, (0) for stay the same, or (?) if the result is unclear based on the evidence. Also, explain your reasons for each.

Event	Demand for Loans	Supply of Loans	Interest Rate
A new electric motor is invented that is expensive but uses only half as much electricity as older motors.			
There is a baby boom, and millions of children are born.			
There is a downturn in the economy and many workers are laid off.			
Many foreigners decide they want to buy more U.S.-made products.			

Digging Deeper

with Economics e-Collection

Access the Gale Economics e-Collection through the URL below. Find a news story that involves the New York Stock Exchange (NYSE), NASDAQ, or the U.S. Securities and Exchange Commission. Summarize the article, and prepare to discuss it in class.

www.cengage.com/school/contecon

oliveromg/Shutterstock.com

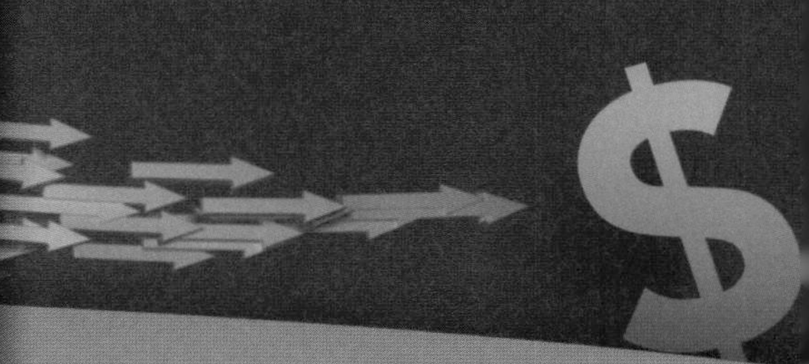

UNIT 4

Personal Financial Literacy

This unit will show how the knowledge you have gained so far about the economy can benefit you, your family, and your community. The focus is on how making wise consumer choices can help boost your sense of well-being, or satisfaction. You will learn about the rights and responsibilities of American consumers, and the ways in which government tries to protect these rights. You also will learn how to monitor and control your spending and saving and the advantages of doing so. Lastly, you will consider a variety of ways to invest your savings. By investing wisely, you may earn a return that will help you achieve your most important life goals.

CHAPTER 11

Consumer Responsibilities and Protections

CONSIDER ...

- How does it feel when your wallet is empty on Tuesday and you don't get paid until Friday?
- What's the downside to buying an expensive sports car you can't really afford?
- Where can you find information about products you are thinking of buying?
- How do you decide when a sales clerk asks, "Will that be cash or charge?"
- If an offer seems too good to be true, is it?
- Would you pay a lot for fashionable jeans without shopping around first?

Point your browser

www.cengage.com/school/contecon

Kalim/Shutterstock.com; Background image: Dibrova/Shutterstock.com

11.1 CONSUMER CHOICE

Learning Objectives

LO1 Understand the importance of setting personal financial goals.

LO2 Describe how making wise spending choices helps you achieve your goals.

Key Terms

In Your World

Every day you consume a wide variety of goods and services, ranging from breakfast cereal, to shampoo, to gas for the family car. Most of these products are things that you, or some other member of your family, purchased. When you buy goods and services, you seek the greatest satisfaction possible from your income. One of the best ways to achieve this goal is to create a budget that sets priorities about how to spend and save your income.

PERSONAL FINANCIAL GOALS

LO1 Understand the importance of setting personal financial goals.

Everyone is a **consumer**. Each time you eat your dinner, ride a school bus, or turn on your lights, you consume. Any use of a good or service is an example of consumption. Your family may not pay directly for your education, but when you attend school you are consuming an educational service. People consume within the limits of their resources. For most people, these limits are determined by their available time and money.

Think about the goals you would like most to achieve in your life. For example, you may want to complete your education, pursue a rewarding career, own a nice home, get married and have children, or travel to a foreign country. No matter what your goals are, to achieve them you will need to make many decisions. Most of these decisions will involve how best to spend your time and money.

The amount of income you can earn is limited. Even if you become a wildly successful entrepreneur with an annual income in the millions, you still will not be able to buy everything you would like to have. For example, you might have to give up a new swimming pool to be able to have the sails on your yacht replaced. The time available to pursue your different interests also would be limited. As noted in the opening chapter, your resources are scarce, but your wants, or desires, are virtually unlimited.

To maximize your utility, or satisfaction, during your life, you need a plan. Your plan should identify the things you most want to achieve and spell out the steps you intend to take to achieve them. You should be sure to include a financial plan within your general life plan. **Personal finance** involves the way you plan to spend or save your income. The satisfaction you achieve in life will depend to some extent on the quality of the financial decisions you make along the way.

consumer Anyone who uses a good or service

personal finance The way you plan to spend or save your income

Set Financial Goals

It is difficult to develop a useful financial plan if you don't know what you want to achieve. For example, would you be willing to set aside $10 each week from your income if you had no idea what to do with the money? Would it be easier to save if you knew that you would use the money to buy a smartphone? Choosing what you want most and setting goals is the first step in creating a financial plan.

Although you must spend money to achieve most goals, not all goals are the same. Short-term goals are things you hope to accomplish within a year or less. Long-term goals take longer than one year to achieve, while your most important life goals can take decades to reach.

Goals often are related. You might set a short-term goal to save $1,500 this year to help pay for college. Then your long-term goal of completing a degree in elementary education could help you achieve your life goal of a career as a second-grade teacher. Along the way you will set many other goals that have little to do with your life goals. You should be careful when you identify these additional goals. For example, buying an expensive sports car may bring you immediate satisfaction, but this choice is not likely to help you achieve career success in elementary education. This does not mean you should give up all choices that bring immediate satisfaction. It does mean you should make sure these choices do not prevent you from achieving the goals you value most in life.

Achieve Financial Goals

A useful skill to develop is the ability to distinguish between things you need and things you want. In Chapter 4, you were reminded that a $139,100 Mercedes Roadster probably is not something you need. You might need transportation between your home and your job, but you could satisfy this need by taking a bus or riding a bicycle. For most people, buying an expensive car or other luxury item is an example of trying to satisfy a want rather than a need.

Questions to Ask When you consider spending part of your income for a product, you should always ask yourself these questions: (1) Do I really need this product? (2) Is this the best deal available for this product? (3) Can I afford this product? (4) Will buying this product now prevent me from buying something else I want more in the future? If you answer "yes" to the first three and "no" to the last, then making the purchase probably is a reasonable choice. If not, you need to reconsider your options.

Seek Expert Advice Another useful strategy is to seek expert advice when considering important purchases. Many products available today are so complex that most consumers do not really understand them. You may know how to operate your computer, but you probably do not understand how it works, except in the most general way. Products change so rapidly that even if you knew how to evaluate a telephone calling plan last year, that knowledge probably is now out of date. As a general rule, it is better to admit your knowledge is limited and to rely on those with better information to help you make your decision.

Expert advice about consumer products can be found in many locations. One of the most useful is *Consumer Reports*, a monthly magazine published by Consumers Union. This magazine reports on a wide variety of consumer products including cars, clothing, cameras, and cooking oil to name only a few. Most libraries subscribe to *Consumer Reports*, or, for a fee, its articles can be found online. Consumer products also are reviewed and evaluated in magazines that include *Money, Kiplinger's Personal Finance Magazine, Popular Science, Popular Mechanics, PC,* and many others. Much of this information can be accessed online for free or for a small fee. You should be careful though, because anyone can place anything on the Internet, regardless of its accuracy.

Ask Other People Seeking advice from people who already own specific products can also be useful. Although products change so rapidly that their information may be out of date, people who have experience with a product may be able to suggest what to look for in it.

Shop at Reputable Businesses It often is a good idea to purchase products from large, established businesses. Because these firms have survived for many years, they are likely to be more reputable and to stand behind the products they sell. There is, of course, no guarantee that a large business will not take advantage of consumers. However, a large business is more likely to be worthy of your trust than Joe who sells computer components out of the trunk of his car.

CHECKPOINT

Why is it important to set personal financial goals?

MAKE WISE CONSUMER DECISIONS

LO2
Describe how making wise spending choices helps you achieve your goals.

More goods and services are offered for sale than anyone could possibly buy. Unless you are very fortunate, after paying for necessary expenses, you probably will have little income left over to buy things you don't really need. *When choosing how to spend your income, make sure each decision is based on reason and logic rather than on emotion and impulse.* Consider making a rule for yourself never to make a major purchase without taking time to consider the alternatives.

Budget Your Income

Have you ever run out of money on Tuesday, when you wouldn't get paid again until Friday? More to the point, do you know where and how you spend your income? Surveys show that for most Americans the answer is "no." Every consumer needs to create a financial plan called a **budget** showing sources and uses of income. Without a budget you may be leaving your financial future to chance.

Suppose that you already have set your life goals. This is no simple task, but a little planning really pays off. You must now decide how to use your expected income to achieve these goals. The most important information you need to get started are up-to-date records of your income and spending. Without this information, any budget you create is likely to be little more than fiction, disconnected from the reality of your life.

Budget Worksheets An important step in creating a budget is to develop a worksheet that contains your expected income, spending, and saving, for a month. A sample one-month budget worksheet appears in Figure 11.1. To create your own worksheet, divide a sheet of paper into four columns. List the sources and amounts of income you expect to receive at the top of the first and second column. Add the

budget A consumer's plan showing the sources and uses of income

FIGURE 11.1 One-Month Budget Worksheet for a Typical Student

Source	Expected Amount	Actual Amount	Difference
Monthly Income			
Allowance	$ 60.00	______	______
After-School Job	$200.00	______	______
Total	$260.00	______	______
Monthly Spending			
Food	$ 35.00	______	______
Entertainment	$ 50.00	______	______
Clothing	$100.00	______	______
Miscellaneous	$ 25.00	______	______
Total Spending	$210.00	______	______
Monthly Saving	$ 50.00	______	______
Total Spending and Saving	$260.00	______	______

Try comparison shopping for items you plan to buy now or in the future. Make a list of three items you wish to purchase. Choose one of the items for this activity. Shop in three or four different types of retail outlets for your item. Write down the characteristics of the alternative products you find in each store, noting the price of each one. Determine which item you would purchase, and list your reasons for doing so. Prepare to discuss your choice in class.

amounts to find your total expected income. For most young people, predicting expected income is relatively easy. The reality is that you are not likely to have all that much income, and it is likely to come at predictable times each month.

Next, list amounts you expect to spend in the first and second columns below the total expected income you have just calculated. This is probably more of a challenge. Many people, both young and old, have only a vague idea where their money goes. There is little point in trying to predict each specific transaction, such as how much you plan to spend on apples or movies in the next month. Estimating totals such as $35 for food and $50 for entertainment is sufficient. Sum the amounts you expect to spend.

Finally, below the expected amount of total spending, list the amount you intend to save. The total you expect to spend and save for the month should equal your total expected income. If these totals differ, adjust your spending or saving until the totals match.

Over the next month, keep track of all your income and spending. List these amounts in the third column of your worksheet. Compare the actual amounts with your expectations, and list positive or negative differences in the fourth column. Use these differences to help adjust your expectations. Then budget for another month. You may decide to adjust your spending if you are not achieving your financial goals. After several months, you should know enough about your spending habits to create a one-year budget.

Keep Your Budget Up to Date Planning a budget will not help you achieve your financial goals unless you follow it. Continue to keep complete records of your income, spending, and saving. Compare your budgeted amounts with your actual income and spending several times each month to be sure your plan is working. *You should review and revise your budget at least once per year or any time your financial circumstances change.*

Comparison Shopping

To get the best product and price, you should comparison shop. **Comparison shopping** is reviewing products and prices charged by different suppliers for similar products before making a purchase. Although it would be difficult and time-consuming to comparison shop for everything you might buy, it's usually not wise to buy the first thing you see. Suppose you notice a pair of jeans selling for $100. You like them, but should you buy them? Spending $100 for new jeans does not fit your budget. Are there other jeans selling for less that you would like as well? Visit online shopping sites to get an idea whether $100 is a competitive price for the jeans you like. Or, visit a few stores at the mall. You may decide that a better use of your income is buying $30 jeans even if they are not as stylish. Comparison shopping can help you stay within your budget.

Rational Consumer Choice

When shopping, your goal should be to make a **rational consumer choice**. This is a choice to buy or not buy a product so that your satisfaction is the greatest possible per dollar spent. Again, suppose you are thinking of buying a new pair of jeans. After considering your alternatives, you might decide that $100 is just too much to spend if you want to stay within your budget. If you spend $30 for the less expensive pair, you have $70 left over to buy things you like more. Put another way, the satisfaction you expect from buying a $30 pair of jeans plus what you could do with the extra $70 could exceed the satisfaction you expect from spending $100 on a pair of jeans. Alternatively, you could decide that your old jeans are still good enough. You save the entire $100, which could help pay for insurance on your car. You have decided that this use of your limited income will bring you the most satisfaction per dollar spent. In this case, not buying jeans is a rational consumer decision for you.

comparison shopping The act of reviewing products and prices charged by different businesses for similar products before making a purchase

rational consumer choice A decision to buy or not to buy a product so that your utility, or satisfaction, per dollar spent is maximized

dlewis33/iStockphoto.com

When making purchase decisions, such as when purchasing clothing for a new school year, what should you keep in mind? Explain your answer using an example.

ESSENTIAL QUESTION

Standard CEE 2: Decision Making

Effective decision making requires comparing the additional costs of alternatives with the additional benefits. Many choices involve doing a little more or a little less of something: few choices are "all or nothing" decisions.

CHECKPOINT Why should consumers always try to make wise spending decisions?

11.1 ASSESSMENT

Think Critically

1. Why is it important to consider your life goals when you decide how to use your income?
2. What are examples of several goods or services you need? What makes them different from things you only want?
3. How can preparing a series of monthly budget worksheets help you create a useful yearly budget?
4. Why is it important to review and evaluate your budget at least once a year?
5. Why is it sometimes difficult or impossible to carry out comparison shopping? What alternative is always available when it is difficult to comparison shop?
6. When is a choice to buy a product a rational decision?

Graphing Exercise

7. Use the data in the table to construct a line graph that shows Jeff's spending for entertainment over the past six months. If Jeff has budgeted $45 for entertainment each month, has he stayed within his budget? What could he do to achieve his budget goals?

JEFF'S ENTERTAINMENT SPENDING

Month	Amount	Month	Amount
July	$36.72	**October**	$37.25
August	$44.28	**November**	$39.21
September	$38.52	**December**	$94.02

Make Academic Connections

8. **Personal Finance** Explain why a couple expecting their first child will need to revise their budget.

TeamWork

Working in teams, construct a monthly worksheet for a hypothetical fellow student who has an expected monthly income of $120. Identify categories of spending, set goals for each type of spending, and decide how much of the student's income should be saved. Each team should explain their work to the class and consider the decisions of other teams.

MOVERS AND SHAKERS

Jeff Taylor

Founder, Monster.com

Phil McCarten/Landov

Jeff Taylor is the founder of the popular job-hunting website Monster.com. Prior to his success with Monster, Taylor owned an ad agency that specialized in helping companies place help-wanted ads. He started thinking about how an electronic bulletin board might work for the human resources business. One night he had a dream. Jeff said, "I woke up from the dream and sketched out the entire idea. The idea for a happy monster logo and the concept of 'big, not scary,' the design of the buyer–seller marketplace which is still in place to this day, and a really important patent all came out of that dream."

Taylor credits "dream mechanics" for helping him come up with groundbreaking ideas that benefit millions of people around the world. To keep track of his ideas Taylor keeps a dream journal by his bed. When he wakes up each morning, he writes down his ideas. He also uses visualization skills. He "sees" success as if it has already happened.

Taylor talks about what it takes to generate ideas. His advice is to

- dive into your ideas, be open and literal.
- be optimistic, expect that things will turn out well.
- use the power of your subconscious mind.

Taylor left Monster in 2005 and started a new project. Eons is a social-networking website that caters to the millions of Americans over the age of 55. In 2008 Jeff also created Tributes.com, a website that offers current local and national obituaries.

Taylor admits he was not a star student in school. He said, "I was the screwball. I couldn't get anywhere on time. One of my most dreaded sounds was the bus going by at 8 a.m. and I wasn't on it." As a freshman at Amherst, Taylor worked in advertising for the campus newspaper. He soon became the business manager supervising a staff of 30 people. He said, "So while most people were going to class, I was actually running a business." He also became an entrepreneur, creating college survival kits for final exams and selling them to parents of freshmen. Although he didn't graduate from Amherst, he ran the campus tour service there. He credits that experience with helping him develop his public speaking skills. Today he gives about 75 motivational talks per year.

Of entrepreneurs Taylor said, "The whole concept behind being an entrepreneur is that you have to have the horsepower, the pride, and the ability to execute (despite the naysayers). You need that passion…When everyone thinks you're crazy and you still think you have a good idea, you're an entrepreneur."

Jeff advises prospective entrepreneurs to

- train like an athlete.
- prepare like a marketer.
- work like an entrepreneur.
- add a pinch of luck.

Ideas and dreams are an important part of success, Jeff said, "One person's idea can change the world… It doesn't matter how you do it; you just have to do it."

Think Critically **As a student, you need spending money. If you aren't the lucky recipient of a parental allowance, you need to come up with a way to generate the money yourself. Jeff Taylor earned money during college as an entrepreneur running the student paper and selling college survival kits. Think of entrepreneurial ways in which you could generate an income as a student. Estimate the amount of income you could generate as well as the costs involved in conducting this venture.**

Sources: http://www.umassmag.com/Fall_2002/What_s_the_big_idea__Jeff_Taylor__355.html; http://www.apbspeakers.com/speaker/jeff-taylor;http://www.leaders.umb.edu/index.php/leaders/news/P15/; and http://www.tributes.com/.

11.2 USE CREDIT RESPONSIBLY

Key Terms

consumer loan 338
consumer sales credit 338
secured loan 339
unsecured loan 339
creditworthiness 340
credit history 341
credit rating 341
credit scoring 342

Learning Objectives

LO1 Understand whether to use cash or credit to pay for purchases.

LO2 Name the two sources of consumer credit.

LO3 Describe how lenders decide who qualifies for credit.

LO4 Explain how you can avoid credit problems.

In Your World

You buy products using either cash or credit. Credit often is more convenient than cash, and it allows you to enjoy some products you could not afford otherwise. The cost of a car or an education, for example, could be too great without using credit. Overuse of credit, however, can create financial problems. To be a responsible consumer, you must learn how credit works and how to use it wisely.

PAYING FOR YOUR PURCHASES

LO1
Understand whether to use cash or credit to pay for purchases.

It would be nice if you always had enough money to pay for anything you might want with cash, a check, or a debit card. Making a purchase with a debit card is like writing a check. It allows you to deduct the price of purchases directly from your checking account.

The reality is that we cannot pay cash, write a check, or use a debit card for all the products we want at the time we want them. In this chapter we will assume that paying for a purchase with a check or a debit card is no different from paying cash. All three options reduce your current spending power. Even when you do have enough cash to pay for a product, there is a temptation to charge your purchase and then use your cash for something else. Millions of consumers every day make the "cash or charge" decision. Sometimes their choices land them in financial trouble that prevents them from achieving their life goals.

Will That Be Cash or Charge?

How often have you heard a store clerk ask, "Will that be cash or charge?" There are costs and benefits of each. Your best alternative depends on your individual financial goals and your situation. Study Figure 11.2 to learn how consumers chose to pay for their purchases in 2005 and how they are expected to make such decisions in 2015. Based on the number of transactions, debit cards ranked fourth in 2005 but are expected to climb to first by 2015. Checks ranked second in 2005, but are expected to drop to fifth by 2015. Based on the total dollar volume of purchases, debit cards are expected to climb from fifth in 2005 to second in 2015. Checks are expected to fall from first to fifth place. Thus, the trend is for a rise in the use of debit cards and a decline in checks, two ways off accessing bank accounts.

Benefits and Costs of Paying Cash Whenever you pay cash for a product, you give up the ability to use that cash for something else. Remember that every consumer decision involves an opportunity cost. Charging a purchase today will limit your ability to spend in the future. You also may have to pay interest or other fees for borrowed funds.

Benefits and Costs of Using Credit Remember that although credit allows you to consume now, you surrender some ability to spend in the future. The amount of future spending you give up will exceed the additional spending you enjoy today if you must pay interest and fees for the borrowed funds.

There are legitimate reasons for using credit to make purchases, particularly for major items such as a home, a car, or a college education. First, your earning power usually increases as you get older, especially if you have a good education. An entry-level employee may earn relatively little. Ten years later this same worker may be a manager with a good salary, and after 30 years he or she may be running the firm. It makes sense for most people to borrow at a young age for major purchases such as a home because they will be better able to pay off their loans when they are older and earn more.

Another reason to borrow is to make major purchases that will increase in value or provide an ongoing benefit over time. Most students borrow at least part of the money they need for college. Data show that college graduates, on average, earn about twice as much over a lifetime as high-school graduates. Borrowing $50,000 to increase your earnings by $500,000 makes economic sense. A similar argument can be made for borrowing to buy a house. Few people can afford to pay cash. Still, owning a house provides much more than a place to live. It eliminates the need to pay rent. Mortgage interest is tax deductible. The resale

FIGURE 11.2 Popularity of U.S. Consumer Payment Systems: 2005 vs. 2015

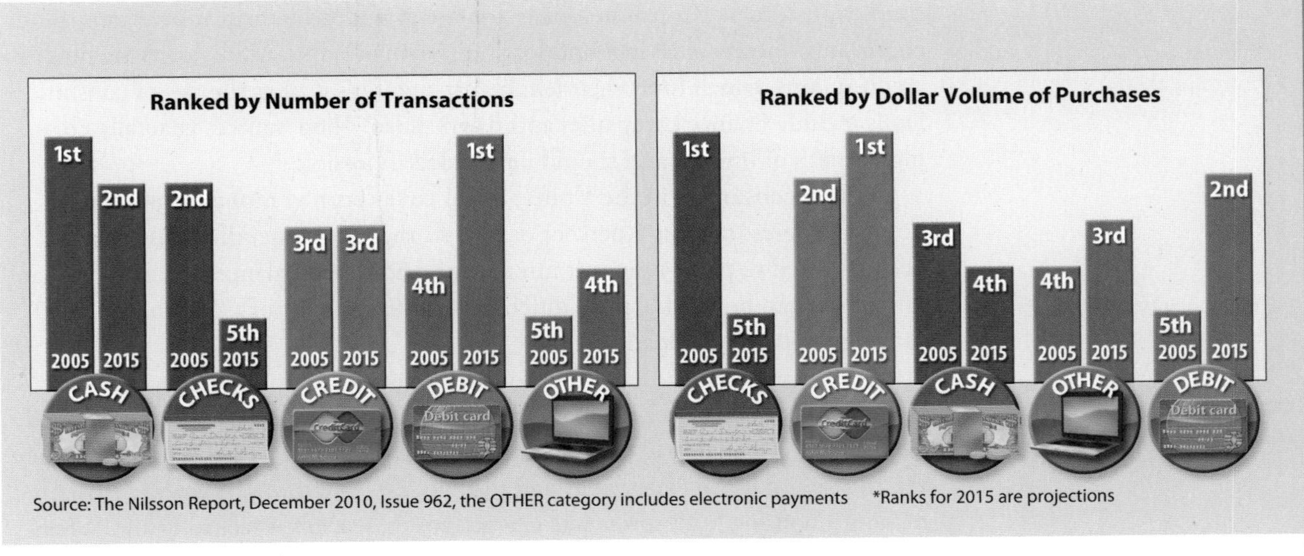

value of a home usually increases over time. (Housing prices declined with the financial crisis of 2008, but that was an exception.) What's more, any appreciation in a home's value when it is sold usually is tax free.

For most people the question is not, "Should I ever use credit?" It is, "How can I use credit responsibly?"

CHECKPOINT **What factors should you consider in determining whether to use cash or credit for a purchase?**

SOURCES OF CONSUMER CREDIT

LO2
Name the two sources of consumer credit.

Most sources of consumer credit can be divided into two basic categories. **Consumer loans** involve borrowing money to be repaid in regular installments over time. Most loans for homes, automobiles, and education fall into this category. On the other hand, **consumer sales credit** refers to amounts charged to an account that involves variable payments over time. Such debts do not have a specific term or time period in which they must be paid. Consumer sales accounts often have no set interest rate, but one that changes with market conditions or the financial situation of the individual borrower. Credit card purchases are examples of consumer sales credit.

Consumer Loans

Consumers may choose from among many sources of credit. Ultimately, most consumer loans are provided by banks. Consumers may apply for a loan directly from a bank, or they may receive their loan through a retail store that borrows the funds from a bank. Consumer loans also are provided by thrift institutions, more commonly known as savings and loans, or savings banks. Many loans are made by credit unions, which limit their lending to members. Other sources of consumer loans include finance companies and pawn shops. These sources generally charge higher rates of interest and should be avoided if possible.

In 2011 consumers in the United States could borrow money to purchase a home at interest rates of 5 percent or less. At the same time, they might have been required to pay 14 percent interest for credit-card balances. Most of the rate differences can be attributed to differences in the amount of risk associated with making the particular loan.

As noted in Chapter 10, when a consumer borrows to buy a house, the house is pledged as collateral for the loan. If the borrower is unable to make the required payments, the lender may take possession of the property and sell it to pay the debt. Houses do not usually lose value, and they do not leave town. There is less risk in making a housing loan, so the rate charged for these loans is relatively low. When

consumer loan
Borrowing money to be repaid in regular installments over time, such as a car loan

consumer sales credit
Amounts charged to an account that involves variable payments over time, such as a credit card

a consumer borrows to buy a car, the car is pledged to back the loan. Again, if the payments are not made, the car can be repossessed and sold to satisfy the loan. Cars lose value as they are driven, however, and they can be stolen. As a result, the interest charged on automobile loans is usually higher than on home loans. Both home and auto loans are **secured loans** because property is pledged to back their repayment.

Photodisc/Getty Images

What type of loan would you need to purchase an automobile, and what property would you pledge to back its repayment?

Consumer Sales Credit

Probably the most common source of credit in the United States involves charging to credit-card accounts. This type of consumer sales credit is used mostly for convenience. It is much easier and safer to shop using a credit card than to carry large amounts of cash, which could be lost or stolen.

Most credit cards are issued through VISA®, MasterCard®, or Discover®. Banks, thrifts, credit unions, and other organizations sign consumers up for these credit cards and receive a share of the fees and interest that consumers pay. *Consumers should be careful when they choose a credit card because of the wide differences from card to card in fees and interest rates charged.*

Credit-Card Fees At one time almost all credit-card organizations charged an annual fee for a card. These fees typically ranged between $20 and $100 per year. In recent years, competition among credit-card issuers has reduced or eliminated such fees. Today there is little reason to use a card that requires an annual fee. For most card users, other fees are more important. These include fees for charging more than your credit limit or for making payments after their due dates. Always keep track of your credit-card spending to avoid exceeding your limit. Also be sure to make payments on time.

Interest on Credit-Card Debt Each month you will receive a statement from your credit-card issuer, itemizing your credit-card purchases, the total you owe, and the minimum payment due that month. There will be a grace period before you must pay your entire balance and owe no interest. The grace period typically is 21 days. If you pay only the minimum due, you will be charged interest on the funds you have borrowed, usually from the time of each credit-card purchase.

The interest rates charged by most credit card issuers are substantial. Although some cards initially offer low rates to attract new cardholders, most eventually raise these rates, ranging from 12 to 20 percent. *It is wise to pay off your credit-card balance each month if you can.* If the balance is large, and you can't pay it off each month, a better choice may be to take out a loan from a bank to pay off credit-card debt. The rate on the loan is usually lower than the rate on the card.

Almost all credit-card borrowing is made up of **unsecured loans**. In these cases, no specific property is pledged by the borrower that can be sold to satisfy the debt if payments are not made. The legal process of obtaining payment for these debts is much more complicated and expensive for lenders than for secured loans. Therefore, unsecured loans require higher interest payments.

secured loan Loan for which property is pledged to back its repayment, such as a home mortgage

unsecured loan Loan for which no specific property is pledged by the borrower that can be used to satisfy the debt if payments are not made, such as credit card debt

CHECKPOINT

What are the two basic sources of consumer credit?

RECEIVE AND USE CREDIT

LO3
Describe how lenders decide who qualifies for credit.

Think about your friends and relatives. Would you be willing to lend $100 to any of them if you had the money? Are there any you would refuse? What if the amount was $1,000 or more? Would that make a difference? What are the differences between people to whom you would be willing to lend money and those you would not? One important difference probably is whether you believe your loan would be repaid on time or at all. Like you, businesses that extend credit to consumers evaluate the creditworthiness of people who want to borrow money.

The Three Cs of Credit

Lenders evaluate the **creditworthiness** of consumers who want to borrow money. That is, they evaluate how likely the borrower is to repay the loan. There are three primary factors, known as the three Cs of credit, that lenders typically consider when they evaluate a consumer's creditworthiness. These are character, capacity, and capital.

creditworthiness The measure of your dependability to repay a loan

Character *Character* is a measure of your financial responsibility. It is determined largely by your credit history, or record of paying bills and debts on time. Lenders reason that consumers who have repaid their debts on time in the past are likely to repay them on time in the future. A record of late, missing, or unpaid debts almost guarantees that a consumer will have difficulty getting credit.

Capacity *Capacity* is a measure of a consumer's ability to repay a debt on time. The amount of income a consumer receives each month is one factor lenders use to determine capacity. Equally important is the amount that a consumer already is obligated to pay. Someone who earns $10,000 each month has little capacity if current debts require monthly payments of $9,500.

Capital *Capital* is a measure of the value of things a consumer owns that could be sold or cashed in to repay a loan. Capital includes savings, stocks, bonds, buildings, and land. The more capital a consumer has, the safer a lender feels in making a loan.

To be creditworthy, you need to possess each of the three Cs of credit. Having a large income has little value to a lender if you have a history of not paying your bills on time. Owning a 1,000-acre ranch won't help you repay a debt if you share your ownership with another person who refuses to sell.

Photodisc/Getty Images

Do you consider yourself creditworthy? Why or why not?

Credit-Reporting Agencies

There are three primary credit-reporting agencies, or credit bureaus, that gather, maintain, and share financial information about almost every adult in the United States. These businesses are Equifax, Experian, and TransUnion. When you apply for a loan to buy a house, apply for a credit card, fail to make a payment on your auto loan on time, or complete virtually any other financial transaction, a record of this event will be sent to one or more of these credit bureaus. Regardless of which one receives the record first, they will all get it soon enough because they share whatever information they gather. The records of a consumer's **credit history** are then offered for sale to other businesses that might extend you credit.

Credit Ratings A consumer's **credit rating** is a measure of the person's creditworthiness. It is based on many factors, including the person's history of making payments on time, her current debt, other credit history, her recent applications for credit, and the type of credit she tends to use. Other factors that could affect a credit rating are the type of job a person holds, how long she has held that job, how long she has lived at her current address, and her level of education. Basically, lenders want to know as much as possible about people who apply for credit. A credit rating provides a written history of your financial transactions. This type of knowledge not only protects lenders but it protects other borrowers as well. If a borrower fails to repay a loan, the lender may be forced to charge other borrowers more, or stop making loans entirely.

credit history A person's record of paying bills and debts over time

credit rating The measure of a person's creditworthiness

Math in Economics

Common Core Ratios and Proportional Relationships

To calculate the percent one number is of another number, divide the number that represents the part by the number that represents the total. After dividing, convert the decimal to a percent. Multiply by 100, or move the decimal point two places to the right.

EXAMPLE What percent of 236 is 47?

SOLUTION The total number is 236. The part is 47. Divide 47 by 236. Move the decimal point two places to the right to write as a percent. Write the percent to the nearest tenth (one decimal point).

$47 \div 236 = 0.199 = 19.9\%$

47 is 19.9% of 236.

Practice the Skill Find each percent. If necessary, write answers to the nearest tenth of a percent.

1. What percent of 1,860 is 93?
2. What percent is 423 of 7,191?
3. If your credit card charges you $6.15 in interest when you carry a $410 debt over from one month to the next, what percent are you being charged each month in interest payments?

Credit Scores In recent years, a method of evaluating consumers' creditworthiness called credit scoring has become much more common. **Credit scoring** is a system that assigns a number, or score, to each consumer indicating whether this person is a good or bad credit risk. It is based on a formula that was originally developed by the Fair Isaac Company in the 1950s. This is the source of its technical name, FICO. FICO scores make it easier for lenders to decide whether or not to extend credit to a specific consumer. Suppose a bank decides that it will make no loans to people with a FICO score below 650. This means that when you apply for a loan with your FICO score of 623, the bank will quickly explain that you do not qualify for their credit. FICO scores also are used to set interest rates on some loans. If your score is below 650, you might have to pay a higher rate than someone with a score of 700. These scores affect your ability to buy a house or a car or rent an apartment. A credit score is a number. A credit rating, on the other hand, offers a history of your financial transactions.

Obviously your credit score can be important to your financial situation. The formula used to calculate these scores is secret. However, there are steps you can take to improve your score. These include paying your bills on time, using credit only in limited amounts, and paying down your debts.

Accessing Your Credit File You have the legal right to see the information credit reporting agencies gather about you. You may access this information for free online once per year at www.annualcreditreport.com, or you may write to each of the three major credit bureaus for a report on your file. (Note that the free reports do not include your credit score.) Other businesses will automatically send you reports including your score for a fee. *Most experts recommend that consumers review their credit files at least once per year to determine whether mistaken information appears in them.*

If you discover a mistake in your credit file, you can write to the credit bureau explaining the mistake and request that the information be corrected. If the bureau disputes your point of view and refuses to remove the information, you have the right to enter a 100-word explanation that will go in your file.

What do lenders want to know about consumers before granting them credit?

AVOID CREDIT PROBLEMS

LO4
Explain how you can avoid credit problems.

Every year millions of consumers experience problems with credit accounts. Most problems are the direct result of poor record keeping, late payments, or excessive borrowing. Lending institutions also may make mistakes that can harm consumers. In either case, it is important for all consumers to be aware of their financial circumstances and to develop financial habits that will establish and protect a good credit history.

credit scoring A system that assigns a number, or score, to each consumer indicating whether this person is a good or bad credit risk

Use Credit Wisely

Credit is dangerous because it is so easy to use. Many consumers use credit without much thought. They walk into a store, see a product they like, slap down their card, and it's theirs. The problem is, the responsibility to pay the debt they have just created also is theirs. Consumers should try to limit their credit purchases to products they need and to situations where using cash or checks are not reasonable methods of payment. Any use of credit should be the result of a rational consumer choice. The best way to avoid credit problems is to limit your credit purchases to those that are absolutely necessary and that can be repaid without requiring other important sacrifices.

Establish a Positive Credit History

Most young people have not lived long enough to have much of a credit history. How can lenders know whether you have the character to repay a loan when you have never borrowed money before? The best way to establish a positive credit history is to start small and avoid making financial mistakes. Here are some steps you can take to create a positive credit history for yourself.

- Be a regular saver. Make deposits every month even if they are small.
- Ask for a credit card from the bank where you save. You might pledge the funds in your savings account to cover the amount you are able to charge on your card. Those under 21 years of age usually require someone, typically a parent, to cosign for a card, unless you can demonstrate you have sufficient earnings to support a credit card.
- Make your payments on time and never exceed your credit limit.

Repair a Damaged Credit Rating

Sometimes bad things happen to good people. You might be injured in an accident. You could be laid off from work. You might have huge medical bills. Your house might be damaged in a fire. Any of these events could prevent you from repaying your debts on time. If this happened, your credit history would show that you had missed payments. You might find it impossible to borrow at the very time when you need credit the most.

If you find that you cannot pay your debts on time, follow these steps to protect your credit history or repair it over time:

- If you find that you will not be able to make a payment on time, contact the lender and explain the situation. Most lenders are willing to work with you to solve your problem if they believe you will eventually pay your debt.
- Do your best to avoid using any additional credit.
- Identify the most important lenders and pay them first. Write other lenders to explain why you can't pay now and how you intend to pay in the future.
- When your financial situation improves, use credit regularly but only in small amounts.
- Pay off your account balances in full every month if you possibly can.
- If you can't pay your balance in full, try to pay more than the minimum.

Although it can take years to repair a damaged credit history, the sooner you take these steps the sooner you will be able to take advantage of the benefits of an improved credit rating.

CHECKPOINT How can you avoid problems with credit?

11.2 ASSESSMENT

Think Critically

1. Why do many consumers use cash to make small purchases and credit for larger ones?
2. Why is the interest rate for secured loans usually lower than that for unsecured loans?
3. What is the major cost involved in using credit, and how can consumers manage this cost effectively?
4. What is the difference between a credit rating and a credit score?

Graphing Exercise

5. The amount of money consumers owe through various types of consumer sales credit has grown in most recent years. In 2010, however, it fell significantly. Use the data in the table to construct a line graph that shows this growth and decline. Evaluate the relationship between the amount of consumer borrowing and the state of the U.S. economy.

TOTAL OUTSTANDING CONSUMER SALES CREDIT

Year	Outstanding Consumer Sales Credit in Billions of Dollars
2002	$738.3
2004	$790.5
2006	$871.0
2008	$957.5
2010	$800.6

Source: *Economic Indicators*, June 2011, p. 29.

Make Academic Connections

6. **History** Before the 1960s, use of consumer credit was limited. Credit cards were issued by individual stores and could be used only in that store. Describe how stores have benefited from the growth of consumers' use of credit cards since the 1960s. What new costs have resulted from this use? Do you think most consumers are better or worse off because of their use of credit cards? Explain your answer.

TeamWork

Obtain a copy of a credit card statement and look for the disclosure information, found on the back of the first page. Find a partner who has a statement for a different credit card. Compare the information disclosed by the two credit-card issuers. Be sure to compare how each issuer calculates interest charges. Report your findings in class.

Connect to History

Credit Cards

Credit cards have their roots in the early twentieth century, when some businesses issued cards to customers with charge accounts. The Flatbush National Bank in Brooklyn, New York, expanded the idea in 1947 when it created the third-party universal credit card. The bank's plan allowed customers to charge purchases at stores within a two-block area around the bank. The concept went national in 1950 with the introduction of the Diners Club® credit card. In its first year, Diners Club enlisted 285 businesses along with 35,000 cardholders. Diners Club quickly spread to other cities and other businesses, making it the first national credit card.

Throughout the 1950s, Diners Club faced little competition. Then in 1958, American Express and Carte Blanche entered the market, soon followed by major banks such as Bank of America. Demand for credit cards grew. To meet this demand, in 1966 Bank of America began to offer its BankAmericard® (renamed Visa® in 1977) to other banks. That same year, a second group of banks formed the Interbank Card Association. It purchased rights to the name Master Charge® in 1969, which later became MasterCard®.

Throughout most of the 1950s, credit cards were used only by the wealthy or by businessmen on expense accounts. This began to change in 1958 when Joe Williams mailed out 60,000 unsolicited BankAmerica cards to residents of Fresno, California (a practice outlawed in 1977). The stunt, known in the industry as the "Great Fresno Drop," was successful. Using their cards, Fresno residents went on a spending spree. Two other major credit-card companies then used mass mailings to get their cards into people's hands. As easy credit came to the middle class, the number of issued credit cards grew. During the 1970s, credit card purchases rose by 1,400 percent.

Well into the 1970s, the nation's largest department stores had their own charge cards, which they viewed as a way of creating customer loyalty and sales. However, a tipping point was reached as millions of customers began holding bank cards rather than store cards. In 1979, J.C. Penney signed a contract with Visa to allow customers to use bank-issued cards. Other stores soon followed.

The next revolution in the credit-card business began in 1988, with the founding of Capital One. Relying on sophisticated computer programs that analyzed consumer purchasing and debt, the new company created an information-based strategy to market the cards. Capital One offered thousands of different combinations of interest rates and incentives as well as innovative ideas such as balance transfers, low introductory rates, and multicolored cards. It soon became one of the nation's largest Visa and MasterCard providers.

Plastic cards have changed how we buy and how we bank. Aided by the use of credit and debit cards, money moves electronically around the world as less and less cash changes hands. For many, the credit card is the financial innovation of the twentieth century. Debit cards may turn out to be the financial innovation of the twenty-first century.

Think Critically What do you think the next major financial innovation will be? Will this change our borrowing, saving, and spending habits? Explain your answer.

Sources: Katrina Brooker, "Just One Word: Plastic; How the Rise of the Credit Card Changed Life for the Fortune 500—and for the Rest of Us," ***50 Years of the Fortune 500***, 2004; Ted Miller and Courtney McGrath, "Power to the People," ***Kiplinger's Personal Finance Magazine***, 54:82, January 2000.

11.3 CONSUMER PROTECTION

Key Terms

Food and Drug Administration (FDA) 348
Federal Trade Commission (FTC) 348
cease and desist order 348
Consumer Product Safety Commission (CPSC) 348
Environmental Protection Agency (EPA) 349
identity theft 351

Learning Objectives

LO1 Explain why consumers sometimes may need the government to protect them from defective or dangerous products.

LO2 Understand how to protect yourself as a consumer.

LO3 Know how to prevent identity theft and know what to do if your identity is stolen.

In Your World

The U.S. government has created agencies to help protect consumers from products that are defective or dangerous. Given the billions of transactions that take place in our economy every day, the government cannot monitor every one. Your best bet is to be careful about what you buy. You also need to protect yourself from identity theft—that is, where someone fraudulently uses your identity to obtain credit or to access your financial accounts.

GOVERNMENT EFFORTS TO PROTECT CONSUMERS

LO1
Explain why consumers sometimes may need the government to protect them.

How often do you buy or use a product you don't really understand? For example, you probably use a computer at home or in school. You may be able to effortlessly surf the Web, download photographs posted by a friend, or maintain complicated financial records on a spreadsheet application. But does your ability to operate a computer mean you understand how it works? You probably are not qualified to repair a computer, and if you wanted to buy a new one, would you know enough to choose the best model to meet your needs and budget?

Consider other products you buy that also are too complicated or technologically advanced for you to really understand. You may take medicines or dietary supplements but have no idea how they cure your illnesses or keep you healthy. And you probably don't know the ingredients in the processed foods you eat. Take a few seconds to read the label of a breakfast cereal box. Can you understand what it means? What are niacin amide, thiamin mononitrate, or riboflavin? These substances are likely to be included in every breakfast cereal you eat. Do you know what they do, and whether they are good for you? What about the preservatives or colorings that many foods contain? Are they safe? How would you know? Most consumers rely on manufacturers to be responsible and on the government to set quality and safety standards to protect them from harm.

The Roots of Government Protection

The federal government has a long history of consumer protection. In the years following the Revolutionary War, the federal government monitored product weights and measures to make sure that consumers received what they paid for. In the late 1800s, laws were passed to keep railroads from charging unreasonable rates and to prevent a large firm from monopolizing the market for specific goods and services such as steel or oil. During the early years of the twentieth century, Congress passed laws intended to assure consumers that products were safe and marketed honestly.

The Pure Food and Drug Act The Pure Food and Drug Act was passed in 1906, possibly in reaction to Upton Sinclair's book *The Jungle.* That classic exposed unsanitary conditions in the meat-packing industry, prompting legislation for the government to improve food safety. The passage of this law, however, resulted in little immediate improvement. Although food processors were required to maintain sanitary conditions, there were no measures in the law to monitor

Span the Globe

Consumers Lack Protection in Developing Economies

In most economies that develop quickly, consumer protections lag behind economic growth. This has been true in China as it transforms into a more consumer-driven economy. As an example, throughout China athletic clubs are closing, causing members who prepaid their fees to lose their money. Due to increased competition, the athletic clubs offered discounted prepaid memberships at a time when other prices were rising. Eventually athletic clubs around the country began to close their doors, victims of rental inflation and high competition. One athletic club, after going out of business, sent a text message to its members saying, "As a private company, we do not have support from the State or any consortium. In a highly competitive marketplace, it has not been easy for us to continue our business." No regulations are in place to protect customers who sign up for prepaid services. When the businesses become unsustainable, the owners simply close down and keep the money.

Think Critically **Why must China improve its consumer protection laws if it wants to continue to transform its economy?**

Source: "Uphold Consumer Rights," ***Business Daily Update*** (China), January 6, 2011, at http://news.xinhuanet.com/english2010/indepth/2011-01/06/c_13678895.htm; and Duan Yan, "Clubs Need to Get Financially Fit" ***Business Daily Update*** (China), January 27, 2011, at http://www.chinadaily.com.cn/business/2011-01/27/content_11929050.htm.

production and punish violators. It wasn't until 1938, when the Food, Drug, and Cosmetic Act was passed, that government gained these powers. Since then the **Food and Drug Administration (FDA)** has set standards for foods and drugs produced or marketed in the United States. The FDA has the power to impose fines and to make businesses withdraw unsafe products from the market. In extreme cases, the FDA can close a business that fails to comply with its orders.

Food and Drug Administration (FDA)
Federal agency that sets standards for foods and drugs produced or sold in the United States

Federal Trade Commission (FTC)
Government agency that tries to ensure that businesses compete and market their products fairly and honestly

cease and desist order
FTC-issued directive to stop a firm from making a false or misleading advertising claim

Consumer Product Safety Commission (CPSC)
Federal agency created to protect consumers from dangerous products they might purchase or use

The Federal Trade Commission In 1914 Congress passed the Federal Trade Commission Act, a measure already discussed in Chapter 7. This law created the **Federal Trade Commission (FTC)**, which tries to ensure that businesses compete and market their products in a fair and honest way. Today the FTC sets standards for product packaging, labeling, and truth in advertising. It also enforces antitrust laws to limit monopoly power. When the FTC determines that an advertising claim is false or misleading, it has the authority to issue a **cease and desist order**, which requires the firm to stop making the claim. If the firm does not stop, it can be fined as much as $10,000 each additional time it makes the dishonest claim.

The Consumer Product Safety Commission In 1972 Congress created the **Consumer Product Safety Commission (CPSC)** to protect consumers from dangerous products they purchase or use. The CPSC has the power to force the manufacturer or marketer of any product it deems dangerous to recall the product and remove it from the market. The CPSC maintains a consumer website that, among other things, lists all products that have recently been recalled. On average, the CPSC orders the recall of about 400 products each year. Figure 11.3 shows the number of recalls during the month of April from 2000 through 2011. Recalls increased by about 50 percent, from an average of 23 per month

FIGURE 11.3 Number of CPSC-Ordered Recalls during the Month of April, 2000–2011

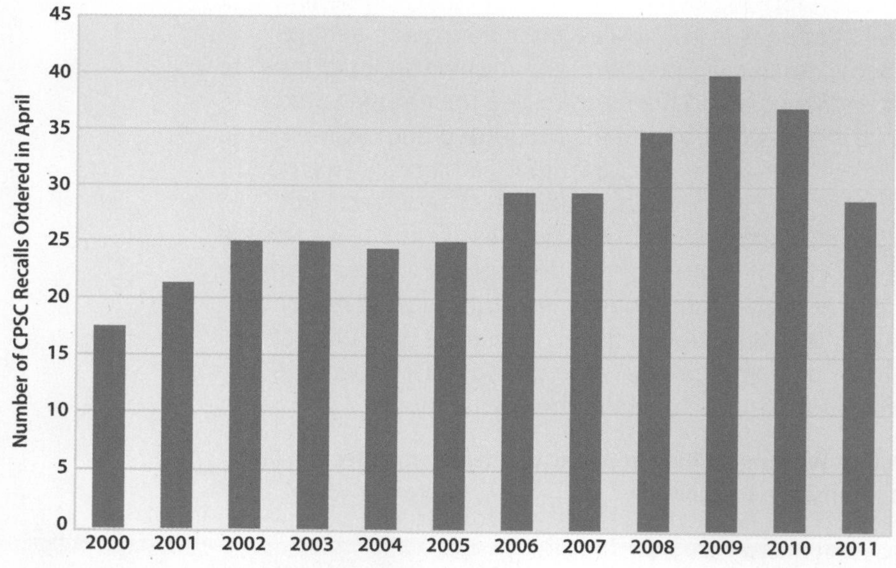

Source: CPSC website: http://www.cpsc.gov/CPSCPUB/PREREL/prerelmar11.html, May 5, 2011.

during the first five years, to 34 per month during the most recent five years. Do you believe that there may be more than 400 consumer products that should be recalled each year? What does this tell you about the importance of using your consumer skills to evaluate products you might purchase?

The Environmental Protection Agency The Environmental Protection Agency (EPA) was established in 1970 to interpret and enforce federal laws that involve the environment. Among its many responsibilities, the EPA enforces standards for toxic emissions into the air and water. Although the laws that give the EPA its powers are enacted by Congress, the EPA recommends standards to Congress that generally are passed into law. The EPA also provides expert advice to help businesses meet environmental standards.

Environmental Protection Agency (EPA)
Federal agency that interprets and enforces laws passed by Congress that involve the environment

Other Government Protections

Further government protections are offered by other federal agencies and agencies at the state and local levels.

Other Federal Agencies Many other federal agencies are responsible for protecting consumers in other ways. The Federal Communications Commission (FCC) regulates television, radio, and cellular communications. The U.S. Securities and Exchange Commission (SEC) enforces laws regarding the marketing and trading of corporate stocks and bonds. The Federal Aviation Administration (FAA) regulates airlines. The Federal Reserve System sets and enforces standards that protect our financial system. The Consumer Financial Protection Bureau (CFPB), which is financed by the Federal Reserve System, oversees and enforces federal laws aimed at fair and nondiscriminatory access to consumer credit. Each of these agencies is designed to provide a degree of safety to consumers they could not reasonably be expected to achieve on their own.

State and Local Protection All state and many local governments also have agencies responsible for protecting consumers. In New York, for example, the Department of Environmental Conservation (DEC) is charged with overseeing the disposal of industrial and toxic waste in a safe and environmentally responsible way. California's Environmental Protection Agency (CEPA) enforces water and air standards that are more strict than those set by the federal government. The Upper Mississippi River System

Photodisc/Getty Images

Which government agency do you think is responsible for ensuring that oil refineries operate in a safe and environmentally responsible way? Explain your answer.

Environmental Management Program coordinates efforts to keep the Mississippi River clean and healthy.

On a local level, city zoning ordinances that keep factories using dangerous chemicals away from residential areas also are a form of consumer protection. The same is true of ordinances that limit the spraying of chemicals on lawns or discarding oil into waste-water systems.

CHECKPOINT **Why do consumers need the government to help protect them from defective or dangerous products?**

TAKE RESPONSIBILITY FOR YOUR PROTECTION

LO2 Understand how to protect yourself as a consumer.

The United States is a big place. Millions of businesses operate in our economy selling hundreds of millions of different goods and services. In any year, consumer transactions number in the hundreds of billions. As a responsible consumer, you need to recognize that it is impossible for the government to protect your interests in every transaction you make. Your best source of protection is your own ability to evaluate products and make rational choices.

Consumer Rights and Responsibilities

As a consumer, you have many rights that protect you in the economy. For example, you have the right to be informed. When you buy a product, its label should tell you what it contains and the directions should explain proper assembly and use. You have a responsibility to read and follow the directions for proper use. When you buy a lawn mower, for example, the directions will tell you never to put your hands or feet under it when it is operating. If you are injured if you do, you have no one to blame but yourself. No law can protect people from their own carelessness or stupidity.

Consumers have the right to return a defective or dangerous product to a seller for replacement, repair, or refund. They also have a responsibility to let a manufacturer or marketer know when a product is defective. This will allow the product to be tested to find out if only yours is defective or if the defect is widespread.

Most businesses want satisfied customers, and they cannot achieve this unless they know when a customer is dissatisfied. Suppose you buy a hair dryer that gives you an electric shock when you plug it in. If you simply throw it away because it wasn't very expensive, other consumers also may receive shocks from the same model of dryer. When you find a product you have purchased is defective or dangerous, you should immediately report the problem to the store where you bought it.

Use Common Sense

Probably your best protection from defective or dangerous products is common sense. When all is said and done, most people are smart enough to use consumer products safely. You don't have to be a trained automobile mechanic to see that one of the tires is getting bald. If you don't replace it, you shouldn't be surprised if it rips apart at 70 miles per hour. Or, suppose you see an ad for dining room furniture offering a table and six chairs for just $99. Should you seriously consider such an offer? If you bought the table and chairs, would you be surprised if the set started falling apart after only a few months of use? As the saying goes, "When an offer seems to be too good to be true, it probably is."

What can you do to protect yourself as a consumer? **CHECKPOINT**

DEALING WITH IDENTITY THEFT

LO3
Know how to prevent identity theft and what to do if your identity is stolen.

In recent years, millions of Americans have suffered financial problems because someone else fraudulently used their identity to obtain credit or to access their financial accounts. This crime is known as **identity theft**. From a criminal's point of view, identity theft can be accomplished easily and there is little risk of getting caught. To steal your identity, all the identity thief really needs is your Social Security number. Other information, such as your address, bank account, and credit card and personal identification numbers (PINs), also would be useful, but not necessary. With this information, criminals may be able to charge purchases to your credit cards or withdraw funds from your accounts. More often these thieves simply open up new accounts in your name that you don't know about until you start receiving bills for things you never bought. At the beginning of 2010 an estimated that 3.5 percent of the U.S. population had been victims of identity theft.

Protect Yourself From Identity Theft

The best way to protect yourself from identity theft is to avoid letting other people see your financial information unless they have a legitimate reason to see it. Never let anyone watch you enter your PIN when you use a debit card. Before you discard them, shred all bank statements, bills, or other documents that include account or Social Security numbers. Don't leave financial documents in plain sight either at home or at work. Be suspicious of anyone who asks for personal financial information for reasons you do not understand. Be especially wary of email or telephone requests for personal information. Although taking these steps can reduce your chances of you becoming a victim of identity theft, there is no way to avoid this possibility entirely. For this reason it is important to always check your financial statements carefully to be sure they do not include transactions you did not make.

identity theft
Crime in which one person fraudulently uses another's identity to obtain credit or to access financial accounts

NET Bookmark

The FTC maintains a web page about identity theft. Access the website shown below and click on the link for Chapter 11. Click to begin taking the ID Theft Faceoff Quiz. Share your results in class.

www.cengage.com/school/contecon

Ilya Andriyanov/Shutterstock.com

When using a debit card, you should be sure that no one else can see the PIN you are entering. What other precautions should you take to protect yourself against identity theft?

What If Your Identity Is Stolen?

If you discover that your identity has been stolen, follow these steps:

- Contact each of the three major credit-reporting agencies to have a "fraud alert" placed in your credit file.
- Contact each business that has extended credit to you and explain what has happened. Ask the business to close your existing accounts and open new accounts with different numbers.
- Report your identity theft to law enforcement agencies.
- Contact the Federal Trade Commission's ID theft hot line at (877) 438-4338 or online. The FTC will give you advice and provide you with an ID Theft Affidavit you may complete and use to identify yourself as a victim of identity theft.

Although victims generally are not financially responsible for fraudulent use of their identity, they are responsible for correcting mistaken information in their credit files. This can take many hours of work and result in significant problems that can cause them to temporarily lose their access to credit. In 2010, the government estimated that the average victim of identity theft spent more than $600 and 40 hours to correct the problem. Even after corrections are made, mistaken records can reappear in a consumer's credit file. If you have been a victim of identity theft, you should review your credit file every few months.

CHECKPOINT What is the best way to protect yourself from identity theft?

11.3 ASSESSMENT

Think Critically

1. Why is the need for government consumer protection unlikely to decrease in the future?
2. What responsibility does the Federal Trade Commission have for advertising, and what power does it have to enforce its decisions?
3. What are two examples of rights and responsibilities consumers have in our economy?
4. What should you do if you become a victim of identity theft?

Graphing Exercises

5. Many who study the Earth's environment worry about the increase in average temperatures called global warming. They suggest that melting of the Earth's ice caps is linked to higher temperatures. A primary cause of global warming is thought to be carbon dioxide gas (CO_2) that is released into the atmosphere from burning fossil fuels. Use data from the table to construct a bar graph that shows the amount of CO_2 released by the United States in recent years. Explain what you think the government should do to protect consumers from global warming. Remember that to reduce CO_2 emissions, Americans would have to reduce their use of fossil fuels (gasoline, coal, and heating oil).

CO_2 EMISSIONS RELEASED BY YEAR, IN MILLIONS OF METRIC TONS

Year	Amount of Carbon Dioxide Released
2005	6,029.0
2006	5,928.7
2007	6,017.0
2008	5,839.3

Source: *Statistical Abstract of the United States, 2011*, p. 228

Make Academic Connections

6. **Government** Congress created government agencies that are responsible for protecting consumers. Some argue that these agencies are weak because many members of Congress receive large campaign contributions from big businesses that do not care for the regulations. Evaluate this point of view. Do you think big businesses exert too much control over government policy? What changes would you propose in the system?

TeamWork

Working in a team, identify a multinational corporation that does business in the United States. Make a list of benefits American consumers receive from this firm and another list of possible costs they pay. On balance, does your team think American consumers are better or worse off because of this firm? What, if anything, do you think the federal government should do to regulate this firm? Compare your answers with those of other teams.

21st Century Skills

CIVIC LITERACY

Responsible Consumers in the 21st Century

Technological developments not only provide consumers with better quality and more useful products, they also create opportunities to exercise civic responsibility. Consider the fact that some new products have proven to be dangerous when used irresponsibly. A good example is talking or texting on handheld cell phones while driving. Thousands of people have been injured or killed in accidents caused by drivers who were distracted by these devices. Many states have passed laws to limit their use. In 2011, eight states outlawed use of handheld cell phones by drivers and 30 states outlawed all texting by drivers. Many other states outlawed the use of these devices by commercial or young drivers.

Various organizations, including the National Safety Council and the American Automobile Association, support restrictions on the use of cellular devices while driving. These organizations have encouraged passage of laws to accomplish this through

- News releases that emphasize the dangers of distracted driving by reporting accident injury and death statistics.
- Programs that make presentations to schools and other public groups.
- Lobbying elected officials to encourage them to pass laws that limit the use of these devices by drivers.
- Circulating printed and electronic publications that explain the dangers of distracted driving and encourage the public to support legislation that outlaws use of these devices by drivers.

What You Can Do

Although you cannot pass laws by yourself, the Constitution guarantees all U.S. citizens the right to petition the government. This means you can give elected officials your opinion on any public situation. You can take advantage of this right by:

- Attending public meetings to voice your opinion.
- Writing letters to the editor of your local newspaper.
- Placing your opinion on social networking websites, such as Facebook.
- Demonstrating outside offices of organizations you support or oppose.
- Sending letters or emails to government officials

You have a right to tell the government what you think is true and what official policies should be. Consider joining an organization that supports your point of view. When you work with like-minded people, together you often are better able to influence government policy. Elected officials, after all, want to protect their jobs, and the best way to do this is to keep voters happy.

Apply the Skill

Suppose a new study has conclusively shown that the number of football injuries suffered by high school players can be reduced by at least 40 percent if they are required to wear a new kind of high-tech protective padding. Each set of padding will cost $500 and must be custom fit to each player. The padding could not be used by other players in the future or by the same player who grows much. Many school districts say they simply cannot afford to pay for the new padding. In addition, many players argue that the padding is too hot and restricts their ability to move quickly.

Decide whether you would support or oppose requiring high schools to provide this padding for players. Then explain three different ways you could use your right to petition the government to try to convince members of your school board that your point of view is correct.

Chapter 11 Summary

11.1 Consumer Choice

A. Anyone who uses a good or service is a consumer. Personal finance involves how consumers choose to spend or save their income. Consumers set personal financial goals in order to accomplish the things they want most out of life.

B. A budget is one important tool consumers can use to help make wise financial decisions. Budgets are financial plans that predict a person's income, spending, and saving for a specific period. Comparison shopping also helps consumers make rational choices.

11.2 Use Credit Responsibly

A. Consumers pay for purchases with either cash or credit. Paying with cash, check, or debit card prevents consumers from accumulating debt, but it requires them to carry cash, checks, or debit cards with them. Credit allows consumers to enjoy some products now they could not otherwise afford. The use of credit may lead to an accumulation of debt that can prevent people from achieving their life goals.

B. There are two sources of consumer credit: consumer loans and consumer sales credit. Consumer loans, such as a car loan, are for a set amount and must be repaid over a specific time period. Consumer sales credit, such as a credit card, involves charging to an account and making variable payments that do not have to be repaid within a specific time period.

C. Secured loans are backed with something of value, such as property or another asset. These loans have lower risk for lenders because the asset can be sold to satisfy the debt. Unsecured loans are not backed with assets. These loans pose higher risk for lenders because getting repaid can be a problem. Lenders evaluate consumers' creditworthiness according to the three Cs—character, capacity, and capital.

D. You should work to develop a positive credit history by making payments on time and never exceeding your credit limit. If you realize you cannot make a payment on time, you should notify the lender and explain the situation before the payment becomes due.

11.3 Consumer Protection

A. The government has passed laws and created many agencies to help protect consumers. Most federal consumer-protection laws were passed in the twentieth century. The first was the Pure Food and Drug Act of 1906. Other laws that followed included the Federal Trade Commission Act of 1914, the Environmental Protection Act of 1970, and the Consumer Product Safety Act of 1972. Each act created agencies or commissions that became responsible for the supervision and enforcement of various consumer protection laws.

B. So many transactions take place within the U.S. economy that it is impossible for the government to protect consumers in every situation. For this reason, you need to take personal responsibility and evaluate choices before you buy.

C. Identity theft occurs when another person fraudulently uses a consumer's identity to obtain credit or withdraw funds from someone else's account. The best way to avoid becoming a victim of identity theft is to protect your personal financial information. If you become a victim of identity theft, contact the three primary credit bureaus immediately to have your files placed on a "fraud alert." You also should notify the police and businesses that have given you credit.

ASK THE EXPERT

www.cengage.com/school/contecon

What's the best thing you can do to increase your value as a worker?

CHAPTER 11 ASSESSMENT

Review Economic Terms

a. budget
b. cease and desist order
c. comparison shopping
d. consumer
e. consumer loan
f. consumer sales credit
g. CPSC
h. credit history
i. credit rating
j. credit scoring
k. creditworthiness
l. EPA
m. FDA
n. FTC
o. identity theft
p. personal finance
q. rational consumer choice
r. secured loan
s. unsecured loan

Match the terms with the definitions. Some terms will not be used.

_____ 1. Federal agency that sets standards for foods and drugs produced or marketed in the United States

_____ 2. A consumer's plan for receiving and using income

_____ 3. A choice to buy or not buy a product so that your satisfaction is the greatest possible per dollar spent

_____ 4. A system that assigns a number or score to each consumer, indicating whether that person is a good or bad credit risk

_____ 5. Borrowing money to be repaid in regular installments over time

_____ 6. Anyone who uses a good or service

_____ 7. Loan for which property or other asset is pledged to back its repayment

_____ 8. The fraudulent use of a consumer's identity to obtain credit or to use that person's financial accounts

_____ 9. Amounts charged to an account that involves variable payments over time

_____ 10. A measure of your dependability to repay a loan

_____ 11. A person's record of paying bills and debts over time

Review Economic Concepts

12. Which of the following should be included as predicted income when you create your personal budget for next year?
    a. the amount you have deposited in your checking account
    b. the amount you expect to earn from working as a lifeguard next summer
    c. the amount your grandmother gave you for your birthday last year
    d. the amount you won as a door prize at a store's grand opening

13. ________?________ goals are things you hope to accomplish within a year or less.

14. Before you buy a product, you should ask yourself each of the following questions except
    a. Do I really need this product?
    b. Can I afford to pay for this product?
    c. Will this product impress my friends?
    d. Is this the best deal available for this product?

15. **True or False** A one-month budget worksheet includes predictions of your expected income, saving, and spending for a month.

16. When you comparison-shop you should choose the product that you think
    a. has the best value per dollar spent.
    b. has the best quality.
    c. has the best style or appearance.
    d. has the lowest price.

17. **True or False** A decision to use cash to make a purchase is always better for a consumer than a decision to use credit.

18. Why is the amount you borrow likely to be less than the amount you must repay?
    a. Prices are likely to go up in the future.
    b. You must pay interest on the funds you borrow.
    c. The money you borrow will be taxed.
    d. Your income is likely to be greater in the future.

19. Which of the following is an example of a consumer loan?
    a. A construction firm borrows $150,000 to build a house.
    b. A worker borrows $2,000 to buy a set of tools he needs to build the house.
    c. A husband and wife borrow $200,000 to buy a house.
    d. A husband and wife charge the price of a table for their new house on their credit card.

20. **True or False** Credit bureaus gather, maintain, and share financial information about almost every adult in the United States.

21. Which of the following is not one of the three Cs of credit?
    a. credit rating
    b. capacity
    c. capital
    d. character

22. Your credit ________?________ is a number assigned to you in your credit file that indicates whether you are a good or bad credit risk.

23. Which of the following is a good way for a young person to begin to establish a positive credit history?
    a. Always save and pay cash for things you buy.
    b. Borrow to buy one expensive item and then pay off the loan over many years.
    c. Save regularly and use your savings to back a small loan that you pay off on time.
    d. Always carry a balance on your account so you pay interest to the bank.

24. **True or False** If you find you cannot make a payment on a loan, you should go on vacation until you have enough money to pay your debt.

25. **True or False** It is a good idea to review your credit file at least once a year.

26. **True or False** All states and many local governments have agencies that are responsible for protecting consumers.

27. Which federal agency tries to ensure that businesses compete and market their products in a fair and honest way?
    a. the Consumer Product Safety Commission (CPSC)
    b. the Food and Drug Administration (FDA)
    c. the Environmental Protection Agency (EPA)
    d. the Federal Trade Commission (FTC)

Apply Economic Concepts

28. **Choose Cash or Credit** You would like to purchase a used car for $4,500. You have $1,000 for a down payment, sales tax, and other fees. You still need to borrow $3,500. The dealer offers to arrange a loan that will require you to pay $110 per month for the next three years. If you agree to this, how much will you end up paying for the loan? Instead, you could put off buying a car until you save enough to pay cash. What factors should you consider when you make your choice?

29. **Decide How Much to Pay** You just received your monthly credit-card statement. The balance you owe is $228.39. You have $239.00 in your checking account and only $4.00 in your wallet. You could pay the entire amount to avoid an interest payment. That would leave you with almost no ready cash for anything else. Or, you could make the minimum payment of $18.43. Your account charges 1 percent per month on unpaid balances. How much would the interest be if you pay only the minimum (you would be charged interest on the entire balance if you don't pay it all)? Should you pay off the entire balance? Explain the benefits and costs of your choice.

30. **Evaluate a Food Label** Copy the nutritional label for a food product you frequently consume, such as a breakfast cereal or frozen pizza. List all items on the label that you recognize and understand along with their definitions. Make a second list of items that you do not recognize or understand. Look up the meaning of each of these items in an encyclopedia or online. How useful is the label to you? Do you believe the food product is a healthy part of your diet?

31. **Write a Letter to the CPSC** Imagine that you recently purchased a Golden Glow gas grill for your patio. You followed the directions carefully when you assembled the grill. But when you went to light it, there was a small explosion and a ball of fire appeared below the grill next to the gas regulator. You quickly turned off the gas at the tank, and the fire went out. Next you reread the instructions to be sure you had made no mistakes. Convinced that you had done it right, you tightened all the fittings on the grill and tried to light it again. This time there was a bigger explosion. You intend to return the grill to the store where you bought it, but you also want to inform the Consumer Product Safety Commission so it can take action to protect other consumers. Write a letter to the CPSC explaining what happened and what you think the agency should do.

32. **21st Century Skills: Civic Leadership** Technological advancements often result in the creation of new products that require consumers to learn and use new skills to make sure they are used safely. Identify a product that first appeared on the market in the past two years and any dangers it may pose if it is used inappropriately. Describe steps groups of citizens could take to encourage consumers to use this product responsibly.

Digging Deeper

with Economics e-Collection

Access the Gale Economics e-Collection through the URL below to find articles about three federal consumer protection agencies discussed in Lesson 11.3. List the agencies you research and write a sentence about the issue reported in each article. Be prepared to share your results in class.

www.cengage.com/school/contecon

CHAPTER 12

Managing Your Money

Point your browser

www.cengage.com/school/contecon

airportrait/iStockphoto.com; Background image: Dibrova/Shutterstock.com

CONSIDER...

→ Why is keeping your savings in a bank a better idea than storing it in a box under your bed?

→ Why should you keep track of the deposits and withdrawals you make from your bank accounts?

→ Why are higher-income families more likely to own corporate stock?

→ Would you rather own blue chip stocks or growth stocks, and what's the difference?

→ You are talking on your cell phone while driving, and you run into your neighbor's car. Who pays for the damages?

12.1 SAVING

Key Terms

saving 360
return 361
compound interest 363
annual percentage yield (APY) 363
certificate of deposit (CD) 363
money market account 365

Learning Objective

LO1 Describe benefits people receive from saving part of their income.

LO2 Identify and describe the types of deposit accounts offered by banks.

In Your World

You save when you spend less than you earn. If you save, you must decide how to store your savings. Cash kept on hand may be lost or stolen, or it may lose value if prices increase. For these reasons, you should deposit your savings in a bank or other financial institution. Banks offer many types of accounts that provide security, combinations of convenience and access to savings, and, in most cases, interest to help protect your savings from inflation. To make rational decisions, you should identify and evaluate your savings alternatives to find those that best suit your individual goals and financial situation.

SAVE FOR YOUR FUTURE

LO1 Describe benefits people receive from saving part of their income.

Each pay period, you, as a worker, will receive income you will either spend or save. Economists define **saving** as the act of choosing not to spend current income. Saving involves a trade-off. By choosing to save, you trade the satisfaction from buying something now for the satisfaction you may receive from buying something in the future. One major benefit of saving is that you can accumulate enough savings to help buy expensive products such as a home or an automobile.

Probably the most important benefit of saving is the security it provides against unexpected events. You have no way of knowing whether you will be struck by a truck, fall down a manhole, become ill, or be injured in some other way. Maybe a storm, earthquake, fire, or natural disaster will destroy your home. Or, you may lose your job through no fault of your own. Any of these events can drop your income to zero. If any of these unfortunate events occur, you will be able to maintain your standard of living and will recover your financial health if you have saved enough money.

Create a Savings Plan

Trading the ability to buy something you want now to buy something in the future usually is not an easy choice. Experts agree that creating and following a savings plan is the best way to save successfully. These steps should help you improve your chance of reaching your savings goals:

saving The act of choosing not to spend current income

- Establish a clear idea why you are saving and how much you want to save. It is easier to save if you have a particular objective in mind, such as buying a car or paying for college.
- Create a saving strategy. You might, for example, decide to set aside $20 from every paycheck before you spend for anything else. Or, if the amount you earn varies from week to week, you might decide to save a percentage of your pay instead or a specific dollar amount.
- Save automatically if you can. Some employers will deposit a portion of your salary into your bank account automatically. Funds you never see may be easier to save.
- Reward yourself when you reach savings goals. If there is something you enjoy that doesn't cost much, you could commit to doing this each time you achieve a savings goal. You might take a hiking trip to a state park each time your save another $500, for example.

Store Your Savings

If you decide not to spend your income, you face another decision: where to store the money you have not spent. Keeping savings in a box under your bed, for example, is one possibility. However, this would not be a wise choice. Money kept at home or in your wallet or purse might be lost or stolen. Inflation poses another hazard. As prices increase, the purchasing power of your savings will fall. It's better to store your savings where it will earn a return. **Return** is income earned from funds that are not spent. Earning a return is another major benefit of having a savings plan.

The return you could earn from your savings depends on how you store it. Obviously, money stored in a box under your bed earns no return. If you deposit your savings in a bank, however, the bank will usually pay you interest. The rate of interest is your return. Interest will help protect your savings against inflation. In addition, a bank provides security for your savings because the FDIC, or a similar government agency insures your deposit up to a maximum of $250,000.

There are choices you could make other than storing your savings in a bank or under your bed. For example, you could lend your savings to a friend who wants to open a bicycle-repair business. She might offer to pay you 10 percent interest. But if her business fails, you might lose your savings. When you decide where to store your savings, there is a trade-off between risk and return. In general, the greater the expected return, the greater the risk of losing your money.

Methods of saving that involve more risk are discussed in Section 12.2 of this chapter, entitled "Investing." Methods of saving that involve lower degrees of risk include depositing money in bank accounts as well as purchasing U.S. savings bonds. The various types of bank accounts will be discussed next.

return Income earned from funds that are not spent

CHECKPOINT

What benefits do people receive from saving some of their income?

TYPES OF BANK ACCOUNTS

LO2 Identify and describe the types of deposit accounts offered by banks.

There are several types of financial institutions that accept deposits from individuals. These include banks, savings and loan associations, savings banks, and credit unions. These institutions provide similar services, and all will be referred to as "banks" in this chapter.

Banks earn income by accepting deposits from savers and then lending these funds to borrowers. Banks pay interest to most depositors. They charge borrowers higher rates of interest. The difference between the interest paid to depositors and the interest charged to borrowers helps banks try to earn a profit. There are many types of deposit accounts in which you may store your savings. These include time deposits, savings accounts, checking accounts, and money market accounts. The balances held by households in various types of bank accounts during the past two decades are presented in Figure 12.1.

Savings Accounts

A savings account allows you to deposit or withdraw your savings at any time and earn a relatively low, fixed rate of interest. The bank records deposits and withdrawals from savings accounts electronically. Depositors are expected to maintain a separate record of their transactions to check against monthly statements they receive from their bank. Banks pay relatively low rates of interest on savings accounts because

FIGURE 12.1 Amounts Deposited in Bank Accounts, 1990–2010

Checking deposits fluctuated between 1990 and 2010 but ended up about where they began. Other bank deposits were higher in 2010 than in 1990.

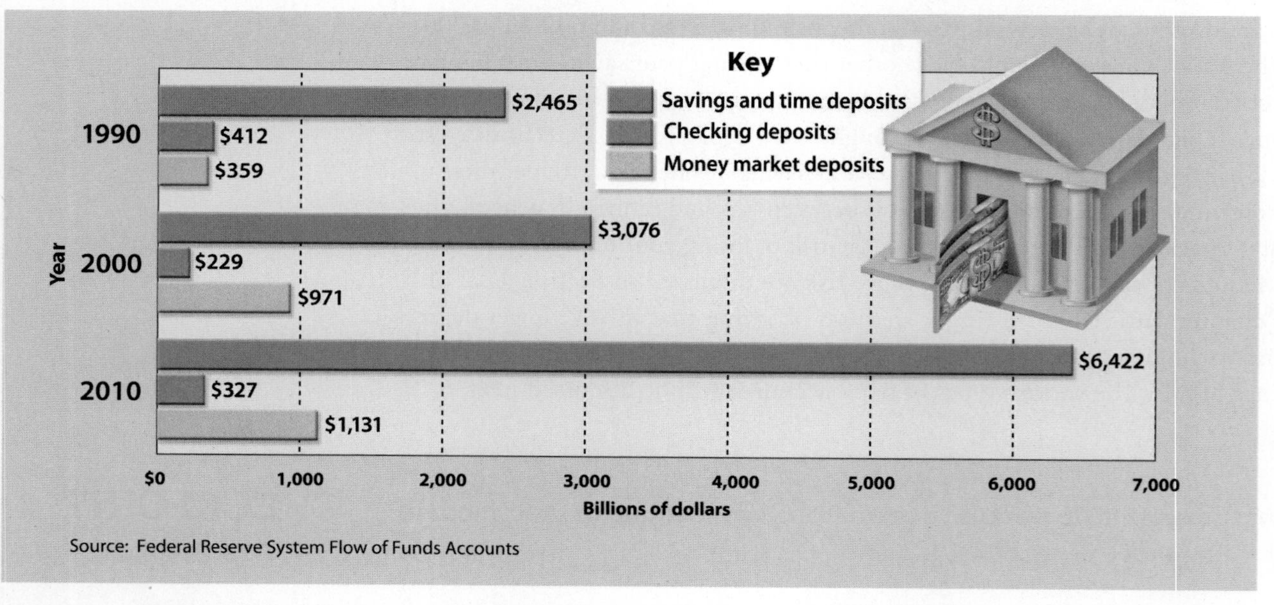

Source: Federal Reserve System Flow of Funds Accounts

banks do not know how long they will have use of the funds. Most savings accounts earned little interest, typically only about 1 percent per year.

Compound Interest Deposits usually earn **compound interest**. Suppose you deposit $100 in a bank account, and the bank agrees to pay 6 percent interest compounded twice a year. After six months, the bank would pay 3 percent of $100, or $3, to increase the value of your deposit to $103. Then, after the next six months, an additional 3 percent interest would be calculated on this new amount. At the end of the year, you would receive an additional $3.09, bringing your deposit to $106.09. The extra nine cents would be the additional interest you earned on the interest you already had been paid.

You might think that nine cents isn't important. But when interest is compounded every day over many years, it can make a sizable difference. Note that a 10 percent interest rate on a deposit of $1,000 will boost the deposit to $2,718 in 10 years!

Banks usually advertise their accounts with names such as "Gold Returns" or "Premium Plus." How can you tell which bank is making the best offer? *Federal law requires that all banks calculate the interest paid on deposits in exactly the same way.* It is called the **annual percentage yield (APY)**. Because all banks must use the same calculation, you know that an account that has an APY of 4.53 percent pays more than one offering an APY of 4.44 percent, no matter what the bank calls its interest rate.

Time Deposits

When you open a time deposit, you commit to leave an amount of money in your account for a specified period of time. This duration may be as short as several days or as long as ten years. Time deposits typically are for six months or for one, two, or five years. The most common type of time deposit is called a **certificate of deposit** or **CD**. A certificate of deposit is a savings instrument with a fixed interest rate and a fixed maturity date.

When you open a CD, you deposit an amount of money and commit to leave it on deposit for a specific period of time. Banks are willing to pay higher interest on CDs because they will have use of these funds for an extended and predictable period of time. This greater certainty allows banks to use these funds in ways that will earn them a greater return. This greater return enables banks to pay depositors more. Recently most CDs paid between 1 and 3 percent, depending on their term. The longer a depositor agrees to leave funds on deposit, the higher the interest paid. The holder of a CD may pay a penalty for early withdrawals, usually equal to six months or more of interest.

Checking Accounts

A checking account allows a depositor to make payments by writing checks or using a debit card that directs the bank to pay someone from the account. There are minor differences between checking accounts offered by different banks, but they all work in about the same way.

Advantages of Checks or Debit Cards Probably the most important advantage of making payments with checks or debit cards is the safety they provide.

compound interest Computed on the amount saved plus the interest previously earned

annual percentage yield (APY) Formula banks must use to calculate interest they pay on deposits

certificate of deposit (CD) Savings instrument with fixed interest rate and fixed maturity date

You do not need to carry large amounts of cash. When you use checks or debit cards, there is no doubt that payment has been made. Banks keep a record of all such transactions.

Checking account statements can be useful when you evaluate your budget or prepare your income tax return. Finally, some checking accounts pay a modest rate of interest on deposits. To earn interest on checking accounts, you usually must have a substantial amount on deposit, at least several thousand dollars.

Open and Maintain a Checking Account The first step in opening a checking account is to visit a bank that is conveniently located. Investigate the checking accounts offered, and compare these with offerings of other banks you might choose. When you decide where to open your account, you will be required to sign papers and deposit funds into the account. Initially, you will be provided with a few checks that you may use immediately. A supply of checks with your name and address printed on them will be mailed to you. In addition, you usually will receive a debit card, which you can use to tap into your checking account balance at ATMs and at a growing number of retailers. You also will receive a check register for recording your transactions, including deposits you make, checks you write, and debit card payments.

Each time you write a check, use your debit card, or make a deposit, enter the amount in your check register and calculate your new balance. At the end of each month, your bank will send you an account statement listing your deposits, checks, and debits. *You should reconcile your checking account each month to catch any mistakes and to avoid overdrawing your account.* Banks may charge an overdraft fee for check or debit payments that exceed your account balance.

To reconcile (or balance) your account, you should compare your records of each deposit, check written, and debit card transaction with those recorded by your bank. Some checks you wrote may not yet have cleared—that is, these checks have not yet been paid by your bank. These outstanding checks should be taken into account when you calculate your balance. You should also make adjustments for any fees charged and interest earned. If your balance still does not match the amount the bank says you have, recheck your calculations. If you are unable to determine the discrepancy, contact your bank for assistance.

Checking Account Fees There are two types of fees that banks charge for most checking accounts. Unless you are able to maintain a substantial balance in your account, you cannot avoid paying them. These fees are a *monthly maintenance charge* and a *service charge* for each check written. Investigate these fees before you open your account because different banks charge different amounts.

The maintenance fee of a few dollars a month is charged to cover the bank's cost of keeping records for your account. Also, a service charge is sometimes imposed on each check you write. It covers the bank's cost of processing your check. Most banks charge from 15 to 30 cents per check you write, though many banks waive these charges if the average account balance meets or exceeds their minimum requirement. Banks usually do not impose a service charge on debit card transactions (though the retailer accepting your debit payment often is charged a small fee by the bank). Your check-writing habits will determine which type of account is best for you. If you write few checks, it is more important to choose an account with a low maintenance fee. If you write many checks, it can be better to choose an account with a low service charge. As noted in the previous chapter, the trend is towards debit card transactions and away from checks. By 2015, debit cards are expected to be the most popular form of payment, with cash second, credit cards third, other electronic payments fourth, and checks last.

Money Market Accounts

Like savings accounts, **money market accounts** allow you to deposit or withdraw funds at any time, though most banks limit the number of transactions per month and the size of transactions. Money market accounts are different from savings accounts because the rate of interest they pay varies from day to day as interest rates throughout the economy change. Money market accounts usually require a minimum deposit of $500 or more to open. The greatest advantage of money market accounts is that they usually pay a slightly higher rate of interest than savings accounts.

money market accounts Bank accounts that allow depositors a limited number of transactions per month; interest is slightly higher than on savings accounts but can vary from from day to day

CHECKPOINT Name and define the four types of bank accounts.

Math in Economics

Common Core Measurement and Data

You can determine the balance in an account that pays interest compounded daily by multiplying the appropriate value in the compound interest table by the amount deposited into the account. To find the amount of the balance that is interest paid, subtract the original amount deposited from the answer to your multiplication problem.

DAILY COMPOUND INTEREST TABLE

	Annual Interest Rate			
Years	1%	2%	3%	4%
1	1.010050	1.020201	1.030453	1.040808
2	1.020201	1.040810	1.061834	1.083282
3	1.030454	1.061835	1.094170	1.127489
4	1.040810	1.093285	1.127491	1.173501
5	1.051270	1.105168	1.161827	1.221389

EXAMPLE Use the compound interest table to determine how much interest would have been paid after two years for a $2,000 deposit that earned interest at a rate of 3% compounded daily. Assume that no additional money was deposited, and no money was withdrawn. Write answers rounded to the nearest cent.

SOLUTION Find the value in the table that corresponds to two years and a 3% annual interest rate. Multiply the value from the table by $2,000.

$1.061834 \times \$2{,}000 = \$2{,}123.67$

Subtract $2,000 to find the amount of interest paid.

$\$2{,}123.67 - \$2{,}000 = \$123.67$

Practice the Skill Use the Daily Compound Interest Table to calculate the interest paid on each deposit. Assume that no additional money was deposited, and that money was withdrawn. Write answers rounded to the nearest cent.

1. $500 for three years at a 2% rate
2. $1,200 for four years at a 4% rate
3. $750 for five years at a 1% rate

12.1 ASSESSMENT

Think Critically

1. Why is it important to set your financial goals before you create a savings plan?
2. Give two reasons why you should not store your savings in a box under your bed.
3. Why do certificates of deposit pay a higher rate of interest than other types of bank accounts?
4. What is the greatest advantage of making payments with checks rather than cash?

Graphing Exercise

5. Use data from the table to construct a line graph that shows the average rate of interest paid on 1-year CDs between 2002 and 2009. Can you think of any reasons why this rate fell in the years following 2007?

Year	Value	Year	Value
2002	1.98%	2006	3.64%
2003	1.20	2007	3.65
2004	1.45	2008	2.36
2005	2.77	2009	1.16

Source: *Statistical Abstract of the United States, 2011*, p. 744.

Make Academic Connections

6. **Mathematics** Calculate the value of a $4,000 deposit that was made two years ago in a CD that has an Annual Percentage Yield (APY) of 5.0 percent. To make this calculation, multiply the original deposit by 1.05 twice (once for each year the funds were on deposit). Complete the same calculation for a CD that pays 5.2 percent. This time, multiply the original deposit by 1.052 two times. How much more will the second CD pay? Why does the requirement that banks report interest rates as APYs help savers earn the most from their deposits?
7. **Personal Finance** Last year you deposited $1,000 in a five-year CD that paid an APY of 4.2 percent. One year later, interest rates have risen and new four-year CDs pay 6.5 percent. If you withdraw your deposit early, you will be charged a penalty equal to all the interest you earned in the past year. But then you could open a new CD and earn the higher rate for the next four years. Determine which choice would result in the higher return for your savings over the five years. Explain your answer.

TeamWork

Working with a partner, investigate the checking account options available at two local banks. Learn what fees, if any, each bank charges for monthly maintenance and the service charges for the number of checks written and for overdrawn checks. Evaluate other considerations involved in choosing a bank for your checking account, such as location, hours of operation, and availability of ATMs. Determine which bank offers the better option for each partner's personal needs

21st Century Skills

Creativity and Innovation

Saving and Investing for the Future

Benjamin Franklin said the only two things you can count on in life are death and taxes. It is possible that a third item, inflation, should be added to this list. Many goods and services will become so expensive in the future that some people will not be able to afford them unless they have created and followed a regular savings plan. Consider these average costs for consumer products in 2010:

- The average cost of a new home was just over $204,000.
- The average price of a new car was slightly more than $29,000.
- The average cost (tuition, books, and fees only) for a year of college at a private institution was $33,300, while at public colleges it was $16,730.
- The average cost for a day of vacation for a family of four was almost $500.
- The average cost for a wedding was nearly $25,000.

In the 21st century, few people will be able to pay for goods or services such as these out of their current income. This leaves three alternatives. They can wait until they have saved all the funds they need. They can borrow the funds they need. Or, they can do a little of both. Most lending institutions are not willing to make large loans to people with little or no savings.

Creative Consumption

An obvious way to increase your ability to save is to find ways to reduce the amount you spend for consumption. Although adjusting your spending habits can take a little creativity, it does not necessarily mean you have to accept a lower standard of living. Which of the following steps could you take to reduce your spending?

- Always compare prices for products you want to purchase, both in physical stores and online.
- Avoid making buying decisions without evaluating alternatives.
- Keep track of products you throw away. If you discard many of your clothes before you wear them out, you may be spending more than you should on new garments.
- Look for opportunities to share expenses. If you and a neighbor work for the same employer, you might be able to reduce your spending by riding together. There are ride-share websites in many cities to help commuters find each other.
- When new product models become available, the models they replace often are sold at reduced prices. Why buy this year's refrigerator model when last year's is selling at a 25 percent discount?
- Keep up with innovations that can reduce your cost of living. Something as simple as replacing your incandescent light bulbs with compact fluorescent bulbs can save the average consumer more than $100 per year in electricity costs.

Apply the Skill

Survey your home to identify ways in which your family could reduce spending without seriously affecting its standard of living. Describe three of these ways and explain how you could encourage the family to implement your ideas.

12.2 INVESTING

Key Terms

investing 368
corporate stock 368
diversification 371
mutual fund 372
corporate bond 373
financial planner 375

Learning Objectives

LO1 Compare and contrast investing in corporate stock versus investing in corporate bonds.

LO2 Examine resources to help you manage your investments.

In Your World

Although most bank accounts pay interest, many savers choose to invest a portion of their funds in ways they hope will earn them a higher return. To achieve this, they must be willing to take more risk. The options include investing in corporate stocks or corporate bonds. These investments offer many combinations of risk and return. To make rational investment decisions, you need to identify and evaluate investment alternatives to find those best suited to your individual goals and financial situations.

INVEST TO EARN A RETURN

LO1
Compare and contrast investing in corporate stock vs. bonds.

As you will learn in Chapter 13, business investment is defined as the purchase of new plants, new equipment, new homes, and net increases in inventories. A discussion of personal finance takes a much broader view of investment. In that broader perspective, **investing** is defined as using your savings in a way that earns a return. When you deposit your savings in a bank account that pays interest, you are investing. However, *investing more generally refers to using your savings to earn a greater return than is paid by banks, and investing usually involves more risk than leaving your funds in a bank account.* There are many ways of investing your savings. Two investments are described here: corporate stocks and corporate bonds.

Invest in Corporate Stock

As introduced in Chapter 10, when corporations are formed they sometimes raise funds by selling shares of ownership, or stock, to the public. Investors purchase shares of **corporate stock** because they hope to earn a return. Stockholders may earn a return from their stock in two ways. They may receive a share of the corporation's earnings as a dividend payment, or they may earn a capital gain if they sell their stock for more than they paid for it. There is no guarantee a corporation will earn a profit or pay dividends. If the firm does not do well, the value of its stock may fall and its stockholders might suffer a capital loss if they sell their shares. You should not buy stocks if you will need that money in the near future. If you have only a few hundred dollars saved, you should keep your savings in a bank account and wait to invest in stocks until you are in a stronger financial position. Consider Figure 12.2, which lists the percentage of U.S. families that own corporate stock according to

investing Using your savings in a way that earns a return

corporate stock Shares of ownership in a corporation

FIGURE 12.2 Percent of Families Owning Corporate Stock by Income Group

Why are higher-income families more likely to own corporate stock?

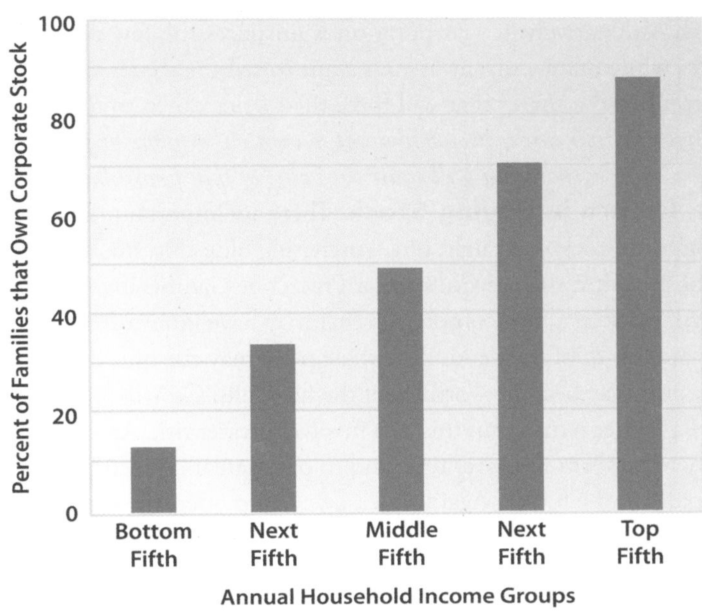

Source: *Statistical Abstract of the United States, 2011*, p. 750.

family income. Note that among the bottom fifth of families based on income, only 14 percent own stocks. Among the top fifth of families, 88 percent own stocks.

Two Types of Corporate Stock There are two types of corporate stock: common and preferred. Although both types represent ownership in the corporation, there are important differences.

Shares of *common stock* give their owners one vote per share when important decisions are made for the firm. These decisions include electing a board of directors to oversee the firm's operations. Owners of common stock do not receive a dividend unless one is declared by the firm's board of directors. The amount of any dividend may change over time, according to other financial needs of the corporation or the amount of profit earned. If the corporation is successful, it could pay large dividends to its common stockholder. If it does poorly, the corporation may pay common stockholders no dividends at all. For these reasons, buying common stock is regarded as relatively risky when compared to other investments you might make.

Shares of *preferred stock* do not give their owners a vote in how the corporation is operated. They do, however, provide a fixed dividend that is equal to a percentage of the original sales price of the stock. A corporation generally will pay this fixed dividend each year unless it suffers a large loss. In such a case, the board of directors may choose not to pay a dividend to preferred stockholders. If the firm later returns to profitability, all missed preferred-stock dividends must be paid before any dividends are paid to common stockholders. For these reasons, buying preferred stock has a lower risk than buying common stock in the same firm.

Why Does the Value of Stock Change? The price of corporate stock changes for the same reason as the price of any other good or service. It is all a matter of demand and supply. If a corporation is successful, many people want to buy shares in that business, but few current owners want to sell their shares. This creates a shortage of the shares that will force their price up to the market-clearing level. Alternatively, if a corporation is unsuccessful, few people want to buy its shares while many current owners want to sell the shares they own. This creates a surplus of the shares that will force their price down to the market-clearing level. *Anything that causes people to want to own either more or fewer shares of stock in a particular corporation will cause the value of that firm's shares to change.*

Risk vs. Return in Buying Stock There are important differences in the nature of common stock you might buy. Purchasing blue chip stock in a large, successful, established firm such as Chevron or Procter & Gamble involves less risk than buying growth stock in a new corporation that may have innovative products, but no record of success or of dividends. The share price may rise quickly if the new firm is successful, or it may become worthless if the firm fails. Growth stocks offer the possibility of a higher return, but this also involves greater risk. An established firm is more likely to perform well over time and to pay regular dividends even if it does not grow rapidly in the future. Again, stock ownership offers the expected positive relationship between risk and return.

Buying and Selling Shares of Stock Most shares of stock that are sold in the United States are traded in one of two ways. They are either sold through a formal stock exchange such as the New York Stock Exchange (NYSE) or they are sold through an electronic market called the National Association of Securities Dealers Automated Quotations (NASDAQ) system.

The New York Stock Exchange The New York Stock Exchange (NYSE) and other formal exchanges in the past have been physical locations where shares of stock were bought and sold. The NYSE sells one-year licenses to trade on the exchange. Major brokerage firms rent seats on the exchange and charge their customers to execute stock transactions for them.

Suppose a person wants to sell 100 shares of IBM. She might call or visit the office of a brokerage firm in Denver, Colorado, to place her sell order. This order would be sent to that firm's office at the NYSE in New York City. About the same time a different person in Sarasota, Florida, might call or visit his broker's office and ask to buy 100 shares of IBM. This time a buy order would be sent to his firm's office at the NYSE. Representatives of these two firms would meet at a desk on the floor of the NYSE that is designated to handle IBM trades. With the help of a specialist who deals in IBM stock, the transaction would be completed. In recent years more trades on the NYSE have been carried out electronically, and still more are likely to be done that way in the future. Those who want to buy or sell stock are now also more likely to do so online, and the transaction is executed within seconds.

The NASDAQ Now imagine that someone wants to sell 100 shares of Microsoft stock, while a different person wants to buy 100 shares. Microsoft stock is listed, or traded, on the NASDAQ. This time the two brokerage firms enter their buy and sell orders in a computer system that electronically matches the orders and completes the transaction. Trades that take place on the NASDAQ are usually much faster than those that occur on the NYSE. This means they are less costly to the brokerage firms. They also can be carried out when formal exchanges are closed. For these reasons, more transactions take place on the NASDAQ than on the NYSE, and that's why the NYSE is moving toward electronic trading.

Create Your Stock Portfolio Suppose you put all your savings in a firm that you believed would be a big success, but you were wrong. The business failed, and you lost everything. Investing in only one firm is seldom a good idea. The rational decision for investors is **diversification**. This means investing in a wide variety of corporations so that if one does poorly, others may succeed, allowing your investments to grow.

When you buy stocks, you are creating a stock portfolio. Your portfolio should be diversified and should reflect your goals and personal financial situation. Suppose you are supporting a family on a limited income and have only a little to invest. Because you can't afford to lose much, you should buy a variety of blue chip stocks that may grow in value over time, pay regular dividends, and face less chance of losing much value. If you are financially established and can afford to lose some of your funds, you might choose to invest in some higher-risk growth stocks. The value of these shares might fall, but you can afford to take the loss. For example, between the end of 2007 and the end of 2008, the market value of all U.S. publicly traded corporations fell from $19,081 billion to $12,050 billion, for a drop of 37 percent and one of the biggest declines in decades. Figure 12.3 shows the decline. Or, stock values might increase sharply, in which case you would benefit from their growth. For example, U.S. corporations made up most of the lost ground, recovering to $17,507 billion by the end of 2010. The best portfolio for one person may not be right for someone else.

Mutual Funds Many people would like to invest in stocks but lack the time or skill to select stocks and keep track of them. Or, they may have so little to invest that they are not able to diversify their choices. For these people, investing through

diversification Investing in a wide variety of firms

FIGURE 12.3 Market Value of Publicly Traded U.S. Corporations at Year End, in Billions

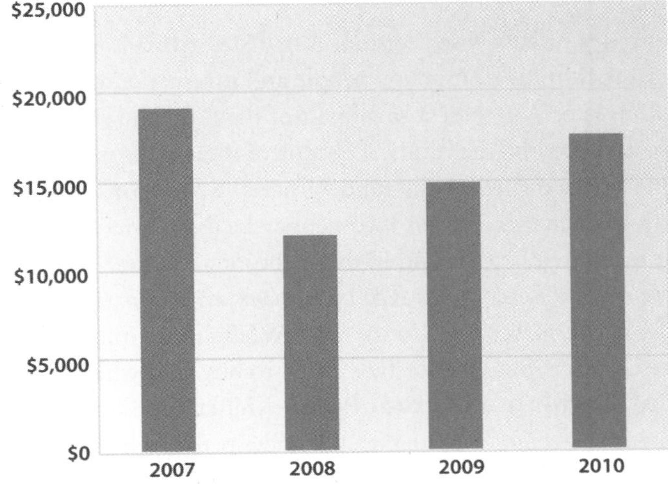

Source: Board of Governors of the Federal Reserve System, *Flow of Funds Guide*, Table L.213 Corporate Equities at http://www.federalreserve.gov/apps/fof/DisplayTable.aspx?t=l.213.

Span the Globe

Stock Exchanges Around the World

From the Athenian *emporion* to Rome's *collegiums mercatorum*, flourishing societies have always had gathering places where important traders came together at established hours to transact business. Today's world is no exception. Stock exchanges, the modern equivalents of the *emporion* and the *collegiums mercatorum*, are popping up all over the globe. South Africa has two, as does Indonesia. Canada and the United Kingdom have six. Russia has eight. Japan has a dozen, and the United States has 31. In the mood for a trading vacation? Stock exchanges in the Bermudas or the Cayman Islands await.

All told, more than 170 stock exchanges are open around the world. The largest is the New York Stock Exchange, showing about $16.7 trillion invested. Tokyo's stock exchange is the second largest at $5 trillion. The London Stock Exchange is $3.5 trillion, with NASDAQ close behind at $3.1 trillion.

The world's newest stock exchange is located in a communist country of six million, previously known as being the most heavily bombed county per capita ever—Laos. The Laos Securities Exchange opened with a listing of two stocks with hopes to quickly add a dozen more as its rulers add additional state-controlled businesses to its exchange.

Because of the ability to shift funds almost instantaneously, stock traders now find they can keep their money busy 24/7, in whatever exchange the sun is shining.

Think Critically **Is the large number of stock exchanges a good or bad sign? Explain your answer.**

Source: Kelsie Brandlee, "Laos Launches Stock Exchange," Center for International Finance & Development at the University of Iowa College of Law currents events blog, January 12, 2011; James Hookway, "Laos Looks to Become a New Market Frontier," *The Wall Street Journal*, January 11, 2011; and "List of Stock Exchanges Around the World" at www.world-stock-exchanges.net.

a mutual fund is often a wise decision. A **mutual fund** is a financial organization that accepts funds from many people and invests them in a variety of stocks. Individual investors purchase a small part of the fund and therefore a tiny fraction of each stock owned by the fund. The value of their investment changes with the value of the stocks owned by the fund. When the fund earns income from dividends or from capital gains, this income may be distributed to the mutual fund owners or reinvested by the fund in more corporate shares. *The big advantage of investing in mutual funds is that such investments are automatically diversified across the many different stocks owned by the fund.* What's more, the fund employs experts to make decisions about what to buy, when to buy, and when to sell.

mutual fund A financial organization that accepts funds from many people and invests them in a variety of stocks

Cost of Owning a Mutual Fund Mutual funds may be either load or no-load funds. *Load funds* are marketed by sales people who receive a commission of roughly 6 percent of the amount invested either when you buy the fund or when you sell it. *No-load funds* do not charge a sales commission. To purchase shares in these funds, you must contact the fund, read literature that is provided by the fund to decide whether it is right for you, and send a check to the fund to purchase its shares. All mutual funds charge an annual maintenance fee that pays for the cost of operating the fund. This can be as little as 0.4 percent of the amount you have invested or as much as 3.0 percent.

Most experts recommend that small investors choose a large no-load fund that has a low maintenance fee. Many funds offered by Fidelity, Vanguard, or other financial organizations fit this description.

Mutual Funds Invest in Different Ways Not all mutual funds make the same types of investments. Some are conservative and buy stocks only in large, well-established firms. Others buy stocks in small firms, while some look for stocks in cutting-edge firms that are creating new technology. In recent years, many mutual funds have invested in foreign stocks or in businesses that specialize in developing eco-friendly energy or new types of pharmaceuticals.

Still other funds do not so much "pick" stocks as simply establish clearly defined rules for selecting stock—rules that remain constant regardless of market conditions. These so-called *index funds* may invest, for example, in all of the 30 corporations in the Dow Jones Industrial Average or in all of the 500 largest U.S. corporations.

By reading a fund's prospectus, you can find out what investment strategy is followed. A prospectus will be provided free of charge when you request one in writing, by telephone, or online.

Invest in Corporate Bonds

In Chapter 10 you learned that a bond is a promise to repay the holder a fixed sum of money on a designated date of maturity plus make annual interest payments until that date. Federal, state, and local governments, and corporations issue bonds to borrow money. Nearly half of the money borrowed by corporations is obtained by selling bonds. Investors who purchase corporate bonds do not thereby become owners of that firm. They have made a loan that entitles them to be repaid at the specified date and receive interest until that date. Investing in **corporate bonds** involves less risk than buying stock in that firm because the bonds must be repaid whether or not the business earns a profit. The only reason a bond would not be repaid is if the business fails. Even then, the firm's bondholders must be paid from the firm's remaining assets before preferred or common stockholders receive a cent.

Most bonds are transferable. This means they can be resold to someone else in the *secondary bond market.* Just like the stock exchanges where "used" shares of stock are traded, previously purchased bonds are traded in the secondary bond market.

The Price of "Used" Bonds Can Change An investor who purchases a newly issued corporate bond and holds it until it matures will be paid the amount originally invested plus interest. However, the market value of a "used" bond will change if it is resold on the secondary market before it matures. Suppose you purchased a corporate bond for $1,000 that promised to pay 6 percent interest ($60) in each of the next 10 years. Four years after you bought the bond, you decide to sell it. In the meantime, prevailing interest rates have fallen and a new bond issued by the same firm pays only 5 percent interest ($50). Your "used" bond pays more interest than a new bond so you can expect a higher price when you sell it. You might be able to get $1,050 for your bond. The person who buys your bond will still receive only $1,000 when the bond matures. But he will

corporate bonds
Loan that entitles an investor to be repaid at the specified date and receive interest until that date

Investigate Your Local Economy

Interview a full-service stockbroker or a financial planner in your area. Find out what types of investments the person recommends and the fees he or she charges. Prepare a short presentation on your findings for your class.

earn $10 more in interest in each of the next six years than he would if he had purchased a new bond paying only $50 in annual interest. This is why he is willing to pay more than $1,000 for it. If prevailing interest rates fall, the value of "used" bonds will increase.

Suppose again you buy a newly issued bond paying 6 percent interest. Again, four years after you bought the bond, you decide to sell it, but this time new bonds issued by the same business pay 7 percent interest ($70). In this case, no one would want to buy your "used" bond, which pays only $60 a year, unless you are willing to accept less than you paid for it. You might be able to sell your bond for $950. The buyer would receive $10 less in each of the next six years than he would from a new bond. However, he would receive $1,000 when the bond matures, giving him $50 more than he paid for the bond. If prevailing interest rates increase, the value of "used" bonds will fall. *Anyone who purchases bonds as an investment should understand that the value of the bond will change inversely with market interest rates until the bond matures.*

Different Bonds, Different Risks Although owning corporate bonds is less risky than purchasing stock in the same firms, there still is risk involved in bond ownership. As noted already, there is a risk that interest rates will increase, causing the value of bonds to fall. There also is a risk of non-payment or default by the issuing corporation. Every year some corporations fail. Bondholders in a failed corporation will probably not receive all they are owed. They might receive nothing if the firm is deep in debt.

If you buy a corporate bond issued by a large successful firm, there is little chance of losing your investment. If you buy bonds from a firm that is in financial trouble, the interest rate will be higher, but you may lose part or all of your investment. Bonds issued by businesses that are in financial trouble are often called *junk bonds.* Junk bonds pay higher rates of interest to compensate investors for the higher risk. In 2011, quality corporate bonds paid about 5 percent interest per year. At the same time, junk bonds paid about 8 to 12 percent per year. Obviously, people who cannot afford to lose the money they invest should avoid junk bonds.

Mutual Funds That Buy Corporate Bonds Many people would like to own corporate bonds but do not have the time or expertise to decide which bonds to buy. Or, they may not have enough money to diversify their investment. There are many mutual funds that purchase corporate bonds instead of stock. Bond funds work exactly the same way as stock mutual funds. Some buy only government bonds; others purchase bonds from only large, successful firms. Still others specialize in buying bonds issued in other nations. The funds that offer the highest returns usually buy junk bonds. Investors should study each fund before choosing the ones that best fit their financial goals.

CHECKPOINT **What similarities and differences do you see between investing in corporate stock and investing in corporate bonds?**

MONEY MANAGEMENT ASSISTANCE

LO2 Examine resources to help you manage your investments.

You may feel overwhelmed by the number and complexity of savings and investment choices you have to make. There is a temptation to simply place your savings in a bank account and forget about it. Although understandable, this choice is almost certain to reduce what you earn from your savings and, over time, to reduce the likelihood of achieving your financial life goals. In recent years, bank account interest has been historically low, close to zero.

Where to Find Investment Information

A good way to begin learning about investment opportunities is to regularly read financial publications such as *The Wall Street Journal.* This newspaper carries a wide variety of articles about businesses, the economy, and investments. Over a period of time, you should come to better understand what is happening in the economy and to identify investment options you might consider. There are many other financial publications available, including *Money, Kiplinger's Personal Finance Magazine, Fortune*, and *Forbes.* All of these are available free at larger public libraries. You also may investigate specific firms or funds online, where a vast amount of information is available.

Where to Find Investment Help

Many people choose to hire experts to help them make investment decisions. One possibility is to talk with a full-service stockbroker. Full-service stockbrokers are trained to explain investment opportunities and to recommend how to allocate funds. Stockbrokers earn income from the fees they charge when transactions are made. Because full-service brokers provide advice for "free," the fees they charge for transactions can be substantial. There also are discount brokers, who help complete transactions without offering much advice. Their fees are lower, but the individual must make investment decisions alone.

Another type of expert you could hire is a **financial planner**. This is a person who gives investment advice for a fee. A financial planner may be self-employed or may work for a bank or other financial institution. If you choose to employ a financial planner, you should be sure that this person spends enough time learning about your financial goals and situation. Financial planners cannot help you achieve your goals unless they know what you hope to achieve and understand what resources you have to achieve your goals.

Financial planners are in business to earn a living. They get paid in three primary ways. Some charge a flat fee to help you create a financial plan. This fee may vary according to the amount you plan to invest and the time they spend helping you create your plan. Alternatively, some planners charge a fixed percent of the amount that is to be invested. A third method is to charge an initial fee plus an amount for each transaction. You probably should avoid employing a planner who uses this third method. It gives the planner an incentive to make more trades, or to "churn" your account. Excessive trading adds to costs and may benefit the planner much more than the investor.

financial planner
Expert who gives investment advice for a fee

Many planners receive a commission from the mutual funds you buy. Some planners may be more interested in their commissions than in making the best investment choices for you. Ask friends or relatives to recommend a financial planner. If others have been satisfied with a planner's advice, you may be satisfied, too.

Present Value of Future Amounts

To weigh costs and benefits of investments accurately, consider when they occur. In general, an amount of money received today is worth more than the same amount received in the future. For example, if you received $100 today, you could save it in a bank and see it grow at the rate of interest. At 4 percent interest, your $100 becomes $104 by the end of a year. So $104 received one year from now would have a value today, a present value, of $100. Alternatively, the present cost of having to make a payment of $104 one year from now is $100. By depositing $100 in an account earning 4 percent interest, you would have $104 after a year, which you could use to make that $104 payment. Thus, the value one year from now is linked to a present value by the interest rate. The relation between future and present values can be expressed as follows:

$$\text{Future value} = (1 + \text{interest rate}) \times \text{Present value}$$

An interest rate of 4 percent is expressed as the decimal 0.04, so

$$\$104 = (1.04) \times \$100$$

CHECKPOINT Where can you turn for assistance with managing your investments?

ESSENTIAL QUESTION

Standard CEE 10: Institutions

Institutions evolve and are created to help individuals and groups accomplish their goals. Banks, labor unions, markets, corporations, legal systems, and not-for-profit organizations are examples of important institutions. A different kind of institution, clearly defined and enforced property rights, is essential to a market economy.

The largest U.S. financial institutions have their headquarters on Wall Street in New York City. What types of goals do financial institutions, such as banks and stock markets, help individuals and groups accomplish?

12.2 ASSESSMENT

Think Critically

1. What are the differences between the two types of corporate stock?
2. What causes the market price of a particular stock to change?
3. Why shouldn't a person invest in only one or two stocks?
4. What would cause the price of a "used" corporate bond to increase on the secondary bond market?
5. Why should people be careful when they choose a financial planner?

Graphing Exercise

6. There are many ways to judge how a stock market is doing. One of the most popular is to examine the Dow Jones Industrial Average (DJIA). This index averages the stock value of 30 large corporations that represent a cross section of the U.S. economy. Use data in the table to make a bar graph that shows the average annual value of the DJIA over ten years. What would have happened if you had invested your savings in stocks in 2003 or in 2007?

VALUE OF THE DOW JONES INDUSTRIAL AVERAGE (DJIA), 2000–2009

Year	Value of the DJIA	Year	Value of the DJIA
2000	10,734	2005	10,849
2001	10,198	2006	11,409
2002	9,226	2007	13,170
2003	8,994	2008	8,876
2004	10,317	2009	10,663

Source: *Economic Indicators*, June 2011, p. 31.

Make Academic Connections

7. **Entrepreneurship** Assume that you have saved $500,000. You want to use your savings and to raise another $1 million to start a business that manufactures and sells baseball bats. You could borrow funds from a bank, form a corporation, and sell stock to the public, or sell corporate bonds that your corporation would eventually be required to repay. Which of these alternatives would you choose? Explain how you would try to convince the bank or investors to provide you with the funds you need. How much risk would your business hold for investors?

TeamWork

Working in small teams, assume your team has inherited $1 million. You have decided to make five $200,000 investments that have different combinations of risk and return. Work together to identify specific investments you would make to achieve diversification along with a reasonable return for your portfolio. Compare your decisions with those made by other teams.

The Rise and Fall of Homeownership

On the eve of the 2008 financial collapse, more Americans owned their own homes (about 70 percent) than ever before. Fueled by easy mortgages, housing prices rose to unrealistic levels. Many people became unable to make their payments.

For most of our nation's history, mortgages required a 50 percent down payment. During the Great Depression, a goal of the New Deal was to create a consumer-friendly atmosphere. To accomplish this, the Federal Housing Administration (FHA) was created to insure mortgage lenders against losses from default, and to encourage them to offer more money for mortgages.

The plan worked: More people were able to afford homes, but increased demand meant there wasn't always enough money to lend. To make more money available, the Federal National Mortgage Association (FNMA)—Fannie Mae—was created in 1938. It bought FHA-insured mortgages, which it then kept or sold. This allowed lenders to get cash for additional mortgages. In 1970, the Federal Home Loan Mortgage Corporation (FHLMC)—Freddie Mac—was created to increase even more the amount of mortgage funds available.

Like previous administrations, President George W. Bush and Congress pushed to expand homeownership after 2000. Government deregulation allowed banks to expand into new financial activities. There was lax enforcement of regulations left in place. There were also low interest rates. In an attempt to stimulate the economy, the Federal Reserve lowered rates and kept them low throughout most of the decade.

Another factor adding demand for housing was the loosening of qualifications for home loans. With Congress pressuring them to help low-income borrowers and investors, Fannie and Freddie plunged into the subprime market, which means lending to those considered poorer credit risks. Looking back, one official observed, "If you were alive, they would give you a loan. Actually, I think if you were dead, they would still give you a loan." After the collapse these risky loans came to be known as "toxic loans."

The subprime mortgage market was profitable because banks and mortgage brokers earned fees based on the number of mortgages sold. This gave them an incentive to approve loans even for people who they knew would never pay them back. This didn't matter to the bankers and mortgage brokers because they simply issued mortgage-backed securities (MBSs) that they sold to investors.

Increasingly, MBSs were owned by individuals, companies, and government agencies, which spread the risk throughout the economy. When the housing bubble burst, investors began to understand that the MBSs would not be paid back, and the real estate backing for the loans would not be worth enough to cover them. Investors lost confidence in the securities and the market for them dried up. They became "toxic assets." Additional losses came in the form of mortgage derivatives, which were essentially bets that the mortgage investments would not suffer a loss. Large banks that had invested in MBSs, and derivatives were on the verge of bankruptcy. Some were allowed to fail. Some were purchased by other institutions. Many got government money to operate until the value of their assets could be determined.

The United States was plunged into its deepest recession since the Great Depression, and the ripple effects were felt around the world. The finger pointing as to "Who caused the Great Recession?" went in all directions.

Think Critically Investing involves risk. What role should the government have in insuring that investors are provided accurate, honest information about a potential investment?

Source: "The Reckoning," *The New York Times* (series), 2008; Sewell Chan, "Financial Crisis Was Avoidable, Inquiry Finds," *The New York Times*, January 25, 2011.

12.3 INSURANCE

Learning Objectives

LO1 Understand the kinds of insurance you can buy to protect yourself against risk.

LO2 Determine the types and amounts of insurance you will need.

Key Terms

In Your World

Most people try to avoid unpleasant surprises. For example, you wouldn't want to find that your property has been lost, stolen, or damaged. Being sued because a delivery person trips on a shovel left on your front steps also is something you would rather avoid. Perhaps most frightening is the prospect of becoming ill or injured, such that you are unable to work, causing you to face enormous medical bills. Unfortunately, there is no way to avoid all risk. Fortunately, there is something you can do to address most risks. You can insure against any losses from events you hope will never occur.

PROTECT YOURSELF WITH INSURANCE

LO1 Understand the kinds of insurance you can buy to protect yourself against risk.

Life is full of risks. Your investments may go sour, causing you to lose part of your savings. A storm might tear the roof off your house, or a tree might fall on your car. You might accidentally break your neighbor's window, or a delivery person might fall over toys left on your sidewalk. You might be injured in an accident or become ill and unable to work. Such events cannot be predicted. You can, however, buy **insurance** to protect yourself against a variety of losses.

People who purchase insurance sign a legal contract, or **policy**. The policy requires them to pay premiums in exchange for an insurance company's promise to pay claims for any insured loss up to a maximum amount. The insurance company receives premiums from all policyholders and uses these funds to pay benefits to the few who actually suffer losses. In this way policyholders share their risk. They all share the cost of large losses by paying the smaller cost of their premiums.

Premiums and Past Events

Insurance companies need two types of information to determine premiums. They need to know the probability of a loss being suffered by an insured policyholder, and they need to know the probable cost of that loss. Suppose the Safety Insurance Company (SIC) insures one million drivers. The company knows from experience that about one out of every 1,000 drivers will cause an accident each

insurance Protection you purchase against losses beyond your ability to withstand

policy Legal contract between an insured person and an insurance company

year by driving into the back of another car. It also knows that the cost of such an accident in the past has averaged $6,000. So, by charging each policyholder $6 a year, SIC can cover policyholders for this type of loss. The firm would collect $6 million from its insured drivers and pay the $6 million to the 1,000 drivers who caused rear-end collisions. Premiums would also add in all the other risks the policy covers, the costs of administration, plus a competitive level of profit. SIC cannot tell which particular policyholders will suffer a loss, but it can be reasonably sure how many will suffer losses and how much those losses will cost.

Insurance companies also receive income when they invest funds they have accumulated in previous years. This revenue makes up for years when insured losses and operating expenses exceed the amount received in premiums.

Consider Figure 12.4, which shows the insurance industry's income and expenses from 2000 through 2009. If insurance companies had not earned income from investments, what might they have been forced to do regarding the premiums they charge?

Types of Insurance

There are three types of insurance: property, liability, and personal. No insurance plan is complete without some of each.

Property insurance protects policyholders against losses to their property. When you buy automobile insurance, for example, your collision coverage will pay for any damage to your car that results from an accident. Your homeowner's policy will protect your home and personal property from theft or fire.

Almost every property insurance policy has a deductible and limits the loss that is covered. A **deductible** is an amount an insured person must pay before the insurance company pays anything. For example, many automobile collision policies have a $500 deductible. If your car suffers an insured loss of $2,500, you will pay the first $500 of repair cost and the insurance company will pay the remaining $2,000. The dollar limit for property insurance is stated in the policy or determined by the value of the insured property. For example, if the policy sets a windstorm damage limit of $4,500, this is the most that your insurance will pay.

property insurance Protects policyholders from losses to their property

deductible The amount an insured person must pay before the insurance company pays anything

FIGURE 12.4 Insurance Industry Income and Expenditures, 2000–2009, Values in Billions of Dollars

	2000	2001	2002	2003	2004	2005	2006	2007	2008	2009
Premiums	$304.3	$327.8	$372.7	$407.6	$425.7	$427.6	$447.8	$447.9	$439.9	$422.9
Investment Income	42.0	38.7	39.8	39.8	40.0	49.7	52.3	54.6	53.1	48.3
Losses and Expenses	321.3	361.8	377.4	390.9	407.7	421.4	401.0	417.6	457.6	424.4
Pretax Earnings	$ 25.0	$ 4.7	$ 35.1	$ 56.5	$ 58.0	$ 55.9	$ 99.1	$ 84.9	$ 35.4	$ 46.8

Source: *The III Insurance Fact Book Annual* and the *Financial Services Fact Book Annual* at http://www.iii.org/financial2/. Figures are for property and casualty insurance.

Liability insurance covers losses from injuries you cause to another person or damage you cause to someone else's property. Suppose, while backing out of your driveway, you are distracted while on your cell phone and fail to see a neighbor driving past. You back into him, damage his car, and break his leg. The liability protection of your automobile insurance policy would pay for his medical care, lost wages, and the cost of repairing his car.

Evgeny Murtola/Shutterstock.com

What type of automobile insurance coverage protects your car from damage that results from an accident?

Liability insurance included in your homeowner's policy protects you from losses suffered by others when they are on your property. For example, if a delivery person was injured when she tripped over toys left on your sidewalk, the cost of her medical care would be paid by your homeowner's policy. The limit on the amount paid by a liability policy is determined by the amount of coverage purchased, or the cost of the loss that is suffered, whichever is less. If your liability coverage is limited to $50,000 and the loss you cause costs $60,000, you will be responsible for $10,000 of the loss.

Personal insurance protects you and your family from financial loss if a family member is injured, becomes ill, or dies unexpectedly. *Medical insurance*, for example, helps pay the cost of your medical care if you are injured or become ill. Typically, medical insurance policies have a deductible that must be paid by the insured person before the insurance company pays any part of the cost of treatment. Your policy might require you to pay the first $500 of medical expenses in any year. After that amount is paid, the insurance company will pay all or a share of the remaining cost. The typical share paid by an insurance company is 80 percent. There usually is a limit to the total amount an insurance company will pay over an insured person's lifetime. This amount often is $1 million or $2 million. A wide variety of medical insurance policies pay different amounts under different circumstances. However, they are all designed to protect insured people from medical costs that are greater than they would be able to pay on their own.

Life insurance is another type of personal insurance. It protects an insured person's family from financial loss if an insured person dies. Life insurance is particularly important for couples with young children. If one parent dies, the other may need to pay the cost of child care at the same time household income falls because of the death. Even people who do not work outside their home should be insured. If a stay-at-home parent dies, the spouse would have to perform extra tasks or hire others to do them. This can be expensive.

liability insurance
Protects against losses from injuries you cause to another person or damage you cause to another's property

personal insurance
Protects against financial loss from injury, illness, or unexpected death of the insured person

CHECKPOINT

What types of property, liability, and personal insurance are available for your household?

YOUR INSURANCE NEEDS

LO2 Determine the types and amounts of insurance you will need.

No combination of insurance protection is right for everyone. Different people have different needs and financial circumstances. This means they also have different insurance needs. When you evaluate your insurance needs, you should keep these ideas in mind.

- It is impossible to eliminate all risk from your life.
- You should try to limit your risks to those you would be able to deal with on your own.
- You should consider buying insurance to cover risks you could not deal with on your own.

Before you decide what insurance protection to purchase, you should first make a list of the losses you might reasonably expect to suffer given your personal situation. If you own a car, for example, you are required by state law to purchase basic liability insurance. You also may decide to buy collision insurance. You may purchase comprehensive insurance as well to protect your car from damage that is not the result of a traffic accident. For example, if your car is destroyed by a fire, comprehensive insurance will help pay for a replacement. People who own a home need to buy homeowner's insurance to protect their property. Homeowner policies usually include liability insurance. If someone is injured on your property, your homeowner's policy will cover the loss. Renter's insurance is important for people who lease an apartment. It pays for losses renters suffer when their possessions are lost, damaged, or stolen. It also provides basic liability protection.

Rank Your Insurance Needs

Once you have a clear idea of the types of losses you need to insure against, you should rank them according to their importance and probability of happening. *You should always purchase liability protection.* In general, automobile and homeowner's policies provide sufficient liability coverage for most people. An additional *umbrella policy* may be purchased for a few hundred dollars per year that will increase liability protection to $1 million or $2 million in losses.

Everyone should have at least some medical insurance. Today most employers who provide medical insurance expect employees to pay part of the cost of coverage. However, even if your employer covers a portion of medical insurance costs, that policy likely will

Everyone who owns or drives a car needs auto insurance, but not everyone knows what they should about the coverage an auto policy includes. Access the website shown below and click on the link for Chapter 12. Read the Insurance Information Institute's web page entitled "What is covered by a basic auto policy?" Study the descriptions of each of the six coverages included in an auto policy. Be prepared to explain each in class.

www.cengage.com/school/contecon

cost you much less than coverage you could purchase on your own.

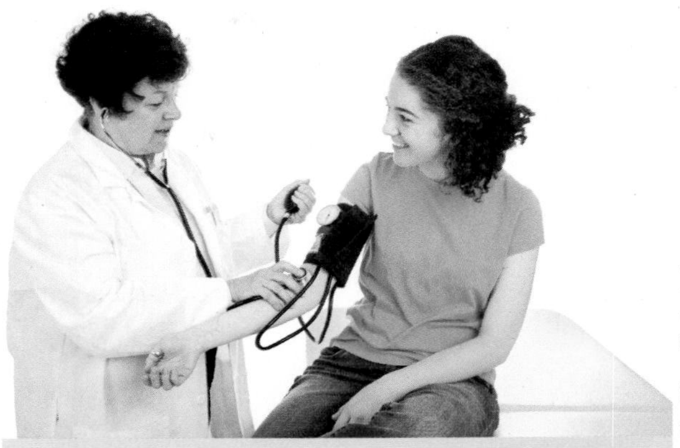
Lisa F. Young/Shutterstock.com

Do you think medical insurance is important for someone your age? Why or why not?

People who are not insured through an employer usually pay dearly for medical insurance. In 2011, a traditional family medical policy cost more than $10,000 per year, depending on location and the amount of coverage. Coverage for a single person cost more than $6,000. Less protection costs less. Some policies have a deductible of as much as $2,500 or more. After that deductible is paid, insurance picks up a share, possibly 80 percent, until the total cost hits some large amount, say $10,000. Then the insurance pays all of the additional medical costs that year. This plan is less costly for those who remain healthy, and more costly for anyone who becomes seriously ill or seriously injured. Still, such a policy protects people from enormous medical costs they couldn't possibly pay on their own. This is only one of hundreds of variations of medical coverage that you can investigate before buying a policy. Recent federal legislation will affect the availability of health insurance during the next decade.

Many people ignore their need for life insurance. No one likes to think about it, but death is unavoidable. *People should protect their families from the financial loss resulting from an unexpected death.*

Life insurance is sold in two basic forms, term and whole. Term life insurance provides a death benefit only if an insured person dies within a specific period of time. These policies, particularly for young people, are relatively inexpensive. In 2011, a 25-year-old non-smoking male could purchase $50,000 in term insurance for 10 years for less than $230 a year. *Whole life insurance policies* are much more expensive because they not only pay when an insured person dies, but also provide a way of saving for the future. When a whole-life policyholder reaches a specific age, the policy will have a value that can be cashed and spent if the policy is surrendered before his or her death occurs. Even without surrendering the policy, you can borrow against its value.

The Decision to Purchase Insurance

A decision to purchase insurance is always a trade off. Buying insurance usually will not increase your ability to consume either now or in the future. When you buy insurance, you trade some of your current income for the security it offers against the possibility of unforeseen loss that may, or may not, occur in the future. No one should spend so much on insurance that he or she is unable to maintain a reasonable standard of living. Only you are qualified to determine the amount and types of insurance that are right for you. Just be sure you gather and evaluate enough information to make your decision a rational one.

CHECKPOINT

What types and amounts of insurance do you think you will need in the future?

12.3 ASSESSMENT

Think Critically

1. Explain how insurance policyholders share their risk.
2. What is the difference between property insurance and liability insurance?
3. What are the two primary types of personal insurance?
4. Why do parents with young children need to purchase at least some life insurance?
5. In what way is buying insurance protection a trade off?

Graphing Exercises

6. Although most financial experts agree that buying life insurance is a wise choice, most Americans do without this type of protection. As a matter of fact, the number of policies in force has fallen in recent years. Use data in the table to draw a line graph that shows the number of new life insurance policies purchased by Americans each year from 2002 through 2009. What does your graph show about new life insurance policies?

NUMBER OF NEW LIFE INSURANCE POLICIES PURCHASED, 2002–2009, VALUES IN THOUSANDS

Year	Number Purchased	Year	Number Purchased
2002	14,692	2006	10,908
2003	13,821	2007	10,826
2004	12,581	2008	10,207
2005	11,407	2009	10,139

Source: *Statistical Abstract of the United States, 2006*, p. 1210, and 2012, p. 754.

Make Academic Connections

7. **Demographics** Drivers are most likely to be involved in automobile accidents when they are relatively young or old. Although drivers are involved in more accidents as they grow old, these accidents usually result in fewer injuries and less property damage than accidents involving young drivers. What reasons can you think of that could explain these facts? As the population of the United States becomes older, what is likely to happen to the number of automobile accidents? What might this do to automobile insurance premiums over time?

TeamWork

Working in small teams, list the types and amounts of insurance protection Joe and Rita should purchase for their family of four, given the following facts:

Rita's yearly income is $42,000. They are buying a home that is worth $180,000. Their car is five years old. Joe's construction job paid him $31,000 last year. The children are in high school. Their employers do not provide health insurance.

MOVERS AND SHAKERS

Genevieve Thiers

Founder, Sittercity®

As the oldest of seven kids, Genevieve Thiers grew up babysitting. Changing her siblings diapers didn't pay much. However, she found a way to turn diapers to dollars. She babysat her way through college and viewed it as a business opportunity rather than a dead-end job.

One day on her college campus, Thiers saw a pregnant mom struggling with stairs and posting flyers about her babysitting needs. Thiers sent the woman home and posted the rest of the flyers herself. Borrowing $80 from her father, she bought a domain name and printed 20,000 flyers and posted them on college campuses around Boston.

Sittercity launched in 2001. It is an online registry for people offering sitting services for the elderly, pets and children, and those seeking the services. She said, "Many women don't realize that the troublesome issues facing them every day are opportunities for big business," she said. "Every time there is an inconvenience for someone, there is an opportunity for someone else. Anything can be your golden ticket—you just have to see it."

Thiers says the most challenging part of being an entrepreneur is "Learning to let go. In the beginning, you want to control everything, and it's small. Learning to hire and trust my amazing team was hard, but now I am in heaven! It's an amazing group of people, all with their own talents."

Sittercity is a privately owned corporation and a certified Women's Business Enterprise (WBE). It currently employs 12 people full-time and lists more than 150,000 babysitters nationwide. Thier's success has landed her a spot on Crain's "40 under 40" list and she was recognized by President George W. Bush as the Small Business Association's Young Entrepreneur of the Year in 2006. Thiers has a master's degree in public relations and also aspires to be a professional opera singer.

When asked how she uses her public relations skills to grow her business, Thiers offered these three "must have" skills:

- **Creativity** "You need unique pitch angles and interesting story ideas, otherwise no one will want to write about you or feature you on-air. You must give them something that has substance, something carefully thought through."

Courtesy of Sittercity

- **Careful strategies** "You must be able to network and foster relationships with producers, editors, and other PR professionals. It's important to think about everything from that person's perspective. . . . It's not just all about you and what kind of coverage you can get. You also have to follow up with these people, be flexible and accommodating (sometimes they'll want an interview at the last minute!), and remain committed to keeping in touch."
- **Brand awareness** "You have to be well aware of what image you want to portray. Sittercity, for example, is a trust-based business. It is absolutely essential that we let people see how trustworthy and safe we are. At the same time, we work in caregiving, so having fun is also a part of our brand. It's important that we showcase the skills and talents of our sitters when talking about our service, but give the impression at the same time that we could get down on the floor and play with your kids or pet."

Think Critically **In building Sittercity, Thiers recognized that families want to hire babysitters they can trust. The statement on the website that "Safety Is Our Number One Priority" addresses this desire. Go to the website, and find the ways Sittercity assures parents that the sitters they hire through Sittercity are trustworthy. Would you be assured of hiring a trustworthy sitter through Sittercity? Why or why not?**

Sources: http://ypwr.blogs.cnn.com/2008/03/01/genevieve-thiers/; http://www.bc.edu/alumni/news/BCM/previous_bcm/thiers.html; and http://www.northwestern.edu/magazine/spring2007/feature/thiers.html

Chapter 12 Summary

ASK THE EXPERT

www.cengage.com/school/contecon

How are banks different from other businesses?

12.1 Saving

A. Saving is the act of not spending current income. The most important reason to save is to achieve financial security. People who save need to choose a way to store their savings. Most people keep their savings in one or more types of bank accounts.

B. Banks offer a variety of accounts. Funds may be deposited or withdrawn at any time from savings accounts that pay a fixed rate of interest. Withdrawals are limited to a few each month from money market accounts. The interest rate paid on such accounts changes over time with market conditions. Time deposits, or certificates of deposit, pay higher rates because the depositor agrees to leave funds on deposit for an extended period of time. Checking accounts give depositors the ability to write checks or use a debit card to make payments, but checking accounts pay little or no interest. Checking accounts usually involve two types of fees: a monthly maintenance fee and a service fee for each check written. Banks provide depositors with monthly statements that report all transactions.

12.2 Investing

A. Investing is using savings to earn a return. People invest their savings in a variety of ways. These include depositing them in a bank account that earns interest, buying shares of corporate stock, or buying corporate bonds. People who invest in corporate stock may earn a return from dividends and from capital gains. They have one vote per share when important decisions are made for the corporation. Owners of preferred stock receive a fixed dividend and have no vote in corporate matters. A corporate bond is a written promise to repay an amount borrowed when the bond matures and to pay annual interest at a specific rate until then.

B. There are many sources of information about investments. These include *The Wall Street Journal* and other financial publications, online sources, or information provided by businesses and stockbrokers. Financial planners help many people make investment choices for a fee. You should always investigate the qualifications of a financial planner before hiring one.

12.3 Insurance

A. Many people buy insurance protection that will directly benefit those who suffer insured losses. An insurance policy is a legal contract that requires people to pay premiums in exchange for the company's promise to pay claims for losses up to a maximum amount. Policyholders share their risk and the costs of losses that occur. Insurers set premiums by projecting the probability of a loss and the expected cost of that loss. If the insurer's projections are accurate, premiums will cover costs and generate a competitive profit.

B. There are three basic types of insurance. Property insurance protects people from property damage. Liability insurance protects them from damage or injuries they cause to others. Personal insurance pays for medical care or an untimely death. Buying insurance involves a trade off between current consumption and future security. The amount and types of insurance that people should purchase varies, depending on their personal and financial situations.

CHAPTER 12 ASSESSMENT

Review Economic Terms

Match the terms with the definitions. Some terms will not be used.

_____ 1. Using savings in a way that earns income to create a return

_____ 2. A financial organization that accepts funds from many people and invests them in a variety of stocks

_____ 3. A formula banks must use to calculate interest they pay on deposits

_____ 4. Interest paid on an amount deposited and on interest that has previously been earned

_____ 5. Income earned from funds that are invested

_____ 6. Investing in a wide variety of firms

_____ 7. Protection against losses you cause by injuring other people or damaging another person's property

_____ 8. Protection against financial loss if an insured person is injured, becomes ill, or dies unexpectedly

_____ 9. The amount an insured person must pay before an insurance company pays any part of a loss

_____ 10. The legal contract between an insured person and an insurance company

a. annual percentage yield (APY)
b. certificate of deposit (CD)
c. compound interest
d. corporate bond
e. corporate stock
f. deductible
g. diversification
h. financial planner
i. insurance
j. investing
k. liability insurance
l. money market account
m. mutual fund
n. personal insurance
o. policy
p. property insurance
q. return
r. saving

Review Economic Concepts

11. **True or False** When you save, you trade the satisfaction of buying something now for the satisfaction you may receive from buying something in the future.

12. It generally is easier to follow a savings plan when
    a. you have set clear goals for your financial future.
    b. your monthly income is less than your monthly expenses.
    c. your bank decreases the interest rate it pays on customer's deposits.
    d. your income has recently changed.

13. Income earned from funds that are not spent is called a(n) ________?________.

14. Which of the following accounts pays interest that changes daily if necessary to reflect changes in the prevailing interest rate in the economy?
    a. savings accounts
    b. money market accounts
    c. checking accounts
    d. certificates of deposit

15. **True or False** In general, the greater the risk you take when you make an investment, the smaller the amount you expect to earn from it.

16. Which of the following refers to the amount banks charge each month to keep a checking account open?
    a. service fee
    b. carrying fee
    c. support fee
    d. maintenance fee

17. You should always ________?________ your accounts by comparing the records you have of the transactions with those printed on the monthly statement you receive from the bank.

18. **True or False** A corporate bond represents partial ownership of a corporation.

19. Investing in a wide variety of firms to reduce the overall risk of owning stock is called ________?________.

20. Which of the following refers to shares of stock in large, successful, established corporations?
    a. growth stock
    b. blue chip stock
    c. venture stock
    d. guaranteed stock

21. Which of the following people should invest in stocks through a mutual fund?
    a. Jose, who enjoys following the stock market and choosing stocks he likes
    b. Keisha, who is a professional full-service stockbroker
    c. Harold, who has a little money to invest
    d. Debbie, who has no money to invest

22. **True or False** A no-load mutual fund is less costly to invest in than a load fund.

23. **True or False** All financial planners must pass a qualifying exam and be licensed by the federal government.

24. **True or False** To set premiums, insurance companies must project the probability of a loss being suffered as well as the probable cost of that loss, should it occur.

25. What type of insurance protects you from losses when you injure other people or damage other people's property?
    a. property insurance
    b. liability insurance
    c. personal insurance
    d. universal insurance

26. What type of insurance protects things you own from loss?
    a. property insurance
    b. liability insurance
    c. personal insurance
    d. universal insurance

27. **True or False** An umbrella policy protects homeowners from floods.

28. A(n) ________?________ insurance policy provides protection for damage to your home and protection if you cause injury to others.

29. What type of insurance is life insurance?
    a. property insurance
    b. liability insurance
    c. personal insurance
    d. universal insurance

30. **True or False** All people need to buy insurance, even if the premiums drastically cut their current standard of living.

31. What does term life insurance provide?
    a. a death benefit as well as a method to save and invest money
    b. only a way to save and invest money
    c. only a death benefit
    d. an amount that can be cashed in when a person reaches a certain age

Apply Economic Concepts

32. **Choose a Medical Insurance Policy** Suppose you are married and have two children. You are a computer consultant and earn a good income. Your spouse stays home to care for the children. Because you are self-employed, you must purchase your own medical insurance. You have narrowed your choice to the two policies described below. Evaluate each policy and choose the one that you believe would be best for your family. Explain your choice.

    Policy A

    This traditional policy allows you to choose your doctor, hospital, or other medical provider. It has a $200 annual deductible. It does not pay for regular physicals. It does pay for prescription medicines, but you must pay the first $10 of each prescription. The maximum it will pay for any insured person is $2 million over that person's life span. This policy would cost $20,000 per year.

    Policy B

    This health maintenance organization (HMO) requires you to choose doctors, hospitals, and other medical providers that belong to its system. When you receive treatment you must pay the first $100 for each insured person. After that, the insurance will pay 80 percent of the cost. This policy covers the cost of regular physicals and pays for prescription drugs after you pay the first $20 for each prescription. The maximum it will pay for any insured person is $1 million over that person's life span. This policy would cost $11,500 per year.

33. **21st Century Skills: Creativity and Innovation** You rent a large apartment for $800 each month. Other expenses add $350 to your housing costs. You feel you need to reduce these costs by at least $150 each month so you can save to buy a car. Create an innovative plan that will allow you to reach your saving goal.

Digging Deeper
with Economics e-Collection

Access the Gale Economics e-Collection through the URL below to find an article or articles that offer advice on saving, investing, or purchasing insurance. After reading the articles, make a list of three to five tips you learned that you can apply in your life. Present the tips in a chart or PowerPoint presentation. Be prepared to share your list in class.

www.cengage.com/school/contecon

NOT IN SERVICE
NO PASSENGERS

UNIT 5

The National Economy

Since 1776, when Adam Smith inquired into the *Wealth of Nations*, economists have been trying to figure out why some economies prosper while others do not. Because a market economy is not the product of conscious design, it does not reveal its secrets readily. There is no clear blueprint of the economy, so policymakers cannot simply push here and pull there to create prosperity for everyone. Still, economists are learning more every day about how the U.S. economy works. You, too, can discover the challenges and opportunities facing the largest and most complex economy in world history.

CONSIDER...

- How is the economy's performance measured?
- What's gross about the gross domestic product?
- What's the impact on gross domestic product if you make yourself a sandwich for lunch?
- How can you compare the value of national production in one year with that in other years if prices change over time?
- What's the business cycle?
- What's the big idea with the national economy?

CHAPTER 13

Economic Performance

Point your browser

www.cengage.com/school/contecon

Brand New Images/Getty Images; Background image: Lukiyanova Natalia/frenta/Shutterstock.com

13.1 ESTIMATING GDP

Learning Objectives

LO1 Describe what GDP measures.

LO2 Learn two ways to calculate GDP, and explain why they are equivalent.

Key Terms

In Your World

As you probably noticed, the economy has its ups and downs. These swings in economic activity, however, were once worse. The Great Depression of the 1930s convinced economists and the government to get a better handle on what was happening with the economy. Economists began assembling huge quantities of data from a variety of sources. The federal government organizes and reports the data periodically. The resulting system for measuring the nation's economy has been hailed as one of the great achievements of the twentieth century.

THE U.S. ECONOMY

LO1 Describe what GDP measures.

Macroeconomics focuses on the overall performance of the *economy.* The term **economy** describes the structure of economic activity in a locality, a region, a country, a group of countries, or the world. You could talk about the Chicago economy, the Illinois economy, the Midwest economy, the U.S. economy, the North American economy, or the world economy.

Gross Domestic Product (GDP)

An economy's size can be measured in different ways. The value of production, the number of people employed, or their total income can be measured. The most commonly used measure is the *gross product.* This is the market value of production in a geographical region during a given period, usually one year.

The **gross domestic product**, or **GDP**, measures the market value of all final goods and services produced in a country during a given period, usually a year. So GDP measures the U.S. economy. GDP includes production carried out by foreign firms in the United States, such as production at a Japanese auto manufacturing plant in Kentucky. It excludes foreign production by U.S. firms, such as a General Motors plant in Mexico.

GDP measures the economy's total production of final goods and services, from trail bikes to pedicures. GDP can be used to track the same economy over time. It also may be used to compare different economies at the same time.

National Income Accounts

National income accounts organize huge quantities of data collected from a variety of sources across America. The federal government summarizes and reports these data periodically. The U.S. national income accounts are the most widely copied and most highly regarded in the world.

economy The structure of economic activity in a locality, a region, a country, a group of countries, or the world

gross domestic product (GDP) The market value of all final goods and services produced in the nation during a given period, usually a year

National income accounts keep track of the value of *final goods and services.* These are goods and services sold to the final, or end, users. A toothbrush, a pair of contact lenses, and a bus ride are examples of final goods and services. Gross domestic product includes the value of only final goods and services. Your purchase of chicken from a grocer is reflected in GDP. When KFC purchases chicken, however, this transaction is not recorded in GDP because KFC is not the final consumer. Only after KFC fries that chicken and sells it is the sale recorded as part of GDP.

No Double Counting

Intermediate goods and services are those purchased for additional processing and resale, such as the chicken purchased by KFC. This additional processing may be minor, as when a grocer buys canned goods to stock the shelves. Or, the intermediate goods may be altered dramatically. For instance, oil paint costing $30 and a canvas costing $50 may be transformed into a work of fine art that sells for $10,000.

Sales of intermediate goods and services are excluded from GDP to avoid the problem of *double counting.* This is counting an item's value more than once. For example, suppose the grocer buys a can of tuna for $0.80 and sells it for $1.00. If GDP counted both the intermediate transaction of $0.80 and the final transaction of $1.00, that can of tuna would be counted twice in GDP. Its recorded value of $1.80 would exceed its final value of $1.00 by $0.80. Therefore, GDP counts only the final value of the product.

GDP also ignores most of the secondhand value of used goods, such as existing homes and used cars. These goods were counted in GDP when they were produced. However, the services provided by realtors and used-car dealers are counted in GDP. For example, suppose a new-car dealer gives you a $1,500 trade-in allowance for your used car. The dealer cleans and repairs the car, and then resells it for $2,500. Only the $1,000 increase in the car's value is included in GDP.

CHECKPOINT **What does the gross domestic product measure?**

CALCULATING GDP

LO2
Learn two ways to calculate GDP, and explain why they are equivalent.

The national income accounts are based on the idea that *one person's spending is another person's income.* This is expressed in a double-entry bookkeeping system of accounting. Spending on final goods and services is recorded on one side of the accounting ledger and income created by that spending is recorded on the other side. GDP can be measured either by total spending on U.S. production or by total income earned from that production.

GDP Based on the Expenditure Approach

The *expenditure approach to GDP* adds up the spending on all final goods and services produced in the economy during the year. The easiest way to understand the spending approach is to divide spending into its four components: consumption, investment, government purchases, and net exports.

consumption Household purchases of final goods and services

Consumption consists of purchases of final goods and services by households during the year. Goods include *nondurable goods*, such as soap and soup, and *durable goods*, such as HDTVs and furniture. Durable goods are expected to last at least three years. Examples of *services* include dry cleaning, haircuts, and air travel. Figure 13.1 shows the composition of U.S. spending since 1960. During the past decade, consumption averaged 70 percent of all spending in the U.S. economy.

Investment consists of spending on new capital goods and on additions to inventories. More generally, investment consists of spending on current production that is not used for current consumption. The most important category of investment is new *physical capital*, such as new buildings and new machinery purchased by firms and used to produce goods and services. Spending by households on new residential construction also counts as investment.

Changes in firms' inventories are another category of investment. Inventories include stocks of goods in process, such as computer parts. They also include stocks of finished goods, such as new computers awaiting sale. Investment changes more from year to year than any other spending component. During the past decade, investment averaged 15 percent of U.S. GDP.

In the national income accounts, investment does not include purchases of existing buildings and machines. Nor does it include purchases of financial assets, such as stocks and bonds. Existing buildings and machines were counted as part of GDP in the year they were produced. Purchases of stocks and bonds sometimes provide firms with the funds to invest. However, stocks and bonds are not investments according to the national income accounts. They are simply indications of ownership.

investment The purchase of new plants, new equipment, new buildings, new residences, and net additions to inventories

FIGURE 13.1 U.S. Spending Components as Percentages of GDP Since 1960

Consumption's share of total U.S. spending increased from 1960 to 2010. During the most recent decade, consumption averaged 70 percent of GDP.

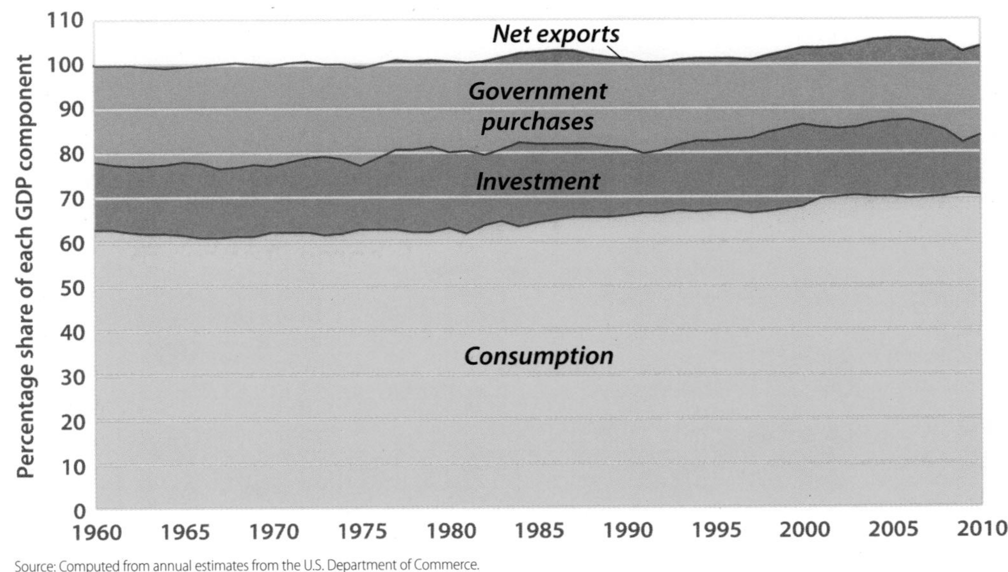

Source: Computed from annual estimates from the U.S. Department of Commerce.

Stockbyte/Getty Images

Photodisc/Getty Images

Which of these consumers are shopping for durable goods?

Government purchases include spending by all levels of government for goods and services—from clearing snowy roads to clearing court dockets, from library books to the librarian's pay. Government purchases at all levels averaged 19 percent of U.S. GDP during the past decade. Government purchases, and therefore GDP, exclude transfer payments such as those for Social Security, welfare, and unemployment compensation. These transfer payments are outright grants from the government to the recipients and are not true purchases by the government or true earnings by the recipients.

The final component of the expenditure approach to GDP is **net exports**. This results from the interaction between U.S. residents and the rest of the world. Some spending for consumption, investment, and government purchases is allocated for imports. However, spending on imports does not count as part of U.S. GDP. On the other hand, purchases of U.S. products by foreigners do count as part of U.S. GDP. To determine the net effect of the rest of the world on GDP, the value of imports must be subtracted from the value of exports. *Net exports* equal the value of U.S. exports of goods and services minus the value of U.S. imports of goods and services.

The expenditure approach considers the nation's *aggregate expenditure.* Any time an economist uses the term *aggregate*, you can substitute the word *total* to determine the meaning. **Aggregate expenditure** equals the sum of consumption, C, investment, I, government purchases, G, and net exports, which is the value of exports, X, minus the value of imports, M, or $(X - M)$. Summing these spending components yields aggregate expenditure, or GDP:

$$C + I + G + (X - M) = GDP$$

The value of U.S. imports has exceeded the value of U.S. exports every year since 1976. This means U.S. net exports $(X - M)$ have been negative. Negative net exports means that the sum of consumption, investment, and government purchases exceeds GDP. You can see negative net exports in red in Figure 13.1. It is that portion of consumption, investment, and government purchases that exceeds 100 percent of GDP.

During the past decade, negative net exports have averaged 4 percent of U.S. GDP. This means that the sum of consumption, investment, and government purchases has exceeded U.S. GDP by an average of 4 percent.

government purchases Spending on goods and services by all levels of government

net exports The value of a country's exports minus the value of its imports

aggregate expenditure Total spending on all final goods and services produced in the economy during the year

aggregate income The sum of all the income earned by resource suppliers in the economy during the year

GDP Based on the Income Approach

The expenditure approach sums, or aggregates, spending on production. The *income approach* sums, or aggregates, income arising from that production. The income approach to GDP adds up the aggregate income earned during the year by those who produce that output. Again, double-entry bookkeeping ensures that aggregate output equals the aggregate income paid for resources used to produce that output. **Aggregate income** equals the sum of all the income earned by resource suppliers in the economy. Thus,

$$\text{Aggregate expenditure} = GDP = \text{Aggregate income}$$

A finished product usually is processed by several firms on its way to the consumer. A wooden desk, for example, starts as raw timber, which usually is cut by a logging company. It is milled by a lumber company, made into a desk by a furniture maker, and sold to you by a retailer. GDP estimates avoid double counting either by focusing only on the market value of the desk when it is sold to the final user or *by calculating the value added at each stage of production.*

The *value added* by each firm equals that firm's revenue minus the amount paid for intermediate goods. Intermediate goods are inputs purchased from other firms. The value added at each stage represents income to individual resource suppliers at that stage. *The sum of the value added at all stages equals the market value of a final good. The sum of the value added for all final goods and services equals GDP based on the income approach.*

For example, suppose you buy a wooden desk for $200, which is the final market value counted in GDP. Consider the production of that desk. Suppose the tree that gave its life for your studies was cut into a log that was sold to a lumber mill for $20. That log was milled into lumber and sold for $50 to a manufacturer, who made your desk and sold it for $120 to a retail store. The retailer then sold it to you for $200. If all these transactions were added up, the total of $390 would exceed the $200 market value of the desk.

To avoid double counting, you include only the value added at each stage of production. In this example, the logger adds $20, the miller $30, the manufacturer $70, and the retailer $80. The total value added is $200, which also is the selling price of the desk. This is illustrated in Figure 13.2.

Figure 13.2 Value Added for a New Desk

The value added at each stage of production is the sale value minus the cost of intermediate goods, or column (2) minus column (3). The sum of the values added at all stages equals the market value of the final good, shown at the bottom of column (4).

(1) Stage of Production	(2) Sale Value	(3) Cost of Intermediate Goods	(4) Value Added
Logger	$20	———	$20
Miller	50	$20	30
Manufacturer	120	50	70
Retailer	200	120	80
	Market value of final good		$ 200

CHECKPOINT What are two ways of calculating gross domestic product, and why are they equivalent?

13.1 ASSESSMENT

Think Critically

1. Why should people care about the amount of production that takes place within the economy?
2. Why wouldn't your efforts add $100 to GDP if you made a table that you sold for $100?
3. Why are the values of spending and income always equal?
4. In what way are investment by businesses and some spending by the government similar?
5. Explain what your teacher meant if he or she said, "The aggregate income of all students in this class was $52,315.28 last year."

Graphing Exercise

6. Use the data in the table to construct two grouped bar graphs showing the percentage of spending for $C + I + G + (X - M)$ for U.S. GDP in 1970 and 2010. The vertical axis should show the percent of GDP spending. Each of the spending types should be represented by bars placed along the horizontal axis. Make a separate bar for each type of spending. Show the negative net exports in 2010 by extending that bar below the horizontal axis of the graph. What conclusions about changes in the economy can you draw from your graphs?

Spending	1970	% of GDP	2010	% of GDP
Consumption	$ 648	62.6%	$ 10,246	70.5%
Investment	$ 150	14.5%	$ 1,795	12.4%
Government	$ 236	22.8%	$ 3,003	20.7%
Net Exports	$ 1	0.1%	$ −517	−3.6%
Total GDP	$1,035	100.0%	$ 14,527	100.0%

Source: *Economic Indicators,* July 1990, July 2011, p. 1

Make Academic Connections

7. **Mathematics** Calculate the price consumers would pay at the pump for a gallon of gasoline given the following costs. How does this example demonstrate the need for calculating value added when measuring GDP?
   - Crude oil is extracted from the ground at a cost of $90 per 40-gallon barrel.
   - Crude oil is transported to a refinery at a cost of 18 cents per gallon.
   - It takes 1.25 gallons of crude oil to produce 1 gallon of gasoline.
   - Crude oil is refined into gasoline at a cost of 20 cents per gallon of gasoline.
   - Gasoline is transported to gas stations at a cost of 18 cents per gallon.
   - Gas station owners add 20 cents to the cost of each gallon sold.

Working in a team, make a list of the activities and materials used by a bakery to produce and market a loaf of bread to consumers. Estimate the value added to production by the bakery. What is the final cost of the bread? How much of this value was produced by other businesses that supplied intermediate products to the bakery? Compare your team's work with that of other teams.

MOVERS AND SHAKERS

Richard Simmons

Health and Fitness Entrepreneur

PRNewsFoto/OCEAN SPRAY/AP Photo

Recognizing America's growing problem with obesity, zany fitness guru Richard Simmons made a business doing what he knows and doing it well, and with heart. He also found his niche market: obese and morbidly obese Americans who are often overlooked by mainstream diet and fitness programs.

Simmons grew up in the French Quarter of New Orleans, the son of two talented chefs. By the time he graduated from high school, Simmons weighed 268 pounds. He went to Italy to study art, and also worked as an actor there. Even though he was overweight, the 5′7″ Simmons landed roles as a *grotesque*—a fat character in Fellini's *Satyricon* and *The Clowns*. He also appeared in 137 commercials, including TV spots for chubby jeans, Dannon® yogurt, and Fruit of the Loom®. One day someone left a note on his car that read, "Dear Richard, you are very funny, but fat people die young, please do not die…"

Stunned by the note Simmons decided to do something about his weight. At first he went about it in dangerous ways. He said, "I ended up looking like a thin Glad bag. My hair fell out, my skin drooped, my breath was foul, and my mood matched." At age 19, after a stay in the hospital because he weighed 119 pounds and couldn't walk, he decided to take charge of his eating. He said, "I sort of felt my way to a healthy balanced diet, and then refined that later with the help of nutritionists."

Simmons realized that Americans were getting fat and he recognized the reasons, including:

- a lack of self-esteem,
- confusion and conflicting information about healthy foods, and
- exercise was not a part of their mindset.

In 1974, Simmons was determined to do something about America's increasing girth. He consulted with doctors and fitness experts and developed safe, effective exercises that anyone could do. Then he opened "Slimmons" in Beverly Hills. It was his first fitness center, still in operation today, and he still teaches there occasionally. Simmons has integrated the two most important components of a weight-loss plan: movement and controlling food intake. He invented Deal-A-Meal and the FoodMover programs to keep track of portions and calories and to manage food intake. To encourage movement, he created and marketed 50 video workouts including "Sweatin' to the Oldies."

Simmons has helped people from around the world lose an estimated 3 million pounds. His net worth is rumored to exceed $15 million, and he is a popular guest on TV shows. But being rich and famous hasn't changed how he feels about the people who come to him for hope and help. He receives and answers hundreds of emails a day. He also phones 50 to 100 people each day to cheer and encourage them in their weight loss efforts.

Simmons has been working to get a bill passed that would make physical fitness mandatory in schools across America. He also develops special programs for people with physical challenges saying, "I am a physically challenged person myself. I was born with a few missing bones in my feet, a deformed femur bone, and severe asthma. So I developed a program called Sit Tight that allows physically challenged people to work out while sitting in a chair."

Passing on the message of diet and exercise is rewarding for Simmons. He said, "My passion is making exercise and healthy eating fun for people so they can help themselves!"

Think Critically **Richard Simmons' market is obese and morbidly obese people who wish to lose weight and become healthy. What types of goods and services does Simmons provide for consumption through his programs?**

Sources: http://www.richardsimmons.com/j15/index.php?option=com_content&view=article&id=15&Itemid=80; https://www.facebook.com/note.php?note_id=10150571988565425; http://www.people.com/people/archive/article/0,,20079026,00.html; http://www.askmen.com/celebs/interview/30b_richard_simmons_interview.html; and http://www.sheknows.com/health-and-wellness/articles/7206/an-interview-with-richard-simmons

13.2 LIMITATIONS OF GDP ESTIMATION

Key Terms

depreciation 401
nominal GDP 403
real GDP 403
consumer price index (CPI) 404

Learning Objectives

LO1 Identify types of production that GDP calculations neglect.

LO2 Determine why and how to adjust GDP for changes in the general price level.

In Your World

Imagine the difficulty of developing an accounting system that must describe such a complex and dynamic economy. In the interest of clarity and simplicity, certain features are neglected. Features that are easier to measure and to explain may get too much attention. The problem is that the more comprehensive the national income accounts become, the more complicated they get. Trackers of the U.S. economy are always making tradeoffs between simplicity and comprehensiveness. As a result, some production is not accounted for in GDP. GDP must also adjust for changes in the economy's price level over time.

WHAT GDP MISSES

LO1
Identify types of production GDP calculations neglect.

With some minor exceptions, GDP includes only those products that are sold in legal markets. GDP thereby neglects all household production and all illegal production. GDP accounting also has difficulty capturing changes in the quality and variety of products, and in the amount of leisure time available.

Household Production

Do-it-yourself household production, such as childcare, meal preparation, house cleaning, and home repair, is not captured in GDP. Consequently, an economy in which each household is more do-it-yourself has a lower GDP than an otherwise similar economy in which households buy these services.

During the 1950s, more than 80 percent of American mothers with small children stayed at home, caring for the family. All this care did not add one cent to GDP. Today more than one-half of all mothers with small children are in the workforce. Their market labor is counted in U.S. GDP. What's more, GDP also has increased because meals, childcare, and the like are now more apt to be purchased in markets than provided by households. In less-developed economies, more economic activity is do-it-yourself or provided by the extended family.

Because official GDP estimates ignore most home production, they understate actual production in economies where families produce more for themselves and buy less in the market.

Underground Economy

GDP also ignores production in the *underground economy*, which includes activity that goes unreported either because it's illegal or because those involved want to evade taxes on otherwise legal activity. The underground economy is also called the black market or "working off the books." An example is a restaurant waiter who fails to report tip income in order to evade paying taxes on that income. A federal study suggests production in the underground economy is the equivalent of 7.5 percent of GDP. This amounted to about $1.1 trillion in 2011.

Leisure, Quality, and Variety

GDP indicates the value of goods and services produced in the economy. This gives economists some idea of the economy's *standard of living*, or its level of economic prosperity. However, GDP fails to capture some features of the economy that also play a part in living standards. For example, more leisure time contributes to a higher standard of living, but GDP offers no information about the amount of leisure available in an economy. If the amount of leisure remained relatively constant over time, then ignoring leisure would not distort the picture.

However, the average U.S. workweek is much shorter now than it was a century ago. This means people work less to produce today's output. People also increasingly retire at an earlier age and, typically, they live longer after retirement. Thus, over the years, there has been an increase in the amount of leisure time available. Yet, leisure is not reflected in GDP because leisure is not explicitly bought and sold in a market. So the standard of living has increased more than GDP indicates.

The quality and variety of products available also have improved over the years because of technological advances and market competition. Recording systems, computers, tires, running shoes, cell phones, and thousands of other products have improved. Also, new products are introduced all the time, such as HDTVs, 3D TVs, smartphones, and wonder drugs. Yet most of these improvements and innovations are not captured in GDP.

GDP fails to capture changes in leisure time. GDP sometimes fails to reflect changes in the quality of existing products and in the availability of new ones. These factors make GDP a less reliable measure of an economy's standard of living.

Depreciation

The nation's *capital stock* consists of the buildings, machines, vehicles, computers, and other physical capital used to produce GDP. In the course of producing GDP, some of that capital wears out, such as the delivery truck that finally dies. A new truck that logs 100,000 miles its first year has been subject to wear and tear. It is now less valuable as a productive resource. Other capital becomes obsolete, such as an aging computer that cannot run the latest software.

Depreciation measures the value of the capital stock that is used up or becomes obsolete in the production process. Gross domestic product is called "gross" because it does not take into account this depreciation. A clearer picture of the net production that actually occurs during a year is found by subtracting this depreciation from GDP. *Net domestic product* equals gross domestic product minus depreciation, the value of the capital stock used up in the production process. By failing to account for depreciation, GDP overstates what's actually produced.

depreciation The value of the capital stock that is used up or becomes obsolete in producing GDP during the year

Economists distinguish between two definitions of investment. *Gross investment* measures the value of all investment during a year. Gross investment is used in computing GDP. *Net investment* equals gross investment minus depreciation. The economy's production possibilities depend on what happens to net investment. If net investment is negative—that is, if depreciation exceeds gross investment—the capital stock declines, so its contribution to output declines as well. If net investment is zero, the capital stock remains constant, as does its contribution to output. If net investment is positive, the capital stock grows, as does its contribution to output. As the names indicate, *gross* domestic product reflects gross investment and *net* domestic product reflects net investment.

Stockbyte/Getty Images

Is the value of what this woman is doing in her home captured in GDP? Explain your answer.

GDP Does Not Reflect All Costs

Some production and consumption degrades the environment. Trucks and cars pump carbon monoxide into the atmosphere. Housing developments gobble up forests and reduce open space. Paper mills pollute lungs and burn eyes. These negative externalities—costs that fall mostly on those not directly involved in the market transactions—are ignored in GDP accounting, even though they diminish the standard of living and may limit future production. To the extent that growth in GDP also involves growth in such negative externalities, a rising GDP may not be as attractive as it would first appear.

Net domestic product captures the depreciation of buildings, machinery, vehicles, and other manufactured capital. Both GDP and net domestic product ignore the depletion of natural resources, such as standing timber, fish stocks, and soil fertility. Some economists argue that the federal government should develop so-called *green accounting*, or green GDP, to reflect the impact of production on air pollution, water pollution, lost trees, soil depletion, and the loss of other natural resources.

Despite the limitations and potential distortions associated with official GDP estimates, measures of GDP over time provides a fairly accurate picture of the overall performance of the U.S. economy. Inflation, however, distorts comparisons of dollar amounts from one year to the next. Adjusting for that problem is discussed next.

CHECKPOINT **What types of production does the calculation of GDP neglect?**

ADJUST GDP FOR PRICE CHANGES

LO2
Determine why and how to adjust GDP for changes over time in the general price level.

The national income accounts are based on the market values of final goods and services produced in a particular year. Gross domestic product measures the value of output in *current dollars*—that is, in the dollar values at the time the output is produced. The system of national income accounting based on current dollars allows for comparisons among income or expenditure components in a particular year. For example, you could say that consumption last year was about four times greater than investment. Because the economy's general price level changes over time, however, current-dollar comparisons across years can be misleading.

Nominal GDP Versus Real GDP

When GDP is based on current dollars, the national income accounts measure the *nominal value* of national output. Thus, the current-dollar GDP, or **nominal GDP**, is based on the prices when the output is produced. Because of inflation, however, focusing on the nominal value of GDP over time distorts the true picture. For example, between 1979 and 1980, nominal GDP increased by about 9 percent. That sounds impressive, but the economy's general price level rose more than 9 percent. So the growth in nominal GDP resulted entirely from inflation. **Real GDP**, or GDP adjusted for inflation, in fact, declined. *Inflation* is an increase in the economy's average price level.

If nominal GDP increases in a given year, part of this increase may simply result from inflation—pure hot air. To make meaningful comparisons of GDP across years, you must take out the hot air, or *deflate* nominal GDP. To focus on real changes in production, you must eliminate changes due solely to inflation.

Price Indexes

To compare the price level over time, you need a point of reference, a base year to which prices in other years can be compared. An *index number* compares the value of something in a particular year to its value in a base year, or reference year. Suppose bread is the only good produced in the economy. As a reference point, consider the price in some specific year. The year selected is called the base year. Prices in other years are expressed relative to the base-year price.

Suppose the base year is 2011, when a loaf of bread sold for $2.50. The price of bread increased to $2.60 in 2012 and to $2.80 in 2013. To construct a price index, each year's price is divided by the price in the base year and then multiplied by 100, as shown in Figure 13.3. For 2011, the base year, the base price of bread is divided by itself, $2.50/$2.50, which equals 1. So the price index in 2011 equals $1 \times 100 = 100$. *The price index in the base year, or base period, is always 100.*

The price index in 2012 is $2.60/$2.50, which equals 1.04, which multiplied by 100 equals 104. In 2013, the index is $2.80/$2.50, or 1.12, which multiplied by 100 equals 112. Thus, when compared to the base year, the price index is 4 percent higher in 2012 and is 12 percent higher in 2013.

The price index permits comparisons between any two years. For example, what if you were presented with the indexes for 2012 and 2013 and were asked what happened to the price level between the two years? By dividing the 2013 price index by the 2012 price index, or 112/104, you find that the price level rose by 7.7 percent.

nominal GDP The economy's aggregate output based on prices at the time of the transaction; current-dollar GDP

real GDP The economy's aggregate output measured in dollars of constant purchasing power; GDP measured in terms of the goods and services produced

FIGURE 13.3 Example of a Price Index (Base Year = 2011)

The price index equals the price in the current year divided by the price in the base year, all multiplied by 100. Here, the base year is 2011.

Year	(1) Price of Bread in Current Year	(2) Price of Bread in Base Year of 2011	(3) Price Index (3) = (1) ÷ (2) × 100
2011	$2.50	$2.50	100
2012	$2.60	$2.50	104
2013	$2.80	$2.50	112

Consumer Price Index

The **consumer price index (CPI)**, measures changes over time in the cost of buying a "market basket" of goods and services purchased by a typical family. For simplicity, suppose that market basket for the year includes 365 pounds of bananas, 200 gallons of fuel oil, and 12 months of cable TV. Prices in the base year are listed in column (2) of Figure 13.4. Multiplying price by quantity yields the total cost of each product in the base year, as shown in column (3). The cost of the market basket in the base year is $1,644.85, shown as the sum of column (3).

Prices in the current year are listed in column (4). Note that not all prices changed by the same percentage since the base year. The price of fuel oil increased by 33 percent, but the price of bananas fell. The cost of purchasing that same basket in the current year is $1,808.35, shown as the total of column (5).

To compute the consumer price index for the current year, you simply divide the total cost in the current year by the total cost of that same basket in the base year, or $1,808.35/$1,644.85, and then multiply by 100. This yields a price index of 109.9. You could say that between the base year and the current year, the "cost of living" increased by 9.9 percent, although not all prices changed by the same percentage.

The federal government uses the years 1982 to 1984 as the base period for calculating the CPI for a market basket of about 80,000 items in more than 200 categories of goods and services. The CPI is reported monthly, based on prices from thousands of sellers across the country.

GDP Price Index

Price indexes are weighted sums of various prices. Whereas the CPI focuses on just a basket of consumer purchases, a more comprehensive price index, the *GDP price index*, includes all goods and services produced. The GDP price index is found by dividing the nominal GDP by the real GDP and then multiplying by 100:

$$\text{GDP Price Index} = \frac{\text{Nominal GDP}}{\text{Real GDP}} \times 100$$

consumer price index (CPI) Measure of inflation based on the cost of a fixed "market basket" of goods and services purchased by a typical family

FIGURE 13.4 Example Market Basket Used to Develop the Consumer Price Index

The cost of a market basket in the current year, shown at the bottom of column (5), sums the quantity of each item in the basket, shown in column (1), times the price of each item in the current year, shown in column (4).

Good or service	(1) Quantity in Market Basket	(2) Price in Base Year	(3) Cost of Basket in Base Year (3) = (1) × (2)	(4) Price in Current Year	(5) Cost of Basket in Current Year (5) = (1) × (4)
Bananas	365 pounds	$ 0.89/pound	$ 324.85	$ 0.79	$ 288.35
Fuel Oil	200 gallons	$ 3.00/gallon	$ 600.00	$ 4.00	$ 800.00
Cable TV	12 months	$60.00/month	$ 720.00	$60.00	$ 720.00
			$1,644.85		$1,808.35

Nominal GDP is the dollar value of this year's GDP measured in current-year prices. Real GDP is the dollar value of this year's GDP measured in base-year prices. If you know both nominal GDP and real GDP, you can find the GDP price index. The federal government most recently has used 2005 as the base year. It moves forward every few years and could be later year by the time you read this.

Economists use the GDP price index to eliminate any year-to-year changes in GDP due solely to changes in the economy's price level. After this adjustment is made, remaining changes reflect changes in real output, or changes in the amount of goods and services produced. After adjusting GDP for price changes, you end up with real GDP.

Why and how is GDP adjusted for changes in the general price level? **CHECKPOINT**

Span the Globe

The UK's "Basket of Goods"

Most countries have a "basket of goods" from which they determine their consumer price index. The mix of goods differs from country to country, reflecting the individual nation's buying patterns and society. Also, goods are added and removed to reflect changes in a nation's buying patterns. For instance, the United Kingdom, which annually revises the 650-item basket it measures, recently added smartphones, such as the iPhone, to the basket. Also, the cost of apps has been added to the list. Another new phenomenon that found its way into the UK's basket is the fee charged by Internet dating services. However, not every item that first finds its way into the basket is cutting edge. Hair conditioner, for instance, which has been around for decades, is newly listed.

Because the overall basket is limited, when items are added others must be removed. So when medium density fiberboard is in, hardboard is out. Other factors can change the mix of goods, as illustrated by the elimination of cigarettes from vending machines due to UK legislation banning such sales.

Think Critically **Consider a consumer price index for your school. Make a list of categories and include the goods and you would use to make your basket of goods.**

Source: Paul Gooding, "Consumer Prices Index and Retail Prices Index: the 2011 Basket of Goods and Services," United Kingdom, Office for National Statistics.

13.2 ASSESSMENT

Think Critically

1. Why wouldn't our nation's GDP grow if you mow your own lawn, but would grow if you were paid to mow your neighbor's lawn?
2. How do many young people participate in the underground economy?
3. Why wouldn't the purchase of a used truck for $20,000 represent a $20,000 addition to GDP?
4. If the value added by a power plant to GDP is $18 million why might the *green accounting* value it adds be less than this amount?
5. If last year's CPI was 216.20 and this year's CPI is 227.01, what was the rate of inflation over the past year, according to the CPI?

Graphing Exercise

6. Americans watch TV for more hours per year than people in any other nation. Although they value their time in front of the "tube," this value is not included in GDP. Why is time watching TV not included in GDP? Construct a bar graph from the data in the table showing the hours the average American spends watching TV. On a separate graph, show for each year the average time spent watching TV per day. What might explain the decline in hours watched after 2008?

AVERAGE HOURS SPENT WATCHING TV PROGRAMMING PER YEAR, 2000–2010

Year	Average Viewing Hours
2000	1,635
2002	1,705
2004	1,792
2006	1,858
2008	1,931
2010	1,793

Make Academic Connections

7. **Government** In 2000, the federal government spent or transferred $1,789 billion when the CPI was 172.2. Ten years later, in 2010, the federal government spent or transferred $3,456 billion when the CPI was 218.0. Did the federal government's real spending and transfers increase in these years? Explain your answer.

TeamWork

Working in teams, each member should identify a different good or service he or she buys regularly that has increased significantly in price over the past year. List these products and rank them in order of their importance to the person's standard of living. Use thes items as examples to explain why adjusting national income account values for inflation is important to understanding what is happening in our economy. Compare your group's work with that of other groups.

21st Century Skills

INFORMATION LITERACY

Keep Up with Economic Change

The federal government spends millions of dollars each year to measure and report current trends in economic activity. It makes this information available to the public in print and over the Internet. Types of economic information the government provides include

- Measures of output and earnings such as Gross Domestic Product, Real Gross Domestic Product, National Income, and Personal Income
- Data on employment, unemployment, hours worked, and average weekly earnings
- Data on new construction, industrial production, business shipments, and inventories.
- Measures of prices and rates of inflation
- Data on the amount of money in circulation, bank loans, and interest rates
- Federal tax receipts and spending

Economic Data Online

Much of the economic data collected by the federal government is available online. One of the most useful sources can be found at the Government Printing Office website. When you reach this website click on the A to Z resource list box and then on E to find a publication titled *Economic Indicators*. This publication reports data for the latest month for each of the categories listed above.

Using Economic Data

Individuals, government leaders, and entrepreneurs pay close attention to economic data gathered and reported by the government. If the government reported that consumer prices had increased at an annual rate of 6 percent last month, each of the following might result:

- Consumers might buy more products now to avoid price increases in the future.
- Businesses might increase prices because they expect their costs to go up.
- Workers might demand higher wages from their employers.
- Politicians might propose measures to slow the rate of inflation.

New Sources of Data

In March 2011, the U.S. Government Printing Office introduced a new system called FDsys. This online system offers a wide variety of economic data for examination and download. In the future, this system will be expanded to provide even more information. People who want to keep up with economic changes will benefit from this readily available information provided by the government.

Apply the Skill

Imagine that data reported in *Economic Indicators* showed that the rate of unemployment increased 0.3 percent last month. Although 0.3 percent may not seem like much, it means there were about 460,000 more people out of work last month. Explain how this might affect decisions made by each of the following people.

1. Retail store managers
2. Bank lending officers
3. Consumers considering the purchase of a new home

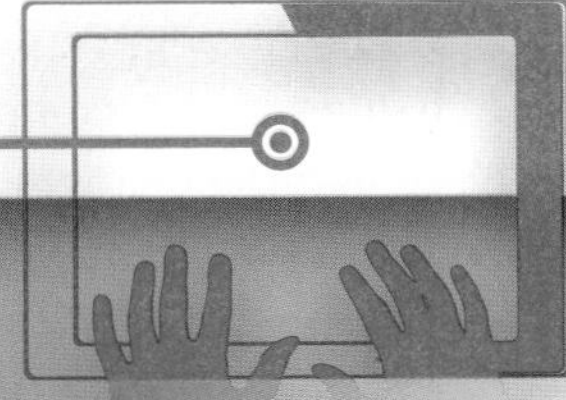

13.3 BUSINESS CYCLES

Key Terms

Learning Objectives

LO1 Distinguish between the two phases of the business cycle.

LO2 Differentiate among the types of economic indicators.

In Your World

Economic activity, like cycles in nature, fluctuates in a fairly regular way. The U.S. economy and other industrial market economies historically have experienced alternating periods of good times and hard times. These ups and downs vary in length and intensity, yet some features appear common to all. They usually involve the entire nation and often the world. They affect nearly all dimensions of economic activity, not simply employment and production. You may recall what came to be known as the Great Recession of 2008–2009. Despite these ups and downs, the U.S. economy has grown dramatically over the long run.

U.S. ECONOMIC FLUCTUATIONS

LO1
Distinguish between the two phases of the business cycle.

The **business cycle** reflects the rise and fall of economic activity relative to the long-term growth trend of the economy. Perhaps the easiest way to understand the business cycle is to examine its components. During the 1920s and 1930s, Wesley C. Mitchell, director of the National Bureau of Economic Research (NBER), noted that the economy experiences two phases: periods of expansion and periods of contraction.

Recessions and Expansions

A contraction might be so severe as to be called a *depression.* This is a sharp reduction in the nation's total production lasting a few years and accompanied by high unemployment. A milder contraction is called a **recession**, which is a decline in total production lasting at least two consecutive quarters, or at least six months. The U.S. economy experienced both recessions and depressions before World War II. Since then, there have been many recessions but no depressions.

Long-Term Growth

Despite these ups and downs, the U.S. economy has grown dramatically over the long run. The economy in 2011 was 14 times larger than it was in 1929, as measured by real gross domestic product, or real GDP. With real GDP, the effects of changes in the economy's price level have been stripped away. Therefore, the remaining changes reflect real changes in the value of goods and services produced.

business cycle Fluctuations reflecting the rise and fall of economic activity relative to the long-term growth trend of the economy

recession A decline in total production lasting at least two consecutive quarters, or at least six months

Production tends to increase over the long run because of

1. increases in the amount and quality of resources, especially labor and capital.
2. better technology.
3. improvements in the *rules of the game* that facilitate production and exchange, such as property rights, patent laws, legal systems, and customs of the market.

Figure 13.5 shows a long-term growth trend in real GDP as an upward-sloping straight line. Economic fluctuations reflect movements around this growth trend. A recession begins after the previous expansion has reached its *peak*, or high point, and then heads down until the economy reaches a *trough*, or low point. The period between a peak and trough is a recession. The period between a trough and subsequent peak is an **expansion**, or the phase of economic activity during which the economy's total output increases. Note that expansions last longer than recessions, but the length of the full cycle varies.

expansion The phase of economic activity during which the economy's total output increases

History of U.S. Business Cycles

Economists at the NBER have been able to track the U.S. economy back to 1854. Between 1854 and 2011, the nation experienced 33 business cycles. No two have been exactly alike. The longest expansion began in the spring of 1991 and lasted ten years. The longest contraction lasted five-and-a-half years, from 1873 to 1879.

Output changes since 1929 appear in Figure 13.6. The figure shows the annual percent change in real GDP, with declines in red bars and increases in green bars. The big decline during the Great Depression of the early 1930s and the sharp jump during World War II stand in stark contrast. Growth since 1929 has averaged 3.3 percent a year. Since the end of World War II in 1945, expansions have averaged just under five years and recessions just under one year. Thus, expansions have averaged five times longer than recessions.

FIGURE 13.5 Business Cycles

Business cycles reflect movements of economic activity around a trend line that shows long-term growth. A recession (shown in pink) begins after a previous expansion (shown in blue) has reached its peak and continues until the economy reaches a trough. An expansion begins when economic activity starts to increase and continues until the economy reaches a peak. A complete business cycle includes both the recession phase and the expansion phase.

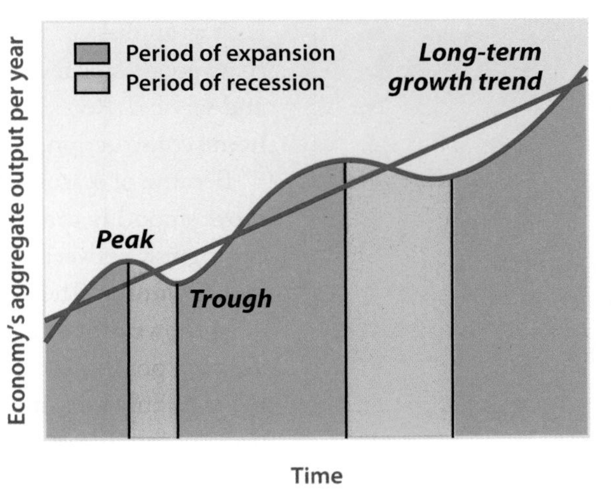

FIGURE 13.6 Annual Percent Change in U.S. Real GDP

Since the end of World War II in 1945, the economy has gone through 11 business cycles. Expansions averaged just under five years. Recessions averaged just under one year. Note: In this chart, declines in real GDP are shown in red and increases, in green.

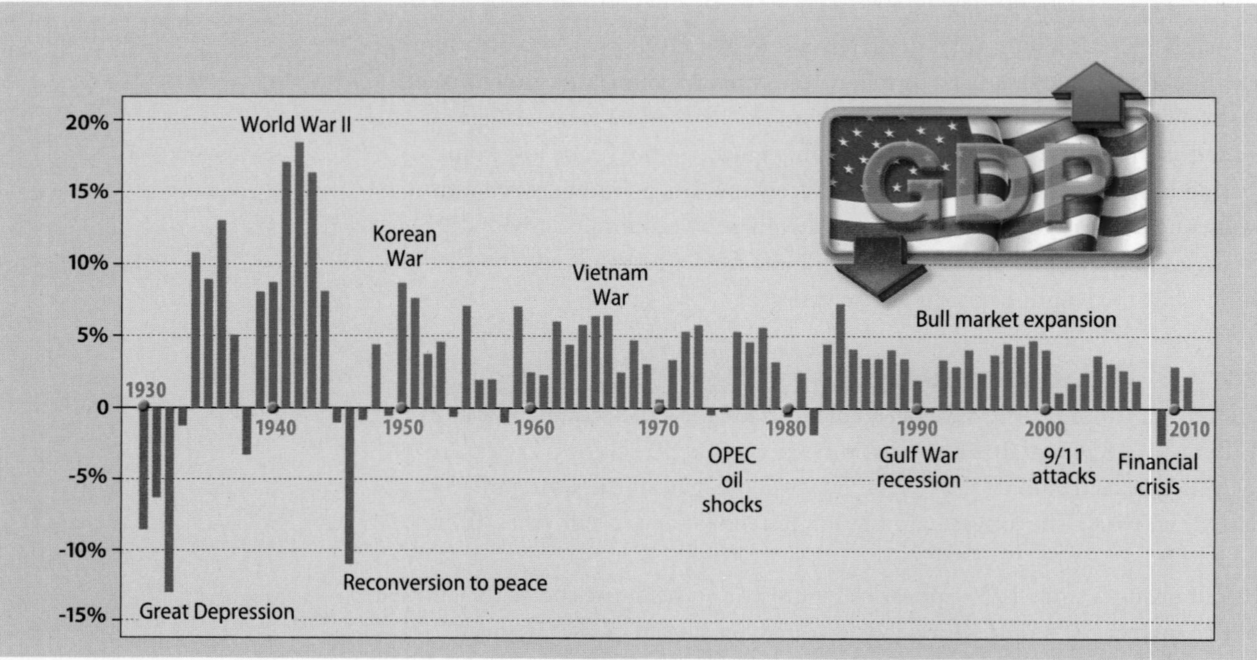

Source: Based on annual estimates from the U.S. Department of Commerce. The growth rate for 2011 is a projection.

Different Impact on States

The intensity of the business cycle varies from region to region across the United States. A recession hits hardest those regions that produce durable goods, such as appliances, furniture, and automobiles. This is because the demand for these goods falls more during hard times than does the demand for other goods and services. Recessions also hit harder those states whose economies rely more on home construction, such as Arizona, California, Florida, and Nevada.

Because of seasonal fluctuations and random events, the economy does not move smoothly through phases of business cycle. Economists cannot always distinguish between temporary setbacks in economic activity and the beginning of a downturn. The drop in production in a particular quarter may result from a big snowstorm or a poor harvest rather than mark the onset of a recession. Turning points—peaks and troughs—are thus identified by the NBER only after the fact, only after more evidence piles up. Because recession means that output declines for at least two consecutive quarters, a recession is not so designated until at least six months after it begins.

Business Cycles Around the Globe

Business cycles usually involve the entire nation. Indeed, market economies around the world often move together. Consider the experience during the last quarter century of two leading economies—the United States and the United Kingdom (which consists of England, Scotland, Wales, and Northern Ireland). Figure 13.7 shows for both economies the year-to-year percent change in their real GDPs. Again, real means that the effects of inflation have been erased. Remaining changes reflect real changes in the total amount of goods and services produced.

If you follow the annual changes in each economy,

The National Bureau of Economic Research maintains a web page devoted to business cycle expansions and contractions. Access this page through the URL shown below. Take a look at the page and see if you can determine how the business cycle has been changing in recent decades. Has the overall length of cycles been changing? Have recessions been getting longer or shorter?

www.cengage.com/school/contecon

FIGURE 13.7 U.S. and U.K. Growth Rates in Real GDP

Growth rates of output in the United States and the United Kingdom are similar.

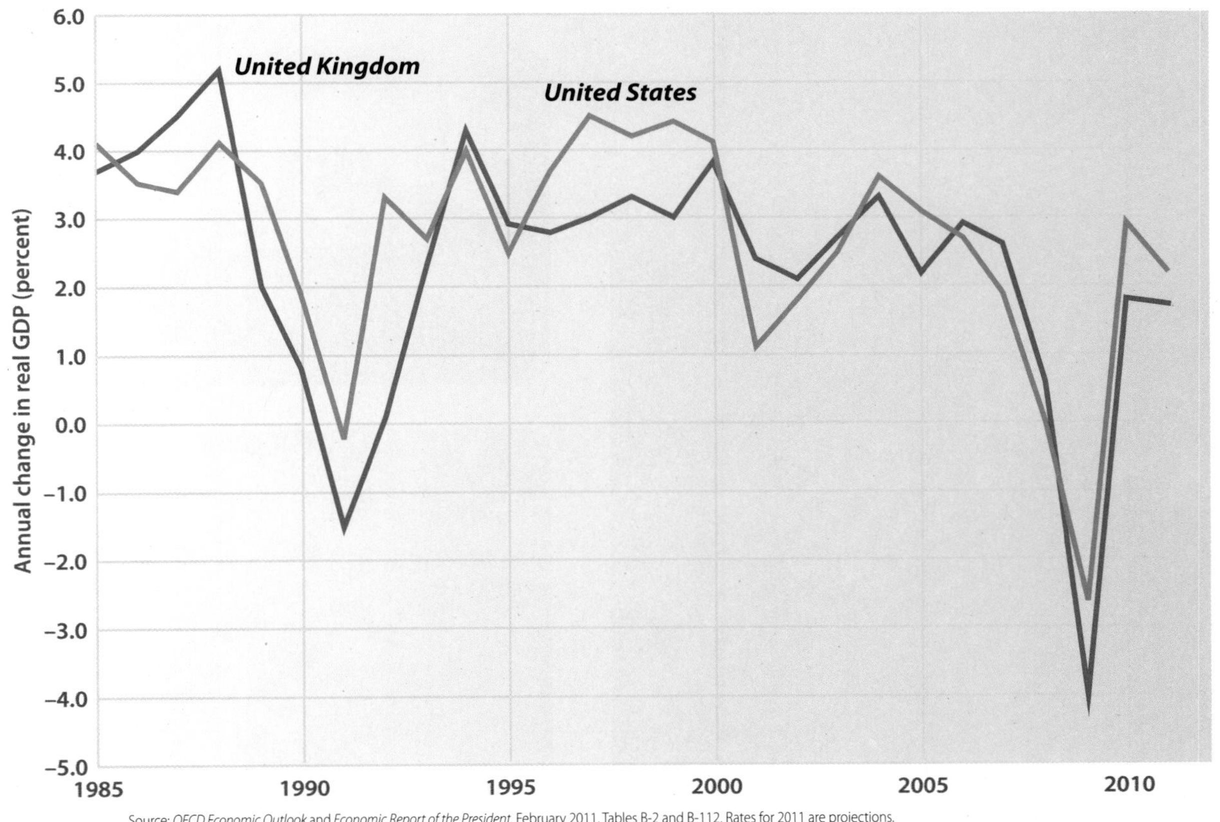

Source: *OECD Economic Outlook* and *Economic Report of the President*, February 2011, Tables B-2 and B-112. Rates for 2011 are projections.

you can notice the similarities. For example, in 1991, U.S. real GDP declined, reflecting a recession. Most noticeably, GDP dropped sharply in both economies because of the Great Recession of 2008–2009.

One problem with the linkage across economies is that a slump in other major economies could worsen a recession in the United States, and vice versa. This occurred during the financial crisis of September 2008, which sent shock waves around the world.

Although year-to-year fluctuations in output are of interest, even more important to an economy's standard of living is the long-term growth trend. U.S. real GDP growth averaged 2.7 percent per year between 1985 and 2011, compared with 2.3 percent in the United Kingdom. This seemingly small difference compounded over the years to raise the level of real GDP much more in the United States. For example, if U.S. GDP had averaged only 2.3 percent

ESSENTIAL QUESTION

Standard CEE 18: Economic Fluctuations

Fluctuations in a nation's overall levels of income, employment, and prices are determined by the interaction of spending and production decisions made by all households, firms, government agencies, and others in the economy. Recessions occur when overall levels of income and employment decline.

iofoto/Shutterstock.com

jondpatton/iStockphoto.com

trekandshoot/Shutterstock.com

What determines the fluctuations in a nation's economic activity?

growth since 1985, output by 2011 would have been $ 1,350 billion below that achieved with its 2.7 percent growth. The lower growth rate would have reduced U.S. production and income in 2011 by about $4,300 per person, or $17,300 for a family of four. Seemingly small differences in growth rates, when compounded for years, result in big differences in GDP.

CHECKPOINT

What are the two phases of the business cycle, and what has been the average length of each since World War II?

ECONOMIC INDICATORS

LO2 Differentiate among the types of economic indicators.

During the Great Depression, economists identified measures that would keep better track of the economy. These economic indicators are classified according to their timing relative to the ups and downs of the business cycle. Those that predict future changes are called *leading indicators.* Those that measure the ups and downs as they occur are called *coincident indicators.* Those that measure the ups and downs after they have already occurred are called *lagging indicators.*

To understand economic indicators better, consider weather indicators as an example. A leading indicator tells you what the weather will be like tomorrow. A coincident indicator tells you what it's like outside right now. A lagging indicator tells you what the weather was yesterday. Leading economic indicators get the most attention because people want to know where the economy is headed.

Leading Indicators

Certain events foretell a turning point in the economy. Months before a recession begins, changes in leading economic indicators point to the coming storm. In the early stages of a recession, business slows, orders for construction and machinery slip, and the stock market, anticipating lower profits, turns down. Consumer confidence in the economy's future also begins to sag. Households cut back on their spending, especially for big-ticket items like new cars and new homes.

All these activities are called **leading economic indicators** because they usually predict, or *lead to*, a downturn. There are ten leading indicators rolled into the *index of leading indicators* and reported monthly. Upturns in leading indicators point to an economic recovery. The index of leading indicators is a closely followed measure of economic activity.

Leading indicators cannot predict precisely when a turning point will occur, or even whether one will occur. Sometimes the leading indicators sound a false alarm. Leading indicators also may not work when there is an external shock to the economy, such as a terrorist attack, financial crisis, drought, earthquake, or hurricane. For example, when Iraq invaded Kuwait in 1990, the price of crude oil jumped 60 percent. This caused an economic downturn throughout the world that could not have been predicted by the leading indicators. The financial crisis of September 2008 turned what, to that point, was an average recession, into the worst one since the Great Depression.

Investigate Your Local Economy

Before new houses may be built, contractors must obtain building permits from local government. Find out the number of building permits issued in your community during the most recent two months of available data. Compare these figures with the same months for the previous year. In light of this information, what will probably happen to the local economy in the next few months?

leading economic indicators Measures that usually predict, or *lead to*, recessions or expansions

Coincident Indicators

Some economic indicators measure what's going on in the economy right now. *Coincident economic indicators* are those measures that reflect peaks and troughs as they happen. There are four coincident indicators combined into the *index of coincident indicators*, including total employment, personal income, and industrial production.

Lagging Indicators

Some economic indicators measure what has already happened. *Lagging economic indicators* follow, or trail, changes in overall economic activity. There are seven economic measures combined into the *index of lagging indicators*, including the interest rate, measures of loans outstanding, and the average duration of unemployment.

This introduction to the business cycle has been largely descriptive, focusing on the history and measurement of these fluctuations. Why economies fluctuate has not been addressed, in part because such a discussion requires a fuller understanding

Math in Economics

Common Core Number and Operations in Base 10

You can round numbers to a number of decimal places and then add or subtract these rounded values to calculate an estimated change.

Civilians Employed in the United States 2001–2010

CIVILIANS EMPLOYED IN THE UNITED STATES 2001–2010

Year	Civilians Employed	Year	Civilians Employed
2001	136,933,000	2006	144,427,000
2002	136,485,000	2007	146,047,000
2003	137,736,000	2008	145,362,000
2004	139,252,000	2009	139,877,000
2005	141,730,000	2010	139,064,000

EXAMPLE Estimate how many million jobs were created in the U.S. economy from 2001 through 2007.

SOLUTION Round the employment values for 2001 and 2007 to the nearest million. Subtract the rounded amount for 2001 from the rounded amount for 2007 to find the estimated number of jobs created in millions.

If the number in the hundred-thousand place is equal to or greater than 5, increase the number in the millions place by 1. If the number in the hundred-thousand place is less than 5, the number in the millions place stays the same. All place values to the right of the millions place are filled with 0.

146,000,000 – 137,000,000 = 9,000,000 jobs

Practice the Skill

1. Estimate how many million jobs were lost in the U.S. economy from 2007 through 2010
2. Estimate how many million jobs were created in the U.S. economy from 2003 through 2005.
3. Estimate how many million jobs there were in 2011 if 1,892,000 jobs were created that year?.

of the economy and in part because the causes are not always clear. The next section begins to build a framework by introducing a key model of the national economy.

CHECKPOINT What are the differences among leading, coincident, and lagging economic indicators?

13.3 ASSESSMENT

Think Critically

1. Decide whether the U.S. economy is currently in an expansion or a recession. Identify and explain the types of information that allow you to make this decision.
2. Do you think a recession would harm your community more than or less than the average of all communities in the United States? Explain your answer.
3. How would a major expansion of the economies in Europe affect the U.S. economy?
4. What would a 10 percent increase in factory construction tell you about the economic conditions that will exist next year? Why might this information be a leading indicator?

Graphing Exercises

5. Use data in the table to construct a bar graph that shows the rate of growth of real GDP from 2001 through 2010. If the long-range growth rate averages 3.0 percent per year, which years exceeded this growth rate and which had lower rates of growth? How does your graph demonstrate the business cycle?

REAL GDP GROWTH RATES, 2001–2010

Year	Real GDP Growth	Year	Real GDP Growth
2001	1.1%	2006	2.7%
2002	1.8%	2007	1.9%
2003	2.5%	2008	−0.3%
2004	3.5%	2009	−3.5%
2005	3.1%	2010	3.0%

Source: *Economic Indicators*, July 2011, p. 3.

Make Academic Connections

6. **History** During the Great Depression of the 1930s, average prices fell in the United States. Did nominal GDP decline? Did real GDP decline? Explain your answers.

TeamWork

Many students would like to have summer jobs. Working in teams, identify factors in your local economy that exist now that might tell you whether it will be easy or difficult for you to find employment next summer. Discuss how these factors are similar to leading indicators for the economy.

13.4 AGGREGATE DEMAND AND AGGREGATE SUPPLY

Key Terms

Learning Objectives

LO1 Explain aggregate output and the economy's price level.

LO2 Describe the aggregate demand curve and aggregate supply curve.

In Your World

In the study of market economics, the focus is on particular markets, such as the market for pizza, cargo shorts, or makeup. However, the national economy is so complex that you need to simplify in order to focus on the big picture. The perspective broadens from individual markets to a giant market for everything produced in the economy. Aggregate demand and aggregate supply curves help you understand how the price and output for the economy as a whole are determined.

AGGREGATE OUTPUT AND THE PRICE LEVEL

LO1 Explain aggregate output and the economy's price level.

Picture a pizza. Now picture food more generally. Food includes not just pizza but thousands of edibles, from apples to ziti. Although food is more general than pizza, you probably have no difficulty picturing food. Now make the leap from food to all goods and services produced in the economy—food, housing, clothing, entertainment, education, transportation, medical care, and so on.

Aggregate Output

aggregate output A composite measure of all final goods and services produced in an economy during a given period; real GDP

aggregate demand The relationship between the average price of aggregate output and the quantity of aggregate output demanded, with other things constant

price level A composite measure reflecting the prices of all goods and services in the economy relative to prices in a base year

Aggregate output is a composite measure of all final goods and services produced in the economy during a given period. The best measure of aggregate output is *real GDP*, which was addressed in a previous section. Just as you can talk about the demand for pizza or the demand for food, you can talk about the demand for aggregate output. **Aggregate demand** is the relationship between the average price of aggregate output and the quantity of aggregate output demanded.

The Price Level

The **price level** is a composite measure reflecting the prices of all goods and services in the economy relative to prices in a base year. You are more familiar than you may think with these aggregate measures. Headlines refer to changes in the growth of aggregate output—as in "Growth Slows in Second Quarter." News accounts also report on changes in the economy's price level—as in "Prices Up Slightly in June." You already have some idea how the economy's price level is computed. What you need to know now is that the price level in any year is an *index number*, or reference number. This compares average prices that year to average prices in some base, or reference, year. If you say that the price level is higher, you mean it's higher compared to where it was. The focus here is on the price level of all goods and services produced in the economy *relative to the price level in some base year.*

As discussed in the section about price indexes, the price level in the base year has a benchmark value of 100. Price levels in other years are expressed relative to the base-year price level. The price level, or price index, is used not only to compare price levels across time but also to make more accurate comparisons of aggregate output over time.

What is aggregate output, and what is the economy's price level? **CHECKPOINT**

AGGREGATE DEMAND AND AGGREGATE SUPPLY CURVES

LO2
Describe the aggregate demand curve and aggregate supply curve.

In Chapters 4 and 5, you learned about the demand and supply of a particular product, such as pizza. Now you will focus on the demand and supply of aggregate output, or real GDP.

The Aggregate Demand Curve

Just as you can talk about the demand for pizza or the demand for movie tickets, you can talk about the demand for aggregate output in the economy. The **aggregate demand curve** shows the relationship between the price level in the economy and real GDP demanded, other things constant. Figure 13.8 shows a hypothetical aggregate demand curve, *AD*. The vertical axis measures an index of the economy's price level relative to a 2005 base-year price level of 100. The horizontal axis shows real GDP, which measures aggregate utput in dollars of constant purchasing power (here, based on 2005 prices).

The aggregate demand curve in Figure 13.8 reflects an inverse relationship between the price level in the economy and real GDP demanded. Aggregate demand sums the demands of the four economic decision makers: households, firms, governments, and the rest of the world. As the price level increases, other things constant, households demand less housing and furniture, firms demand fewer trucks and machines, governments demand less computer software and military hardware, and the rest of the world demands less U.S. grain and U.S. aircraft.

Here's a quick explanation of the inverse relationship between price level and real GDP demanded. Real GDP demanded depends in part on household wealth. Some wealth is typically held in bank accounts and in currency. An increase in

aggregate demand curve A curve representing the relationship between the economy's price level and real GDP demanded per period, other things constant

FIGURE 13.8 Aggregate Demand Curve

The quantity of real GDP demanded is inversely related to the economy's price level, other things constant. This inverse relationship is reflected by the aggregate demand curve *AD*.

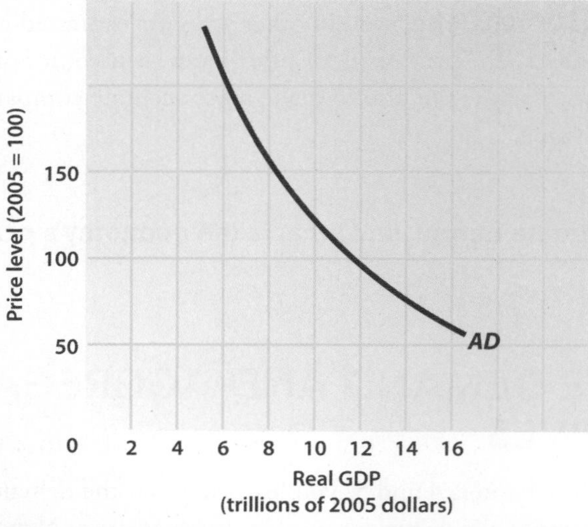

the price level, other things constant, decreases the purchasing power of bank accounts and currency. Households, therefore, are poorer in real terms when the price level increases, so the quantity of real GDP demanded decreases. Conversely, a reduction in the price level increases the purchasing power of bank accounts and currency. *Because households are richer as the price level decreases, the quantity of real GDP demanded increases.*

What happens to a household's demand for goods when the price level increases?

Among the factors held constant along a given aggregate demand curve are price levels in other countries as well as exchange rates between the U.S. dollar and foreign currencies. When the U.S. price level increases, U.S. products cost more relative to foreign products. Consequently, households, firms, and governments both here and abroad decrease the quantity of U.S. real GDP demanded. On the other hand, a lower U.S. price level makes U.S. goods relatively cheap compared with foreign goods, so the quantity of U.S. real GDP demanded increases.

The Aggregate Supply Curve

The **aggregate supply curve** shows how much output U.S. producers are willing and able to supply at each price level, other things constant. How does the quantity supplied respond to changes in the price level? The upward-sloping aggregate supply curve, as in Figure 13.9, shows a positive relationship between the price level and the quantity of aggregate output that producers supply, other factors remaining constant.

Assumed constant along an aggregate supply curve are (1) resource prices, (2) the state of technology, and (3) the rules of the game that provide production incentives, such as patent and copyright laws. Wage rates are typically assumed to remain constant along the aggregate supply curve. With wages constant, firms find a higher price level more profitable, so they increase real GDP supplied. *Whenever the prices firms receive rise faster than the cost of production, firms find it profitable to expand output. Therefore, real GDP supplied varies directly with the economy's price level, other things constant.*

Equilibrium

The intersection of the aggregate demand curve and aggregate supply curve determines the equilibrium price level and real GDP in the economy. Figure 13.9 is a rough depiction of the aggregate demand curve and aggregate supply curve in 2011. Equilibrium real GDP in 2011 was about $13.6 trillion, measured in dollars of 2005 purchasing power. The equilibrium price level in 2011 was 114, compared with a price level of 100 in the base year of 2005. At any other price level, real GDP demanded would not match real GDP supplied.

aggregate supply curve A curve representing the relationship between the economy's price level and real GDP supplied per period, other things constant

FIGURE 13.9 Aggregate Demand and Supply

The economy's real GDP and price level are determined at the intersection of the aggregate demand and aggregate supply curves. The equilibrium point reflects real GDP and the price level for 2011, using 2005 as the base year for prices.

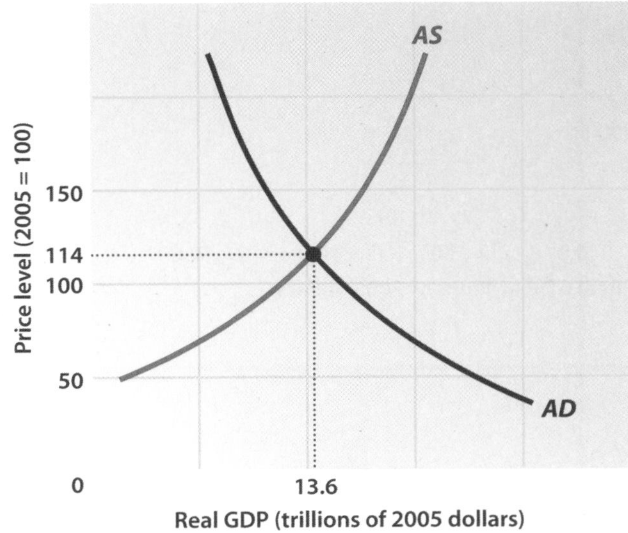

Although employment is not measured directly along the horizontal axis, firms usually must hire more workers to produce more output. Greater levels of real GDP are beneficial because (1) more goods and services are available in the economy and (2) more people have jobs.

Real GDP and Prices Since 1929

Figure 13.10 traces the U.S. real GDP and price level since 1929. Aggregate demand and aggregate supply curves for 2011 are shown as an example, but all points in the series reflect such intersections. Real GDP, measured along the horizontal axis in 2005 constant dollars, grew from $1.0 trillion in 1929 to $13.6 trillion in 2011—nearly a fourteenfold increase and an average annual growth rate of 3.3 percent. The price level also rose, but not as much, rising from only 10.6 in 1929 to 114 in 2011, nearly an elevenfold increase and an average inflation rate of 2.9 percent per year.

Because the U.S. population is growing all the time, the economy must continue to create new jobs just to employ the additional people entering the workforce. For example, the U.S. population grew from 122 million in 1929 to 311 million in 2011, a rise of 155 percent. Fortunately, employment grew even faster, from 48 million in 1929 to 140 million in 2011, for a growth of 191 percent.

FIGURE 13.10 U.S. Real GDP and Price Level Since 1929

Both real GDP and the price level increased since 1929. Blue points indicate years of growing real GDP, and red points are years of declining real GDP. Real GDP in 2011 was nearly 14 times greater than it was in 1929. The price level was nearly 11 times greater.

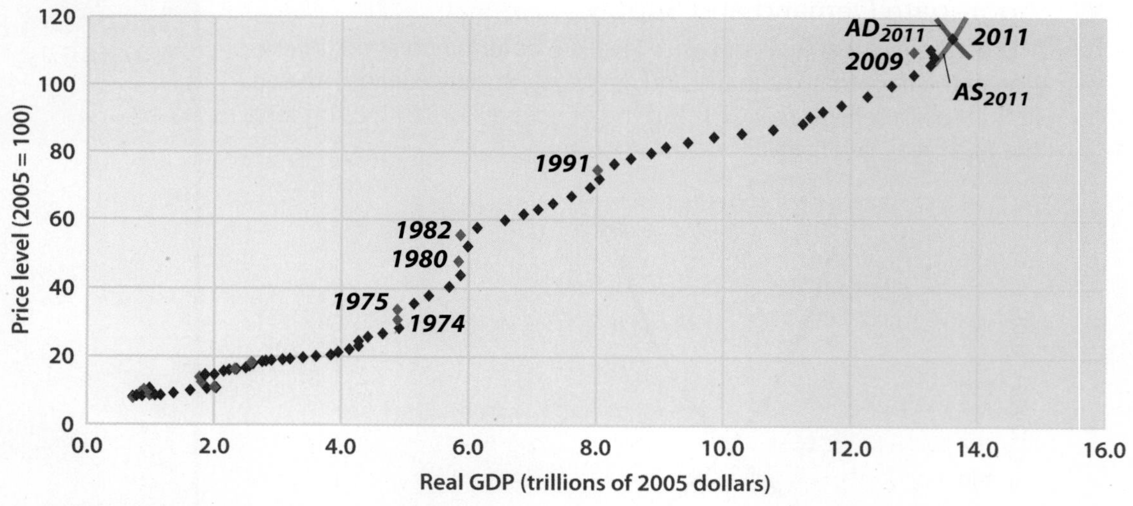

Source: Based on annual estimates from the U.S. Department of Commerce.

During the past seven decades, employment grew more than enough to keep up with a growing population. Not only did the number of people working nearly triple, but workers' average level of education increased as well. Employment of other resources, especially capital goods, also rose sharply. Furthermore, the level of technology improved steadily, thanks to major breakthroughs such as computer chips and the Internet. The availability of more and higher-quality human capital and physical capital increased the productivity of each worker. This contributed to the nearly fourteenfold jump in real GDP since 1929.

Real GDP is important, but the best measure of an economy's standard of living is real GDP per capita, which indicates how much an economy produces on average per resident. U.S. real GDP per capita is found by dividing real GDP by the U.S. population. Because real GDP grew much faster than the population since 1929, real GDP per capita jumped fivefold since 1929. The United States is the largest economy in the world and has been a leader among major economies in real GDP per capita.

CHECKPOINT

What are the aggregate demand and aggregate supply curves, and how do they determine the economy's equilibrium price level and aggregate output?

thelinke/iStockphoto.com

Benis Arapovic/Shutterstock.com

How do improvements in technology affect worker productivity?

13.4 ASSESSMENT

Think Critically

1. Explain how your spending would be affected by a 10 percent average increase in prices. How would this change affect aggregate demand for goods and services throughout the economy?
2. How is it possible for aggregate output to fall at the same time that nominal GDP increases by 2 percent?
3. What effect would an increase in the cost of productive resources have on the aggregate supply curve and on the equilibrium prices of products?
4. What would you need to know to be able to determine whether real GDP per capita increased from last year?

Graphing Exercise

5. Use the data in the table to construct a bar graph that shows the year-to-year *change* in real GDP per capita from 2005 through 2009. Why did the per capita real GDP fall in the years after 2007?

REAL GDP PER CAPITA, 2000–2009, VALUES IN 2005 DOLLARS

Year	Real GDP Per Capita
2005	$42,675
2006	$43,400
2007	$43,789
2008	$43,243
2009	$41,377

Source: *Statistical Abstract of the United States, 2011*, p. 10; *Economic Indicators*, July 2011, p. 2.

Make Academic Connections

6. **History** Study the data in the table. How do you think the lives of many U.S. citizens changed during the Great Depression of the 1930s?

REAL GDP PER CAPITA, 1929–1938, VALUES IN 1929 DOLLARS

Year	Real GDP Per Capita	Year	Real GDP Per Capita
1929	$857	1934	$639
1930	$772	1935	$718
1931	$721	1936	$787
1932	$611	1937	$845
1933	$590	1938	$794

Source: *Historical Statistical Abstract of the United States*, 1957, p. 139.

TeamWork

Working in small teams, identify five important national or international events that have taken place in the past year that either caused aggregate demand to increase—that is, for the *AD* curve to shift rightward, or to decline—that is, for the *AD* curve to shift leftward. Explain how each of these events affected the price you pay for the goods and services you and your family buy. Assume the aggregate supply curve does not shift. Compare your work with that of other teams.

Connect to History

The Panic of 1907

During the 1800s, economic panics were a familiar feature of the American economy. Before 1907, the economy had suffered through four such events in the course of 34 years. In the summer of 1907, the American economy began another downturn. Each fall, the financial system suffered stress because money was needed to move crops from the Midwest to the markets in the East and in Europe. Thousands of banks across the country, needing to maintain their reserves, withdrew cash from the country's 47 regional banks. These banks, in turn, withdrew cash from other banks in one of three cities that acted as central reserves—most notably, New York City. While not unexpected, the situation did cause short-term interest rates to rise. What was different in 1907 was that the money supply did not increase to meet the demand for money. Gold that usually would have flowed into the United States from Europe due to the higher interest rate did not do so. In 1907, the banking system that had been able to contain the earlier financial panics failed.

The panic accentuated an already declining stock market, which bottomed out on November 15 with a decline of 39 percent as people shifted out of stocks and into the safety of cash.

Although the New York banking community pledged to support the New York banks, depositors of the Knickerbocker Trust Company tried to withdraw their deposits. Another bank, not wanting to be stuck with worthless checks, refused to process checks from the Knickerbocker bank. After $8 million was paid out to depositors, and the bank closed it doors. New Yorkers lined up outside their banks, fearing for their deposits.

Financier J.P. Morgan decided to take action to restore confidence and end the panic. He called a committee of bankers, which first decided that the Knickerbocker's finances were in such bad shape that it could not be helped. It would be allowed to fail while more sound banks were helped. The panic spread as bankers around the country worried that New York banks would refuse them loans.

Morgan and his bankers could not contain the crisis. After making a direct plea to President Theodore Roosevelt, Morgan secured the aid of the U.S. government, which agreed to deposit $25 million in New York banks. Industrialist John D. Rockefeller also contributed $10 million in an effort to boost depositor confidence. Morgan was able to get New York bankers to put another $25 million into ailing banks.

Over the next several weeks, the situation slowly improved. By mid-October, the panic had subsided, but the downturn in the business cycle lasted until June 1908. Banks around the country, afraid of being cut off by larger banks, continued to draw down their reserves at larger banks and hoarded what cash they had. They stopped extending credit to customers and stopped making payments in cash. Thousands of firms that depended on short-term loans went bankrupt, and tens of thousands thousands lost their jobs. Much trade in the country ground to a halt.

Think Critically The Federal Deposit Insurance Corporation (FDIC), an agency of the federal government, now insures most bank deposits up to a maximum of $250,000. This means that if a bank fails and is unable to repay its depositors, the FDIC will repay them instead. There essentially is no risk of losing money on deposits up to $250,000 in an FDIC insured bank account. Consider how the panic of 1907 might have turned out differently if the FDIC had existed at that time. Explain how the FDIC reduces the chance of a bank panic in today's economy.

Chapter 13 Summary

ASK THE EXPERT

www.cengage.com/school/contecon

GDP increased between 1973 and 1974, but some say we had a recession. How could this be?

13.1 Estimating GDP

A. Gross domestic product (GDP) measures the market value of all final goods and services produced in a country in a year. GDP can be used to track an economy's performance over time or to compare different economies at a point in time.

B. To measure GDP accurately, it is necessary to avoid double counting. This can be done (1) by totaling the value of final goods and services produced or (2) by summing the value added at each stage of the production process. The expenditure approach to GDP counts all spending on final goods and services produced in the economy. The income approach totals the value of all income earned producing those goods and services.

13.2 Limitations of GDP Estimation

A. Several difficulties must be overcome to measure GDP accurately. Chief among these is the complex nature of production. A number of simplifications are made. GDP includes only products that are sold in legal markets. To calculate net domestic product, GDP is adjusted for depreciation. Finally, GDP ignores any changes in the amount of leisure and changes in the cost of pollution arising from production.

B. GDP must be adjusted for price changes. Without such an adjustment, it is possible for nominal GDP to grow even without an actual increase in the amounts of goods and services produced. The Consumer Price Index (CPI) measures the change in prices charged for a market basket of goods and services purchased by the typical family. The GDP price index is found by dividing nominal GDP by real GDP and multiplying by 100.

13.3 Business Cycles

A. Business cycles involve periods of expansion and periods of recession. During expansions real GDP grows. Recessions occur when real GDP declines for at least two successive quarters, or at least six months.

B. Various factors within the economy change during the business cycle. Factors that change before the overall economy changes are leading indicators. Those that change at the same time as the overall economy are coincident indicators. Those that change after the overall economy are lagging indicators.

13.4 Aggregate Demand and Aggregate Supply

A. The total production of all goods and services in an economy is called aggregate output. The total demand for all goods and services in an economy is called aggregate demand.

B. The aggregate demand curve slopes downward, indicating that the quantity of aggregate output demanded increases as the price level falls. The aggregate supply curve slopes upward, indicating that the quantity of aggregate output supplied increases as the price level increases. The economy's price level is determined by the interaction of the aggregate demand and aggregate supply curves.

C. Since 1929, real GDP in the United States has increased nearly fourteenfold. The best measure of a nation's standard of living is its real GDP per capita. This also has grown sharply thanks to a more educated workforce, more capital, better technology, and improvements in the rules of the game.

CHAPTER 13 ASSESSMENT

Review Economic Terms

Match the terms with the definitions. Some terms will not be used.

_____ 1. The market value of all final goods and services produced in the United States during a given period, usually a year

_____ 2. The structure of economic activity in a locality, a region, a country, a group of countries, or the world

_____ 3. Fluctuations reflecting the rise and fall of economic activity relative to the long-term growth trend of the economy

_____ 4. Measures that usually predict recessions or expansions in the economy

_____ 5. Household purchases of final goods and services except for new residences, which count as investment

_____ 6. Total spending on all final goods and services produced in the economy during the year

_____ 7. The purchase of new plants, new equipment, new buildings, new residences, and net additions to inventories

_____ 8. The value of capital stock that is used up or becomes obsolete in producing GDP

_____ 9. GDP based on prices at the time of the transaction; current-dollar GDP

_____ 10. The economy's aggregate output measured in dollars of constant purchasing power; GDP measured in terms of the goods and services produced

_____ 11. A composite measure reflecting the prices of all goods and services in the economy relative to prices in a base year

_____ 12. A measure of inflation based on the cost of a fixed market basket of goods and services purchased by a typical family

_____ 13. A decline in the nation's total production lasting at least two consecutive quarters, or at least six months

_____ 14. The phase of economic activity during which the economy's total output increases

a. aggregate demand
b. aggregate demand curve
c. aggregate expenditure
d. aggregate income
e. aggregate output
f. aggregate supply curve
g. business cycle
h. consumer price index (CPI)
i. consumption
j. depreciation
k. economy
l. expansion
m. government purchases
n. gross domestic product (GDP)
o. investment
p. leading economic indicators
q. net exports
r. nominal GDP
s. price level
t. real GDP
u. recession

Review Economic Concepts

15. Which of the following would be included in GDP?
    a. the entire value of a used car your family purchased
    b. the amount you received in your paycheck
    c. the weekly allowance your parents give you
    d. the $50 you received from your aunt for your birthday

16. The ________?________ is a method of measuring GDP that adds up all spending on final goods and services produced in the economy.

17. **True or False** If you bake a cake from a cake mix and sell it for $8, you have added $8 to GDP.

18. ________?________ GDP has not been adjusted for changes in price.

19. **True or False** The value of capital depreciation is not considered when GDP is calculated.

20. ________?________ usually predict what is likely to happen to the economy in the near future.

21. If last year's consumer price index was 185.0, and this year's is 192.4 how much inflation has there been in the past year?
   a. 7.4%
   b. 3.8%
   c. 5.0%
   d. 4.0%

22. **True or False** A business cycle will affect all states, people, and businesses equally.

23. The business cycle consists of two phases that are called
   a. expansions and recessions.
   b. recessions and contractions.
   c. inflation and recessions.
   d. expansions and inflation.

24. Aggregate demand and aggregate supply interact to determine
   a. business profits.
   b. government tax receipts.
   c. investment.
   d. real GDP and the price level.

Apply Economic Concepts

25. **Measuring GDP** Identify which of the following activities would be included in the measurement of GDP. For those that would be included, indicate whether they would be used in the income approach or expenditure approach.

Activity	Included in GDP?	Expenditure Approach	Income Approach
Buying a used bicycle	___	___	___
Paying for a movie ticket	___	___	___
Being paid to sell magazines	___	___	___
Buying a new coat	___	___	___
Mending your own shirt	___	___	___
Earning interest on your savings	___	___	___
Earning profit from a business	___	___	___
Paying a toll to use a bridge	___	___	___

26. **Calculate Real GDP** Suppose that the nominal GDP in Germany was 560 billion euros in 2011 but grew to 588 billion euros in 2012. In these years the German CPI increased from 210.0 to 214.2. Use these data to calculate the percent change in real German GDP between 2011 and 2012.

27. **Mathematics** In 2010, real GDP in 2005 dollars was $13,249 billion. Suppose that the real GDP for the United States increased at the following rates in the five years following 2010. Calculate the real value of GDP for each of these years. What would this mean for aggregate demand and supply in our economy?

Year	Rate of Increase in Real GDP	Real GDP in Billions
2011	1.4%	_____
2012	2.6%	_____
2013	3.3%	_____
2014	4.1%	_____
2015	2.5%	_____

28. **21st Century Skills: Information Literacy** You read that the government has reported that the average price of a new home has fallen by 4.0 percent in each of the past three years. You purchased your home three years ago for $240,000. If your home's value has fallen at the same rate as the national average, how much could you sell it for today? Why do people who are involved in making large financial transactions often pay close attention to economic data reported by the government?

29. **Measuring GDP** Explain why each of the following events would, or would not, be included in this year's GDP.
    a. You buy your neighbor's used car for $6,000
    b. A mechanic at a local garage charges you $400 to repair your car's brakes.
    c. You purchase 15 gallons of gasoline for your car.
    d. A car dealership buys tires that it will sell to consumers.

Digging Deeper
with Economics e-Collection

The size of an economy is measured by gross domestic product (GDP). Access the Gale Economics e-Collection through the URL below to find recent information about GDP forecasts and trends in the United States. Conduct a Basic Search by typing "gross domestic product" under the Keyword tab. Read several articles and record any statistics you find about U.S. GDP. Keep a record of the source citation of the articles that contain these statistics. Be prepared to share your results in class.

www.cengage.com/school/contecon

CONSIDER...

- Why is the standard of living so much higher in some countries than in others?
- How can a nation boost its standard of living?
- Why is the economy's long-term growth rate more important than short-term fluctuations in economic activity?
- What is labor productivity, and why has it grown faster in recent years?
- Are firms or are governments better positioned to identify the growth industries of the future?

CHAPTER 14

Economic Growth

Point your browser

www.cengage.com/school/contecon

Dennis Owusu-Ansah/Shutterstock.com; Background image: Lukiyanova Natalia/frenta/Shutterstock.com

14.1 THE PPF, ECONOMIC GROWTH, AND PRODUCTIVITY

Learning Objectives

LO1 Use the production possibilities frontier to analyze economic growth.

LO2 Define labor productivity, and discuss what can increase it.

Key Terms

standard of living 431
productivity 432
labor productivity 432
human capital 432
physical capital 432
capital deepening 433
rules of the game 433

In Your World

Throughout history, economic growth has been the primary way of reducing poverty and raising living standards. Over the past century, there has been an incredible increase in the U.S. standard of living as measured by the goods and services available per person. You may not realize it, but you are now living in the most innovative era in human history. Each day brings faster computers, smarter phones, higher definition video, more sophisticated social networks, better medical treatments, and other breakthroughs that can improve your living standard.

THE PPF AND ECONOMIC GROWTH

LO1
Use the production possibilities frontier to analyze economic growth.

The easiest way to introduce economic growth is to begin with the production possibilities frontier, or PPF. The *production possibilities frontier*, introduced in Chapter 2, shows alternative combinations of goods the economy can produce if available resources are used efficiently. Here are the assumptions used to develop the frontiers shown in Figure 14.1. During the period under consideration, usually a year, the quantity of resources in the economy and the level of technology are assumed to remain unchanged. The rules of the game that enable production and exchange also are assumed fixed. These "rules" are discussed at the end of this section.

In Figure 14.1, production is sorted into two broad categories—consumer goods and capital goods. Capital goods are used to produce other goods. For example, the economy can make both pizzas and pizza ovens. Pizzas are consumer goods, and pizza ovens are capital goods.

The production possibilities frontier *CI* in each panel of Figure 14.1 shows the possible combinations of consumer goods and capital goods that can be produced in a given year. Point *C* depicts the quantity of consumer goods produced if all the economy's resources are employed efficiently to produce them. Point *I* depicts the same for capital goods. Points inside the frontier are inefficient. Points outside the frontier are unattainable, given the resources, technology, and rules of the game. The production possibilities frontier is bowed out because resources are not perfectly adaptable to the production of both goods. Some resources are specialized, or better suited for a particular good. For example, some heavy machinery is better suited to produce capital goods than consumer goods.

FIGURE 14.1 Economic Growth Shown by Outward Shifts of the PPF

An economy that produces more capital goods will grow more, as shown by a shifting outward of the production possibilities frontier. More capital goods and fewer consumer goods are produced at point *B* in panel (B) than at point *A* in panel (A), so the PPF shifts outward more in panel (b).

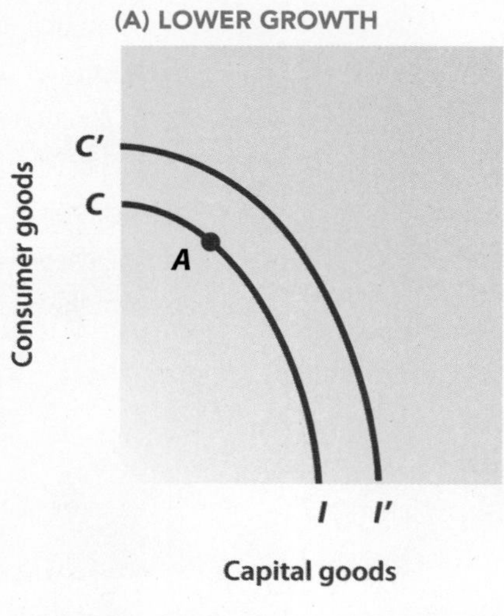

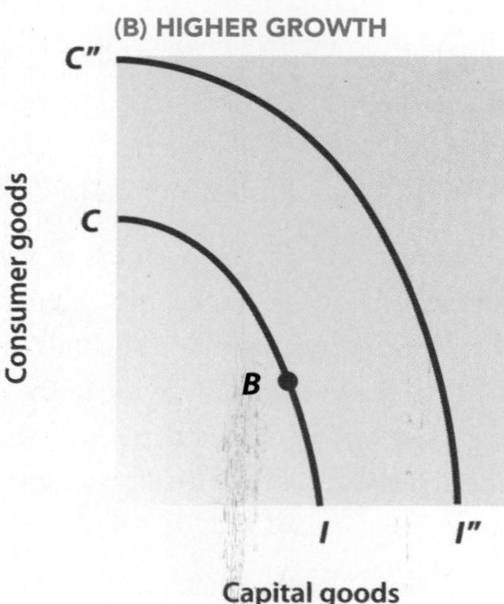

Economic Growth and the PPF

An outward shift of the production possibilities frontier reflects economic growth. Economic growth means the economy can produce more. This is shown in each panel of Figure 14.1. What can generate this growth? Any increase in the availability of resources, such as a growth in the labor supply or in the capital stock, shifts the frontier outward. Labor can increase because of an increase in either the quantity or the quality of labor. For example, growth in the population can increase the number of workers. An increase in education levels can increase the quality of workers. The greater the quantity or quality of workers, the more the economy can grow, as shown by an outward shift of the PPF.

The capital stock grows if the economy produces more capital goods this year. Any improvement in technology also expands the frontier by making more productive use of existing resources. Technological change often improves the quality of capital goods.

Finally, any improvements in the rules of the game that encourage production and exchange will promote growth and expand the frontier. These include tax laws, property rights, patent laws, the legal system, and customs of the market. For example, the economy can grow as a result of a patent law revision that encourages more inventions or legal reforms that lower transaction costs. Extending the years of patent protection could encourage drug companies to invest more in developing new drugs.

In summary, the economy grows because of (1) a greater availability of resources, (2) an improvement in the quality of resources, (3) technological breakthroughs that make more productive use of resources, or (4) improvements in the rules of the game that boost production incentives.

Capital and Growth

The amount of capital produced this year affects the location of the PPF next year. For example, in panel (A) of Figure 14.1, the economy has chosen point *A* from possible points along *CI*. The capital produced this year shifts the PPF next year out to *C'I'*. However, if more capital is produced this year, as reflected by point *B* in panel (B), the economy will grow more. The PPF will shift farther outward next year, to *C"I"*.

An economy that produces more capital this year is said to invest more in capital. As you can see, to invest more in capital goods, people must give up some consumer goods. Thus, the opportunity cost of producing more capital goods this year is producing fewer consumer goods. More generally, to invest in capital, people in the economy must save more now—that is, they must give up some current consumption. Economies that save more can invest and grow more.

How can the PPF be used to show economic growth? **CHECKPOINT**

PRODUCTIVITY

LO2
Define labor productivity, and discuss what can increase it.

Productivity measures how much output is produced from given inputs. In simplest terms, the greater the productivity, the more goods and services can be produced from a given amount of resources. Economies that use resources more productively create a higher standard of living. This means that more goods and services are produced per person. The **standard of living** is an economy's level of prosperity as measured by the value of goods and services produced, on average, per person. The standard of living measures the average material well-being of people in the economy.

standard of living An economy's level of prosperity; best measured by the value of goods and services produced, on average, per person

ESSENTIAL QUESTION

Standard CEE 15: Economic Growth
Investment in factories, machinery, new technology, and in the health, education, and training of people stimulates economic growth and can raise future standards of living.

Rainer Plendl/Shutterstock.com

track5/ iStockphoto.com

What effect does investment in new technology and in employee training have on economic growth and living standards?

NET Bookmark

The Bureau of Labor Statistics (BLS) has a web page on Productivity and Costs. Access the website shown below and click on the link to Chapter 14. Find the latest news release on productivity and costs. Read the information about the manufacturing sector of the U.S. economy. Then summarize the trends in one or two sentences.

www.cengage.com/school/contecon

Labor Productivity

Productivity compares total output to a specific measure of input. It usually reflects an average, expressing total output divided by the amount of a resource employed, such as bushels of grain per acre of farmland. **Labor productivity** is the output per unit of labor. It measures total output divided by hours of labor employed to produce that output.

Economists can focus on the productivity of any resource, such as labor, capital, or land. When agriculture accounted for the bulk of output in the economy, land productivity, such as bushels of grain per acre, shaped the standard of living. Where soil was rocky and barren, people were less well-off than where soil was fertile and fruitful. Even today, in many countries around the world, land productivity determines the standard of living.

Industrialization and trade have freed many economies from dependence on land fertility. Today, some of the world's most productive economies have little land or have land of poor fertility. For example, Japan has only about 2 percent as much land per capita as Russia, but Japan's GDP per capita is more than double that of Russia.

Human and Physical Capital

Labor is the resource most commonly used to measure productivity. Why labor? First, labor accounts for a large share of the cost of production—about 75 percent on average. Second, labor is more easily measured than other inputs, whether measured in hours per week or full-time workers per year. Measures of hours worked and total employment are more readily available and more reliable than measures of other resources.

The resource most responsible for increasing labor productivity is capital. The two broad categories are human capital and physical capital. **Human capital** is the accumulated knowledge, skill, and experience of the labor force. As individual workers acquire more human capital, their productivity and incomes grow. That's why surgeons earn more than barbers, and accountants earn more than file clerks. You are reading this book right now to improve your human capital.

Physical capital, or *capital goods*, includes the machines, buildings, roads, airports, communications networks, and other manufactured creations used to produce goods and services. Think about the difference between digging a ditch with your bare hands and digging it with a shovel. Now compare that shovel to excavating equipment, such as a backhoe. More physical capital obviously makes a digger more productive.

As an economy accumulates more human and physical capital per worker, labor productivity increases and the standard of living grows. The most productive

productivity Compares total output to a specific measure of input; usually reflects an average, such as bushels of grain per acre of farmland

labor productivity Output per unit of labor; measured as total output divided by the hours of labor employed to produce that output

human capital The accumulated knowledge, skill, and experience of the labor force

physical capital The machines, buildings, roads, airports, communications networks, and other manufactured creations used to produce goods and services; also called capital goods

combination of all is abundant human capital combined with the best physical capital. For example, one certified public accountant with a fast computer and sophisticated software can sort out a company's finances more quickly and more accurately than could a hundred high-school-educated file clerks with pencils and paper.

Capital Deepening

Two kinds of changes in capital can improve worker productivity:

1. An increase in the *quantity* of capital per worker, and
2. An improvement in the *quality* of capital per worker, as reflected by technological change.

More capital per worker and better capital per worker generally result in more output per worker.

An increase in the quantity and quality of capital per worker is called **capital deepening**. This is one source of rising labor productivity. *Capital deepening contributes to labor productivity and to economic growth.* Over time, more output per worker translates into more output per person, meaning a higher standard of living.

Changes in the *quantities* of labor and capital account for less than half of economic growth. Most growth comes from improvements in the quality of resources. As technological breakthroughs lead to new and better capital, total output increases. Thus, *capital serves as the primary engine of economic growth.*

capital deepening
An increase in the quantity and quality of capital per worker; one source of rising labor productivity

rules of the game
The formal and informal institutions that provide production incentives and promote economic activity, such as laws, customs, and conventions of the market

Rules of the Game

The most complex ingredients of productivity and growth are the **rules of the game**. These include the formal and informal institutions that provide production incentives and promote economic activity. Rules of the game include the laws, customs, and conventions that encourage people to undertake productive activity. A stable political environment and a system of well-defined property rights are important. Little investment in human or physical capital will occur if people believe the fruits of their investment might be seized by government, stolen by thieves, destroyed by civil unrest, or blown up by terrorists.

Improvements in the rules of the game can affect the incentives that reward successful innovation and investment. Better incentives can boost economic growth and improve the standard of living. For example, a more stable political climate could promote investment in the economy. Conversely, destabilizing events such as civil wars and terrorist attacks can discourage investment and harm productivity and economic growth.

Stockbyte/Getty Images

What "rule" do you think this sign represents? How would it affect productivity in the economy?

CHECKPOINT

What is labor productivity, and what can increase it?

14.1 ASSESSMENT

Think Critically

1. Why does the U.S. production possibilities frontier usually shift outward each year? What does this have to do with the graduation of many students from high school or college?
2. Why is it more difficult for poorer nations to invest in capital goods than it is for wealthier nations?
3. How is capital deepening demonstrated when more students purchase computers to help with their studies?
4. How could a cut in payroll taxes make businesses more productive?

Graphing Exercise

5. Use the data in the table to construct a bar graph of investment in physical capital each year since 2004. Explain how changes in the level of investment in physical capital are likely to affect productivity in the economy.

Year	Gross Private Domestic Investment (in billions of 2005 dollars)
2004	$2,058
2005	$2,172
2006	$2,230
2007	$2,146
2008	$1,989
2009	$1,434
2010	$1,715

Source: *Statistical Abstract of the United States, 2011*, p. 512; and *Survey of Current Business*, Vol. 91 (November 2011), Table 1.1.6.

Make Academic Connections

6. **Management** You are the president of a small corporation. Your firm was profitable last year and could afford to increase dividends. You, however, think those funds should be used to purchase a new computer system to improve your firm's efficiency. Write a letter to your firm's stockholders, explaining the benefits of your proposed use of the firm's profit.
7. **Research** Use newspapers or Internet sources to find information about college programs you might enroll in to improve the quality of your human capital. Explain how completing a college degree could increase your productivity.

TeamWork

Working in groups, identify a professional sports team that members of your group follow. Make two lists of types of human and physical capital the sports team could add that might increase its productivity (number of games it wins next year). If your team had an additional $5 million to spend on acquiring either human or physical capital, how would it spend these funds? Compare your group's work with that of other groups.

MOVERS AND SHAKERS

Larry Page and Sergey Brin

Google founders

KIMBERLYWHITE/Reuters/Landov

Larry Page and Sergey Brin were both Stanford University PhD candidates when they were assigned to work on a team conducting a data-mining experiment. Although they argued a lot, they managed to create an algorithm that would search hypertext for key words.

Their first search engine, called PageRank, quickly became popular with other students. "Pretty soon, we had 10,000 searches a day," Page said, "And we figured, maybe this is really real." The duo spent their own money to buy more computers to handle the demand for searches. Sergey said, "We spent about $15,000 on a terabyte [one million megabytes] of disks. We spread that across three credit cards." Brin and Page tried to license their PageRank technology and sell it to other companies in order to pay off their credit card debt. No one was interested. Another Stanford graduate, David Filo, founder of Yahoo.com, told them they should start their own company. In 1999, after raising money from friends and family, they set up their first office in Mountain View, California. Brin and Page named their new company "Google" after the mathematical term *googol*, which means the number one followed by 100 zeros. By June of 2000, they had indexed more than one billion Internet websites.

Google's corporate culture is legendary. Workers enjoy free Ben and Jerry's ice cream, on-site massages, Ping-Pong, yoga classes, and a staff doctor. Employees are welcome to bring their dogs to work, and the company cafeteria is famous for healthy and varied food choices. Brin said, "Since we started the company, we've grown 20 percent per month. Our employees can do whatever they want." Google's company motto is "don't be evil." Brin said, "We have tried to define precisely what it means to be a force for good—always do the right, ethical thing. Ultimately, "Don't be evil" seems the easiest way to summarize it." While some might argue Google's commitment to that philosophy due to its casual attitude towards privacy issues, no one can argue the company's success.

When Google went public and began trading on the stock market, Brin and Page became instant billionaires. But Google isn't just about profits. The company also offers grants that give advertising to nonprofits. Their free email accounts provide a means of communication to people around the world. "A schoolchild in Cambodia can have a Gmail account," Brin said.

Google has also created a foundation that utilizes its engineering abilities. Some of their projects include:

- **Google Crisis Response** A service that makes important information about natural disasters and humanitarian crisis immediately available to searchers.
- **Google Earth Engine** An online environment monitoring program that allows "high-performance tools to analyze and interpret this information that can then be visualized on a map, ranging from rainforest changes in the Amazon to water resources in the Congo."
- **Google Flu Trends** Provides up-to-date estimates of flu trends around the world.
- **RE<C** A Google project committed to renewable energy, "Our over-arching vision is to one day transform the global economy from one running on fossil fuels to one largely based on clean energy. Our Clean Energy 2030 plan offers a potential path to do just that."
- **All for Good** A community service-based search engine that matches volunteers with volunteer opportunities.

Brin and Page are successful businessmen. They've proven that it is possible to be a part of a large, prosperous company that provides a useful service and at the same time do good in the world.

Think Critically **Page and Brin go to great lengths to make their headquarters an attractive place to work. How does the company benefit from these employee perks? Do you see any disadvantages to offering so many perks? If so, what are they?**

Sources: http://www.notablebiographies.com/news/Ow-Sh/Page-Larry-and-Brin-Sergey.html#ixzz1SUwSJZT2; http://www.google-watch.org/playboy.html; and http://www.google.org/about.html

14.2 LIVING STANDARDS AND LABOR PRODUCTIVITY GROWTH

Key Terms

Learning Objectives

LO1 Explain the large differences among countries in standard of living.

LO2 Evaluate U.S. labor productivity growth, and explain output per capita.

In Your World

The single most important determinant of a nation's standard of living over the long run is the productivity of its resources. A nation prospers by getting more from its resources. Even a relatively small growth in productivity, if continued for years, can have a huge effect on living standards—that is, on availability of goods and services for you and others in the economy. Growing productivity is critical to a rising standard of living. It has kept the United States ahead of every other major economy.

STANDARD OF LIVING

LO1 Explain the large differences among countries in standard of living.

Standards of living differ widely among countries. For example, per capita output in the United States is about 150 times that of the world's poorest countries. With only one-twentieth of the world's population, the United States produces more than the nations making up two-thirds of the world's population combined. You might say that people in a poor country are poor because the country has low labor productivity.

Industrial and Developing Economies

The world's economies can be sorted into two broad groups. **Industrial market countries**, or *developed countries*, make up about 16 percent of the world's population. They include the advanced market economies of Western Europe, North America, Australia, New Zealand, and Japan. Industrial market countries were the first to experience long-term economic growth during the nineteenth century. Today they have the world's highest standard of living, based on abundant human and physical capital.

The rest of the world—the remaining 84 percent of the population—consists of **developing countries**, which have a lower standard of living because they have less human and physical capital. Nearly one-half of the workers in many developing countries are in agriculture. Farming methods in developing countries often are labor intensive because capital is scarce. Labor productivity there is low, and most people barely subsist. In the United States, only about 2 percent of all workers are in agriculture. However, U.S. farmers are so productive that

industrial market countries The advanced market economies of Western Europe, North America, Australia, New Zealand, and Japan; also called developed countries

developing countries Countries with a lower standard of living because they have relatively less human and physical capital

they grow enough to feed the nation and export to other countries. Because developing countries have less human and physical capital, their 84 percent of the world's population produce only 28 percent of the world's output. Put another way, the 16 percent of the world's population in industrial market economies produce 72 percent of the world's output.

Investigate Your Local Economy

Research the average years of education among adults in your state for different years. Then, determine the gross state product per capita for your state for those same years. Is there a correlation? If so, describe it.

Education and Economic Development

An important source of productivity is the quality of labor—the skill, experience, and education of workers. If knowledge is lacking, other resources may not be used efficiently. For example, a country may have fertile land, but farmers may lack knowledge of modern irrigation and fertilization techniques.

How exactly does education contribute to the process of economic development? Education makes workers more aware of the latest production techniques and more receptive to new ideas and methods. Countries with the most advanced educational systems also were the first nations in the world to achieve a high level of economic development.

One distinguishing feature between industrial economies and developing economies is the literacy of the population. *Literacy* is the ability to read and write. Among countries that make up the poorest countries, about one-third of adults are illiterate. In contrast, only 2 percent of adults in industrial market economies are illiterate.

Figure 14.2 shows the percent of those ages 25 to 64 with at least a two-year or four-year college degree for the seven leading industrial market countries. Together

Figure 14.2 Percent of Adults with at Least a Two-Year or Four-Year College Degree: 1998 and 2008

The share of the U.S. population ages 25 to 64, with at least one degree beyond high school, increased from 35 percent in 1998 to 41 percent in 2008. The United States slipped from second to third among major industrial market economies.

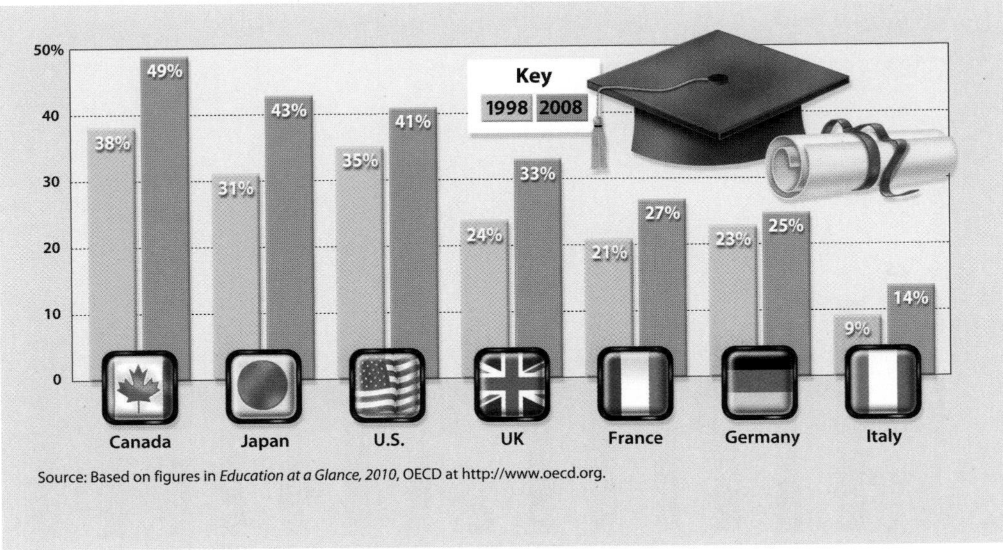

Source: Based on figures in *Education at a Glance, 2010*, OECD at http://www.oecd.org.

these seven economies are called the **Group of Seven** (or **G-7**). (Sometimes Russia is added to form the G-8, but Russia is not yet an industrial market economy and has a per-capita income less than one-half that of any G-7 country). For example, 35 percent of Americans ages 25 to 64 had a college degree in 1998. This ranked the United States second that year, behind Canada, where 38 percent had college degrees. By 2008, 41 percent of Americans ages 25 to 64 had a college degree. The United States slipped to third, behind Canada, at 49 percent, and Japan, at 43 percent.

CHECKPOINT **Why is there such a difference among countries in standards of living?**

U.S. LABOR PRODUCTIVITY AND OUTPUT PER CAPITA

LO2 Evaluate U.S. labor productivity growth, and explain output per capita.

Labor productivity is measured by real output per work hour. The higher the level of labor productivity is, the more output per labor hour, and the higher the standard of living in the economy. Thus, differences across economies in labor productivity determine differences in living standards. The key to a rising standard of living is the growth in labor productivity.

Group of Seven (G-7) The seven leading industrial market economies, including the United States, United Kingdom, France, Germany, Italy, Japan, and Canada

Record Over the Long Run

Figure 14.3 offers a long-run perspective, showing U.S. productivity growth stretching back to the nineteenth century. Annual productivity growth is averaged

FIGURE 14.3 Long-Term Trend in U.S. Labor Productivity Growth: Annual Averages by Decade

For the entire period since 1870, productivity growth has averaged 2.2 percent per year. (The 2000s decade includes 2000 through 2010.)

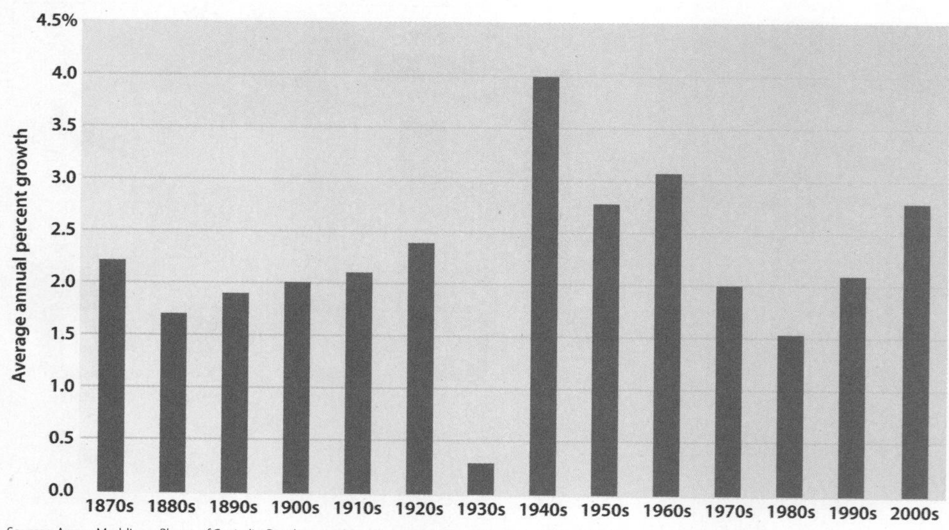

Sources: Angus Maddison, *Phases of Capitalist Development* (New York: Oxford University Press, 1982) and U.S. Bureau of Labor Statistics.

by decade. Note the slowdown during the 1930s because of the Great Depression and the rebound during the 1940s because of World War II. Productivity growth slowed again during the 1970s and 1980s but recovered in the 1990s and 2000s.

For the entire period since 1870, productivity growth averaged 2.2 percent per year. This may not seem like much, but growth has a powerful cumulative effect. Real output per work hour has grown a total of 2,050 percent since 1870. To put this in perspective, if a carpenter in 1870 could build one house in a year, today's carpenter could build 21.5 of those same houses in a year.

Small differences in productivity growth can amount to huge differences in the economy's ability to produce and, therefore, in the standard of living. For example, if productivity growth had averaged only 1.2 percent per year instead of 2.2 percent, output per work hour since 1870 would have increased by only 438 percent, not 2,050 percent. On the other hand, if productivity growth had averaged 3.2 percent per year, output per work hour since 1870 would have jumped 8,400 percent! The wheels of progress seem to turn slowly, but the cumulative effect of compound growth is powerful. Compounding magnifies what seem like small differences in the annual growth rate.

Slowdown and Rebound in Productivity Growth

You can see in Figure 14.3 that productivity growth declined during the 1970s and 1980s and recovered since 1990. To focus on productivity trends since World War II, Figure 14.4 offers the average annual growth for four distinct periods. Labor productivity growth declined from an average of 2.9 percent per year between 1948 and 1973 to only 1.0 percent between 1974 and 1982. The annual rate of growth in

Figure 14.4 U.S. Labor Productivity Growth

Growth in labor productivity in the United States slowed during 1974 to 1982 and then rebounded. Most recently, average productivity growth has nearly reached where it had been during the 1948–1973 period.

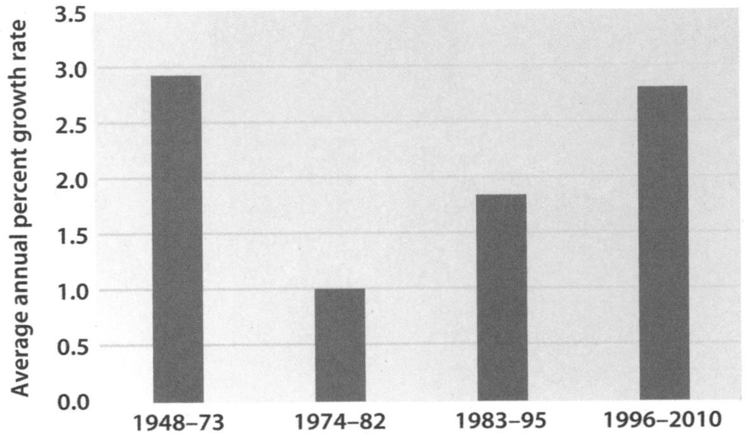

Source: Averages based on annual estimates from the U.S. Bureau of Labor Statistics. For the latest data, go to http://www.bls.gov/lpc/home.htm.

labor productivity from 1974 to 1982 averaged only about one-third the rate during the quarter-century following World War II. The annual rate of growth in labor productivity during 1974 to 1982 was below the annual average for any decade during the previous 140 years, except for the 1930s.

Why the slowdown? First, the price of oil quadrupled from 1973 to 1974 as a result of OPEC actions. Spikes in energy prices fueled inflation during the period. This contributed to three recessions, which slowed productivity growth. Second, in the early 1970s, several laws were passed to protect the environment and improve the quality and safety of the workplace. These measures ultimately led to cleaner air, purer water, and safer working conditions. However, they also required more costly production methods. Productivity growth slowed down as these costlier methods were introduced. Third, high and variable inflation during the period introduced more business uncertainty. Firms had to spend more time coping with inflation, and they were reluctant to invest in productivity-boosting capital. This slowed labor productivity growth.

Fortunately, annual productivity growth rebounded off the lows of 1974 to 1982, growing 1.8 percent from 1983 to 1995 and 2.8 percent from 1996 to 2010. This recent rate was just shy of the 2.9 percent average from 1948 to 1973. Why the rebound? The most dramatic technological development in recent years has been the information revolution powered by computers and the Internet. New technology helps workers produce more. Computers also increase the flexibility of machines, which can be reprogrammed for different tasks.

Higher productivity growth, when compounded over years, can easily make up for output lost during recessions. For example, if, over the next 10 years, U.S. labor productivity grows an average of 2.8 percent per year (the average from 1996

What effect does an investment in new technology have on productivity?

to 2010) instead of 1.8 percent (the average from 1983 to 1995), in the tenth year, real GDP will be $1.6 trillion higher. This is three times the output lost during the recession of 2008–2009, the worst one since the Great Depression. *This cumulative power of productivity growth is why economists are more concerned about long-term growth in productivity.* At the same time, concern about long-term growth should not ignore the fact that job losses from recessions can be devastating for those affected.

Output Per Capita

So far, the focus has been on rising labor productivity as an engine of economic growth—that is, growth achieved by getting more output from each hour worked. Even if labor productivity remained unchanged, real GDP would grow if the quantity of labor increased. Total output can grow as a result of greater labor productivity, more labor, or both.

The best measure of an economy's standard of living is output per person, or per capita. *Output per capita*, or real GDP divided by the population, indicates how much an economy produces on average per resident. Labor productivity in the U.S. economy in 2011 was about $88,000 per worker

FIGURE 14.5 U.S. Real GDP per Capita

Despite the seven recessions in the past half century, U.S. real GDP per capita has nearly tripled. Periods of recession are indicated by the pink-shaded columns.

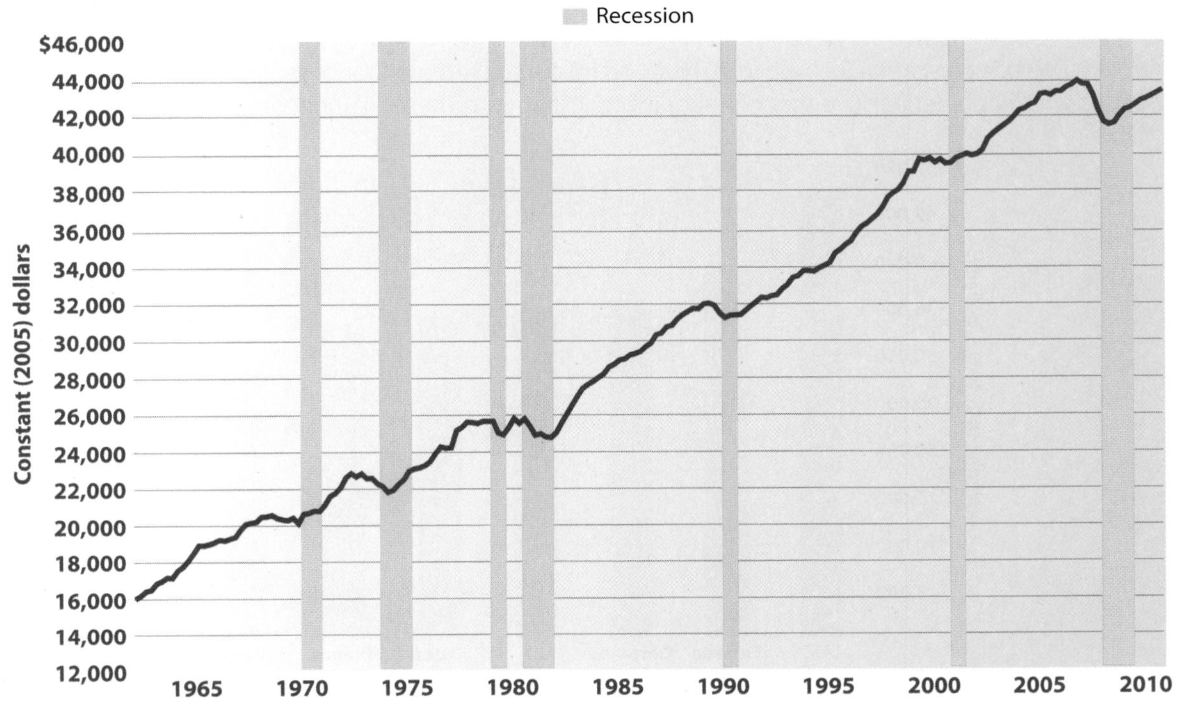

Source: U.S. Department of Commerce. *Survey of Current Business*, 91 (May 2011), p. D-55.

(in 2005 dollars). In the United States, about one of every two people in the economy is a worker. Therefore, *output per capita* equals output per worker divided by two. In this example, output per capita in 2011 would be about $88,000/2, or about $44,000.

Figure 14.5 presents real GDP per capita for the United States during the past half century. Notice the general upward trend, interrupted by seven recessions, indicated by the pink shading. Real GDP per capita nearly tripled (measured in 2005 dollars) from about $16,000 in 1963 to about $44,000 in 2011 for an average annual growth rate of 2.1 percent.

International Comparisons

How does U.S. output per capita compare with that of other major industrial economies? Figure 14.6 compares GDP per capita for the United States in 2010 with the six other leading industrial nations. The United States produced more output per capita than any other major economy, about 20 percent higher than Canada, which ranked second.

What has been the record of U.S. labor productivity growth, and why are even small differences in average growth important?

Figure 14.6 U.S. GDP per Capita in 2010 as Compared to Other Major Economies

The U.S. per-capita income in 2010 stood 20 percent above that of second-ranked Canada and 54 percent above that of Italy, ranked last among these major economies.

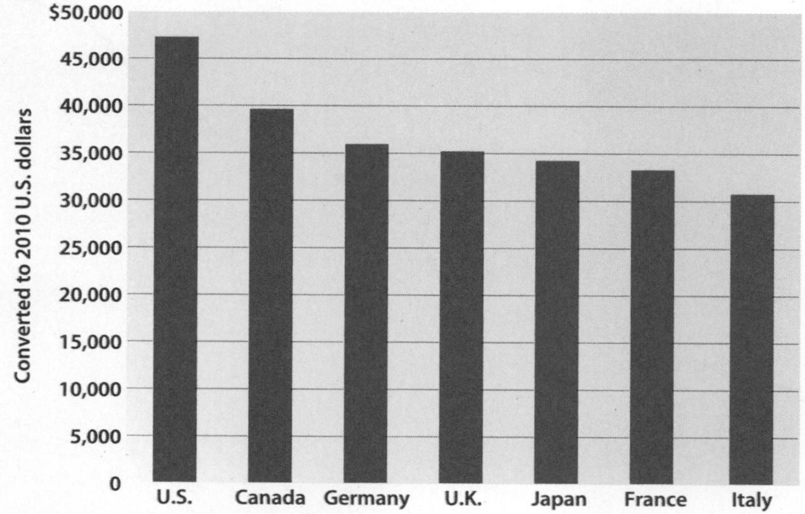

Source: Based on estimates by the Central Intelligence Agency, which are adjusted across countries using the purchasing power of the local currency as of July 1, 2010.

14.2 ASSESSMENT

Think Critically

1. Do you think your standard of living is better than that of your parents when they were your age? Explain your answer.
2. Why is providing education to all residents a difficult task for many developing countries?
3. What if, by earning a high-school diploma, you are able to produce 25 percent more each year than you could have produced without graduating from high school? How important would this extra production be to you, your family, and the economy in general if you work until you are 67 years old?
4. Why are economists now less concerned about short-term output fluctuations due to the business cycle and more concerned about long-term growth in productivity?
5. Measures of output per capita do not consider production that takes place within households. In the past 50 years, a much larger share of U.S. citizens have worked outside the home. How has this affected output per capita?

Graphing Exercise

6. An increase in the value of output per hour worked reflects growth in labor productivity. The data in the table show an index of real output per hour worked for 2003 through 2010. The year 2005 represents the base year value of 100 percent. Use these data to construct a line graph that shows the *change in output per hour* worked for these years. Explain what this information shows about the economy.

INDEX OF REAL OUTPUT PER HOUR WORKED, 2003–2010 (2005 = 100)

Year	Output	Year	Output
2003	95.6	2007	102.5
2004	98.4	2008	103.6
2005	100.0	2009	107.3
2006	100.9	2010	110.7

Source: *Economic Report of the President*, February 2011, Table B-49.

Make Academic Connections

7. **Science** Identify and describe a scientific advancement that has contributed to increases in labor productivity in this country or in other countries of the world.
8. **Literature** Identify and describe advances in communications technology that have changed the way books are written and published in recent years. If Shakespeare had lived today, how might his work have been different?

TeamWork

Working in small teams, prepare a list of five inventions of the past 50 years that have significantly increased labor productivity in the United States. Rank these inventions from the most to the least important. Take notes on how your group agreed to its ranking. Share your work with other teams.

21st Century Skills

INITIATIVE AND SELF-DIRECTION

Staying Competitive in a Changing Economy

The 21st century will see the introduction of many productivity-increasing technologies. Businesses that recognize and take advantage of these opportunities can improve their competitive positions. To remain competitive, firms need to continually assess when to replace their physical capital. To accomplish this, businesses may do the following.

- Regularly review and evaluate processes to find ways to increase efficiency and productivity.
- Monitor any new processes competitors use.
- Find more efficient means of production and develop new products that consumers will demand.
- Notice changes in the demand for their products. There is no advantage in being the most efficient producer of a product that no one wants.

Investing in Human Capital

In a similar way, businesses must be sure their workers know how to use the best technologies. When Intel designed a new microprocessor it called the Core i5, it had to train workers for the exacting standards this production required. This investment in human capital paid off when the new processor was acclaimed "the future of processor design" by reviewer Mat Bettinson in *PCR,* an online computer magazine.* Businesses that take the initiative to invest in new technologies can get the needed human capital by taking one or more of the following steps.

- Require those who developed the new physical capital to train workers to use it effectively.
- Hire professionals to create training programs.
- Hire workers who already possess the needed skills. This may be difficult or impossible when the physical capital is truly new and different.

Balance Physical and Human Capital

Some businesses have lost their competitive edge because they did not keep up with technological changes. Others have been hurt because they failed to employ workers with necessary skills. Although physical capital serves as the primary engine for economic growth, businesses need to achieve the right mix between the physical and human capital they employ.

Apply the Skill

You are the chief operating officer of a corporation that produces batteries for portable computers. Devices that use your firm's batteries hold their charge for up to 10 hours of use. A new type of battery can extend the useful time per charge to 20 hours. Production of these batteries requires an entirely new process including both new physical capital and specially trained workers. Explain steps your firm should take to help it decide whether to produce this new battery.

* Mat Bettinson, *PCR,* "Intel Core i5 2500 k 'Best CPU of 2011,'" 3/21/11, p. 1.

14.3 TECHNOLOGICAL CHANGE

Learning Objectives

LO1 Discuss the impact of research and development on standards of living.

LO2 Explain the relationship between technological change and employment levels.

LO3 Describe industrial policy and the arguments for and against its use.

Key Terms

basic research 445
applied research 445
industrial policy 448
cluster 448

In Your World

A major contributor to productivity growth and a rising standard of living is an improvement in the quality of human and physical capital. Improvement of human capital results from better education and more job training. Improvement of physical capital springs from better technology. Some other issues of technological change include the role of research and development and the relationship between technological change and employment. Could technological breakthroughs put you out of a job?

RESEARCH AND DEVELOPMENT

LO1
Discuss the impact of research and development on standards of living.

Improvements in technology arise from scientific discovery, which is the product of research. Economists distinguish between basic research and applied research.

Basic and Applied Research

The search for knowledge without regard to how that knowledge will be used is called **basic research**. Basic research is a first step toward technological advancement. In terms of economic growth, however, scientific discoveries are meaningless until they are implemented in production, which requires applied research.

Applied research seeks to answer particular questions or to apply scientific discoveries to the development of specific products. Technological breakthroughs may or may not have commercial possibilities. Thus, the payoff from basic research is less immediate than that from applied research.

basic research The search for knowledge without regard to how that knowledge will be used; a first step toward technological advancement

applied research Research that seeks answers to particular questions or applies scientific discoveries to develop specific products

R&D Comparisons Across Countries

Technological change is the fruit of research and development (R&D). Investment in R&D reflects the economy's efforts to improve productivity through technological discoveries. One way to track R&D spending is to measure it relative to gross domestic product, or GDP. Figure 14.7 shows R&D spending as a share of GDP for the United States and six other major economies in the 1980s, 1990s,

FIGURE 14.7 R&D Spending as a Percentage of GDP for Major Economies in the 1980s, 1990s, and 2008

The share of U.S. GDP spent on R&D has remained stable over the past three decades. In Japan, R&D spending has increased steadily.

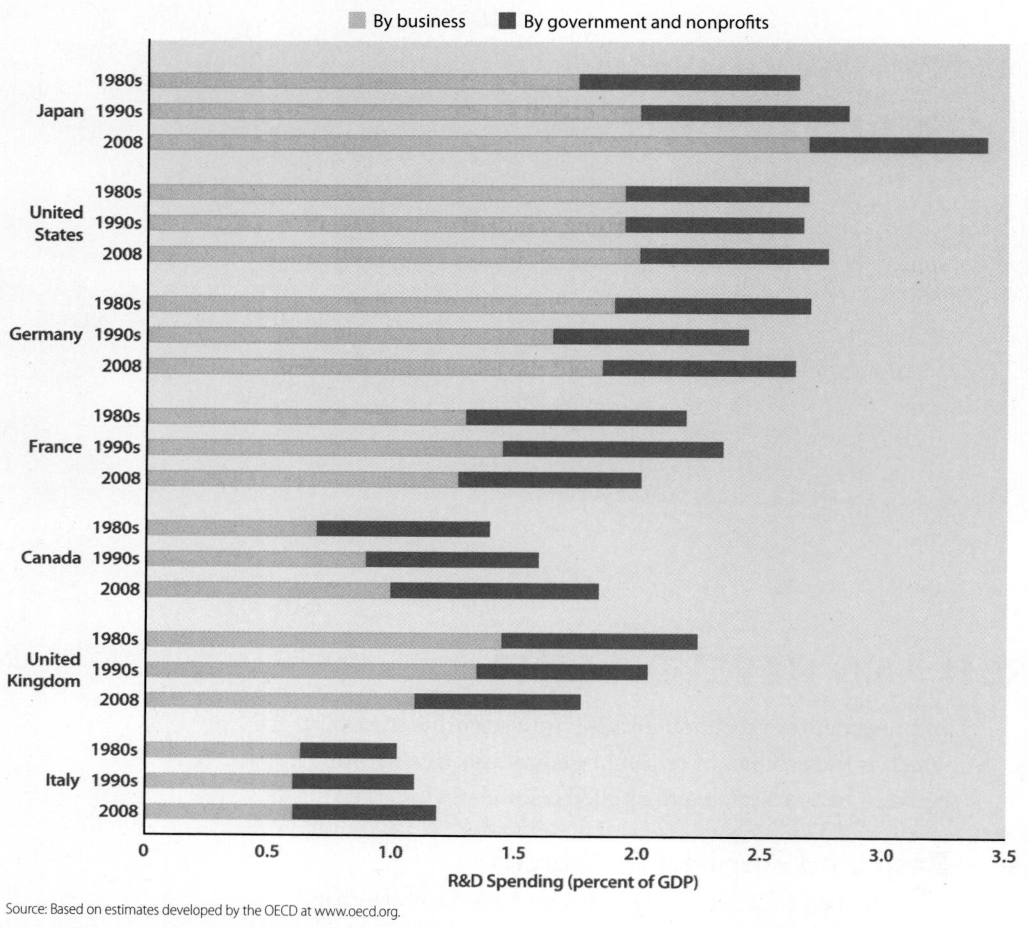

Source: Based on estimates developed by the OECD at www.oecd.org.

and 2008. Overall R&D spending in the United States averaged 2.7 percent of GDP in both the 1980s and the 1990s and was 2.8 percent in 2008. In 2008, R&D as a share of GDP ranked the United States second among these major economies, behind Japan, at 3.4 percent, but well ahead of last-place Italy, at only 1.2 percent.

Bar segments in the chart distinguish between R&D by businesses and R&D by governments and nonprofit institutions. Business R&D is more likely for applied research and innovations. R&D spending by governments and nonprofits, such as universities, is more likely for basic research. This basic research may generate valuable ideas that ultimately have specific applications. For example, the Internet came from U.S. government research into a national defense communications system.

In short, the United States devotes relatively more resources to R&D than most other advanced economies. This contributes to a higher standard of living for Americans.

CHECKPOINT

What is the impact of research and development on standards of living?

TECHNOLOGICAL CHANGE AND EMPLOYMENT LEVELS

LO2
Explain the relationship between technological change and employment levels.

Technological change affects the economy in a variety of ways. Most of these are beneficial. However, technological change usually reduces the number of workers needed to produce a given amount of output. Consequently, some critics charge that new technology throws people out of work.

Technological Change and Labor Productivity

Technological change may increase production and employment by making products more affordable. For example, the introduction of the assembly line made automobiles more affordable to the average household. This stimulated production and employment in the auto industry. The same happened with personal computers and with some other technological breakthroughs.

Technological change also could cost jobs in some industries. But even in industries where some workers are displaced by machines, those who keep their jobs are more productive, so they earn more. As long as human wants are unlimited, displaced workers usually can find jobs producing other goods and services demanded in a growing economy. Sometimes finding another job requires a worker to retrained for a new occupation.

Technological Change and Employment Levels

There is no evidence that unemployment today is any greater than it was in 1870. Since then, however, worker productivity per hour has increased by 2,050 percent. The length of the average workweek has been cut nearly in half. Although technological change may displace some workers in the short run, long-run benefits include higher real incomes on average and more leisure—in short, a higher standard of living.

If technological change increases unemployment, then unemployment should be higher in economies where the latest technology has been introduced, such as in industrial countries. In fact, unemployment levels there generally are much lower than in developing countries, where the latest technology seldom is found. What's more, those in developing countries who are lucky enough to find work earn relatively little because they are not very productive.

Again, there is no question that technological change sometimes creates hardships in the short run, as some workers scramble to adjust to a changing world. Some workers who lose jobs due to advances in technology may not find jobs that pay as well as the ones they lost. These lost jobs are one price of progress. Over time, however, most of these workers find other jobs, often in new industries created by technological change. In a typical month, the U.S. economy sheds about 3.8 million jobs but creates about 4 million new ones. Of course, months during the Great Recession were far from "typical."

How does technological change affect employment levels?

INDUSTRIAL POLICY

industrial policy The view that government—using taxes, subsidies, and regulations—should nurture the industries and technologies of the future, thereby giving domestic industries an advantage over foreign competition

cluster Firms in the same industry or in related industries that group together in a region

LO3 Describe industrial policy and the arguments for and against its use.

Because technological change is so important to a rising standard of living, some argue that governments should become more involved in shaping an economy's technological future. One concern is that technologies of the future require huge sums to develop and implement. An individual firm cannot raise these sums easily and cannot risk failure. Another concern is that individual firms have less incentive to carry out basic research even though that research eventually has a high payoff for the economy as a whole. The fruits of basic research do not immediately show up in something the firm can sell. An individual firm may go bankrupt before applications become marketable.

Photodisc/Getty Images

In the United States, the business of making movies is carried out primarily in Hollywood, California. Why would people working in the movie business benefit from living in or near Hollywood?

Government Involvement

One possible solution to the problem of under-investment is greater government involvement to promote investment in particular industries. **Industrial policy** is the idea that government—using taxes, subsidies, regulations, and coordination in the private sector—could help nurture the industries and technologies of the future. This could give U.S. industries an advantage over foreign competition. U.S. industrial policy over the years was aimed at creating the world's most advanced military production capacity. With the demise of the Soviet Union, however, defense technologies became less important.

Europe has a more aggressive industrial policy. One example is Airbus Industrie, a four-nation aircraft maker. With an estimated $20 billion in government aid, the company has become Boeing's main rival. When Airbus seeks aircraft orders around the world, it can draw on government backing to promise special advantages, such as landing rights at key European airports and an easing of regulatory constraints. Few U.S. producers get such government backing.

Identifying Industry Clusters

Economists have long recognized that firms in particular industries gain a performance advantage by forming a **cluster**. That is, they locate in a region already thick with firms in that same industry or in related industries. Examples of industry clusters include Hollywood

Math in Economics

Common Core Ratios and Proportional Relationships

Calculate the percent return on an investment in a new technology by dividing the change in revenue that results from the investment by the cost of the investment.

EXAMPLE Find the annual percent return on a firm's investment in new physical capital that resulted in an $850,000 per year increase in the firm's revenue. The cost of the equipment, installation, and training for workers totaled $13,500,000.

SOLUTION Divide the change in revenue by the cost. Convert the decimal answer to a percent by multiplying by 100, or moving the decimal point two places to the right. Write the percent to the nearest tenths.

$\$850{,}000 \div \$13{,}500{,}000 = 0.063 = 6.3\%$

Practice the Skill Find the annual percent of return for each investment.

1. A firm purchased new physical capital that costs $940,000 to buy, install, and train workers. The purchase increased the firm's revenue by $52,000 per year.
2. A firm spent $5,872,000 to buy, install and train workers on new equipment. The firm's revenue increased $641,000 per year.
3. A firm's revenue increased $24,000 per year after it purchased new physical capital. The purchase, installation, and worker training cost $2,983,000.
4. Why might the firm in exercise 3 choose to purchase the new physical capital despite its low rate of return?

movies, Broadway theaters, Wall Street finances, Silicon Valley software, and Orlando theme parks.

Clusters aid communication and promote healthy competition among cluster members. The flow of information and cooperation between firms, as well as the competition among firms located together, stimulates regional innovation and promotes growth. By locating in a region that has similar businesses, a firm also can tap into an established customer base and into local markets for specialized labor and for other inputs.

Some state and local governments are trying to identify industries to promote in their area. Governments try to attract firms in favored technologies by adopting favorable tax policies. They also may help to pay for the construction of support facilities and for training programs.

Pitfalls of Trying to Pick Technological Winners

Skeptics of industrial policy wonder whether the government should be trusted to identify emerging technologies and to pick the industry clusters that will lead the way. Critics of industrial policy say that markets allocate scarce resources better than governments do. For example, in the early 1980s, the U.S. government spent $1 billion to help military contractors develop a high-speed computer circuit. However, Intel, a company that received no federal support, was the first to develop the circuit. In an effort to stimulate green energy, the 2009 federal stimulus program included a $527 million loan to Solyndra, a California maker of solar panels. In 2011, the company went bankrupt, leaving taxpayers on the hook for the loan.

Japan has had the most aggressive policy for regulating and supporting favored industries. Its approach includes discouraging competition in these industries and encouraging joint research among firms. Those Japanese industries subject to the most regulation and support, such as chemicals and aircraft manufacturing, became uncompetitive in the world market. Meanwhile, the Japanese industries that received little government backing, such as automobiles, cameras, and video games, turned out to be dynamic world competitors.

There also is concern that government aid would be awarded based on political connections rather than on the promise of the technologies. Most economists would prefer to let private firms bet their own money on the important technologies of the future. Wasting government resources trying to identify industries of the future would be an example of government failure.

CHECKPOINT **What is industrial policy, and what are the arguments for and against its use?**

Span the Globe

Software Piracy

Few industries could withstand the theft of $51 billion worth of their products, yet that is the number given to software piracy worldwide in the latest IDC Global Software Piracy Study. As a result of the growth of the personal computer in markets such as Brazil, India, and China, the software piracy rate worldwide rose to 43 percent. Viewed another way, for every $100 worth of legitimate software sold, an additional $75 was stolen. The nation of Georgia leads the world with a 95 percent piracy rate. At 20 percent, software piracy in the United States was the lowest of any nation in the world. Still, because of the size of its market, the United States leads the world in commercial value of pirated software.

Think Critically **What economic benefits should result from an effective campaign against software piracy?**

Sources: "BSA Reports $51 Billion Worth of Software Theft in 2009," Business Software Alliance / IDC Global Software Piracy Study, March 11, 2011.

14.3 ASSESSMENT

Think Critically

1. Which of the following types of research would have a more immediate impact on our nation's productivity: research into new types of genetically engineered plants or research about how genes control the development of fish embryos? Explain your choice.
2. A good deal of R&D in the United States and other countries is devoted to creating new types of consumer products such as shampoo, dish soap, or frozen pizza. Do you think this type of R&D adds significantly to our nation's productivity? Explain your answer.
3. There are considerably fewer manufacturing jobs in the U.S. economy today than there were in the past. Many people who once held manufacturing jobs have not been able to find new jobs that allow them to earn as much as they did in the past. Do you think government should provide such workers with special benefits? Why or why not?
4. Do you think that government-supported student aid for college students is similar to industrial policy in any way? Explain your answer.

Graphing Exercise

5. Ownership of computers in America has become almost universal in recent years. Although most families and businesses invest in new computers every few years, data in the table show that the amount invested actually has declined in some recent years. Use the data to construct a line graph of the amount spent on new computers. How can you explain the decline in spending your graph shows?

RETAIL SPENDING ON COMPUTERS (IN MILLIONS OF DOLLARS)

Year	Spending	Year	Spending
2004	$37,895	2007	$36,859
2005	$38,386	2008	$37,542
2006	$37,657	2009	$33,013

Source: *Statistical Abstract of the United States, 2011*, p. 648.

Make Academic Connections

6. **Government** In 1981, Congress passed a law that allowed businesses to deduct from their federal income taxes 10 percent of the cost of investments they made. A firm that purchased a $1 million machine could subtract $100,000 from its federal taxes. This law expired in 1986. Why do you think this law Congress passed this law in 1981? What do you think happened when it expired in 1986? Some people think a similar law should be passed today. Would you support such a law? Why or why not?
7. **Science** The federal government has provided many billions of dollars to the National Science Foundation (NSF) to support scientific research and development. Although some of the discoveries made by researchers supported by NSF grants have been of great value to the economy, others have not. Do you think that using several billion dollars each year for NSF research is a good use of your tax payments? Explain your answer.

In small teams, brainstorm to identify any business clusters in your region. Then discuss the influence you think the clusters have on economic growth in the region. Compare your work with that of other teams.

Connect to History

Interchangeable Parts and the Assembly Line

First proposed for the gun industry, the idea of interchangeable parts depended on machinery and precise measurements to build parts that were exactly the same. This allowed lesser-skilled workers to use machines to construct identical parts that could be assembled quickly and easily. The result was that productivity increased and cost declined. The work that took skilled craftspeople half a day now could be completed in just three-and-a-half minutes.

By the 1850s, meat packers in Cincinnati began to combine slaughtering and processing under one roof. Set up as "disassembly" lines, they were noted as models of efficiency. After the hogs were killed, their bodies were hung from hooks and moved along a pulley through the slaughterhouse. Along the line they were bled, scalded, gutted, and cleaned. Finally the carcasses were dismembered in about 35 seconds by a team of butchers.

Ransom Olds was the first person to mass-produce automobiles. Before mass production, the cars remained stationary in the factory. The workers moved from chassis to chassis assembling parts. Other workers would bring the parts to the workers wherever they were needed. Olds manufactured the cars by bringing all the material, including both the chassis and the parts, to the workers, who remained in one place. Henry Ford used the same process. Frames were arranged in a line in the plant, and teams of assemblers moved down the line performing one assembly operation. Parts already delivered to each station were ready for installation when the assemblers arrived. Following a suggestion by scientific management expert Clarence Avery, Ford installed conveyer belts to deliver the parts.

In 1913, Ford adopted the moving assembly line to automobile manufacturing in his Highland Park plant. Assembly time dropped from 17 hours to six. Workers were more productive, and the cost of the automobile fell—making it more affordable to most Americans. Ford was able to give his unskilled workers wages that previously had been available only to skilled workers. In 1914, Ford was selling cars for $440 each. By 1916 the price had dropped to $345. Following World War I, the Model T Roadster was priced at $260.

Think Critically **Look at your own life and home and determine the things that make your life more productive, such as computers, telephones, dishwashers, etc. Ask your parents, grandparents, or both to estimate the time they spent on household tasks when they were young, and compare it to the time you spend doing those same tasks today. What is the effect on everyday life? Describe your findings, and be prepared to compare them to what your classmates have found.**

Stanislaw Tokarski/Shutterstock.com

Chapter Summary

14.1 The PPF, Economic Growth, and Productivity

A. Economic growth is the primary way to reduce poverty and raise living standards. When a greater share of a nation's resources is allocated to the production of capital goods, there are higher rates of economic growth. When this is graphed on a production possibilities frontier, the frontier shifts out over time.

B. Productivity measures how well resources are employed to create goods and services. The more efficiently resources are used, the higher a nation's standard of living. Measures of productivity include labor productivity, capital productivity, and land productivity. Labor productivity can increase through investments in human capital and in physical capital.

C. Investments in physical capital can result in capital deepening, which involves adding more or better physical capital to production. Investment in physical capital also may involve the creation and use of new types of capital. Rules of the game also affect productivity and growth. These include the laws, customs, and conventions that encourage people to undertake productive activity.

ASK THE EXPERT

www.cengage.com/school/contecon

Have computers affected worker productivity?

14.2 Living Standards and Labor Productivity Growth

A. The single most important determinant of a nation's standard of living is the productivity of its resources. There are great differences in the standards of living among nations. Developing countries have a lower standard of living than industrial market countries because they have less human and physical capital.

B. The quality of a nation's labor is an important source of productivity. Over the past 140 years, labor productivity has grown at an average rate of 2.2 percent per year in the United States. Because of the power of compounding, this seemingly small growth rate translated into more than a twentyfold increase in labor productivity.

C. The best measure of an economy's standard of living is its output per capita. Output per capita in the United States is greater than in other major economies.

14.3 Technological Change

A. Improvements in technology arise from scientific discovery, which is the product of basic research and applied research. Basic research investigates general fields of knowledge without regard for its marketability. Applied research seeks to answer particular questions that will assist in the production of specific products. As a greater share of a nation's resources is devoted to research and development, that nation should enjoy a greater increase in its productivity.

B. Technological improvements that are brought about through research lead to increases in labor productivity. Workers trained to use new technologies produce goods and services that have greater value. New technologies, however, can cause some workers who lack needed skills to become unemployed.

C. Some nations have created and implemented industrial policies intended to shape their economies' futures. These nations use taxes, subsidies, and regulations to coordinate business activity in their private sectors to nurture industries and technologies. Although industrial policies have assisted some types of production, they also allocated resources to industries that could not use them efficiently.

ASK THE EXPERT

www.cengage.com/school/contecon

Does technological innovation destroy jobs and lead to unemployment?

CHAPTER 14 ASSESSMENT

Review Economic Terms

- a. applied research
- b. basic research
- c. capital deepening
- d. cluster
- e. developing countries
- f. Group of Seven (G-7)
- g. human capital
- h. industrial market countries
- i. industrial policy
- j. labor productivity
- k. physical capital
- l. productivity
- m. rules of the game
- n. standard of living

Match the terms with the definitions. Some terms may not be used.

_____ 1. The machines, buildings, roads, airports, communications networks, and other manufactured creations used to produce goods and services

_____ 2. An economy's level of economic prosperity

_____ 3. Firms in the same industry or in related industries that group together in a region

_____ 4. The advanced market economies that include Western Europe, North America, Australia, New Zealand, and Japan

_____ 5. Output per unit of labor

_____ 6. The accumulated knowledge, skill, and experience of the labor force

_____ 7. Countries with a lower standard of living because they have relatively little human and physical capital

_____ 8. The search for knowledge without regard to how that knowledge will be used

_____ 9. The ratio of output to a specific measure of input

_____ 10. Research that seeks answers to particular questions or applies scientific discoveries to develop specific products

_____ 11. The view that government—using taxes, subsidies and regulations—should nurture the industries and technologies of the future, thereby giving domestic industries an advantage over foreign competition

_____ 12. The formal and informal institutions—such as laws, customs, and conventions—that provide production incentives and promote economic activity

Review Economic Concepts

13. **True or False** Capital deepening involves adding more or better physical capital to production.

14. ________?________ measures how efficiently resources are employed to create goods and services.

15. **True or False** The more of a nation's resources that are allocated to the production of capital goods, the greater that nation's rate of economic growth will be.

16. ________?________ takes place when there is an increase in the quantity or quality of capital per worker.

17. Which of the following will shift a nation's production possibilities frontier outward over time?
    - a. switching production away from capital goods
    - b. an increase in resources that are devoted to Social Security benefits
    - c. switching production away from consumer goods and towards capital goods
    - d. an increase in resources that are devoted to employee benefits

18. Which of the following is an example of a change in the rules of the game that could increase a nation's productivity?
    a. Farmers are given a tax deduction when they buy new farm equipment.
    b. Lunches are provided free to students at an elementary school.
    c. Taxes on imported automobiles are increased.
    d. Welfare payments are increased for the nation's poor.
19. Labor productivity in most ________?________ countries is very low, so many residents barely subsist.
20. The single most important determinant of a nation's standard of living is the
    a. productivity of its resources.
    b. size of its population.
    c. annual amount of rainfall.
    d. size of its government.
21. Some nations have created and implemented ________?________ that are intended to nurture the industries and technologies of the future.
22. ________?________ investigates general fields of knowledge but has no direct application to production.
23. Which of the following is regarded as the best measure of a nation's standard of living?
    a. total output
    b. output per capita
    c. annual amount of rainfall
    d. size on capital goods
24. ________?________ seeks to answer particular questions or to use scientific discoveries to develop specific products.
25. **True or False** Technological advances will benefit all workers equally.
26. Which of the following is not a common argument against the use of industrial policy?
    a. Industrial policy may result in investments that do not add to productivity.
    b. Industrial policy may give politicians too much control over the economy.
    c. Industrial policy may cause businesses to become uncompetitive in international trade.
    d. Industrial policy may prevent businesses from investing in new technologies.
27. **True or False** Productivity in the United States has increased at a constant annual rate of 2.2 percent per year over the past century.
28. Although technological improvements can lead to increased labor productivity, they also
    a. often reduce the quality of production.
    b. can cause some workers who lack needed skills to lose their jobs.
    c. can weaken a nation's ability to compete in the global economy.
    d. may lower a nation's average standard of living.

Apply Economic Concepts

29. **Calculate Labor Productivity** The ABC Bowling Pin Company employs 20 workers who all work 40 hours per week, 50 weeks per year. Last year ABC produced 480,000 bowling pins that sold for $2.50 each. What was the average hourly value of each ABC worker's production?

30. **Compare Growth Rates Among Nations** Suppose that two nations have exactly the same GDP this year. Country A allocates 10 percent of its resources to producing capital goods, while country B devotes only 6 percent of its resources to this type of production. As a result, country A's production grows at a rate of 2.5 percent per year while country B's growth rate is only 1.8 percent per year. After five more years, how much larger will country A's GDP be than country B's? Make the amount of production in the first year equal to $100 billion in both countries.

31. **Graph Land Productivity** The amount of corn that Sara is able to grow on her farm depends on many things, including the amount of fertilizer she adds to the soil. She has studied her production over many years and has listed her findings in the table. Use these data to construct a bar graph that relates the land productivity per acre of Sara's farm to the amount of fertilizer she applies. Why does production per acre decrease when she applies more than 5 bags of fertilizer per acre?

BAGS OF FERTILIZER AND CORN PRODUCTION PER ACRE

Bags Applied Per Acre	Bushels of Corn Produced Per Acre
0	100
1	130
2	160
3	185
4	200
5	210
6	200

32. **21st Century Skills: Initiative and Self-Direction** Imagine you are the president of a major university. Your funding for investments in new technology has been cut in each of the past three years. You have decided to appeal to a major technology firm to partner in a new technology initiative. You hope to negotiate an agreement whereby the firm provides cutting-edge equipment and training for your students in exchange for an opportunity to hire your best students first. Write a letter to the CEO of a technology firm that explains your proposal. If you were applying to be a student at this university, why might you be interested in this type of partnership?

Digging Deeper

with Economics e-Collection

The economic well-being of the people living in a country is referred to as the country's standard of living. Access the Gale Economics e-Collection through the URL below to find two articles related to standard of living. One article should concern an industrial country and the other article should concern a developing country. After reading the articles, write a one-page paper comparing and contrasting issues related to the standard of living in the two countries. Keep a record of the source citations of the articles you chose.

www.cengage.com/school/contecon

CHAPTER 15

Economic Challenges

Point your browser

www.cengage.com/school/contecon

CONSIDER ...

- → Would a high school senior who is not working be considered unemployed?
- → What type of unemployment might be a healthy sign for the economy?
- → What's so bad about inflation?
- → What's stagflation?
- → Why don't some families benefit from a strong economy?
- → How might government transfer programs affect work incentives?

pressdigital/iStockphoto.com; Background image: Lukiyanova Natalia/frenta/Shutterstock.com

15.1 UNEMPLOYMENT

Key Terms

Learning Objectives

LO1 Distinguish among four types of unemployment.

LO2 Discuss the unemployment rate, and describe how it differs over time and across groups.

LO3 Explain who is eligible for unemployment benefits in the United States.

In Your World

"They scampered about looking for work. … They swarmed on the highways. The movement changed them. The highways, the camps along the road, the fear of hunger and the hunger itself, changed them. The children without dinner changed them, the endless moving changed them." There is no question, as John Steinbeck wrote in *The Grapes of Wrath*, that a long stretch of unemployment profoundly affects the individual and the family. Unemployment also imposes costs on the economy. When unemployment is high, the economy does not achieve its potential. Because teenagers have the highest unemployment rate, this section should be of special interest to you. Not all unemployment harms the economy, however. Even in a healthy economy, some unemployment reflects the voluntary choices of workers and employers seeking the best fit. For example, your search for a summer job may take time. You won't necessarily accept the first offer. You may decide to look around a bit.

TYPES OF UNEMPLOYMENT

LO1 Distinguish among four types of unemployment.

Think about all the ways people can become unemployed. They may quit or be fired from their job. They may be looking for a first job, or they may be reentering the labor force after an absence. A look at the reasons behind unemployment in April 2011 indicates that 59 percent of the unemployed lost their previous jobs, 7 percent quit their previous jobs, 10 percent were entering the labor market for the first time, and 24 percent were reentering the market. The help-wanted section of a big-city newspaper may list thousands of job openings, from accountants to zoologists. Why are people unemployed when so many jobs are available? To understand the answer, take a look at the four types of unemployment: frictional, structural, seasonal, and cyclical.

Frictional Unemployment

Just as employers do not always hire the first applicant who comes through the door, job seekers do not always accept their first offer. Both employers and job seekers need time to explore the job market. Employers need time to learn about the talent available, and job seekers need time to learn about employment opportunities. The time required to bring together labor suppliers and labor demanders creates *frictional unemployment.* Frictional unemployment does not usually last long and results in a better match-up between workers and jobs. The entire economy becomes more efficient. A marketing major who graduated from college in June and is taking the summer to look for the perfect sales position is frictionally unemployed. A high school teacher who quits his job at the end of the school year to look for a job in another field is frictionally unemployed.

Photodisc/Getty Images

What type of unemployment results for members of the ski patrol during spring and summer months?

Structural Unemployment

In a dynamic economy, the demand for some labor skills declines while the demand for other labor skills increases. For example, automatic teller machines have put many bank tellers out of work. At the same time, those with certain computer skills are in greater demand. *Structural unemployment* results when job seekers do not have the skills demanded. Structural unemployment poses more of a problem than frictional unemployment because the unemployed may need to retrain to develop the required skills.

Seasonal Unemployment

Unemployment caused by seasonal changes in labor demand during the year is called *seasonal unemployment.* During cold winter months, for example, demand for farm hands, lifeguards, and construction workers shrinks. Workers in these seasonal jobs know they probably will be unemployed in the off-season. Some may have even chosen a seasonal occupation to complement their lifestyle or academic schedule.

Cyclical Unemployment

As output declines during recessions, firms reduce their demand for inputs, including labor. *Cyclical unemployment* is the increase in unemployment caused by the recession phase of the business cycle. Cyclical unemployment increases during recessions and decreases during expansions.

Full Employment

In a dynamic, growing economy, changes in consumer demand and in technology continually affect the market for particular types of labor. Thus, even in a healthy, growing economy, there is some frictional, structural, and seasonal unemployment. The economy is said to be at **full employment** if there is no cyclical unemployment. When economists talk about "full employment," they do not mean zero unemployment but relatively low unemployment, say between 5 and 6 percent. Even when the economy is at full employment, there is some frictional, structural, and seasonal unemployment.

full employment Occurs when there is no cyclical unemployment; relatively low unemployment

Problems with Official Unemployment Estimates

Official unemployment statistics have limitations. For example, some people may have become so discouraged by a long, unsuccessful job search that they have

Investigate Your Local Economy

Research to find the unemployment rates in your city and state. Compare these rates with the most current unemployment rate for the United States. If these rates differ, propose an explanation for why they differ.

given up looking for work. These *discouraged workers* have, in effect, dropped out of the labor force, so they are not counted as unemployed. Because the official unemployment rate ignores discouraged workers, it may underestimate unemployment in the economy.

Official employment figures also ignore the problem of **underemployment**. This arises because people are counted as employed even if they can find only part-time jobs or are overqualified for their job. For example, if someone with a PhD in English Literature can find work only as a bookstore clerk, that individual would be considered underemployed. Counting the underemployed as employed tends to understate the true amount of unemployment.

On the other hand, there are reasons why unemployment figures may overstate the true extent of employment. For example, to qualify for some government transfer programs, beneficiaries must look for work. If some of these people do not in fact want to find a job, then counting them as unemployed overstates the true unemployment rate. Also, people working in the underground economy may not readily admit they have a job if their intent is to evade taxes or skirt the law. Many of those in the underground economy end up being counted as unemployed even though they are working.

CHECKPOINT What are the four types of unemployment?

THE COST AND MEASURE OF UNEMPLOYMENT

LO2
Discuss the unemployment rate, and describe how it differs over time and across groups.

The most obvious cost of unemployment is the loss of a steady paycheck for the unemployed individual and the family. However, many who lose their jobs also suffer a loss of self-esteem. No matter how much people complain about their jobs, they rely on them not only for income but also for part of their personal identity. A long stretch of unemployment can have a lasting effect on both self-esteem and economic welfare.

In addition to these personal costs, unemployment imposes a cost on the economy as a whole because fewer goods and services are produced. When the economy does not generate enough jobs to employ all who seek work, that unemployed labor is lost forever. *This lost output together with the economic and psychological damage to unemployed workers and their families represents the true cost of unemployment.*

underemployment
Workers are overqualified for their jobs or work fewer hours than they would prefer

Unemployment Rate

The most widely reported measure of the nation's economic health is the unemployment rate. To see what the unemployment rate measures, you need to understand its components. A measurement of unemployment begins with the U.S. *noninstitutional adult population*, which consists of all those 16 years of age and older, except people in the military, in prison, or in psychiatric hospitals. When the expression "adult population" is referred to in this section, it means the noninstitutional adult population.

The **labor force** consists of those in the adult population who are either working or looking for work. *Those with no job who are looking for work are counted as unemployed.* Thus, a high school student at least 16 years of age who wants a job but can't find one would be counted as unemployed. The **unemployment rate** equals the number unemployed—that is, people without jobs who are looking for work—divided by the number in the labor force.

Unemployment rate = Number unemployed ÷ Number in the labor force

Only a fraction of those not working are considered unemployed. People may not be working for all kinds of reasons. They may be full-time students, retirees, homemakers, or disabled. Or they may simply not want to work.

labor force Those in the adult population who are either working or looking for work

unemployment rate The number of people without jobs who are looking for work divided by the number in the labor force

Labor Force Participation Rate

Employment measures are illustrated in Figure 15.1. In this figure, circles represent the various groups, and the millions of people in each category and subcategory are shown in parentheses. The circle on the left depicts the entire U.S. labor force, including both those employed and those looking for work. The circle on the right represents members of the adult population who are not working. Together, these two circles add up to the adult population.

Figure 15.1 Composition of U.S. Adult Population (in millions), April 2011

The labor force consists of employed and unemployed people 16 years or older.

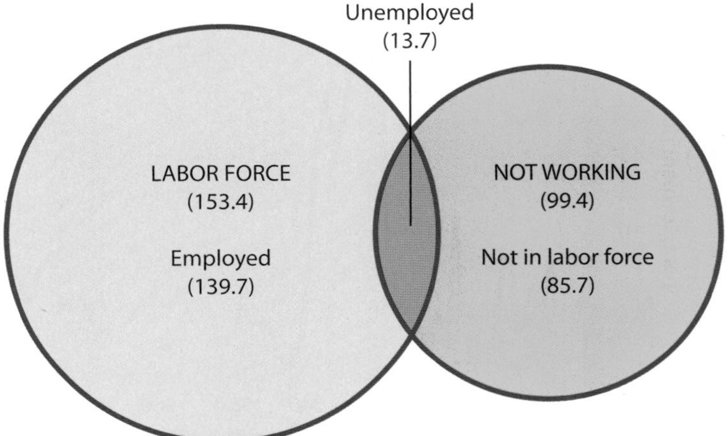

Source: U.S. Bureau of Labor Statistics, "The Employment Situation: April 2011." For the latest figures, go to http://www.bls.gov/news.release/pdf/empsit.pdf.

The overlapping area identifies *unemployed workers*—that is, people in the labor force who are not working but are looking for work. Using the formula given above, in this example 13.7 million people were unemployed in a labor force of 153.4 million. This resulted in a U.S. unemployment rate of 8.9 percent.

The productive capability of any economy depends in part on the proportion of adults in the labor force, measured as *the labor force participation rate.* In Figure 15.1, the U.S. adult population equals those in the labor force (153.4 million) plus those not in the labor force (85.7 million), for a total of 239.1 million. The **labor force participation rate** therefore equals the number in the labor force divided by the adult population. For April 2011, that was 153.4 million divided by 239.1 million, which equals 64 percent. So, on average, about two out of three adults were in the labor force. The labor force participation rate increased from about 60 percent in 1970 to about 64 percent in 2011, mostly because more women joined the labor force.

Changes in the Unemployment Rate

labor force participation rate The number in the labor force divided by the adult population

Figure 15.2 shows the U.S. unemployment rate since 1900, with shading to indicate periods of recession or depression. As you can see, the rate increased during recessions or depressions and fell during expansions. Perhaps the most striking feature of the graph is the dramatic jump that occurred during the Great Depression of the 1930s, when the unemployment rate reached 25.2 percent. More recently, the rate climbed because of the Great Recession of 2008–2009.

Figure 15.2 The U.S. Unemployment Rate Since 1900

Since 1900, the unemployment rate has fluctuated widely, rising during recessions or depressions and falling during expansions. During the Great Depression of the 1930s, the rate rose as high as 25.2 percent.

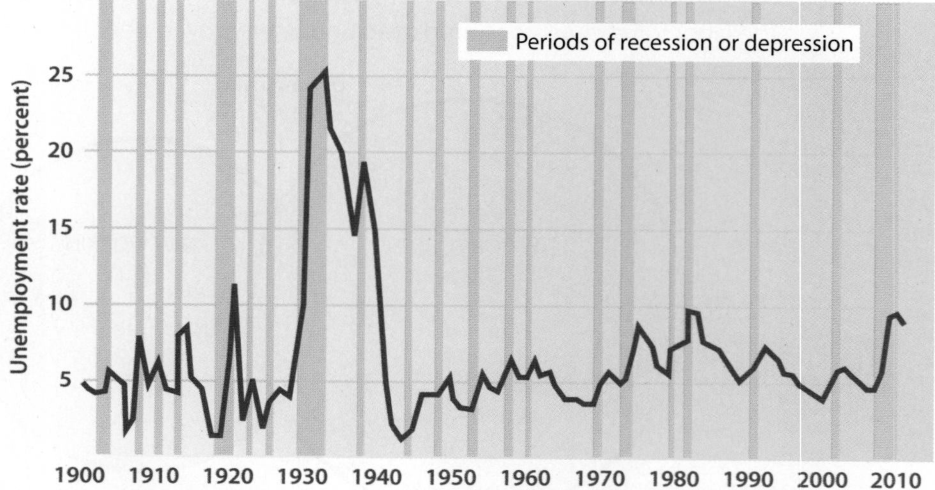

Source: U.S. Census Bureau, *Historical Statistics of the United States: Colonial Times to 1970* (Washington, D.C.: U.S. Government Printing Office, 1975); *Economic Report of the President*, February 2011; and U.S. Bureau of Labor Statistics. Rate for 2011 is a projection based on the first half of the year.

Unemployment for Various Groups

The unemployment rate says nothing about who is unemployed or for how long. Even a low overall rate often hides wide differences in unemployment rates across age, race, gender, and geographic area. For example in April 2011, when the U.S. unemployment rate was 8.9 percent, the rate was 24.9 percent among teenagers, 16.1 percent among blacks or African Americans, 11.8 percent among Hispanics or Latino ethnicity, and 6.4 percent among Asians. These reflect differences in job opportunities, work experience, education, skills, as well as discrimination. For example, with regard to education, those with a college degree had an unemployment rate only half the national average.

FIGURE 15.3 Unemployment Among Various Groups Since 1972

Unemployment affects different groups in different ways. The unemployment rate is higher for blacks than for whites and higher for teenagers than for workers 20 and older.

(A) 20 YEARS OF AGE OR OLDER

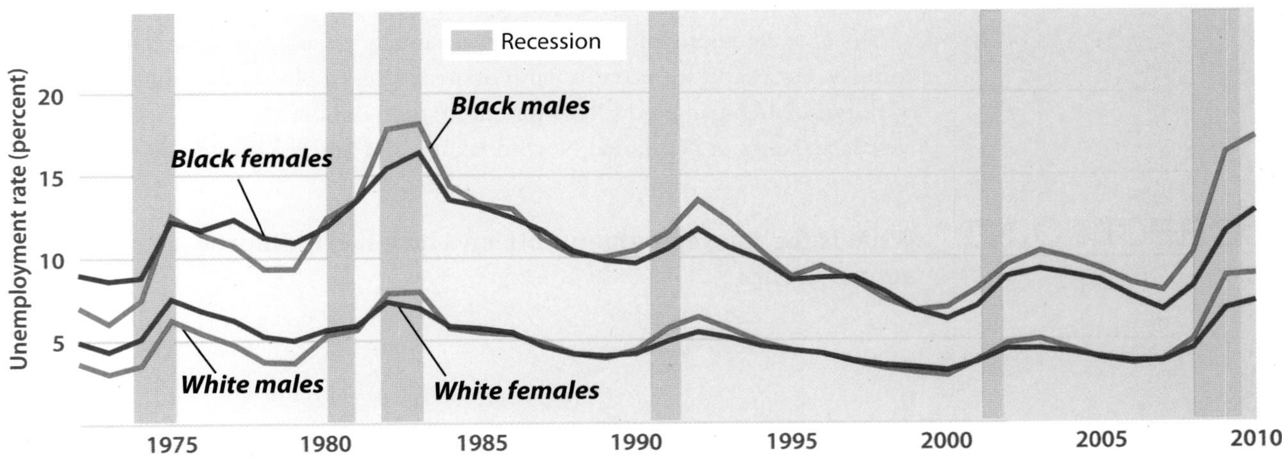

(B) 16 TO 19 YEARS OF AGE

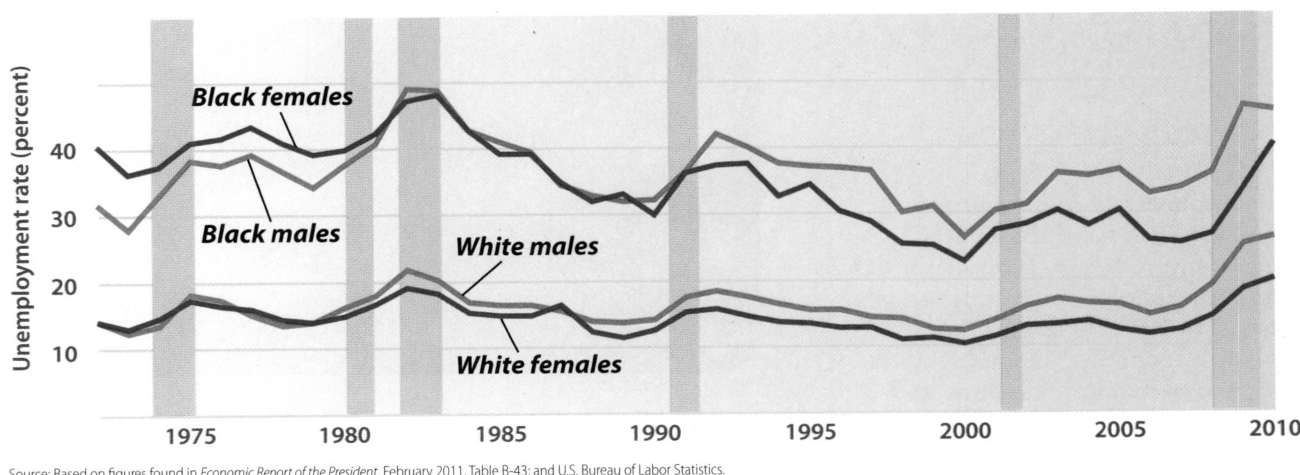

Source: Based on figures found in *Economic Report of the President*, February 2011, Table B-43; and U.S. Bureau of Labor Statistics.

Unemployment rates for some different groups appear in Figure 15.3. As you can see, rates are higher among blacks than among whites. Rates also are higher among teenagers than among those aged 20 and older. During recessions, the rates climbed for all groups. Rates peaked during the recession of 1982, and then trended down. Rates turned up again with the recession of 2001, settled down for a few years, then rose with the recession of 2008–2009.

Why are unemployment rates among teenagers so much higher than among workers age 20 and older? Because young workers enter the job market with little training, take unskilled jobs, and are the first to be fired when the economy slows down. Young workers also move in and out of the job market more frequently during the year, as they juggle school demands. Even those who have left school often shop around for jobs more than older workers do.

Why are unemployment rates higher among black workers than among white workers? The black workforce is on average younger, and younger workers tend to have higher unemployment rates. A smaller percentage of black workers graduated from college. Black workers tend to live in areas harder hit by the recession. Racial discrimination also is a contributing factor.

The U.S. unemployment rate covers up much variation in rates across the country. For example, recent unemployment rates in blue-collar industrial states of Illinois, Michigan, and Ohio were more than double those in the upper-Midwest farm states of Nebraska, North Dakota, and South Dakota.

CHECKPOINT **What is the unemployment rate and how has it differed over time and across groups?**

ESSENTIAL QUESTION

Standard CEE 19: Unemployment and Inflation

Unemployment imposes costs on individuals and the overall economy. Inflation, both expected and unexpected, also imposes costs on individuals and the overall economy. Unemployment increases during recessions and decreases during recoveries.

sjlocke/iStockphoto.com

What are the costs of unemployment for unemployed individuals?

UNEMPLOYMENT BENEFITS

LO3
Explain who is eligible for unemployment benefits in the United States.

As noted earlier, unemployment often imposes both an economic and psychological hardship on the unemployed worker and the family. Today, a large proportion of households have two workers in the labor force, so if one becomes unemployed, another is likely to still have a job that may provide health insurance and other benefits. Having more than one family member in the labor force cushions the economic shock of unemployment.

Unemployment Compensation

Workers who lose their jobs today often receive unemployment benefits. In response to the massive unemployment of the Great Depression, Congress passed the Social Security Act of 1935. This act provides unemployment insurance financed by a tax on employers. Workers who have lost their jobs and who meet certain qualifications can receive **unemployment benefits** for up to six months, provided they actively seek work.

During recessions, unemployment benefits often extend beyond six months in states with especially high unemployment. During the recession of 2008–2009, for example, unemployment benefits stretched up to two years in many states. Insurance benefits go mainly to people who have lost jobs. Individuals just entering or reentering the labor force are not covered, nor are those who quit their last job or those fired for just cause, such as excessive absenteeism or theft. Because of these restrictions, about one-half of all unemployed workers receive unemployment benefits.

Unemployment benefits averaged about $310 per week in 2011. This replaced on average about one-half of a person's take-home pay, with a higher share for those whose jobs paid less.

Unemployment Benefits and Work Incentives

Because unemployment benefits reduce the opportunity cost of remaining unemployed, they also may reduce the incentive to find work. For example, what if you faced the choice of taking a job washing dishes that pays $300 per week or collecting $200 per week in unemployment benefits? Which would you choose?

Evidence suggests that those who receive unemployment benefits tend to search less actively than those who don't. Many of those who receive benefits take jobs as the end of benefits approaches.

Although unemployment benefits provide a safety net for the unemployed, they also may reduce the need to find work. They may increase the average length of unemployment and the unemployment rate as well.

On the plus side, unemployment benefits allow for a more careful job search, because the job seeker has some income and need not take the first job that comes along. As a result of a wider search, there is a better match between job skills and job requirements, and this promotes economic efficiency. In addition, unemployment compensation payments allow the unemployed to continue to spend. This spending reduces the likelihood that other workers will be laid off.

unemployment benefits Cash transfers to unemployed workers who lost their jobs, actively seek work, and meet other qualifications

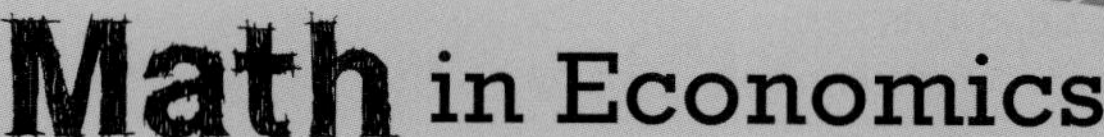

CHECKPOINT Who is eligible for unemployment benefits in the United States?

Math in Economics

Common Core Ratios and Proportional Relationships

You can calculate the number of degrees needed for each section of a circle graph by multiplying each percent expressed as a decimal by 360 degrees. Then, using a compass and protractor, you can construct a pie graph with sections that have central angles that match these values.

DURATION OF UNEMPLOYMENT BY PERCENT 2001 AND 2011

Year	Less than 5 Weeks	5–14 Weeks	15–26 Weeks	27 or more Weeks
2001	42.0%	32.3%	14.0%	11.7%
2011	17.5%	22.6%	16.0%	43.8%

EXAMPLE Construct a pie graph that shows duration of unemployment in 2001.

SOLUTION Multiply the percent represented by each group by 360 to find the number of degrees for each. Use these values to construct a pie graph using a compass and protractor.

Less than 5 weeks: $0.420 \times 360 = 151$ degrees

5–14 weeks: $0.323 \times 360 = 116$ degrees

15–26 weeks: $0.140 \times 360 = 50$ degrees

27 or more weeks: $0.117 \times 360 = 42$ degrees

Duration of Unemployment, 2001

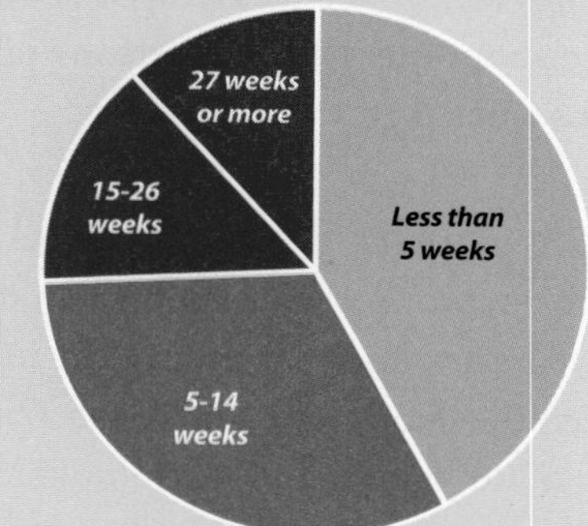

Practice the Skill Construct a pie graph and answer the questions.

1. Construct a pie graph that shows the duration of unemployment in 2011.
2. How much larger was the percentage of people who had been unemployed for 27 or more weeks in 2011 than it had been in 2001?
3. Why could this change in duration of unemployment have been considered important by many economists?

15.1 ASSESSMENT

Think Critically

1. How may people who keep their jobs be harmed by high levels of unemployment?
2. Are you currently a member of the labor force? Explain your answer.
3. Why do you think the government considers as unemployed only those who are without employment but are looking for work?
4. Do you know anyone who has chosen to change jobs? Why did this person make this choice? How long was he or she unemployed? Was this person satisfied with the job he or she eventually accepted? Do you think this person made a rational choice?
5. How can unemployment compensation payments help workers who are not unemployed?

Graphing Exercise

6. In general, unemployment is higher among young people. Use data from this table to construct a double line graph that compares the rates of unemployment for people who are 16 to 19 years of age with the average for all members of the labor force. Identify and explain three possible reasons why young people have higher unemployment rates.

UNEMPLOYMENT RATES, 1990–2010

Year	Unemployment Rate for People 16–19	Unemployment Rate for Entire Labor Force
1990	15.5%	5.6%
1995	17.3%	5.6%
2000	13.1%	4.0%
2005	16.1%	5.1%
2010	25.9%	9.6%

Source: *Economic Indicators*, June, 2011, p. 12.

Make Academic Connections

7. **History** The Great Depression of the 1930s was the deepest and most well-known economic downturn in recent U.S. history. There were other depressions between 1776 and 1929. Years in which depressions occurred include 1837, 1873, and 1893. Investigate one of these events. What happened to employment in the depression you chose to study?

TeamWork

Working with a partner, investigate the current unemployment rates for all members of the labor force and for people who are from 16 to 19 years of age. Make a list of steps that you and your partner think young people could take to improve their chances of finding a job soon. Do you think the government should make a special effort to help unemployed young workers find jobs? Explain your answer.

MOVERS AND SHAKERS

Matias de Tezanos

CEO, BrokersWeb.com

Photo courtesy of Matias de Tezanos

The dot.com industry calls Guatemalan-born Internet entrepreneur Matias de Tezanos a "serial Internet entrepreneur" because of his uncanny ability to take generic key words and create thriving domains. In 1996, at the age of 15, he became curious about how to build web pages and taught himself to code HTML and JavaScript. After high school, de Tezanos attended dental school because it was a "respected" profession. However, after two years he dropped out to pursue what made him happy—website development.

The day after he dropped out of dental school, de Tezanos and two friends started a Web design company. Before long, he was learning how the domain industry worked.

The most popular Internet domains (Internet addresses) are created by the use of generic keywords. Those are the words that you might enter into a search engine first, such as "hotel" when searching for a hotel. The first domain de Tezanos created with a generic keyword was Hoteles.com. He developed it into an aggregate hotel reservation website that listed hotels all over the world and offered discounts for booking rooms through the site. De Tezanos sold Hoteles.com to Internet travel site Expedia.com, and it is now known as Hotels.com. Later, with his partner Julio Gonzales, he started ClickDiario Network which fast became the leader in "Internet advertising for the Spanish-speaking market."

In order to grow his company, de Tezanos went to Miami, Florida, to seek investors, but he got no offers that would leave him in control of his company. De Tezanos and Gonzales then decided to develop LoPeor.com, a site Gonzales already owned, to generate the revenue to grow their company. LoPeor.com, which means "TheWorst.com" in Spanish, was developed to host "the worst"—usually funny videos and photos which users found and submitted as being the worst. Within three months the company was thriving from advertising revenue. The partners used the money to purchase more Spanish generic keywords. Before long, de Tezanos was known as the "ringleader" of the web development world. He has learned that a domain will likely earn more money if it is developed. He said, "In 2003 we bought Deportes.com (Sports.com in Spanish), and then spent $30,000 on development and three months selling sponsorships. We were able to recover our entire investment in the first 12 months."

The Dot.com Bust

De Tezanos admitted the dot.com bust that started in 1995 and lasted through 2001 had been tough on his business, and he almost went bankrupt. His advice on recovery: "Surround yourself with amazing people, that's the best lifesaver you can find. Stay away from those giving you headaches."

Currently de Tezanos is CEO of Miami-based BrokersWeb.com. The company had revenues of more than $15 million in 2010. De Tezanos believes in giving back to the community. He mentors other entrepreneurs and participates in nonprofit projects that make an impact in his community.

Think Critically **Search the Internet to find information about the "dot.com bust." Prepare a short oral report discussing its causes as well as its effects on the economy in general. Conclude your report with the lessons learned from the dot.com bust.**

Sources: http://www.weforum.org/young-global-leaders/matias-de-tezanos/index.html; http://dnjournal.com/cover/2005/december.htm; and Young Entrepreneurs on Facebook: https://www.hs.facebook.com/note.php?note_id=446403078368&comments; and http://www.historyoftheinternet.net/dot_com_bust.html]

15.2 INFLATION

Learning Objectives

LO1 Describe the types of inflation, and identify two sources of inflation.

LO2 Identify the problems that unexpected inflation creates.

Key Terms

inflation 469
demand-pull inflation 469
cost-push inflation 470
nominal interest rate 473
real interest rate 473

In Your World

As a result of incredibly high inflation, Zimbabwe's prices at the end of 2008 averaged 150 million times higher than at the beginning of that year. To put this in perspective, with such inflation in the United States, the price of gasoline would have climbed from $3.00 per gallon at the beginning of 2008 to $450 million per gallon at the end of that year. A pair of jeans that sold for $25 at the beginning of 2008 would have cost $3.8 billion at year's end. With such wild inflation, people had difficulty keeping track of prices. People couldn't carry enough money to make even small purchases. The government kept issuing currency in larger and larger denominations, ultimately printing millions of $100 trillion notes. Inflation, particularly high inflation, makes market transactions much more difficult.

INFLATION BASICS

LO1 Describe the types of inflation, and identify two sources of inflation.

You were introduced to the concept of inflation earlier in this book. **Inflation** is an increase in the economy's average price level. Inflation reduces the value of money and is usually measured on an annual basis. The annual *inflation rate* is the percentage increase in the price level from one year to the next.

Types of Inflation

Extremely high inflation, such as the experience in Zimbabwe, is called *hyperinflation.* A reduction in the rate of inflation is called *disinflation,* as occurred in the United States during the 1980s. A decrease in the price level is called *deflation,* as occurred in the United States during the Great Depression and recently in Japan, Hong Kong, and Taiwan.

Two Sources of Inflation

Inflation is an increase in the economy's price level resulting from an increase in aggregate demand or a decrease in aggregate supply. Panel (A) of Figure 15.4 shows an increase in aggregate demand that raises the price level from P to P'. Inflation resulting from increases in aggregate demand is often called **demand-pull inflation**. In such cases, a rightward shift of the aggregate demand curve *pulls up* the price level.

inflation An increase in the economy's price level

demand-pull inflation Inflation resulting from a rightward shift of the aggregate demand curve; greater demand pulls up the price level

To generate continuous demand-pull inflation, the aggregate demand curve would have to keep shifting out along a given aggregate supply curve. Rising U.S. inflation rates during the late 1960s resulted from demand-pull inflation. At that time, federal spending for the Vietnam War and for expanded social programs boosted aggregate demand.

Alternatively, inflation can arise from reductions in aggregate supply. This is shown in panel (B) of Figure 15.4, where a leftward shift of the aggregate supply curve raises the price level. For example, crop failures and cuts in OPEC oil supplies reduced aggregate supply during 1974 and 1975, thereby raising the price level.

cost-push inflation
Inflation resulting from a leftward shift of the aggregate supply curve; reduced supply pushes up the price level

Inflation stemming from decreases in aggregate supply is called **cost-push inflation**, suggesting that increases in the cost of production *push up* the price level. If the price level increases and real GDP decreases, this combination is called *stagflation*, which is discussed later in this chapter. To generate sustained and continuous cost-push inflation, the aggregate supply curve would have to keep shifting to the left along a given aggregate demand curve.

FIGURE 15.4 Inflation Caused by Shifts of the Aggregate Demand and Aggregate Supply Curves

Panel (A) illustrates demand-pull inflation. A rightward shift of the aggregate demand curve to *AD′ pulls* the price level up from *P* to *P′*. Panel (B) shows cost-push inflation, in which a leftward shift of the aggregate supply curve to *AS′ pushes* the price level up from *P* to *P′*.

(A) DEMAND-PULL INFLATION: INFLATION CAUSED BY AN INCREASE OF AGGREGATE DEMAND

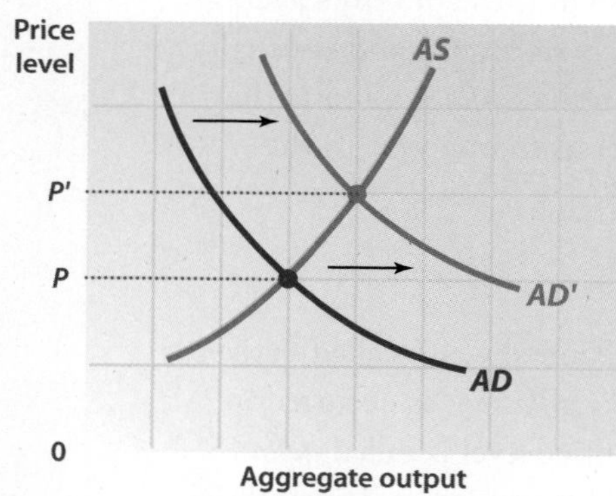

(B) COST-PUSH INFLATION: INFLATION CAUSED BY A DECREASE OF AGGREGATE SUPPLY

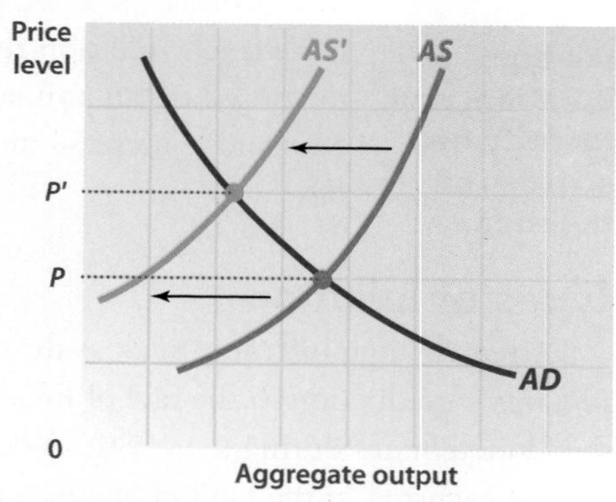

An Historical Look at Inflation and the Price Level

The Bureau of Labor Statistics website includes a home page for the Consumer Price Indexes (CPI). Access the website shown below and click on the link for Chapter 15. Check out the Frequently Asked Questions about the CPI. What goods and services does the CPI cover?

www.cengage.com/school/contecon

The consumer price index is the price measure you most often encounter. As you have already learned, the *consumer price index (CPI)* measures the cost of a "market basket" of consumer goods and services over time. Figure 15.5 shows price levels in the United States since 1913, using the consumer price index. The price level is measured by an index relative to the base period of 1982 to 1984. As you can see, the price level actually was lower in 1940 than in 1920. Since 1940, however, the price level has risen steadily, especially during the 1970s.

Name the types of inflation and identify two sources of inflation. **CHECKPOINT**

FIGURE 15.5 Consumer Price Index Since 1913

Despite fluctuations, the price level, as measured by the consumer price index, was lower in 1940 than in 1920. Since 1940, the price level has risen nearly every year.

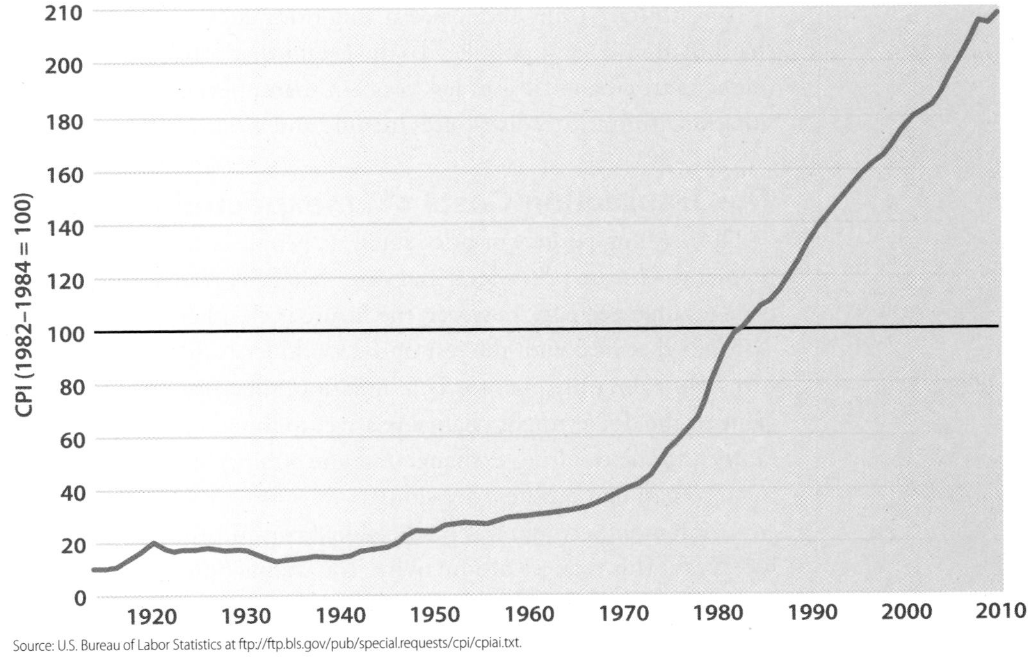

Source: U.S. Bureau of Labor Statistics at ftp://ftp.bls.gov/pub/special.requests/cpi/cpiai.txt.

IMPACT OF INFLATION

LO2
Identify the problems that unexpected inflation creates.

Changes in the price level are nothing new. Prior to World War II, periods of inflation and deflation balanced out over the long run. Therefore, people had good reason to think the dollar would retain its purchasing power over the long term. Since the end of World War II, however, the CPI has increased by an average of 3.8 percent per year. That may not seem like much, but it translates into an *elevenfold* increase in the consumer price index since 1946. Thus, it now takes on average $11 to purchase what $1 bought in 1946. *Inflation reduces the value of the dollar and erodes confidence in the dollar as a store of value over the long term.*

Expected vs. Unexpected Inflation

What is the effect of inflation on the economy's performance? *Unexpected* inflation creates more problems for the economy than does expected inflation. To the extent that inflation is higher or lower than expected, it arbitrarily creates economic winners and losers.

Suppose inflation next year is expected to be 3 percent, and you agree to work next year for a wage that is 4 percent higher than your wage this year. In this case, you expect your real wage—that is, your wage measured in dollars of constant purchasing power—to increase by 1 percent. If inflation turns out to be 3 percent, you and your employer will both be satisfied with your nominal wage increase of 4 percent. After all, that's the wage your employer offered and you accepted.

If, however, inflation turns out to be 5 percent, your real wage will fall. You will be a loser and your employer will be a winner. If inflation turns out to be only 1 percent, your real wage will increase by 3 percent. In this case, you will be a winner and your employer, a loser.

The arbitrary gains and losses arising from unexpected inflation are one reason that inflation is so unpopular. To the extent that inflation is fully expected by market participants, it is of less concern than unexpected inflation. Unexpected inflation arbitrarily redistributes income and wealth from one group to another.

The Transaction Costs of Unexpected Inflation

During long periods of price stability, people correctly think that they can predict the future prices level and can, therefore, plan accordingly. If inflation changes unexpectedly, however, the future is cloudier and planning gets harder.

Firms that deal with the rest of the world face added complications. These firms must not only plan for U.S. inflation, they also must anticipate how the value of the dollar might change relative, to foreign currencies. Inflation uncertainty and the resulting exchange-rate uncertainty increase the difficulty of making international business decisions.

As inflation becomes less predictable, firms must spend more time coping with its effects. This reduces productivity. The transaction costs of market exchange increase. *High and variable inflation interferes with the ability to make long-term plans. It also forces buyers and sellers to pay more attention to prices.* For example, high and variable inflation rates in the United States during the 1970s and early 1980s slowed economic growth during that period.

Goodluz/Shutterstock.com

What effect does the expected inflation rate have on the interest rate that lenders require and that borrowers are willing to pay?

Inflation and Interest Rates

No discussion of inflation would be complete without some mention of interest rates. *Interest* is the cost of borrowing and the reward for lending. The *interest rate* is the interest per year as a percentage of the amount loaned.

The **nominal interest rate** measures interest in terms of current dollars. The nominal rate is the one that appears on the loan agreement and the rate discussed in the news media, such as a home mortgage rate of 5 percent. In contrast, the **real interest rate** measures interest in dollars of constant purchasing power as a percentage of the amount loaned. The real interest rate equals the nominal interest rate minus the inflation rate:

Real interest rate = Nominal interest rate − Inflation rate

With no inflation, the nominal interest rate and the real interest rate would be identical. But with inflation, the real interest rate is less than the nominal interest rate. For example, if the nominal interest rate is 5 percent and the inflation rate is 3 percent, then the real interest rate is 2 percent. Lenders and borrowers are concerned more about the real rate than the nominal rate. The real interest rate, however, is known only after the fact—that is, only after inflation actually occurs.

Because the future is uncertain, lenders and borrowers must form expectations about inflation. They base their willingness to lend and to borrow on these expectations. Lenders and borrowers base their decisions on the *expected* real interest rate, which equals the nominal rate of interest minus the expected inflation rate. Other factors remaining constant, the higher the expected inflation rate, the higher the nominal rate of interest that lenders require and that borrowers are willing to pay.

nominal interest rate The interest rate expressed in current dollars as a percentage of the amount loaned; the interest rate on the loan agreement

real interest rate The interest rate expressed in dollars of constant purchasing power as a percentage of the amount loaned; the nominal interest rate minus the inflation rate

CHECKPOINT

What problems does unexpected inflation create for the economy?

15.2 ASSESSMENT

Think Critically

1. If you think prices will be 10 percent higher one year from now, will your current demand for goods and services be affected? Why or why not?
2. Suppose that the government reduced personal income taxes by 10 percent. At the same time, it increased social insurance payments by 10 percent. Why would these changes tend to cause inflation? Would this inflation be demand-pull or cost-push inflation?
3. Why would a 10 percent increase in prices be bad for an economy if most people expected prices to go up by only 2 percent?

Graphing Exercise

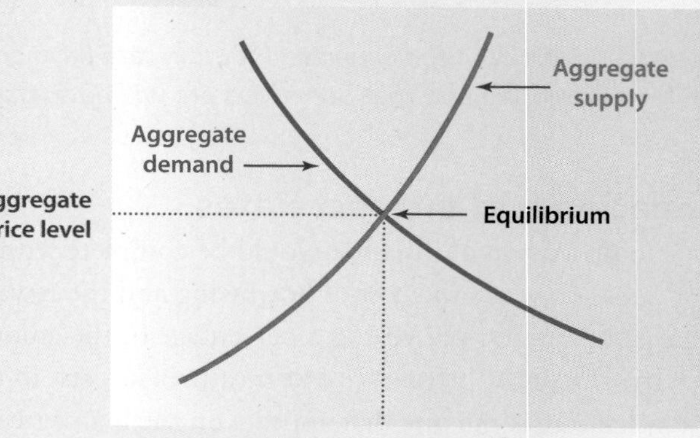

4. Consider this graph of the aggregate demand and aggregate supply curves. What would happen to the location of each of these curves, the average price level, and aggregate output as a result of each of the following events? Would the change in the price level be the result of a demand-pull inflation, cost-push inflation, or deflation in the economy?
   - Many more foreign consumers choose to buy U.S. products.
   - There is a 20 percent increase in the cost of crude oil.
   - A new technology is invented that allows automobiles and trucks to be driven 100 miles per gallon of gasoline.
   - Federal income taxes are increased by 10 percent.

Make Academic Connections

5. **Management** Suppose the inflation rate was 3 percent last year. This year the inflation rate is 5 percent. You are the manager of a large business. It is your job to set the prices your firm will charge next year. How much will you choose to increase prices? Why will you make this choice?

TeamWork

Working in teams, consider this situation. You own a business that manufactures metal ducting for air-conditioning systems. Your business employs six workers. Recently, two of your workers retired and you can't find qualified applicants to replace them at the current wage rate you pay. Make a list of ways you could solve this labor shortage. How would you deal with any resulting increases in your costs? What type of inflation might this cause? Compare your results with the work of other teams.

21st Century Skills

Environmental Literacy

Government Policy, the Economy, and the Environment

It has been said that it is easier to be charitable on a full stomach than on an empty one. Whether or not this is true, the same principle might be applied to the willingness of consumers to support legislation designed to protect the environment. When people are working and have good incomes they are more likely to favor laws that require businesses to install costly pollution control equipment than when they are unemployed and find it hard to pay their bills. Consider the economic recession that took place at the end of the last decade. In 2010 the unemployment rate reached 9.6 percent. Given this fact, it is easy to see why some people were more interested in finding work than in protecting the environment. Consider changes that some individuals, business leaders, and elected officials proposed for environmental protections laws at that time.

- In 2008, the Alliance of Automobile Manufacturers asked Congress to lower required miles per gallon standards.
- In 2010, the California Air Resources Board weakened state air-pollution standards for diesel-powered vehicles.
- In 2011, a resolution was introduced into the U.S. House of Representatives to eliminate some controls for cement plants, thereby undoing a Clean Air Act standard.

Can Government Regulation Create Jobs?

Although many people believe environmental regulations increase costs and discourage employment, others disagree. They argue that when businesses are required to invest in environmental protection they create jobs. After all, someone must design and build the devices that remove pollutants from the environment.

21st Century Skills and Employment

The skills that employers will demand in the 21st century are not the same skills they looked for in the past. In 1960, a mechanic could learn how to "tune up" your car in just a few hours. Today, a mechanic needs to study for months to learn how to use electronic diagnostic equipment. New technologies and government regulations make the same true of many other types of employment. Workers who lack 21st century skills are less likely to find employment. To make sure that you do not become one of the long-term unemployed, you should take the following steps:

- Commit yourself to a life of learning. Never assume that what you know now is all you will need to know in the future.
- Take advantage of training programs offered by your employer.
- Remain aware of technological developments that may affect your employer and, therefore, your job.
- If you become unemployed, be willing to consider and train for other types of work. Don't simply wait for your job to "come back."

Apply the Skill

Imagine that your employer produces engines that power leaf blowers and grass trimmers. The government has proposed stricter pollution controls on these engines. Explain why the future of your job may be in doubt, and name three things you could do to prepare for other employment in the future.

15.3 ECONOMIC INSTABILITY

Key Terms

Learning Objectives

LO1 Use aggregate demand and aggregate supply to analyze the Great Depression.
LO2 Use aggregate demand and aggregate supply to analyze demand-side economics.
LO3 Use aggregate demand and aggregate supply to analyze stagflation.
LO4 Use aggregate demand and aggregate supply to analyze supply-side economics.
LO5 Use aggregate demand and aggregate supply to analyze the Great Recession.

In Your World

The recent history of the U.S. economy can be divided into five economic eras: (1) before and during the Great Depression; (2) after the Great Depression to the early 1970s; (3) from the early 1970s to the early 1980s; (4) from the early 1980s to 2007; and (5) the Great Recession of 2008–2009 and beyond. The first era was marked by recessions and depressions, ending in the Great Depression of the 1930s. The second era was one of strong economic growth, with only moderate increases in the price level. The third era saw high unemployment combined with high inflation. The fourth era showed good growth on average with only moderate increases in the price level. The Great Recession of 2008–2009 began the fifth era. Government leaders during all five eras had to deal with the challenge of economic instability.

THE GREAT DEPRESSION AND BEFORE

LO1
Use aggregate demand and aggregate supply to analyze the Great Depression.

Before World War II, the U.S. economy alternated between periods of prosperity and periods of sharp economic decline. The longest contraction on record lasted five-and-one-half years between 1873 and 1879. During this time, 80 railroads went bankrupt and most of the nation's steel industry shut down. During the depression of the 1890s, the unemployment rate topped 18 percent. In October 1929, the stock market crashed. This began what was to become the deepest—though, at four-and-one-half years, not the longest—economic contraction in the nation's history. This period is known as the Great Depression of the 1930s.

Decrease in Aggregate Demand

In terms of aggregate demand and aggregate supply, the Great Depression can be viewed as a leftward shift of the aggregate demand curve, as shown in Figure 15.6. AD_{1929} is the aggregate demand curve in 1929, before the onset of the depression. Real GDP in 1929 was $977 billion, measured in dollars of 2005 purchasing power. The price level was 10.6, relative to a 2005 base-year price level of 100.

FIGURE 15.6 The Decrease of Aggregate Demand Between 1929 and 1933

The Great Depression of the 1930s can be represented by a leftward shift of the aggregate demand curve, from AD_{1929} to AD_{1933}. In the resulting depression, real GDP fell \$261 billion, or 27 percent. The price level dropped from 10.6 to 7.9, or 26 percent.

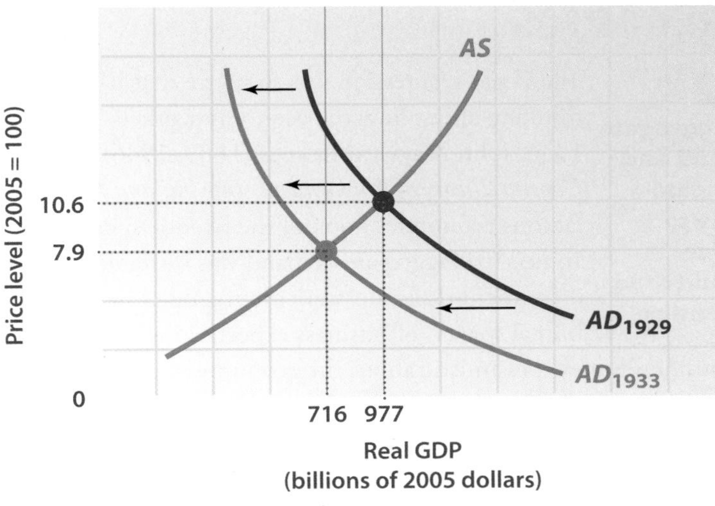

By 1933, aggregate demand had shifted leftward, decreasing to AD_{1933}. Why did aggregate demand decline so much? Though the causes are still debated, the list of suspects is long. It includes the stock market crash of 1929, grim business expectations, a drop in consumer spending, widespread bank failures that wiped out nearly 10 million bank accounts, a sharp decline in the nation's money supply, and severe restrictions on world trade.

Because of the decline in aggregate demand, both the price level and real GDP dropped. Real GDP fell 27 percent, from \$977 billion in 1929 to \$716 billion in 1933, and the price level fell 26 percent, from 10.6 to 7.9. As real GDP declined, the unemployment rate soared, climbing from 3 percent in 1929 to 25 percent in 1933. This remains the highest U.S. unemployment rate ever recorded.

Laissez-Faire

Before the Great Depression, macroeconomic policy was based primarily on the **laissez-faire** doctrine that said government should not intervene in a market economy beyond the minimum required to maintain peace and property rights. This idea dates back at least to Adam Smith. In his 1776 book *The Wealth of Nations*, Smith argued that if people were allowed to pursue their self-interest in free markets, resources would be guided as if by an "invisible hand" to produce the greatest, most efficient level of aggregate output.

Although the U.S. economy had suffered several sharp contractions since the beginning of the nineteenth century, most economists of the day viewed these as a natural phase of the economy—unfortunate, but ultimately self-correcting.

laissez-faire The doctrine that the government should not intervene in a market economy beyond the minimum required to maintain peace and property rights

CHECKPOINT In terms of aggregate demand and aggregate supply, how is the Great Depression viewed on the aggregate demand curve?

FROM THE GREAT DEPRESSION TO THE EARLY 1970S

LO2 Use aggregate demand and aggregate supply to analyze demand-side economics.

The Great Depression was so severe that it stimulated new thinking about how the economy worked—or didn't work. In 1936, John Maynard Keynes (1883–1946) published *The General Theory of Employment, Interest, and Money*, the most famous economics book of the twentieth century. In it, Keynes argued that aggregate demand was unstable, in part because investment decisions were often guided by the unpredictable "animal spirits" of business expectations.

If businesses grew pessimistic about the economy, they would cut investment spending. This, in turn, would reduce aggregate demand. This reduction in aggregate demand would cut output and employment. For example, investment spending dropped more than 80 percent between 1929 and 1933. Keynes saw no natural market forces operating to ensure that the economy would return to a higher level of output and employment.

demand-side economics Macroeconomic policy that focuses on shifting the aggregate demand curve as a way of promoting full employment and price stability

The Image Bank/Getty Images

Day-to-day life during the Great Depression was grim. The unemployment rate reached 25 percent in 1933. Many people could not afford food and gathered in "breadlines" to receive free food from charities. How did the sharp drop in aggregate demand from 1929 to 1933 lead to such high unemployment?

Stimulating Aggregate Demand

Keynes proposed that the government shock the economy out of its depression by increasing aggregate demand. The government could achieve this stimulus directly by increasing its own spending, or indirectly by cutting taxes to stimulate consumption and investment. One problem was that either action could create a federal budget deficit. A *federal budget deficit* measures the amount by which total federal outlays exceed total federal revenues.

To understand what Keynes had in mind, imagine federal budget policies that would increase aggregate demand in Figure 15.6. Ideally, this would shift the aggregate demand curve to the right, back to its original position. After such a shift, the aggregate demand curve would intersect the aggregate supply curve at the original equilibrium point. This would raise real GDP, which would increase employment.

You can think of the Keynesian approach as **demand-side economics** because it focused on how changes in aggregate demand could promote full employment. Keynes argued that government stimulus could jolt the economy out of its depression and back to health. Once investment returned to normal, the government stimulus would no longer be necessary.

World War II and Aggregate Demand

World War II boosted demand for tanks, ships, aircraft, and the like. This increased output and employment. It also seemed to confirm the powerful impact that government spending could have on the economy. The increase in government spending, with no increase in tax rates, created large federal budget deficits during the war.

Immediately after World War II, memories of the Great Depression were still fresh. Trying to avoid another depression, Congress approved the *Employment Act of 1946*, which imposed a clear responsibility on the federal government to foster "maximum employment, production, and purchasing power." The act also required the president to report each year on the state of the economy and to appoint a *Council of Economic Advisers.* This council is a three-member panel of economists, with a professional staff, that offers the president economic advice.

The Golden Age of Keynesian Economics

The economy seemed to prosper during the 1950s, largely without the added stimulus of fiscal policy. Fiscal policy is the federal government's use of taxing and public spending to influence the macroeconomy. The 1960s, however, proved to be the *golden age of Keynesian economics.* During this period, some economists thought they could "fine-tune" the economy to avoid recessions—just as a mechanic could fine-tune a race car to achieve top performance. During the early 1960s, nearly all advanced economies around the world enjoyed low unemployment and healthy growth with only modest inflation. In short, the world economy was booming, and the U.S. economy was on top of the world.

Why is Keynes' approach to stimulating the economy out of depression known as demand-side economics? **CHECKPOINT**

STAGFLATION: 1973–1980

LO3 Use aggregate demand and aggregate supply to analyze stagflation.

During the late 1960s, federal spending increased on both the war in Vietnam and social programs at home. This combined stimulus increased aggregate demand enough that, in 1968, the inflation rate jumped to 4.4 percent, after averaging only 2.0 percent during the previous decade. Inflation climbed to 4.7 percent in 1969 and to 5.3 percent in 1970.

Reduction in Aggregate Supply

Inflation rates were so alarming that, in 1971, President Richard Nixon tried to put a ceiling on price and wage increases. The ceiling was eliminated in 1973, about the time crop failures around the world caused grain prices to climb. To compound these problems, OPEC cut its supply of oil, thus increasing oil prices. Decreases in the supplies of grain and oil reduced aggregate supply in the economy.

This reduction in aggregate supply is shown in Figure 15.7 by the leftward shift of the aggregate supply curve from AS_{1973} to AS_{1975}. This created the **stagflation** of the 1970s, meaning a stagnation, or a contraction, in the economy's aggregate output combined with inflation, or a rise, in the economy's price level. Real GDP declined between late 1973 and early 1975. At the same time, the price level jumped about 20 percent. The unemployment rate climbed from 4.9 percent in 1973 to 8.5 percent in 1975. Stagflation created higher inflation and higher unemployment.

Stagflation Repeats in 1980

stagflation A decline, or stagnation, of a nation's output accompanied by a rise, or inflation, in the price level

Stagflation hit again in 1980, fueled partly by another jump in OPEC oil prices. Real GDP declined, and the price level climbed 9 percent. Because the problem of stagflation was primarily on the supply side, not on the demand side, Keynesian demand-management solutions seemed ineffective. Increasing aggregate demand might reduce unemployment, but it would worsen inflation.

CHECKPOINT **How is stagflation represented on the aggregate demand curve?**

FIGURE 15.7 Stagflation Between 1973 and 1975

The stagflation of the mid 1970s can be represented as a reduction of aggregate supply from AS_{1973} to AS_{1975}. Between late 1973 and early 1975, real GDP fell (stagnation), and the price level rose (inflation).

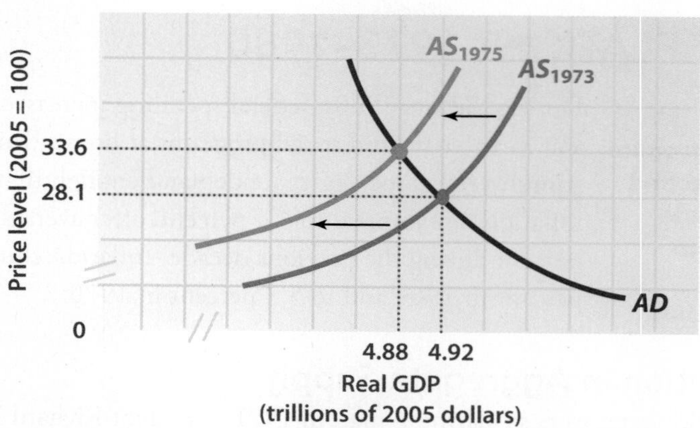

1981–2007: IMPROVING GROWTH, LOWER INFLATION, BUT HIGHER FEDERAL DEFICITS

LO4
Use aggregate demand and aggregate supply to analyze supply-side economics.

Increasing aggregate supply, or shifting the aggregate supply curve rightward, seemed an appropriate way to combat stagflation. Such a move would both lower the price level and increase output and employment. Attention thus turned from aggregate demand to aggregate supply.

Supply-Side Economics

A key idea behind **supply-side economics** was that cutting tax rates would stimulate aggregate supply. Lower tax rates would increase the incentive to supply labor. According to advocates of the supply-side approach, the resulting increase in aggregate supply would expand real GDP and reduce the price level. This, however, was easier said than done.

In 1981, President Ronald Reagan and Congress cut personal income tax rates by an average of 23 percent to be phased in over three years. They hoped the tax cuts would stimulate economic growth enough that the government's smaller share of a bigger pie would exceed what had been its larger share of a smaller pie.

In 1983, the economy began what at the time would become the longest peacetime expansion on record. During the rest of the 1980s, output grew, unemployment declined, and inflation declined. However, the growth in federal spending exceeded the growth in federal tax revenues during this period. Therefore, federal budget deficits swelled.

Large Federal Deficits

During the 1990s, policymakers began to worry more about large federal deficits. To reduce them, President George H.W. Bush increased taxes in 1990. President Bill Clinton increased taxes on the rich in 1993. A newly elected Republican Congress reduced federal spending growth beginning in 1995. *Higher tax rates and a slower growth in federal spending combined with an improving economy to reduce federal deficits. By 1998, the federal budget yielded a surplus.*

By early 2001, the U.S. economic expansion became the longest on record. During the decade-long expansion, 22 million jobs were added, the unemployment rate dropped from 7.5 percent to 4.2 percent, and inflation remained low. After achieving this record, the economy entered a recession in March 2001. Despite the terrorist attacks of September 2001, the recession ended in November 2001. Jobs started coming back in 2003 and beyond, with six million jobs added by early 2006. However, the mounting cost of the wars in Iraq and Afghanistan combined with tax cuts to worsen federal deficits. You will learn more about federal deficits in Chapter 17.

supply-side economics
Macroeconomic policy that focuses on a rightward shift of the aggregate supply curve through tax cuts or other changes that increase production incentives

CHECKPOINT

What was the key idea behind supply-side economics?

THE GREAT RECESSION OF 2008–2009 AND BEYOND

LO5
Use aggregate demand and aggregate supply to analyze the Great Recession.

By late 2007, the expansion, which began in late 2001, had lasted six years, a little longer than average since World War II. So it was not that surprising when the expansion ended in December 2007. This recession was triggered by declining home prices and rising foreclosures, as more borrowers failed to make their mortgage payments. With home prices falling, fewer homes were getting built. This meant fewer jobs in residential construction, furnishings, and other industries that rely on the housing sector. One immediate result of the softer economy was to nearly triple the federal deficit from $161 billion in 2007 to $460 billion in 2008.

The Global Financial Crisis of September 2008

Fears about the effect of rising home foreclosures on the banking system led to a full-scale global financial crisis in September 2008, triggered by the collapse of a Wall Street investment bank. Banks grew reluctant to lend, so credit dried up—a major problem for an economy that relies a lot on credit. Businesses cut their investment sharply. Fear spread to consumers, who cut their spending in the face of sliding home prices, mounting job losses, and a collapsing stock market. You could picture all this as a leftward shift of the aggregate demand curve, just as in Figure 15.6.

The Federal Government's Response

With financial flows drying up around the world, federal officials were emboldened to take some extraordinary measures. The objective was to shore up confidence in financial institutions, open up the flow of credit, and stimulate consumer spending. These measures included two huge programs: (1) the $700 billion Troubled Asset Relief Program, or TARP, aimed at stabilizing banks, and (2) the $787 billion American Recovery and Reinvestment Act, or the stimulus bill, aimed at increasing aggregate demand. The effects of these programs are still being debated and will be discussed in later chapters. What is certain is that these rescue programs helped triple the federal deficit from $460 in 2008 to $1.4 trillion in 2009, the largest ever.

During the 12 months following the financial crisis of September 2008, the economy lost 6.8 million jobs. The country had not experienced job losses on that scale since the Great Depression. By the third quarter of 2009, real GDP was growing again, though job growth did not return until 2010. Events that occurred during the recession of 2008–2009 traumatized the economy; they will be dissected for years, to explore the causes.

CHECKPOINT

How would the events leading to the global financial crisis of September 2008, and consumers' reaction to them, be pictured on the aggregate demand curve?

15.3 ASSESSMENT

Think Critically

1. Before 1929, most economists thought the federal government should always have a balanced budget (government revenues = government spending). When the Great Depression began in 1929, government revenues fell rapidly. The federal government responded by cutting spending. What was the impact of this policy on the economy?
2. People who support the economic theories of Keynes think that a stable economy will result from a steady increase of aggregate demand. Given this idea, what would Keynes have recommended the federal government do if consumption and investment declined because people and business owners started to worry about the future?
3. How could stagflation result from a large increase in the costs of production throughout the economy?

Graphing Exercise

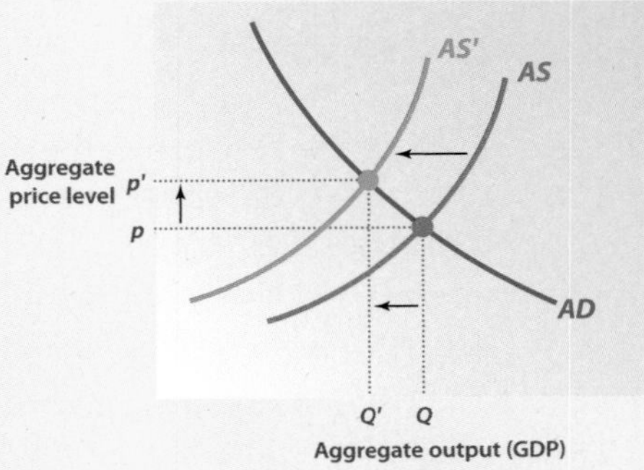

4. Study this graph of aggregate demand and supply. The aggregate supply curve has shifted to the left from *AS* to *AS'* because of an increase in the costs of production. This has increased the average price level and reduced the amount produced. Which of the policies listed below might reduce costs of production and cause the aggregate supply curve to return to its original location at *AS*? Why are these policies examples of supply-side economics?
   a. The government reduces taxes for businesses that buy new technology.
   b. By reducing red tape, the government lowers the cost of hiring new workers.
   c. The government lowers tariffs on imported raw materials.
   d. The government reduces taxes on business profits.
   e. The government gives grants to people who carry out applied research.

Make Academic Connections

5. **History** The U.S. government borrowed most of the money it needed to pay for its military efforts during World War II. The national debt increased by $23.5 billion in 1943, $64.3 billion in 1944, and $10.7 billion in 1945. In these years, the unemployment rate fell from its level of 14.0% in 1940, to 4.4% in 1942, 1.7% in 1943, and 1.0% in 1944. How did these data support Keynes' theory that the way to combat a depression is to have more government spending?

Organize the class into four teams. Each team should work with a different economic era. Analyze the era by drawing an aggregate supply and aggregate demand graph. A representative from each team should then present and explain its graph in class.

The New Deal and the Deficit

During the early years of the Great Depression, those who believed that the economy would correct itself suggested a laissez-faire approach to the business cycle. They viewed depressions as an unfortunate but necessary purge of the economy. They considered budget deficits to be inflationary, and a bad example for the nation's citizens.

Still, from 1929 to 1933, prices dropped severely, and the government deficit increased. Early attempts by President Herbert Hoover to balance the budget, such as sharply increasing tariffs on imports, made matters worse. In the face of increasing deficits, Hoover resisted more government intervention in the economy. He continued to advocate spending cuts and tax increases, telling Congress that "nothing is more necessary at this time than balancing the budget."

When Franklin D. Roosevelt swept into office in 1932, he initiated a host of programs known collectively as the New Deal. Although Roosevelt believed in a balanced budget, he was—unlike Hoover—willing to accept deficits in order to pump government spending into the economy. The Reconstruction Finance Corporation, first begun under Hoover, was beefed up. New programs—such as the Public Works Administration, the Agricultural Adjustment Administration, National Recovery Administration, and later the Works Progress Administration—were designed to boost federal spending to stimulate the economy.

Under the New Deal, the economy began a slow recovery until 1937, when Roosevelt, believing that the nation's economy was strong enough to continue on its own, announced a reduction in federal spending and a plan to balance the budget by 1939. Instead, by the fall of 1937, the economy began to falter and the president called for a resumption of deficit spending in April 1938.

Hulton Archive/Getty Images

John Maynard Keynes

By this time, many in the government had become supporters of the ideas of John Maynard Keynes. Keynes himself, however, believed Roosevelt's latest attempts to build up the economy needed far more government spending than the $3 billion prescribed by the president. Before the results of the Second New Deal could be fully judged, World War II intervened and the country was brought back to full employment. The events of the 1930s, however, changed how many Americans viewed fiscal policy. As deficit spending became more accepted, they saw the government as having a crucial role in the nation's economy.

Think Critically **Evaluate and compare the wisdom of deficit spending by the government from an economic perspective, from a social perspective, and from a political perspective.**

15.4 POVERTY

Learning Objectives

LO1 Describe the link among jobs, unmarried motherhood, and poverty.

LO2 Identify some unplanned results of income-assistance programs.

Key Terms

cycle of poverty 489
welfare reform 490

In Your World

How should the government respond to the challenge of poverty? In a market economy, your income depends primarily on how much you earn, which depends on the productivity of your resources. The problem with allocating income according to productivity is that some people have difficulty earning income. Families where someone has a job are much more likely to escape poverty than are families with no workers. Thus, the government's first line of defense in fighting poverty is to promote a healthy economy, thereby providing job opportunities for those who want to work.

POVERTY AND THE ECONOMY

LO1 Describe the link among jobs, unmarried motherhood, and poverty.

The best predictor of whether a family is poor is whether someone in that family has a job. If no one in the family has a job, the family is more likely to be poor. Thus, the most direct way the government can help reduce poverty is to nurture a healthy economy. The stronger the economy, the greater the job opportunities, and the more likely people can find good jobs.

Poverty and Jobs

The poverty rate is much higher among families with no workers. Figure 15.8 shows the poverty rate based on the type of family and on the number of workers in the family. Overall, the poverty rate is about four times greater in families with no workers than in families with at least one worker. *The poverty rate of families headed by a female and with no workers is 14 times greater than the rate for married-couple families with at least one worker.*

Poverty and Unemployment

Perhaps the best indicator of whether or not job opportunities are readily available is the unemployment rate. The lower the unemployment rate, the greater the

FIGURE 15.8 U.S. Poverty Rates by Family Type and Number of Workers

Regardless of the family structure, poverty rates in the United States are much higher in families with no workers.

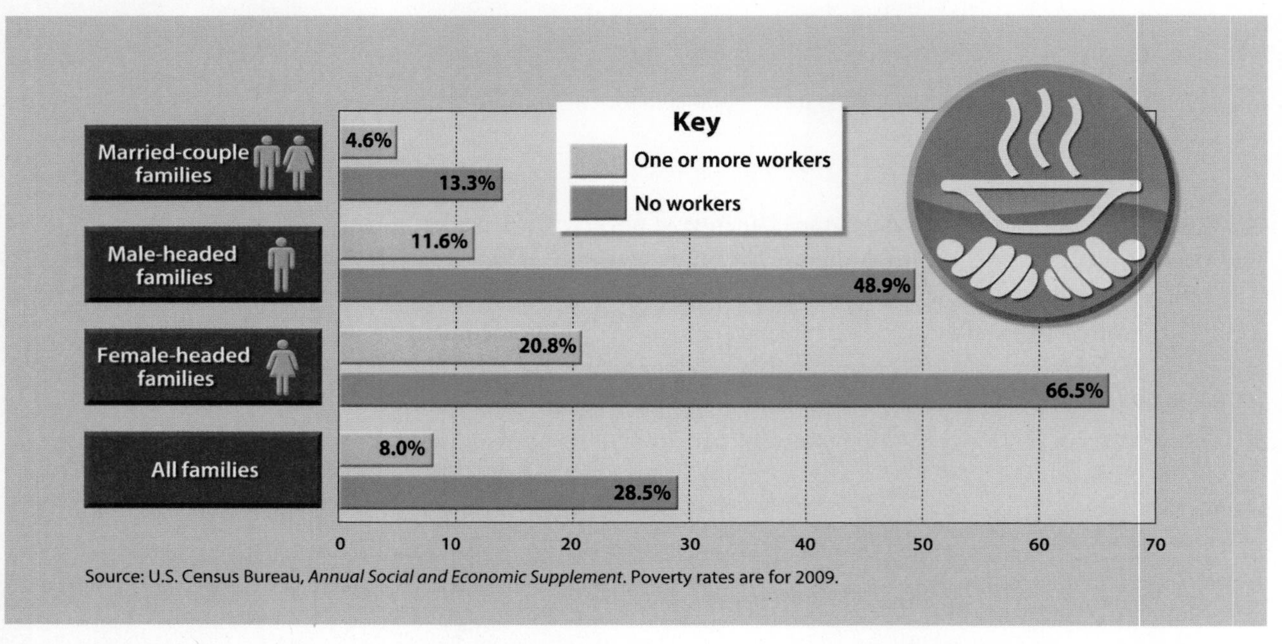

Source: U.S. Census Bureau, *Annual Social and Economic Supplement*. Poverty rates are for 2009.

Photodisc/Getty Images

Why is the government's nurturing a healthy economy important to reducing poverty?

likelihood that someone who wants to work can find a job. The more jobs available in the economy, the lower the poverty rate.

Figure 15.9 shows poverty rates and unemployment rates in the United States each year since 1969. As you can see, the poverty rate tends to rise when the unemployment rate increases and fall when the unemployment rate declines. For example, between 1979 and 1982 the unemployment rate climbed from 5.8 percent to 9.7 percent. During that same period, the nation's poverty rate rose from 11.7 percent to 15.0 percent. More recently, the unemployment rate rose from 4.6 percent in 2007 to 9.6 percent in 2010. During that same period, the poverty rate climbed from 12.5 percent to 15.1 percent.

FIGURE 15.9 U.S. Poverty Rates and Unemployment Rates

The top line shows the percentage of the U.S. population below the official poverty level. The bottom line shows the percentage of the U.S. labor force that is unemployed. Note that the poverty rate and unemployment rate tend to move together.

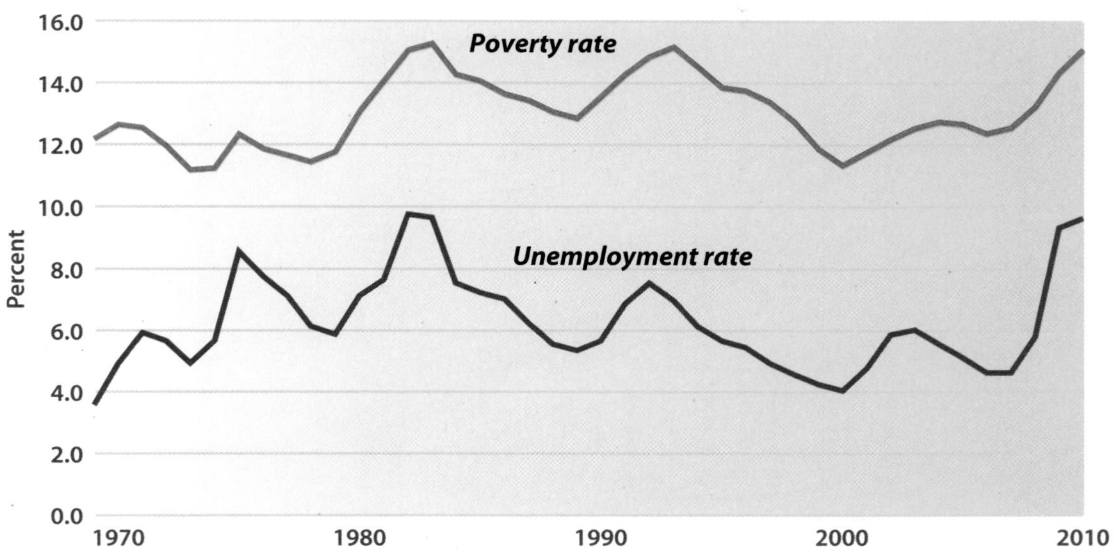

Source: U.S. Census Bureau, *Income, Poverty, and Health Insurance Coverage in the United States: 2010*, Current Population Reports, P60–238(RV), September 2011, Figure 3, p. 13; and U.S. Bureau of Labor Statistics.

Unmarried Motherhood and Poverty

Even when the unemployment rate is low, the poverty rate may remain stubbornly high. A strong economy with low unemployment is little aid to families with nobody in the labor force. Chapter 3 noted that young, single motherhood is a recipe for poverty. Often the young mother drops out of school, which reduces her future earning possibilities when and if she seeks work outside the home.

Because of a lack of education and limited job skills, most young single mothers go on welfare. Before recently imposed lifetime limits on welfare, the average never-married mother had been on welfare for a decade.

Figure 15.10 shows the poverty rates for each of the 50 states. Those states with a deeper shade of pink have the highest poverty rates. States with no shading have the lowest rates. As you can see, poverty rates are highest across the bottom half of the United States. Poverty rates tend to be highest in states where births to single mothers make up a large percentage of all births. For example, New Mexico, Louisiana, and Mississippi have the highest rates of births to unmarried mothers. Nearly one-half of all births in these three states are to unmarried mothers. These three states also have the highest poverty rates.

What is the link between jobs, unmarried motherhood, and poverty? **CHECKPOINT**

FIGURE 15.10 Poverty Rates in the United States

Poverty rates are higher across the southern states. Rates are lower along the Northern Atlantic Coast and across the Midwest.

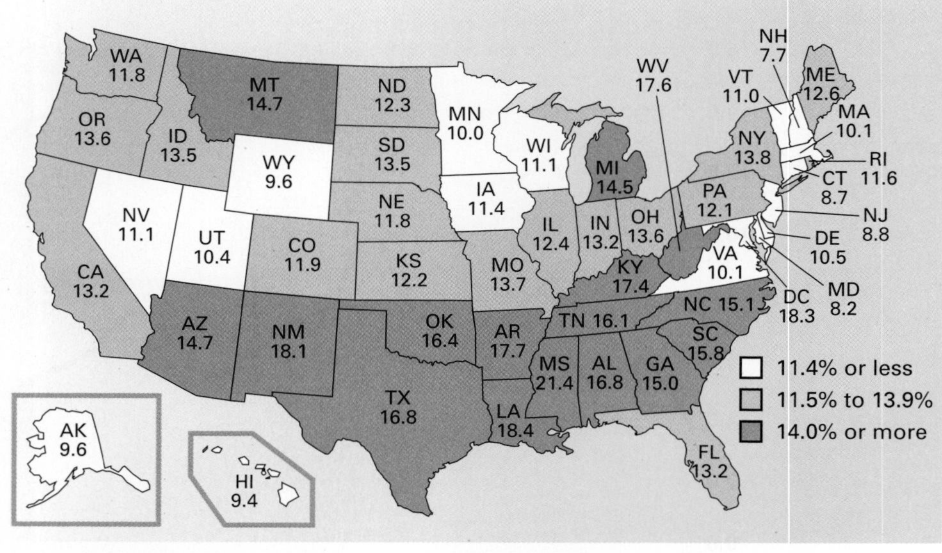

Source: U.S. Census Bureau at http://www.census.gov/hhes/www/poverty/poverty.html. Rates are for 2009.

UNPLANNED RESULTS OF INCOME ASSISTANCE

LO2 Identify unplanned results of income-assistance programs.

On the plus side, antipoverty programs increase the consumption possibilities of poor families. This is important because children are the largest group in poverty. However, programs to assist the poor may have other effects that limit their ability to reduce poverty. Consider some unplanned results of these programs.

Why Work?

Society, through government, tries to provide families with an adequate standard of living, but society also wants to ensure that only the poor receive benefits. Income assistance consists of a combination of cash and in-kind transfer programs. Because these programs are designed to help the poor and only the poor, welfare benefits decline as income from other sources increases. This has resulted in a system in which transfer payments decline sharply as earned income increases.

An increase in earnings reduces benefits from cash assistance, Medicaid, food vouchers, housing assistance, energy assistance, and other programs. In some cases, total welfare benefits are cut by $1 or more as earned income increases by $1. Because welfare benefits decline with earnings, this reduces the incentive to find work. Why work if doing so simply reduces your income and your standard of living? After all, holding even a part-time job involves additional expenses—for work clothes, transportation and childcare, for instance—not to mention the loss of free time. In many cases, the value of welfare benefits would exceed the disposable income resulting from full-time employment. Such a system can frustrate people trying to work their way off welfare. *The high tax rate on each additional dollar earned discourages employment and self-sufficiency.*

Long-Term Dependency

The longer people are out of work, the more their job skills weaken. When those who have been on welfare for years finally do look for work, their productivity and pay are usually lower than when they were last employed. This lowers their expected wage, thus making work even less attractive. Some economists argue that in this way, welfare benefits can lead to long-term dependency on welfare.

Cycle of Poverty

A second and more serious concern is that children in welfare families may end up on welfare themselves when they grow up. This is referred to as the **cycle of poverty**. Children in welfare households may learn the ropes about the welfare system and may come to view it as a normal way of life rather than as a temporary bridge.

cycle of poverty Children in welfare families may end up on welfare themselves when they grow up

Research indicates that daughters from welfare families are more likely than daughters in other families to participate in the welfare system themselves. It

Span the Globe

Pro-Poor Tourism

For many people in the world's poorest countries, poverty is an ongoing fact of life. Tourism is increasingly being used as an answer to some of the problems in these areas. "Pro-poor tourism," as it is called, is the idea of promoting tourism in order to provide jobs and ongoing economic growth without destroying the natural environment. Because many of these countries have no major industry, their undeveloped environments are an attractive draw for tourists. The growth of tourism can come at the expense of the people, however. Some of these projects cut off land and water access without providing enough new jobs to compensate for the loss. Another opportunity cost is that public funds which might otherwise have gone into providing services for the locals would now be spent on facilities for tourists. Still, if properly managed, tourism offers opportunities for participation and income.

Think Critically **Do you think pro-poor tourism is an effective way to help the people in the world's poorest countries? Why or why not?**

Sources: "Pro-Poor Tourism: Harnessing the World's Largest Industry for the World's Poor" International Institute for Environment and Development, May 2001; "Pro-Poor Tourism: Opportunities for Sustainable Local Development," *D&C Development and Cooperation* ,5 (September/October, 2000), pp. 12–14; and Oheneba Akwasi Akyeampong, "Pro-Poor Tourism: Residents' Expectations, Experiences and Perceptions in the Kakum National Park Area of Ghana," *Journal of Sustainable Tourism*, 19 (March,2011), pp. 197–213.

is hard to say whether welfare "causes" the link between mother and daughter, because the same factors that contribute to a mother's welfare status also can contribute to her daughter's welfare status.

Welfare Reforms

Concern about welfare dependency and a cycle of poverty prompted **welfare reform**, or an overhaul of the welfare system in 1996. The reform imposed a lifetime welfare limit of five years per recipient. As a condition of receiving welfare, the head of the household also must participate in education and training programs, search for work, or take some paid or unpaid position. The idea is to help people on welfare learn about the job market. Those who find work are able to maintain some of their welfare benefits, such as free medical care, during a transition period from welfare to work. Those who find jobs also get childcare services. This increases the incentive to work. The earned-income tax credit also boosts pay and thus the attractiveness of work.

welfare reform An overhaul of the welfare system in 1996 that imposed a lifetime welfare limit of five years per recipient and other conditions

Evidence from various states indicates that programs involving mandatory job searches, short-term unpaid work, and training increase employment. Those involved in such programs left welfare rolls sooner. Welfare recipients as a share of the U.S. population fell from 5.5 percent in 1994 to only 1.4 percent in 2010, as you can see in Figure 15.11.

FIGURE 15.11 Welfare Recipients as a Percentage of the U.S. Population

Welfare recipients as a percentage of the U.S. population declined sharply after welfare reform of 1996.

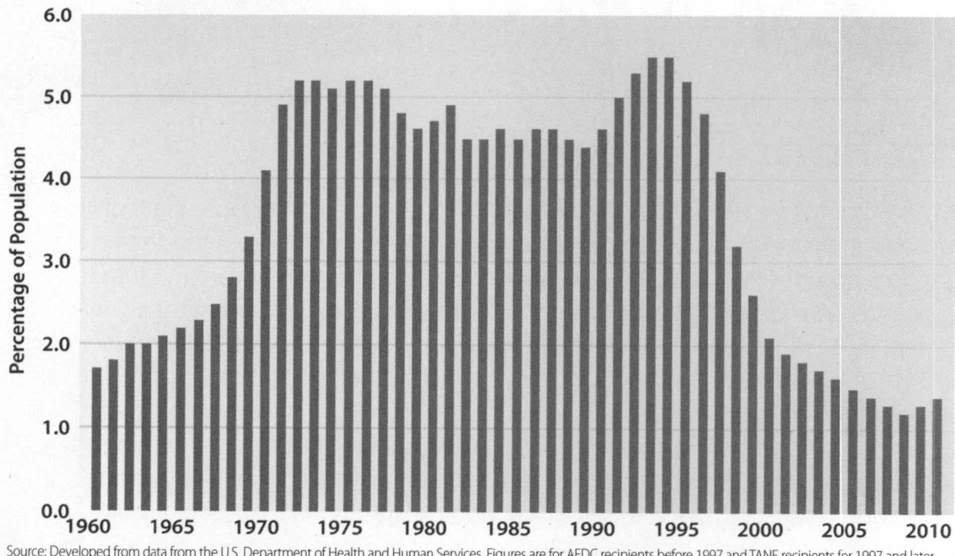

Source: Developed from data from the U.S. Department of Health and Human Services. Figures are for AFDC recipients before 1997 and TANF recipients for 1997 and later. Caseload figures for each year are found at http://www.acf.hhs.gov/programs/ofa/data-reports/index.htm.

CHECKPOINT What are some unplanned results of income-assistance programs?

15.4 ASSESSMENT

Think Critically

1. Why is nurturing a healthy economy the most direct way the government can help reduce poverty?
2. What reasons can you identify to explain why the number of welfare recipients in the United States fell by more than one-half between 1995 and 2010?
3. Does the fact that fewer people are receiving social benefits necessarily mean that fewer people are living in poverty? Explain why or why not.

Graphing Exercise

4. Many people think the bulk of federal government transfers are used to support the poor. This is not the case. In 2009, all federal government transfers to individuals totaled $2,094.1 billion. The table shows how these payments were distributed. Use the data in the table to construct a pie chart that shows how federal transfers were distributed. Is there any information in the graph that you find surprising? Explain why or why not.

FEDERAL TRANSFERS TO INDIVIDUALS BY USE, 2009 (IN BILLIONS OF DOLLARS)

Type of Spending	Amount	Percent of Total
Medical Payments (Medicare and Medicaid)	$813.8	38.9%
Retirement and Disability Insurance (Social Security)	$681.0	32.5%
Other Transfers to Individuals	$161.8	7.7%
Veteran's Benefits	$161.7	7.7%
Income Maintenance (SSI and Welfare)	$156.0	7.4%
Unemployment Insurance Benefits	$119.8	5.7%

Source: *Statistical Abstract of the United States, 2011*, p. 313.

Make Academic Connections

5. **Management** You are the owner of a small business that produces precision parts for specialized machines. If one of your skilled workers were to leave, it would take a long time to find and retrain a replacement. The economy has been in a recession for the past six months, and your firm's sales have fallen by 30 percent. You are having trouble selling enough to pay your workers and keep them busy. You are thinking of laying off three of your 10 workers. What reasons are there for you to do this or not do this? Explain each reason.

In small teams, make a list of additional expenses an unemployed single parent of two might reasonably expect to pay if he or she accepted a full-time job that provided no medical benefits. Estimate the amounts that this person would need to spend on each identified expense. Determine how much he or she would need to earn to make the job worthwhile. Compare your work with that of other teams.

Chapter 15 Summary

ASK THE **EXPERT**

www.cengage.com/school/contecon

What are the principal types of unemployment?

15.1 Unemployment

A. The labor force is made up of all people 16 and older who are either employed or seeking work. The labor force participation rate is the number of people in the labor force divided by the noninstitutionalized adult population.

B. Unemployment is more common among individuals who have less education, experience, or training. It also is more likely to affect young people and minorities. There is always some unemployment in the economy as workers move from job to job.

C. Unemployment compensation is paid to workers who lose their jobs through no fault of their own. The benefits may reduce the incentive to find a job.

15.2 Inflation

A. Inflation is an increase in the economy's general price level. Demand-pull inflation results from an increase in aggregate demand. Cost-push inflation results from a decrease in aggregate supply.

B. Some people are harmed and other people benefit when prices increase more than expected. Higher rates of inflation are associated with higher interest rates.

ASK THE **EXPERT**

www.cengage.com/school/contecon

Which is worse: demand-pull inflation or cost-push inflation?

15.3 Economic Instability

A. Before the Great Depression, most economists held a laissez-faire doctrine that said government's role in a market economy shoud be limited to keeping the peace and protecting property rights. The economic difficulties of the 1930s convinced many people that government intervention in the economy was sometimes necessary for the economy to work better. Keynes argued that the government should adjust its own spending and taxing to assure that there is sufficient aggregate demand in the economy to sustain production and employment.

B. By the 1970s, it became clear that Keynes's theories could not solve all economic problems. In these years, a combination of high rates of unemployment and inflation called stagflation occurred. In the 1980s, some economists suggested stagflation could be reduced or eliminated by implementing government policies that would reduce the costs of production. The tax cuts of 1981–1983 were intended to stimulate investment in the economy and were effective. One result of these and later tax cuts, however, was higher federal deficits and a growing national debt.

C. The financial crisis of September 2008 contributed to the worst recession since the Great Depression. To help stimulate aggregate demand, the federal government introduced some major spending programs. These new programs, along with falling tax revenues due to the poor economy, created the largest federal deficit on record.

15.4 Poverty

A. About one in seven people in the United States lives in poverty. Because poverty goes up when unemployment increases, the government's first line of attack in fighting poverty is supporting a vibrant job market.

B Income-assistance programs help people who live in poverty, but they also may reduce incentives to work. This has caused a long-term dependency on social programs that lead to what has been called a cycle of poverty.

CHAPTER 15 ASSESSMENT

Review Economic Terms

Match the terms with the definitions. Some terms will not be used.

_____ 1. Workers who are overqualified for their jobs or who work fewer hours than they would prefer

_____ 2. An increase in the economy's price level

_____ 3. Macroeconomic policy that focuses on shifting the aggregate demand curve as a way of promoting full employment and price stability

_____ 4. The number of people without jobs who are looking for work divided by the number in the labor force

_____ 5. Macroeconomic policy that focuses on a rightward shift of the aggregate supply curve through tax cuts or other changes that increase production incentives

_____ 6. The doctrine that the government should not intervene in a market economy beyond the minimum required to maintain peace and property rights

_____ 7. Inflation that results from a leftward shift of the aggregate supply curve

_____ 8. A decline of a nation's output accompanied by a rise in the price level

_____ 9. Inflation that results from a rightward shift of the aggregate demand curve

_____ 10. Children in welfare families may end up on welfare themselves when they grow up

_____ 11. The interest rate expressed in current dollars as a percentage of the amount loaned; the interest rate on a loan agreement

_____ 12. Occurs when there is no cyclical employment

a. cost-push inflation
b. cycle of poverty
c. demand-pull inflation
d. demand-side economics
e. full employment
f. inflation
g. labor force
h. labor force participation rate
i. laissez-faire
j. nominal interest rate
k. real interest rate
l. stagflation
m. supply-side economics
n. underemployment
o. unemployment benefits
p. unemployment rate
q. welfare reform

Review Economic Concepts

13. Imagine there are 150 million adults in a country. Of these, 45 million are not seeking work, and 105 million are either working or looking for work. In this case, the labor force participation rate is
    a. 40 percent.
    b. 70 percent.
    c. 30 percent.
    d. 60 percent.

14. **True or False** The labor force is made up of all the people who would like a job but lack employment.

15. Job seekers who lack the skills that are demanded by employers are ________?________.

16. **True or False** Interest rates tend to increase when the inflation rate increases.

17. Which of the following events would cause cost-push inflation?
    a. The price of natural gas increases by 20 percent.
    b. The stock market's value grows by 20 percent.
    c. The federal government cuts income taxes by 20 percent.
    d. The amount of grain produced in the United States grows by 20 percent.

18. ________?________ inflation is particularly harmful to people in businesses because they are not able to plan for it.

19. ________?________ results in higher unemployment and higher inflation.

20. Before the Great Depression, most economists believed that the government should
    a. intervene in the economy when there was a problem.
    b. intervene in the economy only when the federal government had a large debt.
    c. try not to intervene in the economy at any time.
    d. intervene in the economy at all times to make sure there was full employment.

21. **True or False** Poverty is closely associated with unemployment.

22. Which group is less likely to suffer from higher rates of unemployment and poverty than the average for all people?
    a. single parents
    b. minorities
    c. people with limited education
    d. two-parent families

Apply Economic Concepts

Identify items 23 to 27 as examples of

A. structural unemployment

B. cyclical unemployment

C. seasonal unemployment

D. frictional unemployment

E. discouraged worker

23. Rosetta quit her job at the public library to look for a job with better pay.

24. Brandon was laid off from his job as a lifeguard last September.

25. Peter was laid off from his job at Ford when Ford's sales declined.

26. Serena gave up looking for work after she got zero job offers in six months of looking.

27. Walter was laid off from his bookkeeping job after his employer installed a new automated inventory control system.

Calculate the Unemployment Rate Use the following data to calculate the items listed in exercises 28–31.

Total population: 10,000 people

Non-institutionalized adult population: 7,000 people

Adults who do not work and are not looking for work: 2,000 people

People who have employment: 4,750 people

28. the labor force.

29. the labor force participation rate.

30. the number of people who are unemployed.

31. the unemployment rate.

32. **History** Investigate the inflation that took place in Germany after World War I. In 1914, $1 was equal in value to 4.2 marks. By the end of November 1923, $1 had about the same value as 1 trillion marks. What impact did this hyperinflation have on the German economy and German people?

33. **21st Century Skills: Environmental Literacy** Imagine that you are the mayor of a small city that suffers from high unemployment. A large waste disposal firm sends you a letter that says it is interested in building a plant in your city where it would sort and dispose of industrial and residential waste. It would spend $20 million to build the plant and eventually employ from 100 to 120 workers. When you let the public know about the proposal, many people support the idea but others are strongly opposed. How would you try to reach an agreement among local voters for what to do? What else would you like to know about the plant's operation? What decision would you recommend? Explain your point of view.

34. **Graphing Inflation** Use data in the table to draw a line graph that shows the rate of inflation in the United States as measured by the Consumer Price Index (CPI). Why did prices decline in 2009?

RATES OF INFLATION AS MEASURED BY THE CPI, 1990–2010

Year	Inflation	Year	Inflation	Year	Inflation
1990	5.4%	1997	2.3%	2004	2.7%
1991	4.2%	1998	1.6%	2005	3.5%
1992	3.0%	1999	2.2%	2006	3.3%
1993	3.0%	2000	3.4%	2007	2.8%
1994	2.6%	2001	2.8%	2008	3.9%
1995	2.8%	2002	1.6%	2009	−1.0%
1996	3.0%	2003	2.3%	2010	1.7%

Source: *Economic Indicators*, July 2011, p. 23.

Digging Deeper

with Economics e-Collection

Access the Gale Economics e-Collection through the URL below to research unemployment, inflation, or poverty in the United States. Choose one of these three topics and find at least two recent articles related to it. After reading the articles, prepare a short oral presentation about the current status of unemployment, inflation, or poverty in this country. Keep a record of the source citation of the articles you read.

www.cengage.com/school/contecon

Sportstock/Shutterstock.com

UNIT 6

Public Policy and the U.S. Economy

Does the U.S. economy function pretty well on its own, or does it need government intervention to keep on track? According to one view, the economy can get off track quite easily, resulting in falling output and rising unemployment. To get the economy moving again, government must step in to boost employment and output. According to another view, the economy is fairly stable on its own. Even when things do go wrong, the economy can bounce back pretty quickly. If this second view is true, not only is government intervention unnecessary, it could do more lasting harm than good.

CONSIDER...

- → How does the demand for public goods differ from the demand for private goods?
- → How are responsibilities divided among levels of government?
- → How big is the federal budget, and where does the money go?
- → Why do politicians deal so much with special interest groups?
- → Why is it hard to interest the public in the public interest?

CHAPTER 16

Government Spending, Revenue, and Public Choice

Point your browser

www.cengage.com/school/contecon

Photodisc/Getty Images; Background image: Pefkos/Shutterstock.com

16.1 PUBLIC GOODS AND TAXATION

Learning Objectives

LO1 Determine the optimal quantity of a public good.

LO2 Distinguish between the two principles of taxation.

LO3 Discuss a tax's incidence, marginal rate, and effects on behavior.

Key Terms

benefits-received tax principle 501
ability-to-pay tax principle 502
tax incidence 503
proportional taxation 503
progressive taxation 503
regressive taxation 503
marginal tax rate 504

In Your World

Competitive markets are marvelous devices, but they are not perfect. They have limitations and shortcomings. For example, firms have little incentive to supply public goods because such goods, once produced, are available to all, regardless of who pays and who doesn't. Because a firm cannot limit the good just to those who pay for it, firms can't earn a profit selling public goods. Governments attempt to compensate for this market failure by supplying public goods and paying for them with taxes. The effects of government are all around you in ways large and small, from the quality of your education to the labels stitched into your clothing that give you washing instructions.

PUBLIC GOODS

LO1
Determine the optimal quantity of a public good.

You already learned about the market demand for a private good. For example, the market quantity of pizza demanded when the price is $10 is the quantity demanded by Alan, plus the quantity demanded by Maria, plus the quantity demanded by all other consumers in the pizza market. Because private goods are rival in consumption, the amount demanded at each price is the sum of the quantities demanded by each consumer.

The Demand for Public Goods

A public good is nonrival in consumption. A public good is available to all consumers in an identical amount. For example, if the town sprays Alan and Maria's neighborhood for mosquitoes for two hours per week, each resident benefits from fewer mosquito bites. Spraying is a public good that spreads through the neighborhood. The market demand for each hour of spraying reflects Alan's marginal benefit plus Maria's marginal benefit plus the marginal benefit to all others in the community.

For simplicity, suppose the neighborhood consists of only two households, one headed by Alan and the other by Maria. Alan spends a lot more time in the yard and therefore values a mosquito-free environment more than Maria does. Maria spends more time away from home. Alan's demand curve, D_a, is shown in the bottom panel of Figure 16.1. Maria's demand curve, D_m, appears in the middle panel. These demand curves reflect the marginal benefits that each person enjoys from each additional hour of spraying.

Figure 16.1 Market Demand for a Public Good

Because public goods, once produced, are available to all in identical amounts, the market demand for a public good sums up each person's demand at each quantity.

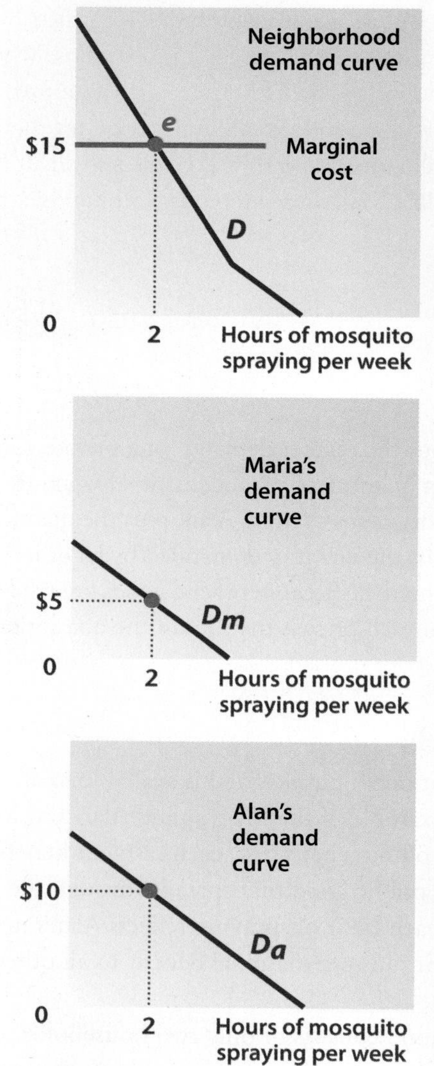

For example, when the town sprays two hours per week, Maria values the second hour at $5 and Alan values it at $10. To derive the sum of the marginal benefits of that second hour for the neighborhood, simply add up each marginal benefit to get $15, as identified by point *e* in the top panel. By vertically summing up marginal benefits at each quantity, you derive the neighborhood demand curve, *D*, for mosquito spraying.

Note again that the demand for private goods is found by horizontally summing quantities across consumers at each price. Pizza and other private goods are rival in consumption. A pizza sold to Alan cannot also be sold to Maria. But public goods are nonrival, so any given quantity of mosquito spraying benefits both Alan and Maria. Each may value that second hour of spraying differently, but the same quantity is available to each.

Optimal Quantity of the Public Good

How much mosquito spraying should the community provide? To determine the optimal level of a public good, compare the sum of the marginal benefits with the marginal cost. Suppose the marginal cost of spraying for mosquitoes is a constant $15 per hour, as shown in the top panel of Figure 16.1.

The efficient level of the public good is found where the sum of the marginal benefits equals the marginal cost of providing the good. This occurs where the neighborhood demand curve intersects the marginal cost curve. These two curves intersect at two hours per week. Thus, two hours is the efficient amount of spraying. That's where the marginal benefit enjoyed by the community just equals the marginal cost. If the town sprayed three or more hours per week, the marginal cost would exceed the marginal benefit.

What is the optimal quantity of a public good? CHECKPOINT

TAX PRINCIPLES

LO2 Distinguish between the two principles of taxation.

Two hours per week is the efficient, or optimal, quantity of the public good. How should the government pay for it? Taxes are the source of most government revenue. The way a tax is imposed often is justified on the basis of one of two general principles: the benefits received and the ability to pay.

Benefits-Received Taxation

The **benefits-received tax principle** relates taxes to the benefits taxpayers receive from a public good. For example, gasoline tax payments increase the more people drive. The more people drive, the more they benefit from roads financed by the gasoline tax. In that sense, the gasoline tax is based on the benefits-received tax principle. In the mosquito-spraying example, the government would impose a tax on each resident based on his or her marginal benefit from the good. In this case Alan would pay $10 per hour of spraying, or $20 in all. Maria would pay $5 per hour of spraying, or $10 in all. This seems simple enough, but there are at least two problems with it.

First, once people realize that their taxes are based on how much the government thinks they value the good, they tend to understate their true valuation. Why admit how much you value the good if, as a result, you get hit with a higher tax bill? Therefore, taxpayers are reluctant to offer information about their true valuation of public goods. This creates the *free-rider problem,* which occurs because people try to benefit from the public good without paying for it, or by paying less than they think it's worth.

Even if the government has accurate information about how much people value the good, the resulting tax may not seem fair if those who value the good more have lower incomes. In this example, Alan values mosquito spraying more than Maria does because he spends more time in the yard than she does. What if Alan is around more because he can't find a job? Maria is around less because she has a job. Should Alan's taxes be double those of Maria? Taxing people according to their marginal benefit may seem reasonable, but it may not be fair if the ability to pay differs sharply across taxpayers.

benefits-received tax principle Those who receive more benefits from the government program funded by a tax should pay more of that tax

Ability-to-Pay Tax Principle

The second approach to taxes is based on the **ability-to-pay tax principle**. Those with a greater ability to pay are taxed more. In the mosquito-spray example, Maria would pay more taxes because she has the greater ability to pay. For example, Maria might pay twice as much as Alan. Income and property taxes usually rely on the ability-to-pay approach. The ability-to-pay tax principle

ability-to-pay tax principle Those with a greater ability to pay, such as those with a higher income, should pay more of a tax

Math in Economics

Common Core Ratios and Proportional Relationships

Taxable income is the part of your income that you actually pay taxes on. It is the amount of your pay left after exemptions, deductions, and exclusions. You can calculate the amount of federal income tax you would have owed in 2010 on your taxable income by multiplying your taxable income (or the appropriate part) times the corresponding values in the table. To find the total amount owed, add the separate answers.

Tax Bracket	Filing Status—Single
10%	\$0–\$8,375
15%	\$8,376–\$34,000
25%	\$34,001–\$82,400
28%	\$82,401–\$171,850
33%	\$171,851–\$373,650
35%	All taxable income over \$373,650

EXAMPLE Find the amount of federal income tax you would have owed in 2010 if your taxable income were \$38,400.

SOLUTION Multiply the amount of your income in each tax bracket by the corresponding tax rate as a decimal. Add these products to find the tax you would have owed.

You pay 10% of the first \$8,375. \$8,375 × 0.10 = \$837.50

You pay 15% on the amount greater than \$8,375 up to \$34,000.

\$34,000 – \$8,375 = \$25,625, \$25,625 × 0.15 = \$3,843.75

You pay 25% on any amount greater than \$34,000 up to \$82,400;

\$38,400 – \$34,000 = \$4,400, \$4,400 × 0.25 = \$1,100

\$837.50 + \$3,843.75 + \$1,100.00 = \$5,781.25

Practice the Skill Find the amount of federal income tax due in 2010 for each taxable income.

1. If your taxable income had been \$21,800.
2. If your taxable income had been \$86,000.
3. Do the federal income tax rates represent a progressive, regressive, or proportional tax system? Explain how you know.

focuses more on taxpayer's income or wealth than on the taxpayer's benefit from the public good. Maria might not think the tax is fair, because she is paying twice as much as Alan, even though she values the good only half as much as he does. Neither the ability-to-pay tax principle nor the benefits-received tax principle can be said to be absolutely fair in all circumstances.

Public goods are more complicated than private goods in terms of what goods should be produced, in what quantities, and who should pay. These decisions are sorted out through public choices, which are examined later in the chapter.

What are the two principles of taxation? **CHECKPOINT**

OTHER REVENUE ISSUES

LO3 Discuss a tax's incidence, marginal rate, and effects on behavior.

Ability-to-pay and benefits-received are two ways of justifying a particular tax. Another way to understand a tax is to focus on its rates across households and over time. For example, how do tax rates differ based on a household's income? What is the top tax rate, and how has that changed over time? Yet another way to understand a tax is to look at its effect on people's behavior. Some taxes aim to discourage consumption, such as taxes on cigarettes or liquor. Other taxes have unintended effects on behavior, for example, by discouraging work or investment. Besides taxes, other revenue sources include user fees, such as admissions to state parks. If revenues fall short of expenditures, governments cover the resulting deficit by borrowing money.

Tax Incidence

Tax incidence indicates who actually bears the burden of the tax. One way to evaluate tax incidence is by measuring the tax as a percentage of income. Under **proportional taxation**, taxpayers at all income levels pay the same percentage of their income toward that tax. A proportional income tax is also called a *flat tax*, because the tax as a percentage of income remains constant, or flat, as income increases.

Under **progressive taxation**, the percentage of income paid in taxes increases as income increases. The federal income tax and most state income taxes are progressive, because tax rates increase as taxable income increases.

Finally, under **regressive taxation**, the percentage of income paid in taxes decreases as income increases, so the tax rate declines as income increases. For example, Social Security taxes in 2010 collected 6.2 percent of the first $106,800 of a workers' earnings. The tax rate imposed on income above that level dropped to zero. The average Social Security tax rate declines as income exceeds $106,800.

tax incidence Indicates who actually bears the burden of a tax

proportional taxation The tax as a percentage of income remains constant as income increases; also called a flat tax

progressive taxation The tax as a percentage of income increases as income increases

regressive taxation The tax as a percentage of income decreases as income increases

Marginal Tax Rate

The **marginal tax rate** is the percentage of each additional dollar of a taxpayer's income that goes to taxes. High marginal rates reduce the after-tax income from working, saving, and investing. Therefore, high rates can reduce people's incentives to work, save, and invest. As of 2012, six marginal rates for those who must pay federal income taxes range from 10 percent to 35 percent, depending on income. Most households in the bottom half of the income distribution pay no income taxes. Because of the earned income tax credit, which was discussed in Chapter 3, more than 20 million people with low earnings receive tax refunds that exceed the amount paid in.

Federal income tax rates are, therefore, progressive. Figure 16.2 shows the top marginal tax rate on federal personal income taxes since the tax was introduced in 1913. Note that most recently the highest rate was relatively low by historical standards. Still, the top 10 percent of tax filers, based on income, pay more than two-thirds of all federal income taxes collected.

marginal tax rate The percentage of each additional dollar of income that goes to pay a tax

Pollution Taxes and Sin Taxes

At times, taxes and fines are imposed to discourage certain activities. For example, government may impose a tax or a fine on pollution emissions. Fines for

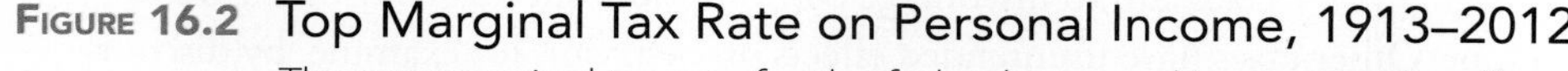

FIGURE 16.2 Top Marginal Tax Rate on Personal Income, 1913–2012

The top marginal tax rate for the federal personal income tax has fluctuated during the past century. The top 10 percent of tax filers, based on income, pay more than two-thirds of all federal income taxes collected.

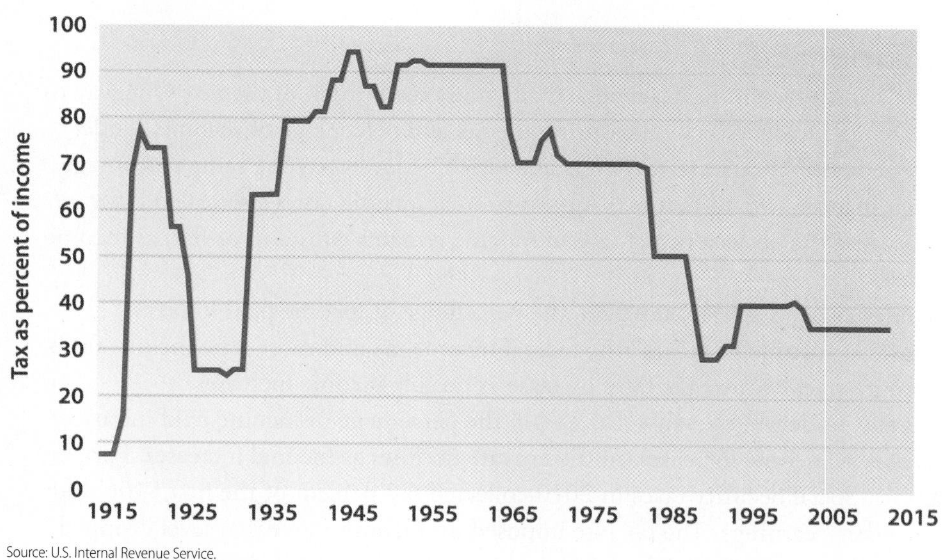

Source: U.S. Internal Revenue Service.

littering, disturbing the peace, and having a defective muffler are designed to reduce these negative externalities. To discourage activities deemed socially undesirable, governments also impose *sin taxes* on cigarettes, liquor, and legal gambling.

Photodisc/Getty Images

Why would the local government of this beach town impose a $1,000 fine for littering?

Unintended Consequences of Taxes

Some taxes have unintended consequences. For example, income taxes can reduce the incentive to work and to invest. Some taxes distort resource allocation in other ways. In Egypt, for example, a property tax is not imposed until a structure is built. To avoid this tax, buildings remain unfinished—missing the top floor, or some windows. Property taxes in Amsterdam and in Vietnam were originally based on the width of the building. As a result, buildings there are extremely narrow but very deep, which results in a poorly designed structure. Such taxes distort the efficient allocation of resources.

User Fees

Sometimes the government can easily exclude those who don't pay for a good and so can charge a user fee. For example, states charge entrance fees at state parks and tuition at public colleges. Those unwilling to pay are not admitted. A user fee is just like the price for a private good except that the user fee usually does not cover the full cost.

Borrowing

Governments sometimes borrow from households, firms, other goverments, and from the rest of the world to fund public programs. Government borrowing can be justified for capital projects that increase the economy's productivity—investments such as highways, airports, and schools. The cost of these capital projects should be borne in part by future taxpayers, who also will benefit from these investments. Governments, especially the federal government, also borrow when revenues fall short of expenditures. Government borrowing is examined in the next chapter.

Name the three ways of evaluating tax incidence. **CHECKPOINT**

16.1 ASSESSMENT

Think Critically

1. Why isn't a campsite you rent in a national park a perfect example of a public good?
2. Suppose your town council has determined that it would need to spend $1 million to repave and widen the road that leads to your school. How should council members decide whether to undertake this project?
3. Why isn't it logical for the government to pay for a welfare program by imposing a benefits-received principle tax?
4. Why aren't property taxes, particularly for older people, always examples of ability-to-pay principle taxes?
5. Why is it difficult for people to agree on a tax structure that is fair for all?
6. How willing would you be to work 10 hours next week at a local store to earn $100? If $25 of your earnings were taken to pay taxes, what would happen to your willingness to work? What if $50 or $75 were taken? How does this example demonstrate the importance of the marginal tax rate to production in the economy?

Graphing Exercise

7. Many residents of Oakwood, a small town, have asked to have the town's swimming pool kept open for eight hours each day during the summer instead of only six hours. The cost of operating the pool is $80 per hour. Draw a graph that shows the efficient level of swimming pool hours per day to be eight hours. Explain how your graph demonstrates that this is the optimal quantity of this public good.

Make Academic Connections

8. **Math** Patty is a loan officer for a bank. She earns $80,000 per year and drives a new Jaguar. Tony is a night janitor who works for the same bank. He earns $20,000 per year and drives an old Ford. Both Patty and Tony buy 1,000 gallons of gasoline for their cars each year. The tax per gallon of gasoline is $0.50. How much does each person pay in gasoline tax? What percent is this payment of each person's income? Is the tax on gasoline proportional, progressive, or regressive? Explain how you know.

Working in teams of three, brainstorm a list of user fees—other than those listed in the text—that you might have to pay. Share your results with the rest of the class.

MOVERS AND SHAKERS

Kathleen Sebelius

Secretary, U.S. Department of Health and Human Services

You might say that politics is in Kathleen Sebelius's blood. When she was young, her father John J. Gilligan, served on the city council in Cincinnati, Ohio; as a U.S. representative; and as governor of Ohio. Kathleen decided to pursue a political science degree from Trinity Washington University in Washington, D.C. Later she earned a master's degree in public administration from the University of Kansas. Along the way, she met and married Gary Sebelius, the son of a former congressman from Kansas.

A Democrat, Kathleen won a seat in the Kansas House of Representatives in 1986 and served for eight years. She then became the Kansas Insurance Commissioner. In 2002 she was elected governor of Kansas and was reelected to a second term in 2006. Sebelius was able to create consensus with Republicans on issues such as school financing and the state budget. In her first year as governor, she ordered a top-down review of the state government resulting in the elimination of a $1.1 billion budget deficit. Her policies also helped improve the Kansas economy and increased jobs.

In her campaign for governor, Sebelius promoted her ability to rid the government of wasteful spending. She said, "I know firsthand you find waste in state government. As Insurance Commissioner, I reduced the department's budget by 19 percent while vastly improving department services." As governor she performed an "in-depth look at government operations and initiated an extensive review of state government, looking for waste and inefficiency. The results of her review added up to nearly $1 billion in savings and efficiencies in just a few years. During her tenure as governor she also fired two state attorneys, who she believed "were double-billing the state and charging exorbitant fees." She lowered the fees paid to other state attorneys and, through these efforts, saved the state more than $4 million.

When Sebelius took over as governor, the Kansas sales tax applied only to tangible goods such as groceries, cars, and clothing. Service providers, such as accountants, beauticians, and veterinarians, were not taxed. Asked if she thought such a tax structure was fair, she said, "I will fight to make sure that no single sector of

UNITED STATES DEPARTMENT OF HEALTH AND HUMAN SERVICES

our economy or group of our citizens bears a disproportionate share of our tax burden."

President Barack Obama appointed her Secretary of the U.S. Department of Health and Human Services (HHS), the government agency responsible for keeping Americans healthy and making sure they get proper health care. She was sworn into that office on April 28, 2009, and worked to implement the health-care reform bills passed by both houses of Congress. On why health care is such an important issue in the United States, Sebelius said, "When we talk about health-care, we always keep in mind that we are not just talking about saving money or increasing efficiency. We are also talking about providing a higher quality of life. When people are healthy, they miss fewer days of work and get more done. They spend more time at home and less time in doctors' offices."

Think Critically **Sebelius promised to "fight to make sure that no single sector of economy or group of our citizens bears a disproportionate share of our tax burden." Do you think this statement supports the benefits-received principle of taxation or the ability-to-pay principle? Explain your answer.**

Sources: http:/ http://www.biography.com/articles/Kathleen-Sebelius-354546; http://topics.nytimes.com/topics/reference/timestopics/people/s/kathleen_sebelius/index.html; http://www.kathleensebelius2012.com/kathleen%20sebelius%20biography.shtml; http://www.grist.org/article/whats-not-the-matter-with-kansas; and The White, Female Obama: Kathleen Sebelius for Obama's VP? | NowPublic News Coverage http://www.nowpublic.com/politics/white-female-obama-kathleen-sebelius-obamas-vp#ixzz1SWBiAum8

16.2 FEDERAL, STATE, AND LOCAL BUDGETS

Key Terms

government budget 508
payroll taxes 510

Learning Objectives

LO1 Identify the top spending category in the federal budget and the top source of revenue.

LO2 Identify the top spending category in state budgets and the top source of revenue.

LO3 Identify the top spending category in local budgets and the top source of revenue.

LO4 Compare the size of government here and abroad.

In Your World

The United States has a federal system of government, meaning that responsibilities are shared across levels of government. State governments grant some powers to local governments and surrender some powers to the national, or federal, government. As the system has evolved, the federal government has assumed primary responsibility for national security and the stability of the economy. State governments fund public higher education, most prisons, and—with grants from the federal government—highways and welfare. Local governments are responsible mainly for local schools—perhaps your school—though much funding for this comes from the state government. Taxes provide most revenue at all levels of government. The federal government relies primarily on the personal income tax. State governments rely on income and sales taxes. Local governments rely on the property tax.

FEDERAL BUDGETS

LO1 Identify the top spending category in the federal budget and the top source of revenue.

A **government budget** is a plan for spending and revenues for a specified period, usually a year. The word *budget* derives from the Old French word *bougette*, meaning "little bag." The federal budget is now about $3,800,000,000,000—$3.8 trillion a year. If this "little bag" contained $100 bills, it would weigh more than 40,000 *tons!* These $100 bills could cover a 22-lane highway stretching from northern Maine to southern California.

government budget A plan for government spending and revenues for a specified period, usually a year

Federal Spending

One way to track the impact of government spending over time is to compare that spending to the U.S. gross domestic product, or GDP. In 1929, the year the Great Depression began, government spending at all levels totaled about 10 percent of GDP. Local government spending accounted for about one-half that total. The federal government played a minor role in the economy. In fact, during the nation's first 150 years, federal spending, except during war years, never exceeded 3 percent of GDP.

The Great Depression, World War II, and a change in economic thinking boosted government spending, particularly at the federal level, to about 40 percent of GDP most recently. The federal portion accounts for nearly two-thirds of the total. Thus, since 1929, government spending relative to GDP has increased fourfold and the federal portion has increased eightfold.

Figure 16.3 shows the share of federal spending by major category since 1960. The share of the budget going to national defense fell from 52 percent in 1960 to only 20 percent in 2011. Redistribution, which consists largely of Social Security, Medicare, and welfare benefits, grew steadily as a share of the total, climbing from 21 percent in 1960 to 48 percent in 2011. In 1960, the federal government focused primarily on national defense. By 2011, spending had shifted to income redistribution.

Interest payments on the federal debt stood at 8 percent of the budget in 1960, grew during the middle years, and then declined (thanks to record low interest rates on government borrowing) to 7 percent by 2011. Spending on all other programs, from federal prisons to the environment, went from 20 percent in 1960 to 25 percent in 2011.

FIGURE 16.3 Composition of Federal Outlays Since 1960

As a share of the federal budget, defense spending has declined and redistribution has increased since 1960.

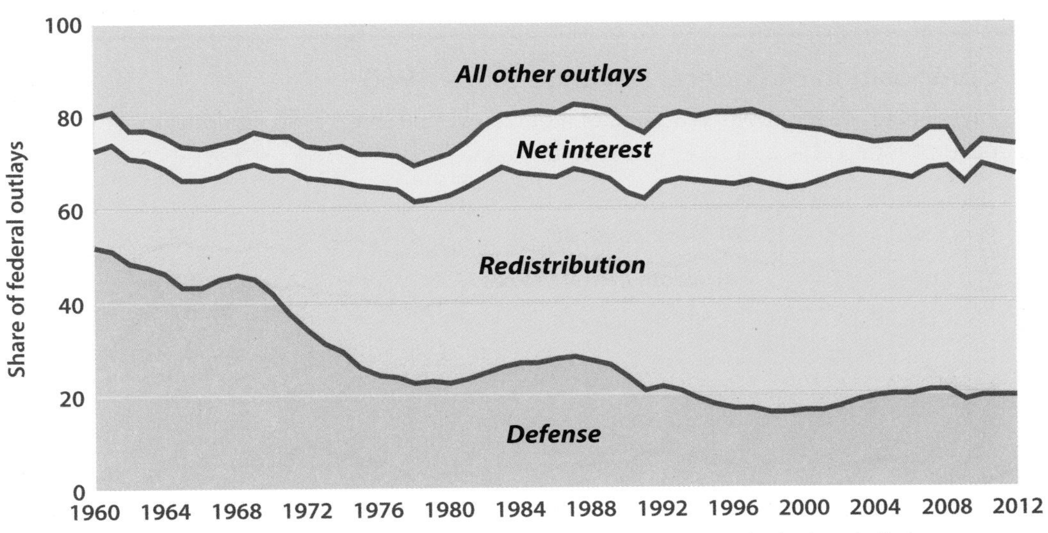

Source: Based on fiscal year outlays from *Economic Report of the President*, February 2011, Table B-80. Figures for 2011 are projections based on the president's budget.

Federal Revenue

During its first century, the federal government raised most of its revenue from taxes on imports, taxes on specific goods, and property taxes. All that changed with the Sixteenth Amendment to the U.S. Constitution. This empowered Congress to levy a tax on personal income. The personal income tax was introduced in 1913. The tax originally affected only the top 10 percent of households based on income. Rates were raised during World War II to help pay for the war. The personal income tax has remained the primary source of federal revenue.

Figure 16.4 shows the composition of federal revenue since 1960. The personal income tax share fluctuated from 42 percent to 50 percent of the total during the period. Income tax cuts in 2001 and 2003 and a slumping economy in 2011 reduced income taxes as a share of all revenue from 50 percent in 2001 to 44 percent in 2011, the same as in 1960.

Because of higher tax rates and an increase in the amount of income to which the tax applies, the share coming from payroll taxes more than doubled from 16 percent in 1960 to 36 percent in 2011. **Payroll taxes** are deducted from paychecks to support Social Security, which is a retirement program, and Medicare, which was introduced in the mid-1960s to fund medical care for the elderly. The abbreviation *FICA* on your paycheck stub refers to these payroll taxes. FICA stands for the Federal Insurance Contributions Act. Corporate income taxes declined as a share of the total from 23 percent in 1960 to 12 percent in 2011. All other sources combined, including tariffs and user charges, fell from 17 percent to 8 percent.

payroll taxes Taxes deducted from pay to support Social Security and Medicare programs

Note that Figure 16.4 shows the composition of revenue sources and ignores borrowed funds. The federal government usually spends more than it takes in and makes up the difference by borrowing from the public. This is discussed in the next chapter.

FIGURE 16.4 Composition of Federal Revenue Since 1960

Payroll taxes have grown as a share of federal revenue since 1960. Personal income taxes have changed little as a share of the total.

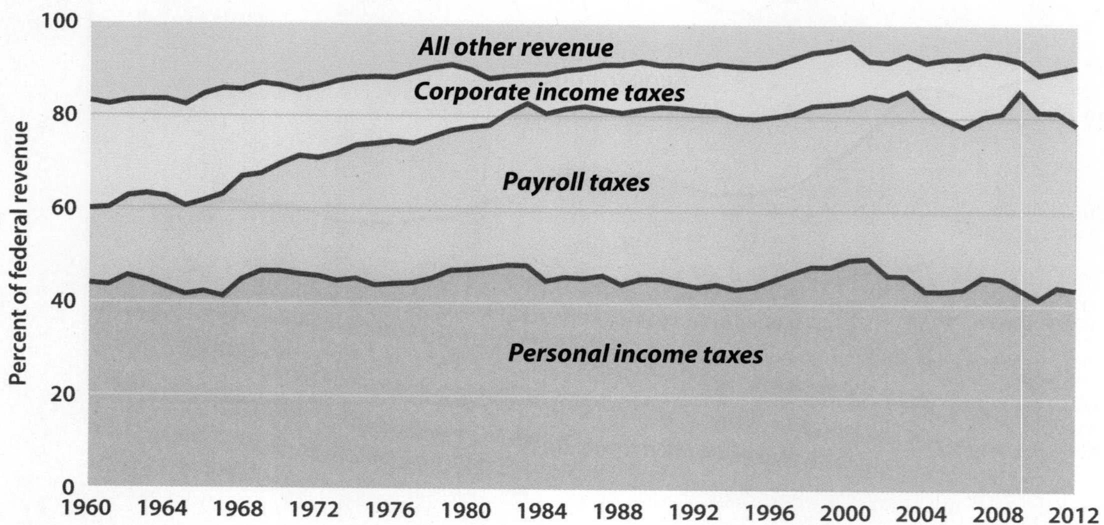

Source: Based on fiscal year revenue figures from the *Economic Report of the President*, February 2011, Table B-80. Figures for 2011 and 2012 are projections based on the president's budget.

What is the top spending category in the federal budget and the top source of revenue?

STATE BUDGETS

LO2 Identify the top spending category in state budgets and the top source of revenue.

You already know something about state government. You travel on state roads, visit state parks, and may be planning to attend a state college. State regulations dictate how old you must be to get a driver's license, how fast you may drive on most roads, and how many days per year school is in session. You pay state excise taxes on certain items, including gasoline and movie tickets. If you earn a paycheck, you may pay state income taxes. You also may pay state sales taxes on most purchases. From the department of motor vehicles to the department of education, state government affects your life in many ways.

State Spending

The pie chart on the left of Figure 16.5 shows the composition of spending by all U.S. states. The largest chunk, 32 percent of the total, goes toward aid to local governments, mostly to help pay for schools. The next largest share, 30 percent, goes to social services, including welfare payments. Most state welfare spending funds medical care for the poor, especially elderly in nursing homes. Education ranks third at 15 percent of the total. The remaining 23 percent pays for highways, state police, prisons, interest on state debt, administration, and other state activities.

FIGURE 16.5 Composition of State Spending and State Revenue

The largest share of state spending goes toward aid to local governments. The largest source of state revenue is aid from the federal government.

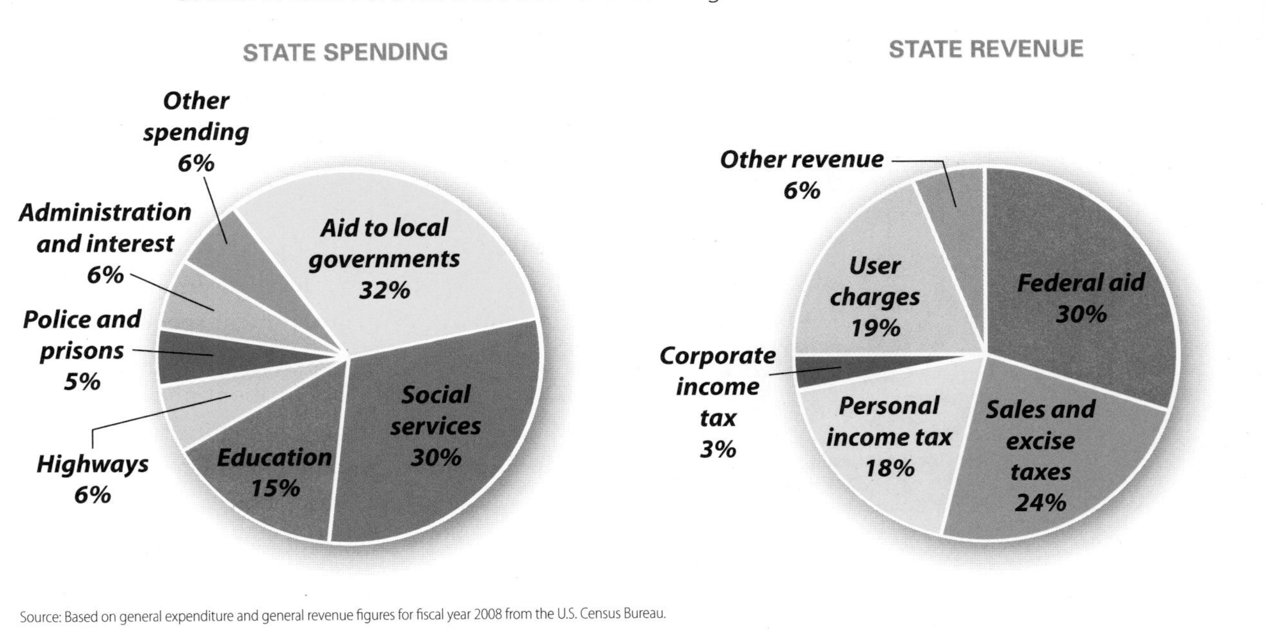

Source: Based on general expenditure and general revenue figures for fiscal year 2008 from the U.S. Census Bureau.

Investigate Your Local Economy

Research to find out the size of your local government's budget and how much of this budget is spent on local schools. What are the other items in the budget, and how much is spent on each? Present your findings in a pie chart.

State Revenue

The pie chart on the right in Figure 16.5 shows the sources of state revenue. The largest source, 30 percent of the total, is aid from the federal government, which covers more than one-half of state welfare costs. The second largest source, sales and excise taxes, makes up 24 percent of state revenue. Sales taxes collect a percentage of the sales price for broad categories of goods. All but five states imposed a sales tax as of 2011. California has the highest rate at 8.25 percent. Does your state have a sales tax? If so, what's the rate and how broad is the tax base (most states exempt food and medicine from sales taxes)? Excise taxes apply to specific goods such as cigarettes and gasoline, which are taxed in all states.

The third largest source of state revenue is user charges, making up 19 percent of the total. Examples include admissions to state campgrounds and tuition at state colleges. The state personal income tax ranks fourth, accounting for 18 percent of state revenue. All but seven states imposed a tax on at least some forms of income as of 2011, and most rates are progressive. Hawaii has the highest marginal tax rate at 11 percent in the top tax bracket. Does your state have an income tax? If so, what are the marginal rates?

CHECKPOINT **What is the top spending category in state budgets and the top source of revenue?**

LOCAL BUDGETS

LO3
Identify the top spending category in local budgets and the top source of revenue.

Of all government levels, you may be most familiar with your local one. You may be attending a public school. You may get to school in a government-funded bus on roads maintained by local government and patrolled by local police. Local schools decide school hours, what you may wear to school, and when you eat lunch. You may stroll on city sidewalks to visit city parks or the local library. Your family pays property taxes either directly as property owners or indirectly as part of the rent. Your family also may pay user fees for water, trash collection, parking, and other local services.

What is the largest spending category for a local government?

Local Spending

Before the Great Depression, local government accounted for one-half of all government spending. However, the growing importance of the federal government has reduced the local share to about one-sixth of the total. The pie chart on the left in Figure 16.6 shows the composition of local spending. No other spending category comes close to education, which accounts for 44 percent of the total. Social services rank a distant second at 12 percent.

FIGURE 16.6 Composition of Local Spending and Local Revenue

The largest category of local spending is education. State and federal aid make up the largest source of local revenue.

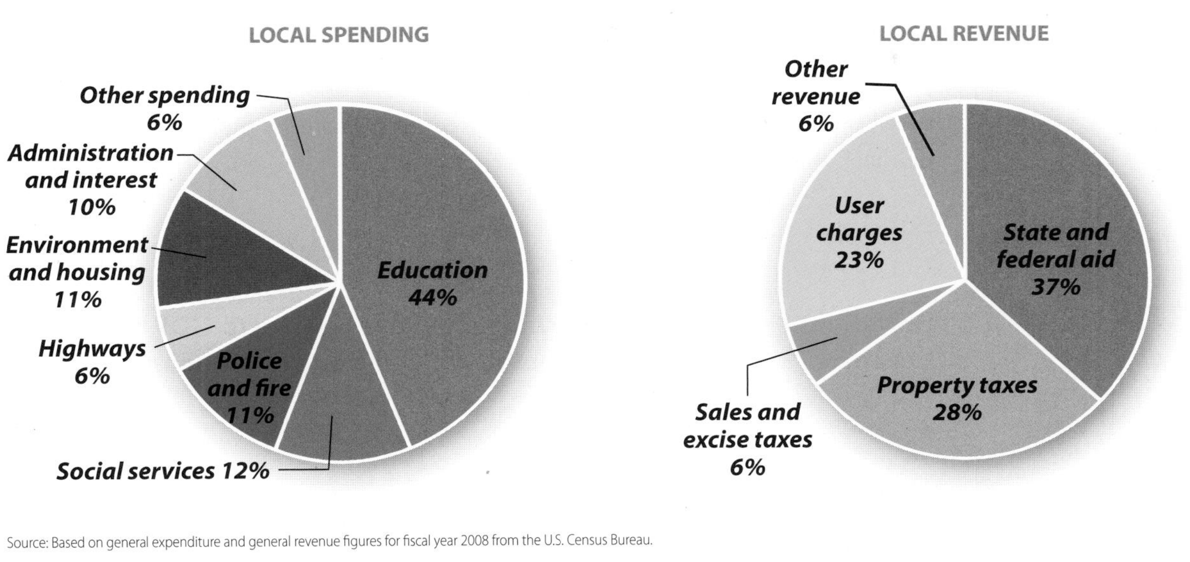

Source: Based on general expenditure and general revenue figures for fiscal year 2008 from the U.S. Census Bureau.

Local Revenue

As the right-hand pie chart in Figure 16.6 shows, state and federal aid make up 37 percent of local revenue, by far the largest source. Most of this aid funds local schools. The property tax accounts for 28 percent of local revenue. User charges rank third at 23 percent. Examples of user charges include charges for water, sewer services, parking meters, and school lunches.

What is the top spending category in the local budget and the top source of revenue?

RELATIVE SIZE AND GROWTH OF GOVERNMENT

LO4 Compare the size of government here and abroad.

So far, the focus has been on each level of government, but a fuller picture includes all three levels. How has the size of government in America changed in recent decades, and how does that compare with other major economies around the world?

An International Comparison

Figure 16.7 shows government outlays at all levels relative to GDP in 10 major industrial economies for 1993 and 2012. Government outlays in the United

States in 2012 were 40 percent relative to GDP, the second smallest share in the group. This is up slightly from 38 percent in 1993, a year when only Japan among the 10 industrial economies had a smaller government share.

Between 1993 and 2012, government outlays relative to GDP decreased in 7 of these 10 industrial economies. The average dropped from 47 percent to 45 percent. Why the drop? The breakup of the Soviet Union in the early 1990s reduced defense spending in major economies. The poor performance of most socialist economies around the world shifted voter attitudes more toward private markets, thus lessening the role of government.

How did the size of U.S. government outlays relative to GDP change between 1993 and 2012 compared with other major economies?

Figure 16.7 Government Outlays as Percent of GDP: 1993 and 2012

Government outlays as percent of GDP declined between 1993 and 2012 in seven of these 10 major industrial economies. That share rose in the United States from 38 to 40 percent.

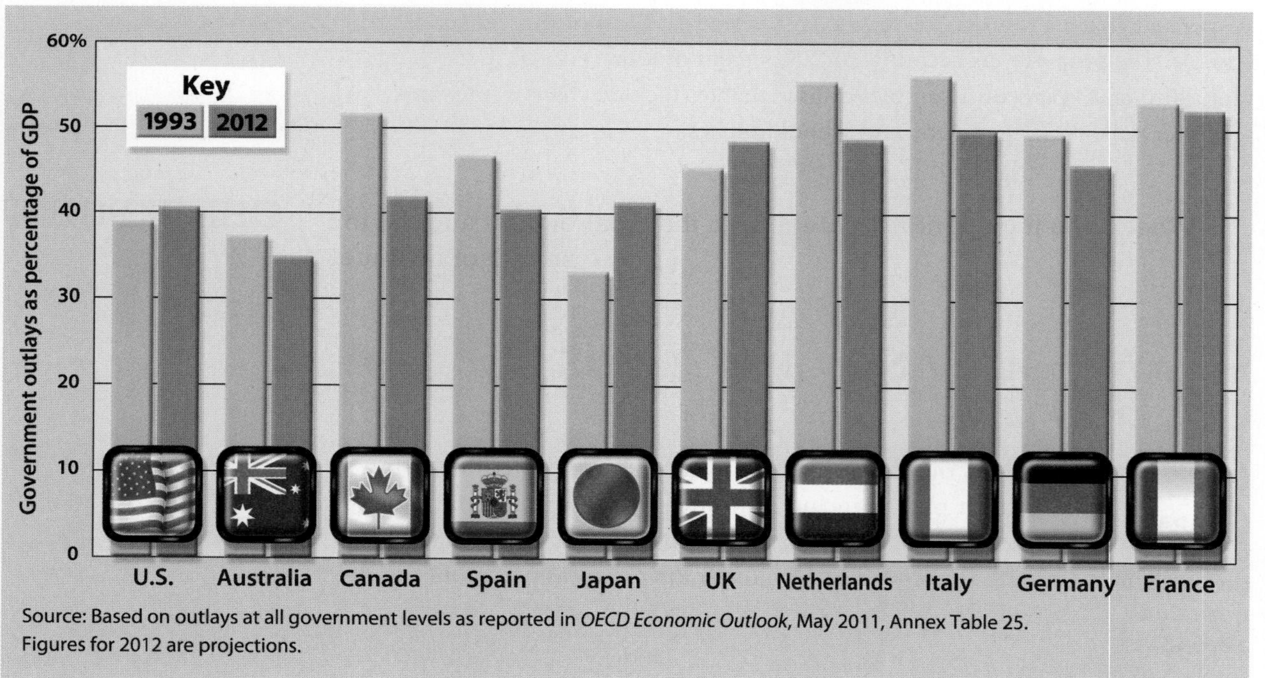

Source: Based on outlays at all government levels as reported in *OECD Economic Outlook*, May 2011, Annex Table 25. Figures for 2012 are projections.

Span the Globe

Why Japan Is Different

In Japan, where the economy suffered for more than a decade, the ratio of government debt to gross domestic product is more than 100 percent. Its minister for economic and fiscal affairs states that, "We face a dreadful dream." Japan's troubles are not new. Beginning with a collapse in real estate values and stock prices in 1990, the crash of wealth crushed consumer confidence and greatly diminished Japanese banks' ability to make loans. With consumers unwilling to spend as much, the government tried to stimulate aggregate demand by increasing spending on government projects. This has led to excessive spending in rural areas, which has done little to stimulate growth. For some, however, government spending is not the major cause of the country's deficit. They see their deficit as largely due to an erosion of the nation's tax base following years of deflation, which caused income and tax revenues to shrink.

Not everyone thinks that Japan is in trouble. They argue that unlike other debt-ridden nations, such as Greece and Ireland, the Japanese economy is still powerful—the world's third largest. In addition, unlike those countries (and the United States), the Japanese debt is largely self-financing, covered by domestic savings and not relying on foreign lenders. They argue that, in reality, government debt will never be paid back and, that as long as its interest payments can be comfortably serviced, no big problems will arise.

Think Critically **Should the Japanese economic policy emphasis spending reductions or efforts to end inflation? Do you agree that it can continue to run a deficit if the interest payments can be managed comfortably?**

Sources: Peter Tasker, "The Japanese Debt Disaster Movie," *Financial Times*, January 27, 2011; and Robert Pozen, "Japan Can Rebuild on New Economic Foundations," *Financial Times*, March 21, 2011.

Photodisc/Getty Images

The Japan Highway Corporation is one area where reform is needed in Japan, because it spends trillions of yen on what some critics charge are wasteful projects.

16.2 ASSESSMENT

Think Critically

1. Why were most Americans willing to accept a larger role for the government in the economy during the Great Depression and World War II?
2. Why would the share of federal revenue that comes from personal income taxes change from year to year, even though the income tax rates remained unchanged?
3. Why is state revenue more responsive to the growth in personal income than is local revenue?
4. Why have some state courts ruled that funding public schools mainly from local property tax receipts results in unequal educational opportunities for school children?
5. Why do governments in countries that experience rapid economic growth often spend smaller portions of GDP?

Graphing Exercise

6. Since its creation in 1965, the Medicare program, which provides medical coverage for our nation's elderly, has claimed a growing share of GDP. Use data in the table to construct a double-line graph that shows the annual rates of growth of real federal Medicare payments and real GDP from 2006 through 2010. What does your graph show about the relative rates of growth during these years? Given the large number of people born during the baby boom years from 1946 through 1964, what will probably happen to the relationship between these amounts in future years?

REAL GROWTH IN FEDERAL MEDICARE PAYMENTS AND IN GDP, 2006–2010

Year	Growth in Real Medicare Payments	Growth in Real GDP
2006	10.8%	2.7%
2007	10.5%	1.9%
2008	13.8%	−0.3%
2009	4.1%	−3.5%
2010	10.1%	3.0%

Source: *Economic Indicators*, July 2011, pp. 2, 23, and 33.

Make Academic Connections

7. **Government** An important part of state government spending is controlled by federal laws that require state governments to provide Medicaid programs for people who are unable to pay for their own medical care. Investigate Medicaid spending in your state. Have these payments grown faster than other types of state government spending? What could explain the growth in your state's Medicaid payments?

TeamWork

Working in small teams, make a comprehensive list of services your local government provides. Choose the five that your group thinks are the most important. For each of these, investigate how the service is funded (local taxes, fees, state or federal aid, etc.). Discuss what would happen if local residents were required to pay for these services without any outside assistance. Compare your work with that of other teams.

21st Century Skills

Health Literacy

Staying Healthy in the 21st Century

Innovations in medical technology in the 21st century hold the promise of longer, healthier, and more satisfying lives for those who are able to take advantage of them. Unfortunately, the cost of many health-related technologies is so great that there is doubt society will be able to provide them to everyone they would benefit. Consider the average costs of the following treatments in 2010.

- Heart transplant operation—$148,000.
- Liver transplant operation—$235,000.
- Year of cancer treatment—$66,000.
- Implanting a pacemaker—$40,000.

Care of the Elderly

Although medical care for young people can be expensive, the average cost of care increases rapidly as people age because older people need more care. Consider the cost of nursing home care as an example. In 2009, the average cost for this type of care exceeded $80,000 per year, not including the costs of medicine or other therapies.

Studies showed that in 2009 more than $40,000 was spent on medical care in the last six months of the average American's life. Roughly 2.5 million Americans die each year. That means the last six months of their care can cost more than $100 billion per year.

Medical Costs Grow as the Nation Ages

The average age of the American population is steadily increasing. The "baby boom" of the late 1940s and 1950s created a bulge in the population of people who are now in their 50s and 60s. Also, people are living longer. In 1970 the average life expectancy for people in the United States was just over 70 years. It is now approaching 80. The longer people live, the more medical care they are likely to need.

Total health-care spending in real terms increased by more than 200 percent in the past 20 years; at the same time, the U.S. population grew by roughly 25 percent. Many people believe that it will be impossible for the United States to sustain these rates of growth in the future. Regardless of what changes take place, American consumers will no doubt have many important health-care decisions to make in the 21st century.

Minimize Health-Care Costs

There are steps you can take to increase your probability of having a long and healthy life. These include:

- Exercise regularly.
- Limit the amount you eat.
- Eat a balanced diet.
- Don't smoke or use drugs.
- Get regular medical checkups.
- Follow your doctor's instructions.
- Keep up with major developments in medicines and medical technology.
- Seek medical attention quickly if you think something is wrong, before it can get worse.

Apply the Skill

Imagine that your employer has offered to pay for medical insurance for all employees who exercise regularly, don't smoke, and keep their weight within guidelines set by the federal government. Decide whether you would make an effort to qualify for this benefit. Explain three reasons for your decision.

Sources: www.chfpatients.com/tx/transplant.htm; www.kaiserhealthnews.org/Daily-Reports/2010/March/17/Cancer-Costs.aspx; and www.bcbst.com

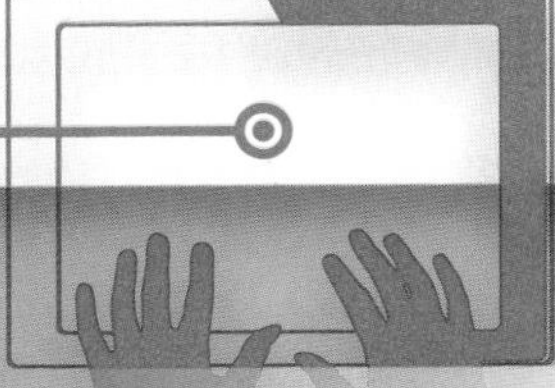

16.3 ECONOMICS OF PUBLIC CHOICE

Key Terms

Learning Objectives

LO1 Explain why representative democracy may favor special interests over the public interest.

LO2 Distinguish between government bureaus and for-profit firms.

In Your World

This book, for the most part, has assumed that governments make optimal adjustments to the shortcomings of the private sector. In other words, when confronted with market failure, governments adopt just the right program to address the problem. However, there are limits to government's effectiveness, just as there are limits to the market's effectiveness. For example, elected officials sometimes may side more with special interests than with the public interest. Government bureaus usually get less consumer feedback and face less competition than for-profit firms. Just as there are market failures, there are also government failures.

REPRESENTATIVE DEMOCRACY

LO1 Explain why representative democracy may favor special interests over the public interest.

In market decisions, each person votes with dollars for what gets produced. The rule is: one dollar, one vote. People with more to spend get more votes and have more influence in the marketplace. In public decisions, each person has a single vote to decide what gets produced. The rule is: one person, one vote, regardless of income. People vote directly on public choices at New England town meetings and on the occasional referendum, but direct democracy is rare. When you consider the thousands of public choices required to run a government, it would be impractical for voters to make all those choices. Instead, voters elect representatives, who—at least in principle—make public choices that reflect constituent views. Delegating choices to representatives is complicated, however.

Maximizing Political Support

Economists assume that households try to maximize utility and firms try to maximize profit, but what about governments—or, more specifically, what about elected representatives? What do they try to maximize? One problem is that the U.S. system of federal, state, and local governments consists of not one government but nearly 90,000 separate governments in all. These range from the federal government down to local school districts.

Even a particular government does not act as a single, consistent decision maker. For example, the federal government relies on a system of checks and balances to limit the executive, legislative, and judicial branches.

Even within the federal executive branch, the many agencies and bureaus seem at times to work at cross-purposes. For example, for decades the U.S. Surgeon General has required health warnings on cigarette packages. During much of that time, however, the U.S. Department of Agriculture subsidized tobacco farmers.

To simplify this tangled web, economists assume that elected representatives try to maximize their political support, including votes and campaign contributions. In this theory, **maximizing political support** guides the decisions of elected officials who, in turn, direct government employees.

Role of Special Interest

Elected representatives often appear to cater to special interests rather than the public interest. Consider only one of the thousands of decisions made by elected representatives: funding an obscure federal program that subsidizes U.S. wool production. Under the wool-subsidy program, the federal government guaranteed sheep farmers a certain price for each pound of wool they produce. This subsidy over the years has cost taxpayers more than $75 million. During deliberations to renew the program, the only person to testify before Congress was a representative of the National Wool Growers Association, who claimed that the subsidy was vital to the nation's economic welfare. Why didn't a single taxpayer challenge the subsidy?

maximizing political support The objective assumed to guide the behavior of elected officials; comparable to profit maximization by firms and utility maximization by households

mifilippo/iStockphoto.com

When do costs of government policies exceed benefits?

ESSENTIAL QUESTION

Standard CEE 17: Government Failure

Costs of government policies sometimes exceed benefits. This may occur because of incentives facing voters, government officials, and government employees; because of actions by special interest groups that can impose costs on the general public; or because social goals other than economic efficiency are being pursued.

NET Bookmark

Access the Center for Competitive Politics website through the URL below. You will find a list of articles about campaign reform. Choose one of these articles and write a paragraph summarizing its message.

www.cengage.com/school/contecon

As a consumer, you do not specialize in woolen goods. You buy thousands of different goods and services, from software to underwear. You have no special interest in wool legislation. Wool producers do have a special interest, because that's how they make a living. As a result of this mismatch of interests, legislation often favors producers rather than consumers. Well-organized producer groups, as squeaky wheels in the legislative machinery, get the most grease in the form of favorable legislation.

Special interest groups spend a lot to secure these advantages. For example, political action committees, known more popularly as PACs, contribute millions to political campaigns. More than 4,000 PACs try to shape federal legislation. The top 20 PACs spent a combined $400 million in 2010. Ten of the top 20 PACs that year represented labor unions.

Rational Ignorance

How do elected officials get away with serving special interests? Why don't voters elect someone else? Sometimes voters do, especially when there is a scandal. However, some people don't bother to vote and even those who do vote consume so many different goods and services that they have neither the time nor the incentive to keep up with public choices that affect any particular product. For example, a $75 million subsidy for wool growers amounts to only about 25 cents per U.S. citizen. Would you make the effort to protest this government subsidy to save yourself 25 cents in taxes? Probably not.

Unless voters have a special interest in the legislation, they adopt a stance of **rational ignorance**. This means the costs and benefits of the thousands of proposals considered by elected officials remain largely unknown to voters. The cost to the typical voter of acquiring and acting on such information usually is greater than any possible benefit. This is why it's hard to interest the public in the public interest.

In contrast, consumers have much more incentive to gather and act on information about their market choices. For example, a consumer in the market for a new car has an incentive to examine the performance records of different models, test-drive a few, and check prices at dealerships and on the Internet. That buyer has complete control over the choice of a new car. *Because information and the time required to acquire and digest it are scarce, consumers focus more on private choices than on public choices. The payoff in making wise private choices usually is more direct, more immediate, and more substantial.*

rational ignorance A stance adopted by voters when they believe that the cost of understanding and voting on a particular issue exceeds the benefit expected from doing so

CHECKPOINT Why does representative democracy favor special interests?

BUREAUS VS. FIRMS

LO2
Distinguish between government bureaus and for-profit firms.

Elected representatives approve legislation, but the task of implementing that legislation typically is delegated to **bureaus**. These are government departments and agencies whose activities are financed through legislative bodies. Examples include the FBI, FDA, FCC, EPA, the Pentagon, your state's department of motor vehicles, and your public school system.

Voluntary Exchange vs. Coercion

Market exchange relies on the voluntary behavior of buyers and sellers making private choices. Don't like tofu? No problem—don't buy any. Nobody can force you to buy something you don't want. In political markets, the situation is different. Only public choices reached by unanimous consent will involve no government coercion. With majority-rule, even if you object to certain government programs, you must still pay the taxes that ultimately fund those programs. Public choices are enforced by the police power of the state. If you fail to pay your taxes, you could go to prison.

Product Prices

For-profit firms sell products for prices that at least cover the cost of production. Bureaus usually offer products for either a zero price or some price below cost. For example, if you plan to attend a public college in your state, your tuition will not cover the state's cost of providing your education.

Because the revenue side of the government budget usually is separate from the expenditure side, there is no necessary link between the marginal cost of a public program and the marginal benefit. Contrast this with the private sector, in which the marginal benefit of a good must at least equal marginal cost. Otherwise, people wouldn't buy it.

Consumer Feedback

Markets offer firms a steady stream of consumer feedback. If prices are too high or too low, surpluses or shortages become obvious. Not only is consumer feedback abundant in markets, but firms have a profit incentive to act on that feedback. The firm's owners stand to gain from any improvement in customer satisfaction or any reduction in the cost of production.

Because public goods and services are not sold in markets, government bureaus receive less consumer feedback. There usually are no prices for public goods and no obvious shortages or surpluses. For example, how would you know whether there was a shortage or a surplus of police protection in your community?

bureaus Government agencies charged with implementing legislation and financed through legislative bodies

Voter Incentives

Voters can move from a jurisdiction if they think the government there is inefficient. This mechanism, whereby people "vote with their feet," promotes some efficiency at the state and local levels. For example, parents might decide to move to a better school district. Voters who are not satisfied with the federal government, however, cannot easily vote with their feet.

In the private sector, competition makes firms more responsive to customers. If a firm's product does not appeal to consumers, that firm either has to shape up or it will go out of business. Bureaus that do not appeal to voters do not necessarily go out of business. A bureau that is inefficient may continue to waste taxpayer resources indefinitely. Thus, bureaus face less pressure to satisfy consumer demand or to operate efficiently. A variety of studies compares costs for products provided by both public bureaus and private firms, such as trash collection. Of those studies that show a difference, most find that private firms are more efficient.

Private vs. Public Production

Just because some goods and services are *financed* by the government does not mean they must be *produced* by the government. Elected officials may contract directly with for-profit firms to produce public output. This could introduce more competition and more efficiency. For example, a city council may seek competitive bids from firms to handle trash collection for the city. For-profit firms in some jurisdictions now provide everything from fire protection to prisons to schools.

Stockbyte/Getty Images

Why do governments sometimes contract with for-profit firms to produce public output, such as highways and bridges?

Elected officials also may use some combination of bureaus and firms to produce the desired output. For example, the Pentagon, a giant bureau, hires and trains military personnel. Yet the Pentagon contracts with for-profit firms to develop and produce weapons systems. State governments typically hire for-profit contractors to build roads but have government employees maintain those roads.

The mix of for-profit firms and bureaus varies over time and across jurisdictions. However, the trend is toward greater production by the for-profit sector of public goods and services. These goods and services are still financed by government, usually with taxes.

When government bureaus produce public goods and services, they are using the *internal organization* of the government—the bureaucracy—to supply the product. When governments contract with for-profit firms to produce public goods and services, they are using *the market* to supply the product. Legislators may prefer dealing with bureaus rather than with firms for two reasons. First, in situations where it is difficult to specify in a contract just what is being produced, as with education or social work, bureaus may be more responsive to the legislature's concerns. Second, bureaus provide legislators with more opportunities to reward political supporters with government jobs.

CHECKPOINT

Why might government bureaus be less responsive to customers than for-profit firms are?

16.3 ASSESSMENT

Think Critically

1. Your class has decided to earn money to fund a class trip. The big question is deciding where the class should go. Some students want to visit Washington, D.C., and some prefer New York City, while others choose Disney World or other destinations. Describe how this decision might be made and why this decision-making process is similar to the way government makes choices.
2. A school's sports director decided to spend $15,000 on new equipment for the football team. Although this decision left only $5,000 to pay for equipment for all of the school's other teams, most of the students didn't complain. Explain how this situation demonstrates the idea of rational ignorance.
3. Why does the saying "the squeaky wheel gets the grease" often describe how government decisions are made?
4. What would happen to a private firm that employed clerks who were rude or unresponsive to customer requests? Why may bureaucracies employ such workers and still survive over many years?
5. Why might parents demand fewer services from public schools if each parent were required to pay for these services directly from that family's own funds?

Graphing Exercise

6. Use data in the table to construct a bar graph that shows the per-student spending in selected states for public schools in 2009. What might explain spending differences across states? Do you think there is a direct relationship between per-student spending and the quality of education? Explain your answer.

PER-STUDENT PUBLIC SCHOOL SPENDING IN SELECTED STATES, 2009

State	Per-Student Spending	State	Per-Student Spending
Rhode Island	$16,127	Texas	$9,143
Connecticut	$14,099	Mississippi	$7,814
Ohio	$10,796	Nevada	$7,777
Indiana	$10,514	Arizona	$6,385

Source: *Statistical Abstract of the United States, 2012*, Table 262, p. 170.

Make Academic Connections

7. **Government** Identify and describe a public policy issue that is important to you. How could you try to influence legislation in a way that would affect government policy. Why might you be more successful acting as a member of a group than as an individual voter?

TeamWork

Working in small teams, identify a specific project that was at least partially funded by your local government such as a new school, road, park, or community center. Investigate how the decision to carry out this project was made. Evaluate this process in terms of efficiency, timeliness, and how well it met the community's needs.

The Evolution of the Federal Income Tax

One trigger of the American Revolution was a tax revolt. It was through trade that England lightly taxed its American colonies. When England attempted to impose a direct tax through the Stamp Act, the American colonists objected. They saw it as a violation of the British Bill of Rights, which historically had held that taxes could not be imposed without the approval of Parliament. Because the colonies had no direct representation in Parliament, they rejected England's right to tax them directly, arguing that "taxation without representation is tyranny."

Following the Revolution, the first American constitution, the Articles of Confederation, did not grant the central government the power to levy taxes. Therefore, taxation was one of the problems addressed at the Constitutional Convention held in Philadelphia. Through the U.S. Constitution, the new government was given the power to "lay and collect Taxes, Duties, imports, and Excises."

During the nation's early days, the federal government relied primarily on tariffs (taxes on imports) and land sales to fund its operations. An early attempt to increase revenue by levying excise taxes on items such as carriages, sugar, salt, and distilled spirits met with armed resistance in Western Pennsylvania. The "Whiskey-Rebellion" was quickly put down. However, with the election of Thomas Jefferson in 1800, most of the excise taxes were repealed.

The government returned to relying on tariffs for revenue until outlays for the Civil War required new sources of revenue. The nation's first income tax was imposed during that war, along with taxes on a variety of goods. Following the war, the high tariffs imposed during the war remained. However, the income tax rate was first reduced, and then the tax was allowed to expire by 1872.

In the 1890s, the idea of an income tax resurfaced, and a new income tax was passed in 1894. The following year, the Supreme Court declared it unconstitutional. A decade later, following the Panic of 1907, a federal income tax once again emerged as an issue. President William Howard Taft, not wanting to directly challenge a Supreme Court decision, suggested a constitutional amendment authorizing an income tax. He also suggested a tax on corporate profits. The corporate profits tax passed a Supreme Court challenge, and Congress and the states passed the Sixteenth Amendment, which was adopted in 1913. Later that year, President Woodrow Wilson signed the personal income tax into law.

The tax burden from the income tax fell on the wealthy. In its first year, only 357,598 tax forms were filed, or about one filing for every 250 people. In 1910, before the income tax, tariffs on imported goods supplied 90 percent of federal revenue. Today that share is about one percent.

Where previously the debate over tariffs pitted regions of the country against each other, today the argument is more between economic classes. The top 10 percent of taxpayers based on income pay about 70 percent of all income taxes collected, and the bottom 50 percent of taxpayers pay about 3 percent of all income taxes collected.

Think Critically **A century ago the United States underwent a fundamental change in how it funds the government—from relying on tariffs to relying on personal and corporate income taxes. Could the country undergo such a change today? What alternate forms of taxation could it employ?**

Chapter 16 Summary

16.1 Public Goods and Taxation

A. Public goods differ from private goods in that they are nonrival in consumption. The market demand for public goods is the sum of the marginal benefits for all community members. The efficient level of a public good is found where the sum of the marginal benefits equals the good's marginal cost.

B. There are two generally recognized principles of taxation: the benefits-received principle and the ability-to-pay principle. According to the benefits-received principle, the tax you pay should be in proportion to the benefit you receive from the public good. According to the ability-to-pay principle, those with more income or more wealth should pay more taxes.

C. Tax incidence indicates who bears the burden of a tax. Under a proportional tax, all would pay the same percent of their incomes in tax. With progressive taxes, people pay a greater share of their incomes in tax as their incomes grow. With regressive taxes, people pay a smaller share of their income in tax as their incomes grow.

D. The marginal tax rate is the percentage of each additional dollar of a taxpayer's income that is paid in taxes. High marginal tax rates reduce a person's after-tax income and can reduce the incentive to earn additional income.

ASK THE EXPERT

www.cengage.com/school/contecon

What is the meaning of public goods?

16.2 Federal, State, and Local Budgets

A. Through the first 150 years of U.S. history, federal outlays amounted to about 3 percent of GDP except during times of war. This share has grown to about 25 percent of GDP, or about $3.8 trillion, in 2011. Nearly half of federal spending goes to income redistribution (48 percent). The largest source of federal revenue is the personal income tax (44 percent).

B. The largest share of state spending goes to aid local governments (32 percent). The largest source of state revenue is federal aid (30 percent).

C. Local governments spend the largest share of their budget for education (44 percent). The largest source of local government revenue is state and federal aid (37 percent).

D. Total government outlays in the United States are smaller, relative to GDP, than government outlays in most other major industrial nations.

16.3 Economics of Public Choice

A. When government leaders make decisions, they do not necessarily try to achieve economic efficiency. They may instead attempt to maximize their political support and their chances of getting reelected. Special interest groups often try to get government to make choices that benefit them.

B. Many laws are implemented or enforced by government bureaus that are not always responsive to interests of the population as a whole. Government bureaus often supply programs that have little link between costs and benefits. However, people won't make market purchases unless the expected benefits at least equal the expected costs.

C. Some governmental units have attempted to supply services more efficiently by contracting with for-profit firms to produce them.

CHAPTER 16 ASSESSMENT

Review Economic Terms

a. ability-to-pay tax principle
b. benefits-received tax principle
c. bureaus
d. government budget
e. marginal tax rate
f. maximizing political support
g. payroll taxes
h. progressive taxation
i. proportional taxation
j. rational ignorance
k. regressive taxation
l. tax incidence

Match the terms with the definitions. Some terms will not be used.

_____ 1. A tax as a percentage of income increases as income increases

_____ 2. Government agencies charged with implementing legislation and financed through legislative bodies

_____ 3. A plan for government spending and revenues for a specified period, usually a year

_____ 4. Those who receive more benefits from a government program funded by a tax should pay more of that tax

_____ 5. A tax as a percentage of income decreases as income increases

_____ 6. Those with a greater ability to pay should pay more of a tax

_____ 7. The percentage of each additional dollar of income that goes to pay a tax

_____ 8. A tax as a percentage of income remains constant as income increases

_____ 9. Taxes deducted from paychecks to support Social Security and Medicare

_____ 10. A stance adopted by voters who find that the cost of understanding and voting on a particular issue exceeds the benefit expected from doing so

Review Economic Concepts

11. Public goods are ________?________ in consumption.

12. **True or False** The efficient level of production of a public good is found where the marginal benefit of additional units of that good is zero.

13. Which of the following is an example of the benefits-received tax principle?
    a. the excise tax on cigarettes
    b. a tariff on imported automobiles
    c. a sales tax on purchases of new clothing
    d. the tax on each gallon of gasoline

14. **True or False** Taxes that fall more heavily on people who earn larger incomes represent the ability-to-pay principle of taxation.

15. An ability-to-pay tax also is likely to be
    a. regressive.
    b. progressive.
    c. proportional.
    d. reactionary.

16. If a tax structure is progressive and we know that Tom pays $1,000 on his $10,000 income, then Alicia, who earns $30,000, must pay
   a. more than $3,000 in tax.
   b. exactly $3,000 in tax.
   c. less than $3,000 in tax.
   d. more than $4,000 in tax.
17. The part of the next dollar you earn that is taken in tax is your ________?________.
18. The largest share of federal spending is allocated to
   a. national defense.
   b. income redistribution.
   c. interest on the national debt.
   d. government employee salaries.
19. **True or False** High marginal tax rates encourage people to work and earn additional income.
20. **True or False** The largest source of federal government revenue is the corporate income tax.
21. The biggest spending category for state governments is ________?________.
22. Which of the following is not a source of revenue for state or local governments?
   a. tariffs on imported goods
   b. aid from the federal government
   c. income taxes
   d. sales taxes
23. **True or False** The largest part of local government spending is for schools.
24. Government outlays in the United States are roughly what percent relative to the nation's GDP?
   a. 25
   b. 33
   c. 40
   d. 47
25. **True or False** Some political leaders appear to be more interested in whether they are reelected than in how well government works.
26. Voters sometimes choose not to learn about how their taxes are spent because
   a. collectively, they are not able to influence government decisions.
   b. there is no information available to them about how their tax money is spent.
   c. they are not affected by government policies.
   d. they think the cost of learning about how tax money is spent is greater than the benefits of working to influence legislation.
27. One theory states that unless voters have a special interest in a piece of legislation, they are likely to adopt a stance of ________?________.
28. **True or False** Bureaus usually offer products for either a zero price or some price below cost.

Apply Economic Concepts

29. **Identify the Optimal Quantity of a Public Good** Residents of a riverside community wish to have a break wall built around the town to protect their homes from flooding. The cost of construction is $100,000 per 100 yards. The break wall must be at least 1,800 yards long in order to surround the entire community. The people of the community have voted to spend up to $1 million for the break wall. How much of this amount should they spend? How does this situation demonstrate a problem of achieving an efficient level of public goods?

30. **21st Century Skills: Health Literacy** You have been offered a job that you would like to accept. The only problem is that the employer requires employees to have an annual physical that includes an evaluation of their weight and physical condition. Any employees judged to be overweight or out of shape will lose their jobs unless they participate in a program designed to improve their condition on their own time. Is this a reasonable demand? Would you take the job? Explain your answers.

31. **Assess a Proportional Income Tax** Some politicians believe that high marginal tax rates discourage people from working. They suggest that if all taxpayers were charged the same percent of their income, the lower marginal tax rates would encourage many people to work and earn more. Estimates show that the same amount of tax revenue could be collected if all taxpayers paid roughly 23 percent of their taxable income. This means that a person with taxable income of $10,000 per year would pay $2,300 in tax while a person with taxable income of $100,000 would pay $23,000. Decide whether you think this is a good or a bad idea. Then write several paragraphs that explain your point of view. Discuss the impact of such a tax structure on the economy, as well as your opinion of its fairness.

32. **Construct a Bar Graph to Show Marginal Income Tax Rates** The federal marginal income tax rates for single filers in 2012 are shown in the table below. Construct a bar graph to show these rates. What, if anything, has happened to these rates since 2012? Why have changes been made in the rates or why have they remained unchanged?

FEDERAL MARGINAL INCOME TAX RATES FOR SINGLE FILERS, 2012

Taxable Income in 2012	Marginal Tax Rate
$0–$8,700	10%
$8,701–$35,350	15%
$35,351–$85,650	25%
$85,651–$178,650	28%
$178,651–$388,350	33%
$388,351 or more	35%

Digging Deeper

with Economics e-Collection

Access the Gale Economics e-Collection through the URL below. Read several recent articles about the U.S. federal budget. Make a list of five facts you learned about the budget. Bring your list of facts to class and be prepared to share it with your classmates.

www.cengage.com/school/contecon

CHAPTER 17

Fiscal Policy, Deficits, and Debt

Point your browser

www.cengage.com/school/contecon

CONSIDER ...

- What is your normal capacity for academic work, and when do you usually exceed that effort?
- Can fiscal policy reduce swings in the business cycle?
- Why has the federal budget been in deficit most years?
- How is a strong economy like a crowded restaurant?
- How high will the federal debt be when it becomes the responsibility of your generation?

17.1 THE EVOLUTION OF FISCAL POLICY

Key Terms

potential output 530
natural rate of unemployment 531
classical economists 533
annually balanced budget 534
multiplier effect 535

Learning Objectives

LO1 Identify the economy's potential output.

LO2 Distinguish between fiscal policy before and after the Great Depression.

In Your World

Federal spending for national defense, education, the environment, and other programs aims to achieve specific objectives, such as national security, a more educated workforce, cleaner air, and the like. Fiscal policy has a broader focus. Fiscal policy considers the overall impact of the federal budget on the economy, especially on employment, output, and prices. Fiscal policy tries to promote full employment and price stability by targeting changes in aggregate demand.

FISCAL POLICY AND POTENTIAL OUTPUT

LO1 Identify the economy's potential output.

Fiscal policy aims to use government taxing and spending to move the economy toward full employment with price stability. The focus is mainly on shifts of the aggregate demand curve. If unemployment is high, as it was because of the Great Recession of 2008–2009, fiscal policy tries to increase aggregate demand as a way of boosting output and employment. If aggregate demand is already so strong that it threatens to trigger higher inflation, fiscal policy tries to relieve that pressure by reducing aggregate demand.

Potential Output

Fiscal policy aims to move the economy to its potential output level. **Potential output** is the economy's maximum sustainable output in the long run, given the supply of resources, the state of technology, and the rules of the game that nurture production and exchange. Potential output also is referred to as the full-employment output. When the economy produces its potential output, it is operating on its production possibilities frontier.

Suppose potential output equals a real GDP of $15 trillion. This is shown in Figure 17.1 as the vertical line where real GDP is $15 trillion. If potential output is achieved, the economy reaches full employment with no inflationary pressure. At full employment, the economy is doing as well as possible in the long run. In theory, fiscal policy can be used to ensure that the economy achieves its potential, with full employment and price stability.

potential output The economy's maximum sustainable output in the long run

The unemployment rate that occurs when the economy is producing its potential GDP is called the **natural rate of unemployment**. At this rate, there is no cyclical unemployment. Generally accepted estimates of the natural rate of unemployment are in the range of 5 to 6 percent of the labor force.

Output Below Potential

If the aggregate demand curve and aggregate supply curve intersect in the pink-shaded area of Figure 17.1, then output is less than the economy's potential. The economy is not producing as much as it can. Unemployment exceeds its natural rate. The amount by which short-run output falls short of the economy's potential output is called a *recessionary gap*. Faced with this gap, policy makers often decide to reduce taxes or increase government spending. The idea is to stimulate aggregate demand as a way of increasing output to its potential.

Output Exceeding Potential

If the aggregate demand curve and aggregate supply curve intersect in the blue-shaded area of Figure 17.1, then output exceeds the economy's potential. Unemployment is below its natural rate. The amount by which actual output in the short run exceeds the economy's potential output is called the *expansionary gap*.

natural rate of unemployment The unemployment rate when the economy is producing its potential level of output

FIGURE 17.1 Fiscal Policy and Potential Output

Potential output is the economy's maximum sustainable output in the long run. The pink-shaded area indicates real GDP below the economy's potential. The blue-shaded area indicates real GDP exceeding the economy's potential. When the economy reaches potential output, there is full employment and price stability.

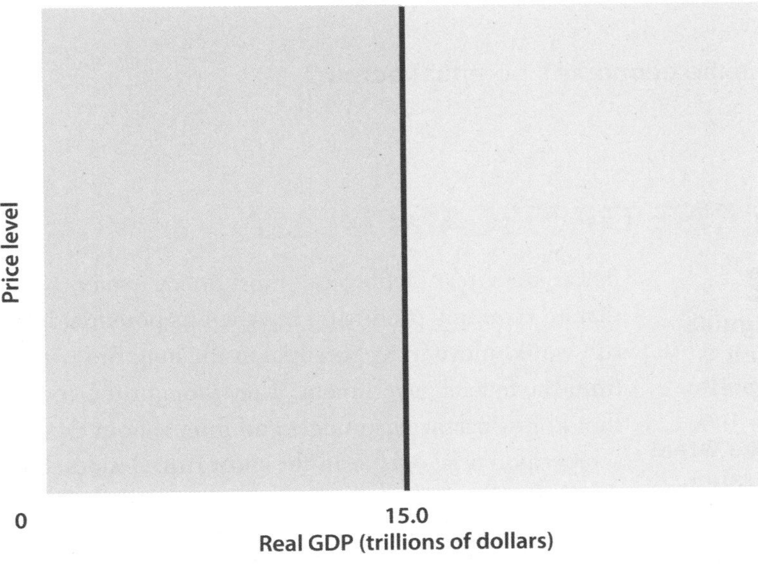

This seems like a good outcome. However, production beyond the economy's potential creates inflationary pressure in the economy. Production exceeding the economy's potential is not sustainable in the long run. The result is higher inflation and a return to the economy's potential output. To head off this higher inflation, policy makers sometimes increase taxes or reduce government spending to reduce aggregate demand.

How Can Output Exceed the Economy's Potential?

You probably have no problem understanding that output may fall short of its potential. But how can output exceed its potential? Remember, potential output does not mean zero unemployment but the natural rate of unemployment—about 5 to 6 percent. Even an economy producing its potential output has some unemployed labor and some unused production capacity.

If you think of potential output as the economy's *normal production capacity*, you get a better idea of how the economy can temporarily exceed that capacity. Consider your own study habits. During most of the school year, you display your normal capacity for academic work. As the end of a grading period draws near, however, you may step it up a notch to finish long-standing assignments. You may study more than usual and make an extra effort trying to pull things together. During these brief stretches, you study beyond your normal capacity, beyond the schedule you follow on a regular or sustained basis.

Producers, too, can exceed their normal capacity in the short run to push output beyond the economy's potential. For example, during World War II, businesses pulled out all the stops to win the war. The unemployment rate fell below 2 percent. However, in the long run, the economy does not exceed its potential, just as you don't boost your study effort permanently. Output in the long run gravitates back to the economy's potential. *Production beyond the economy's potential usually leads only to inflation in the long run.* For example, despite price controls put in place during World War II, inflation was still relatively high.

CHECKPOINT **What is the economy's potential output?**

THE RISE OF FISCAL POLICY

LO2
Distinguish between fiscal policy before and after the Great Depression.

Before the Great Depression, most policy makers believed that an economy producing less than its potential in the short run would move to its potential in the long run without help from the federal government. They thought the government should just balance its budget and forget about trying to achieve potential output in the short run. Besides, before the Great Depression, the federal government itself played a relatively minor role in the economy. At the onset of the Great Depression, for example, federal spending was less than 3 percent of GDP, compared to about 25 percent today.

Views of Classical Economists

Before the 1930s, fiscal policy was seldom used to influence the overall performance of the economy. Prior to the Great Depression, public policy was shaped by the views of **classical economists**. They advocated *laissez-faire*, the belief that free markets without government intervention were the best way to achieve the economy's potential output.

Classical economists did not deny the existence of depressions and high unemployment. They argued, however, that the sources of such crises lay outside the market system, in the effects of wars, tax increases, poor growing seasons, and the like. Such external events could shock the economy, reducing output and employment in the short run. Yet classical economists believed that natural market forces, such as declining prices, wages, and interest rates, would end any recession in a short time by encouraging consumers and businesses to spend more.

Simply put, classical economists argued that if the economy's average price level was too high to sell all that was produced, prices would fall until the quantity supplied equaled the quantity demanded. If wages were too high to employ all who wanted to work, wages would fall until the quantity of labor supplied

classical economists A group of laissez-faire economists who believed that economic downturns corrected themselves in the long run through natural market forces

Span the Globe

Laissez-Faire Policies in France

The French term *laissez-faire* literally means "allow to do." The exact origins of the term are unknown. It was first associated in the late 1700s with a group of French economists called the Physiocrats. Physiocrats believed economies worked best if grounded in agriculture and allowed to run freely based on natural laws, not regulation by the government. They strongly opposed the growing European policies of mercantilism, in which governments heavily regulated trade and manufacturing more for their own good than that of individual property owners. Physiocrats also believed that land and the products grown from it were a nation's source of wealth. Mercantilists believed that hard currency and precious metals were a nation's source of wealth. In the end, even though mercantilism itself did not survive long, the mercantilist theories of wealth became more widely accepted than the Physiocrat theories. Nevertheless, many people embraced the Physiocrats' laissez-faire ideas. When the French Revolution began in 1789, the new government instituted a number of reforms aimed at easing regulations on trade. The French government today is far from laissez-faire. Modern France has a mixed economy, which includes heavy regulation over the economy but not complete control of private property.

Think Critically **Why do you think the French government moved away from applying the ideas of the Physiocrats to its economy? With which philosophy regarding wealth—the mercantilist or the Physiocrat—do you most agree? Justify your answer.**

equaled the quantity demanded. If interest rates were too high to invest all that had been saved, rates would fall until the amount invested equaled the amount saved.

The classical approach claimed that natural market forces, through flexible prices, wages, and interest rates, would move the economy toward its potential GDP in the long run. Classical economists saw no need for changes in government spending or taxing to "correct" the economy.

Instead, fiscal policy prior to the Great Depression pursued an **annually balanced budget**, except during wartime. This means that the government aimed to match annual spending with annual revenue. Tax revenues tend to rise during expansions and fall during recessions. Therefore, with an annually balanced budget, spending increased during expansions and declined during recessions. One problem with this approach was that such a pattern magnified fluctuations in the business cycle. It overheated the economy during expansions and increased unemployment during recessions.

The Great Depression and Keynes

Classical economists acknowledged that market economies could produce less than potential in the short run. The prolonged depression of the 1930s, however, strained belief in the economy's ability to correct itself. The Great Depression was marked by unemployment reaching 25 percent and much unused plant capacity. With vast unemployed resources, output and income fell far short of the economy's potential for several years.

The market adjustments predicted by classical theory and the years of unemployment experienced during the Great Depression represented a clash between theory and fact. In 1936, John Maynard Keynes of the University of Cambridge, England, published *The General Theory of Employment, Interest, and Money.* This book challenged the classical view and touched off what would later come to be called the Keynesian revolution. *Keynesian theory and policy were developed to address the problem of unemployment during the Great Depression.*

Keynes's main quarrel with the classical economists was that prices and wages did not appear to be flexible enough, even in the long run, to ensure the full employment of resources. According to Keynes, prices and wages were somewhat inflexible—they were "sticky." So if unemployment was high, natural market forces would not return the economy to full employment in a timely fashion. Keynes also believed business expectations might, at times, become so grim that even very low interest rates would not be enough to encourage firms to invest.

The Multiplier Effect

Keynes also argued that any change in taxing or government spending had a magnified effect on aggregate demand. For example, suppose the government spends $100 million on a new presidential jet, Air Force One. Workers and other resource suppliers at Boeing, the manufacturer of the 747, see their incomes rise by $100 million. These people will spend at least part of that higher income on products such as food, clothing, housing, cars, appliances, and the like. As a result, the people who make all those products also will have more income. They will spend some of that higher income on yet more goods and services.

annually balanced budget Matching annual spending with annual revenue, except during war years; the approach to federal budgeting prior to the Great Depression

Each round of income and spending increases aggregate spending a little more. This is called the **multiplier effect** of fiscal policy, which claims that any change in fiscal policy affects aggregate demand by more than the original change in spending or taxing. The multiplier effect also could result from a change in business investment and even a change in consumption. However, Keynes focused on changes in government spending and taxing.

The Rise of Fiscal Policy

Three developments in the years following the Great Depression promoted the use of fiscal policy in the United States. The first was the influence of Keynes's *General Theory.* Keynes thought the economy could get stuck at a level of output that was well below its potential, well below the full-employment level. He argued that increasing government spending or cutting taxes could have a multiplier effect on aggregate demand. According to Keynes, fiscal policy should be used in times of high unemployment to increase aggregate demand enough to boost output and employment.

The second development giving credibility to Keynesian fiscal policy was the powerful impact World War II had on output and employment. The demands of war greatly increased production and cut unemployment to less than 2 percent, ending the depression.

The third development, largely a consequence of the first two, was the passage of the Employment Act of 1946, which gave the federal government the responsibility for promoting full employment and price stability.

Again, prior to the Great Depression, the dominant fiscal policy was a balanced budget. Indeed, in 1932, when the economy was in the depths of the Depression, federal taxes were increased to help reduce a budget deficit. This made things worse. In the wake of Keynes's *General Theory* and World War II, however, policy makers

multiplier effect A theory that claims any change in fiscal policy affects aggregate demand by more than the original change in spending or taxing

Time & Life Pictures/Getty Images

How did World War II help end the Great Depression?

grew more receptive to the idea that fiscal policy could improve the economy's performance. The objective of fiscal policy was no longer to balance the budget but to promote full employment with price stability, even if this resulted in budget deficits.

Figure 17.2 illustrates Keynesian fiscal policy in a modern setting. The aggregate demand curve *AD* and the aggregate supply curve *AS* intersect at point *e*. Output of $14.5 trillion falls short of the economy's potential of $15.0 trillion. The result is a recessionary gap of $0.5 trillion, meaning that unemployment exceeds the natural rate. According to Keynes, this gap could be closed by discretionary fiscal policy that increases aggregate demand by just the right amount. An increase in government spending, a decrease in taxes, or some combination of the two could shift aggregate demand to *AD**, moving the economy to its potential level of output at *e**. This was the idea behind the "stimulus bill" of 2009, which aimed to increase aggregate demand in the face of a global financial crisis and recession. Unfortunately, the unemployment rate remained stubbornly high for years.

CHECKPOINT **How did the Great Depression change fiscal policy?**

FIGURE 17.2 **Discretionary Fiscal Policy to Close a Recessionary Gap**

The aggregate demand curve *AD* and the aggregate supply curve *AS* intersect at point *e*. Output of $14.5 trillion falls short of the economy's potential of $15.0 trillion. The result is a recessionary gap of $0.5 trillion. This gap could be closed by discretionary fiscal policy that increases aggregate demand by just the right amount. An increase in government spending, a decrease in taxes, or some combination of the two could shift aggregate demand to *AD**, moving the economy to its potential level of output at *e**.

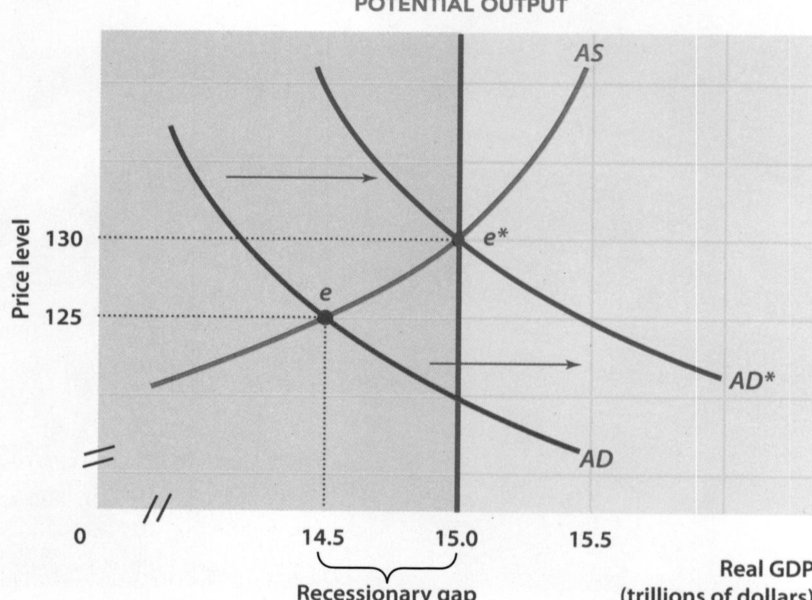

17.1 ASSESSMENT

Think Critically

1. How close do you think the U.S. economy is currently to its potential output? Explain your answer.
2. Why can the economy still have a 5 to 6 percent unemployment rate when it is at its natural rate of unemployment?
3. In 2008–2009, the U.S. economy was in recession. Why would classical economists have believed that this downturn in the economy would not last very long?
4. According to Keynes, if the federal government borrows and spends an additional $50 billion, why are aggregate demand, production, and income likely to grow by more than $50 billion?

Graphing Exercise

5. Draw a bar graph to show five rounds of the multiplier effect on spending when the federal government implements fiscal policy by borrowing and spending an additional $10 million. Remember that all spending becomes someone else's income. Assume that each person who receives additional income saves 10 percent and spends 90 percent of these funds, as shown in the table below. According to Keynes, how does your graph demonstrate the power of government spending?

FIVE ROUNDS OF THE MULTIPLIER EFFECT

Round	Additional Spending	Additional Income	Amount Saved
1	$10,000,000	$10,000,000	$1,000,000
2	$ 9,000,000	$ 9,000,000	$ 900,000
3	$ 8,100,000	$ 8,100,000	$ 810,000
4	$ 7,290,000	$ 7,290,000	$ 729,000
5	$ 6,561,000	$ 6,561,000	$ 656,100

Make Academic Connections

6. **History** When Keynes first asserted that the government could stabilize the economy by adjusting its spending and taxing, his ideas were met with skepticism from many economists and politicians. Events during World War II, however, caused most people to change their minds and come to believe that his ideas had merit. Investigate government borrowing and spending that took place during World War II and explain how they supported Keynes's ideas.

TeamWork

Working with a partner, perform a role-play. Acting as a classical economist, one partner will explain how that economic approach should have been used in the Great Recession of 2008–2009. Acting as a Keynesian economist, the other partner will explain that approach to the Great Recession. Make a list of the issues about which these two schools of thought disagree.

21st Century Skills

Critical Thinking and Problem Solving

Take Advantage of Fiscal Policy

When the economy turns down, the federal government often adjusts its spending and taxing in an effort to stimulate the economy and bring about an economic recovery. If this happens, there are opportunities for individual taxpayers to take advantage of the government's fiscal policy. Consider the programs below that were implemented during the Great Recession of 2008–2009.

- Energy tax credits were offered to people who insulated their homes, had new windows installed, or replaced their heating or air-conditioning units with more efficient models. Some of these credits reduced the cost of these products by as much as 30 percent.
- Tax credits of up to $1,500 were offered to people who purchased hybrid automobiles. Those who purchased electric cars could receive a tax break of as much as $7,500.
- Tax credits of 30 percent of the purchase price were offered for wood-burning stoves that met federal standards.
- Tax credits for 30 percent of the purchase price were offered for the purchase and installation of solar and wind powered home heating or electric generation devices.
- Federal grants were made to states to help them purchase land where they could build high-speed rail lines
- First-time home buyers received a tax credit of up to $8,000.
- A $2,500 per year tax credit was offered to help families pay college tuition costs.
- Financial assistance was provided to help pay for medical insurance for workers who lost their jobs.

A Dual Purpose

Each of the programs listed above had a dual purpose. They were intended to benefit both the economy as a whole and taxpayers as individuals. Many were designed to reduce our nation's energy consumption, dependence on foreign sources of energy, and global warming and at the same time create jobs for people employed in the companies making the energy-efficient products. The tax credits also saved individual taxpayers money that they could then save or spend on other products to create even more jobs.

Fiscal Policy in the Future

To make rational consumer decisions in the 21st century, you need to stay aware of federal programs to keep the economy running. You also should realize that many states sponsor similar programs that can offer even more advantages to taxpayers who keep up with opportunities that are available to them.

Apply the Skill

Imagine that it is 20 years from now and you own a home built in the year 2000. Although it isn't really old, it could use some fixing up. How could you find out if there are any government programs that could help you pay for improvements to your home? List three steps you could take and explain how each would work.

17.2 FISCAL POLICY RECONSIDERED

Learning Objectives

LO1 Identify two tools of fiscal policy.

LO2 Evaluate discretionary fiscal policy in light of the time lags involved.

LO3 Explain how fiscal policy was used during the Great Recession.

Key Terms

In Your World

From the Great Depression through the 1960s, fiscal policy appeared to be the miracle drug for what ailed the economy. Policy makers would adopt the necessary spending and tax policies to move the economy to its potential. The 1970s brought a new set of problems—problems of both unemployment and inflation that seemed beyond the reach of fiscal policy. Policy makers also face the challenge of lags between the time they select and implement a policy and when it actually has an effect on the economy. All this forced policy makers to reconsider the role of fiscal policy. The largest fiscal policy measure in decades was President Obama's Recovery Act of 2009. The effectiveness of this measure is still being debated, as you will see.

FISCAL POLICY TOOLS

LO1
Identify two tools of fiscal policy.

The tools of fiscal policy sort into two broad categories: discretionary fiscal policy and automatic stabilizers.

Discretionary Fiscal Policy

This chapter so far has focused mostly on discretionary fiscal policy. **Discretionary fiscal policy** requires congressional and presidential action to change government spending or taxing. These actions are designed to promote macroeconomic goals such as full employment and price stability. President Obama used discretionary fiscal policy in his Recovery Act of 2009.

discretionary fiscal policy Legislative changes in government spending or taxing to promote macroeconomic goals

automatic stabilizers Government spending and taxing programs that year after year automatically reduce fluctuations in disposable income, and thus in consumption, over the business cycle

Automatic Stabilizers

Once adopted, a discretionary fiscal policy usually becomes an ongoing part of the federal budget. Most taxing and spending programs, once implemented, become **automatic stabilizers**. They automatically adjust with the ups and downs of the economy to help stabilize *disposable income*, the income available after taxes. By smoothing fluctuations in disposable income, automatic stabilizers also smooth fluctuations in consumption and in aggregate demand.

NET Bookmark

In the United States, fiscal policy is determined jointly by the President and Congress. The Congressional Budget Office provides analysis to Congress. The Office of Management and Budget does the same for the executive branch. Access the websites for these offices through the URL below to get a sense of the kind of analysis provided, and how this research might be used to shape fiscal policy. Write a one-page essay describing your findings.

www.cengage.com/school/contecon

One automatic stabilizer is unemployment insurance. During a recession, payments automatically flow to the unemployed. This increases disposable income and props up consumption and aggregate demand. Likewise, welfare payments automatically increase as more people become eligible during hard times.

The progressive income tax is an example of an automatic stabilizer that works to cool off the economy. Such a tax takes a bigger bite as incomes increase. During an economic expansion, income taxes claim a growing percentage of income. This slows the growth in disposable income, which slows the growth in consumption. Therefore, the progressive income tax relieves some of the inflationary pressure that might otherwise arise when output increases during an economic expansion.

On the other hand, when the economy enters a recession, real GDP declines, but taxes decline faster. Therefore disposable income does not fall as much as real GDP does. This props up consumption and aggregate demand during recessions.

ESSENTIAL QUESTION

Standard CEE 20: Fiscal Policy

Federal government budgetary policy influences the overall levels of employment, output, and prices.

How does the federal government's fiscal policy influence the levels of employment, output, and prices in the economy?

auremar/Shutterstock.com

Digital Vision/Getty Images

fotofrog/iStockphoto.com

The progressive income tax helps insulate the economy against declines in disposable income, in consumption, and in aggregate demand.

Automatic stabilizers smooth fluctuations in disposable income over the business cycle. They boost aggregate demand during periods of recession and dampen aggregate demand during periods of expansion. Automatic stabilizers do not eliminate economic fluctuations, but they do reduce their magnitude. The stronger and more effective the automatic stabilizers, the less need there is for discretionary fiscal policy. Because of automatic stabilizers introduced during the Great Depression, *the economy is more stable today than it was during the Great Depression and before.* Without much fanfare, automatic stabilizers have been quietly doing their work, keeping the economy on a more even keel.

What are the two tools of fiscal policy? **CHECKPOINT**

PROBLEMS WITH DISCRETIONARY FISCAL POLICY

LO2
Evaluate discretionary fiscal policy in light of the time lags involved.

Discretionary fiscal policy is a type of demand-management policy. The idea is to enact specific measures that increase or decrease aggregate demand to smooth economic fluctuations and move the economy toward its potential output. This seemed to work between the Great Depression and the 1960s. The 1970s, however, turned out to be different.

Stagflation

The problem during the 1970s was stagflation. A decrease in aggregate supply created the double trouble of higher inflation and higher unemployment. The aggregate supply curve shifted to the left because of crop failures around the world, sharply higher oil prices, and other adverse supply shocks. Demand-management policies are not suited to solving the problem of stagflation. This is because in the short run, it is impossible to fight unemployment and inflation at the same time with fiscal policy. An increase in aggregate demand through increased government spending or reduced taxation would worsen inflation, whereas a decrease in aggregate demand would worsen unemployment.

Calculating the Natural Rate of Unemployment

As noted earlier, the unemployment rate that occurs when the economy is producing its potential output is called the *natural rate of unemployment.* Before adopting discretionary fiscal policies, public officials must correctly estimate this natural rate. That's no easy task, and they may get it wrong.

For example, suppose the economy is producing its potential output of \$15.0 trillion, as shown by point *a* in Figure 17.3, where the natural rate of unemployment is 5 percent. Also suppose that public officials mistakenly think the natural rate of unemployment is 4 percent. They then attempt to increase output and reduce unemployment through discretionary fiscal policy. In the short run, the aggregate demand curve would shift out from *AD* to *AD′*, moving the equilibrium point from *a* to *b*. The economy is exceeding its potential output. Some workers find that their agreed-upon wage is not high enough for the extra effort that's expected of them. What's more, their agreed-upon wage would be eroded by the increase in the price level. In the long run, these workers would negotiate higher wages and this would shift aggregate supply from *AS* back to *AS.′* Equilibrium would move from *b* to *c*. Thus, this policy of increasing aggregate demand to stimulate the economy would lead only to inflation in the long run.

FIGURE 17.3 When Discretionary Fiscal Policy Underestimates the Natural Rate of Unemployment

If public officials underestimate the natural rate of unemployment, they may attempt to stimulate aggregate demand even if the economy is already producing its potential output, as at point *a*. In the short run, this expansionary policy yields a short-run equilibrium at point *b*. At this point the price level and output are higher and unemployment is lower. The policy appears to be working. But at point *b*, output exceeds the economy's potential, and this creates inflationary pressure that shifts the economy's aggregate supply curve from *AS* back to *AS.′* Thus, attempts to increase production beyond potential GDP lead only to inflation in the long run.

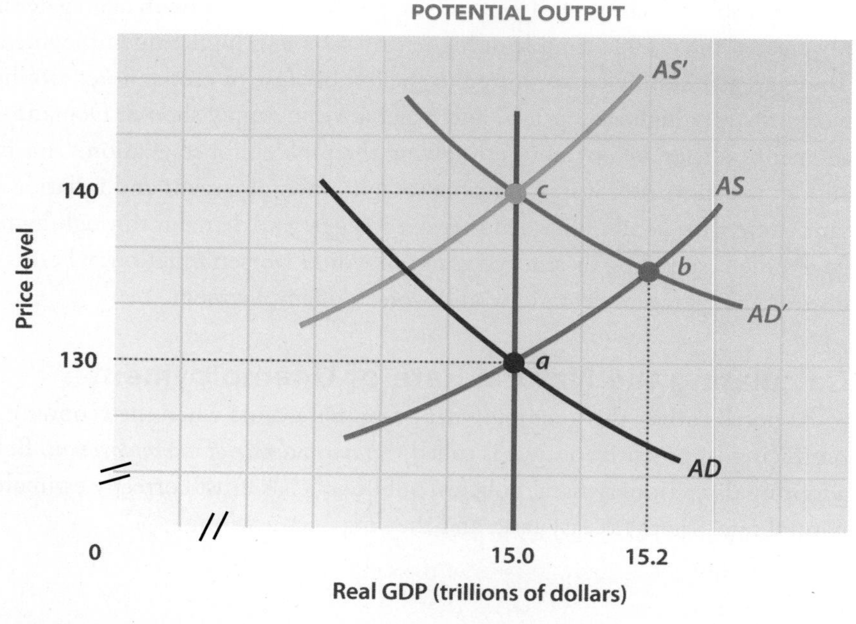

The Problem of Lags

So far the discussion has ignored the time required to implement discretionary fiscal policy. The assumption has been that the desired policy is selected and implemented in no time. The presentation also has assumed that, once implemented, the policy works quickly. Actually, there may be long, sometimes unpredictable, lags at several stages in the process. These lags may reduce the effectiveness of discretionary fiscal policies.

Recognition Lag First, there is a recognition lag, which is the time it takes to identify a problem and determine how serious it is. Because a recession is not identified until more than six months after it begins and the average recession lasts less than a year, a typical recession is more than half over before it is officially recognized as such.

Decision-Making Lag Even after it becomes clear that the economy is in trouble, Congress and the President must develop and agree on an appropriate course of action. Because policy makers usually take time deciding what to do, there is a decision-making lag. Changes in fiscal policy usually take months to approve, but they could take more than a year.

Implementation Lag Once a decision is made, the new policy must be introduced and executed. This often involves an implementation lag. For example, in early 2009, President Obama proposed a $787 billion program of tax cuts and spending increases to stimulate an economy reeling from the global financial crisis and the recession. Although Congress passed the measure relatively quickly, it took years to fully implement some parts of the program. President Obama later acknowledged that many of the spending projects were not as "shovel-ready" as he thought they would be.

Effectiveness Lag Once a policy has been implemented, there is an effectiveness lag before the full impact of the policy registers on the economy. Fiscal policy, once implemented, takes between 9 and 18 months to register its full effect.

These lags make it difficult to carry out discretionary fiscal policy. Discretionary fiscal policy to address a recession could take hold only after the economy has recovered on its own. Thus, discretionary fiscal policy aimed at increasing output and employment may end up just fueling inflation. These lags are reasons why policy makers need to be careful with discretionary fiscal policy.

recognition lag The time needed to identify a macroeconomic problem

decision-making lag The time needed to decide what to do once the problem has been identified

implementation lag The time needed to execute a change in policy

effectiveness lag The time needed for changes in policy to affect the economy

JustASC/Shutterstock.com

Once government decision makers implement a policy, there is a lag before the full impact of the policy registers on the economy. What is this lag called and how long does it usually last?

Fiscal Policy and Aggregate Supply

The discussion of fiscal policy thus far has been limited to effects on aggregate demand. Fiscal policy also can affect aggregate supply, although often that effect is unintentional. For example, suppose the government increases unemployment benefits by imposing higher taxes on the employed. This redistributes income from workers to the unemployed. These offsetting effects may leave aggregate demand unchanged.

What about the possible effects of these changes on aggregate supply? Those who receive higher unemployment benefits have less incentive to find work, so they may search at a more leisurely pace. On the other hand, the higher marginal tax rate on those who have jobs makes work less attractive. In short, the supply of labor could decrease as a result of offsetting changes in taxes and transfers. A decrease in the supply of labor would decrease aggregate supply, reducing output and employment.

Both automatic stabilizers, such as unemployment insurance and the progressive income tax, and discretionary fiscal policies, such as changes in tax rates, may affect individual incentives to work, spend, save, and invest, although these effects are usually unintended. Policy makers should keep these secondary effects in mind when they consider fiscal policies.

CHECKPOINT **What are the various lags involved with discretionary fiscal policy?**

FISCAL POLICY DURING THE GREAT RECESSION

LO3 Explain how fiscal policy was used during the Great Recession.

After peaking in December 2007, the U.S. economy entered a recession. Congress and President Bush enacted a $168 billion plan in early 2008 to stimulate the softening economy. The centerpiece was a one-time tax rebate of up to $600 for individual tax filers and up to $1,200 for joint filers. Probably because the tax cuts were temporary, the results were disappointing and the stimulation, minimal. Surveys showed that most households saved the rebate or used it to pay off debt. They spent less than one-third of the rebate.

After a quiet start, the recession gathered steam. Job losses jumped to 190,000 per month in the second quarter of 2008. Then things got worse. In the third quarter, monthly job losses averaged 334,000.

The Recovery Act of 2009

With the economy bleeding jobs, policy makers had a sense of urgency, if not panic. In February 2009, newly elected President Barack Obama signed the **Recovery Act of 2009**, a $787 billion stimulus package of tax benefits and spending programs aimed at stimulating aggregate demand. The President called the measure "the most sweeping economic recovery package in our history." He predicted the measure would "create or save 3.5 million jobs over the next two years."

Recovery Act of 2009 At $787 billion, the largest stimulus measure in U.S history; enacted in February 2009 and projected to last two years

Thirty-seven percent of the total went for various tax benefits, 28 percent funded entitlements (such as Medicaid), and 35 percent was for grants, contracts, and loans. Most of the tax benefits were one-time reductions for individuals. Again, one-time cuts are not likely to have much of an effect on spending. Grants, contracts, and loans included some so-called "shovel ready" infrastructure projects, such as bridges and roads, but these projects were slow to get underway and they represented just a small fraction of stimulus spending.

Rationale for Deficit Spending

The stimulus package was all deficit spending, so it increased the federal debt. The rationale for deficit spending is that unemployed labor and idle capital would be put to work. And if the multiplier exceeds one, a dollar of government spending would result in more than a dollar of new output and income. Thus, the effectiveness of any stimulus program depends on the size of the multiplier. During the debate on the measure, one group of economists argued that the multiplier was one or less and another group, including the president's economists, argued they were greater than one. Unfortunately, research was inconclusive.

Two years after passage of the measure, some of the stimulus money still had not been spent. The White House claimed that the program was on track to create or save the 3.5 million jobs promised. Employment actually fell by 3.0 million between February 2009, when the stimulus package was approved, and February 2010, for a decline of 2.1 percent. The White House argued that those losses would have been a lot worse without the stimulus. That's difficult to prove or disprove. The unemployment rate remained stubbornly high, hovering around 9 percent deep into 2011.

© Todd Bannor/Alamy

Explain the rationale for how the "shovel-ready" infrastructure projects, financed through deficit spending, would benefit the economy.

Two years after the stimulus package was passed, there were still debates about its effectiveness. Those supporting the stimulus program said that it was effective as far as it went, but it should have been bigger to counter the huge hit to the economy from the financial crisis. Critics of the stimulus program argued that it did little to boost the economy. They claimed that the only obvious results were larger budget deficits and a mountain of debt.

It is said that geologists learn more about the nature of the Earth's crust from one major upheaval, such as a huge earthquake or major volcanic eruption, than from a dozen lesser events. The recession of 2008–2009 traumatized the economy. Events will be dissected for years to develop a clearer understanding of how the economy works and what went wrong.

How was fiscal policy used during the Great Recession? **CHECKPOINT**

17.2 ASSESSMENT

Think Critically

1. Why is the unemployment insurance program an example of an automatic stabilizer for the economy?
2. Inflation often results when the economy is growing rapidly. Why is it politically difficult for Congress to use discretionary fiscal policy by passing tax increases or reducing its spending that could slow economic growth and reduce inflation?
3. If the government decided to extend unemployment benefits for an extra 13 weeks beyond the 26 that normally are paid, what would happen to the incentive unemployed people have to find work? How might this affect the economy?
4. Why do some economists believe that the decision-making lag is the longest of the lags involved with discretionary fiscal policy?

Graphing Exercise

5. The so-called *misery index* is found by summing the unemployment rate and the inflation rate by year. Draw a line graph of the misery index based on data in the table. How does the misery index appear to be related to the economic conditions of the country? What would you expect to happen to the misery index if the economy begins to grow rapidly?

INFLATION, UNEMPLOYMENT, AND THE MISERY INDEX, 2001–2010

Year	Unemployment	Inflation	Misery Index
2001	4.7%	2.8%	7.5
2002	5.8%	1.6%	7.4
2003	6.0%	2.3%	8.3
2004	5.5%	2.7%	8.2
2005	5.1%	3.4%	8.5
2006	4.6%	3.2%	7.8
2007	4.6%	2.8%	7.4
2008	5.8%	3.8%	9.6
2009	9.3%	−0.4%	8.9
2010	9.6%	1.6%	11.2

Source: *Economic Indicators*, July 2011, pp. 12 and 24.

Make Academic Connections

6. **Government** An important part of state government spending is governed by federal laws that require state governments to provide Medicaid programs for people who are unable to pay for their own medical care. Investigate Medicaid spending in your state. Have these payments grown more rapidly than other types of state government spending? What could explain the growth in your state's Medicaid payments?

TeamWork

Working in small teams, make a comprehensive list of services your local government provides. Choose the five that your team thinks are most important. For each of these, investigate how the service is funded (local taxes, fees, state or federal aid, etc.). Discuss what would happen if local residents were required to pay for these services without any outside assistance. Compare your work with that of other teams.

MOVERS AND SHAKERS

Ron Paul

U.S. Congressman

Evan Meyer/Shutterstock.com

Dr. Ron Paul is a 12-term representative from Texas in the U.S. House of Representatives. Paul first won his seat in Congress in 1976. Known for his strict adherence to Constitutional principles, critics have nicknamed him "Dr. No" because he insists he will "never vote for legislation unless the proposed measure is expressly authorized by the Constitution." Paul is a former flight surgeon with the Air Force and has had a private medical practice.

Paul's position on government spending has made him unpopular with liberal politicians and other proponents of the federal government's "tax and spend" policies. He is a strong advocate of Austrian School economics, a modern adaptation of classical economics, which touts the value of an unregulated free market. The main concept of the Austrian School is that individuals make better decisions without the interference of government. Freedom of association and individual rights, abolition of central banks and the Internal Revenue Service, and a return to the gold standard are all tenets of the Austrian School.

Paul is a noted Libertarian. The Libertarian Party emphasizes personal freedom and independence and believes that government's only role is "to help individuals defend themselves against force and fraud." However, because third-party candidates rarely are taken seriously, he made his third attempt for the office of President in 2012 as a Republican candidate. His determination to bring attention to runaway spending and government intrusion into private lives has gained him an audience. He said, "Time has come around to the point where the people are agreeing with much of what I've been saying for 30 years. So, I think the time is right." Paul feels strongly that the states, not the federal government, should regulate issues such as abortion, gay marriage, and drug use. During his presidential run, he argued that defense spending should be curbed, and that U.S. armed conflicts at the time were hurting the viability of the U.S. dollar—which he believed to be on the verge of a collapse.

A fiscal conservative, Paul believes that ideas should succeed or fail on their own merit without interference from government. He thinks bad investments should be punished by loss (via market forces) and should not be insured by the government. Under his administration, the government would not "bail out" banks, firms, and people who make bad investments. On why his views are gaining in popularity, he said, "The country is entirely different. The credibility of what I've been saying has been growing by leaps and bounds." Paul believes the federal budget should be balanced, and that spending should be capped and programs cut. He said, "If you don't get rid of programs and you don't change this attitude that we have to be the policemen for the whole world, the demand will be there to spend the money." He believes that unless the United States stops spending money it does not have, our country will default on its debt and go bankrupt. He said, "Defaults occur when you don't pay your debt, but if you pay somebody the bill back again with money that has less value, you've defaulted again, too. If the dollar is worth 50 cents on the dollar, then we've defaulted on real value. So the default is ongoing."

Think Critically **Go online and research the Austrian and Keynesian schools of economics. Write a brief paper comparing and contrasting the main tenets of each school. Include your opinion of each school of thought.**

Sources: http://www.businessdictionary.com/definition/Austrian-School-of-Economics.htm; http://www.realclearpolitics.com/articles/2010/01/06/ron_paul_transcript_interview_with_ron_paul_99810.html; http://www.lp.org/introduction/what-is-the-libertarian-party; http://www.mlive.com/politics/index.ssf/2011/05/ron_paul_announces_third_run_a.html; http://salem-nh.patch.com/articles/campaign-qa-ron-paul; and http://transcripts.cnn.com/TRANSCRIPTS/0712/18/gb.01.html

17.3 FEDERAL DEFICITS AND FEDERAL DEBT

Key Terms

crowding out 552
crowding in 553
debt ceiling 556

Learning Objectives

LO1 Discuss why federal budget deficits have been common since the Great Depression.

LO2 Distinguish between crowding out and crowding in.

LO3 Discuss changes in the relative size of the federal debt since World War II.

LO4 Explain who bears the burden of the federal debt.

LO5 Evaluate whether deficits are sustainable and understand how serious a debt default would be.

In Your World

When governments spend more than they take in, budget deficits result. These deficits can have their own effect on the economy, beyond the stimulus provided by changes in spending and taxing. These deficits add to the federal debt, which also can have its own effect on the economy. Policy makers usually focus on the immediate impact of a policy and mistakenly ignore the long-term effects. Huge federal deficits accumulate into a giant federal debt that will claim a growing portion of the federal budget. Eventually, a giant federal debt could cripple the government's ability to function. Because you and your classmates will one day inherit responsibility for the federal debt, you have a particular interest in this material.

BUDGET DEFICITS

LO1 Discuss why federal deficits have been common since the Great Depression.

When government spending exceeds government revenue, the result is a *budget deficit.* The federal budget deficit measures the amount by which total federal spending for the year exceeds total federal revenues. The federal government finances a deficit by selling U.S. government securities, such as bonds or other government IOUs. U.S. households, businesses, other levels of government, and foreigners buy them because they earn interest and the U.S. government has long been considered the most trustworthy borrower in the world.

Federal Deficits Over the Years

Between 1789, when the U.S. Constitution was officially adopted, and 1930, the first full year of the Great Depression, the federal budget was in deficit 33 percent of the years. Federal deficits during that stretch occurred primarily during war years. Because wars involved much personal hardship, public officials were understandably reluctant to increase taxes to finance war-related spending. After a war, government spending dropped more than government revenue. Thus, deficits arising during a war were largely self-correcting once the war ended.

Since the Great Depression, the federal budget has been in deficit 85 percent of the years. Figure 17.4 shows federal deficits and surpluses as a percentage of GDP since 1934. Unmistakable are the huge deficits during World War II. Also notable are the sizable deficits in recent years because of the financial crisis of 2008 and the Great Recession.

The federal budget experienced a surplus from 1998 to 2001. Aside from that brief surplus, the budget has been in deficit every year but one since 1960. The average annual deficit grew from less than 1 percent relative to GDP in the 1960s to nearly 10 percent from 2009 to 2012. Except for World War II, these were the largest deficits in the nation's history. During the period from 2009 to 2012, about 40 cents of every dollar of federal spending had to be borrowed.

FIGURE 17.4 Federal Deficits and Surpluses as Percent of GDP Since 1934

Between 1934 and 2012, the federal budget was in deficit in all but 12 years. The largest deficits relative to GDP occurred during World War II.

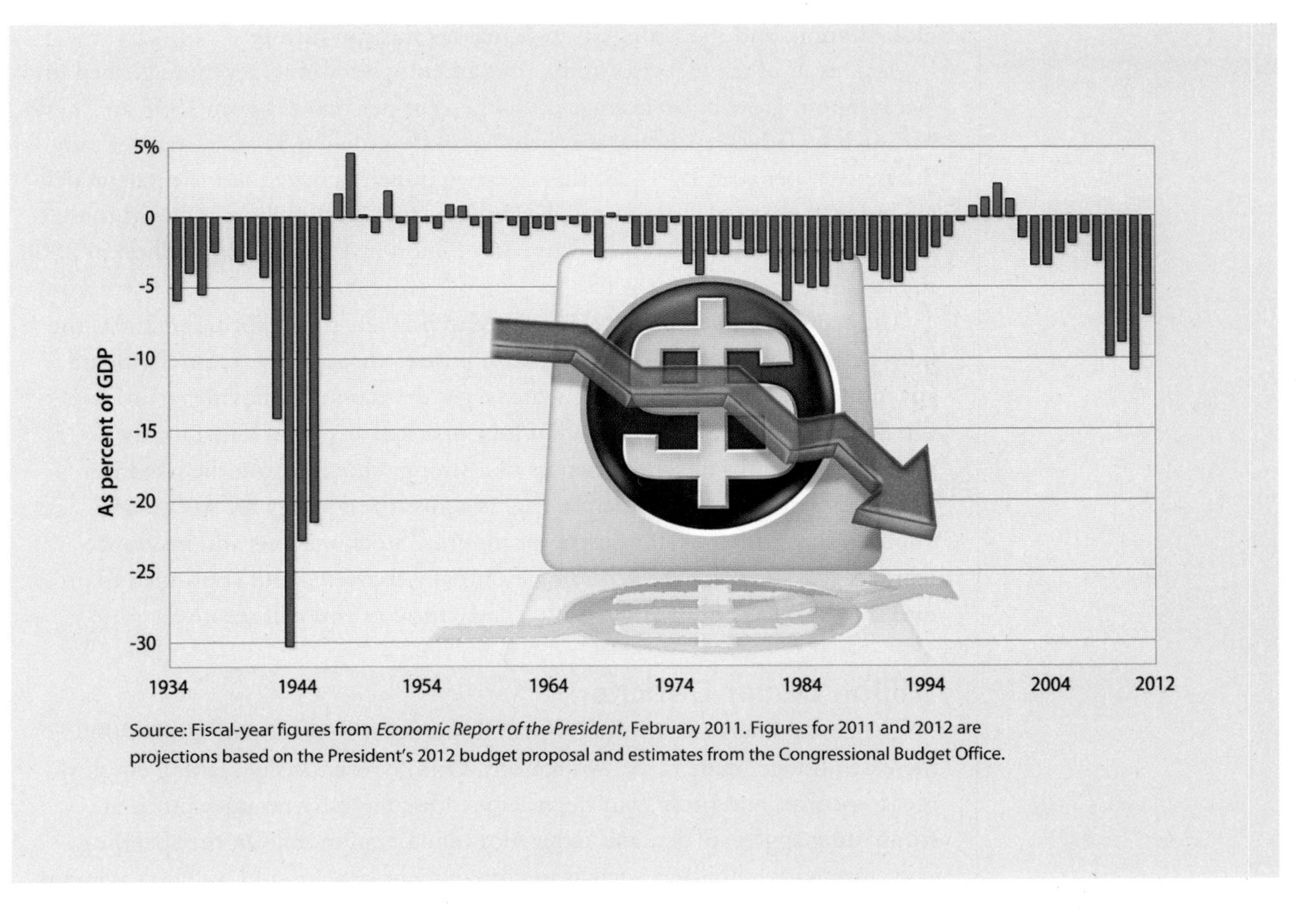

Source: Fiscal-year figures from *Economic Report of the President*, February 2011. Figures for 2011 and 2012 are projections based on the President's 2012 budget proposal and estimates from the Congressional Budget Office.

Investigate Your Local Economy

Interview three or four adults about the federal budget deficit. Ask if they know the size of the federal deficit. Ask if they think having a budget deficit is a good idea or a bad idea for the economy, and why. Then compare the answers you receive with the answers your classmates receive. Did you uncover any trends? If so, what are they?

Why Is the Federal Budget Usually in a Deficit?

Why has the federal budget been in deficit so often? One obvious reason is that, unlike the legislatures in 49 states, the U.S. Congress is not required to balance the budget. Why does Congress approve budgets with deficits most years?

One widely accepted model of the public sector discussed in the previous chapter argues that elected officials try to maximize their political support. Voters like public spending programs but hate paying taxes. Therefore, spending programs win voters' support and taxes lose it. Elected officials try to maximize their political support by spending more than they tax. This results in chronic deficits. Why were deficits more common after the Great Depression? The answer can be traced back to Keynes and his followers, who thought deficits were a justifiable result of fiscal policy. They were less worried about the long-run consequences of deficits. As Keynes once observed, "In the long run, we are all dead."

The Federal Surplus of 1998–2001

What about the federal budget surpluses from 1998 to 2001? Where did they come from? Concern about rising deficits during the 1980s led to two tax hikes in the early 1990s. The Republican Congress elected in 1994 imposed more discipline on federal spending. Meanwhile, the economy experienced a healthy recovery resulting from technological innovation, the collapse of communism, market globalization, and the strongest stock market surge in history.

As a result of tax increases and a strengthening economy, revenues gushed into Washington, growing an average of 8.3 percent per year between 1993 and 1998. Meanwhile, federal spending was held in check, growing by an average of only 3.2 percent per year. By 1998, that one-two punch knocked out the federal deficit, a deficit that only six years earlier had reached $290 billion, a record to that point. The federal surplus grew from $69 billion in 1998 to $236 billion in 2000, the largest ever.

The economy entered a recession in March 2001. In the spring of 2001, the newly elected President George W. Bush pushed through an across-the-board cut in income tax rates to, in his words, "get the economy moving again." On September 11, 2001, 19 men in four hijacked airplanes killed nearly 3,000 people and squelched chances of a strong rebound from the recession. The attacks grounded commercial flights across the country for weeks, and knocked down the travel industry for months. Stock markets and insurance markets also suffered. The economy eventually recovered and continued to grow into 2007. The economy then took a nasty turn, as you will see next.

Trillion Dollar Deficits

The global financial crisis of 2008 and the Great Recession of 2008–2009 increased budget deficits for two reasons. On the revenue side, falling employment, income, and profits cut tax receipts. Discretionary tax cuts aimed at stimulating aggregate demand reduced revenue even more. On the spending side, automatic stabilizers such as unemployment benefits and welfare payments increased federal outlays, as did discretionary spending increases resulting from

President Obama's $787 billion Recovery Act of 2009, known more popularly as the "stimulus bill." The federal deficit climbed from $161 billion in 2007 to $1.4 trillion in 2009 and $1.3 trillion in 2010.

President Obama's budgets projected deficits of $1.6 trillion in 2011 and $1.1 trillion in 2012. Deficits between 2009 and 2012 were the first trillion dollar deficits in the nation's history. By 2011 the fiscal policy focus had shifted from how to revive the economy to how to reduce these huge deficits.

Why have federal deficits been so common since the Great Depression?

Math in Economics

Common Core Expressions and Equations

You can follow the problem-solving plan below to help you solve a word problem.

1. Read the problem carefully to be sure you understand what it is asking you to find.
2. Determine the method you will use to find the answer.
3. Carry out your plan to find the answer to the problem.
4. Check that your answer is reasonable in the context of the problem.

EXAMPLE

If the federal government expects to spend $3,729 billion next year and expects to receive $2,627 billion from taxes and other revenue, how much does the government expect next year's deficit to be?

SOLUTION

The question asks for the amount of next year's expected federal deficit. Plan to find this value by subtracting the expected federal government revenue from the amount of it expects to spend.

$3,729 billion – $2,627 billion = $1,102 billion

The government expects a $1,102 billion deficit.

Practice the Skill

Use the problem solving plan to solve each problem.

1. If the federal government increases tax rates next year and therefore increases its tax receipts by 10%, how much will the expected deficit be? Assume that federal spending remains unchanged.
2. If the federal government cuts spending next year by 15%, instead of increases tax receipts, how much will the expected deficit be? Assume government revenue remains unchanged.
3. If the federal government both increases revenue by 10% and cuts spending by 15% next year, how much will the expected deficit be?
4. Do you believe the federal government could increase its revenue by 10% and cut its spending by 15% to reduce, but not eliminate, its expected deficit?

DEFICITS AND INTEREST RATES

LO2
Distinguish between crowding out and crowding in.

What effect do federal deficits have on interest rates? Recall that interest rates affect investment, a critical component of economic growth. Year-to-year fluctuations in investment are the primary source of instability in GDP. Figure 17.5 compares the percent change in real investment and the percent change in real GDP since 1960. As you can see, investment fluctuates much more than GDP.

Crowding Out

How do federal deficits affect investment? Here's a way of looking at the question. Were you ever unwilling to go to a particular restaurant because it was too crowded? You simply did not want to put up with the hassle and long wait. You were "crowded out." Some version of this also can result from federal deficits.

The larger the deficit, the more the government must borrow. This increased demand for borrowed funds can drive up the market rate of interest. Higher interest rates discourage, or *crowd out,* some private investment. **Crowding out** occurs when larger government deficits drive up interest rates and thereby reduce private investment. Decreased investment spending reduces the effectiveness of federal deficits that are intended to stimulate aggregate demand.

crowding out Private investment falls when larger government deficits drive up interest rates

FIGURE 17.5 Annual Percent Changes in Real GDP and in Real Investment Since 1960
Investment fluctuates much more from year to year than does GDP.

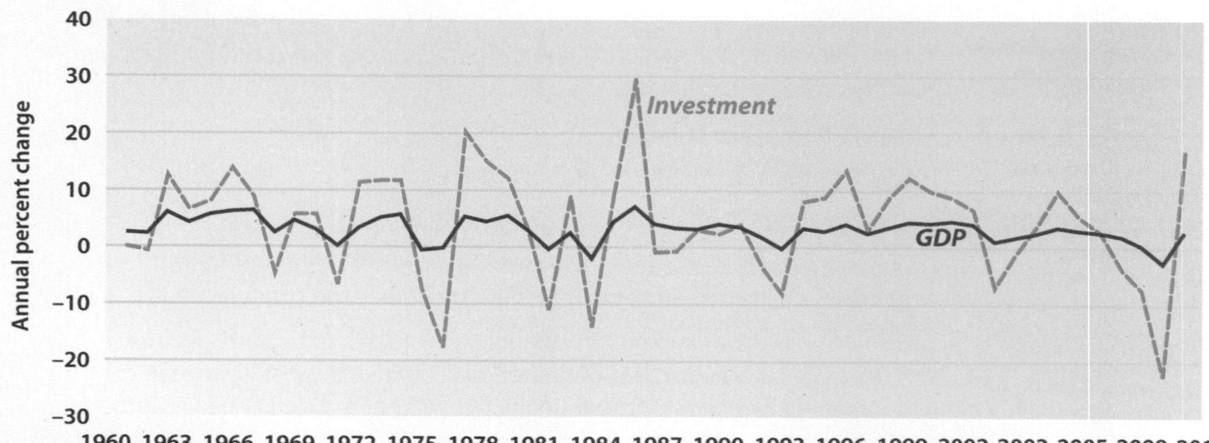

Source: U.S. Department of Commerce. Investment and GDP are in real terms—that is, adjusted for changes in the price level.

Crowding In

Did you ever pass up an unfamiliar restaurant because the place was practically empty? If you had seen just a few more customers, you might have stopped in—you might have been willing to "crowd in." Similarly, businesses may hesitate to invest in a seemingly lifeless economy.

If government stimulates a weak economy, the business outlook may improve. As expectations grow more favorable, firms could become more willing to invest. This possibility of government deficits to stimulate private investment is sometimes called **crowding in**.

What's the difference between crowding out and crowding in? **CHECKPOINT**

FEDERAL DEBT

LO3 Discuss changes in the relative size of the federal debt since World War II.

The federal deficit measures the amount by which annual spending exceeds annual revenue. Federal deficits add up. It took 39 presidents, seven wars, the Great Depression, and more than 200 years for the federal debt to reach $1 trillion, as it did in 1981. It took only five presidents and another 30 years for that debt to reach $15 trillion, as it did by late 2011. The federal debt reflects the accumulation of past deficits, the total amount owed by the federal government. Federal debt adds up all federal deficits and subtracts federal surpluses.

Gross Debt vs. Debt Held by the Public

In discussing the federal debt, economists often distinguish between gross debt and debt held by the public. The gross debt includes U.S. Treasury securities purchased by various federal agencies. Because this is debt the federal government owes to itself, economists often ignore it and focus instead on debt held by the public. Debt held by the public includes U.S. Treasury securities purchased by households, by firms, by banks (including the Federal Reserve bank), by other levels of government, by non-profit institutions, and by foreign entities. As of late 2011, gross federal debt totaled $15 trillion, and debt held by the public totaled $11 trillion. Public debt in 2011 averaged about $36,000 per U.S. citizen.

Debt Relative to GDP

One way to measure debt over time is relative to the economy's production and income, or GDP. In a sense, GDP shows the economy's ability to carry debt, just as household income shows that family's ability to carry a mortgage.

Figure 17.6 shows the federal government's public debt relative to GDP. The cost of World War II spiked the debt to more than 100 percent relative to GDP

crowding in Government spending stimulates private investment in an otherwise stagnant economy

FIGURE 17.6 Federal Debt Held by the Public as Percent of GDP, 1940 to 2012

The federal debt held by the public relative to GDP increased sharply in recent years because of the financial crisis and Great Recession.

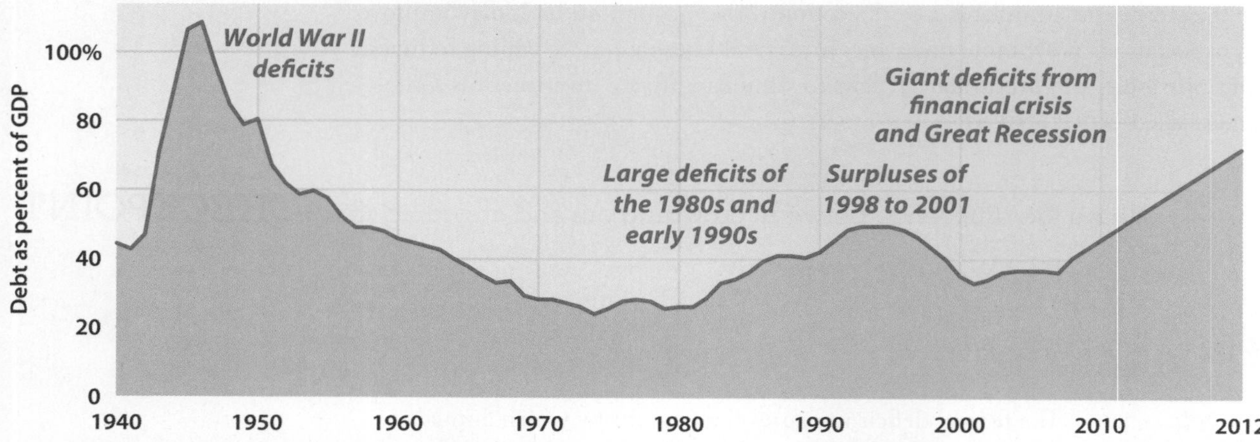

Source: Fiscal year figures from *Economic Report of the President*, February 2011, Table 79, and the President's budget submission. Figures for 2011 and 2012 are projections.

by 1946. After the war, this percentage trended lower, reaching 35 percent by 2000. The financial crisis and Great Recession of 2008–2009 cut federal revenue and increased federal outlays. By 2012 public debt climbed to 75 percent relative to GDP, the highest since 1950.

Note that the usual measures of the federal debt do not capture all future government liabilities. Social Security and other federal retirement programs promise benefits that must be paid from taxes or further borrowing.

CHECKPOINT **What has happened to federal debt levels relative to GDP since World War II?**

ECONOMIC IMPACT OF FEDERAL DEBT

LO4
Explain who bears the burden of the federal debt.

In light of the giant deficits in recent years, the growing federal debt has become a key part of the debate about the use and effectiveness of fiscal policy. What is the impact of a large federal debt on the economy?

Debt and Interest Rates

The federal government seldom pays off any debt. When bonds mature, the government simply sells more bonds to pay off holders of maturing bonds. That's like you paying one credit card bill by charging another credit card. Debt service payments are quite sensitive to changes in interest rates. Based on a $11 trillion debt held by the public in 2011, a one-percentage point increase in the interest rate on government debt would eventually raise the federal government's annual interest cost by $110 billion.

Interest payments on the federal debt were about 8 percent of the federal budget in 1978. Thanks to record-low interest rates, interest payments in 2011 were only about 6.5 percent of the federal budget. If interest rates rise from their low levels, so will the cost of servicing the federal debt.

Who Bears the Burden of the Federal Debt?

Deficit spending is a way of billing future taxpayers for current spending. The federal debt raises questions about the morality of one generation's passing on to the next generation the burden of its borrowing. To what extent do budget deficits shift the burden to future generations?

We Owe It to Ourselves It is often argued that the debt is not a burden to future generations because, although future generations must service the debt, those same generations will receive the debt service payments. In that sense, the debt is not a burden on future generations. It's all in the family, so to speak.

Foreign Ownership of Debt But the "we-owe-it-to-ourselves" argument does not apply to that portion of the federal debt purchased by foreigners. Foreigners who buy U.S. government bonds forgo present consumption. Thus, they sacrifice now for a future payoff. As foreigners buy more government bonds, this increases the burden of the debt on future generations of Americans because future debt service payments no longer remain in the country. Foreigners owned about 46 percent of the federal government's public debt in 2011, compared to 20 percent in 1994. Thus, the burden of the debt on future generations of Americans is growing, both because of the growing size of the federal debt and because a rising share of debt interest and repayments will go to foreigners.

Photodisc/Getty Images

Do you think the federal government is acting responsibly in passing debt on to future generations? Why or why not?

CHECKPOINT Who bears the burden of the federal debt?

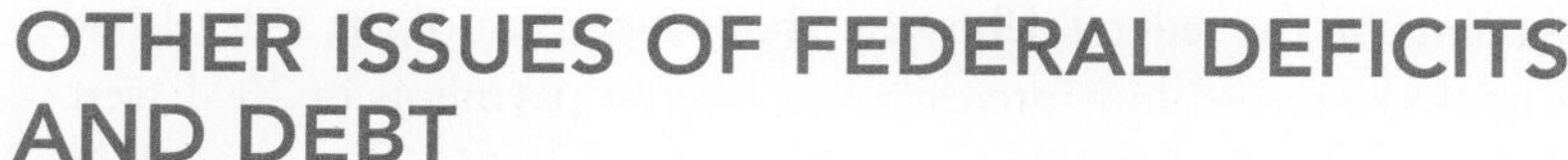

OTHER ISSUES OF FEDERAL DEFICITS AND DEBT

LO5 **Evaluate whether deficits are sustainable and understand how serious a debt default would be.**

Large federal deficits will add to a mounting federal debt for years to come. Federal debt has become the dominant issue in federal budgeting. How sustainable are large deficits? What has been the role of the debt ceiling? And what would happen if the nation defaults on its debts?

Are Persistent Deficits Sustainable?

Given that deficits have been with us so long, we might ask: How long can the country run a large deficit? The short answer is: As long as lenders are willing to finance those deficits at low interest rates. That depends on the confidence that lenders have in getting repaid. At some point, chronic deficits may accumulate into such a debt that lenders lose confidence in the country's ability to repay them. These lenders will demand extremely high interest rates or refuse to lend at all. As interest rates rise, debt service costs grow and could overwhelm the budget.

U.S. government securities have long been considered the safest investment in the world, and this has helped America finance chronic deficits and rising debt. Ironically, the global financial crisis encouraged investors around the globe to buy U.S. government securities as they sought safety. This "flight to quality" drove down the interest rate on government bonds, thus reducing the cost of servicing the federal debt in the years following the global financial crisis.

That favorable set of circumstances could change. The Greek government had little trouble borrowing until 2010, when the financial community decided that Greek debt had become too large and, therefore, too risky. As a result, Greece had to promise borrowers 20 percent interest to sell its bonds. If America ever faced that same high rate on the public debt, interest payments would top $2 trillion a year, swamping the budget.

Countries can continue to run deficits as long as the cost of servicing the resulting debt remains manageable. Suppose that debt service, which consists entirely of interest payments, remains at 10 percent or less of the federal budget. Something like that would appear to be sustainable (since 1960, U.S. debt service payments have averaged about 10 percent of federal outlays). But trillion dollar deficits quickly accumulate into an unsustainable debt.

The Debt Ceiling and Debt Default

debt ceiling A limit on the total amount of money the federal government can legally borrow

The **debt ceiling** is a limit on the total amount of money the federal government can legally borrow. About a century ago, Congress set the first debt ceiling and raised it whenever necessary, more than 80 times in all. The ceiling was largely a formality.

Until early 2011, that is, when the federal government faced sharply rising debt from giant deficits for years to come. In early 2011, the gross debt ceiling stood at $14.3 trillion. The federal government actually hit that ceiling on May 16 of that year, but the U.S. Treasury was able to buy time by suspending payments to some retirement funds. At the time the government was borrowing about 40 cents of each dollar spent, so without additional borrowing, the Treasury would run out of money. The limit would start to bite in early August.

If the debt ceiling had not been raised, the U.S. government would have missed some debt-service payments and would have been in default. This would have triggered a cascade of troubles, not the least of which would be a sharply higher cost of borrowing or even an inability to borrow. Difficulty in rolling over more than $200 billion of debt that would come due each month would cripple federal finances.

A default on what had been considered the securest investment in the world would be catastrophic for world financial markets. Not only would the federal cost of borrowing increase sharply. Market interest rates would spike to reflect a riskier economy, so everything from car loans to home loans would rise. Credit flows would dry up. Unemployment would jump as businesses cut jobs in the face of growing uncertainty.

Both Democrats and Republicans in Congress agreed that the debt ceiling should be raised. Before approving a higher debt ceiling, Republicans focused on reducing future deficits by cutting spending. Democrats focused more on tax increases, especially on high-income households. In the end, the two sides came together enough to raise the debt ceiling and avert a crisis for a while.

CHECKPOINT

How long are large federal deficits sustainable, and what would happen if the nation defaulted on its debt?

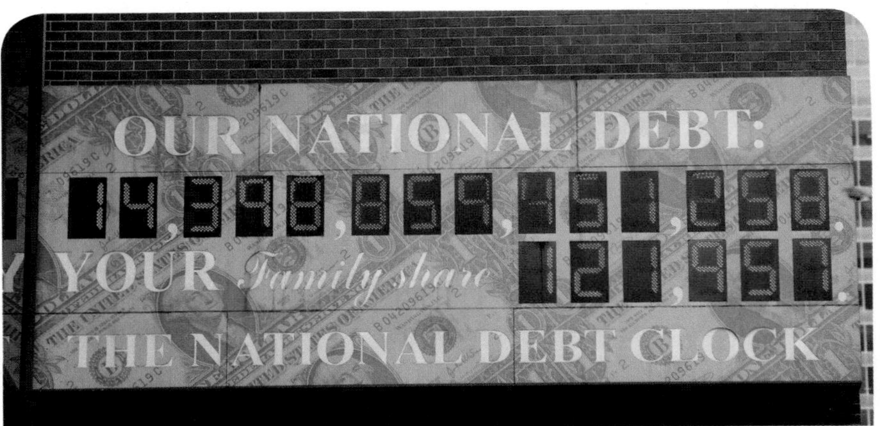

JUSTIN LANE/EPA/Landov

The National Debt Clock near Times Square has been keeping track of the federal debt since 1989. How has the country managed to sustain its debt?

17.3 ASSESSMENT

Think Critically

1. In 1930, the federal debt was slightly more than $16.8 billion. Why doesn't this fact provide much information about the size or importance of this debt? What other information would you need in order to evaluate the debt's importance?
2. Why didn't the tax cuts of 2008 and 2009 immediately cause people to spend more and get the economy moving?
3. The Social Security system has purchased billions of dollars of U.S. Treasury bonds. Some economists believe this is simply a matter of taking money from one of the government's pockets and putting it in another. Others disagree. When the Social Security system cashes in its bonds to pay benefits to retired workers in the future, where will the funds come from? Do these bonds really impose less of a burden on Americans than do other types of debt such as bonds issued by state and local governments or bonds issued by corporations?
4. If interest rates increased by 3 percent across the board, what would happen to annual interest payments on the federal debt owned by the public?

Graphing Exercise

5. From 1985 to 2010, tax payments received by the Social Security system far exceeded the amount paid to beneficiaries. Money that the system accumulated was invested in government bonds and held in the Social Security Trust Fund to be used to make future payments. Use the data in the table to draw a line graph that shows the growth in this trust fund. Why will this trend toward larger balances in the Social Security Trust Fund be reversed in the future?

SOCIAL SECURITY TRUST FUND ACCUMULATED BALANCE, 1985–2010 (IN BILLIONS OF DOLLARS)

Year	Balance
1985	$35.8
1990	$214.2
1995	$488.5
2000	$931.8
2005	$1,663.0
2010	$2,609.0

Source: http://www.ssa.gov/oact/progdata/assets.html

Make Academic Connections

6. **Math** The gross federal debt was approximately $15 trillion dollars in late 2011. If this debt grew at a rate of 3 percent per year in each of the following 5 years, how much would the debt total in 2016? Do the same for a growth rate of 7 percent per year. Should such an increase in the debt be a concern for U.S. citizens? Why or why not?

TeamWork

Most economists agree that the national debt cannot be reduced significantly without reducing entitlement programs such as Social Security. Working in small teams, choose the best alternative to control the cost of Social Security. (1) Increase Social Security taxes paid by workers and employers by 2 percent. (2) Make Social Security taxes apply to all types of income instead of only wages. (3) Increase the retirement age to receive full Social Security benefits by two years. (4) Reduce benefits by an average of 10 percent. (5) Other. Explain the reasons for your choice. Compare your group's work with that of other groups.

Connect to History

Alexander Hamilton and the National Debt

Economic issues played a major role in the American Revolution, and the United States emerged from the struggle in poor financial shape. It had fought the war on borrowed money. It stopped paying interest on its bonds. It was behind in paying soldiers. It also had issued more than $200 million in near worthless paper money, or "continentals." When representatives from the various states met in Philadelphia during the summer of 1787 to address these problems, the result was a new constitution. The new U.S. Constitution gave the federal government certain powers to tax, borrow, and spend.

ConstanceMcGuire/iStockphoto.com

Alexander Hamilton etching

President George Washington appointed Alexander Hamilton as the new nation's first secretary of the treasury in 1789. Hamilton was not the first choice. Robert Morris, the "financier of the Revolution," turned Washington down and recommended Hamilton. Hamilton realized he needed to establish the country's credit by resolving the problems of the nation's debt. The United States and its credit were held in low esteem around the world, and no one was willing to lend money to the country. Hamilton realized that establishing the nation's credit would enhance the nation's prosperity and provide an incentive for individuals and nations to invest in the United States. For Hamilton, federal debt was desirable, as he felt it would bind the moneyed class to the new government. Hamilton had written to Morris, "A national debt, if not excessive, will be to us a national blessing."

Three types of debt sprang from the Revolution: (1) federal debt owed to foreigners, (2) federal debt owed to Americans, and (3) state debts. There was no question about paying the foreign debt at face value. Domestic debt had depreciated to about 25 cents on the dollar, but Hamilton proposed to pay it at face value, or full value, as well. Because many speculators who had purchased the depreciated certificates would stand to profit, some in Congress resisted this solution. They felt it would enrich speculators rather than those who originally had purchased the debt. Despite the opposition, Hamilton's solution prevailed. He proposed to repay the debt by issuing new bonds for the full amount of the old debts. The new debt would be repaid over time from tariff revenues.

Hamilton also proposed that the federal government assume, or promise to repay, state debts. Much of that debt had been incurred during the Revolution for the benefit of all the states. In addition, wealthy residents held many state bonds. If their investments could be shifted from the states to the federal government, he believed their long-term interests in the nation's success would be ensured. Southern states defeated these proposals four times, putting Hamilton's entire financial plan in danger. It was only when he gained Thomas Jefferson's support by agreeing to locate the capital to the south—in the area of Washington, D.C.—that Hamilton secured enough votes to pass his plan.

Hamilton was successful, and the nation's credit was insured. By 1794, the United States had a good credit rating and its bonds were highly sought.

Think Critically **The perfect solution at one time in history may not be the best solution in another. Hamilton saw that the national debt could be a positive factor in the nation's economy. How does that differ from attitudes today?**

Chapter 17 Summary

ASK THE EXPERT

www.cengage.com/school/contecon

In theory, how does a tax cut work to stimulate the economy?

ASK THE EXPERT

www.cengage.com/school/contecon

What is fiscal policy, and what is it supposed to accomplish?

17.1 The Evolution of Fiscal Policy

A. Fiscal policy is intended to move the economy toward full employment at its potential output with price stability. It does this primarily by working to shift aggregate demand. Potential output is the economy's level of production that is sustainable in the long run.

B. If output is below its potential, the federal government may try to use fiscal policy to stimulate production by increasing federal spending or cutting taxes. If, on the other hand, output exceeds its potential, this creates inflationary pressure in the economy.

C. Prior to the Great Depression, classical economists believed natural market forces would help the economy recover from recessions in the long run without government intervention. During the Great Depression, problems with classical economic theory became apparent.

D. Keynes developed a theory in the 1930s that argued prices, wages, and interest rates were "sticky" and would not quickly fall in a recession to bring about economic growth. Keynes believed that government had the responsibility of getting the economy moving again by increasing government spending and/or reducing taxes.

17.2 Fiscal Policy Reconsidered

A. Fiscal policy may either be discretionary or automatic. Discretionary fiscal policy requires legislative actions to promote macroeconomic goals. Automatic fiscal policy gets built into spending and taxing measures because of prior discretionary policy.

B. There are limitations on the effectiveness of fiscal policy. Because fiscal policy is designed to influence aggregate demand, it is not effective in fighting stagflation, when there is both higher unemployment and higher inflation.

C. Fiscal policy decisions may have unintended effects on aggregate supply.

D. Economists are still debating the effects of the Recovery Act of 2009. Those who support the idea say a bigger stimulus was needed. Others say the measure's primary result was larger federal deficits and growing debt.

17.3 Federal Deficits and Federal Debt

A. Before the Great Depression, federal spending equaled federal revenue, except in time of war. Since the 1930s, spending has exceeded revenues in 85 percent of the years. The annual deficits accumulated to create a public debt of $11 trillion by 2011.

B. In most of the 1980s and 1990s, the federal deficit averaged about 4 percent relative to GDP. This trend was reversed between 1998 and 2001, when tax hikes of the early 1990s and reduced spending growth temporarily erased annual deficits. The Great Recession of 2008–2009 spiked federal deficits to more than a trillion dollars a year, or nearly 10 percent relative to GDP, levels not seen since World War II.

C. Deficit spending may contribute to higher interest rates. When the federal government borrows additional money to fund a deficit, interest rates often increase. These higher interest rates can discourage borrowing and spending by businesses and consumers.

D. The federal debt should be evaluated in terms of the nation's ability to carry it, as reflected by GDP. Because of trillion dollar deficits in recent years, the federal debt relative to GDP more than doubled from 35 percent in 2000 to 75 percent in 2012.

CHAPTER 17 ASSESSMENT

Review Economic Terms

Match the terms with the definitions. Some terms will not be used.

_____ 1. Private investment falls when larger government deficits drive up interest rates

_____ 2. The unemployment rate when the economy is producing its potential level of output

_____ 3. Congressional changes in spending or taxing to promote macroeconomic goals

_____ 4. The economy's maximum sustainable output in the long run

_____ 5. The time needed for changes in government policy to affect the economy

_____ 6. A group of laissez-faire economists, who believed that economic downturns were short-run problems that corrected themselves in the long run through natural market forces

_____ 7. The time needed to execute a change in government policy

_____ 8. Matching annual spending with annual revenue, except during war years

_____ 9. The time needed for the government to decide what to do once an economic problem has been identified

_____ 10. Any change in fiscal policy affects aggregate demand by more than the original change in spending or taxing

_____ 11. Government spending and taxing programs that, year after year, automatically reduce fluctuations in disposable income and thus in consumption over the business cycle

_____ 12. The time needed to identify a macroeconomic problem

_____ 13. Government spending stimulates private investment in an otherwise lifeless economy

a. annually balanced budget
b. automatic stabilizers
c. classical economists
d. crowding in
e. crowding out
f. debt ceiling
g. decision-making lag
h. discretionary fiscal policy
i. effectiveness lag
j. implementation lag
k. multiplier effect
l. natural rate of unemployment
m. potential output
n. recognition lag

Review Economic Concepts

14. An economy's potential output is reached
    a. when there is no unemployment.
    b. at the natural rate of unemployment.
    c. when there is only cyclical unemployment.
    d. at the frictional rate of unemployment.

15. **True or False** Output can exceed the potential rate only in the short run.

16. When output is less than the potential rate, there is a(n) ________?________ gap in the economy.

17. Classical economists believed that the federal government should have a(n) ________?________ budget.

18. **True or False** Classical economists believed that, in a recession, prices, wages, and interest rates would fall, and this would bring the recession to an end.

19. Keynes developed a theory that was intended to address which problem during the Great Depression?
    a. unemployment
    b. inflation
    c. government deficits
    d. high interest rates

20. Keynes believed that the ________?________ would cause an increase in government spending or reduction in taxes to have a larger impact on aggregate demand.

21. Which of the following is an automatic stabilizer for the economy?
    a. Congress decides to increase welfare benefits during a recession.
    b. An increase in income tax rates is passed by Congress during a period of inflation.
    c. More welfare compensation is paid because more people are unemployed in a recession.
    d. Congress decides to require people to work until they are 68 years old to collect their full Social Security benefit.

22. **True or False** According to Keynes, prices and wages are inflexible;they are "sticky."

23. Which of the following is an example of discretionary fiscal policy?
    a. Income tax payments grow during an economic expansion.
    b. Congress legislates an extra $20 billion to provide jobs for unemployed workers.
    c. Fewer workers receive unemployment compensation payments in an expansion.
    d. More people apply for and receive welfare benefits in a recession.

24. **True or False** Keynes believed that it was necessary for the government to balance its budget every year.

25. ________?________ takes place when there are both a high rate of inflation and high unemployment.

26. **True or False** Because of lags, it is difficult for the government to implement discretionary fiscal policy effectively.

27. Which of the following situations would indicate that the economy is below its potential output?
    a. Many workers have been laid off because of a decline in aggregate demand.
    b. A large number of construction workers are unemployed each February.
    c. In June, many graduating students spend several months looking for jobs.
    d. There are many people who need to be trained to qualify for job openings.

28. The time that it takes the government to realize that there is a problem in the economy is called the ________?________.

29. **True or False** Crowding out refers to people and businesses choosing to borrow and spend less money because of higher interest rates that result from greater federal borrowing.

Apply Economic Concepts

30. **Calculate the Impact of the Multiplier Effect** In 2009, President Obama and Congress approved an additional $100 billion in spending for the nation's transportation and infrastructure. Assume that each person who received any of this extra spending as income spent 60 percent of it. Describe how the multiplier effect would have increased the total increase in spending by far more than the original $100 billion. What does this show about the changes in government spending?

31. **Explain the Benefits of Unemployment Compensation** When there is a downturn in the economy, unemployment grows and more workers receive unemployment compensation. How do these payments also benefit workers who have not lost their jobs?

32. **Graphs of Interest on the National Debt** Interest on the national debt is an important part of the federal budget. The amount of this cost depends on the size of the federal debt and the interest rate the government pays on the debt. Use the data in the table to construct three pie graphs showing the part of the federal budget that was devoted to paying interest in 1950, 1980, and 2010. Why didn't the burden of the debt increase in 2010? Why is it likely to be greater in the future?

INTEREST ON THE NATIONAL DEBT AS A PERCENT OF THE FEDERAL BUDGET

Year	Interest Payment as a Percent of the Federal Budget
1950	14.5%
1980	11.8%
2010	7.8%

Source: *Economic Indicators*, July 2011, p. 33; and *Economic Report of the President*, February 2011, Table B-84.

33. **21st Century Skills: Critical Thinking and Problem Solving** Imagine that you are a member of your community's governing body. The mayor has suggested lowering taxes on businesses to encourage growth and employment in your community. If this happens, the lost revenue will require cuts in government programs, increases in taxes on residents, or increased borrowing. Assume his proposal is approved. Which of the three alternatives do you believe would be the best way to deal with the tax revenue decline? Explain your choice.

Digging Deeper

with Economics e-Collection

Access the Gale Economics e-Collection through the URL below. Browse through the collection to find recent statistics for the United States on one of the topics in Lesson 17.2 or 17.3. Possible topics include the unemployment rate, deficit spending, budget deficits (or surpluses), debt relative to GDP, and the debt ceiling. Make a poster or chart to present the statistics you find. Label the statistics clearly and be ready to explain them to your classmates.

www.cengage.com/school/contecon

CONSIDER...

- Why is paper money more efficient than gold coins?
- Why was a Montana bank willing to cash a check written on a clean, but frayed, pair of underpants?
- How do banks create money?
- When and why did thousands of different currencies circulate in the U.S. economy?
- Why is there so much fascination with money, anyway?

CHAPTER 18

Money and Banking

Point your browser

www.cengage.com/school/contecon

18.1 ORIGINS OF MONEY

Learning Objectives

LO1 Trace the evolution from barter to money.

LO2 Describe the three functions of money.

LO3 Identify the properties of ideal money.

Key Terms

medium of exchange 566

commodity money 566

In Your World

The word *money* comes from *Moneta*, the name of the Roman goddess in whose temple coins were minted. Money has come to symbolize personal and business finance. You can read *Money* magazine and the "Money" section of *USA Today*. You can watch TV shows such as *Your Money, Mad Money, Fast Money,* and *Strictly Money*. You can also visit online sites about money (a Google search of "money" turned up more than three billion results, such as www.moneyfactory.gov, the website for the federal agency that prints money). With money, you can express your preferences—after all, money talks. When it talks, it says a lot, as in "Put your money where your mouth is."

THE EVOLUTION OF MONEY

LO1
Trace the evolution from barter to money.

In the beginning, there was no money. The earliest families were self-sufficient. Each family produced all it consumed and consumed all it produced, so there was no need for exchange. Without exchange, there was no need for money. When specialization first emerged, as some families farmed and others hunted, farmers and hunters began to trade. Thus, the specialization of labor resulted in exchange. The kinds of goods traded were limited enough that people easily could exchange their products directly for other products. This is a system called *barter*, first discussed in Chapter 2.

Problems with Barter

As long as specialization was limited to just a few goods, mutually beneficial trades were easy to discover. As the economy developed, however, greater specialization increased the kinds of goods produced. As the variety of goods increased, so did the difficulty of finding mutually beneficial trades. For example, a surgeon in a barter economy would have to find people who needed surgery in exchange for what the surgeon wanted to buy. Barterers also had to agree on an exchange rate. Negotiating such exchanges every time the surgeon needed to buy something would be difficult and time consuming. *Greater specialization increased the transaction costs of barter.*

A huge difference in the values of the units to be exchanged also made barter difficult. For example, suppose a hunter wanted to exchange 2,000 hides for a home. A hunter would be hard-pressed to find a home seller in need of that many hides.

The Birth of Money

The high transaction costs of barter gave birth to money. Nobody actually recorded the emergence of money, so we can only speculate about how it developed. Through barter experience, traders may have found that certain goods always had ready buyers. If a trader could not find a good that he or she desired, some good with a ready market could be accepted instead.

Thus, traders began to accept certain goods not for personal use but because the goods were readily accepted by others and so could be held for exchange later. For example, corn might have become accepted because traders knew that corn was always in demand. As one good became generally accepted in return for all other goods, that good began to function as money. *Money* is anything that is widely accepted in exchange for goods and services.

CHECKPOINT How did money evolve from barter?

THREE FUNCTIONS OF MONEY

LO2 Describe the three functions of money.

Money fulfills three important functions. It is

1. a medium of exchange, which is the most important function
2. a unit of account, and
3. a store of value.

Medium of Exchange

If a society, by luck or by design, can find one good that everyone accepts in exchange for whatever is sold, traders can save time, disappointment, and sheer aggravation. Suppose corn plays this role—a role that clearly goes beyond its role as food. Corn becomes a medium of exchange because it is accepted in exchange by all buyers and sellers, whether or not they want corn to eat. A **medium of exchange** is anything that is generally accepted as payment for goods and services. Serving as a medium of exchange is the most important function of money. The person who accepts corn in exchange for some product believes corn can be used later to purchase whatever is desired.

In this example, corn is both a *commodity* and *money*, so corn is called **commodity money**. The earliest money was commodity money. Gold and silver have served as money for at least 4,000 years. Cattle were used as money, first by the Greeks, and then by the Romans. In fact, the word *pecuniary* (meaning "of or relating to money") derives from the Latin word for cattle, *pecus.* Salt also served as money. Roman soldiers received part of their pay in salt. The salt portion was called the *salarium*, the origin of the word *salary.* Commodity money used at various times included wampum (polished shells strung together) and tobacco in colonial America, tea pressed into small cakes in Russia, and palm dates in North Africa.

medium of exchange Anything generally accepted by all parties in payment for goods or services; the most important function of money

commodity money Anything that serves both as money and as a commodity, such as gold

Unit of Account

As one commodity, such as corn, became widely accepted, it also served as a *unit of account*, a standard on which to base all prices. The price of shoes or pots or hides could be measured in bushels of corn. Thus, corn became a common denominator, a yardstick, for measuring the value of all goods and services. Rather than having to determine the exchange rate between each good and every other good, as was the case in a barter economy, buyers and sellers could price everything using a common measure, such as corn.

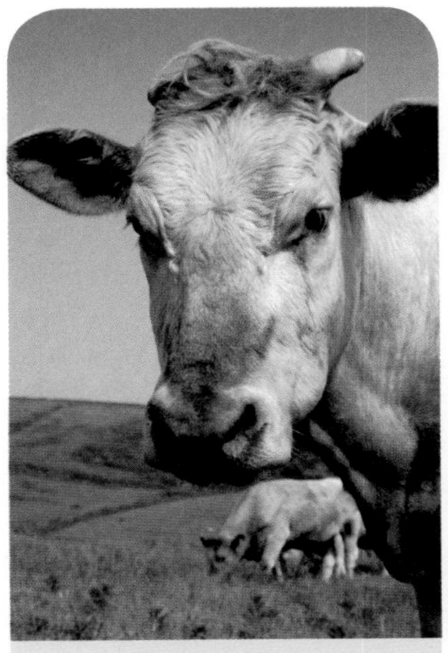

Photodisc/Getty Images

Why were cattle of limited use as commodity money?

Store of Value

Because people do not want to buy something every time they sell something, the purchasing power acquired through a sale must somehow be preserved. Money serves as a *store of value* when it retains purchasing power over time. The better it preserves its purchasing power, the better money serves as a store of value.

To understand the store-of-value function of money, consider the distinction between a stock and a flow. A *stock* is an amount measured at a particular point in time, such as the amount of food in your refrigerator this morning or the amount of money you have with you right now. In contrast, a *flow* is an amount received or expended within a period of time, such as the calories you consume per day or the income you earn per week.

Income, a flow, has little meaning unless the period is specified. For example, you would not know whether to be impressed that a friend earns $300 unless you know whether this is earnings per month, per week, per day, or per hour. Don't confuse money with income. *Money* is a stock measure, and *income* is a flow measure. The store-of-value function focuses on money as a stock.

CHECKPOINT What are three functions of money?

COMMODITY MONEY

LO3 Identify the properties of ideal money.

The introduction of commodity money reduced the transaction costs of exchange compared with barter. Commodity money does involve some transaction costs, however. These transaction costs are reflected by the following limitations of commodity money.

Limitations of Commodity Money

The ideal money is durable, portable, divisible, and of uniform quality. It has a low opportunity cost, does not fluctuate wildly in value, and is in limited supply. As you will see, most commodity money falls short of these ideals.

Durable If the commodity money is perishable, as is corn, it must be properly stored or its quality deteriorates. The ideal money is *durable.*

Portable If the commodity money is bulky, exchanges for major purchases are difficult. For example, if a house costs 5,000 bushels of corn, many cartloads would be needed to purchase it. The ideal money is *portable.*

Divisible Some commodity money is not easily divisible into smaller units. For example, when cattle served as money, any price involving a fraction of a cow posed an exchange problem. The ideal money is *divisible.*

Uniform Quality If bushels of corn are all worth the same in exchange, regardless of quality, people will keep the best corn and trade away the rest. Over time, the quality remaining in circulation deteriorates and becomes less acceptable. The ideal money is of *uniform quality.*

Low Opportunity Cost Commodity money usually ties up valuable resources, so it has a high opportunity cost compared with, say, paper money. For example, corn that is used for money cannot at the same time be eaten. The ideal money has a *low opportunity cost.*

Supply or Demand Must Not Fluctuate Erratically The supply and demand for commodity money determine the prices of all other goods. A record harvest would increase the supply of corn. An increase in the popularity of corn as food would increase the demand for corn. Each change would alter the price level measured in corn. Erratic fluctuations in the supply or demand for corn limit its usefulness as money, particularly as a unit of account and as a store of value. The supply or demand for the ideal money *should not fluctuate wildly.*

Limited Supply Because the value of money depends on its limited supply, anything that can be gathered or produced easily, for example, tree leaves or street pebbles, would not serve well as commodity money. The ideal money should be in limited supply. Figure 18.1 summarizes the seven desirable qualities of ideal money, along with good examples and bad examples of each.

Figure 18.1 Seven Desirable Qualities of Ideal Money

Quality	Rationale	Good Examples	Bad Examples
1. Durable	Money should not wear out quickly.	Paper money; coins; sea shells	Strawberries; seafood
2. Portable	Money should be easy to carry, even large sums.	Diamonds; paper money	Lead bars; potatoes; corn
3. Divisible	Market exchange is easier if denominations support a wide range of possible prices.	Honey; paper money; coins	Cattle; diamonds
4. Uniform Quality	If money is not of uniform quality, people will hoard the best and spend the rest, reducing the quality of money in circulation.	Salt bricks; paper money; coins	Diamonds
5. Low Opportunity Cost	The fewer resources tied up in creating money, the more available for other uses.	Iron coins; paper money	Gold coins; diamonds; corn
6. Stable Value	People are more willing to accept and hold money if they believe it will keep its value over time.	Anything whose supply can be controlled by the issuing authority, such as paper money.	Farm crops; gold
7. Limited Supply	Anything that can be easily gathered or produced would not serve well as money.	Gold and silver are produced with great effort.	Leaves; rocks

Coins

Measuring a unit of commodity money often was quite natural, as in a bushel of corn or a head of cattle. When rock salt served as money, it was cut into bricks. Because salt was usually of consistent quality, a trader could simply count the bricks to determine the amount of money. However, when silver and gold were used as money, both their quantity and quality were open to question. When these precious metals were combined with cheaper metals, their quality lessened. Thus, the quantity and the quality of the metal had to be determined before each exchange.

This quality-control problem was solved by coining silver and gold. *Coinage determined both the amount and quality of the metal.* The earliest known coins appeared in the seventh century BC in Asia Minor to assist sea trade. The use of coins allowed payment by count rather than by weight. The table on which money was counted came to be called the *counter,* a term still used today. Coins were attractive as money because they were durable and easy to carry. They also contained precious metals, so they were valuable as commodities even aside from their value as money.

Originally, the power to coin was vested in the feudal lord, or *seignior.* If the exchange value of a coin exceeded the cost of minting it, minting coins became a source of revenue to the seignior. Revenue earned from coinage is called *seigniorage* (pronounced "seen'-your-edge").

Token money is money whose exchange value exceeds its cost of production. Coins and paper money now in circulation in the United States are token money. For example, a quarter (a 25-cent coin) costs the U.S. Mint only about 10 cents to make. Coin production alone nets the U.S. Mint about $400 million per year in seigniorage. Paper money is a far greater source of seigniorage, as you will learn later.

What seven properties would an ideal money exhibit?

ESSENTIAL QUESTION

Standard CEE 11: Money and Inflation

Money makes it easier to trade, borrow, save, invest, and compare the value of goods and services. The amount of money in the economy affects the overall price level. Inflation is an increase in the overall price level that reduces the value of money.

Blend Images/Jupiter Images

What is the role of money in the economy?

18.1 ASSESSMENT

Think Critically

1. Why could it be difficult for you to exchange your collection of 500 vintage baseball cards for a good-quality used car in a world without money?
2. Why have wheat and corn been used as commodity money in the past, while strawberries and lettuce have not?
3. On the Pacific island of Yap, commodity money took the form of donut-shaped pieces of stone that could weigh one ton or more. In what ways did these stones fall short of being ideal forms of money?
4. At certain times in history, the value of the gold or silver in coins has been greater than the face value of the coins themselves. What did this give people an incentive to do? How would this have affected the economy?
5. What would happen if there were more than one type of commodity money in use—one that people trusted and one they did not? If you had some of both types of money, which would you spend and which would you save? How would this affect the economy?

Graphing Exercise

6. Fred has an electric saw he would like to trade for a tire for his boat trailer. Mary has a tire for a boat trailer that she would be willing to trade for an electric lawn mower. Rachel has an electric lawn mower she would like to trade for a portable TV. Tony has a portable TV he would be willing to trade for an electric saw. Draw a chart that shows the trades that must take place for each of these people to obtain the product he or she wants. Explain why barter is not an efficient way to carry out complicated transactions.

Make Academic Connections

7. **History** When gold and silver coins were the primary type of money in circulation, merchants often weighed the coins before accepting them. Why do you think they did this? What problem of using gold or silver coins as money does this situation demonstrate?
8. **English** You probably have either read or seen a television production of *A Christmas Carol*, a short novel written by Charles Dickens. In his book, Dickens told the story of Ebenezer Scrooge, a miser who accumulated wealth more for the sake of having money than to be able to use it to buy goods or services. Scrooge was regarded as a sour old man who hated Christmas. However, after being visited by the ghosts of Christmas Past, Christmas Present, and Christmas Yet to Come, Scrooge came to view his wealth in a different way. Write an essay in which you explain Scrooge's original point of view about the three functions of money. How did the three Christmas ghosts change his perspective on money?

TeamWork

Working with a partner, role-play a barter situation. One partner will have an iPad to barter. The other student will barter another item or items for the iPad. After completing your role-play barter, compare your results with those of other students. Were the items bartered for the iPad of comparable value?

MOVERS AND SHAKERS

Jim Cramer

Host of CNBC's *Mad Money*

Jim Cramer is the over-the-top host of *Mad Money*—a TV show that offers stock market advice on the financial news network CNBC. He provides commentary for TheStreet.com, a multimedia provider of financial commentary, analysis, and news, which he co-founded. Cramer also writes investment columns for various other websites and newspapers, and is the author of several books.

A graduate of both Harvard College and Harvard Law School, Cramer's grades were not high enough to land him a job in a top law firm, so he turned to reporting the news. He started dabbling in the stock market in college, using his college loan money to buy stocks. His brokerage account began to grow and he started to leave stock tips on his answering-machine message. Finding his tips useful, people began asking him for investment advice. Cramer parlayed his stock savvy into a career. At one time his picks on *Mad Money* showed gains of almost three times the S&P's 2.5 percent gain and seven times the small 0.9 percent advance of the Dow Jones industrial average.

Cramer also has been a successful money manager. His Cramer Berkowitz hedge fund was worth $450 million by the time he sold it in 2000. However, questions have been raised as to how he gained success in an area in which many others lost a great deal.

In a controversial interview with TheStreet.com's Executive Editor Aaron Task on the "Wall Street Confidential" webcast, Cramer boasted about manipulating the price of an expensive stock downward when he was running his hedge fund. He said, "A lot of times when I was short at my hedge fund...When I was positioned short—meaning I needed it down—I would create a level of activity beforehand that could drive the futures....It's a fun game. . . .No one else in the world would ever admit that, but I don't care." He also encouraged other hedge funds to do this because it is, "a very quick way to make money." Cramer admitted the strategy was illegal, but possible to get away with because, he said, "the Securities and Exchange Commission never understands this."

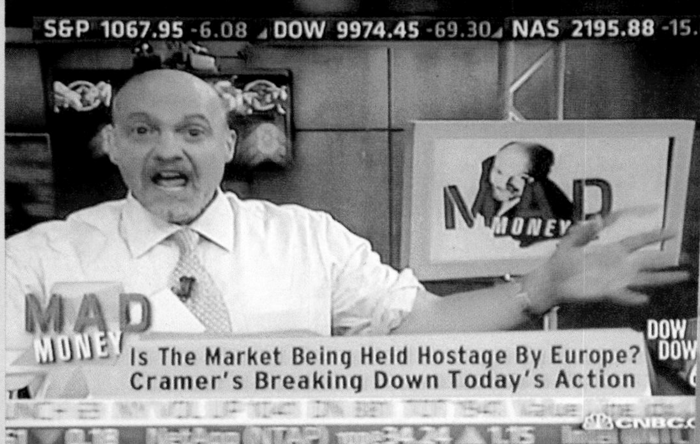

When he was president of Cramer & Company, a private New York-based money management firm, and editor for *Smart Money*, Cramer publicly praised three small companies his firm held large stock positions in. Not long after the publication, stocks in those companies, which normally are lightly traded, rose substantially in value and were traded heavily.

Fred W. Frailey, deputy editor of *Kiplinger's Personal Finance Magazine*, a *Smart Money* competitor, said this was a legal form of "front running," a practice in which stockbrokers buy shares ahead of their clients. Frailey said, "He bought right in front of publication in grotesque quantities." Cramer's stock purchases would have been in clear violation of the conflict of interest rules of Dow Jones, the publisher of *The Wall Street Journal*. These rules "strictly prohibit employees of the company's publications from profiting, or even appearing to profit, from an upcoming article."

Think Critically **Cramer's actions raised ethical and legal questions about investment advice that have long troubled financial journalism. Restate in your own words the legal and ethical lines Jim Cramer crossed as reported in this article.**

Sources: http://www.nypost.com/p/news/business/item_kjjrj8uuhaiw1dsusv4fyi#ixzz1ypikemyo; http://www.thestreet.com/video/cramermarketupdates/10329438.htm; http://www.nytimes.com/1995/02/20/business/smart-money-rethinks-conflict-rule.html?pagewanted=print&src=pm; http://www.cnbc.com/id/29601234; and http://www.bizography.org/biographies/jim-cramer.html

18.2 ORIGINS OF BANKING AND THE FEDERAL RESERVE SYSTEM

Key Terms

Learning Objectives

LO1 Describe how the earliest banks made loans.

LO2 Based on whom they lend to, identify two types of banks.

LO3 Explain when and why the Federal Reserve System was created.

In Your World

You have been familiar with banks all your life, so you know more about them than you may realize. You may even have your own bank account. The word *bank* comes from the Italian word for bench, *banca.* Italian moneychangers originally conducted their business on benches. Banking spread from Italy to England, where London goldsmiths offered people "safekeeping" for their gold, or commodity money. When people needed to make purchases, they would visit the goldsmith to withdraw some money. Deposits by some people tended to offset withdrawals by others, so the amount of money in the goldsmith's vault remained relatively constant over time. Goldsmiths found they could earn interest by lending some of these idle deposits. Today's banks still try to earn a profit by lending out some of the money deposited with them.

THE EARLIEST BANKS

LO1 Describe how the earliest banks made loans.

Keeping money, such as gold coins, on deposit with a goldsmith was safer than carrying it around or leaving it at home, where it could be easily stolen. Still, visiting the goldsmith every time you needed money was a nuisance. For example, a farmer might visit the goldsmith to withdraw enough gold to buy a horse. The farmer would then pay the horse trader, who would promptly deposit the receipts with the goldsmith. Thus, money made a round trip from goldsmith to farmer to horse trader, back to goldsmith.

Bank Checks

Depositors eventually grew tired of visiting the goldsmith every time they needed cash. They began writing notes instructing the goldsmith to pay someone, such as the horse trader, a certain amount from the depositor's account. This payment amounted to moving gold from one stack (the farmer's) to another (the horse trader's). These written instructions to the goldsmith were the first bank checks. A **check** is a written order instructing the bank to pay money from amounts deposited.

Checks have since become official-looking instruction forms. However, they need not be, as evidenced by the actions of a Montana man who paid his speeding fine by writing payment instructions on a clean but frayed pair of underpants. The Western Federal Savings and Loan of Missoula cashed the check.

check A written order instructing the bank to pay someone from money on deposit

Bank Loans

By combining the ideas of cash loans and checks, goldsmiths soon discovered how to make loans by check. Rather than lend idle cash, a goldsmith could simply create a checking account for the borrower. *The goldsmith could extend a loan by creating an account against which the borrower could write checks. In this way goldsmiths, or banks, were able to create a medium of exchange, to "create money."* This money, based only on an entry in the bank's ledger, was accepted because of the public's confidence that the bank would honor these checks.

The total claims against the bank consisted of claims by people who had deposited their gold, plus claims by people for whom the bank had created deposits. So, both groups held deposits. Because the claims by those with deposits at the bank exceeded the value of gold on reserve, this was the beginning of a **fractional reserve banking system**. In this system, the goldsmith's reserves amounted to just a fraction of the claims by depositors.

The *reserve ratio* measures bank reserves as a share of deposits. For example, if the goldsmith had gold reserves valued at $40,000 but deposits totaling $100,000, the reserve ratio would be 40 percent.

Bank Notes

Another way early banks could create money was by issuing bank notes. *Bank notes* were pieces of paper promising the bearer a specific amount of gold or silver when the notes were redeemed at the issuing bank. In London, goldsmiths introduced bank notes about the same time they introduced checks. *Checks could be redeemed for gold only if endorsed by the payee. Bank notes, however, could be redeemed for gold by anyone who presented them to the issuing bank.*

A bank note was "as good as gold," because the bearer could redeem it for gold. In fact, this paper money was more convenient than gold because it was more portable. Bank notes that exchanged for a specific commodity, such as gold, were called **representative money**. The paper money *represented* gold in the bank's vault. Initially, these promises to pay were issued by banks. Over time, governments took a larger role in printing and circulating bank notes.

fractional reserve banking system Only a portion of bank deposits is backed by reserves

representative money Bank notes that exchange for a specific commodity, such as gold

fiat money Money of no value in itself and not convertible into gold, silver, or anything else of value; declared money by government decree

Fiat Money

Once representative money became widely accepted, governments began issuing fiat money (pronounced "fee'at"). **Fiat money** is not of value in itself and is not convertible into gold, silver, or anything else of value. Fiat money is money because the government says it is. People came to accept fiat money because they believed that others would accept it as well. You can think of fiat money as mere paper money. The currency issued by the U.S government and nearly all other governments throughout the world today is fiat money. A well-regulated system of fiat money is more efficient than commodity money or even representative money. Fiat money requires only some paper and a printing press. Commodity money and even representative money tie up more valuable resources, such as gold.

How did the earliest banks make loans?

Investigate Your Local Economy

Research a depository institution in your area to learn something about its history. When was it established, and by whom? In which category of depository institution does it fit now? Write a one-page report explaining your findings.

DEPOSITORY INSTITUTIONS

LO2 Based on whom they lend to, identify two types of banks.

Banks evolved from London goldsmiths into a wide variety of institutions that respond to the economy's demand for financial services. *Depository institutions* accept deposits from the public and make loans from these deposits. These institutions, modern-day versions of London goldsmiths, are classified broadly into commercial banks and thrift institutions.

Commercial Banks

Commercial banks are the oldest, largest, and most diversified of depository institutions. They are called *commercial banks* because, historically, they lent primarily to *commercial* ventures, or businesses, rather than to households. There are about 6,500 commercial banks in the United States, holding more than two-thirds of all bank deposits. Until 1980, commercial banks were the only depository institutions that offered demand deposits, or checking accounts. *Demand deposits* are so named because a depositor with such an account can write a check *demanding* those deposits.

Thrifts

Thrift institutions, or *thrifts,* include savings and loan associations, mutual savings banks, and credit unions. Historically, savings and loan associations and mutual savings banks specialized in making home mortgage loans. Credit unions, which tend to be small, are the most common thrift institutions. They extend loans only to their "members" to finance homes or other major consumer purchases, such as new cars.

nano/iStockphoto.com

What is the difference between commercial banks and thrift institutions?

Dual Banking System

Before 1863, commercial banks in the United States were chartered, or authorized, by the states in which they operated, so they were called *state banks.* These banks, like the English goldsmiths, issued their own bank notes. Thousands of different notes circulated at the same time, and nearly all were redeemable for gold or silver.

The National Banking Act of 1863 and its later amendments created a new system of federally chartered banks called *national banks.* Only national banks were authorized to issue notes and were regulated by the Office of the Comptroller of the Currency, part of the U.S. Treasury. The state banks survived by substituting checks for bank notes. To this day, the United States has a *dual banking system* consisting of both state banks and national banks.

CHECKPOINT

Based on whom they lend money to, what are the two types of depository institutions?

Math in Economics

Common Core The Number System

You can find the balance for a checking account using addition and subtraction. For each deposit made, add to the previous balance to find the new balance. For each check, debit card payment, or fee charged, subtract from the previous balance to find the new balance.

EXAMPLE

Find the current balance in a checking account that had a balance last month of $352.15. A deposit of $200.00 was made and three checks were written in the amounts of $23.46, $51.00, and $137.89. Charges for the month were a maintenance fee of $5.00 and $0.25 per-check written.

SOLUTION

Add the deposit to the previous balance.

$\$352.15 + \$200.00 = \$552.15$

Subtract the amounts of the checks written and fees from the new balance.

$\$552.15 - \$23.46 - \$51.00 - \$137.89 - \$5.00 - (3 \times \$0.25) = \$334.05$

Practice the Skill

Find the current balance for each problem.

1. Balance last month: $690.21. Deposits: $121.00 and $43.50. Checks written: $28.00, $43.29, $104.32, and $26.75. Charges: monthly maintenance fee: $5.00 and per-check fee of $0.30.
2. Balance last month: $431.56. Deposit: $152.00 Checks written: $35.62, $28.94, and $64.50. Charges: monthly maintenance fee: $6.00 and per-check fee of $0.20
3. What could explain the discrepancy if the bank statement for the account in Exercise 2 showed the balance was $512.60?

THE FEDERAL RESERVE SYSTEM

LO3 Explain when and why the Federal Reserve System was created.

During the nineteenth century, the economy experienced a number of panic "runs" on banks by depositors seeking to withdraw their funds. A panic was usually set off by the failure of a prominent bank. As depositors became alarmed, they tried to withdraw their money. But they couldn't do so because each bank held only a fraction of its deposits as reserves, using the rest to earn interest, as in making loans.

Birth of the Federal Reserve System

The failure of a large New York City bank set off the Panic of 1907. During this banking calamity, thousands of depositors lost their savings and many businesses failed. The situation so inflamed public wrath that Congress began developing what would become the **Federal Reserve System**, or **the Fed** for short. The Fed was established in 1913 as the central bank and monetary authority of the United States.

By that time nearly all industrialized countries had established central banks, such as the Bundesbank in Germany, the Bank of Japan, and the Bank of England. The American public's suspicion of monopolies initially led to the establishment of 12 separate banks, one in each of 12 Federal Reserve districts around the country. The banks were named after the cities in which they were located—the Federal Reserve Banks of Boston, New York, Chicago, San Francisco, and so on, as shown in Figure 18.2. Later legislation passed during the Great Depression left the 12 Reserve Banks in place but centralized the power of the Federal Reserve System with a Board of Governors in Washington, D.C.

All national banks became members of the Federal Reserve System and were thus subject to new regulations. For state banks, membership was voluntary. Most state banks did not join the Federal Reserve System because they did not want to face tighter regulations.

Federal Reserve System (the Fed) Established in 1913 as the central bank and monetary authority of the United States

Powers of the Federal Reserve System

The founding legislation directed the Federal Reserve Board of Governors "to exercise general supervision" over the Federal Reserve System to ensure sufficient money and credit in the banking system. The power to issue bank notes was taken away from thousands of national banks and turned over to the Federal Reserve Banks. (Take a look at paper currency and you will read "FEDERAL RESERVE NOTE" across the top.) These notes actually are printed by the U.S. Bureau of Printing and Engraving, which is part of the U.S. Treasury. The Treasury prints the notes, but the Fed has responsibility for putting them into circulation.

NET Bookmark

For an online introduction to the Federal Reserve System, access the New York Federal Reserve Bank website through the link shown below. The New York Federal Reserve Bank site provides an overview of the Fed's structure and operations. Click on "What We Do" and "Introduction," and read the article. What three activities set the New York Federal Reserve Bank apart from the other district banks in the system?

www.cengage.com/school/contecon

FIGURE 18.2 The 12 Federal Reserve Districts

The 12 Federal Reserve districts are named after the cities in which they are located. Which district are you in?

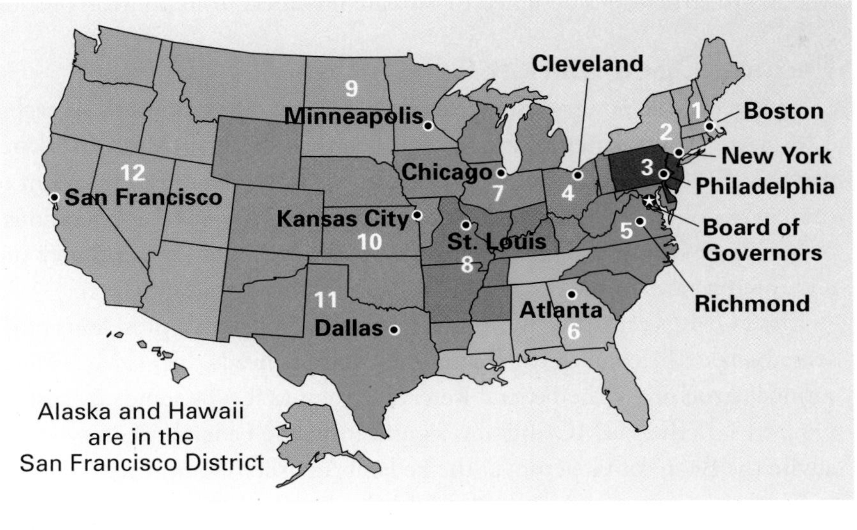

Source: Federal Reserve Board.

Federal Reserve Banks do not deal with the public directly. Each may be thought of as a bankers' bank. Reserve Banks hold deposits for member banks, just as commercial banks and thrifts hold deposits for the public. The name "Reserve Bank" comes from the responsibility to hold member-bank reserves on deposit.

Reserves consist of cash that banks have on hand in their vaults or on deposit with Reserve Banks. By holding reserves of member banks, a Reserve Bank can clear a check written by a depositor at one bank, such as Bank of America, and deposited in another bank, such as your bank. This check-clearance process is, on a larger scale, much like the goldsmith's moving gold from the farmer's pile to the horse trader's pile.

Reserve Banks also extend loans to member banks. The interest rate charged for these loans is called the **discount rate**. By making loans to banks, the Fed can increase reserves in the banking system.

Directing Monetary Policy

The Federal Reserve's Board of Governors is responsible for setting and carrying out the nation's monetary policy. *Monetary policy* is the regulation of the economy's money supply and interest rates to promote macroeconomic objectives such as full employment, price stability, and economic growth.

The Board of Governors consists of seven members appointed by the president and confirmed by the Senate. Each member serves one 14-year nonrenewable term, with one governor appointed every two years. One member is also appointed to chair the Board of Governors for a four-year renewable term. Board

discount rate Interest rate the Fed charges banks that borrow reserves

members tend to be economists. In 2011, most of the governors held degrees in economics, including Chairman Ben Bernanke.

Board membership is relatively stable because a new U.S. president can be sure of appointing or reappointing only two members in a single presidential term. The Board structure is designed to insulate members from political pressure.

Federal Open Market Committee

Federal Open Market Committee (FOMC) Twelve-member group that makes decisions about open-market operations

open-market operations Buying or selling U.S. government securities as a way of regulating the money supply

Originally, the power of the Federal Reserve System was vested in each of the 12 Reserve Banks. Later reforms established the **Federal Open Market Committee (FOMC)** to consolidate decisions regarding the most important tool of monetary policy—**open-market operations**. Open-market operations consist of buying or selling U.S. government securities to influence the money supply and interest rates in the economy. More on that in the next chapter.

The FOMC consists of the 7 governors plus 5 of the 12 presidents of the Reserve Banks. The chair of the Board of Governors heads the FOMC. The organizational structure of the Federal Reserve System as it now stands is presented in Figure 18.3. The FOMC and, less significantly, the Federal Advisory Committee advise the Board of Governors. The Federal Advisory Committee consists of one commercial banker from each of the 12 Reserve Bank districts.

CHECKPOINT

When and why was the Federal Reserve System created?

FIGURE 18.3 Organization Chart for the Federal Reserve System

The Federal Reserve's Board of Governors is responsible for setting and carrying out the nation's monetary policy.

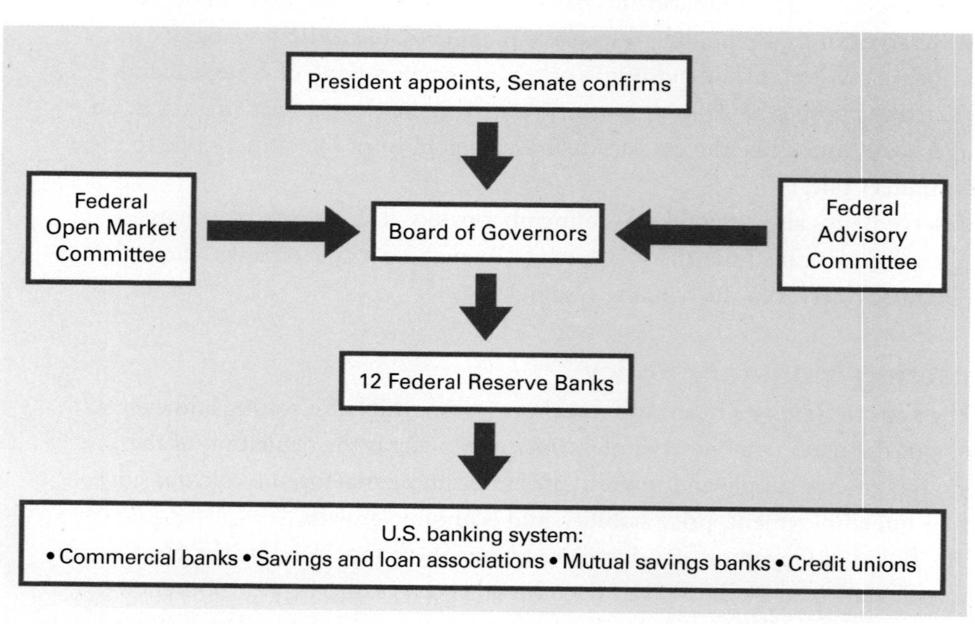

ASSESSMENT 18.2

Think Critically

1. How would you feel about taking $10,000 in cash to an automobile dealership to purchase a used car? Why might you prefer to complete this type of transaction with a check instead?
2. In what way is the Fed insulated from political pressure?
3. Why are you willing to accept Federal Reserve notes (fiat money) in payment for your labor? Remember, these notes are backed by nothing other than the government's statement that they are money.
4. Why is it important to the economy that people who save and deposit money in banks can be sure that they will be able to withdraw their savings anytime in the future without suffering a loss?
5. How may banks obtain extra cash on short notice if an urgent need arises?

Graphing Exercise

6. Although there were about 6,500 commercial banks in the United States in 2010, most were relatively small. Most of the business in the banking industry was dominated by a few large banks. Use data in the table to construct a two pie charts that show the number of commercial banks of different sizes and the amount of assets held by each group in 2010. Do you think the smaller banks could compete successfully with the larger banks? Why were there fewer than 6,500 commercial banks by 2011?

COMMERCIAL BANKS BY ASSET SIZE, 2010

Asset Size of Banks	Number of Banks in Group	Total Assets for Group in Billions
Less than $100 million	2,325	$ 132
$100 million to $1 billion	3,694	$1,059
$1 billion to $10 billion	424	$1,090
Greater than $10 billion	86	$9,787

Source: *Statistical Abstract of the United States: 2012*, p. 737.

Make Academic Connections

7. **Government** Investigate the Banking Act of 1935 to find out how the creation of the Board of Governors changed the nature of the Federal Reserve System. Why do you think the government was willing to concentrate so much economic power in the hands of only seven people?

TeamWork

As a team, choose an important transaction that team members can expect to make over the next few years, such as paying college tuition, buying a car, or financing a wedding. List and explain ways in which the banking system could make this transaction easier to complete. Compare your team's work with that of other teams.

Early Banking in the United States

In 1791, Congress approved a 20-year charter for the First Bank of the United States, there were only three commercial banks in the country. The First Bank was 20 percent owned by the government. It immediately functioned as a central bank with a stabilizing influence on the nation's economy, especially in controlling the over-issuance of private bank notes. Still, many distrusted such a large institution. In 1811, its congressional charter failed to be renewed by only one vote. The lapse was short lived, as the War of 1812 demonstrated to many the need for a strong central bank. In 1816, the Second Bank of the United States, chartered under the same basic rules, was formed.

The Second Bank of the United States also was unpopular in some parts of the country. For many, the bank seemed to serve the wealthy Eastern establishment at the expense of the Southern and Western parts of the country. When Andrew Jackson became president in 1829, he brought a dislike of banks in general and the Second Bank of the United States, in particular. Jackson believed that, because the U.S. Constitution did not explicitly give the government the power to operate a bank, it was unconstitutional. He also believed that the bank's issuance of paper money not backed by gold or silver hurt the economy. Rather than wait for the Bank's 20-year charter to expire in 1836, supporters of the bank pushed for renewal in 1832. Renewal passed Congress, but Jackson vetoed the bill. Wanting to "kill the monster" (the bank), he ordered the government to begin depositing its funds into various state-chartered banks, or "pet banks." The Second Bank of the United States, devoid of government deposits, limped along until 1849, when it finally went out of business.

Without the restraint imposed by a central bank, banks began to issue too much currency, and so the value of each piece of currency fell. By 1836, Jackson became alarmed that people who owed the government money were repaying in currency of declining value. He ordered the Specie Circular, which stated that debts owed to the government could be paid only in "hard currency"—that is, in gold or silver coins. The result was a contraction of the money supply and the "Panic of 1837."

Nationally, Jackson's actions marked the beginning of the so-called "free-banking era." Hundreds of state-chartered banks sprang up around the country. Many were established in such out-of-the-way places that they were called "wildcat banks." They were located in remote areas (where wildcats lived) to discourage people from redeeming their bank notes for gold. Each loosely controlled bank issued its own currency, thus flooding the nation with more than 9,000 denominations and types. People had no way of telling if a particular currency was sound or not. They resorted to "note detectors," which rated the currency according to the soundness of the bank that issued it. Many merchants refused to accept currency coming from outside their state or region.

The banking and currency problems were left unaddressed until the Civil War forced the passage of the National Banking Act in 1863. It wasn't until 1913 that the country formed the Federal Reserve System.

Think Critically **Even today, historians debate Jackson's actions. Based on your understanding of banks and banking, examine Jackson's opposition to the Second Bank of the United States and his support for "hard money." Were his concerns valid and his veto justified? Are the same concerns about central banking and currency relevant today? Why or why not?**

18.3 MONEY, NEAR MONEY, AND CREDIT CARDS

Learning Objectives

LO1 Describe the narrow definition of money.

LO2 Explain why distinctions among definitions of money have become less meaningful over time.

Key Terms

M1 581

checkable deposits 582

M2 583

In Your World

When you think of money, what probably comes to mind is currency—notes and coins. Notes and coins, however, are only part of the money supply. If you deposit currency in a checking account, the amount in that checking account also is money. Currency and checking accounts are money because each serves as a medium of exchange, a unit of account, and a store of value. Some other bank accounts also perform the store-of-value function and sometimes readily converted to cash. These bank accounts are sometimes viewed as money, based on a broader definition.

NARROW DEFINITION OF MONEY: M1

LO1 Describe the narrow definition of money.

Money aggregates are various measures of the money supply. The narrow definition, called **M1**, consists of currency (including coins) held by the nonbanking public, checkable deposits, and traveler's checks. The money supply at any given time is a stock measure, just as is the amount of cash you have with you right now.

Currency in Circulation

Dollar bills and coins in circulation are part of the money supply as narrowly defined. Money in bank vaults or on deposit at the Fed is not in circulation as a medium of exchange and so is not counted in the money supply. Currency makes up about one-half of M1.

The paper currency circulating in the United States consists of Federal Reserve notes. These notes are issued by, and are liabilities of, the Federal Reserve System. Because Federal Reserve notes are redeemable for nothing other than more Federal Reserve notes, they are fiat money. The other component of currency is coins. Like paper money, any U.S. coin is token money because its value in exchange exceeds its value as a commodity.

U.S. Currency Abroad

More than one-half the value of all Federal Reserve notes, particularly $100 notes, are in foreign hands. People around the world, especially in unstable countries or countries that have experienced high inflation, often hoard U.S. currency as insurance against hard times. Some countries, such as Panama, Ecuador, and El Salvador, even use U.S. dollars as their own currency, a process called *dollarization.*

M1 The narrow definition of the money supply; consists of currency (including coins) held by the nonbanking public, checkable deposits, and traveler's checks

It's actually a good deal for Americans to have U.S. currency held abroad. Think about it this way: A $100 note that costs only about 10 cents to print can be "sold" to foreigners for $100 worth of their goods and services. It's as if these foreigners were granting the United States essentially free goods or services as long as that currency remains abroad, usually for years.

Checkable Deposits

Currency, or cash, makes up about one-half of M1, the money supply narrowly defined. Suppose you have some cash with you right now—notes and coins. If you deposit this cash in a checking account, you can then write checks directing your bank to pay someone from your account. **Checkable deposits**, or deposits against which checks can be written, are part of the narrow definition of money.

Checkable deposits also can be tapped with a debit (bank or ATM) card. Banks hold a variety of checkable deposits. In recent years, banks have developed other types of checking accounts, which carry check-writing privileges but also earn modest interest. Checkable deposits of all types make up about one-half of M1.

checkable deposits
Deposits in financial institutions against which checks can be written and ATM, bank, or debit, cards can be applied

Traveler's Checks

If you have ever planned a vacation, you may have visited the bank to buy traveler's checks. You signed the checks at the bank, and then signed them again when you spent them. This allowed a merchant to compare your two signatures as the rightful owner of these checks.

Span the Globe

The U.S. Dollar as a World Currency

Most Americans do not realize that more than half of the U.S. dollars in circulation are held overseas. Unlike domestic demand for currency, which takes the form of smaller denomination notes ($1s through $20s), foreign demand for U.S. currency often is influenced by the political and economic uncertainties associated with certain foreign currencies. Because foreigners demand U.S. currency primarily as a store of value, they tend to hold high-denomination U.S. notes, especially $100 notes. The amount of U.S. currency in foreign hands fluctuates as the value of the dollar changes against other currencies, as reliance on electronic payments increases, and as global financial instability increases. The foreign demand for U.S. currency has increased significantly since the 1980s.

Think Critically **Why do you think the U.S. dollar is so popular around the world? Do you think this helps the United States? Why or why not?**

Source: Sources: Board of Governors of the Federal Reserve System, Economic Research and Data, www.federalreserve.gov/; *Money Stock*, Bank of Japan, www.boj.or.jp/en/type/stat/boj_stat/ms/ms0601.htm; and *Monetary Developments in the Euro Area*, European Central Bank, January 2006, www.ecb.int/press/pdf/md/md0601.pdf.

If your cash is stolen, you are out of luck. However, if your traveler's checks are stolen, you can get them replaced. Therefore, traveler's checks are safer than cash. Traveler's checks are a tiny part of the money supply, accounting for only a fraction of 1 percent of M1.

What is the narrow definition of money? **CHECKPOINT**

BROADER DEFINITION OF MONEY: M2

LO2 Explain why distinctions among definitions of money have become less meaningful over time.

M1 serves as a medium of exchange, a unit of account, and a store of value. Some other bank accounts can be converted readily into M1. Recall that M1 consists of cash held by the nonbanking public, checkable deposits, and traveler's checks. **M2** includes M1 as well as savings deposits, small-denomination time deposits, and money market mutual fund accounts owned by households. Because these other accounts are so close to M1, they are considered to be money when using M2 as a broader definition. Here are details of those bank accounts included in M2.

M2 A broader definition of the money supply, consisting of M1 plus savings deposits, small denomination time deposits, and money market mutual fund accounts owned by households

Savings Deposits

Savings deposits earn interest but have no specific maturity date. This means that you can withdraw them any time without a penalty. Banks often allow depositors to shift funds from savings accounts to checking accounts by using a phone, an ATM, or online banking. Because savings can be converted so easily into checkable deposits and cash, distinctions between narrow and broad definitions of money have become blurred. Still, saving deposits are not counted as part of the money supply when narrowly defined. Savings deposits alone total nearly three times the size of M1.

Time Deposits

Time deposits earn a fixed rate of interest if held for a specified period. The holding period ranges from several months to several years. Holders of time deposits are issued certificates of deposit, or CDs for short. Early withdrawals are penalized by forfeiture of several months' interest. Neither savings deposits nor time deposits serve directly as media of exchange, so they are not included in M1, the narrow definition of money.

Time deposits of less than $100,000 are called small-denomination time deposits and are included in M2.

Photodisc/Getty Images

Using an ATM is a convenient way to access your checking account. Can you think of any disadvantages of using an ATM?

Money Market Mutual Fund Accounts

Money market mutual fund accounts are another component of the money supply more broadly defined as M2. Funds deposited in these accounts are used to purchase a collection of short-term interest-earning assets by the financial institution that administers the fund. Depositors are then able to write checks against the value of their deposited funds. Because of restrictions on the minimum balance, on the number of checks that can be written per month, or on the minimum amount of each check, these popular accounts are not viewed as part of M1, but are part of M2. Only retail money market accounts, or those held by households, are counted as part of M2. Accounts held by businesses and governments are not part of M2.

The size and the relative importance of each definition of money are presented in Figure 18.4. As you can see, M2 is more than four times M1. Again, distinctions between M1 and M2 become less meaningful as banks make it easier for depositors to transfer funds from one type of account to another.

Debit Cards but Not Credit Cards

Why do the definitions of money include funds accessible by debit (bank or ATM) cards but not credit cards, such as VISA and MasterCard? Most sellers accept credit cards as readily as they accept cash or checks. Online purchases and mail orders usually require credit cards.

FIGURE 18.4 M1 and M2: Alternative Measures of the Money Supply, Week of June 20, 2011

M2 is more than four times larger than M1.

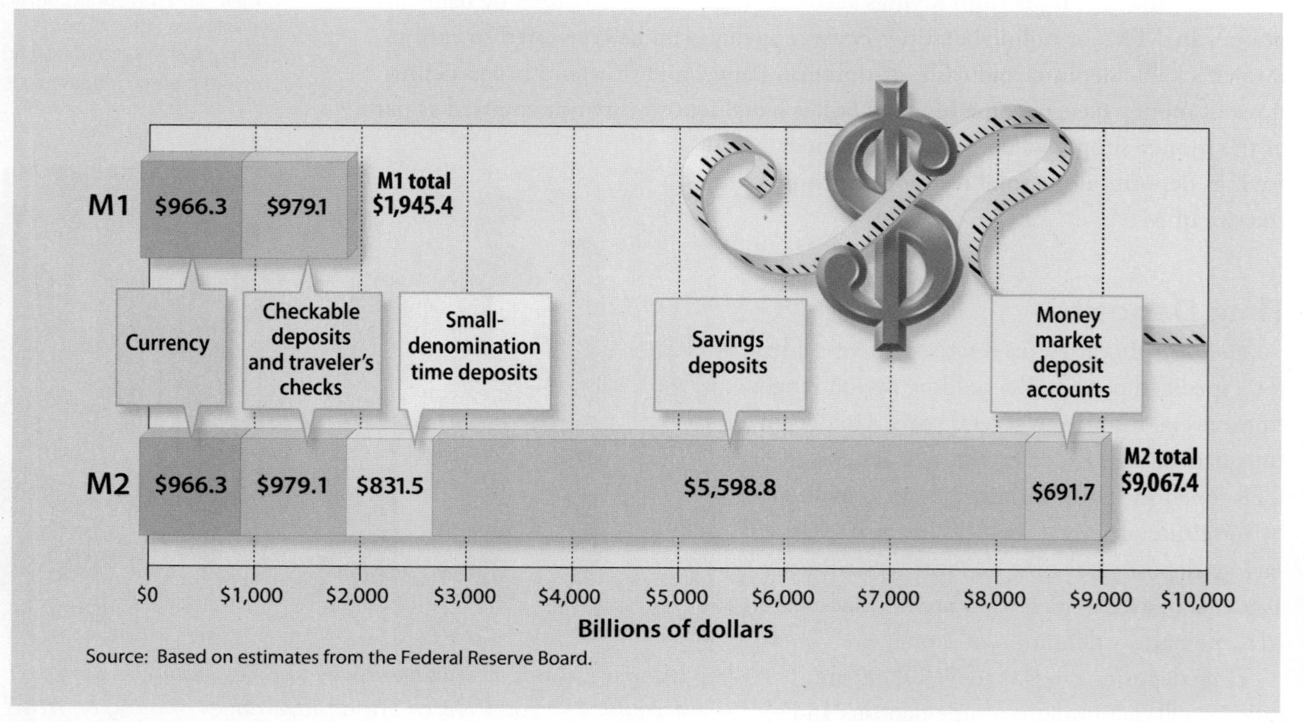

Source: Based on estimates from the Federal Reserve Board.

A credit card itself is not money. Using a credit card, however, is a convenient way of obtaining a short-term loan from the card issuer. If you buy an airline ticket with a credit card, the card issuer lends you the money to pay for the ticket. You don't use money until you pay your credit card bill. The credit card has not eliminated your use of money. It has merely delayed it. On the other hand, when you use a debit card at a grocery store, a drugstore, or any number of other retailers, you draw down your checking account—part of M1.

Electronic Money

Money has grown increasingly more abstract over time, moving from commodity money to paper money that represented a claim on some commodity such as gold, to paper money of no value in itself, to an electronic entry at a bank that can be tapped with a debit card. Much of modern money consists of electronic entries in bank computers. So, money has evolved from a physical commodity to an electronic entry. This evolution is depicted in Figure 18.5. Money today not so much changes hands as it changes computer accounts through electronic funds transfers. Debit cards have become so popular that people now need less cash, so less currency is being printed.

FIGURE 18.5 Evolution of Money

Stockbyte/Getty Images

1. Commodity Money

Stockbyte/Getty Images

2. Representative Money

J.Helgason/Shutterstock.com

3. Fiat Money

Photobac/Shutterstock.com

4. Electronic Money

CHECKPOINT

Why have distinctions among the broad aggregates of money become less meaningful over time?

18.3 ASSESSMENT

Think Critically

1. Explain the differences among checkable deposits, savings deposits, and time deposits.
2. If you had $100, would you be more likely to spend it if you held it in cash, had it deposited in a checking account, or had a traveler's check in that amount? Are these forms of money all equally easy to spend?
3. How would buying a $50 shirt with a credit card be different from buying the same shirt with a debit card?

Graphing Exercise

4. Use data in the table to construct two bar graphs to show the components of M1 and M2 on December 2010. Calculate the percent each component represented of the total for these two measures of the money supply. Do any of these percentages surprise you? Why or why not??

COMPONENTS OF M1 AND M2 IN DEC. 2010, VALUES IN BILLIONS

M1		M2	
Currency	$ 915.7	M1	$1,828.5
Traveler's Checks	$ 4.7	Savings Deposits	$5,355.9
Checkable Deposits	$ 908.1	Small Time Deposits	$ 923.0
		Money Market Funds	$ 706.5
Total	$1,828.5	Total	$8,813.9

Economic Indicators, July, 2011, p. 27.

Make Academic Connections

5. **Mathematics** Calculate the changes in M1 and M2 that would result from each of the following. Explain how you found your answers. Why don't the values of M1 and M2 always change when the value of their components change?
   a. The Fed buys a $10,000 bond from a person who then deposits the funds in her checking account.
   b. A depositor has $500 transferred from his checking account to his savings account.
   c. A depositor withdraws $1,000 in cash from her savings account.
   d. A depositor transfers $2,000 from her savings account to a time deposit.

TeamWork

Assume that banks are paying 0% on checking deposits, 1.0% on savings deposits, 1.5% on money market deposits, and 2.0% on 1-year CDs. Imagine that your team has received $10,000 from an uncle. The only requirement is that you must deposit the gift in a bank for at least one month. Select the type of account the group would use and explain why you made this choice. If the difference in the rates these accounts pay was much greater how much difference would it make? Compare your team's work with that of other teams.

21st Century Skills

INFORMATION AND COMMUNICATIONS TECHNOLOGY

Managing Money in an Electronic Age

In the early 1900s, people received their wages and paid for purchases with cash or checks. Or, if they were trusted, they could put their purchases on a "tab" provided by a retailer and pay later. In the 21st century, you have many choices for how to receive and spend your income. Some employers will deposit your wages directly into your bank account. If you want cash, you withdraw it from your bank either by visiting the bank, using an automatic teller machine (ATM), or getting "cash back" with a debit card purchase. You also probably use electronic funds transfers (EFTs) to spend your income almost as often as you use cash, especially for purchasing higher-ticket items. You may use EFT transactions to

- Make purchases with debit cards that electronically deduct funds from your checking account and credit them to the accounts of stores where you shop.
- Transfer funds to pay bills electronically using your computer.
- Arrange for your bank to pay your bills automatically each month.

Using credit cards acts much the same as putting purchases on a "tab." The biggest difference is you owe a debt to your bank instead of the store where you made the purchase.

New Ways to Save

Income that is not spent is saved. New methods of saving that involve the use of EFTs include:

- Having funds transferred automatically from your checking account to your savings account each month by your bank.
- Having your employer automatically deposit part of your earnings in a savings account each pay period.
- Transferring funds from your checking account into a savings account on your computer or at an ATM.

Use EFTs and Credit Cards Responsibly

Using EFTs or credit cards to spend or save your income does not reduce your need to be responsible. Although credit cards make it easy to spend funds you have not yet earned, they do not increase your purchasing power in the long run. In fact, irresponsible use of credit can result in financial penalties, large fees, and an inability to borrow funds when you really need credit.

Smart Cards

New electronic methods for spending and saving income are available, including the use of "smart cards" to charge purchases. A smart card is a plastic card with a built-in microcomputer chip and integrated circuit that can store data. The data can be read without running the card through a scanner. Some people believe that information transmitted by smart cards will eventually include the card owner's photograph, name, address, and other types of personal information such as employer and credit history. Proponents of smart cards believe the cards will reduce identity theft. Critics regard this technology as an invasion of privacy, as anyone with access to a smart card reader also has access to the information stored on the card.

Apply the Skill

Assume that your bank has offered you a smart card similar to the one described above. Would you accept the offer or refuse it? List and explain three reasons for your choice.

Chapter 18 Summary

ASK THE EXPERT

www.cengage.com/school/contecon

What are the functions of money?

18.1 Origins of Money

A. The earliest families were self-sufficient and did not need money. When people began to specialize, exchanges were carried out through barter at first. Barter involved large transaction costs that gave birth to money. People began to accept goods that they did not expect to use themselves but rather to trade later for other products they wanted. The goods that served as money became known as commodity money.

B. Money must fulfill three functions. (1) It must be accepted as a medium of exchange. (2) It must serve as a unit of account. (3) It must provide a store of value over time. An ideal form of money would be durable, portable, divisible, of uniform quality, have a low opportunity cost of use, have a supply and demand that does not fluctuate wildly, and exist in limited quantity.

C. Coins made of precious metals replaced other types of commodity money in early commerce. They were more portable, durable, and divisible than most types of commodity money. Gradually, most minted coins became token money, which means that the value stamped on them exceeded their metallic value.

18.2 Origins of Banking and the Federal Reserve System

A. The earliest businesses that served as banks were goldsmiths who stored gold for their customers. Depositors often wrote checks to have gold transferred from one account to another. Goldsmiths learned that they could lend part of these funds on deposit to earn interest. Goldsmiths came to operate under the fractional reserve banking system. Paper money was first issued in the form of notes printed by banks. These notes could be redeemed at the issuing bank for gold or silver. Governments eventually issued paper money that was backed by nothing other than the government's assertion that it was money.

B. Depository institutions are classified broadly into commercial banks, which hold most bank deposits, and thrift institutions, which include mutual savings banks and credit unions. Banks may be chartered either by a state or by the federal government in the United States.

C. The Federal Reserve System, or Fed, was established in 1913 to stop runs on banks. The Fed is responsible for supervising banking in the United States and for making and implementing monetary policy. The Fed may lend money to banks and charge them the discount rate of interest.

18.3 Money, Near Money, and Credit Cards

A. The Fed measures the money supply in the U.S. economy through two money aggregates. M1 includes currency in circulation, checkable deposits, and traveler's checks. The measurement of M1 is complicated by U.S. currency that is held abroad.

B. M2 is the broader definition of the money supply. It includes M1 plus savings and time deposits, as well money market mutual fund accounts.

C. Electronic fund transfers carried out through debit cards have made it easier for people to spend their money. When people use credit cards to purchase goods or services, they are effectively taking out short-term loans.

CHAPTER 18 ASSESSMENT

Review Economic Terms

Choose the term that best fits the definition. Some terms may not be used.

_____ 1. Money not of value in itself and not convertible into gold, silver, or anything else of value

_____ 2. Anything generally accepted by all parties in payment for goods or services

_____ 3. Buying or selling U.S. government securities as a way of regulating the money supply

_____ 4. Narrow definition of the money supply

_____ 5. A written order instructing a bank to pay someone from the amount deposited

_____ 6. Bank notes that exchange for a specific commodity, such as gold

_____ 7. Interest rate the Fed charges to banks that borrow reserves

_____ 8. Central bank and money authority of the United States

_____ 9. Deposits in financial institutions against which checks can be written

_____ 10. Anything that serves both as money and as a commodity, such as gold

a. check
b. checkable deposits
c. commodity money
d. discount rate
e. Federal Open Market Committee (FOMC)
f. Federal Reserve System
g. fiat money
h. fractional reserve banking system
i. M1
j. M2
k. medium of exchange
l. open-market operations
m. representative money

Review Economic Concepts

11. Without ________?________ there is no need for money.

12. **True or False** The high transaction cost of money gave birth to barter.

13. Which of the following is not a function of money?
    a. medium of exchange
    b. unit of account
    c. standard of deposit
    d. store of value

14. Gold, silver, salt, and tobacco have all served as ________?________ at some time in the past.

15. **True or False** Fiat money is accepted when people trust the issuing agency.

16. Which of the following is probably the greatest limitation on the usefulness of diamonds as commodity money?
    a. They are not durable.
    b. They are not portable.
    c. They do not have value.
    d. They are not easily divisable.

17. Paper documents issued by banks that promised the bearer a specific amount of gold or silver were called ________?________.

18. Cattle make poor money because they
    a. are not durable.
    b. are not divisible.
    c. have no value.
    d. exist in almost unlimited quantities.

19. **True or False** Money is a stock while income is a flow.

20. Federal Reserve notes are examples of
    a. fiat money.
    b. representative money.
    c. commodity money.
    d. full-bodied money.

21. **True or False** Banks in the United States may be chartered only by state governments.

22. In the past, savings and loans and mutual savings banks specialized in
    a. issuing credit cards.
    b. extending credit to businesses.
    c. maintaining checking accounts.
    d. extending credit to households.

23. When the Fed lends money to banks, it charges them the ________?________.

24. Which of the following statements about the Federal Reserve's Board of Governors is not true?
    a. Its members are responsible for setting monetary policy.
    b. Its members are elected by commercial bank presidents.
    c. Its members also serve on the Federal Open Market Committee.
    d. Each member serves a 14-year term.

25. **True or False** The FOMC was established to coordinate the Fed's open-market operations.

26. M1 includes each of the following except
    a. checkable deposits.
    b. currency.
    c. small savings account deposits.
    d. traveler's checks.

27. A part of a collection of short-term interest-earning assets that individuals are able to purchase is called a ________?________.

28. True or False The use of a debit card will immediately affect your checking account balance while the use of a credit card will not.

29. ________?________ carried out through debit cards make it easier for people to spend their money.

Apply Economic Concepts

30. **Decide When to Use Cash** Which of the following transactions would you complete with cash and for which would you write a check? Explain each of your choices. What generalizations can you make about when people choose to use cash to make their payments?
    - Pay your $850 rent.
    - Buy two $8 movie tickets for your friend and yourself.
    - Make a $199 monthly payment for your car loan.
    - Purchase your lunch for $5.99 at a fast-food restaurant.
    - Repay your uncle the $300 he loaned you last year.

31. **Assess What Makes a Piece of Paper Money** Some resort communities issue guests special pieces of paper that may be used to purchase goods or services within the resort. Guests may spend 50 credits to rent a small sailboat, 75 credits to purchase a meal, or 100 credits to play a round of golf or take a tennis lesson. In what ways are these pieces of paper similar to money, and in what ways are they different?

32. **Calculate the Money Supply** The table lists amounts of money held in a variety of forms in January 2011. Use these values to calculate M1 and M2 at that time.

MONEY HELD IN JANUARY 2011, VALUES IN BILLIONS OF DOLLARS

Savings Deposits	$5,377.8
Checkable Deposits	925.8
Currency	920.1
Small Time Deposits	905.2
Money Market Funds	704.9
Traveler's Checks	4.6

Source: *Economic Indicators*, July 2011, p. 27.

33. **Describe What Happens When the Fed Lends Money** Banks that are short on cash may ask to borrow funds from the Federal Reserve System. This sometimes happens when banks located in rural areas need money to make loans in the spring to farmers who are preparing to plant crops. These loans are repaid the following fall, after farmers have harvested and sold their crops. Write an essay that describes what would happen to the money supply if a bank borrowed $10 million from the Fed and used this money to make loans to farmers.

34. **Identify Depository Institutions** Make a list of all the depository institutions that have offices or branches in your community. Identify them as commercial banks, savings and loans, mutual savings banks, credit unions, or other. How much difference is there in the services that they offer typical consumers?

35. **Illustrate Limitations on Commodity Money** Construct a grid that has five columns and eight rows. List the seven qualities of ideal money in cells 2 through 8 of the first column and four types of commodity money—apples, diamonds, cotton, and chickens—in cells 2 through 5 of the first row. Write "yes" or "no" in each of the remaining cells, depending on whether the corresponding type of commodity possesses the indicated quality. Which of these types of commodity money would probably be most useful in completing transactions? Explain your answer.

36. **21st Century Skills: Information and Communications Technology** Imagine that in a few years your bank offers a new type of credit card that allows customers to enter their personal budget objectives in a memory chip it contains. It then keeps a record of spending and automatically warns users when they start to make a purchase that does not fit in with their objectives. What are the advantages and disadvantages of using this card? Would you want to own such a card? Why might parents want their children to use this type of card?

Digging Deeper

with Economics e-Collection

Access the Gale Economics e-Collection through the URL below. Find an article that discusses one of the topics in this chapter, such as monetary policy, the Federal Reserve System, or the money supply. Read the article and explain its main points to your class in a one- or two-minute oral presentation.

www.cengage.com/school/contecon

CONSIDER...

- How does the banking system create money?
- Why don't you demand all the money you can get your hands on?
- What's the price of holding money?
- How does the supply of money in the economy affect your chances of finding a job, your ability to finance a new car, and the interest rate you pay on credit cards?
- What's the impact of changes in the money supply on the economy in the short run and in the long run?

CHAPTER 19

Money Creation, the Fed, and Monetary Policy

Point your browser

www.cengage.com/school/contecon

19.1 HOW BANKS WORK

Learning Objectives

LO1 Discuss what needs to be done to get a new bank up and running.

LO2 Describe how the banking system can expand the money supply.

Key Terms

net worth 593
asset 593
liability 594
balance sheet 594
required reserve ratio 594
required reserves 594
excess reserves 595
money multiplier 597

In Your World

Coins and paper money account for only part of the money supply in the U.S. economy. The narrow definition of money also includes checking accounts, which consist mostly of electronic entries in bank computers. The Federal Reserve System creates money by circulating more Federal Reserve notes and by having banks do what they do best—accept deposits and lend out some of those deposits to borrowers. Bank reserves provide the raw material banks use to make loans, and these loans are how banks add to the money supply.

OPERATING A BANK

LO1 Discuss what needs to be done to get a new bank up and running.

Suppose some business leaders in your community want to establish a bank. The following section discusses how they would get their new bank up and running. These considerations would apply to the operation of any depository institution—that is, any institution that accepts customer deposits—such as a commercial bank, a savings and loan, a mutual savings bank, or a credit union.

Getting a Charter

The bank founders first need to obtain a *charter*, or the right to operate. They would apply to the state banking authority to start up a state bank or to the U.S. Comptroller of the Currency to start up a national bank. In considering the application, the chartering agency would review the quality of management, the need for another bank in the community, the initial investment, and the likelihood of success.

The founders plan to invest $1 million of their own money in the bank, and they indicate this on their charter application. Once a charter is granted, they incorporate, issuing themselves shares of stock, or certificates of ownership. Thus, they exchange $1 million for shares of stock in a bank they name Home Bank. These shares are called the *owners' equity*, and represent the **net worth** of the bank.

The owners invest this $1 million in building and furnishing the bank. These purchases become the bank's assets. An **asset** is any physical property or financial claim that is owned. The bank is now ready for business.

net worth Assets minus liabilities; also called owners' equity

asset Any physical property or financial claim that is owned

Bank Balance Sheet

Opening day is a lucky one for Home Bank because the first customer opens a checking account and deposits $100,000 in cash. The cash becomes the bank's asset.

In accepting this deposit, the bank promises to repay the depositor that amount. That promise becomes the bank's **liability**, which is an amount that is owed.

As a result of this deposit, the bank's assets increase by $100,000 in cash and its liabilities increase by $100,000 in checkable deposits. At this point, the money supply has not changed. The depositor simply converted $100,000 in cash to $100,000 in checkable deposits, which becomes part of the money supply. The bank's vault now holds the cash, which is no longer in circulation and so is no longer considered part of the money supply.

Look at the bank's **balance sheet**, presented in Figure 19.1. As the name implies, a balance sheet shows an equality, or a balance, between the two sides of the bank's account. The left side lists the bank's assets. At this point, assets include the $1 million in building and furnishings owned by Home Bank and the $100,000 in vault cash.

The right side shows two claims on the banks assets: claims by the owners, or net worth, amounting to $1 million, and claims by nonowners, or liabilities which, at this point, consist of checkable deposits of $100,000. The two sides of the ledger must always be equal, or be in *balance*, which is why it's called a *balance sheet*. Assets must equal liabilities plus net worth.

Assets = Liabilities + Net Worth

liability An amount owed

balance sheet A financial statement showing assets, liabilities, and net worth at a point in time; assets must equal liabilities plus net worth, so the statement is in balance

required reserve ratio A Fed regulation that dictates the minimum fraction of deposits each bank must keep in reserve

required reserves The dollar amount that must be held in reserve; checkable deposits multiplied by the required reserve ratio

Reserve Accounts

The Fed requires Home Bank to set aside, or to hold in reserve, a fraction of checkable deposits. The **required reserve ratio** dictates the minimum fraction of deposits the bank must keep in reserve. The dollar amount that must be held in reserve is called **required reserves**—checkable deposits multiplied by the required reserve ratio.

All banks and thrifts are subject to the Fed's reserve requirement. Reserves are either held as cash in the bank's vault or deposited at the Fed. In neither case are those reserves in circulation, so they are not counted as part of the money supply. Vault cash earns Home Bank no interest, but some reserves on deposit at the Fed do earn Home Bank modest interest. If the required reserve ratio on checkable

FIGURE 19.1 Home Bank's Balance Sheet After $100,000 Deposit in Checking Account

The two sides of a balance sheet are always equal, or "in balance." Assets equal liabilities plus net worth.

Assets		Liabilities and Net Worth	
Cash	$ 100,000	Checkable Deposits	$ 100,000
Building and Furniture	$ 1,000,000	Net Worth	$ 1,000,000
Total	$ 1,100,000	Total	$ 1,100,000

deposits is 0.1, as it has been in recent years, Home Bank must hold $10,000 as required reserves. That equals 0.1 times $100,000.

Home Bank's reserves now consist of $10,000 in required reserves and $90,000 in **excess reserves**, which are bank reserves that exceed required reserves.

So far Home Bank earns interest only on its excess reserves on deposit with the Fed, and that interest is tiny (only 0.25 percent in 2011). Home Bank can use its excess reserves to acquire other assets that pay more interest. The bank's alternatives assets are limited primarily to loans and to government securities. Suppose Home Bank uses the $90,000 excess reserves to make loans and buy government securities.

CHECKPOINT

What needs to be done to get a new bank up and running?

MONEY MULTIPLIER

LO2

Describe how the banking system can expand the money supply.

Home Bank has used all its excess reserves to make loans and buy U.S. government securities, assets that earn interest. The bank now has no excess reserves. What if, in addition to Home Bank having no excess reserves, there are no excess reserves in the entire banking system? In this setting, how can the Fed increase the money supply?

The Fed Makes a Move

To get the ball rolling, suppose the Fed buys a $10,000 U.S. government bond from Home Bank. This is called an open-market operation, and it's the primary way the Fed can alter the money supply. To pay for the bond, the Fed increases Home Bank's reserve account by $10,000. Where does the Fed get these reserves? It makes them up—creates them out of thin air!

In the process, Home Bank has exchanged one asset, a U.S. bond, for another asset, reserves held at the Fed. A U.S. bond is not money, nor are reserves, so the money supply has not yet changed. But Home Bank now has $10,000 in excess reserves, and excess reserves are the fuel for money creation.

Round One

What will Home Bank do with those excess reserves? Suppose Megan comes in and applies for a $10,000 car loan. Home Bank approves her loan and increases her checking account by $10,000. Home Bank has converted her promise to repay, her IOU, into a $10,000 checkable deposit. *Because her newly created checkable deposit is money, this loan increases the money supply by $10,000.*

She writes a $10,000 check for the car, and the car dealer promptly deposits it in the company's checking account at Fidelity Bank. Fidelity Bank increases the car dealer's account by $10,000, and sends Megan's check to the Fed. The Fed transfers $10,000 in reserves from Home Bank's account to Fidelity Bank's account. The Fed then sends the check to Home Bank, which reduces Megan's checkable deposits by $10,000. The Fed has thus "cleared" her check by settling the claim that Fidelity Bank had on Home Bank.

excess reserves Bank reserves in excess of required reserves

courtneyk/iStockphoto.com

Explain how a bank, by granting a loan for a car, increases the money supply.

At this point, the $10,000 in checkable deposits has simply shifted from Megan's account at Home Bank to the car dealer's account at Fidelity Bank. The increase in the money supply in this first round remains at $10,000.

Round Two and Beyond

Because the required reserve ratio is 0.1, Fidelity Bank sets aside $1,000 of the new deposit as required reserves and lends the remaining $9,000 to a family remodeling their kitchen. Home bank increases the family's checking account by $9,000. Thus, the money supply has increased by an additional $9,000, and the cumulative increase to this point is $19,000.

An individual bank can lend no more than its excess reserves. When the borrower spends the amount loaned, reserves at one bank usually fall. However, total reserves in the banking system do not fall because the money spent usually gets deposited in the recipient's bank account, and can fuel more loans. The potential expansion of checkable deposits in the banking system equals some multiple of the initial increase in excess reserves.

This cycle of borrowing, spending, and depositing continues round after round. As a result of the Fed buying this $10,000 bond, the money supply could eventually increase by a multiple of the excess reserves created by the Fed. Because this money-creation process began with the Fed's open-market operation, the Fed can rightfully claim, "The buck starts here." This slogan appeared on a large plaque in the Federal Reserve chairman's office.

Reserve Requirements and Money Expansion

The banking system as a whole eliminates excess reserves by expanding the money supply. With a required reserve ratio of 0.1, the Fed's initial injection of \$10,000 in fresh reserves could support up to \$100,000 in new checkable deposits.

The **money multiplier** is the maximum multiple by which the money supply could increase as a result of an increase in the banking system's excess reserves. The money multiplier equals 1 divided by the required reserve ratio. If r stands for the required reserve ratio, then the money multiplier is $1/r$. In this example, the required reserve ratio is 0.1, so the money multiplier is 1/0.1, which equals 10. The formula for the multiple expansion of checkable deposits can be written as:

$$\text{Change in checkable deposits} = \text{Change in excess reserves} \times 1/r$$

The greater the fraction of deposits that must be held as reserves, the smaller the money multiplier. A required reserve ratio of 0.2 instead of 0.1 would mean each bank would have to set aside twice as much in required reserves. The money multiplier in this case would be 1/0.2, which equals 5. The maximum possible increase in checkable deposits resulting from an initial \$10,000 increase in fresh reserves would be \$10,000 × 5, or \$50,000.

money multiplier The multiple by which the money supply can increase as a result of an increase in excess reserves in the banking system

Math in Economics

Common Core Ratios and Proportional Relationships

You can find the amount of interest that will be paid after several years by multiplying the amount of the debt times 1 plus the rate of interest for the series of years, and then subtracting the original loan from the total.

EXAMPLE Find the interest that must be paid on a \$2,000.00 loan taken out for three years at an annual interest rate of 8%, with interest compounded annually and repaid at the end of the three years.

SOLUTION Multiply the amount of the loan times 1 plus the rate of interest, expressed as a decimal.

\$2,000.00 × 1.08 = \$2,160.00

Multiply this product times 1 plus the rate of interest.

\$2,160.00 × 1.08 = \$2,332.80

Multiply this product times 1 plus the rate of interest.

\$2,332.80 × 1.08 = \$2,519.42

Subtract the amount of the loan from this product to find the interest.

\$2,519.42 – \$2,000.00 = \$519.42

Practice the Skill Find the interest paid for each loan. Assume interest is compounded annually and paid at the end of the loan period.

1. A \$500.00 loan taken out for two years at an annual interest rate of 10%.
2. A loan of \$1,200.00 taken out for four years at an annual interest rate of 6%.
3. Why do people who borrow or lend funds use tables or computers to calculate the amount of interest that will be paid for a loan?

Excess reserves fuel the expansion of checkable deposits. A higher reserve requirement drains this fuel from the banking system, thereby reducing the amount of new money that can be created. The fractional reserve requirement is the key to the multiple expansion of checkable deposits. If each $1 deposit had to be backed by $1 in required reserves, the money multiplier would be cut to 1, which would be no multiplier at all.

Contraction of the money supply works similarly, but in reverse. It begins with the Fed selling a $10,000 U.S. bond to Home Bank. Therefore, the Fed increases the money supply by buying bonds and decreases it by selling bonds.

Limitations on the Money Multiplier

For a given required reserve ratio, the multiplier is greatest if

1. banks do not allow excess reserves to sit idle;
2. borrowed funds do not sit idle in checking accounts, but are spent; and
3. the public does not choose to hold some of the newly created money as cash.

If excess reserves remain idle or if borrowed funds sit around in checking accounts, they are less able to fuel an expansion of the money supply. If people stash away some of the newly created money as cash rather than spend it, or leave it in checking accounts, then that portion of borrowed funds held as idle cash cannot fuel additional reserves in the banking system.

For the money multiplier to operate, a particular bank need not use excess reserves just to make loans. It could just as well use them to pay all its employees a Christmas bonus. As long as that spending ends up as checkable deposits in the banking system, the money multiplier can operate.

CHECKPOINT **How can the banking system expand the money supply by a multiple of excess reserves?**

Mike Truchon/Shutterstock.com

What is the effect on the money supply if someone borrows money but then leaves it in a checking account or holds it as cash rather than spending it?

19.1 ASSESSMENT

Think Critically

1. Why are people who organize a bank required to invest their own funds as owner's equity in the new business? How does this help to protect the bank's depositors?
2. Why is a loan made by a bank counted as an asset of that bank, while a deposit made by a customer is counted as a liability to the bank?
3. Bank ABC holds $100 million in deposits upon which it must maintain a required reserve ratio of 0.1. The bank currently has $12 million in reserve. How much excess reserves does the bank hold? Why would it want to invest or loan these reserves as quickly as possible?
4. Why doesn't the money multiplier work as effectively if people decide to hold additional funds they receive in idle cash?

Graphing Exercise

5. Construct a bar graph to show four rounds of the money-creation process that would result from a new deposit of $2,000 in a checking account when the required reserve ratio is 0.1.

EXPANSION OF A NEW $2,000 CHECKABLE DEPOSIT

	New Deposit	Required Reserve	New Loan
Round 1	$2,000.00	$200.00	$1,800.00
Round 2	$1,800.00	$180.00	$1,620.00
Round 3	$1,620.00	$162.00	$1,458.00
Round 4	$1,458.00	$145.80	$1,312.20

Make Academic Connections

6. **Math** Recalculate the table in exercise 5 above, assuming that the Fed increased the required reserve ratio from 0.1 to 0.12. Why is the required reserve ratio an important factor in determining the amount of money that banks are able to lend? What would happen to consumers' ability to borrow funds from banks if the required reserve ratio was increased?

TeamWork

Working in six-member teams, role-play the expansion of a new deposit of $5,000 in cash in a checking account if the reserve requirement is 20 percent. Team members should assume the following roles: (1) the banker who accepts the $5,000 deposit, (2) a person who wants to borrow $4,000 to buy new furniture, (3) the owner of a furniture store where the $4,000 is spent, (4) a banker who accepts the $4,000 deposit from the furniture store owner, (5) a person who wants to borrow $3,200 to have her car fixed after an accident, (6) the owner of a body shop who accepts $3,200 for repairing the car. Each person should explain what he or she is doing and how it would affect the money supply.

AND MOVERS SHAKERS

Elizabeth Warren

Harvard Law School Professor and Consumer Advocate

Consumer advocate and Harvard Law professor Elizabeth Warren wants to make the lending environment in the United States friendlier to consumers. In 2010 Congress passed the Dodd-Frank Wall Street Reform and Consumer Protection Act, which established the Consumer Financial Protection Bureau (CFPB). Warren was the principal architect of the CFPB, which aims "to give consumers the information they need to understand the terms of their agreements with financial companies….and to make regulations and guidance as clear and streamlined as possible so providers of consumer financial products and services can follow the rules on their own."

Warren, author of six academic books and more than 100 scholarly articles on personal finance, also has written several best-selling books with daughter Amelia Warren Tyagi. In their book, *The Two-Income Trap: Why Middle-Class Mothers and Fathers Are Going Broke,* Warren and Tyagi argue that today a full-time worker earns less income, adjusted for inflation, than the full-time employee of 30 years ago. They discovered that some middle-class families are finding education, healthcare, and safe, clean neighborhoods increasingly out of their reach financially.

Warren says it is too simplistic to assume that consumers are losing ground solely due to overspending. She said "…families aren't going broke because of ordinary consumption…. Today's family has put two people into the workforce…but by the time they make those four basic purchases—the mortgage, their health insurance, their cars and their child care—they have less money to spend on everything else than their parents had a generation ago…."

Warren believes the U.S. credit industry went astray when lending money to bad credit risks became more profitable than lending to good credit risks. She said, "And as soon as they figured that out, consumer credit goes through the roof, and so do profits. That's the effect of a deregulated industry." Bad customers take longer to pay and end up paying big fines for late payments. Lenders can "write off" bad debt from their taxes, further increasing their income.

ZHANG JUN/Xinhua/Landov

Warren has testified many times before the House and Senate committees on banking and financial issues. When asked where people should focus their attention on financial reform, Warren said, "To restore some basic sanity to the financial system, we need two central changes: fix broken consumer-credit markets and end guarantees for the big players that threaten our entire economic system. If we get those two key parts right, we can still dial the rest of the regulation up and down as needed. But if we don't get those two right, I think the game is over. I hate to sound alarmist, but that's how I feel about this."

In 2011 Warren announced she would run, as a Democratic Party candidate, for the U.S. Senate seat held by Scott Brown (R-Mass.).

Think Critically **Research to find the specific issues the Consumer Financial Protection Bureau is addressing. Choose one of the issues and write a one-page paper describing it.**

Sources: http://www.huffingtonpost.com/2011/09/13/elizabeth-warren-senate-massachusetts_n_960510.html; http://www.salon.com/news/elizabeth_warren/index.html; http://transcripts.cnn.com/TRANSCRIPTS/1107/18/sitroom.01.html; and http://www.pbs.org/wgbh/pages/frontline/shows/credit/interviews/warren.html#ixzz1YQMExrBT

19.2 MONETARY POLICY IN THE SHORT RUN

Learning Objectives

LO1 Describe the slope of the money demand curve.

LO2 Explain how changes in the money supply affect interest rates and real GDP in the short run.

LO3 Discuss the federal funds rate and why the Fed uses this rate to pursue monetary policy goals.

Key Terms

In Your World

So far the focus has been on how the banking system creates money. A more fundamental question is how the money supply affects the economy as a whole. When the Fed expands the money supply, this drives down interest rates in the short run. Because the cost of borrowing falls, firms tend to borrow more to buy capital goods and households tend to borrow more to buy cars, homes, and other "big ticket" items. Thus, an increase in the supply of money usually increases aggregate demand, output, and employment in the short run. Monetary policy affects the interest you pay on a car loan and the interest you earn saving for college.

MONEY DEMAND

LO1 Describe the slope of the money demand curve.

Recall the distinction between a *stock* and a *flow*. A stock measures something at a point in time, such as the amount of money you have with you right now. A flow measures something over an interval of time, such as your income per week. **Money demand** is the relationship between how much money people want to hold and the market interest rate. It may seem odd to even talk about the demand for money. You might think people would demand all the money they could get their hands on. Remember, however, that *money*, the stock, is not the same as *income*, the flow. People express their demand for money by holding some of their wealth as money rather than holding their wealth in other assets. People express their demand for income by selling their labor and other resources to earn income.

A Medium of Exchange

Why do people demand money? Why do people have checking accounts and have cash in their pockets, purses, wallets, desk drawers, lockers, and coffee cans? The reason is obvious. *People demand money to carry out market transactions.* Money is a convenient medium of exchange.

Your demand for money is based on your expected spending. If you plan to buy lunch tomorrow, you will carry enough money to pay for it. You may also have

money demand The relationship between how much money people want to hold and the market interest rate

What is the advantage of holding your wealth in money as opposed to other types of financial assets such as bonds?

extra money on hand in case of an emergency or in case you come across something else you want to buy. You may have a little extra cash with you right now for who knows what. Even you don't know.

A Store of Value

The demand for money is related to money's role as a medium of exchange. However, money also is a store of value. People save for a car, for a home, for college, for retirement. People can store their purchasing power as money or as other financial assets, such as corporate and government bonds. The interest rate indicates the cost of borrowing and the reward for lending.

The Cost of Holding Money

The demand for any asset is based on the services it provides. The big advantage of money is its general acceptance in market exchange. In contrast, other financial assets, such as corporate bonds, government bonds, and some bank accounts, must first be *liquidated,* or exchanged for money, before they can fund market transactions.

Money, however, has one major drawback when compared with other financial assets. Money in the form of currency, some checking accounts, and travelers checks earns no interest. Those checking accounts that do earn interest earn much less than other financial assets. In recent years, the interest earned on checking accounts has been tiny—just a fraction of one percent.

Holding wealth in the form of money means passing up some interest that could be earned by holding some other financial asset. For example, suppose a business could earn 4 percent more interest by holding some financial asset other than money. Holding $1 million in money would have an opportunity cost of $40,000 per year. *The interest given up is the opportunity cost of holding money.*

Investigate Your Local Economy

Research interest rates offered on savings accounts at local banks or online banks. Would these rates motivate people to deposit their money in these accounts? Record the interest rates you find, and write a paragraph to explain your answer.

Money Demand and the Interest Rate

Money demand is the relationship between how much money people want to hold and the market rate of interest. The interest earnings that are given up are the cost of holding money. When the market interest rate is low, other things constant, the cost of holding money is low. People hold more of their wealth as money. When the market interest rate is high, the cost of holding money is high. People hold less of their wealth as money and more in financial assets that earn the market rate of interest. Thus, other things constant, the quantity of money demanded varies inversely with the market interest rate.

The money demand curve, D_m, in Figure 19.2 shows the quantity of money people demand at various market interest rates, other things constant. *The quantity of money demanded is inversely related to the price of holding money, which is*

Figure 19.2 Demand for Money Curve

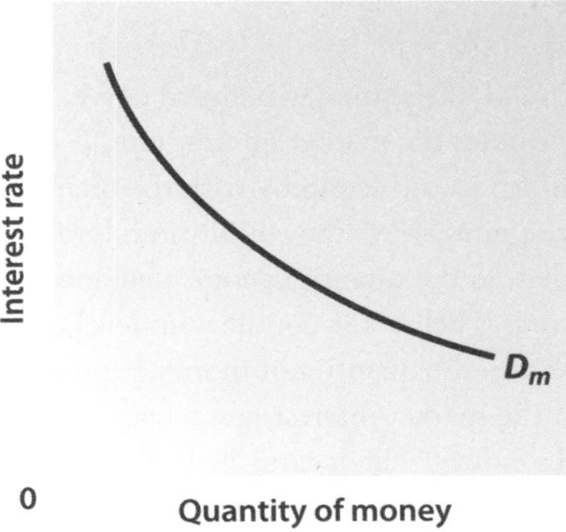

The money demand curve, D_m, slopes downward. As the interest rate falls, so does the opportunity cost of holding money. The quantity of money demanded increases.

the interest rate that could be earned by holding other assets. Movements along the curve reflect the effects of changes in the interest rate on the quantity of money demanded, other things constant.

CHECKPOINT Describe the slope of the money demand curve.

MONEY SUPPLY AND THE MARKET INTEREST RATE

LO2 Explain how changes in the money supply affect interest rates and real GDP in the short run.

The money demand curve has the usual downward slope of other demand curves. The only difference is that the price is measured not by dollars but by the market interest rate, which is the opportunity cost of holding money. What about the supply of money?

Money Supply

Money supply is the stock of money available in the economy at a particular time. Money supply is determined primarily by the Fed through its control over currency and excess reserves in the banking system. The *money supply curve* does not have the usual upward slope of other supply curves. The supply of money, S_m, is depicted as a vertical line in Figure 19.3. Vertical supply indicates that the quantity of money in the economy is fixed by the Fed

money supply The stock of money available in the economy at a particular time; determined by the Fed

at any given time and is therefore independent of the market interest rate. The assumption is that the Fed determines the money supply.

Market Interest Rate

The intersection in Figure 19.3 of the money demand curve, D_m, with the money supply curve, S_m, determines the market interest rate, *i.* That rate equates the quantity of money demanded in the economy with the quantity of money supplied by the Fed. At interest rates above the equilibrium level, the opportunity cost of holding money is higher, so the quantity people demand is less than the quantity supplied. At interest rates below the equilibrium level, the opportunity cost of holding money is lower, so the quantity of money people demand exceeds the quantity supplied. Again, the market interest rate reflects the opportunity cost of holding money. By holding money, which earns little or no interest, people give up the chance to earn the market rate of interest on some other asset, such as bonds.

An Increase in the Money Supply

If the Fed increases the money supply, by, for example, purchasing U.S. bonds, the money supply curve shifts to the right, as shown by the movement from S_m to S'_m in Figure 19.3. The interest rate must fall to encourage people to hold the increased supply of money. The interest rate falls until the quantity of money demanded just equals the quantity supplied. With the decline in the interest rate to i' in Figure 19.3, the opportunity cost of holding money falls enough that the public is willing to hold the now-larger supply of money. *For a given money demand curve, an increase in money supply pushes down the market interest rate, and a decrease in the supply of money pushes up the market interest rate.*

FIGURE 19.3 Effect of an Increase in the Money Supply

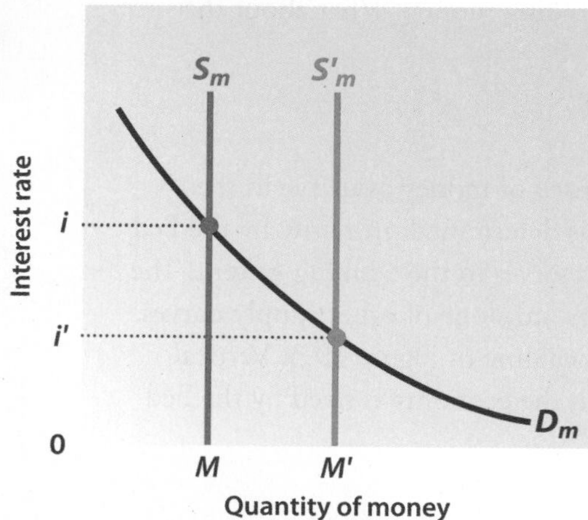

Because the Federal Reserve determines the supply of money, supply can be represented by a vertical line. The intersection of the supply of money S_m and the demand for money D_m determines the equilibrium interest rate, *i*. With an increase in the money supply to S'_m, the interest rate falls enough to encourage people to hold the increased supply of money. With the decline in the interest rate, the opportunity cost of holding money falls as well.

Now that you have some idea how money demand and supply determine the market interest rate, you are ready to see how money fits into the economy in the short run. Specifically, how do changes in the supply of money affect aggregate demand and real GDP?

Effect of Lower Interest Rates

Suppose the Federal Reserve believes that the economy is operating below its potential and decides to stimulate output and employment by increasing the money supply, as it did in response to the Great Recession of 2008–2009. The Fed can try to expand the money supply by

1. purchasing U.S. government securities,
2. reducing the *discount rate* (the rate at which banks can borrow from the Fed), or
3. lowering the required reserve ratio to increase excess reserves.

An increase in the money supply reduces the market interest rate. A lower interest rate encourages consumers to save less and borrow more. A lower rate also encourages businesses to invest more in capital goods. Thus, a lower interest rate usually stimulates consumption and investment. This greater aggregate demand increases real GDP in the short run, as shown by the movement from *Y* to *Y'* in Figure 19.4. Note that the price level also increases.

Thus, an increase in the money supply reduces the market interest rate in the short run. This stimulates aggregate demand and increases real GDP. *In the short run, changes in the money supply affect the economy through changes in the interest rate.*

FIGURE 19.4 Effects of a Lower Interest Rate on Real GDP and the Price Level

A lower interest rate encourages households to borrow more and save less. It also encourages businesses to invest more. More consumption and investment increases aggregate demand. Therefore, a lower interest rate shifts the aggregate demand curve to the right, thereby increasing employment and output in the short run. In the short run, this increases real GDP and the price level.

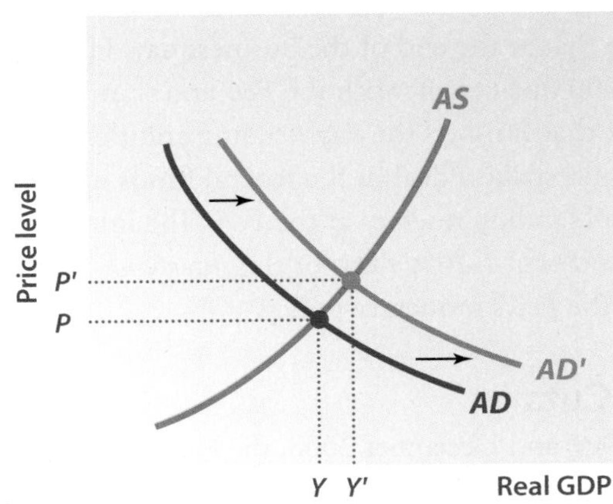

Increasing Interest Rates

Now consider the effect of an increase in the interest rate. Suppose Fed officials decide to reduce the money supply to cool down an overheated economy. The Fed can try to reduce the money supply by

1. selling U.S. government securities,
2. increasing the discount rate, or
3. raising the required reserve ratio to reduce excess reserves.

A decrease in the money supply would increase the market interest rate. At the higher interest rate, businesses find it more costly to finance plants and equipment. Households find it more attractive to save and more costly to finance new homes and other major purchases. Thus a higher interest rate reduces aggregate demand, and this reduction in aggregate demand reduces real GDP in the short run.

How do changes in the money supply affect interest rates and real GDP in the short run?

THE FEDERAL FUNDS RATE

LO3 Discuss the federal funds rate and why the Fed uses this rate.

At 2:15 P.M. on June 22, 2011, immediately following a meeting, the Federal Open Market Committee (FOMC) announced that it would keep its target for the federal funds rate unchanged at a record low of 0 to 0.25 percent. What is the federal funds rate, and how does the Fed's action affect the economy?

Federal Funds Market

Because vault cash earns no interest, banks usually try to keep such cash to a minimum. Banks continuously "sweep" their accounts to find excess reserves that can be put to some interest-earning use. Banks do not let excess reserves remain idle even overnight. The **federal funds market** provides for overnight lending and borrowing among banks of excess reserves on account at the Fed.

For example, suppose that at the end of the business day, Home Bank has excess reserves of $100,000 on account with the Fed and wants to lend that amount to another bank that finished the day needing additional reserves of $100,000. These two banks make a deal in the federal funds market—that is, the market for borrowing and lending reserves at the Fed. The interest rate paid on such loans is called the **federal funds rate** or the *interbank loan rate.* This is the interest rate targeted by the Fed's monetary policy.

federal funds market
A market for overnight lending and borrowing of reserves held by the Fed for banks

federal funds rate
The interest rate banks charge one another to borrow reserves overnight; the Fed's target interest rate

Aggressive Rate Cuts

Between September 2007 and December 2008, the Fed cut the federal funds rate by a total of more than 5.0 percentage points in 10 steps. This was an aggressive effort to boost the economy. The Fed left its target rate unchanged at such a low rate that June 2011 afternoon "to promote the ongoing economic recovery and to help ensure that inflation, over time, is at levels consistent with its mandate." The Fed's mandate is "to foster maximum employment and price stability." To keep the federal funds low, the FOMC continued to carry out open-market operations to provide sufficient reserves to the banking system.

NET Bookmark

Access the web page for the Federal Open Market Committee through the website below. Click on "Meetings and Proceedings of the FOMC," to find a calendar of meetings. Click on "Statement" next to one of the months in the current year. Write a paragraph summarizing the decisions the FOMC made regarding the federal funds rate for that meeting.

www.cengage.com/school/contecon

Why Target This Rate?

For nearly one-half of a century, the Fed has influenced the money supply by focusing mostly on changes in the federal funds rate. There are many interest rates in the economy—for credit cards, new car sales, mortgages, home equity loans, personal loans, and so on. Why does the Fed choose to focus on the federal funds rate? First, by changing bank reserves through open-market operations, the Fed has a direct lever on this rate. The Fed's ability to influence this rate is stronger than it is for any other interest rate. For example, as of June 2011, the Fed had already maintained the target rate at 0 to 0.25 percent for 30 straight months. Second, the federal funds rate serves as a benchmark in the economy for determining many other interest rates. For example, after the Fed announces any change in its target federal funds rate, major banks around the country typically change their prime interest rate by the same amount. The prime rate is the rate banks charge their most trustworthy customers.

Recent History of Federal Funds Rate

Figure 19.5 shows the federal funds rate since 1996. Consider what was going on in the economy during the period. Between early 1996 and late 1998, the economy grew nicely with low inflation, so the FOMC kept the federal funds

fstockfoto/Shutterstock.com

Which interest rate does the Fed focus on to influence the money supply?

FIGURE 19.5 Ups and Downs in the Federal Funds Rate Since 1996 To understand the fluctuations of the federal funds rate, consider what was going on in the economy during the periods shown here.

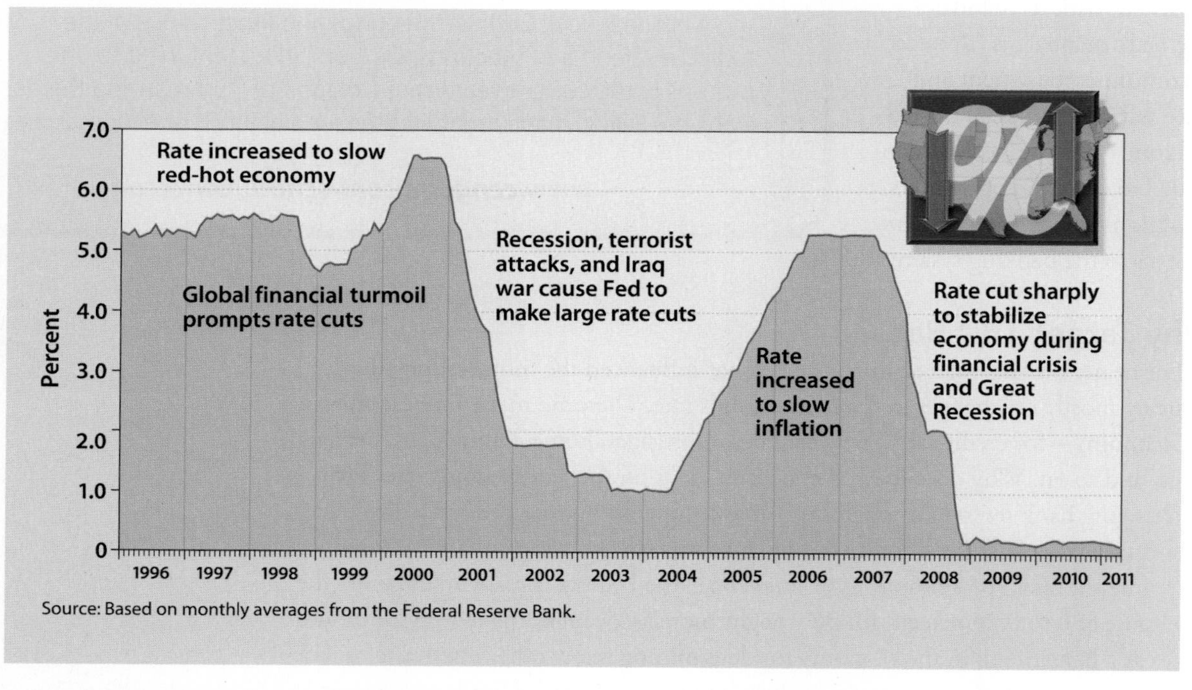

Source: Based on monthly averages from the Federal Reserve Bank.

rate relatively stable in a range of 5.25 percent to 5.5 percent. In late 1998, global financial problems prompted the FOMC to drop its target rate to 4.75 percent.

By the summer of 1999, those fears had subsided, and the FOMC instead became more concerned that robust economic growth would trigger higher inflation. In a series of six steps, the FOMC raised the federal funds rate from 4.75 percent to 6.5 percent. In early 2001, declining consumer confidence, weaker capital spending, falling manufacturing output, and a sinking stock market prompted the FOMC to reverse course. That began a series of rate cuts into 2003.

The rate then remained at 1.0 percent for about one year. In mid-2004 the FOMC, concerned again about inflation, began hiking the rate 0.25 percent at each meeting over the next two years. As you can see, by mid-2006, after 17 hikes, the federal funds rate reached 5.25 percent.

The rate was then kept at 5.25 percent for about one year. Beginning in September 2007, a rising number of mortgage defaults, a worsening economy, and then a global financial crisis prompted a series of rate cuts. After 10 cuts over 15 months, the federal funds rate in late 2008 bottomed out at between 0 and 0.25 percent. The Fed announced the rate would remain at that level at least through 2012.

CHECKPOINT **What is the federal funds rate, and why does the Fed use it to set monetary policy?**

19.2 ASSESSMENT

Think Critically

1. The demand for money normally grows when there is economic growth. What effect does this growth in the demand for money have on interest rates? Explain your answer.
2. If something happened to cause savers to lose faith in the safety of banks, what might happen to the economy? Explain your answer.
3. Of all the interest rates in the economy, why does the Fed focus on the federal funds rate? Why not the prime rate or the mortgage rate?
4. If the Fed purchased $2 billion in government bonds, what would happen to the money supply and interest rates in the economy? Why might the Fed implement such a policy?
5. Why might the Fed set a target for the federal funds rate that is 1 percent higher than its current rate? What steps would the Fed be likely to take to accomplish its goal?

Graphing Exercise

6. Use data in the table to construct a double line graph that shows changes in the federal funds rate and in the prime interest rate over the years from 2000 through 2010. Do you notice a relationship between these interest rates? Would you expect to find similar relationships between the federal funds rate and other interest rates? Why or why not?

AVERAGE ANNUAL FEDERAL FUNDS RATE AND PRIME INTEREST RATE, 2000–2010

Year	Federal Funds Rate	Prime Interest Rate
2000	6.24%	9.23%
2001	3.88%	6.91%
2002	1.67%	4.67%
2003	1.13%	4.12%
2004	1.35%	4.34%
2005	3.22%	6.19%
2006	4.97%	7.96%
2007	5.02%	8.06%
2008	1.92%	5.09%
2009	0.16%	3.25%
2010	0.18%	3.25%

Source: *Economic Indicators*, June 2011, p. 30.

Make Academic Connections

7. **Government** Investigate the policies of the Reagan administration that were intended to stimulate the economy in 1981 and 1982. Compare these policies with the monetary policy implemented at the same time under the Federal Reserve's Chairman Paul Volcker. How does this show that government policies are not always coordinated?

TeamWork

Work in teams of three to four students to research the federal funds rate on the Federal Open Market Committee web page, as directed in the Net Bookmark activity. Each team member should choose a different year to research. Compare and discuss your findings as a team, referring to the line graph in Figure 19.5.

21st Century Skills

FLEXIBILITY AND ADAPTABILITY

Changing Interest Rates

Interest rates have varied widely in recent decades. In the early 1980s, rates for a fixed-rate home mortgage reached 17 percent. In 2011 interest rates for the same mortgage fell to about 4 percent. For a $100,000 mortgage, this means a difference of more than $13,000 in the amount of interest paid each year. The lower rates also apply to rates banks paid depositors. In 1981, you could buy a CD that paid 14 percent per year. In 2011 few CDs paid more than 2 percent.

The changes in interest rates were caused primarily by actions taken by the Federal Reserve System. In the early 1980s, the Fed forced interest rates up to reduce demand and fight inflation. In 2011 the Fed forced interest rates to record lows to encourage spending and recovery in the economy.

Fed Actions

There are three actions the Fed can take with short-term interest rates. It can increase them, lower them, or keep them at current levels.

- An increase in interest rates is intended to discourage borrowing and spending while it encourages saving.
- A decrease in interest rates is intended to encourage borrowing and spending while it discourages saving.
- Leaving interest rates unchanged is intended to keep borrowing and spending steady and have little effect on saving.

Adjust to Changing Rates

As interest rates change, you need to adjust your spending and saving decisions.

- Suppose your mortgage has a high rate of interest. If interest rates decline enough, you should consider refinancing your loan to get a lower rate. Even after paying the costs of this transaction, refinancing could save you many thousands of dollars in the long run.
- When interest rates are abnormally high, consider placing any funds you have saved in a long-term deposit or investment to "lock in" these high rates.
- When interest rates are abnormally low, you should avoid making long-term deposits or investments that will continue to pay a low rate for many years.
- When interest rates are abnormally high, you should avoid taking out long-term loans unless you are able to renegotiate their interest rates in the future.

Keeping Up With the Fed's Plans

At one time, the Fed kept its plans for the immediate future secret. Federal Reserve governors believed that if the Fed told people what it planned to do, they would anticipate decisions so the decisions would then have less impact on the economy. However, the Fed now makes public reports of its decisions soon after they are made. It also announces its expectations for policy changes in the near future. By keeping up with the Fed's public statements, you will have a good idea about what is likely to happen to interest rates in the near future.

Apply the Skill

Imagine you have saved $30,000 that you plan to use for a down payment on a house. The Fed recently has increased interest rates by 2 percent. Would this make you more or less likely to buy a house now or wait until later? Explain your answer.

19.3 MONETARY POLICY IN THE LONG RUN

Learning Objectives

LO1 Understand why changes in the money supply affect only prices in the long run, not real GDP.

LO2 Examine the historical link between money supply growth and inflation.

LO3 Understand why political independence of central banks results in lower inflation.

LO4 Describe how the Fed responded to the Great Recession of 2008–2009.

Key Terms

euro 617
too big to fail 618
stress test 619

In Your World

In the short run, money influences aggregate demand and real GDP through its effect on interest rates. In the long run, the impact of money on aggregate demand is more direct. If the Fed increases the money supply, people will try to spend more. However, because the economy's potential output remains fixed at a point in time, this greater spending simply increases the price level in the long run. There is just more money chasing after the same output. Thus, if the economy is already producing its potential output, increases in the money supply result only in inflation in the long run.

LONG-RUN EFFECT OF MONEY SUPPLY CHANGES

LO1
Understand why changes in the money supply affect only prices in the long run, not real GDP.

Monetary authorities try to keep the economy on an even keel by smoothing fluctuations in the economy over the business cycle. These are based mostly on short-run adjustments in the federal funds rate. What happens in the long run?

Production in the Long Run

In the short run, the aggregate supply curve slopes upward. Thus, an increase in aggregate demand increases both real GDP and the price level, as was shown in Figure 19.4. In the long run, the economy produces its potential level of output, which is the economy's maximum sustainable output. Potential output is determined by the supply of resources in the economy, the state of technology, and the rules of the game that nurture production and exchange. Potential output is the economy's normal capability on a regular or sustained basis. The economy can't produce any more than potential output in the long run.

An increase in the money supply doesn't change potential output. An increase in the money supply means only that there is more money chasing after the same potential output.

FIGURE 19.6 Effect of an Increase in the Money Supply in the Long Run

An increase in the supply of money in the long run results in a higher price level, or inflation. Because the long-run aggregate supply curve is fixed at potential output, increases in the money supply affect only the price level, not real output.

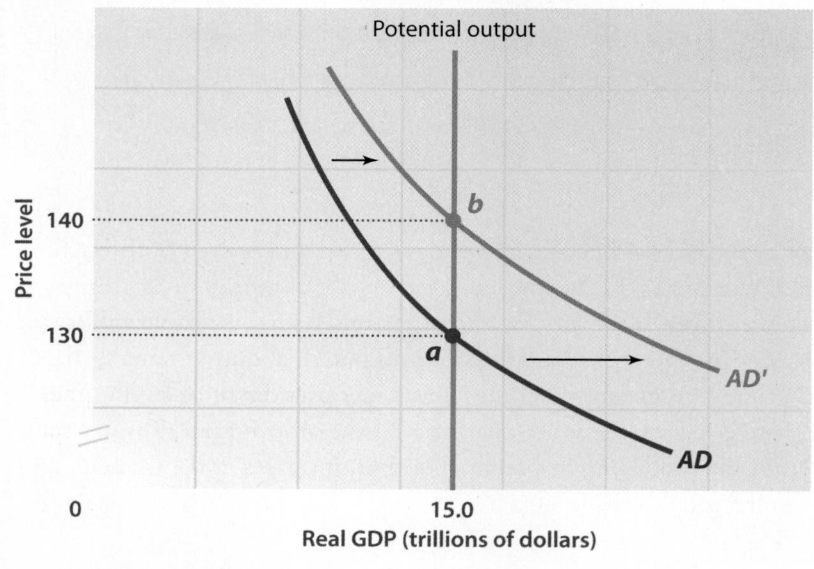

Changes in Aggregate Demand

The economy cannot produce more than its potential output in the long run, You could think of the economy's long-run supply curve as a vertical line drawn at the economy's potential level of output, as shown in Figure 19.6. That figure also shows the long-run effect of an increase in the money supply. An increase in the money supply causes a rightward shift of the aggregate demand curve from *AD* to *AD′*. Because output in the long run is fixed at the economy's potential output, the rightward shift of the aggregate demand curve leads only to a higher price level. Output remains unchanged at its potential level. The economy's potential output level is not affected by changes in the money supply. *In the long run, increases in the money supply result only in higher prices.*

Why do changes in the money supply affect only the price level in the long run, not real GDP?

LONG-RUN EVIDENCE OF MONEY AND INFLATION

LO2
Examine the historical link between money supply growth and inflation.

In the United States and around the world, what has been the long-run relationship between increases in the money supply and inflation?

Money Supply Growth and Inflation in U.S. History

Since the Federal Reserve System was established in 1913, the United States has suffered three bouts of high inflation. These periods occurred from 1913 to 1920, 1939 to 1948, and 1967 to 1981. Each U.S. episode of high inflation was related to a rapid growth in the money supply.

Money Supply Growth and Inflation Around the World

What has been the link around the world between changes in the money supply and inflation in the long run? Again, monetary theory points to a relationship in the long run between the percent change in the money supply and the percent change in the price level. Figure 19.7 illustrates this using the average annual growth rate in M2 over a 10-year period, and the average annual inflation rate during that same period, for dozens of countries around the world. As you can see, the points fall rather neatly along the line, showing a positive relation between money growth, measured along the horizontal axis, and inflation, measured along the vertical axis.

Extremely high inflation, or *hyperinflation*, became a problem for some countries. In every case, hyperinflation has been accompanied by extremely rapid growth in the supply of paper money. For example, Argentina—which had the highest average annual inflation rate over the 10-year period in the sample, at 395 percent—also had the highest average annual growth rate in the money supply, at 369 percent. Note more generally that several Latin American countries had problems with hyperinflation during the period.

These countries all managed to tame inflation. Households in these countries, perhaps mindful of their experience with hyperinflation, still hoard a lot of U.S. currency. The latest victim of hyperinflation is Zimbabwe, where inflation in 2008 averaged 480 percent per month. Not surprisingly, Zimbabwe's currency collapsed, forcing all transactions to be conducted in foreign currencies, such as U.S. dollars.

Another famous hyperinflation during the past century was in Germany, between August 1922 and November 1923, when inflation averaged 322 percent per month. Inflation was halted when the German government created an independent central bank that issued a limited supply of new currency convertible on demand into gold.

FIGURE 19.7 Inflation and Money Growth Worldwide During the Decade of 1980–1990

Inflation was higher in countries where the money supply grew faster. Figures are annual averages between 1980 and 1990.

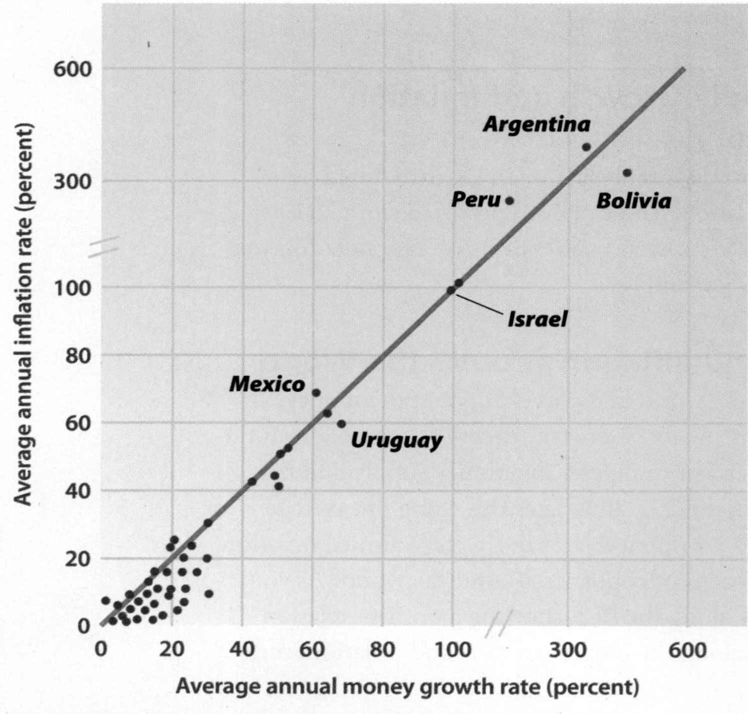

Source: The World Bank, *World Development Report 1992* (New York: Oxford University Press, 1992), Table 13.

CHECKPOINT What has been the link between money growth and inflation in the United States and around the world?

OTHER ISSUES IN MONETARY POLICY

LO3
Understand why political independence of central banks results in lower inflation.

Four issues remain with regard to monetary policy:

1. the relationship between inflation and the central bank's independence from political pressure,
2. the problem of deflation,
3. the lags involved with monetary policy, and
4. monetary policy during the Great Recession of 2008–2009.

Fed Independence

Some economists argue that the Fed would do better in the long run if it were committed to the single goal of price stability. To focus on price stability, a central bank would have to remain insulated from political pressure. Elected officials usually urge the Fed to stimulate the economy whenever it is performing below its potential. All this short-run stimulation, however, can lead to inflation in the long run.

Span the Globe

How Fake Money Saved Brazil

Twenty-five years ago, the inflation rate in Brazil reached 80 percent a month. That meant that if bread cost $1 one day, a month later it would cost $1.80. If the inflation rate remained at 80 percent per month for one year, a loaf of bread would cost $1,157 by year end. Stores were changing their prices every day. In grocery stores, a "sticker man" would walk the aisles putting new prices on food, as customers ran ahead of him trying to buy their food at the previous day's prices.

The inflationary spiral began in the 1950s, when the Brazilian government printed money to build a new capital in Brasilia. Despite the efforts of successive governments, inflation continued for decades. When a new finance minister was appointed in 1992, he called on Edmar Bacha who, along with three of his Yale graduate school buddies, had been studying Brazilian inflation.

For Bacha and his friends, the solution was twofold: slow down the creation of money and restore the people's faith in it. To do this, they wanted to trick people into believing their money would hold its value. Part of the illusion involved the creation of a new fake currency—there would be no coins or bills. They called this fake money a "Unit of Real Value," or URV. It was a virtual currency.

The sleight of hand occurred in that, while people would still use Brazil's existing currency, the *cruzeiro*, prices, wages and taxes would be listed in the fake currency or URVs, which would be kept stable. The only thing that changed would be how many *cruzeiros* each URV was worth. So, that loaf of bread, which now would be listed as 1 URV with a URV worth 5 *cruzeiros*, a month later would still be 1 URV, even though a URV might then be worth 9 *cruzeiros*. The success of the trick depended upon getting the Brazilian people to focus on URVs and not *cruzeiros*.

Like any good trick, it worked. Inflation did end as prices stabilized within six months. The government then declared that the virtual URV currency was now a real currency and the *cruzeiro* was going to disappear. The result set the foundation for additional reforms that turned Brazil's economy around.

Think Critically How did the creation of a new currency help the government implement its policy to control inflation?

Sources: "How Fake Money Saved Brazil," *All Things Considered*, National Public Radio, Robert Siegel and Mary Louise Kelly, hosts, October 4, 2010; Chana Joffe-Walt, "How Fake Money Saved Brazil," Planet Money Blog at http://www.npr.org/blogs/money/, October 4, 2010.

When the Fed was established in 1913, several features insulated it from politics, such as the 14-year terms with staggered appointments for the seven board governors. Also, the Fed does not rely on a Congressional appropriation. The Fed has its own source of income.

Here's how the Fed earns a profit. The Fed, like any other bank, has a balance sheet. More than one-half of the Fed's assets are U.S. government securities. The Fed bought them through open-market operations. They are IOUs from the federal government, and they earn interest for the Fed. The Fed also owns many other assets that earn interest.

More than one-third of the Fed's liabilities are Federal Reserve notes held by the public, These notes—U.S. currency—are IOUs from the Fed and are therefore liabilities of the Fed. However, the Fed pays no interest on Federal Reserve notes. One-half of the Fed's liabilities are reserves held for banks. The Fed pays no interest on required reserves and only a tiny amount of interest on excess reserves.

Most of the Fed's assets earn interest for the Fed. Nearly all of the Fed's liabilities require little or no interest payments by the Fed.

The Fed also earns income from various services it provides member banks. After covering its operating costs, the Fed turns over any remaining income to the U.S. Treasury. In 2010, the Fed turned over about $80 billion. You might think of this as profit resulting from the Fed's ability to issue notes and create bank reserves.

Central Bank Independence and Inflation

Does a central bank's independence from political pressure affect its performance? In one study, the central banks of 17 advanced industrial countries were ranked from least independent to most independent. It turned out that inflation during the 15-year span studied was lowest in countries with the most independent central banks and highest in countries with the least independent central bank. The U.S. central bank is considered relatively independent, and inflation here averaged about halfway between the most independent and least independent groups of banks.

Independence Trend

The trend around the world is toward greater central bank independence from political pressure. For example, Australia and New Zealand, two countries that had problems with inflation, amended laws governing their central banks to make price stability the primary goal. Chile, Colombia, and Argentina—developing countries that experienced hyperinflation—have legislated more central bank independence.

The framework that established the common European currency, the **euro**, identified price stability as the main objective of the new European Central Bank. That bank announced a policy of keeping inflation under 2 percent. In fact, the bank came under criticism for appearing reluctant to cut its target interest rate even though a recession loomed and the unemployment rate exceeded 8 percent. The European Central Bank feared that a cut in its target interest rate would fuel inflation.

Could Deflation Pose a Problem?

Hyperinflation can bring an economy to its knees. But deflation, a decline in the average price level, is no picnic either. Falling prices during the Great Depression caused consumers to delay major purchases, waiting for prices to drop even more. This reduced aggregate demand, output, and employment. Investment also tanked because lower prices erased profits. Further, borrowers found it more difficult to pay off their debts as their incomes fell.

In recent years, Japan has suffered from deflation averaging about 1 percent per year. Germany also feared deflation. Fed Chairman Ben Bernanke voiced concern about the possibility of deflation in the United States. He said the Fed would fight deflation as fiercely as it fights high inflation. Most economists, including Bernanke, don't think the nation will experience deflation. Regardless, you should know that deflation can create as much havoc in an economy as high inflation.

euro The European common currency

Falling prices in the housing market between 2007 and 2011 show how destabilizing deflation in that sector can be. In many cases, housing prices fell below the amount households still owed on the mortgage. A house worth less than the mortgage on it is said to be "under water" or "upside down." That development created an incentive for households to stop making mortgage payments and simply surrender the property to the bank. After all, why continue paying on a house that's worth less than what you still owe on it? As mortgage defaults grew, banks that extended

asiseeit/iStockphoto.com

Explain how deflation in the housing market between 2007 and 2011 prompted some homeowners to default on their mortgages.

these loans faced financial difficulties, and many went broke. Bank failures in the United States jumped from only 3 in 2007 to 157 in 2010.

Lags and Monetary Policy

Recall that one problem with fiscal policy involves lags at several stages of the process. How do the lags involved with monetary policy compare with those involved with fiscal policy?

The *recognition lag*, the time required to identify a problem with the economy, is probably about the same for both policies. Monetary and fiscal decision makers are each supported by a competent team of economists tracking the economy.

With regard to the *decision-making lag*, monetary policy has the advantage, because the FOMC can make a decision during one meeting. Once a decision is made, monetary policy also has the advantage because the FOMC can begin executing open-market operations within minutes. Fiscal policy may take months to implement, so the *implementation lag* is shorter for monetary policy, and that's an advantage.

Finally, with regard to the *effectiveness lag*, it may be a toss-up. Market interest rates can move quickly in response to a change in Fed policy, but there is no way to know how long it will take businesses and consumers to react to changed interest rates. The full effect of changes in the money supply may take a year or more, about as long as it may take fiscal policy to show its full effects.

CHECKPOINT **What is the relationship between inflation and the political independence of central banks?**

MONETARY POLICY DURING THE GREAT RECESSION OF 2008–2009

LO4 Describe how the Fed responded to the Great Recession of 2008–2009.

In response to the Great Recession of 2008–2009, the Fed influenced financial markets in a variety of other ways. You already learned about the Fed's reduction of the federal funds rate to record low levels as a way to stimulate aggregate demand. Here are some other measures undertaken by the Fed to ease the flow of credit and calm the financial panic during that troubled period. The Fed:

too big to fail A financial institution becomes so large and so interconnected with other financial institutions that its failure would be a disaster for the wider economy

1. Invested billions in AIG, a giant insurer considered **too big to fail** because it was so interconnected with other financial institutions that its collapse would trigger a cascade of other business failures
2. Invested more than $1 trillion in securities that financed home mortgages to keep mortgage rates low and offer liquidity to a market in turmoil

3. Worked with the U.S. Treasury and with other regulators to stabilize banks and thaw frozen credit lines, and
4. Helped conduct a **stress test** of the 19 largest banks to determine which ones needed to raise more financial capital to weather a bad economy.

All these efforts could be summed up as the *Fed trying to do whatever was necessary to keep financial markets from freezing up and to stabilize the economy.* Critics charged that the Fed was bailing out those same financial institutions that created most of the problems in the first place. Chairman Bernanke responded that the Fed tried to protect workers and consumers, who would be hurt most by a collapse of the financial system. He also noted that the Fed's investments that seemed like bailouts actually paid off well enough that the Fed sent $80 billion in "profit" to the U.S. treasury in 2010. Fed officials did not want a repeat of the Great Depression, when they dropped the ball by not supplying the liquidity that the banking system needed. Some 10,000 banks failed during the Great Depression.

stress test Bank regulators assessed the soundness of large banks to determine which ones needed more financial capital to weather a bad economy

How did the Fed respond to the Great Recession of 2008–2009? **CHECKPOINT**

Photos: Shutterstock.com; business people: Yuri Arcurs; conveyor belt: Stephen Mahar; shopper: Yuri Arcurs

ESSENTIAL QUESTION

Standard CEE 20: Monetary Policy

The Federal Reserve System's monetary policy influences the overall levels of employment, output, and prices.

What aspects of the U.S. economy does monetary policy influence?

19.3 ASSESSMENT

Think Critically

1. If the Fed attempted to keep the unemployment rate at 3 percent by increasing the money supply year after year, what would happen to prices? Would the Fed be successful in reaching its goal in the long run? Why, or why not?
2. Why would deflation be harmful to the economy?
3. Why might it take many months or possibly more than a year for people and businesses to respond to a change in the money supply? What does this tell you about the usefulness of monetary policy?

Graphing Exercise

4. Use data in the table to create a double line graph of interest rates and changes in real GDP from 2000 through 2010. Does there seem to be a relationship between these values? Which do you think is the cause and which is the effect? Explain your answer.

ANNUAL INTEREST RATES ON 3-YEAR GOVERNMENT BONDS AND ANNUAL CHANGE IN REAL GDP, 2000–2010

Year	Interest Rate on 3-Year Government Securities	Percentage Growth in Real GDP
2000	6.22%	4.1%
2001	4.09%	1.1%
2002	3.10%	1.8%
2003	2.10%	2.5%
2004	2.78%	3.5%
2005	6.19%	3.1%
2006	7.96%	2.7%
2007	8.06%	1.9%
2008	5.09%	−0.3%
2009	3.25%	−3.5%
2010	3.25%	3.0%

Source: Interest rates are from *Economic Indicators*, August 2011, p. 30. GDP growth rates are from the U.S. Bureau of Economic Analysis at http://bea.gov/national/index.htm#gdp.

Make Academic Connections

5. **Management** Business owners cannot be sure what the Fed's policy will be in the future. Wrong guesses could have devastating effects. In 1978, the owners of a small steel mill borrowed $50 million to purchase new equipment. They agreed to pay a flexible rate of interest set at the prime rate plus 1 percent. The prime rate in 1978 was 8 percent. Three years later, actions of the Federal Reserve System had spiked the prime rate to 20 percent, forcing the steel mill to pay 21 percent interest on its loan. The firm was unable to make these payments and in 1983 went bankrupt. If you owned a firm and were considering borrowing funds, how concerned would you be with the future course of monetary policy?

TeamWork

As a team, consider the following situation. You own a flooring store and would like to open a new branch in another town. To do so, you need to borrow $2 million to be repaid over 10 years. Last year, you earned just over $500,000 in profit, so you believe that repaying the loan would not be a financial hardship for your business. Make a list of things that might possibly go wrong over the next year that could make it difficult to make payments on your loan. How could the Fed reassure you to borrow the money and make the investment? Compare your team's answers with those of other groups.

Connect to History

Deflation in the Nineteenth Century

Following the Civil War, prices in the United States, especially for agricultural products, began to decline. In the decade following 1866, wheat prices dropped from $2.06 a bushel to $1.00. Fifteen years later, farmers received only 60 cents a bushel for wheat. Over the same period, corn prices dropped from 66 cents a bushel to 30 cents. Prices declined in part due to the introduction of new techniques and equipment. Farmers became more productive, thus supply increased faster than demand. Farmers, however, wanted higher prices for their crops. Many had run up debts to buy or expand farms, to buy equipment, or to support themselves after a bad year. While the cost of repaying their loans remained the same, lower crop prices meant they had to produce more to earn enough money to make the payments.

Farmers saw one solution to their problem in the government's issuance of Greenbacks, or paper money the government had issued during the Civil War. Greenbacks had no backing in gold or silver. After the War, the government had been withdrawing Greenbacks, thereby leaving less money in circulation. This resulted in fewer dollars chasing more goods, thus lower prices. Farmers wanted the government to issue as many Greenbacks as it took to raise prices. This idea was so appealing that a political party—the Greenback Party—formed around it. However, business interests opposed this solution, and most politicians pursued a policy of "sound money."

In 1873 the government passed the Coinage Act, which said that the government would no longer buy silver to turn into coins. The cost of silver was more than the government was willing to pay. Farmers were outraged because they believed more silver purchases would increase the money supply, resulting in inflation and higher prices for their products. Farmers and now silver miners, referring to the Act as the "Crime of '73," demanded the government to resume buying and coining silver. The government responded by passing the Bland Allison Act (1878) and the Sherman Silver Purchase Act (1890). These acts authorized a limited amount of silver to be purchased and turned into coins. Neither act created the inflation the farmers and silver miners desired.

In the election of 1896, which pitted William Jennings Bryan for the Democratic and Populist parties against Republican William McKinley, a major issue was the gold standard. Bryan argued against the government policy and demanded an increased money supply. Despite his defeat, Bryan's "cross of gold" speech stands as one of the most famous in American history. However, by the turn of the century, the farmers got their wish, and prices stopped declining. This had nothing to do with their efforts to change government policy, however. Additional deposits of gold were discovered in Alaska and other parts of the world that doubled the world's supply of gold.

Think Critically **Write a paragraph to explain the effect deflation had on farmers' incomes and their ability to meet their fixed costs (mortgages, etc.). Assume that farmers' incomes and fixed costs are both $1,000 and that there is 10 percent deflation each year. What would the deflation do to a farmer's ability to meet his debts? Next, assume income and fixed costs of $1,000 and a 10 percent inflation rate. What would this do to the farmer's ability to meet his debts? In what way is the homebuyer of today similar to the farmer of the late 1800s?**

Chapter 19 Summary

19.1 How Banks Work

A. To establish a bank, a group of people must obtain a charter from either the federal or a state government. The bank will report its financial status on a balance sheet, which lists its assets on one side and its liabilities and the amount of the owners' equity on the other. The totals on both sides must be equal. Under the fractional reserve system, banks are required to maintain a fraction of checkable deposits on reserve.

B. New funds deposited in a bank can be multiplied by the banking system into a large increase in total deposits over time. When the Fed buys a bond from a bank or the public, the money paid is new to the economy. The bond purchase increases excess reserves, which the bank can lend. When the borrower spends the checkable deposit, the money is received by someone else, who usually deposits it back into a bank. That bank then can make additional loans based on excess reserves. This cycle of deposits, excess reserves, loans, spending, and more deposits can be repeated, causing the money supply to grow.

C. The money multiplier is limited by the required reserve ratio. When banks are required to keep more deposits on reserve, they are less able to make loans.

ASK THE EXPERT

www.cengage.com/school/contecon

Why should we care how fast the money supply grows?

19.2 Monetary Policy in the Short Run

A. People demand money (1) to carry out financial transactions and (2) to have on hand as a store of value. The amount they wish to hold at any time depends on many factors, including the market interest rate, which is the opportunity cost of holding money.

B. The Federal Reserve System controls the supply of money to the economy. The money supply can be viewed as independent of the interest rate. The intersection of demand for money with the supply of money determines the market interest rate in the economy. An increase in the money supply leads to a lower interest rate while a decrease in the money supply causes the interest rate to rise. Lower interest rates stimulate the economy in the short run while higher rates slow its growth.

C. The Fed targets the federal funds rate, which is the rate banks charge each other for borrowing bank reserves. When the Fed changes the federal funds rate, most other interest rates change, too.

19.3 Monetary Policy in the Long Run

A. Production in the long run cannot be sustained above the economy's potential. Efforts to expand aggregate demand and production beyond potential output can succeed in the short run. In the long run trying to push output beyond the economy's potential leads to inflation.

B. Most nations have a monetary authority similar to the Fed. In some nations, it is independent of the political process. In others, it is controlled by politicians. Inflation rates tend to be higher in nations where the monetary authority is controlled by politicians.

C. Deflation creates instability because falling price levels cause consumers to delay major purchases and cause businesses to put off investments.

D. There are lags in the effectiveness of monetary policy. It takes time for the Fed to recognize a problem, and for the economy to respond to the changed policy.

E. During the Great Recession, the Fed executed policies to unfreeze credit markets and restore financial stability.

CHAPTER 19 ASSESSMENT

Review Economic Terms

Match the terms with the definitions. Some terms will not be used.

_____ 1. Bank reserves in excess of required reserves

_____ 2. The stock of money available in the economy at a particular time

_____ 3. Any physical property or financial claim that is owned

_____ 4. The dollar amount of deposits that a bank must hold in reserves

_____ 5. The interest rate charged in the federal funds market

_____ 6. Bank regulators assessed the soundness of large banks to determine which ones needed more financial capital to weather a bad economy

_____ 7. A Fed regulation that dictates the minimum fraction of deposits each bank must keep in reserve

_____ 8. A financial statement showing assets, liabilities, and net worth at a point in time

_____ 9. An amount owed

_____ 10. The multiple by which the money supply increases as a result of an increase in excess reserves in the banking system

a. asset
b. balance sheet
c. euro
d. excess reserves
e. federal funds market
f. federal funds rate
g. liability
h. money demand
i. money multiplier
j. money supply
k. net worth
l. required reserve ratio
m. required reserves
n. stress test
o. too big to fail

Review Economic Concepts

11. **True or False** Anyone who has enough money has the legal right to start a banking business.

12. A bank's balance sheet lists its assets on one side and its liabilities and the amount of the owner's ________?________ on the other.

13. The required reserve ratio is the
    a. amount of money a bank's owners must invest in the bank.
    b. share of its deposits that a bank may lend.
    c. amount of its deposits that a bank must hold on reserve.
    d. fraction of its deposits that a bank must hold on reserve.

14. **True or False** If the Fed bought a $100,000 government bond from a bank, the money supply would immediately grow by more than $100,000.

15. If the Fed lowered the required reserve ratio from 10 percent to 8 percent, the money ________?________ would increase from 10 to 12.5.

16. If people choose to hold a smaller share of income they receive in cash and deposit more of their earnings in checking accounts, the money expansion will be
    a. greater than it was in the past.
    b. the same as it was in the past.
    c. smaller than it was in the past.
    d. carried out more slowly than it was in the past.

17. **True or False** The demand for money is a measure of a stock. It shows the quantity of money people demand at various interest rates.

18. Which of the following events would reduce the impact of the money multiplier?
   a. The Fed purchases additional government bonds.
   b. Banks allow excess reserves to sit idly in the bank vault.
   c. The Fed lowers the required reserve ratio.
   d. The federal government borrows and spends more money.

19. If the Fed increases the money supply, the demand curve for money will
   a. remain unchanged.
   b. immediately shift to the right.
   c. immediately shift to the left.
   d. eventually shift to the left.

20. **True or False** The opportunity cost of holding cash is the interest that could have been earned but is forgone.

21. Lower interest rates stimulate the economy, while higher rates slow its ________?________

22. The Fed could increase interest rates by
   a. buying additional government bonds.
   b. lowering the required reserve ratio.
   c. lowering the discount rate.
   d. selling some of its government bonds.

23. The Fed's interest rate target is ________?________

24. **True or False** Inflation is likely to occur if the Fed increases the money supply when the economy is already at its potential level of output.

25. By increasing the money supply, the Fed can sometimes
   a. increase output beyond the economy's potential in the short run.
   b. increase output beyond its potential in the long run.
   c. decrease output to its potential in the short run.
   d. decrease output below its potential in the long run.

26. Countries that have experienced high rates of inflation also have usually had
   a. totalitarian forms of government.
   b. independent monetary authorities.
   c. rapid growth in their money supplies.
   d. large government budget surpluses.

27. ________?________ may result from a decline in aggregate demand that forces the price level to fall.

Apply Economic Concepts

28. **Calculate the Impact of a Change in the Reserve Ratio** Suppose that the Fed decided to increase the reserve ratio from 10 to 12.5 percent. How would this change the value of the money multiplier? What would this do to the amount of each checking deposit that banks could lend? How would this decision affect interest rates and the economy? Explain your answer.

29. **Decide How Much Cash to Hold** Imagine that it is 10 years in the future. You are married and have two young children. Every month you pay $800 for your rent, $300 for your car loan, and at least $1,900 in other costs of living. You are trying to save $300 from every paycheck to make a down payment on a house in a few years. You earn a salary that provides you with a take-home pay of $2,000 every two weeks. Your savings account currently pays 2 percent interest. How much of your biweekly pay would you take in cash, deposit in your checking account, and put in your saving account? How would your decision change if the interest rate on your saving account increased to 10 percent?

30. **Choose When to Borrow** Imagine that you have a job that pays you a good wage. You have decided to borrow $20,000 to buy a new car. The current interest rate on a new-car loan is 6 percent. You have read in the newspaper that the Fed is likely to lower interest rates soon because many workers are being laid off and unemployment is on the rise. You believe that if you wait a few months, you might be able to borrow the money you need at only 4 percent interest. Should you buy the car now or wait for lower interest rates? What else should concern you? Explain your answers.

31. **21st Century Skills: Flexibility and Adaptability** When you bought your home five years ago you took out a 30-year mortgage for $150,000 at 6 percent interest. Since then interest rates for mortgages have fallen to 4.5 percent. What could you do to reduce your monthly mortgage payments? What costs would you pay to do this?

32. **Construct a Graph of Demand and Supply for Money** The hypothetical data in the table represent the demand and supply for money in the U.S. economy. Construct a graph from these data, What is the equilibrium interest rate in this example? What are two events that might cause the equilibrium interest rate to increase? What are two events that might cause the equilibrium interest rate to fall?

DEMAND AND SUPPLY FOR MONEY (IN BILLIONS)

Amount Demanded	Amount Supplied	Interest Rate
$ 500	$1,000	10.0%
$ 750	$1,000	8.0%
$ 1,000	$1,000	6.0%
$ 1,250	$1,000	4.0%
$ 1,500	$1,000	2.0%

33. **Diagram the Check-Clearing Process** When you deposit your paycheck into your bank account, the check must clear before your bank will credit funds for your use into your account. Here are the steps that take place.

- You deposit your check for $250 in Bank ABC. The check was drawn on Bank XYZ, which is located in a different community in your state.
- Your bank tentatively credits your account for $250 and sends the check to the nearest Federal Reserve Bank.
- The Federal Reserve Bank credits Bank ABC's account for $250 and deducts this amount from Bank XYZ's account.
- The Federal Reserve Bank sends the cancelled check to Bank XYZ, which will draw down your employer's checkable deposits by the amount of the check, keep a record of the check, and possibly send the cancelled check to your employer. After receiving the funds from Bank XYZ, your bank makes those funds available in your checking account.

Draw and label a diagram to show this process.

Digging Deeper

with Economics e-Collection

Access the Gale Economics e-Collection through the URL below. Find an article that discusses a recent action taken by the Federal Reserve. Actions taken might include purchase of government securities or changes to the money supply, the discount rate, or the required reserve ratio. Describe the action in a paragraph and prepare to discuss it in class.

www.cengage.com/school/contecon

Digital Vision/Getty Images

UNIT 7

The International Economy

Comparative advantage, specialization, and exchange help people get the most from their scarce resources. Despite the clear benefits from free international trade, trade restrictions date back centuries. Pressure from domestic producers on governments to erect trade barriers continues to this day. Still, the overall trend is towards fewer trade restrictions and freer trade. The United States plays a key role in the world economy, not only as the largest importer but also as one of the largest exporters. While the U.S. dollar remains the currency of choice in world trade, all nations face the challenge of achieving greater stability in their global finances.

CONSIDER ...

- If the United States is such a rich and productive nation, why do Americans import so many goods and services?
- Why isn't the United States self-sufficient?
- If free trade is such a good idea, why do many domestic producers try to restrict foreign trade?
- What's up with the euro?
- Is a growing U.S. trade deficit a growing worry?
- What figure guarantees that the balance-of-payments accounts do, in fact, balance?

CHAPTER 20

International Trade and Finance

Point your browser

www.cengage.com/school/contecon

©Simon Rawles/Almay; Background image: Dibrova/Shutterstock.com

20.1 BENEFITS OF TRADE

Learning Objectives

LO1 Identify sources of comparative advantage.

LO2 Discuss gains from trade, even without comparative advantage.

LO3 Describe important U.S. exports and imports.

Key Terms

world output 629

European Union (EU) 631

In Your World

This morning, you put on your Levi jeans made in Mexico, pulled on your Benetton sweater from Italy, and laced up your Timberland boots from China. After a breakfast that included bananas from Honduras and bacon from Canada, you strapped on your JanSport backpack from Indonesia and headed for school in a Swedish Volvo fueled by Venezuelan oil. The world is a giant shopping mall, and Americans are big spenders. Foreigners buy American products, too—products such as grain, personal computers, aircraft, movies, trips to Disney World, and thousands of other goods and services.

COMPARATIVE ADVANTAGE

LO1 Identify sources of comparative advantage.

Recall the discussion in Chapter 2 about how you and your neighbor could increase output by specializing. The law of comparative advantage says that the individual with the lowest opportunity cost of producing a particular good should specialize in that good. Just as individuals benefit from specialization and exchange, so do businesses, regions, and nations.

To reap the gains that arise from specialization, countries engage in international trade. *To maximize the benefits of trade, each country specializes in the goods that it produces at the lowest opportunity cost.* As a result, all countries can become better off than if each tried to go it alone. **World output**, the combined GDP of all nations in the world, increases when countries specialize. Because of the global financial crisis, world output, or world GDP, declined 0.7 percent in 2009. This was the first drop since 1946. World output rebounded to $74.4 trillion in 2010, a growth of 4.6 percent. The United States, which made up 5 percent of the world's population in 2010, accounted for 20 percent of world output. How does a country decide what to produce? In other words, how does it determine its comparative advantages? Trade based on comparative advantage is usually prompted by differences in the quantity and quality of resources across countries. These resources include labor and capital, soil and seasons, and mineral deposits.

world output The combined GDP of all nations in the world

How does a well-educated labor force benefit a country's economy?

Labor and Capital

Two key resources are labor and capital. Countries differ not only in their availability of labor and capital but also in the qualities of these resources. Countries with a well-educated and well-trained labor force specialize in products that require this talent—products such as medical breakthroughs and software development. Similarly, countries with state-of-the-art manufacturing technologies specialize in products that require high-tech capital—products such as precision equipment and lightning-fast computer chips.

Some countries, such as the United States and Japan, have an educated labor force and abundant high-tech capital. Both resources increase productivity per worker. This makes each nation quite competitive globally in producing goods that require skilled labor and technologically advanced capital.

Soil and Seasons

Some countries are blessed with fertile soil and favorable growing seasons. The United States, for example, has been called the "bread basket of the world." The country's rich farmland is ideal for growing corn, wheat, and other grains. Coffee grows best in the climate and elevation available in Colombia, Brazil, and Jamaica. Honduras has the ideal climate for growing bananas. Thus, the United States exports grain and imports coffee and bananas.

Seasonal differences across countries also create gains from trade. For example, during America's winter months, Americans buy fruit from Chile, and Canadians travel to Florida for sun and fun. During the summer months, Americans sell Chileans fruit and Americans travel to Canada for fishing and camping.

Mineral Deposits

Mineral resources often are concentrated in particular parts of the world, such as oil in Saudi Arabia, uranium in Australia, and diamonds in South Africa. The United States has abundant coal deposits but not enough oil to satisfy domestic demand. Thus, the United States exports coal and imports oil.

In summary, countries export what they can produce at the lowest opportunity cost and import what other countries can produce at the lowest opportunity cost. As a result of this trade, all countries can produce and consume more. Countries increase their consumption possibilities.

What are the sources of a country's comparative advantage? **CHECKPOINT**

OTHER REASONS FOR TRADE

LO2 Discuss gains from trade, even without comparative advantage.

If each country had identical labor and capital, soil and seasons, and mineral deposits, and each country combined those resources with equal efficiency, then there would be no comparative advantage. Yet, even then, international trade could still benefit all participants. Here are two reasons why.

Economies of Scale

If their producers experience *economies of scale*—that is, if the average cost of output declines as a firm expands its scale of production—countries can gain from specialization and trade. Such specialization allows firms in each nation to increase output enough to experience economies of scale. For example, one country can make computer chips, which are sold to many countries, and another country can make cars, which are sold to many countries.

The **European Union**, or **EU**, consists of 27 nations joined to enhance economic cooperation. A primary reason for establishing one single market in Europe was to offer producers there a large, open market of more than 500 million consumers. European producers have been able to increase production, experience economies of scale, and sell for less. In the process, these producers also become more competitive sellers outside of Europe.

Differences in Tastes

Even without comparative advantage or economies of scale, countries can gain from trade as long as tastes differ across countries. Consumption patterns do differ across countries, and some of these differences likely stem from differences in tastes. For example, the Danes eat twice as much pork as Americans do. Americans eat twice as much chicken as Hungarians do.

Soft drinks are four times more popular in the United States than in Western Europe. The English like tea. Americans like coffee. Algeria has an ideal climate for growing grapes, but its large Muslim population abstains from alcohol. Thus, Algeria exports wine.

Comparative advantage stimulates trade, but countries still may benefit from international trade even if all countries have identical resources and even if all countries produce with identical efficiency.

European Union (EU)
Twenty-seven nations joined to enhance economic cooperation

How could countries benefit from trade even if there is no comparative advantage? **CHECKPOINT**

Investigate Your Local Economy

Research to find an example of a good or service produced in your local economy that is exported. If possible, find out the annual dollar value of the exported good or service. Share your results in class.

U.S. EXPORTS AND IMPORTS

LO3 Describe important U.S. exports and imports.

Countries trade with one another—or, more precisely, people, firms, and governments in one country trade with those in another—because each side expects to gain from the exchange. Traders expect to increase their consumption possibilities.

U.S. Exports

Just as some states are more involved in interstate trade than others, some nations are more involved in international trade than others. For example, exports account for about one-quarter of the gross domestic product (GDP) in Canada and the United Kingdom; about one-third of the GDP in Germany, Sweden, and Switzerland; and about one-half of the GDP in the Netherlands. Despite the perception that Japan has a giant export sector, exports there make up only about one-seventh of GDP.

In the United States, exports of goods and services amounted to 13 percent of GDP in 2010. Although a small share compared to most other countries, exports play a growing role in the U.S. economy.

The left-hand panel of Figure 20.1 shows the composition of U.S. exports by major category in 2010. Services accounted for the largest share of U.S. exports, at 31 percent of the total. U.S. service exports include air transportation, insurance,

FIGURE 20.1 Composition of U.S. Exports and Imports in 2010

Services are the largest category of U.S. exports, while industrial supplies and materials, including crude oil, are the largest category of imports.

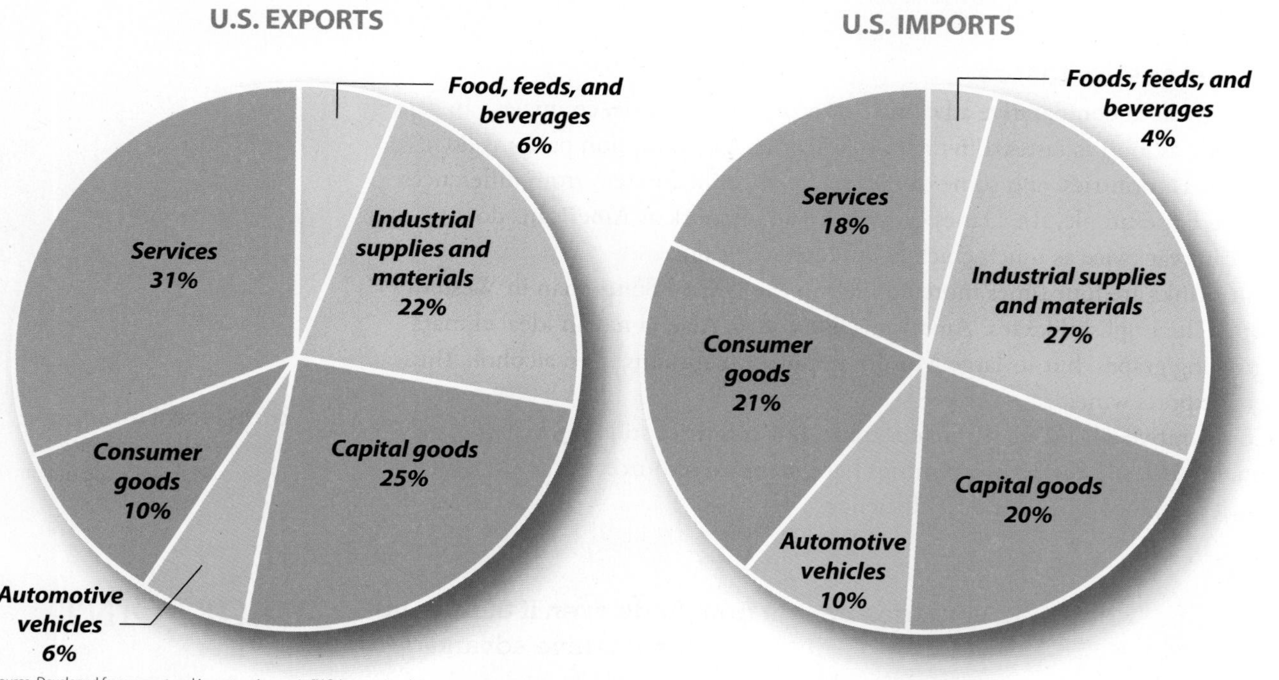

Source: Developed from export and import estimates in "U.S. International Transactions," Survey of Current Business, U.S. Department of Commerce, April 2011, Table F.1. p. D-62.

ESSENTIAL QUESTION

Standard CEE 5: Trade

Voluntary exchange occurs only when all participating parties expect to gain. This is true for trade among individuals or organizations within a nation, and among individuals or organizations in different nations.

Photos: Shutterstock.com; farmer: Darrin Henry; woman: Elena Elisseeva

Who benefits from the international trade of coffee beans?

banking, higher education, consulting, and tourism. Capital goods ranked second at 25 percent of all exports. Capital goods include high-tech products, such as computers and jet aircraft. Next most important is industrial supplies and materials, at 22 percent of the total, with chemicals and plastics leading the category. Together, capital goods and industrial supplies and material made up 47 percent of U.S. exports. So nearly one-half of U.S. exports in 2010 helped foreign manufacturers make things.

U.S. Imports

Americans spend more on imports than foreigners spend on U.S. exports. *U.S. imports of goods and services were 16 percent relative to GDP in 2010.* The right-hand panel of Figure 20.1 breaks out the composition of U.S. imports. The largest category, accounting for 27 percent of U.S. imports, is industrial supplies and material, which includes crude oil. The dollar value of this category more than doubled between 2000 and 2010, due to a spike in crude oil prices. Whereas consumer goods accounted for only 10 percent of U.S. exports, they are the second largest category of U.S. imports at 21 percent of the total. Imported consumer goods include electronics from Taiwan, shoes from Brazil, and kitchen gadgets from China. The next most important category of imports is capital goods, at 20 percent of the total, such as printing presses from Germany.

The top 10 destinations in 2010 for U.S. goods in order of importance are Canada, Mexico, China, Japan, United Kingdom, Germany, South Korea, Brazil, Netherlands, and Singapore. The top 10 sources of U.S. imports in order of importance are China, Canada, Mexico, Japan, Germany, United Kingdom, South Korea, France, Taiwan, and Ireland.

CHECKPOINT

What are the most important categories of U.S. exports and imports?

20.1 ASSESSMENT

Think Critically

1. Why does the United States have a comparative advantage over Chile selling apples during September and October, while Chile enjoys a similar comparative advantage over the United States during the months of March and April?
2. Why wouldn't acquiring the most advanced technology necessarily provide a nation with a comparative advantage relative to other nations?
3. In China, most people consider chicken feet a delicacy. How does this give nations in which people who do not share this taste an export opportunity?
4. In wealthy nations there is a larger proportion of imported goods consumed than in poorer nations. Why do you think this is so?
5. Why doesn't it make sense for the United States to try to export coffee or bananas?

Graphing Exercise

6. One of the most important categories of goods imported into the United States is energy in the form of oil and natural gas. Use data in the table to construct a line graph that shows changes in the value of these imports from 2005 through 2009. Although the value of imported oil and gas fluctuated and finally increased by more than 26 percent over these years, the actual amounts of these products that were imported grew by only about 8 percent over these years. Explain how this was possible.

VALUE OF OIL AND NATURAL GAS IMPORTS, 2005–2009

Year	Value of Oil and Natural Gas Imports (In Millions of Dollars)
2005	$ 48,725
2006	$ 61,758
2007	$ 69,394
2008	$ 104,091
2009	$ 61,700

Source: *Statistical Abstract of the United States, 2009* and *2011*, p. 787 and p. 804, respectively.

Make Academic Connections

7. **Biology** In recent years, genetically engineered foods have been developed and marketed in the United States. These products include tomatoes that are firmer and easier to ship, corn and wheat more resistant to fungal diseases, and fruit that can be stored longer without spoiling. It would be reasonable to assume that the development of these products would give the U.S. a comparative advantage over nations that do not grow genetically engineered foods. Investigate these products to see whether this assumption is accurate. What do you find? Why does a comparative advantage benefit a nation only when there is a willingness by potential customers to purchase the product?

TeamWork

Working in small teams, brainstorm a list of examples of specific products imported from the top 10 sources of U.S. imports: China, Canada, Mexico, Japan, Germany, United Kingdom, South Korea, France, Taiwan, and Ireland. Use the Internet to confirm your lists. Present your team's list of examples in class.

21st Century Skills

Productivity and Accountability

Find a Better Deal

Trade among nations in the 21st century will affect how consumers shop and the way businesses produce goods and services. The results of this can be seen in the U.S. economy today. In the United States, it is almost impossible to purchase a truly American-Made vehicle. When you buy a GMC or Ford product, for example, some of the parts used in its manufacture will be imported from other nations. When the earthquake of March 2011 interrupted production in Japan, a factory in Louisiana that produced GMC trucks was temporarily closed because it couldn't get needed parts from suppliers in Japan.

Businesses buy products from, or produce products in, other countries because they believe it will help them control their costs of production. Consider the following reasons an American business might choose to buy foreign products or produce products in a foreign nation.

- There might be lower labor costs in the foreign nation.
- There might be cheaper power or abundant natural resources in the foreign nation.
- There might be lower taxes in the foreign nation.
- There might be less strict environmental regulations in the foreign nation.
- There might be lower transportation costs for products produced and sold in foreign nations.

Effects of Buying Foreign Products

There are many ways in which the U.S. economy is affected when American consumers or businesses purchase products made in other nations. These include:

- Foreign competitors that have lower costs of production and, therefore, offer lower prices, may harm some U.S. producers and workers.
- U.S. consumers may be able to purchase imported goods at lower prices than those marketed by U.S. firms. This leaves consumers with more money for other purposes.
- Some U.S. workers and businesses benefit from being able to distribute and market foreign products in this country.
- The U.S. government may receive less tax revenue from those hurt by foreign competition, while at the same time it has a greater responsibility to help them.

Weigh Benefits and Costs

When you shop, there are many factors you may evaluate before you make a purchase. Clearly you should look for the best quality products that are priced at a level you are willing and able to pay. In the 21st century, you will find that many of these products have been imported. Should you ignore where products were manufactured or should you make an effort to purchase goods and services that were made in the United States when possible? Do you feel any sense of responsibility or accountability to "buy American." If you do, you will find that this personal choice will make your shopping experience more of a challenge.

Apply the Skill

Choose a type of apparel you would like to buy. Briefly describe your preferences—the design, color, and fabric you are looking for. Now go shopping either in a store or online to find three different examples of the product sold by different retailers. Is it easy for you to determine whether the garment was manufactured in the United States unless you go to a store to read its labels? If you find that one or all of the products you identify were manufactured in other countries, will this fact affect your buying decision? Explain why or why not.

20.2 TRADE RESTRICTIONS AND FREE-TRADE AGREEMENTS

Key Terms

Learning Objectives

LO1 Identify the two key trade restrictions and evaluate their affect on U.S. prices.

LO2 Explain why nations seek free-trade agreements.

In Your World

International trade expands your consumption possibilities and increases your standard of living. Despite the benefits of free trade, nearly all countries, at one time or another, have erected trade barriers across national borders. Trade restrictions usually benefit some domestic producers but harm you and other domestic consumers. The losses to consumers typically exceed the gains to producers. If free trade is such a good deal, why do most nations restrict it? Producer groups are well organized and are able to encourage governments to restrict imports. You and other consumers are disorganized and don't realize that trade restrictions increase many of the prices you pay. The good news is that trade restrictions are diminishing around the world.

TRADE RESTRICTIONS

LO1
Identify the two key trade restrictions and evaluate their affect on U.S. prices.

For an internationally traded good, such as wheat, oil, gold, or steel, a price is established on the world market. The **world price** of any product is determined by world supply and world demand. With free trade, any U.S. consumer can buy any amount desired at the world price.

Tariffs

U.S. producers would like to be able to sell their products in the United States for more than the world price. To achieve this, they often try to persuade legislators to restrict competition from abroad. One way the government can put foreign producers at a disadvantage is to impose a tariff on imports. Simply put, a **tariff** is a tax on imports. The tariff reduces the quantity of imports supplied. With fewer imports, the supply of goods to the U.S. market declines, so the price goes up. As a result, U.S. producers get to sell their products in the U.S. market for more than the world price. A tariff on U.S. imports benefits U.S. makers of those products. However, a tariff harms U.S consumers, who must pay that higher price. The harm to U.S. consumers exceeds any possible gain to U.S. producers. The revenue from tariffs goes to the government.

world price The price at which a good is traded internationally; determined by the world supply and world demand for the good

tariff A tax on imports

Quotas

Another way domestic producers try to limit foreign competition is by getting the government to impose import quotas. A **quota** is a legal limit on the amount of a particular commodity that can be imported. Quotas usually target imports from particular countries. For example, a quota may limit the quantity of automobiles from Japan or the quantity of shoes from Brazil. *By limiting imports, a quota reduces the supply in the U.S. market, which raises the U.S. price above the world price.* Again, this helps U.S. producers, but harms U.S. consumers. Foreign producers who get to sell their goods for the higher U.S. price also benefit.

Producer support for quotas, coupled with a lack of opposition from consumers (who remain mostly unaware of all this), has resulted in quotas that have lasted for decades. For example, sugar quotas have been in effect for more than eight decades. For the past three decades, U.S. sugar prices have averaged double the world price, costing U.S. consumers billions each year.

Tariffs and Quotas Compared

Consider the similarities and differences between a tariff and a quota. Both restrict supply, thereby increasing the domestic price, which hurts U.S. consumers and helps U.S. suppliers of those products. The primary difference is that the revenue from a tariff goes to the U.S. government, whereas the revenue from the quota goes to whoever has the right under the quota to sell foreign goods in the U.S. market. Usually the beneficiary of a quota is a foreign exporter.

Perhaps the worst part about tariffs and quotas is that foreign governments typically respond with tariffs and quotas of their own, thus hurting U.S. producers that sell abroad. This retaliation shrinks the U.S. export market, reducing specialization and exchange around the world.

Other Trade Restrictions

Besides tariffs and quotas, a variety of other measures restricts free trade. To promote exports, a country may provide subsidies to exporters or low-interest loans to foreign buyers. Some countries impose *domestic content requirements* specifying that at least some component of a final good must be produced domestically.

Other requirements concerning health, safety, or technical standards often discriminate against foreign goods. For example, some European countries restrict meat from hormone-fed cattle, a measure aimed at U.S. beef. Food purity laws in Germany prohibit many non-German beers.

Until the European Union adopted uniform standards, differing technical requirements forced manufacturers to offer as many as seven different models of the same TV set for that market. Sometimes exporters voluntarily limit exports, as when Japanese automakers agreed to cut exports to the United States. *The point is that tariffs and quotas are only two of many tools that restrict imports, raise prices, and reduce the benefits of specialization and comparative advantage.*

quota A legal limit on the quantity of a particular product that can be imported

Problems with Trade Restrictions

Trade restrictions raise a number of problems beyond the higher prices. The biggest one is that other countries often respond with trade restrictions of their own, thus shrinking the gains from trade. This can trigger still greater trade restrictions, and lead to an outright trade war as trade restrictions escalate.

Second, protecting one stage of production from international competition often requires protecting other stages of production. For example, protecting the U.S. textile industry from foreign competition raises the cost of cloth to U.S. garment makers. This reduces the competitiveness of U.S. garments compared to foreign ones. As a result, the domestic garment industry might need protection as well.

Third, the cost of protection also includes spending for lobbying fees, industry propaganda, and legal actions to secure and maintain this favorable treatment from government. All these outlays are, for the most part, a social waste, for they reduce competition but produce nothing besides trade restrictions.

A fourth problem with trade restrictions is the high transaction costs of enforcing quotas, tariffs, and other restrictions. The U.S. Customs Service operates 24 hours a day, 365 days a year, inspecting the luggage of more than 500 million people who enter the country each year via air, sea, and more than 300 border crossings. On highway I-35 in Laredo, Texas, for example, about 10,000 trucks roll in from Mexico every day. Policing and enforcement costs add up.

Span the Globe

Games with Trade Restrictions

Besides tariffs, there are more subtle ways to restrict trade. For example, a proposal by the United States aimed at protecting consumers would require that all companies importing into the United States have a U.S. representative. The proposal came after public outcry over the importation of defective Chinese drywall. It would burden importing companies with an additional layer of bureaucracy.

Some foreign producers and shippers find creative ways to get around trade restrictions. For example, because Nepal was not subject to a U.S. clothing quota but India was, Indian manufacturers would ship clothing to the United States through Nepal. To get around U.S. quotas on sugar imports, Brazil exports molasses to Canada, and it is then brought into the United States without a quota. The higher the tariffs and the stricter the quota, the more incentive foreign producers have to work around them.

Think Critically **What would happen if countries did not impose trade restrictions on imports?**

Source: James Cowan, "Is America Bringing Us Down?" *Canadian Business*, October 11, 2010.

Finally, research indicates that trade barriers slow the introduction of new goods and better technologies. So, rather than simply raising domestic prices and reducing the gains from specialization, trade restrictions also slow economic progress.

CHECKPOINT

What are the two main types of trade restrictions and how do they affect U.S. prices?

FREE-TRADE AGREEMENTS

LO2
Explain why nations seek free-trade agreements.

International trade arises from voluntary exchange among buyers and sellers pursuing their self-interest. Since 1950, world output has risen sevenfold, but world trade has increased seventeenfold. World trade offers many advantages to the trading countries. These include increased consumption possibilities, access to a greater variety of products around the world, lower costs through economies of scale, improved quality as a result of competitive pressure, and lower prices. Because of these advantages, the trend around the world is towards freer trade. One way to ensure freer trade is for nations to enter multilateral trade agreements. These are agreements entered into by more than two nations.

General Agreement on Tariffs and Trade (GATT)

Trade restrictions introduced during the Great Depression contributed to that economic disaster. To avoid a return to such dark times, after World War II the United States invited its trading partners to negotiate lower tariffs and quotas. The result was the **General Agreement on Tariffs and Trade (GATT)**, an international trade agreement adopted in 1947 by the United States and 22 other countries. Each signer of GATT agreed to reduce tariffs through multinational negotiations; reduce quotas; and treat all member nations equally with respect to trade.

Since then, a series of trade negotiations among many countries, called trade rounds, has continued to lower trade barriers. Trade rounds offer a package approach to trade negotiations rather than an issue-by-issue approach. A particular industry might object less to freer trade when it sees that other industries also agree to freer trade.

The most recent round of negotiations was completed in Uruguay in 1994. More than 140 countries signed this agreement, called the **Uruguay Round**. This was the most comprehensive of the eight multilateral trade rounds completed under GATT. The Uruguay Round phased in tariff reductions on 85 percent of world trade and will eventually eliminate quotas.

Figure 20.2 on page 640 shows tariff revenue as a percentage of the value of imported goods since 1821. You can see that tariffs have varied widely over time. Note that during the Great Depression of the 1930s, tariffs spiked. These high tariffs contributed to the global economic troubles of that period. Thanks to trade agreements such as the Uruguay Round, average tariffs are lower now than at any time in U.S. history.

General Agreement on Tariffs and Trade (GATT) An international tariff-reduction treaty adopted in 1947 that resulted in a series of negotiated "rounds" aimed at freer trade

Uruguay Round The most recently completed and most comprehensive of the eight postwar multilateral trade negotiations under GATT; created the World Trade Organization

FIGURE 20.2 U.S. Tariff Revenue as a Percentage of Merchandise Imports Since 1821

Over the years, tariffs have been up and down, spiking during the Great Depression. Overall, however, the trend after the Great Depression has been toward lower tariffs.

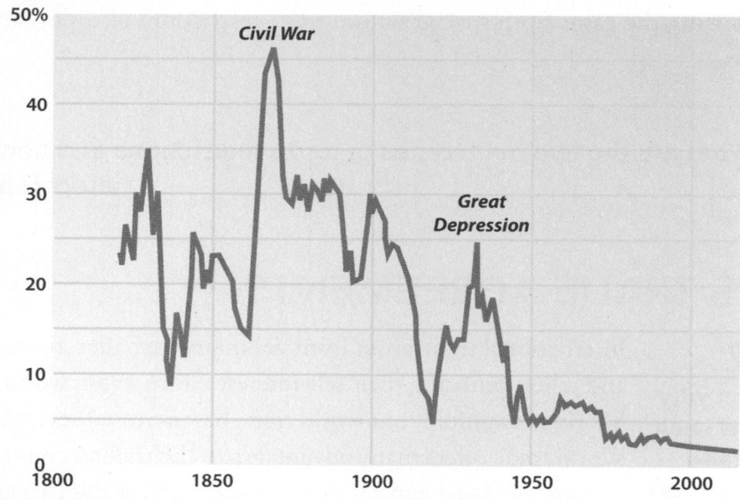

Source: 1821–1970: U.S. Dept. of Commerce, Bureau of Census, *Historical Statistics of the United States, Part 2, 1976*, and *Economic Report of the President*, February 2011, Table B-81.

World Trade Organization (WTO)

The Uruguay Round also created the World Trade Organization (WTO) as the successor to GATT. The **World Trade Organization (WTO)** now provides the legal and institutional foundation for world trade. GATT was a multilateral agreement with no staff or permanent location. The WTO is a permanent institution in Geneva, Switzerland, staffed mostly by economists. Whereas GATT involved only merchandise trade, the WTO also deals with services and intellectual property, such as books, movies, and software. The first round of WTO negotiations began in Doha, Qatar, in November 2001. The objective of the so-called **Doha Round** is to make trade fairer to developing countries by reducing barriers that harm their exports, especially agricultural products.

World Trade Organization (WTO) The legal and institutional foundation of the multilateral trading system that succeeded GATT in 1995

Doha Round The first trade round negotiated under the WTO; aims to help poorer countries by reducing barriers that harm their exports

Common Markets

Some countries have looked to the success of the U.S. economy, which is essentially a free-trade zone across 50 states, and have tried to develop free-trade zones of their own. The largest and best known is the European Union, which began in 1958 with six countries and had expanded to 27 by 2011. The idea was to create a barrier-free European market in which goods, services, people, and capital flow freely to their highest-valued use. Seventeen of the 27 members of the European Union have also adopted a common currency, the euro, which replaced national currencies in 2002.

The United States, Canada, and Mexico also have developed a free-trade pact called the North American Free Trade Agreement (NAFTA). Around the world, the trend is toward free-trade agreements.

CHECKPOINT

Why have nations signed free-trade agreements?

20.2 ASSESSMENT

Think Critically

1. Why do many fruit farmers in the United States think tariffs should be placed on fruit imported from South America and China? Whom would such tariffs benefit, and whom would they harm?
2. If a quota was placed on the number of automobiles that could be imported into the United States, how would U.S. consumers be affected?
3. Many nations require imported car models to be crash-tested before they can be marketed to consumers. They refuse to accept the results of crash tests performed in other countries. This process is expensive for firms involved in trade. How is such a requirement a barrier to trade? How are consumers in these nations affected by such laws?

Graphing Exercise

4. Nations are most likely to impose either tariffs or quotas on trade for products for which they do not have a comparative advantage. Study the data in the table, and use it to construct a double bar graph that shows the value of U.S. imports and exports for these classifications of goods. In which types of production would there have been the greatest pressure from U.S. businesses and labor organizations for the imposition of either tariffs or quotas? Explain your answer.

U.S. EXPORTS AND IMPORTS OF SELECTED COMMODITY GROUPS, 2010 (IN MILLIONS)

Commodity Group	Exports	Imports
1. Soybeans	$18,589	$220
2. Fruits and Vegetables	$15,712	$20,915
3. Clothing	$3,197	$78,518
4. Footwear	$728	$20,907
5. TVs, VCRs, etc.	$21,511	$137,305

Source: *Statistical Abstract of the United States: 2012*, p. 812.

Make Academic Connections

5. **Government** The creation of a free-trade organization requires a formal treaty. Approval of such treaties often involves political issues that go beyond economic considerations. The treaty that created the European Union, for example, was debated by governments in Europe for many years. Some nations, such as Norway and Switzerland, chose not to join the organization. What reasons could these nations have had for their choice? Why might they change their decision in the future?

TeamWork

Working in teams of five, role-play the following situation. A law has been proposed in Congress that would increase tariffs on imported clothing by 50 percent. Students should take the following roles. (1) a consumer, (2) a domestic manufacturer of clothing, (3) a union leader of workers who produce domestic clothing, (4) a member of Congress who is up for reelection, and (5) a leader of the country that currently exports clothing to the United States. Summarize each person's position on the proposed law and compare your team's answers with the work of other teams.

AND MOVERS SHAKERS

Howard Schultz

Chairman, Chief Global Strategist, Starbucks Corporation

Howard Schultz's family lived in a Brooklyn, New York, housing project. Thanks to a football scholarship, Howard was able to attend Northern Michigan University. After graduating, he worked a variety of jobs until becoming the manager of U.S. operations for Hammarplast, a Swedish maker of stylish kitchen equipment.

While at Hammarplast, Schultz noticed that a company in Seattle seemed to be purchasing an unusual number of specialty coffee makers. So, in 1981, he traveled there to see what the company, called Starbucks, was doing with them. He fell in love with the rich aroma of the Starbucks coffee bean store and with the extraordinary care the owners put into selecting and roasting the beans. "I walked away . . . saying, 'What a great company, what a great city. I'd love to be a part of that.'"

BOBBY YIP/Rruters/Landov

Schultz convinced Starbucks' owners to hire him, and he became director of marketing and operations. During a trip to Italy, Schultz noticed the popularity of Italian coffee bars. There were, in fact, 200,000 such coffee bars in Italy at the time. Unlike his bosses, Schultz couldn't shake his enthusiasm for opening coffee bars in the United States. He opened one of his own, called "Il Giornale," the name of a newspaper in Milan, Italy. A year later, with backing from local investors, he bought Starbucks for $3.8 million. By year's end, he established 17 Starbucks coffee bars. Within five years, the company opened 165 Starbucks in such cities as San Francisco, San Diego, and Denver.

Starbucks began to sell common stock in 1992 under the trading symbol SBUX. Schultz said, "Our stock market listing provided the liquidity that has allowed many people at Starbucks, including me, to cash in stock options and buy things we need or have long wished for. It has likewise served as a great incentive to attract talented people, who join us not only because of the excitement of building a fast-growing company but also because of the value we are creating."

In 2011 Starbucks operated about 17,000 stores in 50 countries and employed approximately 140,000 people. In 2010, the company posted $10.7 billion in revenue. Although Starbucks does not offer franchises, it does license stores in limited or restricted access spaces such as airports and grocery stores

Starbucks has been the target of protestors who claim that the company is not making enough progress in fair-trade policies, labor relations, environmental impact, and anti-competitive practices. In 2000 Starbucks started offering Fair Trade coffee, but research revealed that, by 2006, less than 6 percent of the beans purchased that year were certified Fair Trade. Of the 300 million pounds of coffee beans Starbucks purchased in 2006, only 18 million pounds could be certified as Fair Trade. In 2011, about 153 million pounds could be certified as Fair Trade. Starbucks says that its customers do not care about where their coffee comes from and that taste is the primary concern. (Read more about Fair Trade certification in the Movers and Shakers feature in Chapter 21.)

Think Critically It's hard to imagine U.S. culture without coffee, yet coffee is a product we could not enjoy without international trade. Go online and research the history of coffee and the coffee industry. Create a timeline poster with your findings.

Sources: http://www.guardian.co.uk/environment/green-living-blog/2011/feb/28/coffee-chains-ethical; http://www.hoovers.com/company/Starbucks_Corporation/rhkchi-1.html; http://www.wikinvest.com/stock/Starbucks_%28SBUX%29/Filing/10-K/2010/F91012509; and http://online.wsj.com/article/SB10001424053111904772304576468392023889306.html.

20.3 BALANCE OF PAYMENTS

Learning Objectives

LO1 Describe the components of a nation's current account.

LO2 Describe the components of a nation's financial account.

Key Terms

In Your World

Money doesn't grow on trees. In the course of a week, a month, or a year, the amount you spend, save, and give away must equal the amount you earn, borrow, or are given. You, like everyone else in the world, face a budget constraint. Your outflow of money cannot exceed your inflow. Just as you must make ends meet, so too must families, businesses, and even countries. For example, the flow of receipts into the United States from the rest of the world must equal the outflow of payments to the rest of the world. There's no getting around it. True, governments can run deficits year after year as long as they can borrow enough money at reasonable interest rates. However, governments that borrow too much, such as Greece or Italy, get into financial difficulty and can create economic instability around the world.

CURRENT ACCOUNT

LO1
Describe the components of a nation's current account.

The U.S. **balance of payments** is the record of all economic transactions between U.S. residents and residents of the rest of the world. Because it reflects all the transactions that occur during a particular period, usually a year, the balance of payments is a *flow* measure. Balance-of-payments accounts are maintained according to the principles of *double-entry bookkeeping*, in which entries on one side of the ledger are called *credits*, and entries on the other side are called *debits*. Because total credits must equal total debits, there must be a balance of payments when all the separate accounts are added together.

The balance of payments is divided into two broad accounts: the current account and the financial account. The **current account** keeps track of trade in goods and services, the flow of interest and profits across international borders, and the flow of foreign aid and cash gifts. The most important of these is the trade in goods, also called merchandise trade.

balance of payments A record of all economic transactions between residents of one country and residents of the rest of the world during a given period

current account That portion of the balance of payments that records exports and imports of goods and services, net investment income on foreign assets, and net unilateral transfers

merchandise trade balance The value of a country's exported goods minus the value of its imported goods during a given period

The Merchandise Trade Balance

The **merchandise trade balance** equals the value of merchandise exports minus the value of merchandise imports. Merchandise trade reflects trade in goods, or tangible products, such as Irish sweaters and U.S. computers. The merchandise trade balance usually is referred to in the media as simply the *trade* *balance.* Global merchandise international trade was about $15 trillion in 2010, or about 20 percent of world output that year.

The value of U.S. merchandise exports is listed as a credit in the U.S. balance-of-payments account because U.S. residents must *be paid* for the exported goods. The value of U.S. merchandise imports is listed as a debit in the balance-of-payments account because U.S. residents must *pay* foreigners for imported goods.

If the value of merchandise exports exceeds the value of merchandise imports, there is a *surplus* in the merchandise trade balance, or a **trade surplus**. If the value of merchandise imports exceeds the value of merchandise exports, there is a *deficit* in the merchandise trade balance, or a **trade deficit**. The merchandise trade balance, which is reported monthly, influences the stock market, currency exchange rates, and other financial markets.

trade surplus The amount by which the value of merchandise exports exceeds the value of merchandise imports during a given period

trade deficit The amount by which the value of merchandise imports exceeds the value of merchandise exports during a given period

The U.S. trade balance depends on a variety of factors, including the strength and competitiveness of the U.S. economy compared with other economies, the value of the dollar compared with other currencies, and the economic vitality of the U.S. economy. The U.S. merchandise trade balance since 1960 is depicted in Figure 20.3, where exports (the blue line) and imports (the red line) are expressed as percentages of GDP. In the 1960s, exports exceeded imports, so the United States experienced trade surpluses, shaded in blue. Since 1976, imports have exceeded exports every year, resulting in trade deficits, shaded in pink. Trade deficits as a percentage of GDP have trended higher from 1.3 percent in 1991 to 4.4 percent in 2010, when the U.S. trade deficit reached $647 billion. Note the recession of 2008–2009 slowed U.S. imports more than U.S. exports, so the trade deficit in 2009 relative to GDP fell slightly.

FIGURE 20.3 U.S. Merchandise Imports and Exports Relative to GDP Since 1960

U.S. imports of goods have exceeded U.S. exports of goods since 1976, and trade deficits have widened.

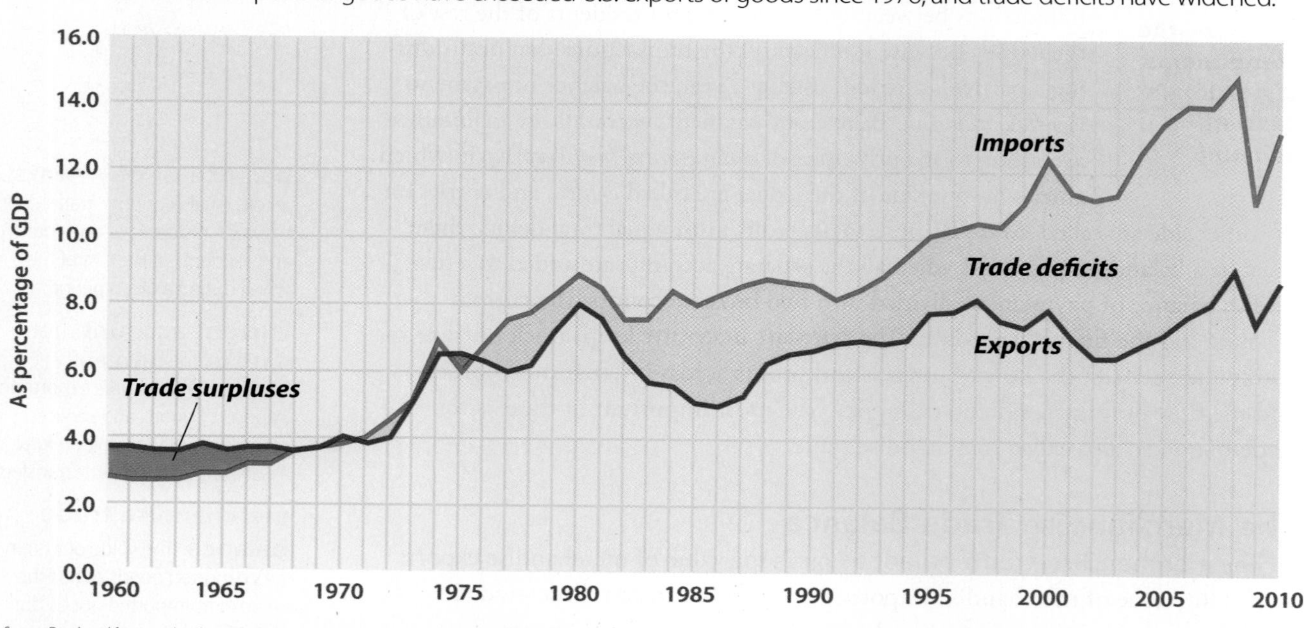

Source: Developed from merchandise trade data in the *Economic Report of the President*, February 2011, and the U.S. Bureau of Economic Analysis. Imports and exports are shown relative to GDP.

The United States imports more from each of the world's major economies than it exports to them. Figure 20.4 shows U.S. trade deficits with major economies or regions of the world in 2010. The $273 billion trade deficit with China was by far the largest with any country in U.S. history. China bought $92 billion in U.S. goods in 2010, but Americans bought $365 billion in Chinese goods. Chances are, most of the utensils in your kitchen came from China.

FIGURE 20.4 U.S. Trade Deficits in 2010 by Country or Region

The United States has merchandise trade deficits with most of the world's major economies because it imports more goods from them than it exports to them.

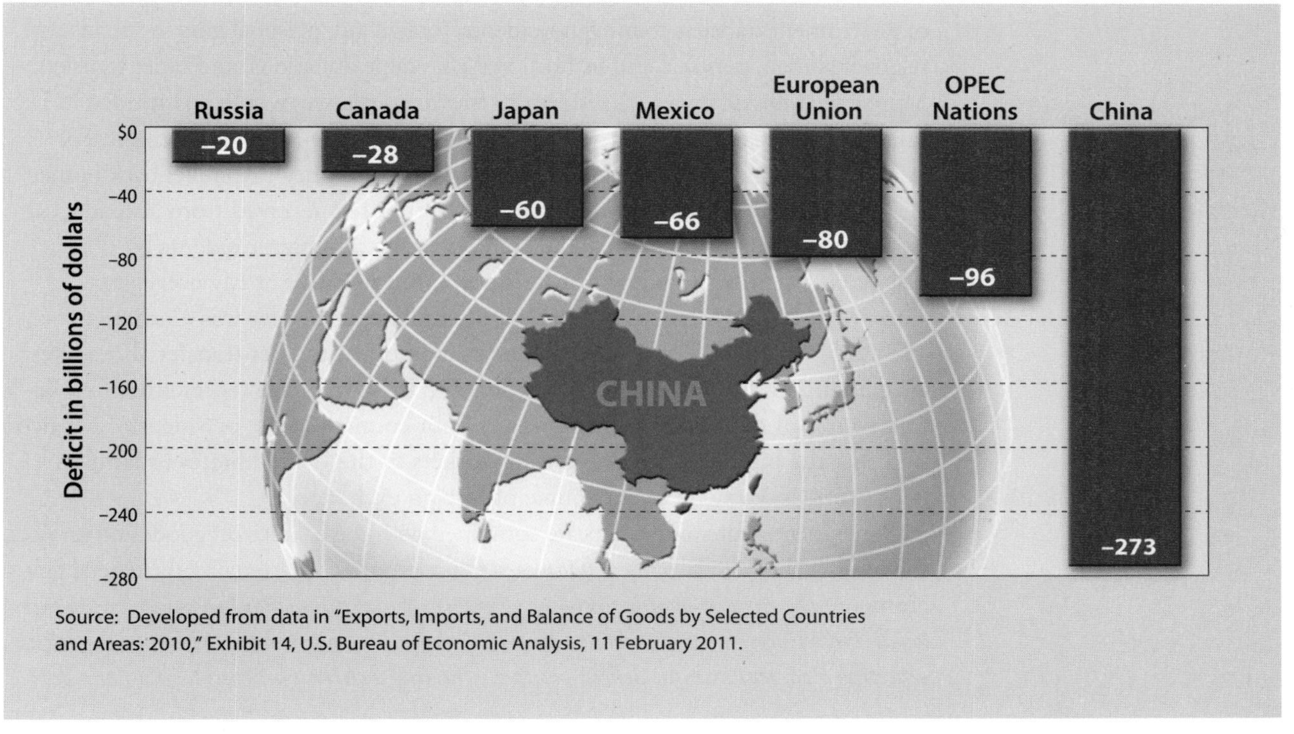

Source: Developed from data in "Exports, Imports, and Balance of Goods by Selected Countries and Areas: 2010," Exhibit 14, U.S. Bureau of Economic Analysis, 11 February 2011.

The Balance on Goods and Services

The merchandise trade balance focuses on the flow of goods, but some services also are traded internationally. *Services* are intangible products, such as transportation, insurance, banking, consulting, higher education, and tourism.

The value of U.S. service exports, such as when an Italian tourist visits Chicago, is a credit in the U.S. balance-of-payments account because U.S. residents receive payments for these services. The value of U.S. service imports, such as when a computer specialist in India enters data for a Connecticut insurance company, is a debit in the balance-of-payments account because U.S. residents must pay for the imported services. Because the United States exports more services than it imports, the balance on services has been in surplus for the past three decades.

NET Bookmark

Access the Bureau of Economic Analysis data reports on U.S. international accounts through the website shown below and click on the link for Chapter 20. Click on "Current releases" under "News" in the left column. Then click on one of the articles under "International." Write a paragraph summarizing the information in the release.

www.cengage.com/school/contecon

The *balance on goods and services* is the value of exports of goods and services, minus the value of imports of goods and services. Because the service account has been in surplus, the balance on goods and services has not been as negative as the merchandise trade balance.

Unilateral Transfers

Unilateral transfers consist of government transfers to foreign residents, foreign aid, personal gifts to friends and relatives abroad, personal and institutional charitable donations, and other transfers. Money sent abroad by a U.S. resident to friends or relatives would be included in U.S. unilateral transfers and would be a debit in the balance-of-payments account. For example, immigrants to the United States often send money to families back home.

Net unilateral transfers equal the unilateral transfers received from abroad by U.S. residents, minus unilateral transfers sent to foreign residents by U.S. residents. U.S. net unilateral transfers have been negative nearly every year since World War II. In 2010, the U.S. net unilateral transfer was a negative $138 billion. To give you some feel for that amount, the net transfer abroad averaged about $1,200 for each U.S. household. These transfers represent an important source of spending power for many poor countries. The president of Mexico said that the billions sent by Mexican workers in the United States to families back home is Mexico's major source of foreign exchange.

When net unilateral transfers are combined with the balance on goods and services, the result is the *current account balance*, a figure reported quarterly by the federal government. *The current account includes all international transactions in currently produced goods and services, flows of interest and profit, plus unilateral transfers. It can be negative, reflecting a current account deficit; positive, reflecting a current account surplus; or zero.*

CHECKPOINT What is included in a nation's current account?

FINANCIAL ACCOUNT

LO2 Describe the components of a nation's financial account.

The United States has been running a current account deficit for years. How can it pay for all the imports and all the transfers? The United States gets the foreign exchange by selling foreigners financial assets, such as stocks and bonds, and by selling them real assets such as land, housing, factories, and other property. When the current account comes up short, asset sales to the rest of the world make up the difference.

financial account That portion of the balance of payments that records international transactions involving financial assets, such as stocks and bonds, and real assets, such as factories and office buildings

The **financial account** tracks the flow of financial capital by recording international transactions involving financial and real assets. For example, if U.S. residents buy foreign assets, money flows from the United States to pay for these assets. Money flows into the United States when foreigners buy U.S. assets, such as U.S. stocks and bonds, an office building in New York City, or a ski chalet in Colorado. The financial account deals with buying and selling assets across international borders.

History of the Financial Account

Between 1917 and 1982, the United States ran a deficit in the financial account, meaning that U.S. residents purchased more foreign assets than foreigners purchased assets in the United States. Since 1983, however, the financial account has been in surplus nearly every year. This means foreigners have been buying more U.S. assets than Americans have been buying foreign assets. Foreign purchases of assets in the United States contribute to America's productive capacity and promote employment. However, the return on these investments flows to foreigners, not to Americans.

The Statistical Discrepancy

Again, the U.S. balance of payments records all transactions between U.S. residents and foreign residents during a specified period. It is easier to describe the balance of payments than to compile it. Despite efforts to capture all international transactions, some are nearly impossible to trace. For example, the government can't easily monitor spending by an American tourist in Europe or illegal drug trafficking. But as the name *balance of payments* suggests, the entire balance-of-payments account must, by definition, be in balance—debits must equal credits.

To ensure that the two sides balance, the *statistical discrepancy* was created. An excess of credits in all other accounts is offset by an equivalent debit in the statistical discrepancy, or an excess of debits in all other accounts is offset by an equivalent credit in the statistical discrepancy.

The statistical discrepancy provides analysts with both a measure of the error in the balance-of-payments data and a means of satisfying the double-entry bookkeeping requirement that total debits equal total credits. In 2010, the current account and the financial account combined for a deficit of $250 billion. To offset that deficit, the statistical discrepancy added $250 billion back into the balance. The statistical discrepancy was especially large in 2010 because the global financial crisis and Great Recession caused unusual fluctuations in international accounts. Thus, the balance of payments for all accounts, including the statistical discrepancy, sums to zero.

Photodisc/Getty Images

The government has difficulty tracking cross-border transactions, such as when an American visiting Italy purchases gold jewelry. How does the government try to make up for any errors in estimating such purchases?

What is included in a nation's financial account? **CHECKPOINT**

20.3 ASSESSMENT

Think Critically

1. Nearly half of the U.S. national debt is owed to foreigners. How is the U.S. current account affected by interest payments made by the federal government on its debt?
2. Why must the total value of all nations' trade surpluses and deficits be balanced?
3. If you received a gift of 100 euros from a relative who lives in Germany, how would this gift affect the U.S. balance of payments?
4. Suppose the value of stocks in the United States increased, causing many foreigners to sell their U.S. stock to earn a profit. They then have their funds sent to them in their own nations. What would this do to the U.S. financial account?

Graphing Exercise

5. When foreigners purchase or build businesses in the United States, their payments for these investments flow into this country. Construct a line graph from the data in the table, which shows the growth in foreign investment in U.S. businesses from 2003 through 2008. What does your graph tell you about this investment? How did this investment affect the U.S. economy? Who earns the return on these investments?

VALUE OF U.S. BUSINESSES ACQUIRED OR ESTABLISHED BY FOREIGN INVESTORS, 2003–2008 (MILLIONS)

2003	$63,591
2004	$86,219
2005	$91,390
2006	$165,603
2007	$251,917
2008	$260,362

Source: *Statistical Abstract of the United States: 2012*, p. 799.

Make Academic Connections

6. **Accounting** Determine whether each of the following would be a credit or a debit for America's balance of payments and how each would affect the nation's economy. Why is it difficult for government officials to keep track of some of these transactions?
   a. There is a $500 million increase in the nation's exports of computers.
   b. U.S. residents send $30 million more to their relatives in other countries.
   c. Foreigners invest an additional $450 million in U.S. businesses.
   d. There is an $800 million increase in the nation's imports of automobiles.
   e. Americans spend $40 million more on foreign travel.
   f. Businesses in the U.S. pay $25 million more in dividends to foreigners.

TeamWork

Working in small teams, make a list of transactions that involve a flow of goods, services, or money between nations that would be difficult or impossible for the government to include in its measures of international trade and finance. Do not use examples already included in this lesson. Provide an explanation for why each transaction would probably not be included in these measures.

20.4 FOREIGN EXCHANGE RATES

Learning Objectives

LO1 Analyze what determines the exchange rates between the dollar and other currencies.

LO2 Identify the participants in the market for foreign exchange.

LO3 Distinguish between flexible and fixed exchange rates.

Key Terms

foreign exchange 649
exchange rate 649
flexible exchange rates 653
fixed exchange rates 653

In Your World

Now that you have some idea about international trade and the balance of payments, you can take a closer look at the forces that determine the rates of exchange between the U.S. dollar and other currencies. When Americans buy foreign goods or travel abroad, these transactions involve two currencies—the U.S. dollar and the foreign currency. What is the dollar cost of a peso, a yen, a pound, or a euro? As you will learn, the exchange rates between the dollar and other currencies usually are determined just like other prices—by demand and supply.

THE MARKET FOR FOREIGN EXCHANGE

LO1
Analyze what determines the exchange rates between the dollar and other currencies.

Foreign exchange is foreign money people need to carry out international transactions. Typically, foreign exchange is made up of bank deposits in the foreign currency. When foreign travel is involved, foreign exchange may consist of foreign paper money. The exchange rate is the dollar price of purchasing a unit of another currency. The **exchange rate**, or price of another currency, is determined by the interaction of all those who buy and sell foreign exchange. The exchange rate between two currencies is set through the interaction of demand and supply for these currencies.

The Euro

The foreign exchange market involves all the arrangements used to carry out international transactions. This market is not so much a physical place as it is a network of telephones and computers connecting electronic accounts among large financial institutions worldwide. The foreign exchange market is like an all-night diner—it never closes. A trading center is always open somewhere in the world.

Consider the market for a particular foreign currency, the euro. For decades, the nations of Western Europe have tried to increase their economic cooperation and trade. These countries believed they would be more productive and more competitive with the United States if they acted more like the 50 United States and less like

foreign exchange Foreign money needed to carry out international transactions

exchange rate The price measured in one country's currency of purchasing one unit of another country's currency

many separate economies, each with its own trade regulations, trade barriers, and currency. Imagine the hassle involved if each of the 50 states had its own currency, which you had to exchange every time you wanted to buy something in another state—such as buying gas, meals, and lodging during a cross-country road trip.

In January 2002, *euro notes* and coins entered circulation and, by 2011, 17 European countries had adopted the new currency. The euro is now the common currency in the eurozone, as the 17 countries are usually called. The price, or exchange rate, of the euro is the dollar price of one euro. The exchange rate, like any other price, is determined by demand and supply. *The equilibrium price of foreign exchange is the one that equates quantity demanded with quantity supplied.*

Demand for Foreign Exchange

U.S. residents need euros to pay for goods and services from the eurozone, to buy assets from there, to make loans to the eurozone, or simply to send cash to friends or relatives there. Whenever U.S. residents need euros, they must buy them in the foreign exchange market, which could be as near as the local bank.

Figure 20.5 depicts a market for foreign exchange—in this case, euros. The horizontal axis shows the quantity of foreign exchange, measured here in millions of euros per day. The vertical axis indicates the dollar price of one euro. The demand curve *D* for foreign exchange shows the relationship between the dollar price of the euro and the quantity of euros demanded, other things assumed constant. Some of the factors assumed constant along the demand curve are the incomes and preferences of U.S. consumers, the expected inflation rates in the United States and in the eurozone, and interest rates in the United States and in the eurozone.

Photodisc/Getty Images

Why do you think adoption of the euro as a common currency in Europe has increased trade among the 17 countries in the euro area?

FIGURE 20.5 The Foreign Exchange Market for Euros

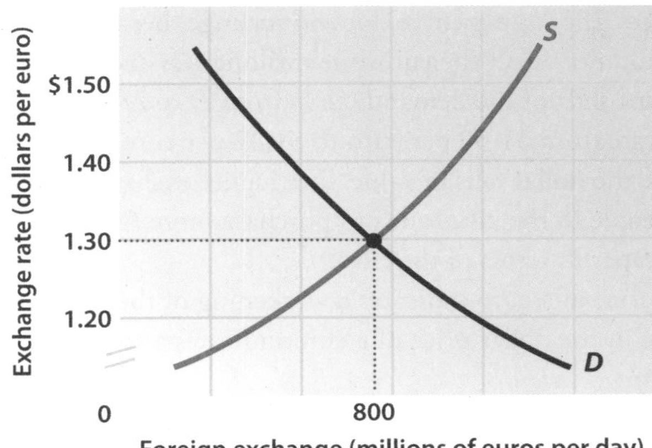

The fewer dollars needed to purchase one euro, the lower the price of European goods and the greater the quantity of euros demanded. On the supply side, an increase in the dollar cost of a euro makes U.S. products cheaper for Europeans. Their increased demand for U.S. goods increases the quantity of euros supplied.

People have many reasons for demanding foreign exchange; but, in the aggregate, the lower the dollar price of foreign exchange, the greater the quantity of foreign exchange demanded. The cheaper it is to buy euros, the lower the dollar price of eurozone products, so the greater the quantity of euros demanded by U.S. residents. For example, a cheap-enough euro might persuade you to tour Rome, climb the Austrian Alps, or wander the museums of Paris.

Supply of Foreign Exchange

The supply of foreign exchange is generated by the desire of foreign residents to acquire dollars—that is, to exchange euros for dollars. Residents of the eurozone want dollars to buy U.S. goods and services, to buy U.S. assets, to make loans in dollars, or to make cash gifts in dollars to their U.S. friends and relatives. Europeans supply euros in the foreign exchange market to acquire the dollars they need.

An increase in the dollar-per-euro exchange rate, other things constant, makes U.S. products cheaper for foreigners. More euros will be supplied on the foreign exchange market to buy dollars. Figure 20.5 shows the upward-sloping supply curve for foreign exchange (again, euros in this example). The supply curve is drawn assuming other things remain constant. These include the eurozone's incomes and tastes, inflation expectations in the euro zone and in the United States, and interest rates in the eurozone and in the United States.

Determining the Exchange Rate

Figure 20.5 brings together the supply and demand for foreign exchange to determine the exchange rate. At a rate of $1.30 per euro, the quantity of euros demanded equals the quantity supplied—in this example, 800 million euros per day.

What if this equilibrium exchange rate is upset by a change in one of the underlying forces that affect demand or supply? For example, suppose an increase in U.S. income causes Americans to increase their demand for all normal goods, including those from the eurozone. An increase in U.S. income shifts the U.S.

demand curve for euros to the right, as Americans seek euros to buy more German cars and European vacations.

This increased demand for euros is shown in Figure 20.6 by a rightward shift of the demand curve for euros. The supply curve does not change, because an increase in U.S. income should not affect the eurozone's willingness and ability to supply euros. The rightward shift of the demand curve from *D* to *D′* leads to an increase in the exchange rate from $1.30 per euro to $1.32 per euro. Thus, the euro increases in value, while the dollar falls in value. The higher exchange value of the euro prompts some people in the eurozone's to purchase more American products, which are now cheaper in terms of the euro.

An increase in the dollar price of a euro indicates a weakening of the dollar, or *dollar depreciation.* A decrease in the dollar price of a euro indicates a strengthening of the dollar, or a *dollar appreciation.*

FIGURE 20.6 Effect on the Foreign Exchange Market of an Increase in Demand for Euros

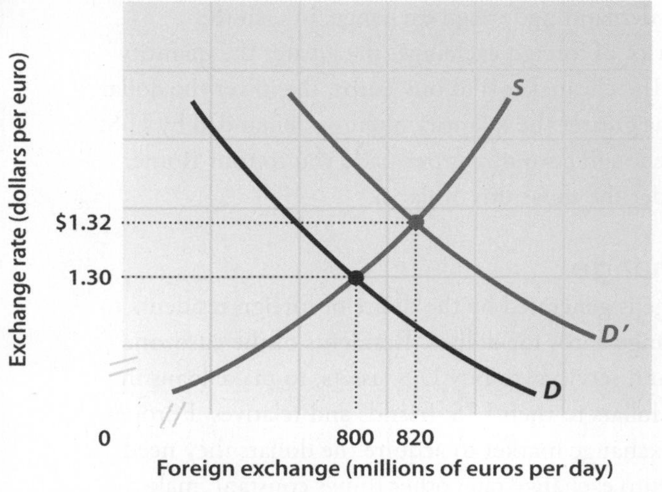

The intersection of supply curve *S* and demand curve *D* determines the exchange rate. An increase in the demand for euros from *D* to *D′* leads to an increase in the equilibrium quantity from 800 million euros to 820 million euros per day. The market exchange rate increases from $1.30 to $1.32 per euro.

CHECKPOINT What determines the exchange rate between the dollar and the euro?

WHO BUYS FOREIGN EXCHANGE?

LO2 Identify the participants in the market for foreign exchange.

Foreign exchange is purchased mainly by those who buy foreign products or invest abroad, such as importers and exporters, investors in foreign assets, central banks, and tourists. Other groups also regularly participate in foreign exchange markets as well, including speculators, arbitrageurs, and people seeking a safe haven for their money.

Speculators

Speculators buy or sell foreign exchange in hopes of profiting later by trading the currency at a more favorable exchange rate. By taking risks, speculators aim to profit from market fluctuations—that is, they try to buy low and sell high.

Arbitrageurs

Exchange rates between specific currencies are nearly identical at any given time in markets around the world. For example, the dollar price of a euro is nearly the same in New York, Paris, Tokyo, London, Zurich, Hong Kong, Istanbul, and other financial centers. *Arbitrageurs* are money dealers who take advantage of tiny differences in exchange rates between markets. Their actions help ensure that exchange rates are the same across markets. For example, if one euro trades for $1.30 in New York but for $1.31 in Paris, an arbitrageur could buy, say, $1,000,000 worth of euros in New York and at the same time sell them in Paris for $1,007,692, thereby earning $7,692 minus the transaction costs of the trades.

Arbitrageurs take less risk than speculators because they simultaneously buy currency in one market and sell it in another. In this example, the arbitrageur increases the demand for euros in New York and increases the supply of euros in Paris. These actions increase the dollar price of euros in New York and decrease it in Paris.

Those Seeking a Safe Haven for Their Money

Finally, people in countries suffering from economic and political turmoil may buy more stable currencies as a hedge against the depreciation and instability of their own currency. For example, the dollar has long been accepted as an international medium of exchange. It is also the currency of choice in world markets for oil, gold, and illegal drugs.

The euro may some day challenge the dollar as the key world currency, in part because the largest euro denomination, the 500 euro note, is worth about seven times a 100 dollar note, the top U.S. note. So it would be seven times easier to smuggle currency or conduct cash transactions using euros rather than dollars.

Who participates in the market for foreign exchange? **CHECKPOINT**

EXCHANGE RATE SYSTEMS

LO3
Distinguish between flexible and fixed exchange rates.

So far the discussion has been about **flexible exchange rates**, with the rate determined by supply and demand. A flexible, or *floating*, exchange rate adjusts continually to the many forces that affect the foreign exchange market. When the exchange rate is flexible, government officials usually have only an indirect role in foreign exchange markets.

However, if government officials try to set, or fix, the exchange rate, active and ongoing central bank intervention is often necessary to establish and maintain this **fixed exchange rate**. For example, prior to World War II, the value of

flexible exchange rates Exchange rate determined by the forces of supply and demand without government intervention

fixed exchange rate Exchange rate fixed within a narrow range and maintained by central banks' ongoing purchases and sales of currencies

each major currency was fixed in relation to gold. This was called the *gold standard.* Because currencies were fixed in relation to gold, they also were fixed in relation to each other (think about that for a minute).

From the end of World War II until 1971, the dollar became the world's key currency. The dollar price of gold was fixed at $35 per ounce. Thus the dollar was fixed in relation to gold, but other countries could adjust their exchange rates relative to the dollar if they experienced chronic balance-of-payments problems. Foreigners could also convert any surplus dollars into gold at $35 per ounce. In 1971, the United States experienced a trade deficit and stopped selling gold to foreigners. No longer tied to gold, the value of the dollar began to float. Exchange rates among major world currencies became flexible, and they remain so today. Some economies, notably China, still try to fix the value of their currency in terms of U.S. dollars. By choosing an exchange rate that undervalues its own currency, China makes foreign products more costly to Chinese consumers and makes Chinese products cheaper abroad. That's one reason why the U.S. trade deficit with China is so large.

CHECKPOINT **Compare a system of flexible exchange rates to one of fixed exchange rates.**

Math in Economics

Common Core Expressions and Equations

You can multiply a price expressed in one currency by an exchange rate to find the price in a different currency.

EXAMPLE An Apple Computer sells for $899.00. Find the price in euros when the exchange rate of dollars to euros is $1.00 = €0.79. Write answer rounded to the nearest hundredths.

SOLUTION Multiply $899.00 × 0.79 = €710.21

Practice the Skill Convert each amount to the given currency.

1. A barrel of oil sells for $123.32. Find the price in Japanese yen when the exchange rate of dollars to yen is $1.00 = ¥83.
2. In yen, a pair of shoes sells for ¥12,363. Find the price in pounds when the exchange rate of yen to pounds is ¥1.00 = £0.0079.
3. Find the lower price for a pair of shoes that sells for €97.00 in Italy or $129.00 in the United States when the exchange rate is €1.00 = $1.27.

20.4 ASSESSMENT

1. What effect would each of the following events have on the exchange rate for the U.S. dollar, relative to other currencies? Explain each of your answers. (a) A new sports car is produced in Japan that many U.S. consumers choose to purchase. (b) U.S. banks offer depositors higher interest rates. This causes many people in other nations to deposit funds in U.S. banks. (c) Many U.S. businesses choose to invest in other nations.
2. Why didn't the conversion by many European nations to the euro at the start of 2002 eliminate all trade problems between nations in the eurozone?
3. How may the conversion by many European nations to the euro have helped U.S. firms that trade with these nations?
4. How are arbitrageurs able to affect the exchange rates for different currencies?
5. Why did the fixed exchange rate system often result in imbalances in trade among nations?

Graphing Exercise

6. In September of 2011, exchange rates for the U.S. dollar, in terms of other currencies, varied widely. Suppose you were considering taking a package vacation in one of the nations listed below. Divide each price by the appropriate exchange rate to calculate the number of U.S. dollars you would have to pay for each trip. Construct a bar graph to show the dollar cost of each trip. What other factors would you consider when choosing among these trips?

Exchange Rate for U.S. Dollar in Selected Currencies, September 8, 2011

$1 = 0.993 Canadian dollars	$1 = 77.789 Japanese yen
$1 = 0.724 euros	$1 = 12.601 Mexican pesos

- A one-week trip to Canada costs 1,360.80 Canadian dollars.
- A one-week trip to Japan costs 230,980 Japanese yen.
- A one-week trip to Germany, a eurozone country, costs 1,259.20 euros.
- A one-week trip to Mexico costs 15,486.80 Mexican pesos.

Make Academic Connections

7. **Math** Toward the end of 2000, the exchange rate was 1.10 euros to the U.S. dollar. By September of 2011, the euro had become more valuable at 0.724 euros per dollar. What percentage increase was this in the value of the euro? How did this euro appreciation affect the ability of U.S. firms to sell their products to European Union member nations?

TeamWork

Working in pairs, students will find the current value of the U.S. dollar compared with the currency of ten different countries. Pairs should first determine the countries to research, and then working alone, go online to find the information for five countries each. In comparing their findings, pairs should determine whether the U.S. dollar is trending up or down as compared to these currencies. They should record their answers and be prepared to share them in class.

Connect to History

Tariffs and Trade, Part I

Alexander Hamilton served as our country's first Secretary of the Treasury from 1789 to 1795. His vision for the United States included manufacturing. To protect the nation's young industries, he proposed a tariff. Because most Americans were doing well in agriculture, there was little incentive in the United States to engage in manufacturing. Therefore, Congress, which had passed a modest tariff in 1789 for revenue purposes, did not support Hamilton's proposal. Still, the tariff remained the federal government's chief source of revenue until 1913.

The Napoleonic Wars (1799–1815) provided the spark for American manufacturing and a move toward protective tariffs. This pattern, repeated during each war in the country's early history, triggered protectionism. Tariff rates were increased for revenue purposes during the War of 1812, and they were not reduced when the war ended.

Throughout the nineteenth century, the tariff was the nation's most important economic policy and became a huge political issue. The South, as buyers of manufactured goods and exporters of cotton, wanted low tariffs. The North favored higher, more protective rates. Tariff rates inched up until the crisis caused by the 1828 "Tariff of Abominations." The South, believing the tariff favored the more industrial North, claimed the theory of "nullification," by which it could invalidate federal laws within its borders. President Andrew Jackson threatened to collect the tariffs by force. Henry Clay defused the situation by negotiating a reduction of rates. The South did not renounce the theory of nullification, and the rift between the North and the South opened.

wynnter/Stockphoto.com

Alexander Hamilton

When the split erupted into the Civil War, the United States' tariff policy changed. Strapped for money, the federal government raised tariff rates by passing the 1861 Morrill Tariff, and tariffs were kept high until 1913, as was shown in Figure 20.2. Following the Civil War, the South's political power diminished. As the United States began a period of rapid industrialization and became more self-sufficient, the importance of international trade declined. The nation's industrialists, supported by the Republican Party, were able to maintain high tariffs. Advocates of low tariffs feared that higher tariffs would cause manufacturing to grow, giving that sector more political power than the agricultural sector.

When tariff rates were finally reduced in 1913, they were replaced by an income tax so as to maintain (and shift the burden of) revenues. Still, the reductions of 1913 had less effect than predicted, primarily because of World War I. The return of higher tariffs reached a peak with the Smoot-Hawley Tariff. This tariff, enacted in 1930 at the outset of the Great Depression, further decreased world trade, thereby worsening the Depression.

Think Critically **Imagine you are a member of Congress immediately after the Civil War. Take a position for or against keeping tariffs high. Then write a paragraph justifying your point of view.**

Chapter 20 Summary

20.1 Benefits of Trade

A. Residents of one country trade with those of another because all try to improve their standard of living. Through international trade, people benefit from comparative advantage by specializing in those products that involve the lowest opportunity cost.

B. People can benefit from international trade even if no nation enjoys a comparative advantage. When a nation specializes in certain products and trades for other products, firms can experience economies of scale.

C. In 2010, U.S. exports of goods and services amounted to 13 percent of GDP and imports were 16 percent of GDP.

ASK THE EXPERT

www.cengage.com/school/contecon

What are some arguments for restricting trade with other nations?

20.2 Trade Restrictions and Free-Trade Agreements

A. The flow of trade in the global economy is restricted by government barriers including tariffs, quotas, and other devices. A tariff taxes an imported good. A quota limits the amount of a good that may be imported from particular countries. When one nation imposes trade restrictions, other nations are likely to retaliate with their own restrictions.

B. World trade offers many advantages to the trading countries including increased consumption possibilities, access to more markets, a greater variety of products, lower costs through economies of scale, improved quality from competitive pressure, and lower prices. GATT is an international trade agreement that reduced tariffs and quotas. Participating nations agreed to treat all other members equally. The World Trade Organization, or WTO, succeeded GATT.

20.3 Balance of Payments

A. The balance of payments is the record of all economic transactions between U.S. residents and the rest of the world. Two broad accounts are included in each nation's balance of payments: the current account and the financial account.

B. Some people send money to friends and relatives in other countries. This outflow of money is a debit in the balance-of-payments account. Net unilateral transfers combine with the balance of goods and services and net investment income make up the current account balance.

C. The financial account tracks the flow of financial capital resulting from international transactions. Any discrepancy between credits and debits in the current account and the financial account is "balanced" by including an offsetting statistical discrepancy.

20.4 Foreign Exchange Rates

A. Foreign exchange is the foreign money used to carry out international transactions. The exchange rate is the dollar price of one unit of foreign currency. By 2011, 17 European nations had adopted the euro as their nation's common currency.

B. Foreign exchange is most often purchased by U.S. residents to buy foreign products or to invest abroad.

C. Before 1971, the dollar price was fixed in terms of gold, and other nation's could fix their exchange rates in terms of the dollar. This system of relatively fixed exchange rates was replaced in 1971 with a floating exchange rate system.

CHAPTER 20 ASSESSMENT

Review Economic Terms

a. balance of payments
b. current account
c. exchange rate
d. financial account
e. fixed exchange rate
f. flexible exchange rate
g. foreign exchange
h. General Agreement on Tariffs and Trade (GATT)
i. merchandise trade balance
j. quota
k. tariff
l. trade deficit
m. trade surplus
n. Uruguay Round
o. world price
p. World Trade Organization (WTO)

Match the terms with the definitions. Some terms will not be used.

_____ 1. The amount by which the value of merchandise exports exceeds the value of merchandise imports during a given period

_____ 2. A tax on imports

_____ 3. A record of all economic transactions between residents of one country and residents of the rest of the world during a given period

_____ 4. Foreign money needed to carry out international transactions

_____ 5. The portion of the balance of payments that records exports and imports of goods and services, net investment income, and net transfers

_____ 6. An exchange rate determined by the forces of supply and demand without government intervention

_____ 7. The amount by which the value of merchandise imports exceeds the value of merchandise exports during a given period of time

_____ 8. A legal limit on the quantity of a particular product that can be imported

_____ 9. An exchange rate fixed within a narrow range of values and maintained by central banks' ongoing purchases and sales of currencies

_____ 10. The portion of the balance of payments that records international transactions involving financial and real assets

Review Economic Concepts

11. **True or False** The law of comparative advantage states that the individual or firm with the lowest opportunity cost of producing a particular good should specialize in that good.

12. A nation could enjoy a comparative advantage as a result of possessing each of the following except
    a. superior labor.
    b. superior resources.
    c. superior capital.
    d. superior consumers.

13. Countries can gain from specialization and trade if that trade results in ________?________ for producers in that country. That is, the producers' average costs of output decline as they expand their scale of production to meet the increased demand.

14. **True or False** Without comparative advantage, international trade has no point.

15. The category of exports from the United States that has the greatest value is
    a. capital goods.
    b. consumer goods.
    c. industrial supplies.
    d. services.

16. The ________?________ for a good or service is determined by world supply and world demand for the product.

17. The category of U.S. imports with the greatest value is
    a. capital goods.
    b. consumer goods.
    c. industrial supplies and materials.
    d. services.

18. A tariff that is placed on an imported good will ________?________ of the taxed product.
    a. harm consumers and domestic producers
    b. harm consumers and benefit domestic producers
    c. benefit consumers and domestic producers
    d. benefit consumers and harm domestic producers

19. **True or False** A tariff on imported goods will have no effect on the price of products made in that country.

20. A(n) ________?________ is a legal limit on the amount of a product a nation may import.

21. Trade restrictions cause
    a. the value of international trade to grow.
    b. the price of products consumers purchase to decline.
    c. the selection of products from which consumers may choose to grow.
    d. the number of people employed in export industries to decline.

22. The ________?________ provides the legal and institutional foundation for the world's multilateral trading system.

23. **True or False** When one nation sets trade restrictions, other nations are unlikely to respond with their own restrictions.

24. Trade of goods is measured by the merchandise trade balance that is equal to
    a. the value of a nation's exported goods plus the value of its imported goods.
    b. the value of a nation's imported goods less the value of its exported goods.
    c. the value of a nation's exported goods less the value of its imported goods.
    d. the value of a nation's exported goods.

25. **True or False** The current account keeps track of trade in goods and services, the flow of interest and profits across international borders, and the flow of foreign aid and cash gifts.

26. Which of the following would appear as a credit in a nation's balance of payments?
    a. Businesses in that country purchase resources from other nations.
    b. Banks in that country lend money to people in other nations.
    c. Farmers in that country sell grain to firms in other countries.
    d. Residents of that country send cash to their relatives in other countries.

27. When the unilateral transfers are combined with the balance of goods and services, the result is the ________?________.

28. **True or False** The exchange rate for the U.S. dollar relative to other currencies is set and controlled by the U.S. government.

Apply Economic Concepts

29. **Determine the Price of an Imported Good** You have decided to buy a new camera while traveling in Germany. The price is 275 euros. If the exchange rate for euros is 0.78 per U.S. dollar, how many dollars will the camera cost? What other costs should you consider?

	Amount of Resource Required		Cost of Resource	
Type of Resource	**Country A**	**Country B**	**Country A**	**Country B**
Labor	2 hours	6 hours	$10 per hour	$6 per hour
Raw materials	20 lbs	20 lbs	$1.00 per lb	$.80 per lb
Power	150 kwh	80 kwh	$.03 per kwh	$.04 per kwh
Tools	1 robot system	1 hand tool	$3 per chair	$1 per chair

30. **Determine Comparative Advantage** In the table above, countries A and B are able to produce similar chairs from the resources shown. Determine which nation has a comparative advantage in this type of production. What should the other nation do to maximize the value of its production?

31. **21st Century Skills Productivity and Accountability** Imagine you are the president of an American business that produces special valves used by oil refineries. Your firm employs 50 highly skilled workers. You have always tried to buy American when it was possible. Recently you have experienced strong competition from a foreign firm that offers valves similar to yours for about 20 percent less. You could purchase an imported machine for $10 million that would allow you to eliminate 20 of your workers and reduce your costs enough to lower your price to match the foreign firm. Would you do this? Why or why not? Do you have all the information you need to make this decision? If not, what more would you like to know?

Digging Deeper

with Economics e-Collection

Access the Gale Economics e-Collection through the URL below. Find current articles from magazines, newspapers, and academic journals that contain information about foreign exchange. Topics to look for include exchange rates for specific foreign currencies such as the euro (European Union), yen (Japan), renminbi (China), peso (Mexico), and others, and information about parties who buy foreign exchange, including importers, exporters, investors, central banks, tourists, speculators, arbitrageurs, and people seeking a safe haven for their money. Write down five facts or statistics you learned, and be prepared to share them in class.

www.cengage.com/school/contecon

CHAPTER 21

Economic Development

Point your browser

www.cengage.com/school/ contecon

CONSIDER ...

- Why are some countries poor while others are rich?
- What determines the wealth of nations?
- Does foreign aid help poorer countries?
- How does terrorism affect economic development?
- What's the "brain drain," and how does it affect poorer countries?
- Why are birthrates higher in poorer countries?
- Are poorer countries catching up with the rest of the world?

iodrakon/Shutterstock.com; Background image: Dibrova/Shutterstock.com

21.1 DEVELOPING ECONOMIES AND INDUSTRIAL MARKET ECONOMIES

Key Terms

developing countries 662
industrial market countries 662
fertility rate 664

Learning Objectives

LO1 Distinguish between developing countries and industrial market countries.

LO2 Explain why labor productivity is so low in developing countries.

In Your World

People around the world face the day under quite different circumstances. Many of you rise from a comfortable bed in your own home, select the day's clothing from a wardrobe, choose from a variety of breakfast foods, and ride to school in one of the family's automobiles. In contrast, most of the world's 7 billion people have less housing, clothing, and food. They own no automobile, and many have limited educational opportunities. Some can't read or write.

WORLDS APART

LO1 Distinguish between developing countries and industrial market countries.

Countries can be classified in a variety of ways, based on their level of economic development. The yardstick used most often is to compare living standards across nations. The most common measure of living standards is a nation's *GDP per capita.* Recall that GDP per capita measures how much an economy produces on average per resident. Based on that measure, countries can be sorted into two broad categories:

1. developing countries, which have lower levels of GDP per capita income
2. industrial market countries, which have higher levels of GDP per capita.

Developing and Industrial Market Countries

Developing countries not only have lower GDP per capita, they also usually have low rates of literacy, high unemployment rates, extensive underemployment, and rapid population growth. On average, nearly one-half of the labor force in developing countries works in agriculture. Because farming methods are relatively primitive there, and farms are small, farm productivity is low, and most people barely subsist.

developing countries Nations with low GDP per capita, low rates of literacy, high unemployment rates, and high fertility rates

industrial market countries Economically advanced market countries of Western Europe, North America, Australia, New Zealand, Japan, and the newly industrialized economies of Asia

Most of the world's 7 billion people live in developing countries. China and India, the two population giants, together account for nearly one-half of the developing world's population.

Industrial market countries not only have higher GDP per capita, they also have higher rates of literacy, lower unemployment, and slower population growth. **Industrial market countries** consist of the economically advanced nations of Western Europe, North America, Australia, New Zealand, Japan, and the newly

FIGURE 21.1 GDP per Capita for Selected Countries in 2010

There is a wide range of productive performance around the world.

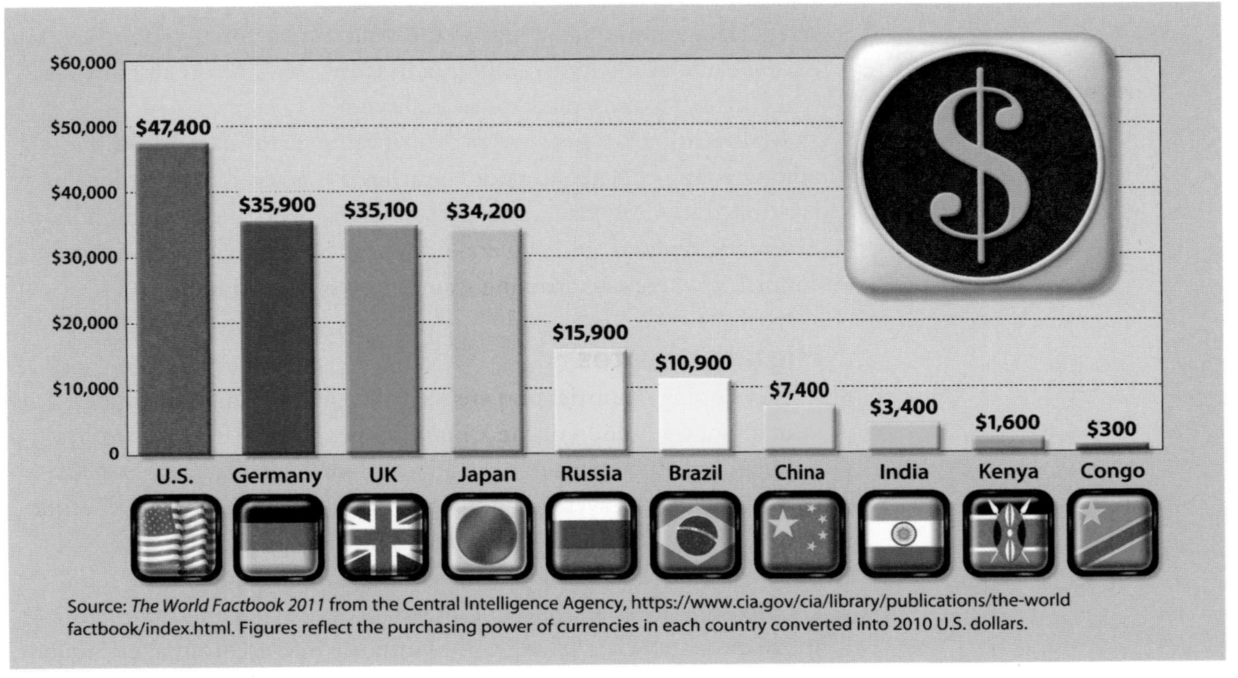

Source: *The World Factbook 2011* from the Central Intelligence Agency, https://www.cia.gov/cia/library/publications/the-world factbook/index.html. Figures reflect the purchasing power of currencies in each country converted into 2010 U.S. dollars.

industrialized economies of Asia. Most were the among the first countries to experience long-term economic growth during the nineteenth century. About 1.5 billion of the world's 7 billion population live in industrial market countries.

Figure 21.1 shows 10 representative countries based on GDP per capita. GDP has been adjusted to reflect the actual buying power of currency in each economy. The United States, Germany, the United Kingdom, and Japan are industrial market economies. The rest are developing economies.

The United States had a GDP per capita in 2010 that was six times that of China, a developing country. But GDP per capita in China, in turn, was about 25 times that of the Democratic Republic of the Congo, one of the poorest countries on Earth. Thus, developing countries are not uniformly poor. They vary much more based on per capita income than do industrial market economies. Residents of China likely feel poor relative to industrial market countries such as the United States, but they are well off compared to the poorest developing countries. Thus, there is a wide range of productive performance around the world. World per capita income in 2010 was about $10,800, roughly that of Brazil.

Life Expectancy

Differences in stages of development among countries are reflected in a number of ways besides GDP per capita. For example, many people in developing countries suffer from poor health because of malnutrition and disease. HIV/AIDS is devastating some developing countries, particularly those in Africa and the Caribbean.

The average life expectancy around the world ranges from about 55 years in the poor African country of Congo, to 82 years in the industrial market economy of Japan. The world average is 67 years. Countries with the shortest life expectancies also have the highest child mortality rates. The mortality rate refers to the death rate before a certain age. For example, about one in five children in Congo dies before reaching age five. This is 25 times the U.S. mortality rate.

Malnutrition is a primary or contributing factor in most deaths among young children in poor countries. Diseases that are easily controlled in industrial economies—malaria, whooping cough, polio, dysentery, typhoid, and cholera—can become deadly epidemics in poor countries, where safe drinking water often is hard to find.

High Birthrates

Developing countries also are identified by their high birthrates. This year, about 65 million of the 75 million people added to the world's population will be born in developing countries. In fact, the **fertility rate**, which is the average number of births during a woman's lifetime, is an easy way of distinguishing between developing and industrial countries. Few developing countries have a fertility rate of less than 2.2 births per woman, but no industrial country has a fertility rate above that rate. After taking child mortality into account, a fertility rate of 2.1 would keep the population constant over time. The world average is 2.5 births per woman. In some developing countries, the population growth rate has exceeded the growth rate in total production, so the standard of living as measured by GDP per capita has declined. Thus, high fertility rates can put pressure on the standard of living.

fertility rate The average number of births during each woman's lifetime

Figure 21.2 presents fertility rates for the 10 countries introduced in Figure 21.1. As you can see, rates are lower in industrial countries and higher in developing countries. The exceptions are China and Russia. China's official policy limits families to one child. Russian officials, on the other hand, are so troubled by the nation's falling fertility rate that the government is offering $9,200 to any woman who has a second child. Sub-Saharan African countries are the poorest in the world and have the highest fertility rates.

Fertility rates are high in developing countries for a variety of reasons. Among these is that parents there view children as a source of farm labor. Also, most

NET Bookmark

The CIA World Factbook website is a great source for information about countries throughout the world. Access the website shown below and click on the link for Chapter 21. Select a country that interests you. Find the following facts about that country: infant mortality rate, life expectancy at birth, and total fertility rate. Then read the "Economy—Overview" paragraph and the economic statistics included. Relate the facts you found to the information about the economy. Write a paragraph that explains the relationship between the two sets of information.

www.cengage.com/school/contecon

FIGURE 21.2 Fertility Rates for Selected Countries as of 2011

Fertility rates are lower in industrial countries and higher in developing countries.

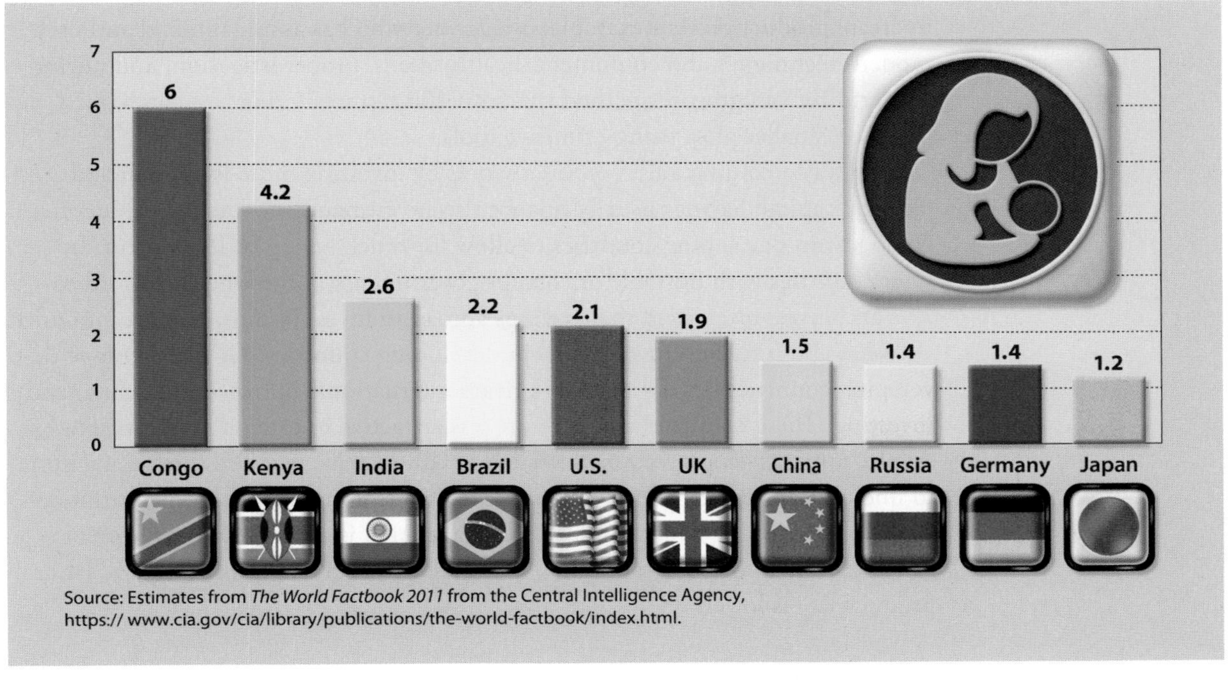

Source: Estimates from *The World Factbook 2011* from the Central Intelligence Agency, https:// www.cia.gov/cia/library/publications/the-world-factbook/index.html.

developing countries have no social security systems, so parents have more children to support them in old age. Higher child mortality rates also lead to higher birthrates, as parents strive to achieve sufficiently large families.

Attitudes about family size are changing, however, even in the poorest countries. According to the United Nations, the birthrate during a typical woman's lifetime in a developing country has fallen from six in 1965 to fewer than three children today. As women become better educated, they earn more. Women who are pregnant or who have young children are less able to work. Because their opportunity cost of child bearing has increased, women choose to have fewer children.

What are some clear differences between developing economies and industrial market economies? CHECKPOINT

PRODUCTIVITY AND ECONOMIC DEVELOPMENT

LO2
Explain why labor productivity is so low in developing countries.

You have examined some symptoms of poverty in developing countries. However, you have yet to explore why poor countries are poor. Simply put, poor countries are poor because they do not produce many goods and services.

Low Labor Productivity

Labor productivity, measured as output per worker, is low in developing countries. Why? Labor productivity depends on the quality of the labor and on the amount of capital, natural resources, and other resources that combine with labor to create production. For example, one farmer who has abundant land and uses modern techniques and equipment, healthy seeds, proper irrigation, and nurturing fertilizer can grow more food than can 100 farmers trying to scratch out a living on smaller plots using primitive tools.

One way a country raises productivity is by investing more in human and physical capital. Savings usually finance this investment. Income per capita often is too low in developing countries to allow for much saving or investment. In poor countries with unstable or corrupt governments, those who can afford to save and invest often send their savings abroad to invest in more stable economies.

What about foreign investments in developing countries? Governments of developing countries heavily regulate private international borrowing, lending, and investing. These countries are therefore less attractive to foreign investors. For example, some developing countries, such as China, have required foreign investors to find a local partner who must be granted controlling interest in the business. Thus, in developing countries, less financial capital is available for investment in either human or physical capital. With less physical and human capital, labor productivity is lower.

Less Education

Education enables workers to use modern production techniques and technology. Education also makes workers more receptive to new ideas and production methods. Countries with the most advanced educational systems also were the first to develop economically. For example, the United States has been a world leader in free public education and in economic development.

In the poorest countries, many adults can't read or write. For example, more than one-third of adults in Sub-Saharan Africa are illiterate. When knowledge is lacking, other resources are not used as efficiently. A country may be endowed with fertile land, but farmers may not adopt the best means of irrigation, fertilization, and crop rotation. In industrial economies, only two percent of adults can't read or write.

Child labor in developing countries reduces educational opportunities there. In Pakistan, for example, there are classrooms and teachers for less than one-half of the country's school-age children. School fees can be prohibitive for poor families. Millions of Pakistani children work full-time, usually in agriculture. Nearly one-half of the adults there are illiterate.

Inefficient Use of Labor

Another feature of developing countries is that they use labor less efficiently than industrial nations do. Unemployment and underemployment reflect the inefficient use of labor. Recall that underemployment occurs when skilled workers are employed in low-skill jobs or when people are working less than they would like—such as working only part time when a full-time job is preferred. Only a small proportion of the workforce in developing countries have what you would call a regular job with normal hours and a steady paycheck. Most work as day laborers in the informal economy, or scratch out a living in agriculture.

Few Entrepreneurs

In order to develop, a market economy must have entrepreneurs who are able to bring together resources and take the risk of profit or loss. Many developing countries, particularly those in Africa, were once under colonial rule, where a foreign country governed. Under this system, the local population had few opportunities to develop leadership or entrepreneurial skills, so such talent is in short supply.

Reliance on Agriculture

In some developing countries, the average farm is as small as two acres, so the average farmer does not grow much. Even where more land is available, a lack of physical capital limits the amount of land that can be farmed efficiently. Nearly one-half of the labor force in developing countries works in agriculture. However, because farm productivity is low there, only about one-quarter of the GDP in those countries comes from agriculture. For example, 60 percent of the labor force in India works in agriculture, but these workers account for less than 20 percent of that country's GDP.

In contrast, modern equipment helps a U.S. farmer to work hundreds or even thousands of acres. Though accounting for only 2 percent of the U.S. labor force, American farmers grow enough to feed the nation and to lead the world in agricultural exports.

Photodisc/Getty Images

On rice plantations in Indonesia, much of the labor is performed by people with hand tools rather than with modern farming equipment. How does this affect the productivity of Indonesian agriculture?

Vicious Cycle of Low Income and Low Productivity

Low productivity obviously results in low income, but low income, in turn, affects worker productivity. Low income means low saving, and low saving means low investment in human and physical capital. These difficult beginnings are made even worse by poor diet and insufficient healthcare. Therefore, as children grow into adults, they are not well suited for regular employment. Thus, *low income and low productivity may reinforce each other in a vicious cycle of poverty.*

Why is labor productivity low in developing countries? **CHECKPOINT**

21.1 ASSESSMENT

Think Critically

1. Do you think it was easier for the United States to become an industrialized market economy in the nineteenth century than it is for developing countries today? Why or why not?
2. Why don't reductions in child mortality rates necessarily cause an improvement in the standard of living in developing countries?
3. Why is labor productivity likely to be low in nations that have rapid population growth?
4. Many developing countries rely on parents to teach their children how to produce goods and services. How does this limit their ability to increase production?
5. Why is 2 percent of the U.S. workforce able to produce more food than our nation needs, while many developing nations cannot grow enough food for themselves, even with one-half of their population working in agriculture?

Graphing Exercise

6. There are many indicators of a nation's economic wealth and development. One of these is the number of personal computers per 1,000 residents. Industrial countries have many more computers per capita than developing countries. Use data in the table to draw a bar graph that shows computer ownership rates in the identified nations. Do you believe computer ownership is a good indicator of a nation's economic wealth and development? Explain your answer.

PERSONAL COMPUTER OWNERSHIP PER 1,000 RESIDENTS IN 2008

Country	PC Ownership	Country	PC Ownership
Switzerland	976	Morocco	57
Taiwan	835	Cuba	56
Hong Kong	693	Egypt	39
Estonia	256	Honduras	25

Source: *Statistical Abstract of the United States, 2011*, p. 869.

Make Academic Connections

7. **Management** Assume you own a small business in a developing country that produces aluminum cooking pots. Through hard work and thrift, you have been able to save enough money to purchase a machine that can produce cooking pots twice as fast. In order to use this machine, however, you would need to hire someone to train your workers. This training would cost as much as the machine itself. Under these conditions, would it make sense for you to purchase the machine? What alternatives do you have if you want your business to become more efficient and grow?

TeamWork

Working in small teams, make a list of skills that you would not possess if you had not been able to attend school. Discuss how the lack of these skills would affect your productivity. What might happen to the economy of the United States if our government stopped providing free public education and abolished requirements to attend school? Compare your team's answers with those of other teams.

MOVERS AND SHAKERS

Joe Whinney

Founder and CEO, Theo Chocolate

Joe Whinney wants you to think about where your chocolate comes from. He wants you to consider that whenever you buy a chocolate bar, you may be buying into an oppressive system that has allegedly used child and forced labor on some cocoa plantations. His company, Theo Chocolate, offers an alternative. Theo Chocolate is the first organic, Fair Trade and Fair for Life certified bean-to-bar chocolate factory in the United States.

As a child, Whinney loved chocolate. As an adult, he began working with cocoa growers in Central America and Africa. He learned about the dietary, cultural, and historical significance of chocolate. He also learned about the social, environmental, and economic problems associated with cocoa growing. He observed that the use of child labor was widespread on the cocoa plantations.

Whinney noticed the extreme poverty of the cocoa growers. He said, "…I was absolutely amazed at the level of poverty… there were farmers who had never seen chocolate…They had no idea what it tasted like…then they asked me how much does a chocolate bar cost. And I told them…one response was, 'Well, I could feed my family for a week for that.'… that redefined what it meant to me to participate in producing a luxury product —that is, chocolate." Whinney explained that the average cocoa farmer makes about a dollar a day. He said, "It's a terrible situation, but there is a business solution to this if consumers are willing to pay a little more for higher quality chocolate that's grown organically and sourced in a way that also benefits the farmers." Whinney says that consumers who wish to purchase products that are not made using child labor should look for products labeled Fair Trade and Fair for Life certified.

In 1994, at age 25, Whinney led the way in the importation of organic Fair Trade certified cocoa beans into North America. Whinney explains, "Fair Trade chocolate is chocolate that certifies that all the way back to the farm the workers are treated fairly, that they have safe working conditions, that children of cocoa farmers have access to education. Farmers benefit from fair prices based on quality and can then choose how the Fair Trade premium is spent within their family, community, or organization."

Courtesy of Joe Whinney

Theo is a "vertically integrated company," meaning it controls the entire chocolate manufacturing process, from bean sourcing through to the final molding process. Whinney knows that Theo Chocolate costs more than conventional chocolate products. He said, "We're more expensive because our product reflects the real cost of doing this right. The farmers need to be guaranteed an ongoing buyer committed to these more expensive beans, or else they just go back to using pesticides and other chemical additives in order to do it as cheaply as possible."

Whinney wants consumers to remember that they have the power to reform the "dark side of the chocolate and cocoa industry". He said, "If you want to help poor farmers and stop the abuses, take a hard look at what you're buying and where it came from. If you don't want to take the time to investigate, just stick with buying Fair Trade and Fair for Life certified and organic chocolate."

Think Critically **Go online to research the process a company must follow to use the Fair Trade Certified™ label on it products. As a consumer, do you feel responsible for buying imported products only from companies that treat workers fairly and humanely? Why or why not?**

Sources: http://transfairusa.org/certification; http://www.myacpa.org/pd/sustainability/whinney.cfm;http://www.huffingtonpost.com/regina-varolli/valentines-chocolate-plea_b_818362.html; http://www.seattlepi.com/local/article/Theo-Chocolate-hopes-to-start-cocoa-revolution-1291912.php#ixzz1ZDZBicYx; http://www.csmonitor.com/The-Culture/Food/2009/0211/p17s01-lifo.html/%28page%29/2; http://www.ilo.org/public//english//standards/ipec/themes/cocoa/download/2005_02_cl_cocoa.pdf; and http://www.laborrights.org/stop-child-labor/cocoa-campaign

21.2 FOREIGN TRADE, FOREIGN AID, AND ECONOMIC DEVELOPMENT

Key Terms

import substitution 670
export promotion 671
brain drain 672
foreign aid 672
bilateral aid 673
multilateral aid 673
U.S. Agency for International Development (USAID) 673

Learning Objectives

LO1 Identify two foreign-trade strategies and assess their impact on economic development.

LO2 Assess the effect of foreign aid on economic development.

In Your World

To boost labor productivity, developing countries must make the most efficient use of their resources. Some developing countries try to speed development by importing better capital goods. To import capital and technology, developing countries first must acquire the foreign exchange needed to pay for them.

FOREIGN TRADE AND MIGRATION

LO1
Identify two foreign-trade strategies and assess their impact on economic development.

What is the role of international trade in economic development? The least-developed economies rely on farming and on natural resources, such as wild game, timber, and mining. Economic development usually involves a shift from agricultural products and raw materials to manufacturing more complex products. If a country is fortunate, this transformation occurs gradually through natural market forces. Sometimes government pushes along the shift. How quickly an economy develops a manufacturing base depends in part on its trade relations with the rest of the world.

Import Substitution

Many developing countries, including Argentina and India, have, in the past, pursued a trade policy called **import substitution**, whereby the country begins manufacturing products that until then had been imported. Often the packaging and even the name of the product were quite similar to the imported good, such as "Crust" toothpaste instead of "Crest" toothpaste. To insulate domestic producers from foreign competition, the government usually imposed high tariffs, stiff import quotas, or other trade restrictions.

Import substitution became a popular development strategy for several reasons.

1. Demand already existed for these products, so the "what to produce" question was easily answered.
2. By reducing imports, the approach addressed a common problem among developing countries—the shortage of foreign exchange.
3. Import substitution was popular with those who supplied labor, capital, and other resources to the protected domestic industries.

import substitution
A development strategy that emphasizes replacing imports with domestic production

Like all protection measures, however, import substitution wiped out the gains from specialization and comparative advantage among countries. Often the developing country replaced low-cost foreign goods with high-cost domestic goods. Domestic producers, insulated from foreign competition, usually failed to become efficient. They produced goods at a higher cost and of inferior quality, compared to the imports they replaced.

Even the balance-of-payments picture did not improve, because other countries typically retaliated with their own trade restrictions. Import substitution protected some domestic industries but hurt consumers with higher prices and lower quality.

Export Promotion

Critics of the import-substitution approach claim that export promotion is a more certain path to economic development. **Export promotion** is a development strategy that focuses on producing for the export market. This approach begins with making relatively simple products, such as textiles. As a developing country builds its educational and technological base, producers can then manufacture and export more complex products.

Economists favor export promotion over import substitution because the emphasis is on comparative advantage and trade expansion, rather than trade restriction. Export promotion also forces producers to become more efficient in order to compete in world markets. Research shows that global competition increases domestic efficiency. What's more, export promotion involves less government intervention in the market than import substitution does.

export promotion
A development strategy that concentrates on producing for the export market

Export promotion has been the more successful development strategy. For example, the newly industrialized "Asian Tigers" (Taiwan, South Korea, Hong Kong,

ESSENTIAL QUESTION

Standard CEE 6: Specialization

When individuals, regions, and nations specialize in what they can produce at the lowest cost and then trade with others, both production and consumption increase.

Photodisc/Getty Images

Stephen Coburn/Shutterstock.com

How do U.S. exports of textile machinery to Italy boost production and consumption of the men's suits that country produces?

and Singapore) have grown much more quickly using export promotion than have import-substituting countries such as Argentina, India, and Peru.

Most Latin American nations, which for decades favored import substitution, are now pursuing free-trade agreements with the United States. India is in the process of dismantling trade barriers, especially for high-technology capital goods such as computer chips. Trade barriers in India, however, still remain in place for many consumer goods. Indian tariffs are the highest in the world. When it comes to imports, one slogan of Indian trade officials is "Microchips, yes! Potato chips, no!"

International Migration

International migration also affects developing economies. Because unemployment and underemployment are high in developing countries, job opportunities are better in industrial economies. This is a big reason why people in poorer countries try to move to richer countries. Millions of Mexicans, for example, have risked their lives trying to migrate to the United States.

A major source of foreign exchange in many developing countries is the money sent home by migrants who find jobs in industrial countries. For example, Salvadoran migrants in the United States account for a significant portion of spending power in El Salvador—about 10 percent of the GDP there. In fact, the Salvadoran economy now uses the U.S. dollar as legal tender, and no longer prints its own currency. Migration also provides a valuable safety valve for many poor countries.

There is a downside to migration for the developing country, however. Sometimes the best and the brightest professionals, such as doctors, nurses, and engineers, migrate from developing countries to industrial countries. The financial incentives can be powerful. For example, a nurse would start at just $6,000 a year in the Philippines, where many nurses remain unemployed, compared to $36,000 in the United States, where nursing jobs are abundant. Because human capital is such a key resource, this **brain drain** may hurt the developing economy in the long run.

CHECKPOINT What are two foreign trade strategies, and what is the impact of each on economic development?

FOREIGN AID

LO2 Assess the effect of foreign aid on economic development.

Because poor countries usually do not generate enough savings to fund an adequate level of investment, these countries often rely on foreign sources of financial capital. What is the role of foreign aid in economic development?

brain drain A developing country's loss of educated migrants to industrial market countries

foreign aid An international transfer of cash, goods, services, or other assistance to promote economic development

What Is Foreign Aid?

Foreign aid is any international transfer made on especially favorable terms, for the purposes of promoting economic development. Foreign aid includes grants, which need not be repaid. It also includes loans extended on more favorable terms than the recipient could receive otherwise. These loans have lower interest rates, longer repayment periods, and sometimes are wiped off the books entirely. Foreign aid can take the form of cash grants, cash loans, capital goods, technical advice, food, and other assistance.

Some foreign aid is granted by one country, such as the United States, to another country, such as the Philippines. Country-to-country aid is called **bilateral aid**. Other foreign aid goes through international bodies, such as the World Bank. Assistance provided by organizations that get funds from a number of countries is called **multilateral aid**. For example, the *World Bank* provides grants and loans to benefit development. This includes aid for health and education programs or for basic infrastructure projects like dams, roads, and communications networks. The *International Monetary Fund* extends loans to countries that have trouble with their balance of payments. The terms of these loans are more favorable to the countries than would be offered by regular banks.

During the past four decades, the United States has provided more than $400 billion to aid developing countries. Most U.S. aid has been coordinated by the **U.S. Agency for International Development (USAID)**. Its mission is

1. to further America's foreign-policy interests in expanding democracy and free markets
2. to improve living standards in the developing world.

USAID concentrates primarily on health, education, and agriculture. It provides both technical assistance and loans.

Foreign aid is a controversial, though small, part of the federal budget. In the past decade, official U.S. aid has been less than 0.2 percent of the U.S. GDP, compared to an average of 0.3 percent given by other advanced industrial nations.

Does Foreign Aid Promote Economic Development?

In general, foreign aid provides additional purchasing power to the country that receives it. It's not clear whether foreign aid simply increases consumption rather than increasing investment. What is clear is that foreign aid often benefits not so much the poor as the government officials, who decide how to allocate the funds. More than 90 percent of the funds distributed by USAID has been dispersed by local governments. There is reason to believe that much of this aid has been diverted from its intended purpose by government officials in recipient nations.

Much bilateral funding is tied to purchases of goods and services from the donor nation, and such programs can sometimes be counterproductive. For example, in the 1950s, the United States began the Food for Peace program, which required recipient nations to purchase food from the United States. Although this helped sell U.S. farm products abroad, it did little to help these nations develop their own agricultural base. It also did not help them to become less dependent on imported food. Worse yet, the availability of low-priced food from abroad drove down farm prices in the developing countries, hurting farmers there.

The same is true for clothing. Used clothing donated to thrift shops and charitable organizations in industrial countries typically winds up for sale in Africa, where the low price discourages local production of clothing. Before all this used

bilateral aid Development aid from one country to another

multilateral aid Development aid from an international organization, such as the World Bank, that gets funds from many countries

U.S. Agency for International Development (USAID) The federal agency that coordinates U.S. aid to the developing world

Math in Economics

Common Core Ratios and Proportional Relationships

You can use values in the table to convert metric measures to customary measures. Multiply the amount of the metric measure by the conversion factor given in the table.

METRIC MEASURE TO COMMON MEASURE CONVERSION TABLE

Metric Measure = Conversion Factor	Metric Measure = Conversion Factor
1 kilometer = 0.621 miles	1 liter = 0.264 gallons
1 meter = 3.28 feet	1 gram = 0.035 ounces
1 square meter = 1.195 square yards	1 kilogram = 2.202 pounds

EXAMPLE A British recipe calls for 500 grams of baking chocolate. How many ounces of chocolate should you use?

SOLUTION Multiply the number of grams times the gram to ounces conversion factor from the table. $500 \times 0.035 = 17.5$ ounces

Practice the Skill Convert each amount to the given currency.

1. A German car is advertised as having a top speed of 180 kilometers per hour. How many miles per hour can the car travel?
2. The German car weighs 1,150 kilograms. How much does the car weigh in pounds?
3. The German car uses 7.9 square meters of upholstery fabric for its seats. How many square yards of fabric are in the car?
4. The German car is able to get 18 kilometers per liter of gasoline. How many miles per gallon does the car get?

clothing swamped the continent, Africa had its own textile industry. Unfortunately, textile production is often the first rung on the ladder to developing a broader manufacturing base.

Foreign aid may have raised the standard of living in some developing countries. However, it has not necessarily increased their ability to become self-supporting at that higher standard of living. Many countries that receive aid are doing less of what they had done well. In some cases, foreign aid has helped corrupt governments stay in power. Agricultural sectors have suffered the most. For example, per capita food production in Africa has fallen since 1960.

Because of disappointment with the results of government aid, the trend is now towards channeling funds through private nonprofit agencies such as CARE. More than half of all foreign aid now goes through private channels. The privatization of foreign aid matches a larger trend toward privatization of state enterprises around the world. This important development is discussed later in the chapter.

CHECKPOINT

What has been the effect of foreign aid on economic development?

21.2 ASSESSMENT

Think Critically

1. In the 1980s, many U.S. automobile manufacturers introduced smaller, more fuel-efficient cars to compete with the flood of small foreign cars that many consumers were buying. Was this an example of import substitution? Explain your answer.
2. What are the pros and cons for a developing country when its people migrate to industrial market economies to obtain employment? Does this depend on whether a migrant is a skilled professional or an unskilled worker? Why or why not?
3. If the United States sent every person in a developing country enough food to eat for free, what would happen to farmers in that country? Why can foreign aid be a mixed blessing?
4. Why do some leaders in developing countries argue that the most effective aid they could receive would be a guarantee from industrial market economies that they will purchase imports from these countries at prices that allow their producers to earn a profit?

Graphing Exercise

5. The United States provides foreign aid to many developing countries. The amount given, however, is not constant or equally distributed among nations or regions. Construct a multiple bar graph using data in the table to show how U.S. foreign assistance was provided between 2006 and 2010. Why do you think the amounts of aid awarded changed from year to year?

U.S. FOREIGN ASSISTANCE PROVIDED THROUGH GRANTS AND CREDITS, 2006–2010 (VALUES IN MILLIONS)

Region	2006	2007	2008	2009	2010
Africa	$1,261	$3,546	$4,778	$6,425	$7,315
Near East & South Asia	$4,767	$9,947	$9,038	$11,780	$14,413
Eastern Europe	$266	$1,089	$2,010	$1,644	$1,490
Western Hemisphere	$1,512	$1,398	$2,087	$4,311	$2,977

Source: *Statistical Abstract of the United States: 2012*, Table 1297.

Make Academic Connections

6. **History** After World War II, the United States provided about $85 billion (in 2010 dollars) in aid through the Marshall Plan to help the nations of Western Europe rebuild from the war. This effort was a great success. Between 1948 and the end of 1952, the nations of Western Europe increased their collective GDPs by well over 100 percent. What advantages did these nations have in rebuilding that are not shared by developing countries today?

TeamWork Working in teams of six or eight students, debate the pros and cons of the import substitution trade strategy versus the export promotion strategy. Divide the team into two smaller teams. One will represent import substitution and the other, export promotion. Spend about 10 minutes in your small teams studying the textbook in preparation for the debate. Start the debate by presenting your team's strategy to the other team. Then debate the effectiveness of the strategies.

21st Century Skills

Global Awareness

Citizens of the World

People who live in industrial market economies often wonder what they can do to help those who live in developing economies. Some possibilities, along with their potential limitations, include:

- Send gifts of food, clothing, and materials to construct homes. These contributions may help to resolve current problems, but they do little to encourage production or eliminate the problems in the long run.
- Send tools to help people become more productive and self-sufficient. Unless people are taught how to use these tools, they may not become more productive.
- Send medicine and health-care professionals to improve medical care. Sending medical assistance will reduce the number of people who become ill or die, but it has a limited impact on productivity , at least in the near term.
- Fund infrastructure improvements. Better roads, irrigation, and communication systems could help the economy but are likely to have limited effect if investments in business capital and education do not take place as well.

Problems Related to International Trade

Many developing nations export products that have relatively low value, while those they import are quite expensive. Further, when there is a downturn in the world's economy, the prices for products from developing nations are likely to fall much more than those from industrial nations. In the economic downturn that began in 2008, for example, the price of metals such as iron ore, copper, and aluminum fell by an average of about 35 percent. Nations in Africa and South America that sold these products suffered a substantial loss in their earnings because smaller amounts of these metals were demanded at the same time that their prices declined. In these same years the price of machinery and electrical equipment they imported fell by less than 5 percent. This situation made it difficult for many developing nations to be economically successful or pay their debts on time.

Can We Help?

People who live in developed nations could help by going out of their way to buy products made in developing countries. Many organizations, such as Ten Thousand Villages, encourage economic growth in developing nations by marketing products made there to people in developed nations. Even greater help could result if businesses based in developed countries choose to manufacture products in developing nations. This type of long-term commitment would provide a steady flow of jobs and income to these countries that would help them make ongoing investments in their economies. Ultimately, there is no single action that will provide developing nations with success. There needs to be a combination of many factors to bring about economic growth and stability.

Apply the Skill

Imagine that you have $500 that you have decided to use to help people in a developing nation. You can simply send the cash to a charity in that country or you could help pay for tools, education, medical care, or anything else that you believe would help. State what use you would make of these funds and why you would make your choice.

21.3 RULES OF THE GAME, TRANSITION ECONOMIES, AND CONVERGENCE

Learning Objectives

LO1 Assess the effect of a nation's physical infrastructure and rules of the game on its economic development.

LO2 Discuss why many command economies are trying, with difficulty, to introduce market forces.

LO3 Explain the convergence theory.

Key Terms

In Your World

Economic systems may be classified based on the ownership of resources, the way resources are allocated to produce goods and services, and the incentives used to motivate people. Laws regarding resource ownership and the role of government in resource allocation determine the "rules of the game"—the incentives and constraints that guide the behavior of you and other individual decision makers. Resources in command economies are owned mostly by the government and are allocated by central planners. Resources in market economies are owned mostly by individuals and are allocated through market coordination. Regardless of the economic system, economic development depends in part on establishing a trusted and reliable framework for productive activity.

INFRASTRUCTURE AND RULES OF THE GAME

LO1
Assess the effect of a nation's physical infrastructure and rules of the game on its economic development.

Key ingredients for economic development that have not yet been discussed are the physical infrastructure and rules of the game that support the economic system. Whether the system involves central planning or competitive markets, all economies benefit from a stable and supportive institutional framework.

Physical Infrastructure

Production and exchange rely on the economy's **physical infrastructure**, which are transportation, communication, energy, water, and sanitation systems provided by or regulated by government. Roads, bridges, airports, harbors, and other transportation facilities are vital to production. Reliable mail, Internet, and phone services, along with a steady supply of electricity and water, also are essential for advanced production techniques. Imagine how difficult it would be to run even a personal computer if electricity and phone service were not available or were continually interrupted, as is often the problem in developing countries.

Many developing countries have serious deficiencies in their physical infrastructures. As just one measure, Figure 21.3 shows the number of fixed and mobile

physical infrastructure
Transportation, communication, energy, water, and sanitation systems provided by or regulated by government

FIGURE 21.3 Fixed and Mobile Telephone Lines per 1,000 Population by Country in 2009

Many developing countries have serious deficiencies in their physical infrastructures.

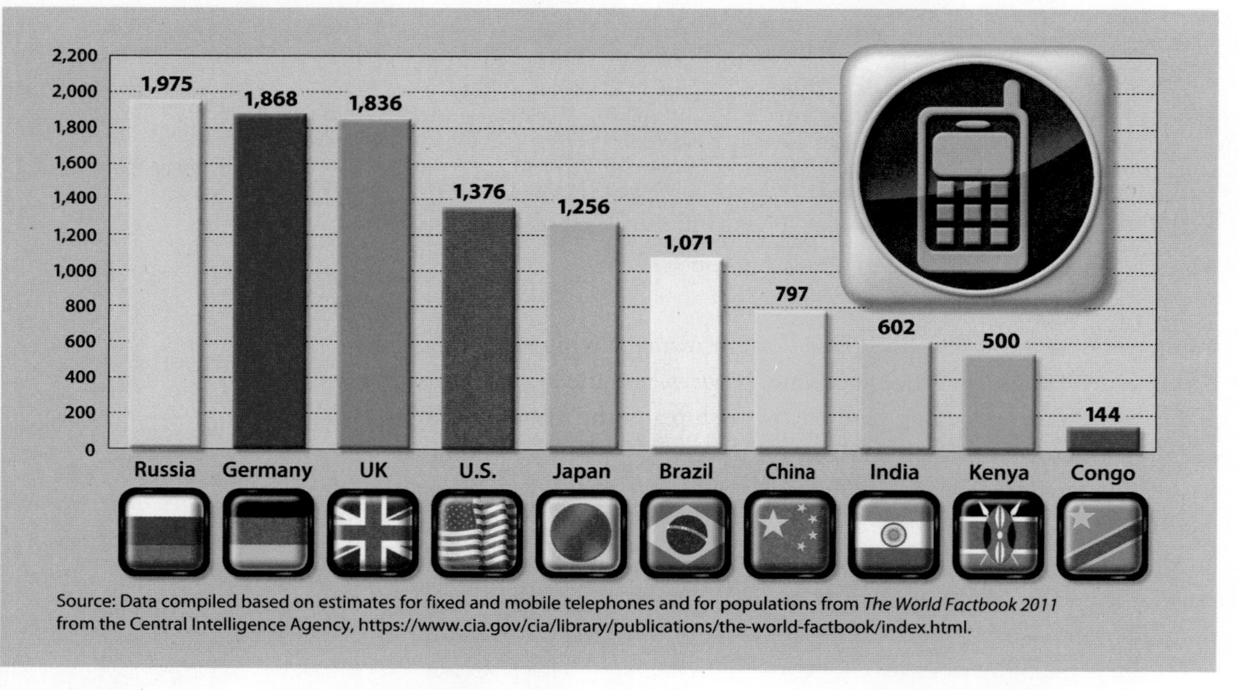

Source: Data compiled based on estimates for fixed and mobile telephones and for populations from *The World Factbook 2011* from the Central Intelligence Agency, https://www.cia.gov/cia/library/publications/the-world-factbook/index.html.

telephone lines per 1,000 population in 2009 for the 10 countries examined earlier. Russia, the top-rated country in this category, had 1,975 phone lines per 1,000 people. Bottom-ranked Congo had only 144 phones lines per 1,000 people. Worldwide, there were 950 phone lines per 1000 people.

Worse still for the infrastructure, some of the poorest countries in Africa have been ravaged by civil war, internal political strife, and government corruption. For example, Congo's civil war has killed more than five million people in recent years. In Sudan, civil war has lasted a quarter of a century. Wars not only kill people, they destroy bridges, roads, electrical systems, water works, schools, and other capital goods vital for economic development. Poverty and government corruption are other reason why some nations have inadequate infrastructures.

Rules of the Game

Reliable and trusted rules of the game also are important for economic development. Recall that the rules of the game are the formal and informal institutions that promote production incentives and economic activity. They include the laws, property rights, customs, conventions, and other social and political elements that encourage people to undertake productive activity.

On the *formal* end of the spectrum, rules of the game include a country's codified rules and laws, along with the system for establishing and enforcing those rules and laws. On the *informal* end of the spectrum, rules of the game include the customs and informal mechanisms that help coordinate production.

Rules of the game are critical for economic development. When operating properly, they allow people to work, spend, and save to build a better future for themselves and their families. When rules are weak, corrupt, or operate unfairly, people lack confidence in the economic system. Weak or corrupt rules also encourage people to "take" rather than to "make." This means they may find it more attractive to steal what others created, rather than to produce something of value themselves. When taking becomes more attractive than making, total production declines and average incomes fall. Such economies suffer a downward spiral.

Better incentives can boost productivity and improve the standard of living. For example, a more stable political climate promotes investment in the economy. Conversely, destabilizing events such as wars and terrorist attacks discourage investment, harm productivity, and reduce the standard of living.

CHECKPOINT

What is the effect of a nation's physical infrastructure and rules of the game on its economic development?

ECONOMIES IN TRANSITION

LO2
Discuss why many command economies are trying to introduce market forces.

From the breakup of the Soviet Union to China's move toward more economic freedom, markets are replacing central plans in countries around the world. The attempt to replace central planning with markets is one of the greatest economic experiments in history. Economists involved in structuring the transition from central planning to market systems are learning as they go.

Prices and Profit in Command Economies

In command economies, most resources are owned by the government and production is directed by the central plans of government. Most prices in command economies are established not by market forces but by central planners. Once set, prices tend to be inflexible. As a result, consumers have little say in what's produced. Consumer goods often are priced below the market-clearing level, so shortages are common. For example, just prior to the collapse of the Soviet Union in 1991, the price of bread had not changed since 1954. That price amounted to only 7 percent of bread's production cost. Some rents had not changed in 60 years. Thus, prices had little relation to supply and demand. Prices were usually far below what they would be with free markets, so shortages were common.

Evidence of shortages of consumer goods included long waiting lines at retail stores. Shoppers in the former Soviet Union sometimes would wait in line all night and into the next day. Consumers often relied on "connections" through acquaintances to obtain many goods and services. Scarce goods were frequently diverted to the black market, where prices reflected market conditions and were much higher.

Investigate Your Local Economy

Think about the infrastructure in your area, such as transportation, communication, energy, water and sanitation systems. For systems you think need to be improved, research to find out if there are plans underway to do so. If so, write a paragraph describing these plans. If not, write a letter to a political leader describing the problem and asking for help in resolving it.

Prices did not allocate products very well in command economies. To make matters worse, state enterprises faced little pressure to cover costs. With central planning, any "profit" earned by a state enterprise was appropriated by the state. Any "loss" was covered by a state subsidy. Thus, covering costs was not important for a state enterprise nor was earning a profit. Such enterprises faced what has been called a **soft budget constraint**. Managers could ignore market forces, could allocate resources inefficiently, and could make poor investment decisions—yet still survive year after year.

Privatization

One necessary step in the move from a command economy to a market economy is **privatization**, which is the process of turning government enterprises into private enterprises. It is the opposite of *nationalization*, which is turning private enterprises into government enterprises.

soft budget constraint In command economies, the budget condition faced by state enterprises that are subsidized when they lose money

privatization The process of turning government enterprises into private enterprises

The problem is that most command economies that are trying to privatize have no history of market interaction. They also have no established record of codified law or rules of conduct for market participants. For example, Russian privatization began in 1992 with the sale of municipally owned shops. Most property in countries of the former Soviet Union was owned by the state. Thus, it often remained unclear who had the authority to sell the property and who should receive the proceeds from the sale. This uncertainty resulted in cases in which different buyers purchased the same property from different public officials. Yet there was no clear legal process for resolving title disputes to establish property rights. Russia did not have a reliable legal system.

Worse still, self-serving managers stripped some enterprises of their assets. The process of privatization does not work well when the general population perceives it to be unfair. Thus, establishing a market system is easier said than done. Many command economies have little experience with laws and customs that are trusted, reliable, and fair.

CHECKPOINT **Why are centrally planned economies trying to introduce market forces, and what has been slowing down the process?**

ARE THE WORLD'S ECONOMIES CONVERGING?

LO3 Explain the convergence theory.

Given enough time, will poor countries eventually catch up with rich ones? The **convergence theory** argues that developing countries can grow faster than advanced ones and should eventually close the gap.

convergence theory A theory predicting that the standard of living in economies around the world will grow more similar over time, with poorer countries gradually closing the gap with richer ones

Reasons for Convergence

Countries that are far behind economically can grow faster by adopting new technology. It is easier to adopt new technology once it is developed than to develop that technology in the first place. For example, it's easier to buy a smartphone than to invent one. Advanced economies, which are already using the latest technology, can boost productivity only with a steady stream of technological breakthroughs.

Advanced countries, such as the United States, find their growth limited by the rate of creation of new knowledge and improved technology. Follower countries can grow more quickly by, for instance, adding computers where they had none before. For example, the United States makes up just 5 percent of the world's population. But in 1995, Americans owned most of the world's personal computers. By 2001, most PC purchases were outside the United States.

Some Convergence

What is the evidence for convergence? Some poor countries have begun to catch up with richer ones. For example, the newly industrialized Asian economies of Hong Kong, Singapore, South Korea, and Taiwan have invested heavily in technology and in education. These Asian Tigers have moved from the ranks of developing countries to the ranks of industrial market economies.

Not long ago, the world was one-sixth rich and five-sixths poor. Now, due to impressive growth in places like the Asian Tigers and China, the world is closer to one-fifth rich, with most of the rest not rich, but improving. So, most developing economies are experiencing a rising standard of living. Still, about one billion people are trapped in poor economies that are going nowhere.

Photodisc/Getty Images

Photodisc/Getty Images

Singapore, one of the so-called Asian Tigers, is a highly developed and successful free market economy. Due to investments in factories, machinery, new technology, and the health, education, and training of people, the population of Singapore enjoys a high standard of living. The country boasts one of the highest per capita GDPs in the world. Singapore is an island nation. How has this helped Singapore to successfully develop its economy?

Higher Birthrates and Less Human Capital

One reason per-capita consumption has grown so slowly in the poorest economies is that birthrates there are double those in richer countries. Therefore, poor economies must produce still more just to keep up with a growing population. Another reason why convergence has not taken hold, particularly for the poorest billion, is the vast difference in the amount of human capital across countries. Whereas technology is indeed portable from industrial economies to developing economies, the knowledge, skill, and training usually required to take advantage of that technology are not portable.

Some poor countries, such as most of those in Africa, simply do not yet have the human capital needed to identify and absorb new technology. Consider Internet use, which requires both online access and some ability to read and write. Figure 21.4 shows Internet users as a percent of the population for the 10 nations examined earlier. In the United Kingdom, 84 percent of the population use the Internet. In Congo, only a fraction of 1 percent uses the Internet. There is a clear digital divide between the richest and poorest economies. Worldwide, 30 percent of the population uses the Internet.

Reasons for Optimism

Despite all that, working conditions and living standards in most poor countries are improving, thanks to greater trade opportunities and pressure from international

FIGURE 21.4 Internet Users as Percent of Population in 2009

Some countries do not have the human capital needed to identify and use new technology.

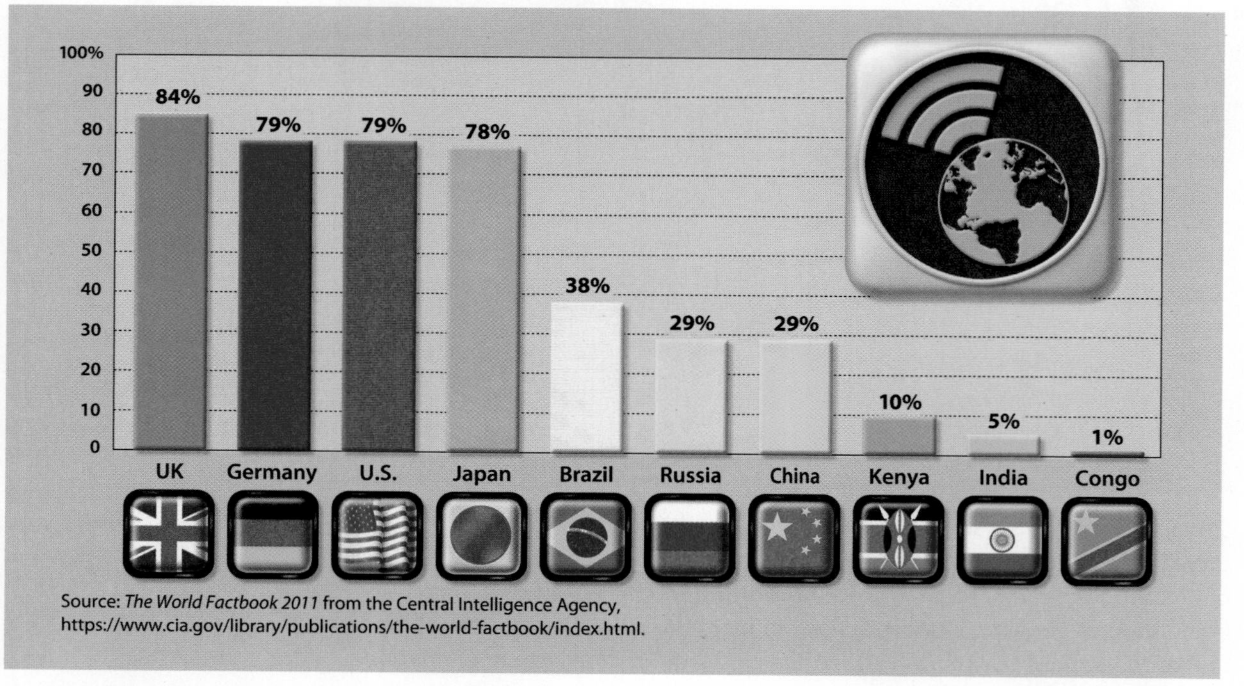

Source: *The World Factbook 2011* from the Central Intelligence Agency, https://www.cia.gov/library/publications/the-world-factbook/index.html.

bodies such as the World Trade Organization. For example, Cambodia is still poor, but the highest wages in the country are earned by those working in the export sector. These workers make products for companies such as Nike and Gap. Though pay is low by U.S. standards, workers in the export sector earn more than twice what judges and doctors average. Child labor is still a problem in poor countries, but because of world pressure on manufacturers, fewer and fewer are hiring children.

The reduction in trade barriers resulting from the Uruguay Round, the latest completed round of trade negotiations, is projected to boost world income by more than $500 billion per year. This amounts to an increase of about $400 per year for each household on Earth. That payoff may not impress those who object to greater globalization through freer trade, but for households in poor countries, it can be a lifesaver.

CHECKPOINT

What does the convergence theory predict, and why hasn't the reality yet matched that prediction?

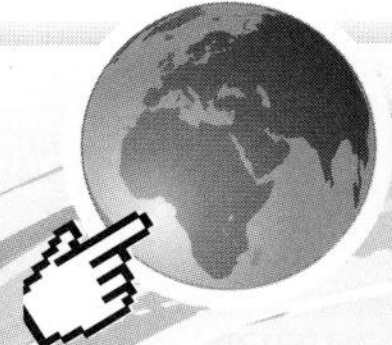

Span the Globe

The Poorest Billion

Not long ago, the world was one-sixth rich and five-sixths poor. Now, thanks to impressive growth in places like China, the world is more like one-sixth rich, two-thirds not rich but improving, and one-sixth poor and going nowhere. Most developing economies are experiencing a rising standard of living. But that still leaves about a billion people trapped in economies that are not only extremely poor, but staying the same or getting worse. About 45 countries fit into this poorest-billion category, including 30 countries in sub-Saharan Africa and Cambodia, Haiti, Laos, and North Korea.

An economist at Oxford University in England has examined what went wrong with these countries. He identified three *poverty traps*: (1) ethnic conflict, or civil war, (2) the misuse of natural resource wealth by government, and (3) a dysfunctional or corrupt government. Corrupt government officials who pursue their own self-interests do serious harm. For example, a recent survey that tracked government funds for rural health clinics in Chad found that less than 1 percent of the money reached the clinics.

Can these poorest billion be helped? The Oxford economist argues that what these countries need most is about ten years of domestic peace, backed by an outside force, if necessary, such as the UN.

Think Critically **Aside from unconditional foreign aid and supporting UN forces to keep the peace, can you think of any specific ways in which the rest of the world could help the billion people trapped and going nowhere in these poor nations?**

Sources: Paul Collier. *The Bottom Billion: Why the Poorest Countries Are Failing and What Can Be Done About It*, (Oxford University Press, 2007); and Paul Collier, *The Plundered Planet*, (Oxford University Press, 2010).

21.3 ASSESSMENT

Think Critically

1. Choose a business in your community that employs many workers. How would this business be affected if suddenly there were no local roads or bridges, electric power, telephone service, water supplies, and waste removal services? Why is a country that lacks basic physical infrastructure unlikely to have a comparative advantage in manufacturing?
2. Many developing countries have created laws to regulate the production of goods and services. Regardless of this fact, many businesses in these nations largely ignore these laws and carry out production as they choose. What do these nations need in addition to their laws? Explain your answer.
3. Why do people who live in nations that once relied on government ownership and control of businesses often find it difficult to operate in a competitive market economic system?
4. Will giving individuals the right to own and operate businesses with little government interference guarantee a nation's smooth transition from a command economy to a free market economy? Why or why not? What other conditions need to be created for this to take place?
5. Some people think that investments made in developing countries by businesses from industrial market economies help the developing nations improve their production efficiency and standard of living. Others think this investment will not improve the lives of these people. Which of these points of view do you believe is nearer to the truth? Explain your answer.

Graphing Exercises

6. U.S. businesses invest billions of dollars every year in developing countries. Draw a line graph showing the total accumulated value of U.S. investments in Latin America in the years from 2005 through 2010. Why do businesses make these investments? How do such investments benefit people in Latin America?

ACCUMULATED VALUE OF U.S. DIRECT INVESTMENTS IN LATIN AMERICA, 2004–2010 (MILLIONS)

Year	Value of Total U.S. Direct Investments in Latin America
2005	$379,582
2006	$418,429
2007	$556,160
2008	$591,363
2009	$678,956
2010	$724,405

Source: *Statistical Abstract of the United States: 2012*, p. 800.

Make Academic Connections

7. **Sociology** You have learned that poverty in the United States is frequently found in households led by single parents. These households often include young children. In what ways are the problems of these households in the United States similar to those faced by people who live in developing countries? In what ways are their problems different?

TeamWork

Working in small teams, make a list of examples of infrastructure that exist in your community that help local businesses to be more productive. For each example listed, explain how it was funded. Why are many developing nations unable to make similar investments in their infrastructure? Compare your team's answers with those of other teams.

Connect to History

Tariffs and Trade, Part II

The Reciprocal Trade Agreement Act of 1934 and its 12 extensions through 1962 ushered in an era of tariff reductions worldwide. The Act authorized the U.S. president to negotiate lower tariffs and give its trading partners "most favored nation status."

In 1947, following World War II, 23 nations negotiated the General Agreement on Tariffs and Trade (GATT). The goal was to encourage nations to lower tariffs and other trade barriers. For the United States, lowering tariffs also had a foreign-policy component of helping to rebuild Europe and develop poor nations. While the general principle is for a country to treat all members equally, some exceptions were allowed for developing countries to protect necessary industries. GATT also allowed for free-trade areas to be created, such as the European Community and the North American Free Trade Agreement (NAFTA). The first five trade agreements, or "rounds," were characterized primarily by countries negotiating tariff reductions. They would then apply the agreement to all members on a "most favored nation" basis.

During the 1964 Kennedy Round, the United States proposed across-the-board tariff reductions to all 62 member nations. Over the years, average tariff rates, at 47 percent in 1947, dropped to 9 percent in 1972, and to under 4 percent by 2011. Following the Kennedy Round, discussions began to focus more on non-tariff barriers and other exclusionary practices.

By the Uruguay Round (1986–1994), membership in GATT had grown to 123 countries. This round created the World Trade Organization (WTO). The WTO now has about 150 members, accounting for more than 97 percent of the world's trade. Fifty additional nations are negotiating membership.

The WTO operates principally under the rules formed by GATT. Documentation of those rules runs to 50,000 pages and incorporates 30 agreements, called schedules. WTO decisions are not put to a vote. In fact, voting rarely was used under GATT. Decisions typically are made by consensus, and then agreements are ratified by member-country legislative bodies.

The system allows countries to bring disputes to the WTO if they believe that their rights or agreements are being infringed. The organization encourages disagreements to be settled by consultation. Since 1995, the WTO has reviewed more than 300 cases before it. This exceeds the number dealt with by GATT from 1947 to 1994.

With 75 percent of its membership consisting of developing countries, the WTO faces huge challenges. The latest round of negotiations (the Doha round, begun in Doha, Qatar, in 2001) was still underway in 2012. During that round of negotiations, developing countries, which typically depend on agriculture for a large portion of their exports, were trying to eliminate export subsidies. The agricultural sectors in industrialized nations, however, rely on these subsidies to stay afloat. Therefore, ending export subsidies on agricultural goods is politically difficult for industrialized countries.

Think Critically Given a world economy, do you think a country can both promote free trade and protect its domestic industries at the same time? What would be the advantages to a country of doing both?

ASK THE EXPERT

www.cengage.com/school/contecon

Why are some nations rich but others poor?

Chapter 21 Summary

21.1 Developing Economies and Industrial Market Economies

A. Countries may be classified in a variety of ways based on their levels of economic development. Developing countries have lower levels of GDP per capita and higher rates of illiteracy, unemployment, underemployment, and population growth than industrial market countries. People in developing countries also have shorter life expectancies and higher birth rates.

B. Developing countries suffer from low labor productivity. Workers often lack a basic education and have health problems that reduce productivity. Income per capita is low in developing countries and does not allow individuals to invest much in their human and physical capital.

21.2 Foreign Trade, Foreign Aid, and Economic Development

A. Developing countries have used many techniques to try to speed their economic growth. One method is import substitution. This policy blocks imports and fills that demand with domestic production. Domestic producers then are able to sell products in a proven market without foreign competition. Another method used to speed growth is export promotion. This policy encourages production of goods targeted for the export market. Export promotion has proven to be the more powerful engine of economic growth.

B. Industrial market economies have attempted to assist developing countries through various programs that encourage investment in human and physical capital. Foreign aid has been extended through bilateral agreements, which are between individual countries, and through multilateral organizations. Over the past 40 years, the United States has given more than $400 billion in assistance to developing countries. Most of this aid was coordinated by the U.S. Agency for International Development (USAID). Foreign aid provides additional purchasing power in developing countries. There is, however, a question about its effectiveness.

21.3 Rules of the Game, Transition Economies, and Convergence

A. For a country to produce goods and services efficiently and to experience economic growth, its economy must provide both a physical infrastructure and a stable business climate. Many developing countries lack sufficient roads, bridges, airports, harbors, and other transportation facilities. They lack reliable mail, Internet access, phone service, or a steady supply of electricity, water, and other essential services.

B. Inefficiencies in command economies led most of them to convert to market-based economies. However, privatization, converting government enterprises to private enterprises, does not necessarily ensure that these new owners have the entrepreneurial skills needed to run them efficiently.

C. Some economists and politicians believe that poor economies will eventually catch up with rich economies—a theory called convergence. A reduction in trade barriers, increased international investments, and a spread of technology and education may allow many to escape poverty in the future.

CHAPTER 21 ASSESSMENT

Review Economic Terms

Match the terms with the definitions. Some terms will not be used.

_____ 1. The process of turning public enterprises into private enterprises

_____ 2. Development aid from one country to another

_____ 3. Nations with low GDP per capita, high rates of illiteracy, high unemployment, and high fertility rates

_____ 4. Transportation, communication, energy, water, and sanitation systems provided by or regulated by government

_____ 5. Development aid from an organization, such as the World Bank, that gets funds from a group of countries

_____ 6. A developing country's loss of educated migrants to industrial market countries

_____ 7. The average number of births during each woman's lifetime

_____ 8. Economically advanced market countries of Western Europe, North America, Australia, New Zealand, and Japan, and the newly industrialized countries of Asia

_____ 9. A development strategy that concentrates on producing for the export market

_____ 10. A development strategy that emphasizes replacing imports with domestic production

a. bilateral aid
b. brain drain
c. convergence theory
d. developing countries
e. export promotion
f. fertility rate
g. foreign aid
h. import substitution
i. industrial market countries
j. multilateral aid
k. physical infrastructure
l. privatization
m. soft budget constraint
n. U.S. Agency for International Development (USAID)

Review Economic Concepts

11. **True or False** Developing countries typically have low GDP per capita, high rates of illiteracy, high unemployment rates, and rapid population growth.

12. Developing countries are likely to have each of the following except
    a. a limited physical infrastructure.
    b. few educational opportunities for students.
    c. easy access to high-quality medical care.
    d. a low savings rate.

13. A country's ________?________ is the average number of children born during each woman's lifetime.

14. **True or False** Countries with low life expectancies also have high child mortality rates.

15. People in developing countries
    a. are all equally poor.
    b. vary in income.
    c. are able to support their families because their prices are low.
    d. are provided with free medical care by their governments.

16. Countries that use tariffs or quotas to encourage the production of products that were formerly imported are following a policy of ________?________.

17. **True or False** Like all protection measures, export promotion reduces the gains from specialization and comparative advantage.

18. Farms in developing countries are often inefficient for each of the following reasons except
    a. they are too small to be efficient.
    b. they lack tools and fertilizer that could make them more efficient.
    c. the farmers do not work hard enough to be efficient.
    d. the farmers do not employ the latest technology.

19. When skilled workers leave developing countries to find employment in industrial market countries, there is a(n) ________?________

20. Foreign assistance extended by one nation to another nation is called
    a. bilateral aid.
    b. unilateral aid.
    c. multilateral aid.
    d. quadrilateral aid.

21. Most U.S. government assistance provided to developing countries in the past 40 years has been coordinated by the ________?________.

22. Which of the following is an example of physical infrastructure?
    a. savings used to purchase machinery
    b. land upon which crops are grown
    c. roads upon which products are moved
    d. good weather that helps crops to grow

23. **True or False** For rules to be effective in regulating production, they must be written into laws.

24. ________?________ in command economies allows inefficient producers to continue to operate over long periods of time, even when their costs were greater than the income they received from products they sold.

25. In the past decade, there has been
    a. a steady convergence of the world's economies.
    b. some evidence that the world's economies are converging.
    c. a narrowing of gaps in productivity among all the world's countries.
    d. no growth in productivity by any of the world's developing countries.

Apply Economic Concepts

26. **Evaluate the Cost of Education** In many of the world's poorest countries, nearly 50 percent of the population is under 15 years of age. If these people are going to help improve the productivity of their economies, they must be trained in modern methods of production. Explain why it would be difficult for many of these children to be educated and become productive members of a growing economy.

27. **Determine the Best Type of Aid** Imagine that you have been given control of the USAID program. You have the power to decide how to use the funds provided to this organization by the U.S. government. Unfortunately, there is a limit to what you can spend, and there are many

nations that need assistance. You have allocated $20 million to a developing country. These funds may be spent to do any of the following. How would you spend this money to do the most good? Explain your choice.

- Spend the money to provide an additional year of education for 20,000 students.
- Spend the money to provide better healthcare for 200,000 people for a month.
- Spend the money to purchase better farm equipment for 10,000 farmers.
- Spend the money to build a 20-mile highway that links the rest of the country to to the country's only port.
- Spend the money to provide 1 million people with better nutrition for two months.

28. **Analyze Visuals** Study the table below and evaluate the information it provides about cellular telephone subscribers. Does it show which countries are still developing and which are established industrial market economies? Explain your answer.

CELLULAR PHONE SUBSCRIBERS PER 1,000 RESIDENTS, 2008

Ethiopia	24
Cuba	29
Haiti	324
Pakistan	497
Brazil	785
United States	868

29. **21st Century Skills: Global Awareness** Search the Internet to identify a famous person who was born in a developing country but has chosen to immigrate to the United States. Investigate this person's history and summarize his or her reasons for coming to this nation. How has this person benefited from this decision? How has the United States benefited? Has this person's native country been harmed by this person leaving? Do you think it is appropriate for the United States to encourage talented people to immigrate? Explain your answers.

Digging Deeper

with Economics e-Collection

Access the Gale Economics e-Collection through the URL below. Search for recent articles about U.S. foreign aid policy. Use the phrase "foreign aid" as your search term, and then refine your search using terms from this chapter including bilateral aid, multilateral aid, USAID, World Bank, International Monetary Fund, and economic development. Find articles from magazines, newspapers, and academic journals. Choose one of the articles, and write a summary of its main points. Be prepared to discuss your article in class.

www.cengage.com/school/contecon

GLOSSARY

A

ability-to-pay tax principle Those with a greater ability to pay, such as those with a higher income, should pay more of a tax

absolute advantage The ability to make something using fewer resources than other producers require

aggregate demand The relationship between the average price of aggregate output and the quantity of aggregate output demanded, with other things constant

aggregate demand curve A curve representing the relationship between the economy's price level and real GDP demanded per period, other things constant

aggregate expenditure Total spending on all final goods and services produced in the economy during the year

aggregate income The sum of all the income earned by resource suppliers in the economy during the year

aggregate output A composite measure of all final goods and services produced in an economy during a given period; real GDP

aggregate supply curve A curve representing the relationship between the economy's price level and real GDP supplied per period, other things constant

allocative efficiency Occurs when a firm produces the output most valued by consumers

annual percentage yield (APY) Formula banks must use to calculate interest they pay on deposits

annually balanced budget Matching annual spending with annual revenue, except during war years; the approach to federal budgeting prior to the Great Depression

antitrust activity Government efforts aimed at preventing monopoly and promoting competition in markets where competition is desirable

antitrust laws Laws that reduce anticompetitive behavior and promote competition in markets where competition is desirable

applied research Research that seeks answers to particular questions or applies scientific discoveries to develop specific products

articles of incorporation A written application to the state seeking permission to form a corporation

asset Any physical property or financial claim that is owned

automatic stabilizers Government spending and taxing programs that year after year automatically reduce fluctuations in disposable income, and thus in consumption, over the business cycle

B

balance of payments A record of all economic transactions between residents of one country and residents of the rest of the world during a given period

balance sheet A financial statement showing assets, liabilities, and net worth at a point in time; assets must equal liabilities plus net worth, so the statement is in balance

barriers to entry Restrictions on the entry of new firms into an industry

barter A system of exchange in which products are traded directly for other products

basic research The search for knowledge without regard to how that knowledge will be used; a first step toward technological advancement

behavioral economics An approach that borrows insights from psychology to help explain economic choices

benefits-received tax principle Those who receive more benefits from the government program funded by a tax should pay more of that tax

bilateral aid Development aid from one country to another

binding arbitration When labor negotiations break down and the public interest is involved, a neutral third party is brought in to impose a settlement that both sides must accept

bond A contract promising to repay borrowed money on a designated date and to pay interest along the way

bounded rationality There are limits to the amount of information that people can comprehend and act on

brain drain A developing country's loss of educated migrants to industrial market countries

budget A consumer's plan showing the sources and uses of income

bureaus Government agencies charged with implementing legislation and financed through legislative bodies

business cycle Fluctuations reflecting the rise and fall of economic activity relative to the long-term growth trend of the economy

C

capital deepening An increase in the quantity and quality of capital per worker; one source of rising labor productivity

capital goods All human creations used to produce goods and services; for example, factories, trucks, and machines

cartel A group of firms that agree to act as a single monopolist to increase the market price and maximize the group's profits

cease and desist order FTC-issued directive to stop a firm from making a false or misleading advertising claim

certificate of deposit (CD) Savings instrument with fixed interest rate and fixed maturity date

check A written order instructing the bank to pay someone from money on deposit

checkable deposits Deposits in financial institutions against which checks can be written and ATM, bank, or debit, cards can be applied

classical economists A group of laissez-faire economists who believed that economic downturns corrected themselves in the long run through natural market forces

cluster Firms in the same industry or in related industries that group together in a region, such as Wall Street, Hollywood, or Silicon Valley

collateral An asset owned by the borrower that can be sold to pay off the loan in the event the loan is not repaid

collective bargaining The process by which representatives of a union and an employer negotiate wages, employee benefits, and working conditions

commodity A product that is identical across sellers, such as a bushel of wheat

commodity money Anything that serves both as money and as a commodity, such as gold

comparison shopping The act of reviewing products and prices charged by different businesses for similar products before making a purchase

compound interest Computed on the amount saved plus the interest previously earned

conglomerate merger One firm combines with another firm in a different industry

consumer Anyone who uses a good or service

consumer loan Borrowing money to be repaid in regular installments over time, such as a car loan

consumer price index (CPI) Measure of inflation based on the cost of a fixed "market basket" of goods and services purchased by a typical family

Consumer Product Safety Commission (CPSC) Federal agency created to protect consumers from dangerous products they might purchase or use

consumer sales credit Amounts charged to an account that involves variable payments over time, such as a credit card

consumer surplus The difference between the most that consumers are willing and able to pay for a given quantity of a good and what they actually pay

consumption Household purchases of final goods and services

convergence theory A theory predicting that the standard of living in economies around the world will grow more similar over time, with poorer countries gradually closing the gap with richer ones

cooperative An organization consisting of people who pool their resources to buy and sell more efficiently than they could independently

corporate bonds Loan that entitles an investor to be repaid at the specified date and receive interest until that date

corporate stock Shares of ownership in a corporation

corporation A legal entity with an existence that is distinct from the people who organize, own, and run it

cost-push inflation Inflation resulting from a leftward shift of the aggregate supply curve; reduced supply pushes up the price level

credit The ability to borrow now, based on the promise of repayment in the future

credit history A person's record of paying bills and debts over time

credit rating The measure of a person's creditworthiness

credit scoring A system that assigns a number, or score, to each consumer, indicating whether this person is a good or bad credit risk

creditworthiness The measure of your dependability to repay a loan

crowding in Government spending stimulates private investment in an otherwise stagnant economy

crowding out Private investment falls when larger government deficits drive up interest rates

current account That portion of the balance of payments that records exports and imports of goods and services, net investment income on foreign assets, and net unilateral transfers

cycle of poverty Children in welfare families may end up on welfare themselves when they grow up

D

debt ceiling A limit on the total amount of money the federal government can legally borrow

decision-making lag The time needed to decide what to do once the problem has been identified

decrease in demand Consumers are willing and able to buy less of the product at each price

decrease in supply Producers are willing and able to sell less of the product at each price

deductible The amount an insured person must pay before the insurance company pays anything

demand A relation showing the quantities of a good that consumers are willing and able to buy per period at various prices, other things constant

demand curve A curve or line showing the quantities of a particular good demanded at various prices during a given time period, other things constant

demand for loans curve A downward-sloping curve showing the negative relationship between the interest rate and the quantity of loans demanded, other things constant

demand-pull inflation Inflation resulting from a rightward shift of the aggregate demand curve; greater demand pulls up the price level

demand-side economics Macroeconomic policy that focuses on shifting the aggregate demand curve as a way of promoting full employment and price stability

depreciation The value of the capital stock that is used up or becomes obsolete in producing GDP during the year

deregulation A reduction in government control over prices and firm entry in previously regulated markets, such as airlines and trucking

derived demand The demand for a resource that arises from the demand for the product that resource produces

developing countries Countries with a lower standard of living because they have relatively less human and physical capital; nations with low GDP per capita, low rates of literacy, high unemployment rates, and high fertility rates

discount rate Interest rate the Fed charges banks that borrow reserves

discretionary fiscal policy Legislative changes in government spending or taxing to promote macroeconomic goals

disequilibrium A mismatch between quantity demanded and quantity supplied as the market seeks equilibrium; usually temporary, except when government intervenes to set the price

diversification Investing in a wide variety of firms

dividends That portion of after-tax corporate profit paid out to shareholders

division of labor Organizes the production process so that each worker specializes in a separate task

Doha Round The first trade round negotiated under the WTO; aims to help poorer countries by reducing barriers that harm their exports

E

economic growth An expansion of the economy's production possibilities, or ability to produce

economic system The set of mechanisms and institutions that resolves the what, how, and for whom questions for an economy

economic theory A simplification of economic reality used to make predictions about the real world

economics The study of how people use their scarce resources to satisfy their unlimited wants

economies of scale Forces that reduce a firm's average cost as the firm's size, or scale, increases in the long run

economy The structure of economic activity in a locality, a region, a country, a group of countries, or the world

effectiveness lag The time needed for changes in policy to affect the economy

efficiency Producing the maximum possible output from available resources, meaning the economy cannot produce more of one good without producing less of the other good

elasticity of demand Measures how responsive quantity demanded is to a price change; the percent change in quantity demanded divided by the percent change in price

elasticity of supply A measure of the responsiveness of quantity supplied to a price change; the percent change in quantity supplied divided by the percent change in price

entrepreneur A profit seeker who develops a new product or process and assumes the risk of profit or loss

Environmental Protection Agency (EPA) Federal agency that interprets and enforces laws passed by Congress that involve the environment

equilibrium interest rate The only interest rate at which the quantity of loans demanded equals the quantity of loans supplied

equilibrium wage The wage at which the quantity of labor firms demand exactly matches the quantity workers supply

euro The European common currency

European Union (EU) Twenty-seven nations joined to enhance economic cooperation

excess reserves Bank reserves in excess of required reserves

exchange rate The price measured in one country's currency of purchasing one unit of another country's currency

expansion The phase of economic activity during which the economy's total output increases

export promotion A development strategy that concentrates on producing for the export market

F

featherbedding Union efforts to force employers to hire more workers than demanded for the task

federal funds market A market for overnight lending and borrowing of reserves held by the Fed for banks

federal funds rate The interest rate banks charge one another to borrow reserves overnight; the Fed's target interest rate

Federal Open Market Committee (FOMC) Twelve-member group that makes decisions about open-market operations

Federal Reserve System (the Fed) Established in 1913 as the central bank and monetary authority of the United States

Federal Trade Commission (FTC) Government agency that tries to ensure that businesses compete and market their products fairly and honestly

fertility rate The average number of births during each woman's lifetime

fiat money Money of no value in itself and not convertible into gold, silver, or anything else of value; declared money by government decree

financial account That portion of the balance of payments that records international transactions involving financial assets, such as stocks and bonds, and real assets, such as factories and office buildings

financial capital Money needed to start or expand a business

financial intermediaries Banks and other institutions that serve as go-betweens, accepting funds from savers and lending them to borrowers

financial planner Expert who gives investment advice for a fee

firm A business unit or enterprise formed by a profit-seeking entrepreneur who combines resources to produce goods and services

fiscal policy The federal government's use of taxing and public spending to influence the macroeconomy

fixed cost Any production cost that is independent of the firm's output

fixed exchange rate Exchange rate fixed within a narrow range and maintained by central banks' ongoing purchases and sales of currencies

flexible exchange rate Exchange rate determined by the forces of supply and demand without government intervention

Food and Drug Administration (FDA) Federal agency that sets standards for foods and drugs produced or sold in the United States

foreign aid An international transfer of cash, goods, services, or other assistance to promote economic development

foreign exchange Foreign money needed to carry out international transactions

fractional reserve banking system Only a portion of bank deposits is backed by reserves

full employment Occurs when there is no cyclical unemployment; relatively low unemployment

G

General Agreement on Tariffs and Trade (GATT) An international tariff - reduction treaty adopted in 1947 that resulted in a series of negotiated "rounds" aimed at freer trade

general partnership Partners share both in the responsibility of running the business and in any liability from its operation

good An item you can see, feel, and touch that requires scarce resources to produce and satisfies human wants

government budget A plan for government spending and revenues for a specified period, usually a year

government purchases Spending on goods and services by all levels of government

gross domestic product (GDP) The market value of all final goods and services produced in the nation during a given period, usually a year

Group of Seven (G-7) The seven leading industrial market economies, including the United States, United Kingdom, France, Germany, Italy, Japan, and Canada

H

horizontal merger One firm combines with another firm making the same product

household The most important economic decision maker, consisting of all those who live together under one roof

human capital The accumulated knowledge, skill, and experience of the labor force

human resources The broad category of human efforts, both physical and mental, used to produce goods and services

I

identity theft Crime in which one person fraudulently uses another's identity to obtain credit or to access financial accounts

implementation lag The time needed to execute a change in policy

import substitution A development strategy that emphasizes replacing imports with domestic production

income-assistance programs Government programs that provide money and in-kind assistance to poor people

increase in demand Consumers are willing and able to buy more of the product at each price

increase in supply Producers are willing and able to sell more of the product at each price

individual demand The demand of an individual consumer

industrial market countries The advanced market economies of Western Europe, North America, Australia, New Zealand, and Japan; also called developed countries; economically advanced market countries of Western Europe, North America, Australia, New Zealand, Japan, and the newly industrialized economies of Asia

industrial policy The view that government—using taxes, subsidies, and regulations—should nurture the industries and technologies of the future, thereby giving domestic industries an advantage over foreign competition

Industrial Revolution Development of large-scale production during the eighteenth century

inflation An increase in the economy's price level

initial public offering The initial sale of corporate stock to the public

innovation The process of turning an invention into a marketable product

insurance Protection you purchase against losses beyond your ability to withstand

interest rate Annual interest expressed as a percentage of the amount borrowed or saved

investing Using your savings in a way that earns a return

investment The purchase of new plants, new equipment, new buildings, new residences, and net additions to inventories

L

labor The physical and mental effort used to produce goods and services

labor force Those in the adult population who are either working or looking for work

labor force participation rate The number in the labor force divided by the adult population

labor productivity Output per unit of labor; measured as total output divided by the hours of labor employed to produce that output

labor union A group of workers who join together to seek higher pay and better working conditions by negotiating a labor contract with their employers

laissez-faire The doctrine that the government should not intervene in a market economy beyond the minimum required to maintain peace and property rights

law of comparative advantage The worker, firm, region, or country with the lowest opportunity cost of producing an output should specialize in that output

law of demand The quantity of a good demanded per period relates inversely to its price, other things constant

law of diminishing marginal utility The more of a good an individual consumes per period, other things constant, the smaller the marginal utility of each additional unit consumed

law of diminishing returns As more of a variable resource is added to a given amount of fixed resources, marginal product eventually declines and could become negative

law of increasing opportunity cost Each additional increment of one good requires the economy to give up successively larger increments of the other good

law of supply The quantity of a good supplied during a given time period is usually directly related to its price, other things constant

leading economic indicators Measures that usually predict, or lead to, recessions or expansions

liability The legal obligation to pay any debts of the business; an amount owed

liability insurance Protects against losses from injuries you cause to another person or damage you cause to another's property

limited liability company (LLC) Business with limited liability for some owners, single taxation of business income, and no ownership restrictions

limited liability partnership (LLP) Like a limited liability company but more easily converted from an existing partnership

limited partnership At least one general partner runs the business and bears unlimited personal liability; other partners provide financial capital but have limited liability

limited willpower Limited self-discipline in following through with decisions that are in one's self-interest, especially one's long-term interest

line of credit An arrangement with a bank through which a business can quickly borrow cash as needed

long run A period during which all of a firm's resources can be varied

long-run average cost curve A curve that indicates the lowest average cost of production at each rate of output when the firm's size is allowed to vary

M

M1 The narrow definition of the money supply; consists of currency (including coins) held by the nonbanking public, checkable deposits, and traveler's checks

M2 A broader definition of the money supply, consisting of M1 plus savings deposits, small denomination time deposits, and money market mutual fund accounts owned by households

macroeconomics Study of the economic behavior of the economy as a whole, especially the national economy

marginal Incremental, additional, extra, or one more; refers to a change in an economic variable, a change in the status quo

marginal cost The change in total cost resulting from a one-unit change in output; the change in total cost divided by the change in output

marginal product The change in total product resulting from a one-unit change in a particular resource, all other resources constant

marginal revenue The change in total revenue from selling another unit of the good

marginal tax rate The percentage of each additional dollar of income that goes to pay a tax

marginal utility The change in total utility resulting from a one-unit change in consumption of a good

market demand The sum of the individual demands of all consumers in the market

market economy Describes the U.S. economic system, where markets play a relatively large role

market equilibrium When the quantity consumers are willing and able to buy equals the quantity producers are willing and able to sell

market for loans The market that brings together borrowers (the demanders of loans) and savers (the suppliers of loans) to determine the market interest rate

market power The ability of a firm to raise its price without losing all sales to rivals

market structure Important features of a market, including the number of buyers and sellers, product uniformity across sellers, ease of entering the market, and forms of competition

markets The means by which buyers and sellers carry out exchange

maximizing political support The objective assumed to guide the behavior of elected officials; comparable to profit maximization by firms and utility maximization by households

median income The middle income when a group of incomes is ranked from lowest to highest

mediator An impartial observer brought in when labor negotiations break down, to suggest how to resolve differences

medium of exchange Anything generally accepted by all parties in payment for goods or services; the most important function of money

merchandise trade balance The value of a country's exported goods minus the value of its imported goods during a given period

merger The joining of two or more firms to form a single firm

microeconomics Study of economic behavior in particular markets, such as the market for computers or for unskilled labor

minimum wage law Establishes a minimum amount that an employer must pay a worker for each hour of labor

mixed economy An economic system that mixes central planning with competitive markets

monetary policy The Federal Reserve System's attempts to control the money supply to influence the macroeconomy

money Anything that everyone is willing to accept in exchange for goods and services

money demand The relationship between how much money people want to hold and the market interest rate

money market accounts Bank accounts that allow depositors a limited number of transactions per month; interest is slightly higher than on savings accounts but can vary from day to day

money multiplier The multiple by which the money supply can increase as a result of an increase in excess reserves in the banking system

money supply The stock of money available in the economy at a particular time; determined by the Fed

monopolistic competition A market structure with low entry barriers and many firms selling products differentiated enough that each firm's demand curve slopes downward

monopoly The sole supplier of a product with no close substitutes

movement along a demand curve Change in quantity demanded resulting from a change in the price of the good, other things constant

movement along a supply curve Change in quantity supplied resulting from a change in the price of the good, other things constant

multilateral aid Development aid from an international organization, such as the World Bank, that gets funds from many Countries

multinational corporation (MNC) A large corporation that makes and sells its products around the world

multiplier effect A theory that claims any change in fiscal policy affects aggregate demand by more than the original change in spending or taxing

mutual fund A financial organization that accepts funds from many people and invests them in a variety of stocks

N

natural monopoly One firm that can serve the entire market at a lower per-unit cost than two or more firms can

natural rate of unemployment The unemployment rate when the economy is producing its potential level of output

natural resources So-called "gifts of nature" used to produce goods and services; includes both renewable and exhaustible resources

negative externalities By-products of production or consumption that impose costs on third parties

net exports The value of a country's exports minus the value of its imports

net worth Assets minus liabilities; also called owners' equity

neuroeconomics The mapping of brain activity while subjects make economic choices to develop better models of economic decision making

nominal GDP The economy's aggregate output based on prices at the time of the transaction; current-dollar GDP

nominal interest rate The interest rate expressed in current dollars as a percentage of the amount loaned; the interest rate on the loan agreement

not-for-profit organizations Groups that do not pursue profit as a goal; they engage in charitable, educational, humanitarian, cultural, professional, or other activities, often with a social purpose

O

oligopoly A market structure with a small number of firms whose behavior is interdependent

open-access goods Goods that are rival in consumption but exclusion is costly

open-market operations Buying or selling U.S. government securities as a way of regulating the money supply

opportunity cost The value of the best alternative passed up for the chosen item or activity

P

partnership Two or more people agree to contribute resources to the business in return for a share of the profit

payroll taxes Taxes deducted from pay to support Social Security and Medicare Programs

perfect competition A market structure with many fully informed buyers and sellers of an identical product and ease of entry

personal finance The way you plan to spend or save your income

personal insurance Protects against financial loss from injury, illness, or unexpected death of the insured person

physical capital The machines, buildings, roads, airports, communications networks, and other manufactured creations used to produce goods and services; also called capital goods

physical infrastructure Transportation, communication, energy, water, and sanitation systems provided by or regulated by government

policy Legal contract between an insured person and an insurance company

positive externalities By-products of consumption or production that benefit third parties

potential output The economy's maximum sustainable output in the long run

price ceiling A maximum legal selling price above which a product cannot be sold

price floor A minimum legal price below which a product cannot be sold

price level A composite measure reflecting the prices of all goods and services in the economy relative to prices in a base year

prime rate The interest rate lenders charge for loans to their most trustworthy business borrowers

private corporation Ownership limited to just a few people, sometimes only family members; shares are not publicly traded

private goods Goods with two features: (1) the amount consumed by one person is unavailable to others, and (2) nonpayers can easily be excluded

private property rights Legal claim that guarantees an owner the right to use a resource or to charge others for its use

privatization The process of turning government enterprises into private enterprises

productive efficiency Occurs when a firm produces at the lowest possible cost per unit

production possibilities frontier (PPF) Shows the possible combinations of the two types of goods that can be produced when available resources are employed efficiently

productive resources The inputs used to produce the goods and services that people want

productivity The value of output produced by a resource; compares total output to a specific measure of input; usually reflects an average, such as bushels of grain per acre of farmland

progressive taxation The tax as a percentage of income increases as income increases

property insurance Protects policyholders from losses to their property

proportional taxation The tax as a percentage of income remains constant as income increases; also called a flat tax

public goods Goods that, once produced, are available to all, but the producer cannot easily exclude nonpayers

publicly traded corporation Owned by many shareholders; shares can be bought or sold on stock exchanges

pure command economy An economic system in which all resources are government-owned and all production is directed by the central plans of government

pure market economy An economic system with no government so that private firms account for all production

Q

quantity demanded The amount demanded at a particular price

quota A legal limit on the quantity of a particular product that can be imported

R

rational consumer choice A decision to buy or not to buy a product so that your utility, or satisfaction, per dollar spent is maximized

rational ignorance A stance adopted by voters when they believe that the cost of understanding and voting on a particular issue exceeds the benefit expected from doing so

real GDP The economy's aggregate output measured in dollars of constant purchasing power; GDP measured in terms of the goods and services produced

real interest rate The interest rate expressed in dollars of constant purchasing power as a percentage of the amount loaned; the nominal interest rate minus the inflation rate

recession A decline in total production lasting at least two consecutive quarters, or at least six months

recognition lag The time needed to identify a macroeconomic problem

Recovery Act of 2009 At $787 billion, the largest stimulus measure in U.S history; enacted in February 2009 and projected to last two years

regressive taxation The tax as a percentage of income decreases as income increases

representative money Bank notes that exchange for a specific commodity, such as gold

required reserve ratio A Fed regulation that dictates the minimum fraction of deposits each bank must keep in reserve

required reserves The dollar amount that must be held in reserve; checkable deposits multiplied by the required reserve ratio

resource complements One resource works with the other in production; a decrease in the cost of one increases the demand for the other

resource substitutes One resource can replace another in production; an increase in the cost of one resource increases the demand for the other

retained earnings That portion of after-tax corporate profit reinvested in the firm

return Income earned from funds that are not spent

right-to-work law State law that says a worker at a union company does not have to join the union or pay union dues to hold a job there

rules of the game The laws, customs, manners, conventions, and other institutional underpinnings that encourage people to pursue productive activity

S

S corporation Organization that offers limited liability combined with the single taxation of business income; must have no more than 100 stockholders and no foreign stockholders

saving The act of choosing not to spend current income

scarcity A condition facing all societies because there are not enough productive resources to satisfy people's unlimited wants

secured loan Loan for which property is pledged to back its repayment, such as a home mortgage

securities Corporate stock and corporate bonds

service Something not physical that requires scarce resources to produce and satisfies human wants

shift of a demand curve Increase or decrease in demand resulting from a change in one of the determinants of demand other than the price of the good

shift of a supply curve Increase or decrease in supply resulting from a change in one of the determinants of supply other than the price of the good

short run A period during which at least one of a firm's resources is fixed

shortage At a given price, the amount by which quantity demanded exceeds quantity supplied; a shortage usually forces the price up

social insurance Cash transfers for retirees, the unemployed, and others with a work history and a record of contributions to the program

soft budget constraint In command economies, the budget condition faced by state enterprises that are subsidized when they lose money

sole proprietorship The simplest form of business organization; a firm that is owned and run by one person who sometimes hires other workers

specialization Occurs when individual workers focus on single tasks, enabling each worker to become more efficient and productive

stagflation A decline, or stagnation, of a nation's output accompanied by a rise, or inflation, in the price level

standard of living An economy's level of prosperity; best measured by the value of goods and services produced, on average, per person

stress test Bank regulators assessed the soundness of large banks to determine which ones needed more financial capital to weather a bad economy

strike A labor union's attempt to withhold labor from a firm

sunk cost A cost you have already paid and cannot recover, regardless of what you do now

supply A relation showing the quantities of a good producers are willing and able to sell at various prices during a given period, other things constant

supply curve A curve, or line, showing the quantities of a particular good supplied at various prices during a given time period, other things constant

supply of loans curve An upward-sloping curve showing the positive relationship between the interest rate and the quantity of loans supplied, other things constant

supply-side economics Macroeconomic policy that focuses on a rightward shift of the aggregate supply curve through tax cuts or other changes that increase production incentives

surplus At a given price, the amount by which quantity supplied exceeds quantity demanded; a surplus usually forces the price down

T

tariff A tax on imports

tastes A consumer's likes and dislikes

tax incidence Indicates who actually bears the burden of a tax

too big to fail A financial institution becomes so large and so interconnected with other financial institutions that its failure would be a disaster for the wider economy

total cost The sum of fixed cost and variable cost

total product The total output of the firm per period

total revenue Price multiplied by the quantity demanded at that price

trade deficit The amount by which the value of merchandise imports exceeds the value of merchandise exports during a given period

trade surplus The amount by which the value of merchandise exports exceeds the value of merchandise imports during a given period

traditional economy An economic system shaped largely by custom or religion

transaction costs The costs of time and information needed to carry out market exchange

transitional economy An economic system in the process of shifting from central planning to competitive markets

U

underemployment Workers are overqualified for their jobs or work fewer hours than they would prefer

unemployment benefits Cash transfers to unemployed workers who lost their jobs, actively seek work, and meet other qualifications

unemployment rate The number of people without jobs who are looking for work divided by the number in the labor force

unsecured loan Loan for which no specific property is pledged by the borrower that can be used to satisfy the debt if payments are not made, such as credit card debt

Uruguay Round The most recently completed and most comprehensive of the eight postwar multilateral trade negotiations under GATT; created the World Trade Organization

U.S. Agency for International Development (USAID) The federal agency that coordinates U.S. aid to the developing world

utility A household's level of satisfaction, happiness, or sense of well-being

V

variable cost Any production cost that changes as output changes

vertical merger One firm combines with another from which it had purchased inputs or to which it had sold output

W

welfare reform An overhaul of the welfare system in 1996 that imposed a lifetime welfare limit of five years per recipient and other conditions

world output The combined GDP of all nations in the world

world price The price at which a good is traded internationally; determined by the world supply and world demand for the good

World Trade Organization (WTO) The legal and institutional foundation of the multilateral trading system that succeeded GATT in 1995

SPANISH GLOSSARY

A

ability-to-pay tax principle *habilidad de pagar el principal del impuesto* Aquellos con más habilidad de pagar, tal como aquellos con ingresos más altos, deberían de pagar más del impuesto

absolute advantage *ventaja absoluta* La habilidad de poder hacer algo usando menos recursos que lo que requieren otros productores

aggregate demand *demanda global* La relación entre el precio promedio de la producción total y la cantidad de producción total exigida, otras cosas constantes

aggregate demand curve *curva de demanda total* Una curva que representa la relación entre el nivel de precio de la economía y el verdadero PIB exigido por período, otras cosas constantes

aggregate expenditure *gasto total* El gasto total en todos los bienes y servicios terminados producidos en la economía durante el año

aggregate income *ingreso total* La suma de todos los ingresos ganados por los proveedores de recursos en la economía durante el año

aggregate output *producción total* Una medida mezclada de todos los bienes y servicios terminados producidos en una economía durante un período determinado; el verdadero PIB

aggregate supply curve *curva de oferta total* Una curva que representa la relación entre el nivel de precio de la economía y el verdadero PIB ofrecido por período, otras cosas constantes

allocative efficiency *eficiencia distributiva* Ocurre cuando una empresa produce el producto más preferido por los consumidores

annual percentage yield (APY) *rendimiento del porcentaje anual* La fórmula que los bancos deben utilizar para calcular el interés que pagan sobre los depósitos

annually balanced budget *presupuesto anual equilibrado* Igualando gastos anuales con ingresos anuales, excepto durante años de guerra; método de preparación del presupuesto federal antes de la Gran Depresión

antitrust activity *actividad antimonopolista* Los esfuerzos del gobierno dirigidos a prevenir monopolios y promover la competencia en los mercados donde la competencia es deseable

antitrust laws *leyes de antimonopolio* Las leyes que reducen el comportamiento anticompetitivo y promueven la competencia en los mercados donde la competencia es deseable

applied research *investigación aplicada* Investigación que busca respuestas a las preguntas en particular o aplica descubrimientos científicos para desarrollar productos específicos

articles of incorporation *acta constitutiva de una sociedad* Una solicitud por escrita al estado, solicitando permiso para la formación de una corporación

asset *activo* Cualquier propiedad física o reclamo financiero que sea poseído

automatic stabilizers *estabilizadores automáticos* Programas de gastos e impuestos por el gobierno que año tras año automáticamente reducen fluctuaciones en los ingresos disponibles, y por lo tanto en el consumo, durante el ciclo de negocios

B

balance of payments *balance de pagos* Un registro de todas las transacciones económicas entre residentes de un país y residentes del resto del mundo durante un período determinado

balance sheet *balance general* Un informe financiero que muestra los activos, las obligaciones y el valor neto en una fecha determinada; los activos deben de igualar a las obligaciones más el valor neto, para que el estado de cuentas esté balanceado

barriers to entry *restricciones de entrada* Las restricciones para la entrada de una nueva empresa a una industria

barter *trueque/intercambiar* Un sistema de intercambio en el cual los productos se intercambian directamente por otros productos

basic research *investigación básica* La búsqueda de conocimiento sin prestar atención de cómo se usará ese conocimiento; un primer paso hacia avances tecnológicos

behavioral economics *economía conductual* Un método que adopta entendimientos de la psicología para ayudar a explicar las opciones económicas

benefits-received tax principle *beneficios recibidos del principal del impuesto* Aquellos que reciben más beneficios del programa gubernamental financiado por un impuesto deberían de pagar más de ese impuesto

bilateral aid *asistencia bilateral* Asistencia de desarrollo de un país a otro

binding arbitration *arbitraje obligatorio* Cuando las negociaciones laborales han fracasado y está involucrado el interés público, un tercer partido neutral es involucrado para imponer un acuerdo el cual ambos lados deben aceptar

bond *bono* Un contrato prometiendo pagar dinero prestado en una fecha designada y de pagar intereses en el proceso

bounded rationality *racionalidad limitada* Hay límites en la cantidad de información que la gente puede comprender y sobre la cual actuar

brain drain *drenaje cerebral* La pérdida de migrantes educados de un país en desarrollo a países con mercados industriales

budget *presupuesto* El plan de un consumidor que muestra las fuentes y usos de sus ingresos

bureaus *agencias* Agencias gubernamentales encargadas de implementar legislación y que son financiadas mediante cuerpos legislativos

business cycle *ciclo de negocio* Fluctuaciones que reflejan el aumento y reducción de actividad económica en relación con la tendencia de crecimiento de largo plazo de la economía

C

capital deepening *intensificación del uso de capital* Un aumento en la cantidad y la calidad del capital por trabajador; una fuente del aumento en productividad laboral

capital goods *bienes de capital* Toda creación humana usada para producir bienes y servicios; por ejemplo, fábricas, camiones y máquinas

cartel *cartel* Un grupo de empresas que acuerda en actuar como un monopolista para aumentar el precio en el mercado y maximizar las ganancias del grupo

cease and desist order *orden de cesar y desistir* Orden emitida por la FTC *(Comisión Federal del Comercio)* para que una empresa cese de publicar anuncios falsos o engañosos

certificate of deposit (CD) *certificado de depósito* Instrumento de ahorros con tasa de interés fija y fecha de madurez fija

check *cheque* Una orden escrita instruyendo al banco de pagarle a alguien de los fondos depositados

checkable deposits *depósitos de cuentas de cheques* Depósitos en instituciones financieras contra los cuales se puede escribir cheques y transacciones de tarjetas de cajero automático, tarjetas bancarias, o de débito se pueden aplicar

classical economists *economistas clásicos* Un grupo de economistas laissez-faire, que creían que las fases de bajas en la economía se corregían por sí mismos a largo plazo mediante las fuerzas naturales del mercado

cluster *grupo* Empresas en la misma industria o en industrias relacionadas que se agrupan en una región, tal como Wall Street, Hollywood o el Valle de Silicón

collateral *garantía* Un activo del prestatario que se puede vender para pagar el préstamo en caso de que el préstamo no se pague

collective bargaining *negociación colectiva* El proceso por el cual representantes del sindicato y del empleador negocian los salarios, beneficios de empleados y condiciones de trabajo

commodity *producto básico* Un producto que es idéntico entre vendedores, tal como un costal de trigo

commodity money *dinero de producto básico* Cualquier cosa que sirve tanto como dinero y producto básico, tal como el oro

comparison shopping *comparación de compras* El acto de comparar productos y precios cobrados por diferentes negocios por productos similares antes de hacer una compra

compound interest *interés compuesto* Calculado sobre la cantidad ahorrada más el interés previamente ganado

conglomerate merger *fusión de conglomerados* Una empresa se combina con otra empresa de una industria diferente

consumer *consumidor* Cualquiera que use un bien o servicio

consumer loan *préstamo al consumidor* Pedir dinero prestado que puede ser pagado en plazos regulares con el tiempo, tal como un préstamo para automóvil

consumer price index (CPI) *índice de precios al consumidor* Medida de inflación basada en el costo fijo de una "cartera de mercado" de bienes y servicios que son comprados por una familia común

Consumer Product Safety Commission (CPSC) *Comisión para la Seguridad de los Productos de Consumo* Agencia federal creada para proteger al consumidor de productos peligrosos que puedan comprar o utilizar

consumer sales credit *crédito de ventas al consumidor* Las cantidades cobradas a una cuenta que involucra pagos variables sobre el transcurso del tiempo, tal como una tarjeta de crédito

consumer surplus *excedente del consumidor* La diferencia entre la cantidad máxima que los consumidores están dispuestos y capaces de pagar por una cantidad determinada de un bien y lo que pagan en realidad

consumption *consumo* Compras del hogar de bienes y servicios terminados

convergence theory *teoría de convergencia* Una teoría que predice que el nivel de vida en economías por todo el mundo será más similar con el paso del tiempo, con los países más pobres gradualmente cerrando el espacio con los países más ricos

cooperative *cooperativa* Una organización que consiste de personas que unen sus recursos para comprar y vender más eficientemente de lo que pudieran hacer de forma independiente

corporate bonds *bonos corporativo* Préstamo que le da derecho a un inversionista de ser reembolsado en la fecha especificada y recibir intereses hasta dicha fecha

corporate stock *acciones corporativas* Las acciones de la propiedad en una corporación

corporation *corporación* Una entidad legal con una existencia que es distinta de aquellas personas que son dueñas, que la organizan y la dirigen

cost-push inflation *inflación de costos* Inflación que resulta de un desplazamiento hacia la izquierda de la curva de oferta total; la reducción en oferta hace subir el nivel de precio

credit history *historial de crédito* El registro de una persona de sus pagos de deudas y cuentas sobre el tiempo

credit rating *clasificación crediticia* La medida de la capacidad crediticia de una persona

credit scoring *calificación de crédito* Un sistema que asigna un número, o calificación a cada consumidor indicando si esta persona es un buen o mal riesgo de crédito

credit *crédito* La habilidad de pedir prestado ahora basada en la promesa de pagar en el futuro

creditworthiness *capacidad crediticia* La medida de su confiabilidad de volver a pagar un préstamo

crowding in *atracción* Los gastos del gobierno estimulan la inversión privada en una economía estancada

crowding out *desplazamiento o exclusión* La inversión privada se cae cuando los déficits más grandes del gobierno hacen subir los intereses

current account *cuenta actual* La porción del balance de pagos que registra las exportaciones e importaciones de bienes y servicios, ingresos netos de inversión en activos extranjeros, y transferencias netas unilaterales

cycle of poverty *ciclo de pobreza* Los niños de familias con asistencia pública pueden terminar con asistencia pública ellos mismos cuando crezcan

D

debt ceiling *limite de deudas* Un límite en la cantidad total de dinero que legalmente el gobierno federal puede pedir prestado

decision-making lag *lapso para tomar una decisión* El tiempo necesitado para decidir qué hacer ya cuando el problema se ha identificado

decrease in demand *reducción en la demanda* Los consumidores están dispuestos y capaces de comprar menos del producto a cada precio

decrease in supply *reducción en la oferta* Los productores están dispuestos y capaces de vender menos del producto a cada precio

deductible *deducible* La cantidad que una persona asegurada debe pagar antes de que la compañía de seguros pague cualquier cantidad

demand *demanda* Una relación que muestra las cantidades de un bien que los consumidores están dispuestos y capaces de comprar por período a diferentes precios, otras cosas constantes

demand curve *curva de demanda* Una curva o línea que muestra las cantidades de un bien en particular en demanda a varios precios durante un período determinado, otras cosas constantes

demand for loans curve *curva de demanda por préstamos* Una curva con inclinación hacia abajo mostrando la relación negativa entre la tasa de interés y la cantidad de préstamos exigidos, otras cosas constantes

demand-pull inflation *inflación impulsada por la demanda* Inflación que resulta por el desplazamiento hacia la derecha de la curva de demanda total; la gran demanda impulsa el nivel de precio hacia arriba

demand-side economics *economía de lado de la demanda* Política de macroeconomía que se enfoca en desplazar la curva de demanda total como una forma de promover el empleo total y la estabilidad de precio

depreciation *devaluación* El valor de la acción de capital que es agotado o se vuelve obsoleto al producir el PIB durante el año

deregulation *desregulación* Una reducción en el control del gobierno sobre los precios y entradas de empresas en mercados previamente regulados, tal como las aerolíneas y el transporte de carga por carretera

derived demand *demanda derivada* La demanda por un recurso se deriva de la demanda por el producto que ese recurso produce

developing countries *países en desarrollo* Países con un nivel de vida más bajo porque tienen relativamente menos capital humano y físico; naciones con un menor PIB por persona, bajos índices de alfabetismo, altos índices de desempleo, y altos índices de fertilidad

discount rate *tasa de descuento* La tasa de interés que el gobierno federal le cobra a los bancos a quienes les presta de las reservas

discretionary fiscal policy *política fiscal discrecional* Cambios legislativos en gastos o impuestos del gobierno para promover metas macroeconómicas

disequilibrium *desequilibrio* Una desigualdad entre la cantidad demandada y la cantidad ofrecida mientras que el mercado busca equilibrio; usualmente temporal, excepto cuando el gobierno interviene y fija el precio

diversification *diversificación* Invirtiendo en una gran variedad de empresas

dividends *dividendos* La porción que se paga a los accionistas, del beneficio de una corporación después de impuestos

division of labor *división de labores* Organiza el proceso de producción para que cada trabajador se especialice en una labor por separada.

Doha Round *Ronda de Doha* La primera ronda de negociaciones de la WTO; con el objetivo de reducir las barreras que dañan las exportaciones de los países pobres

E

economic growth *crecimiento económico* Una expansión en las posibilidades de producción en la economía o en la habilidad de producir

economic system *sistema económico* Un conjunto de mecanismos e instituciones que responde a las preguntas del ¿qué? ¿cómo? y ¿para quién? para una economía

economic theory la *teoría de economía* Una simplificación de la realidad de la economía usada para hacer predicciones sobre el mundo verdadero

economics *economía (ciencia)* El estudio de cómo la gente usa sus recursos escasos para satisfacer sus deseos ilimitados

economies of scale *economías de escala* Las fuerzas que reducen el costo promedio de una empresa mientras que el tamaño o escala de la empresa crece a largo plazo

economy *economía* La estructura de actividad económica en una localidad, región, país, un grupo de países, o el mundo

effectiveness lag *lapso en eficacia* El tiempo necesitado para que los cambios en política afecten la economía

efficiency *eficiencia* Producir la máxima producción posible de los recursos disponibles, es decir que la economía no puede producir más de un bien sin producir menos de otro

elasticity of demand *elasticidad de la demanda* Mide que tan sensible es la cantidad demandada a un cambio de precio; el cambio de porcentaje en la cantidad demandada dividida por el cambio de porcentaje en precio

elasticity of supply *elasticidad de la oferta* Una medida de la receptividad de la cantidad ofrecida a un cambio de precio; el cambio de porcentaje en la cantidad ofrecida dividido por el cambio de porcentaje en el precio

Environmental Protection Agency (EPA) *Agencia de Protección Ambiental* Agencia federal que interpreta y hace cumplir las leyes que involucran al ambiente aprobadas por el Congreso

entrepreneur *empresario* Un buscador de ganancias que desarrolla un nuevo producto o proceso y asume el riesgo de beneficio o pérdida

equilibrium interest rate *tasa de interés en equilibrio* La única tasa de interés a la cual la cantidad de préstamos exigidos es igual a la cantidad de préstamos otorgados

equilibrium wage *salario balanceado* El salario al cual la cantidad de labor en demanda por las empresas iguala exactamente a la cantidad que los trabajadores ofrecen

euro *euro* La moneda común europea

European Union (EU) *Unión Europea* Veintisiete naciones unidas para mejorar la cooperación económica

excess reserves *reservas en exceso* Las reservas del banco en exceso de las reservas requeridas

exchange rate *tasa de cambio* El precio de la moneda de un país medido en términos de una unidad de moneda de otro país

expansion *expansión* La fase de actividad económica durante la cual aumenta la producción total de la economía

export promotion *promoción de exportaciones* Una estrategia de desarrollo que se concentra en producir para el mercado de exportación

F

featherbedding *sinecura* Esfuerzos de un sindicato de forzar a empleadores de contratar a más trabajadores de los que se necesitan para la labor

federal funds market *mercado de fondos federales* Un mercado de las reservas para hacer préstamos de un día para el otro que mantiene el gobierno federal para los bancos

federal funds rate *tasa de fondos federales* La tasa de interés que los bancos se cobran unos a otros por los préstamos de un día para otro; la tasa de interés objetivo del gobierno federal

Federal Open Market Committee (FOMC) *Comité Federal de Mercado Abierto* Un grupo de doce miembros que toma decisiones sobre las operaciones de mercado abierto

Federal Reserve System (the Fed) *Sistema de la Reserva Federal* Establecido en 1913 como el banco central y autoridad monetaria de los Estados Unidos

Federal Trade Commission (FTC) *Comisión Federal del Comercio* Agencia gubernamental que intenta asegurar que los negocios compitan y comercialicen sus productos de manera justa y honesta

fertility rate *índice de fertilidad* El promedio en el número de partos durante la vida de cada mujer

fiat money *dinero fiduciario* Dinero que no tiene en si un valor y que no puede ser convertido en oro, plata, o cualquier otra cosa de valor; declarado dinero por decreto de gobierno

financial account *cuenta financiera* La porción del balance de pagos que registra las transacciones internacionales que involucran activos financieros, tal como acciones y bonos, y activos verdaderos, tal como fábricas y oficinas

financial capital *capital financiero* Dinero necesario para comenzar o crecer un negocio

financial intermediaries *intermediarios financieros* Bancos y otras instituciones que sirven como intermediarios, aceptando fondos de los ahorradores y prestándolos a los prestatarios

financial planner *consejero financiero* Un experto que da consejos de inversión a cambio de honorarios

fiscal policy *política fiscal* La influencia del gobierno federal en la macroeconomía mediante los impuestos y gastos públicos

firm *empresa* Una unidad de negocio o empresa formada por un empresario que busca ganancias el cual combina recursos para producir bienes y servicios

fixed cost *costo fijo* Cualquier costo de producción que es independiente de la producción de la empresa

fixed exchange rate *tasa de cambio fija* Tasa de cambio fija dentro de un límite estrecho y mantenida por las continuas compras y ventas de moneda por un banco central

flexible exchange rate *tasa de cambio flexible* Tasa de cambio determinada por las fuerzas de la oferta y demanda sin la intervención del gobierno

Food and Drug Administration (FDA) *Administración de Alimentos y Medicamentos* Agencia federal que impone los estándares para la producción y venta de alimentos y medicamentos en los Estados Unidos

foreign aid *asistencia extranjera* Una transferencia internacional de efectivo, bienes, servicios u otra asistencia para promover el desarrollo económico

foreign exchange *cambio de divisas* Dinero extranjero necesitado para llevar a cabo las transacciones internacionales

fractional reserve banking system *sistema bancario de reserva fraccional* Solamente una porción de los depósitos del banco está respaldada por las reservas

full employment *empleo completo* Ocurre cuando no hay un desempleo cíclico; relativamente bajo desempleo

G

General Agreement on Tariffs and Trade (GATT) *Acuerdo General sobre Aranceles Aduaneros y Comercio* Un tratado internacional de reducción de aranceles aduaneros adoptado en 1947 que resultó en una serie de rondas de negociaciones con la meta de un comercio más libre

general partnership *sociedad colectiva* Los socios comparten tanto en la responsabilidad de administrar el negocio como en cualquier responsabilidad que surge en su operación

good *bien* Algo que se puede ver, sentir y tocar que requiere escasos recursos y satisface los deseos humanos

government budget *presupuesto del gobierno* Un plan para gastos e ingresos del gobierno por un plazo específico, generalmente un año

government purchases *compras del gobierno* Los gastos en bienes y servicios por parte de todos los niveles del gobierno

gross domestic product (GDP) *producto interno bruto (PIB)* El valor de mercado de todos los bienes y servicios producidos y terminados en los Estados Unidos durante un plazo determinado, generalmente un año

Group of Seven (G-7) *el grupo de siete* Las siete economías de mercado industrial principales, incluyendo los Estados Unidos, el Reino Unido, Francia, Alemania, Italia, Japón y Canadá

H

horizontal merger *consolidación horizontal* Una empresa se combina con otra empresa que fabrica el mismo producto

household *hogar* El más importante tomador de decisiones económicas, consistiendo en todos aquellos que viven bajo un mismo techo

human capital *capital humano* El conocimiento, habilidad, y experiencia acumulada de una fuerza laboral

human resources *recursos humanos* La amplia categoría de esfuerzos humanos, tanto físicos como mentales, usada para producir los bienes y servicios

I

identity theft *robo de identidad* Crimen en el cuál una persona usa fraudulentamente la identidad de otra persona para obtener crédito o tener acceso a cuentas financieras

implementation lag *lapso de implementación* El tiempo necesitado para ejecutar un cambio en la política

import substitution *sustitución de importaciones* Una estrategia de desarrollo que enfatiza reemplazar las importaciones con la producción doméstica

income-assistance programs *programas de asistencia de ingresos* Programas del gobierno que provee dinero y asistencia real a la gente pobre

increase in demand *aumento en la demanda* Los consumidores están dispuestos y capaces de comprar más producto a cada precio

increase in supply *aumento en la oferta* Los productores están dispuestos y capaces de ofrecer más producto a cada precio

individual demand *demanda individual* La demanda de un consumidor individual

industrial market countries *países de mercado industrial* Los países económicamente avanzados en mercados del Oeste de Europa, Norteamérica, Australia, Nueva Zelanda, Japón, y las nuevas economías industrializadas de Asia

industrial policy *política industrial* La perspectiva que el gobierno - usando impuestos, subsidios y regulaciones - debe nutrir las industrias y tecnologías del futuro, de modo de darles una ventaja a las industrias domésticas sobre la competencia extranjera

Industrial Revolution *Revolución Industrial* El desarrollo de producción a grande escala durante el siglo dieciocho

inflation *inflación* Un aumento en el nivel de precio de la economía

initial public offering *oferta pública inicial* La venta inicial de acciones de una corporación al público

innovation *innovación* El proceso de convertir una invención en un producto comercializable

insurance *seguro* Protección que compras contra la perdida más allá de lo que puedas soportar

interest rate *tasa de interés* Interés anual expresado como un porcentaje de la cantidad prestada o ahorrada

investing *invertir* Usando tus ahorros de manera que genere un retorno

investment *inversión* La compra de nuevas plantas, nuevo equipo, nuevos inmuebles, nuevas residencias, y adiciones netas al inventario

L

labor *labor* El esfuerzo físico y mental usado para producir bienes y servicios

labor force *fuerza laboral* Aquellos en la población adulta que están trabajando o buscando empleo

labor force participation rate *índice de participación de la fuerza laboral* El número en la fuerza laboral dividida por la población adulta

labor productivity *productividad laboral* La producción por cada unidad laboral; medida como la producción total dividido por las horas de trabajo empleadas para sacar esa producción

labor union *sindicato laboral* Un grupo de trabajadores que se unen en busca de mayor pago y mejores condiciones de trabajo al negociar un contrato laboral con sus empleadores

laissez-faire *laissez-faire* La doctrina de que el gobierno no debe intervenir en una economía de mercado más allá del requerimiento mínimo para mantener la paz y los derechos de propiedad

law of comparative advantage *ley de ventaja comparativa* El trabajador, empresa, región, o país con el costo de oportunidad más bajo de sacar una producción debería de especializarse en esa producción

law of demand *ley de la demanda* La cantidad de un bien demandado por periodo se relaciona inversamente con su precio, otras cosas constantes

law of diminishing marginal utility *ley de utilidad marginal disminuida* Entre más consuma un individuo un bien por período, otras cosas constantes, es menor la utilidad marginal de cada unidad consumida

law of diminishing returns *ley de los rendimientos decrecientes* Entre más de un recurso variable se agrega a una cantidad específica de recursos fijos, el producto marginal eventualmente se reduce y puede llegar a ser negativo

law of increasing opportunity cost *ley del costo de oportunidad creciente* Cada incremento adicional de un bien requiere que la economía sucesivamente cede incrementos mayores del otro bien

law of supply *ley de la oferta* La cantidad de un bien ofrecido en un período determinado es generalmente relacionado directamente con su precio, otras cosas constantes

leading economic indicators *indicadores principales de la economía* Las acciones que por lo general predicen, o llevan a recesiones o expansiones

liability *responsabilidad* La obligación legal de pagar cualquier deuda del negocio; una cantidad que se debe

liability insurance *seguro de responsabilidad* Protege contra las pérdidas debido a lesiones que causas a otra persona o el daño a la propiedad de otro

limited liability company (LLC) *compañía con responsabilidad legal limitada* Un negocio con responsabilidad legal limitada para algunos dueños, imposición de impuestos sencillo de los ingresos del negocio, y sin restricciones de titularidad

limited liability partnership (LLP) *sociedad con responsabilidad legal limitada* Como una compañía con responsabilidad legal limitada pero más fácilmente convertida de una sociedad que exista

limited partnership *sociedad limitada* Por lo menos un socio general administra el negocio y carga con la responsabilidad legal personal ilimitada; otros socios proveen capital financiero pero tienen responsabilidad legal limitada

limited willpower *fuerza de voluntad limitada* Autodisciplina limitada en darle seguimiento a las decisiones que están en el mejor interés propio, en especial el interés propio a largo plazo

line of credit *línea de crédito* Un acuerdo con un banco mediante el cual un negocio puede conseguir dinero necesitado rápidamente

long-run average cost curve *curva de costo promedio a largo plazo* Una curva que indica el menor costo promedio de producción a cada índice de la producción cuando al tamaño de una empresa se le permite variar

long run *a largo plazo* Un período durante el cual todos los recursos de una empresa pueden variar

M

M1 *M1* La definición estrecha del abastecimiento de dinero; consiste en moneda (incluyendo las monedas) que tiene el público no bancario, depósitos de cuentas de cheques, y cheques de viajero

M2 *M2* Una definición más ancha del abastecimiento de dinero que consiste del M1 más los depósitos de ahorros, depósitos de tiempo en denominaciones pequeñas, y fondos comunes del mercado monetario de los hogares

macroeconomics *la macroeconomía* El estudio del comportamiento de la economía en la economía total, en especial la economía nacional

marginal *marginal* Incremental, adicional, extra, o uno más; se refiere a un cambio en un variable de la economía, un cambio en el statu quo

marginal cost *costo marginal* El cambio en el costo total resultando de producir una unidad más en la producción; el cambio del costo total divido por el cambio en la producción

marginal product *producto marginal* El cambio en el producto total resultando de un cambio de una unidad en un recurso en particular, los demás recursos constantes

marginal revenue *ingreso marginal* El cambio en el ingreso total al vender otra unidad de un bien

marginal tax rate *índice de impuesto marginal* El porcentaje de cada dólar adicional de ingresos con el que se paga el impuesto

marginal utility *utilidad marginal* El cambio en la utilidad total resultando del cambio en una unidad en el consumo de un bien

market demand *demanda del mercado* La suma de la demanda individual de todos los consumidores en el mercado

market economy *economía de mercado* Describe el sistema de economía de los Estados Unidos, en donde los mercados juegan un papel relativamente grande

market equilibrium *equilibrio de mercado* Cuando la cantidad que los consumidores están dispuestos y capaces de comprar iguala la cantidad que los productores están dispuestos y capaces de vender

market for loans *mercado para préstamos* El mercado que une a los prestadores (los que exigen los préstamos) y los ahorradores (los proveedores los préstamos) para determinar la tasa de interés del mercado

market power *poder de mercado* La habilidad de una empresa de aumentar su precio sin perder todas las ventas a sus rivales

market structure *estructura del mercado* Las características importantes de un mercado, incluyendo el número de compradores y vendedores, la uniformidad de productos entre vendedores, la facilidad de entrar al mercado, y las formas de competencia

markets *mercados* Los medios por los cuales los vendedores y compradores llevan a cabo el comercio

maximizing political support *maximizar el apoyo político* El objetivo que se asume dirige el comportamiento de los funcionarios elegidos; comparable a maximizar las ganancias por las empresas y maximizar servicios públicos por los hogares

median income *ingreso medio* El ingreso medio cuando un grupo de ingresos son clasificados del más bajo al más alto

mediator *mediador* Un observador imparcial que se trae para sugerir como resolver las diferencias cuando las negociaciones laborales se deterioran

medium of exchange *medio de intercambio* Cualquier cosa generalmente aceptada por todos los partidos como pago de bienes y servicios

merchandise trade balance *balance de mercancía de comercio* El valor de los bienes exportados de un país menos el valor de los bienes importados durante un período determinado

merger *fusión* La combinación de dos o más empresas para formar una sola empresa

microeconomics *la microeconomía* El estudio del comportamiento de la economía en mercados en particular, tal como el mercado de las computadoras o por la labor no especializada

minimum wage law *ley de salario mínimo* Establece una cantidad mínima que un empleador debe pagar a un trabajador por cada hora de trabajo

mixed economy *economía mixta* Un sistema económico que mezcla la planificación central con los mercados competitivos

monetary policy *política monetaria* Los esfuerzos del Sistema de la Reserva Federal por controlar el suministro de dinero para influir la macroeconomía

money *dinero* Cualquier cosa que todos están dispuestos a aceptar a cambio de bienes y servicios

money demand *demanda de dinero* La relación entre cuánto dinero la gente desea quedarse y la tasa de interés del mercado

money market accounts *cuentas de mercado monetario* Cuentas bancarias que permiten una cantidad limitada de transacciones por mes a los consumidores; los intereses son un poco más elevados que una cuenta de ahorros, pero puede variar día a día

money multiplier *multiplicador de dinero* El múltiple por el cual el abastecimiento de dinero puede aumentar como resultado de un aumento en el exceso de las reservas en el sistema bancario

money supply *abastecimiento de dinero* La reserva de dinero disponible en la economía en un tiempo determinado; determinado por el Sistema Federal de Reserva

monopolistic competition *competencia monopolística* Una estructura de mercado con pocas barreras para entrar y muchas empresas vendiendo productos que son lo suficientemente diferentes que la curva de demanda de cada empresa se inclina hacia abajo

monopoly *monopolio* Un solo proveedor de un producto sin sustitutos cercanos

movement along a given demand curve *movimiento a lo largo de una cierta curva de demanda* Cambio en la cantidad demandada resultando de un cambio en el precio de un bien, otras cosas constantes

movement along a supply curve *movimiento a lo largo de una curva de oferta* Cambio en la cantidad ofrecida resultando de un cambio en el precio del bien, otras cosas constantes

multilateral aid *asistencia multilateral* Asistencia en el desarrollo por parte de una organización internacional, tal como el Banco Mundial, que obtiene fondos de varios países

multinational corporation (MNC) *corporación multinacional* Una corporación grande que fabrica y vende sus productos en todo el mundo

multiplier effect *efecto multiplicador* Una teoría que afirma que cualquier cambio en la política fiscal afecta la demanda total por más del cambio original en gastos o impuestos

mutual fund *fondo mutuo* Una organización financiera que acepta fondos de mucha gente y las invierte en una variedad de acciones

N

natural monopoly *monopolio natural* Una empresa que puede prestar servicio a un mercado entero a un menor costo por unidad que el de dos o más empresas

natural rate of unemployment *índice natural de desempleo* El índice de desempleo cuando la economía está produciendo su nivel potencial de la producción

natural resources *recursos naturales* Llamados "regalos de la naturaleza", usados para producir bienes y servicios; incluye los recursos renovables y agotables

negative externalities *externalidades negativas* Subproductos de producción o consumo que imponen costos a terceros partidos

net exports *exportaciones netas* El valor de las exportaciones de un país menos el valor de sus importaciones

net worth *valor neto* Los activos menos las obligaciones; también llamado la equidad del dueño

neuroeconomics *neuroeconomía* La representación de actividad cerebral mientras que los individuos hacen elecciones económicas para desarrollar mejores modelos de toma de decisiones económicas

nominal GDP *PIB nominal* La producción total de una economía basado en precios en el momento de la transacción; PIB del dólar actual

nominal interest rate *tasa de interés nominal* La tasa de interés expresado en dólares actuales como un porcentaje de la cantidad prestada; la tasa de interés en el acuerdo del préstamo

not-for-profit organizations *organizaciones sin fines de lucro* Los grupos que no buscan ganancias como su objetivo; estos se dedican a actividades de caridad, de educación, humanitarias, culturales, profesionales u otras actividades con una razón social

O

oligopoly *oligopolio* Una estructura de mercado con un pequeño número de empresas cuyo comportamiento es interdependiente

open-access goods *bien de acceso abierto* Un bien que es un rival en su consumo pero costoso en la exclusión

open-market operations *operaciones de mercado abierto* El comprar o vender valores del gobierno de los Estados Unidos como forma de regular el abastecimiento de dinero

opportunity cost *costo de oportunidad* El valor de la mejor alternativa que se descarta por el artículo o actividad elegida

P

partnership *sociedad* Dos o más personas acuerdan de contribuir recursos al negocio a cambio de una parte de las ganancias

payroll taxes *impuestos de nómina* Los impuestos deducidos de los sueldos para apoyar a los programas de Seguro Social y Medicare

perfect competition *competencia perfecta* Una estructura de mercado con muchos compradores y vendedores bien informados de un producto idéntico y facilidad de entrada

personal finance *finanzas personales* La manera en la cual planeas gastar o ahorrar tus ingresos

personal insurance *seguro personal* Protege en contra de la pérdida económica a causa de lesión, enfermedad, o la muerte inesperada de la persona asegurada

physical capital *capital físico* Las máquinas, los edificios, carreteras, aeropuertos, redes de comunicación, y otras creaciones fabricadas que se usan para producir bienes y servicios; también llamados bienes de capital

physical infrastructure *infraestructura física* La transportación, comunicación, energía, agua, y sistemas de higiene que el gobierno facilita y regula

policy *póliza* Contrato legal entre una persona asegurada y la compañía de seguros

positive externalities *externalidades positivas* Subproductos de consumo o de producción que benefician a terceros partidos

potential output *el potencial de la producción* La producción máxima de la economía sostenible a largo plazo

price ceiling *precio máximo* Un precio máximo legal alto sobre el cual un producto no se puede vender

price floor *precio mínimo* Un precio mínimo legal debajo del cual un producto no se puede vender

price level *nivel del precio* Una medida de combinación que refleja los precios de todos los bienes y servicios de la economía relativos a precios en un año base

prime rate *tasa preferencial* La tasa de interés que cobran los prestamistas por préstamos a sus prestatarios de negocios más confiables

private corporation *corporación privada* La propiedad limitada a sólo algunas personas, a veces sólo miembros de familia; las acciones no son vendidas públicamente

private goods *bienes privados* Bienes con dos características: (1) la cantidad consumida por una persona no está disponible para otros, y (2) a los que no pagan se les puede excluir fácilmente

private property rights *derechos de propiedad privada* Reclamo legal que le garantiza al dueño el derecho de utilizar un recurso o de cobrarle a otros por su uso

privatization *privatización* El proceso de transformar las empresas públicas a empresas privadas

productive efficiency *eficiencia productiva* Ocurre cuando una empresa produce al costo más mínimo posible por unidad

production possibilities frontier (PPF) *fronteras de posibilidades de producción* Muestra las posibles combinaciones de dos tipos de bienes que se pueden producir cuando se emplean eficazmente los recursos disponibles

productive resources *recursos productivos* Los factores que se usan para producir los bienes y servicios que la gente quiere

productivity *productividad* El valor de la producción producido de un recurso; compara la producción total con una medida específica; generalmente refleja un promedio, tal como costales de grano por acre agrícola

progressive taxation *impuestos progresivos* Aumenta el impuesto como un porcentaje de ingresos al paso que los ingresos aumentan

property insurance *seguro de propiedad* Protege al asegurado de pérdidas a su propiedad

proportional taxation *impuestos proporcionales* El impuesto como un porcentaje de ingresos se mantiene constante al paso que los ingresos aumentan; también llamado un impuesto fijo

public goods *bienes públicos* Bienes, que ya producidos, están disponibles para todos, pero el productor no puede excluir fácilmente a los que no pagan

publicly traded corporation *corporación que cotiza en la bolsa* Propiedad de varios accionistas; las acciones se pueden comprar y vender en las bolsas de valores

pure command economy *economía planificada absoluta* Un sistema económico en el cual todos los recursos son del gobierno y la producción es coordinada por los planes centrales del gobierno

pure market economy *economía de mercado puro* Un sistema económico gobierno para que las empresas privadas se responsabilicen de toda la producción

quantity demanded *cantidad en demanda* La cantidad en demanda a un precio en particular

quota *cuota* Un límite legal de la cantidad de un producto en particular que puede ser importado

R

rational consumer choice *elección racional del consumidor* Una elección de comprar o de no comprar un producto para que su utilidad, o satisfacción se maximice por cada dólar gastado

rational ignorance *ignorancia racional* Una postura adoptada por los votantes cuando ellos creen que el costo de comprender y votar sobre un tema en particular excede el beneficio esperado de hacerlo

real GDP *PIB verdadero* La producción total de una economía medido en dólares del constante poder de compra; PIB medido en términos de los bienes y servicios producidos

real interest rate *tasa de interés real* La tasa de interés expresado en dólares del constante poder de compra como un porcentaje de la cantidad prestada; la tasa de interés nominal menos el índice de inflación

recession *recesión* Un descenso en producción total que dura por lo menos dos trimestres consecutivos, o por lo menos seis meses

recognition lag *lapso de reconocimiento* El tiempo necesitado para identificar un problema macroeconómico

Recovery Act of 2009 *La Ley de Recuperación y Reinversión de 2009* La medida de estímulo más grande en la historia de los Estados Unidos, a $787 mil millones; promulgada en Febrero del 2009 y proyectada a durar dos años

regressive taxation *impuestos regresivos* El impuesto como un porcentaje de ingresos se reduce al paso que los ingresos aumentan

representative money *dinero representativo* Notas bancarias que se intercambian por una materia prima específica, tal como el oro

required reserve ratio *proporción de reserva requerida* Una regulación de la Reserva Federal que dicta la mínima fracción de depósitos que cada banco debe mantener en reserva

required reserves *reservas requeridas* La cantidad en dólares que debe mantenerse en reserva; depósitos de cuentas de cheques multiplicado por la proporción de reserva requerida

resource complements *complementos de recursos* Un recurso trabaja con el otro en producción; una reducción en el precio de un recurso aumenta la demanda por el otro

resource substitutes *sustitutos de recurso* Un recurso puede remplazar otro en producción; un aumento en el precio de un recurso aumenta la demanda por el otro

retained earnings *ganancias retenidas* La porción del beneficio de una corporación después de impuestos que se reinvierte en la empresa

return *rendimiento* Ingresos ganados sobre fondos que no son gastados

right-to-work law *ley de derecho al trabajo* Ley estatal que estipula que un trabajador en una compañía con sindicato no tiene que unirse al sindicato o pagar cuotas del sindicato para mantener un trabajo allí

rules of the game *reglas del juego* Las leyes, costumbres, maneras, convenciones, y otras instituciones fundamentales que animan a la gente a buscar actividad productiva

S

S corporation *corporación S* Organización que ofrece responsabilidad legal limitada combinada con el sistema de impuestos sencillo sobre los ingresos del negocio; no debe de tener más de 100 accionistas y ningún accionista extranjero

saving *ahorro* El acto de decidir el no gastar el ingreso actual

scarcity *escasez* Una condición que enfrentan todas las sociedades porque no hay suficientes recursos productivos para satisfacer los deseos ilimitados de las personas

secured loan *préstamo garantizado* Préstamo en el cual se compromete alguna propiedad que pueda respaldar el reembolso del préstamo, tal como una hipoteca

securities *valores* Acciones y bonos de corporativos

service *servicio* Algo no físico que requiere recursos escasos y satisface los deseos humanos

shift of a demand curve *desplazamiento de una curva de demanda* Aumento o reducción en la demanda resultando de un cambio en uno de los determinantes de la demanda aparte del precio del bien

shift of a supply curve *desplazamiento de una curva de oferta* Aumento o rebaja en la oferta resultando de un cambio en uno de los determinantes de oferta aparte del precio del bien

short run *a corto plazo* Un período durante el cual por lo menos uno de los recursos de la empresa es fijo

shortage *déficit* A un precio determinado, la cantidad por la cual la cantidad en demanda excede la cantidad ofrecida; un déficit por lo general forzará que el precio suba

social insurance *seguro social* Transferencias de efectivo para los jubilados, los desempleados y a otros con historial de trabajo y de contribuciones al programa

soft budget constraint *limitación presupuestaria poco restrictiva* En economías planificadas, las condiciones del presupuesto que enfrenta las empresas estatales que son subsidiadas cuando pierden dinero

sole proprietorship *propietario único* La forma más sencilla de una organización de negocio; una sola persona es dueña y dirige la empresa quien a veces contrata otros trabajadores

specialization *especialización* Ocurre cuando los trabajadores individuales se enfocan en labores individuales, permitiendo que cada trabajador sea más eficaz y productivo

stagflation *estanflación* Una caída o estancamiento, de la producción de una nación acompañado de un aumento o inflación en el nivel de precio

standard of living *nivel de vida* El nivel de prosperidad de una economía; mejor medida por el valor de bienes y servicios producidos, en promedio, por persona

stress test *prueba de estrés* Los reguladores de bancos examinan la solidez de los grandes bancos para determinar cuáles necesitaban más capital financiero para pasar por una mala economía

strike *huelga* El intento de un sindicato de trabajo de retener la labor de una empresa

sunk cost *costo hundido* Un costo el cual ya has pagado y no puedes recuperar, independiente de lo que hagas ahora

supply *oferta* Una relación mostrando las cantidades de un bien que los productores están dispuestos y capaces de vender a varios precios durante un periodo determinado, otras cosas constantes

supply curve *curva de oferta* Una curva o línea que muestra las cantidades de un bien en particular ofrecido a varios precios durante un período determinado, otras cosas constantes

supply of loans curve *curva de oferta de préstamos* Una curva con inclinación hacia arriba mostrando la relación positiva entre la tasa de interés y la cantidad de préstamos ofrecidos, otras cosas constantes

supply-side economics *economía del lado de la oferta* Política de macroeconomía con un desplazamiento hacia la derecha de la curva de oferta total por medio de una reducción de impuesto u otros cambios que aumenten los incentivos de producción

surplus *excedente* A un precio determinado, la cantidad por la cual la cantidad ofrecida excede la cantidad en demanda; un excedente usualmente forzará que el precio disminuya

T

tariff *arancel* Un impuesto sobre las importaciones

tastes *gustos* Los gustos y desagrados del consumidor

tax incidence *incidencia de impuesto* Indica a aquellos quién lleva la carga del impuesto

too big to fail *demasiado grande para fracasar* Una institución financiera se vuelve tan grande y tan interconectado con otras instituciones financieras que su fracaso sería un desastre para la economía extendida

total cost *costo total* La suma de costo fijo y costo variable

total product *producto total* La producción total de una empresa por período

total revenue *ingreso total* El precio multiplicado por la cantidad en demanda a ese precio

trade deficit *déficit de comercio* La cantidad por la cual el valor de mercancías de importación excede el valor de mercancías de exportación durante un período determinado

trade surplus *exceso de comercio* La cantidad por la cual el valor de mercancías de exportación excede el valor de mercancías de importación durante un período determinado

traditional economy *economía tradicional* Sistema económico formado en su mayor parte por costumbre o religión

transaction costs *costo de transacciones* El coto de tiempo e información necesaria para llevar a cabo el comercio en el mercado

transitional economy *economía en transición* Sistema económico en proceso de cambio de planificación central a mercados competitivos

U

underemployment *subempleo* Los trabajadores están sobre calificados para sus trabajos o trabajan menos horas de lo que prefieren

unemployment benefits *beneficios de desempleo* Transferencias de dinero a trabajadores desempleados que perdieron su trabajo, o están buscan trabajo y que llenan otros requisitos

unemployment rate *índice de desempleo* El número de personas buscando trabajo divido por el número en la fuerza laboral

unsecured loan *préstamo sin garantía* Préstamo en la cual el prestatario no compromete ninguna propiedad específica que pueda satisfacer la deuda si los pagos no se hacen, tal como un deudor de tarjeta de crédito

Uruguay Round *La Ronda de Uruguay* La más reciente y la más completa de las ocho negociaciones de comercio multilaterales después de la guerra bajo GATT; creó la Organización Mundial de Comercio (WTO)

U.S. Agency for International Development (USAID) *Agencia de los Estados Unidos para el Desarrollo Internacional* La agencia federal que coordina la asistencia de los Estados Unidos para al mundo en desarrollo

utility *utilidad* La satisfacción de consumo en el hogar, felicidad, o sensación del bienestar

V

variable cost *costo variable* Cualquier costo de producción que cambia al paso que cambia la producción

vertical merger *fusión vertical* Una empresa se combina con otra de la cual compra aportaciones o a la cual vende la producción

W

welfare reform *reforma de asistencia pública* Una revisión en 1996 del sistema de asistencia pública que impuso un límite de cinco años en asistencia pública de por vida por beneficiado y otras condiciones

world output *la producción mundial* La combinación del PIB de todas las naciones del mundo; en el 2010 la producción mundial alcanzo un total de $74.4 trillones

world price *pecio mundial* El precio al cual un bien se comercializa internacionalmente; determinado por la oferta mundial y la demanda mundial por el bien

World Trade Organization (WTO) *Organización Mundial de Comercio* La fundación legal e institucional del sistema multilateral de comercio que siguió a GATT en 1995

INDEX

A

B

C

D

E

H

I

J

K

L

M

N

O

P

Q

R

S

T

U

V

W

Z